IF LOVE WE

John Campbell's books include *Lloyd George:
The Goat in the Wilderness*, *Edward Heath* (for
which he was awarded the NCR Award) and an
acclaimed two-volume biography of Margaret
Thatcher.

JOHN CAMPBELL

If Love Were All . . .

The Story of Frances Stevenson
and David Lloyd George

VINTAGE BOOKS
London

For Kirsty, with my love

Published by Vintage 2007

2 4 6 8 10 9 7 5 3

Copyright © John Campbell 2006

John Campbell has asserted his right under the Copyright, Designs
and Patents Act 1988 to be identified as the author
of this work

Letters and diaries written by Lloyd George and Frances Stevenson
copyright © 1971, 1975, 2006 The Beaverbook Foundation

First published in Great Britain in 2006 by
Jonathan Cape
Random House, 20 Vauxhall Bridge Road,
London SW1V 2SA

www.vintage-books.co.uk

Addresses for companies within The Random House Group
Limited can be found at: www.randomhouse.co.uk/offices.htm

The Random House Group Limited Reg. No. 954009

A CIP catalogue record for this book
is available from the British Library

ISBN 9781844137565

Penguin Random House is committed to a sustainable future for
our business, our readers and our planet. This book is made from
Forest Stewardship Council® certified paper.

Printed and bound in Great Britain by Clays Ltd, St Ives plc

CONTENTS

ACKNOWLEDGEMENTS

My greatest debt in writing this book has been to Frances Stevenson's daughter and granddaughter, Jennifer Longford and Ruth Nixon, for supporting the project so generously when they might easily have felt that enough had already been written on the subject. Jennifer and her late husband twice entertained me most kindly at their house near Churt, and Jennifer drove me around the lanes to show me what can still be seen of Bron-y-de, Avalon and other places associated with her mother and Lloyd George. She was unfailingly helpful with her time and extraordinarily open in answering questions about her early life and allowing me to read documents and papers still in her possession. Ruth, too, though she was away in America most of the time I was writing the book, was immensely helpful, despite the fact that my book was obviously going to overlap ground that she had covered in her own book, published in 1996. I am grateful to both of them for allowing me to quote from copyright material and print private photographs. I was very pleased that Thomas Tweed's grandson, Barry Saunders, got in touch with me after the publication of the hardback. I thank him for supplying some additional information and two new photographs for the paperback.

I am very grateful to the Beaverbrook Foundation for allowing me to quote so substantially from Lloyd George's letters and from Frances's letters and diary – not only material already published by A. J. P. Taylor in *Lloyd George: A Diary by Frances Stevenson* (Hutchinson, 1971) and *My Darling Pussy: The Letters of Lloyd George and Frances Stevenson, 1913–1941* (Weidenfeld & Nicolson, 1975), but also material not previously published. I am also grateful to the National Library of Wales for permission to quote from A. J. Sylvester's diary; and to the Churchill Archives Centre at Churchill College, Cambridge, for permission to quote from the diary of Lord Hankey.

I would like to thank the librarians and archivists at the House of Lords Record Office, the National Library of Wales, the British Library, and Churchill College for their help in providing the primary sources for my research. I am grateful to that wonderful institution, the London Library, for convenient access to other sources – not least for being the only place I know where one can still read *The Times* in the original bound volumes instead of on microfilm. In case there is any thought of discontinuing this priceless facility, may I beg that it should long continue? I should also pay tribute to the Royal Borough of Kensington & Chelsea for maintaining a high quality public library in a difficult climate for library services.

I must thank Sian Collins for translating Lloyd George's Welsh for me – even though most of his honeyed endearments turned out to be nearly untranslatable; and also Liz Jensen for checking my translation of Philippe Berthelot's French – though I confess that in one ambiguous sentence I dared to prefer my version to hers! Once again I am grateful to Liz for allowing me to rent her lovely house in France – a wonderfully peaceful place to write. I must also thank Peter Sheppard for allowing me to see the interior of Frances Stevenson's former flat in Morpeth Mansions – greatly changed though it was from her day.

I am grateful to Dan Franklin at Jonathan Cape for his support of the book, and to Mandy Greenfield and Alex Milner for their eagle-eyed editing; and as always to my agent, Bruce Hunter of David Higham Associates, for his constant support and encouragement. As with all my previous books I pay tribute to Alison Campbell for her support over thirty years, and to my children Robin and Paddy.

Finally I owe an enormous debt to Kirsty Hogarth, who entered into the project with extraordinary enthusiasm. She twice came with me to Aberystwyth to help me read A. J. Sylvester's diary – the first time I have ever enjoyed the luxury of a research assistant. She also visited Criccieth and Llanystumdwy with me, and helped me explore various sites around London where Frances lived and the nursing home where Jennifer was born. She put up with endless discussions about the possibilities and probabilities of Frances's relationships with LG on the one hand and Thomas Tweed on the other, lending an invaluable female perspective to balance my perhaps too male approach to such matters.

Finally she read the typescript, chapter by chapter, as it came off the computer; and even came up with the title. In short she has given me wonderful support and encouragement throughout; and the book is dedicated to her in love and gratitude.

ILLUSTRATIONS

Photograph no. 5 is reproduced by courtesy of the National Library of Wales; no. 29 is reproduced by courtesy of Popperfoto.

INTRODUCTION

The story of Frances Stevenson's thirty-year relationship with David
Lloyd George has been told before, in one form and another over the
past forty years, but never fully brought together in a single narrative
drawing on all the sources now available.

Frances herself told the bare outline of her life with Lloyd George
in her autobiography, *The Years That Are Past*, published in 1967. But
this was a discreet account that left out all the ups and downs, the
heartbreak and the quarrels: she omitted her love for another man and
made no mention of her daughter, Jennifer, born in 1929. In 1971 she
collaborated with A. J. P. Taylor on a published edition of her diary,
which she had kept intermittently from 1914 to 1944. But this, as its
title suggests – *Lloyd George: A Diary by Frances Stevenson* – concentrated largely on LG's political career and excluded most of the more
personal material. After Frances died in 1972, Taylor revealed more of
the full story by publishing their love letters – those that survived, at
any rate – in a volume entitled *My Darling Pussy*. He revealed for the
first time Frances's simultaneous affair with LG's campaign manager,
Thomas Tweed, but nevertheless believed he had established beyond
doubt that LG was Jennifer's father. Yet Taylor cut some letters, overlooked others and missed some conflicting evidence. He disclosed LG's
bizarre scheme to have Frances marry another man who would act as
cover for their relationship; but he ignored one of the most fascinating
documents in Frances's papers, an uncompleted draft of a novel based
closely on her own experience.

Part of the problem has been that Frances's papers are dispersed in three different places. The bulk were included with LG's papers that Frances sold to Lord Beaverbrook in 1949 and are now in the House of Lords Record Office in London. But a second collection, which she retained, was subsequently given by her daughter to the National Library of Wales in Aberystwyth; while Jennifer still holds some letters and other memorabilia in her own possession – including a second version of Frances's novel and two crucial letters from Thomas Tweed. These furnished the principal new material for a biography of Frances by her granddaughter Ruth Longford: *Frances: More Than a Mistress*, published in 1996. This was a book that Ruth had promised Frances she would write, and it is explicitly Frances's story, told from her point of view with the emphasis on her sacrifice, heartache and divided loyalties. It is an excellent filial book, with important input from Jennifer; but it makes relatively little use of the extensive material already published by Taylor.

In addition to bringing all these sources together for the first time, I have also drawn on LG's letters to his wife and children (held at Aberystwyth) and the diaries of A. J. Sylvester (also at Aberystwyth), Lord Riddell (in the British Library) and Maurice Hankey (at Churchill College, Cambridge). All of these have been published, in more or less heavily edited versions; but in every case I have gone back to the originals to restore details, or whole entries, which the editors for reasons of tact or libel omitted. Their emphasis was usually on LG's politics, with Frances occasionally glimpsed in the background: my interest is frankly in their relationship – the emotions, the deceptions, the crises and vicissitudes – but also in how it was *possible* for the Prime Minister of the most powerful country in the world at the height of a great war to conduct a long-term adulterous affair, and for an ex-Prime Minister to shuttle for years between his wife and mistress in a state of effective bigamy, without anyone – his political opponents, the press or tattling servants – blowing the whistle on him. I believe the social context and the practical logistics of the relationship cast a vivid light on the political world that LG and Frances inhabited between 1910 and 1945. It was a world in some ways similar to, but in others very different from, today's media-driven and scandal-hungry circus.

I have been inspired, if that is not too strong a word, by the example of Claire Tomalin's *The Invisible Woman*, which brilliantly revealed the hidden life of Charles Dickens's mistress, Ellen Ternan. Of course the two cases are not the same. Dickens covered his tracks far more thoroughly than LG did, and Ellen's very existence had almost been obliterated before Claire Tomalin's meticulous detective work recovered her. As the first woman to serve as private secretary to a Prime Minister, Frances could never be invisible, though the true nature of her services to LG was not generally known. She finished up as the Countess Lloyd-George; and A. J. P. Taylor revealed most of the facts of her secret life thirty years ago. Nevertheless Frances lived most of her life in half-shadow, ever-present at LG's side as he waged war and peace, but unacknowledged: the long-term established mistress who still came second to his wife, whom he had no intention of leaving; the 'other woman' who had to make herself invisible whenever Margaret Lloyd George chose to assert herself. There are still many gaps, inconsistencies and puzzles in her story. We have a lot of her letters to LG, and more of his to her; but at least as many, particularly from the early years, are lost. As a result we still know tantalisingly little about Frances's other love for Thomas Tweed – though enough to know that it was serious and enduring; and too little about Tweed himself, who is an interesting figure in his own right. There are question marks – one of them disturbing – about LG's affairs with other women. And there is the still-open question of the paternity of Frances's daughter.

I initially wrote about Lloyd George thirty years ago. My first book – *Lloyd George: The Goat in the Wilderness*, published in 1977 – was a study of LG out of office in the nine years between his leaving Downing Street in 1922 and the illness that unluckily kept him out of the National Government in 1931. With – as I still believe – only slight exaggeration, I maintained that LG remained the central figure in British politics in those years, and that much of the energy of his successors Stanley Baldwin and Ramsay MacDonald (not great to begin with) was devoted to preventing his return to office. I have tried not to repeat that argument here; but the reader needs to be aware that LG was the dominant personality on the political stage from the turbulent Edwardian period of the People's Budget and the House of Lords crisis (1909–11), right through his wartime and post-war premiership (1916–22) and well into the inter-war period. Thirty years ago Lloyd George and Churchill were acknowledged as the twin – and equal – giants of twentieth-century British history: we debated which was the more influential politician, which the greater war leader, which the greater *man*. Nowadays in the public mind there is no contest. Churchill, the hero of 1940, is the Man of the Century, and LG is relatively forgotten. To have been the Prime Minister who presided over the slaughter of Passchendaele and the Somme – even though LG strove hard to mitigate the carnage – is no longer a recommendation to greatness. But that was not a criticism made at the time. In 1918 Lloyd George was The Man Who Won the War – and, unlike Churchill, he won his victory election as well. Domestically, too, LG was the most creative politician of the century: the architect of progressive social policies before 1914 that formed the foundation of the post-1945 Welfare State, and then one of the first to grasp the potential of Keynesian economics to relieve the Depression of the 1920s and 1930s, had he only been given the chance to apply them. Of course he had his faults: his methods were often tricky and his famous charm eventually inspired more distrust than confidence. His post-war government was a disappointment. Through all the twists of his career, however, his heart was invariably on the side of the underdog and the oppressed; while simply as a human being he was much less self-absorbed, less ponderous and much more *fun* than Churchill.

This – as well as the glamorous world of power to which he introduced her – was what attracted Frances. When they met, she was just twenty-three, he forty-eight. She fell instantly under his spell, and remained dazzled by him, despite everything, for the rest of his life, another thirty-four years. She had an enormous amount to put up with, since he was exceptionally demanding and became more so as he got older; but he could also be enchantingly sensitive and considerate. This extraordinary sixth sense, applied equally to political allies and opponents, was part of his armoury as a politician, but all his life he could also deploy it with irresistible effect on women. For all his many infidelities, his wife always forgave him. Frances, too, had a good deal to forgive over the years, but whenever she was tempted to leave him he could always win her back by pleading his need of her. Margaret and Frances both knew that there was simply no one like him. His longtime secretary and intimate assistant A. J. Sylvester, who observed him more closely and judged him more harshly than anyone else over the latter part of his life, at work and at play, wrote that the normal rules did not apply to LG: he had a double endowment of every quality, good and bad, compared with a normal man.[1] Generally speaking, the good outweighed the bad. With all his faults, he was the most exhilarating company, the most life-enhancing individual whom most of those who knew him had ever encountered.

Of course, there was hypocrisy in keeping a mistress for thirty years while ostensibly happily married. But at the same time LG was unusually honest with both his women. He made it clear to Frances from the beginning of their affair that he would never leave Margaret; while to Margaret he undertook that there should be no public scandal. He genuinely needed both in his life: he had energy enough for both. Maggie, his boyhood sweetheart and the mother of his five children, represented his roots in north Wales, which were always essential to him, emotionally and politically – constricting though he found it to spend much time there. He never ceased to love her – more than Frances could ever acknowledge; but even as a young wife in the 1890s she had refused to join him in London. From that moment she tacitly accepted that he would have another life in England while she stayed most of the time in Wales. He found other substitutes before Frances, who gave him the emotional and sexual comfort on which his nature depended; but in Frances he found the perfect complement to Maggie. Politicians frequently fall in love with their secretaries: it is an occupational hazard, particularly if their constituency is far from London. While the wife stays at home in the constituency, remote from the pressures of Westminster, the secretary shares the excitement and the daily crises with intense intimacy. LG is almost the paradigm of this now familiar pattern – except that Frances became his secretary specifically to be his lover, rather than evolving gradually from one into the other.

She was a remarkable woman, who was able without fuss to step into the position of secretary to the Chancellor of the Exchequer – at a time when women in the Civil Service in any capacity more responsible than typist were unknown – and then secretary to the Prime Minister during the greatest war in history, without anyone ever suggesting that she was not up to the job or held it on anything other than merit. She was young; but she was highly intelligent, and she went into the situation with her eyes open. Her draft novel shows how painfully she felt the sacrifice she was required to make – of respectability, of marriage, of children – by devoting her life to LG; but she accepted his terms not only because she loved him, but because she also loved sharing in the exercise of his power, because she believed in him and believed that by helping him achieve his ambitions she was serving her country and helping him to make history. For Frances their relationship was not just a love affair – it was her vocation. Like all lovers, she did not believe she was doing anything wicked: she persuaded herself that Margaret had virtually abdicated her position as his wife, and therefore that patriotism required her to dedicate herself to helping the great leader who would save his nation in war and peace.

It was a romantic adventure, made up of love, sacrifice and destiny. After LG had ceased to be Prime Minister, as the long years of frustration unrolled when the prospect of his return to power and influence receded and eventually died, Frances suffered all sorts of conflicting heartaches. LG became ever more demanding, the indignities of her position greater and the rewards fewer; her heart was torn by love for another man who also could not marry her; and at the age of forty she bore a child whose paternity she could not acknowledge and probably did not know herself. Since Maggie was younger than LG, Frances had no reason to expect that he would ever be free to marry her. Yet she stuck with him to the end: she had invested too much of her life to abandon him now. Even when Maggie died, she had a bruising battle – in the face of his children's hostility – to make him do the right thing by her at last; and though she bore his name in the end through nearly thirty years of widowhood, she was denied, even then, the full honour of her hard-earned position.

'Love justifies many audacities,' Frances wrote in 1915. 'If love were all . . .', she reflected at the time of Edward VIII's abdication twenty-one years later. Between these two positions she lived her life. She knew – she learned the hard way – that love was not all. But audacity brought considerable rewards.

PART ONE

NEW WOMAN

Frances Stevenson's beginnings were modest and outwardly unremark-
able, but her family background was actually more exotic than her
name and upbringing implied.

Her father, John Stevenson, was a Lowland Scot, descended from a
line of Lanarkshire farmers, whose father had moved south to better
himself. John too showed enterprise as a young man by going to France,
where he learned to speak the language well; but he soon returned to
England to work for a firm of French import agents. On his daughter's
birth certificate he is described as a commercial clerk; at the end of his
life his occupation was given as 'retired accountant'. By all accounts
he was an upright but somewhat dour man, a Presbyterian so strict
that in later years his family wondered how he had managed to father
five children. In her memoirs Frances wrote that she did not think he
could have broken one of the Ten Commandments in the whole of his
life. 'To us children,' she wrote loyally, 'he was perfection – the embodi-
ment of truth, justice and kindness . . . Our home was filled with the
love which he generated.'[1] Nevertheless she could not wait to escape
this perfect home and spread her wings.

The more ambitious and romantic side of her inheritance came from
her mother's family. Her maternal grandfather was an Italian artist
named Leopold Armanino, the son of Genoese merchants specialising
for generations in the manufacture of playing cards, who had moved
to Paris – as all aspiring painters did in those days – in the 1860s; then
left hurriedly in 1870 to escape the Paris Commune and moved with
his French wife and young family to London, where he settled in

Kennington. Frances's mother – Louise Augustine – thus grew up in England; yet she remained thoroughly Latin in both appearance and character. She was dark-haired and olive-skinned – 'more typically Italian than French' – passionate, proud and temperamental. At the same time, however, she too was oddly prudish. 'Sex,' her daughter wrote, 'was a thing which she seemed to regard with horror.'[2]

How the nineteen-year-old Louise Armanino came to meet John Stevenson is not recorded. They could scarcely have been more different. 'Where simplicity was the keynote of my father's character, my mother's Latin blood made her complex, mercurial, sometimes difficult,' Frances wrote.[3] Yet some attraction of opposites drew them together and they married in 1888, before Louise was twenty – despite a fifteen-year age gap and the opposition of John's family, who were horrified at his marrying a foreign Catholic. Though John's salary was small they managed, jointly with her parents, to rent a substantial terraced house in Kennington, a few minutes from the Oval cricket ground, with room at the top for Leopold to have a studio: he had taken up colour lithography and was now making a living designing advertisements for firms such as Cadbury and Rowntree; and it was here, at 62 Doddington Grove, that Frances was born on 7 October 1888.* Over the next few years Louise produced two more daughters and a son – Janet, Ninette and Paul – followed after a gap by a fourth daughter, Muriel, born in 1902.

Frances describes her upbringing as 'poor'; but it was so only by the standards she later came to enjoy. Though certainly not affluent, the Stevensons were thoroughly respectable, if slightly bohemian. The London street register for 1890 shows only eight other residents of Doddington Grove with listed occupations: they were a surgeon, an architect, a sculptor, a piano teacher and four clergymen. Like other middle-class housewives, Louise had to budget carefully, keep an eye out for bargains at the Army & Navy Stores, and make and mend their clothes. But they never went short; and Leopold – nostalgic for Italy – usually managed to keep a bottle of wine on the table. In other ways, too, Frances grew up with a strong sense of her European inheritance. Her grandmother (whose own grandfather was said to have fought

---

*Though she was always known as Frances, and signed herself F. L. Stevenson, she was actually christened the other way round: Louise Frances. One might imagine the change was to avoid confusion with her mother, except that Louise too was known – at least by her husband – by her second name, Augustine.

under Napoleon) taught her French, and the house was full of French books and periodicals, so that she was effectively bilingual from an early age. It was also a highly political household, with furious arguments conducted simultaneously in French and English about the rights and wrongs of the Dreyfus case (which rocked France in the 1890s) and the Boer War. Louise and her father were passionately pro-Boer, while John Stevenson patriotically took the British side. No doubt the merits of the most outspoken opponent of the war – the rising young Welsh Liberal, David Lloyd George – were much discussed over the dinner table.

At some point in Frances's childhood the family moved from Kennington a couple of miles further out to a terraced house in Alderbrook Road, just south of Clapham Common.* She and her siblings went initially to the council school; but at the age of fifteen Frances took her first step to greater things by winning a scholarship to Clapham High School for Girls. Here, she wrote, she tasted for the first time 'real happiness and freedom from inhibitions'.[4] Moreover she continued to shine academically, particularly in Classics; she passed her matriculation in the fifth year – a year earlier than normal – and dreamed of going on to Cambridge. Her headmistress, Mrs Woodhouse, however, insisted that she should sit the scholarship exam for London University; and when she passed, persuaded her to settle – 'almost broken-heartedly' – for Royal Holloway instead. She went up four days before her nineteenth birthday, in October 1907.

If this was a disappointment, it also proved another step in her emancipation. It was Frances's first experience of living away from home, and an escape from the dominating influence of her mother – not least in the matter of men, where Louise had strong views.

With a Puritanism strange in a Frenchwoman, she strongly discouraged any ideas we might have on making ourselves attractive to the other sex. We were told that 'a good man' would love us for ourselves alone, and that if we were to dress ourselves in the plainest and most unattractive way, indulge in no feminine wiles whatever, but preserve a prim and even forbidding countenance, the right sort of man (how dull he would have been, I fear!) would somehow discern beneath this very unprepossessing appearance

*They actually moved twice, first to No. 17, and then – by the time Frances went to university – further up the same street to 59 Alderbrook Road. Later they moved further still into suburbia, to Wallington in Surrey.

qualities of sterling worth which would place us on a pedestal above all
other women. But for myself I did not *want* to be put on a pedestal: what
I was beginning to want was a little male company.[5]

Since Royal Holloway was a female college, there was still not much
of that. Still, she wrote, 'the heady wine of freedom, congenial friends,
and lovely surroundings' so distracted her that she did little work, at
least in her first two years. 'I was not an ideal student – I think I was
too full of the joy of life for that.' She and her similarly emancipated
fellow-students often used to bicycle to Windsor – where they once
came upon King Edward VII and the Kaiser in the Great Park. 'We
must have looked very prim with our long skirts, our stiff collars and
our boaters, but there was no primness in our hearts.'[6] In her third
year she buckled down sufficiently to graduate, but after the promise
she had shown at school she only achieved a Third.

When she had gone down and was applying for a teaching job in a
girls' school, the Senior Staff Lecturer in Classics nevertheless wrote
her a glowing reference which, allowing for the conventions of such
writings, still gives a convincing picture of Frances's emerging personality, ability and interests.

> Miss F. Stevenson was a student of this College for three years . . . Her
> work has shown steady progress, and the advance was particularly marked
> in her third year. She has good taste and considerable feeling for style, which
> shows itself both in her English translations and in her Latin and Greek
> prose composition. She is specially interested in Greek sculpture, a subject
> to the study of which her artistic bias naturally led her. She has also shown
> determination in grappling with the thornier and less congenial parts of her
> work.
>
> Miss Stevenson has taken an active part in College life, especially on the
> lighter side. Her talents have been much in request for dramatic perform-
> ances, and her singing has given general pleasure. She has charming manners,
> makes friends readily, and is much liked by her fellow students. I have no
> doubt that she would get on well with girls, and would be an extremely
> pleasant colleague.[7]

A less formal glimpse of Frances's character at this time survives in
a letter from her younger sister Ninette, then nineteen, who wrote to
'My dearest Fran' in May 1910 with some girlish boyfriend talk, wonder-

fully redolent of the conventions of the time. She did not know whether to reply to an 'awfully ducky postcard' from an admirer, since she had already sent him one the previous week and did not like to send another so soon.

> I don't know what Mamma would say . . . She'd think I was arranging to elope with him or something of the sort! What would you do? I can pretty well guess what you'd do though. You've got enough nerve for anything! . . .
>
> Fondest love from Nin.[8]

This is a fascinating snapshot, from the pen of an admiring sister, of a spirited young woman willing to defy convention. But Ninette could never have imagined how far Frances would soon go in that direction.

By now, having cast off her mother's strictures about plain dress and modesty, she had grown into an extremely attractive girl. Taking after her father rather than her mother, she was fair and blue-eyed, with an exceptionally gentle manner disguising her sharp intelligence and a streak of steely determination. All her life she had no difficulty commanding male attention, yet at the same time she retained a deceptively demure appearance, which perfectly camouflaged the irregular life she was leading.

As a graduate of Royal Holloway, Frances was one of what was still a very small class of university-educated women, self-consciously the vanguard of a new generation of their sex, demanding new opportunities and new rights.* Frances was naturally a strong supporter of the campaign for women's suffrage, then just gathering momentum under the leadership of Emmeline Pankhurst and her daughters, Christabel and Sylvia, though she drew the line at violence: she was a suffragist, not a suffragette. She was also, though still very innocent, keenly interested in the sexual emancipation of women. In this respect she could almost have been the prototype of H. G. Wells's 'New Woman' as portrayed in his influential novel *Ann Veronica*, published in 1909, which she devoured in her final year.

'Her manner was one of quiet reserve,' Wells wrote of his heroine, but 'behind this mask she was wildly discontented and eager for freedom and life.'[9] That describes Frances exactly. *Ann Veronica* was very

---

* Founded in 1886, Royal Holloway still had only 165 students in 1909.

shocking in its day – and very thrilling: a feminist declaration almost
as scandalous as Ibsen's *A Doll's House* a generation earlier. It tells the
story of a rebellious young woman who defies her parents, runs away
from home and has an illicit affair with a married man. Read today,
nearly a century later, it is surprisingly tame, specifically in the matter
of the relationship between the sexes. Ann Veronica desires the freedom
to love whom she wants; but she also expects to look up to and be
dominated by the man of her choice. In the end she is conveniently
able to marry her lover after all and the book's ending would do credit
to Mills & Boon. It is full of passages that uncannily anticipate Frances's
relationship with Lloyd George. At one point Ann Veronica, debating
with herself, draws a distinction between 'women who are and women
who are not hostile to men'.

> 'The real reason why I am out of place here,' she said, 'is because I like
> men. I can talk with them. I've never found them hostile. I've got no
> feminine class feeling. I don't want any laws or freedoms to protect me
> from a man like Mr Capes. I know that in my heart I would take what-
> ever he gave . . .
>
> 'A woman wants a proper alliance with a man, a man who is better stuff
> than herself. She wants that and needs it more than anything else in the
> world. It may not be just, it may not be fair, but things are so. It isn't law,
> nor custom, nor masculine violence settled that. It is just how things happen
> to be. She wants to be free – she wants to be legally and economically free,
> so as not to be subject to the wrong man; but only God, who made the
> world, can alter things to prevent her being slave to the right one.'[10]

Wells was not only a man, but a compulsive womaniser – in this
respect very like Lloyd George. Nevertheless his assumption of a natural,
unalterable imbalance between men and women expressed precisely the
philosophy by which Frances – feminist though she thought herself –
would live her life. As an early woman graduate, and then as private
secretary first to the Chancellor of the Exchequer and then to the Prime
Minister, Frances was a 'New Woman' indeed, in the front line of
women's advancement in education and the workplace. Yet in her
private life she was an unashamed romantic, happy – no, not always
happy, but in the end content – to sacrifice her independence to what
she saw as a woman's overriding vocation of Love.

Her first need, on leaving Royal Holloway in the summer of 1910, was to get a job. However lofty her ambitions, the only thing she was qualified for was teaching. Yet she was keen to see something of the world. She had reckoned without her mother, who wrote to her on 10 October:

> My darling,
>
> I hope you have not thought seriously of the Calcutta post. You can certainly get something equally as good nearer home, & we certainly should not sanction you accepting such a post. You are much too young & inexperienced, apart from the fact that we have no wish for you to spend the next few years away entirely from us . . .
>
> Write at once, as Daddy is quite upset that you should have even entertained the idea of going abroad for such a long time . . .
>
> Goodbye darling, loving wishes,
>
> from Mother.[11]

Frances bowed to this emotional blackmail, but still hankered to leave home. She enrolled with an agency and applied for a job at a council school in Hull, but when she travelled up for the interview she was so terrified by the size of the place – and the smell of fish – that she was relieved to be turned down on the grounds of age and inexperience. When she was offered a position at a girls' boarding school in Wimbledon she accepted it gratefully. A college friend envied her luck, fearing that she herself might be driven to take up shorthand typing.[12] Frances was not to know that her job would soon lead her to learn typing – and much else besides.

She started at Allenswood School in January 1911. She was initially set to teach the younger girls, which she thought a waste of her degree; but at least this was an easier introduction, since the older girls were barely younger than she was, and many of them much more sophisticated. Soon she was allowed to teach the senior girls as well, and became a confidante to some of them. It was they who first called her 'Pussy' – a name that stuck. It referred to her softness, not her sharp claws, if one can judge from a saccharine poem that two of them addressed to her on her twenty-fourth birthday in 1912:

> Frances, dear, the gods have blessed thee
> With a nature just and sweet,
> While we poor and timid mortals
> Grovel humbly at your feet.

> Honour, glory, might and merit
> Be to thee, who these inherit.[13]

A rather less cloying note is struck by a letter written to her by another girl during the summer holidays that year:

> Dear Pussy,
>   How I hate you giving me that Latin . . .
>   I hope you have ripping holidays. 'Ripping' isn't slang – Miss Moreson says so . . .
>   Love from Margaret.[14]

Frances wrote in her memoirs that she was not a good teacher. 'I was not nearly strict enough; I saw the children's point of view too well and too easily.'[15] For this very reason, however, she was clearly a popular one. Perhaps for the same reason she was not so popular in the staff room. She was not only the youngest member of staff, but her politics were advanced for an expensive private school. Brought up in the French republican tradition, her instincts were Liberal, if not socialist. She not only defended the Pankhursts and attended some of their meetings, which provoked some 'spiteful banter' from her older, spinsterish colleagues; she also joined the Fabian Society and attended lectures by Shaw and Wells whenever she could. There were after all certain advantages in having stayed near London.

Towards the end of her first summer term the school housekeeper, who was Welsh, persuaded Frances to go with her on Sunday morning to hear Lloyd George speak, as he did from time to time, at the Welsh Baptist chapel in Castle Street, just off Oxford Circus. Frances had given up any belief in Christianity some time before – something else she had to be careful to disguise at school; but she was very interested in the chance to hear the leading radical in the Liberal Cabinet and author of the famous 'People's Budget' of 1909; he was also the senior minister most sympathetic to the women's movement, though he disappointed the suffragists by failing to support their cause more positively. Frances went to Castle Street and 'instantly fell under the sway of his electric personality'.

I listened to his silver voice, observed his mastery over his audience. He seemed to establish a personal relationship immediately with every member of it, and although he spoke almost entirely in Welsh, I felt myself in some mysterious way drawn into the orbit of his influence.[16]

Of course this was written more than half a century later: the memory was clearly gilded by everything that followed. Frances was by no means the only one to be bowled over by the Chancellor's silver tongue in these years. She might have remained just one among thousands of distant admirers, had it not been for an extraordinary stroke of fortune that gave her the chance of a closer acquaintance with him.

It so happened that Lloyd George and his wife were looking for a girl to tutor their youngest daughter, Megan, then aged nine, over the summer holidays in Wales; and that their eldest daughter Mair had attended Clapham High School at the same time that Frances was there. Though Mair was actually a little younger than Frances, they had been friends; Mair used to help Frances with her maths. Frances remembered her as 'a very sweet and gentle girl, and clever too – much loved by all at school'.[17] But Mair had died of appendicitis at the age of seventeen soon after Frances left – a loss from which her father never fully recovered. Three years later, however, needing a tutor, Margaret Lloyd George turned to Mair's old headmistress to see if she could recommend one.

Dear Mrs Woodhouse . . .

My object in writing today is to ask if you know of any nice girl that would be suitable for a temporary governurse [sic] during the Holidays for my little girl. We want one to teach her music & French, one that can talk French well. She had a governurse in the mornings for 2 years, but during this last term she had no lessons at all because she suffered from enlarged tonsils. I fear she will forget all unless she has some lessons during August & September.

If you know of anyone could you let me know.

With kindest regards

Yours very sincerely,

Margaret Lloyd George[18]

The first girl Mrs Woodhouse thought of was unavailable. The second was Frances: not only did she speak French, but she played the piano too. She sent Margaret's letter to Frances on 26 July.

Dear Frances

Would you like to apply for this holiday post? If so please write direct to Mrs Lloyd George, stating your qualifications – especially as regards French.

Mrs Lloyd George has not mentioned salary, but she will probably tell you this in answer to your application.

Please let me know at once if you *are* applying & if not, return the letter at once as I must show it to someone else.

With kind love,

Yours affectly,

E. Woodhouse[19]

Meanwhile Lloyd George, with the help of his second daughter Olwen – known in the family as Llwydyn, then aged nineteen – thought he had found a suitable girl, as he wrote to Margaret in Wales.

Believe Llywdyn & I are on the track of an excellent Governess for Megan. A nice German-Swiss – simple, straight, kind-looking but not good looking.[20]

Evidently Margaret, knowing her husband's susceptibility to pretty girls, did not want anyone too attractive. She had another candidate; but LG did not like the sound of this one. 'I don't know Miss Jones's sister,' he wrote on 26 July. 'But if she is as surly a creature as Miss Jones then I don't like her for Megan' – or, he might have added, for himself.[21] Meanwhile Frances nearly missed her opportunity, as is apparent from a letter written by Olwen from 11 Downing Street two days later.

Dear Miss Stevenson,

I was sorry not to have found you in this afternoon.

I've consulted Father & inasmuch as you have to be away for a fortnight in August it does not quite fit in with our arrangements.

We want someone who can be with my sister for the whole of August and September.

So I do not think it necessary for you to come here tomorrow.

I'm very sorry as otherwise I'm sure you would satisfy us.

Believe me,

Yrs truly

Olwen Lloyd George[22]

Frances must have quickly rearranged her plans, since the next day she did go to Downing Street for a momentous interview.

Nervous and pale, and looking, I think, much younger than I was, I was shown into the large drawing room upstairs. Soon the door opened and I found myself confronting, but this time at nearer quarters, the man whom I had seen in the Welsh chapel a few weeks before. My nervousness was dispersed in a few moments by the warmth of his voice and the kindliness of manner which put me entirely at my ease.

Her memory of the encounter continues rhapsodically:

His image as I saw him then is graven on my mind: the sensitive face, with deep furrows between the eyes: the eyes themselves, in which were all knowledge of human nature, grave and gay almost simultaneously – which, when they scrutinised yours, convinced you that they understood all the workings of your heart and mind, sympathised with all your difficulties, set you in a place apart. The broad brow, the beautiful profile – straight nose, neat insolent chin, and a complexion as young and fresh as a child's . . .

But there was something more than this which distinguished him from all other men I had ever met . . . a magnetism which made my heart leap and swept aside my judgment, producing an excitement which seemed to permeate my entire being . . .

We discussed the job and my qualifications for it, and he must have seen how eager I was to be given it. It was quickly arranged that I should go down to Criccieth almost immediately and spend the summer there . . . I left Downing Street under the impression that I was a free and independent person: in truth, I was enslaved for the rest of my life.[23]

Olwen's recollection suggests that she was present at the interview, and that her father was already taken with something more than Miss Stevenson's academic qualifications.

After I had talked to them both, Father came in. Later I asked him, 'Well, what do you think?' and added, 'I rather like the Swiss girl.' Father said, 'I think the other girl is more intelligent and speaks better French.'

But Olwen was writing more than seventy years later, by which time events had long since soured her memory.

Frances wore a little flowered hat for the interview and looked very sweet. She was certainly prettier than the Swiss girl and obviously appealed to Father. She got the job and came to Criccieth for the summer, but frankly, we children thought she was dull, and we certainly never learned any French from her.[24]

This is unfair – Frances was not hired to teach the older children, who were all practically grown up – and inaccurate. That summer and for some time afterwards all the Lloyd Georges loved her.

Writing to Margaret, LG was careful to associate Olwen with his decision.

You know we have engaged Miss Stevenson for Megan. I liked her when I saw her. She has a kind face. She is half-French & can play. You will like her.

She will go there on Tuesday.[25]

That gave Frances just three days to get ready. On the back of Olwen's letter she scribbled a shopping list – or perhaps a packing list – comprising some of the things she would need for a summer in north Wales:

notepaper
spongebag
sulphur tablets
muslin dress
sunshade
indoor shoes
hat
coat and skirt [crossed out]
camisole[26]

She also wrote 'Tuesday 11.30' – the time appointed when the Chancellor would send his ministerial car to Clapham to bring her to Downing Street for lunch, before taking her to Paddington to catch the train to Wales. This, very precisely, was the beginning of a new life to which Frances would quickly become accustomed. Not only had she never before been in a private car; lunch at No. 11 plunged her into a political world that was quite new to her and deeply exciting. The great barrister Rufus Isaacs was there – one of Lloyd George's closest friends, at that time Attorney-General – 'full of raillery and charm, handsome and debonair . . . I had never before listened to such witty and stimulating conversation'.[27]

As she sat on the train that afternoon – 1 August 1911, less than a week after Mrs Woodhouse had sent her Margaret's letter – Frances must have reflected on the stunning transformation in her circumstances. Just six days earlier she had been a restless schoolteacher, following politics only through the newspapers. Of course it was only a summer holiday job: it might have led her nowhere. In fact it led her very quickly to the heart of British government. Within a few months Downing Street – first No. 11, later No. 10 itself – was to be her place of work, and the company of Cabinet ministers, Prime Ministers, generals and foreign statesmen would be her everyday experience at breakfast, lunch and dinner for the next eleven years. Her life would never be the same again.

2

THE WIZARD – AND HIS WIFE

In 1911 David Lloyd George was forty-eight and at the height of his powers. He was the most colourful and controversial politician of the day, an electrifying speaker, loathed by the Tories for his socialistic policies and rabble-rousing diatribes against the House of Lords, but at the same time, behind the platform rhetoric, an exceptionally creative and constructive minister, fertile in the solution of problems, with an uncanny ability to get opponents round a table to charm or bully them to do his will. The press, from a mixture of admiration for his magical abilities and distrust of his sometimes devious methods, dubbed him 'the Welsh Wizard'.* Already Chancellor of the Exchequer since 1908, he was indisputably the second man in the Liberal Cabinet and the clear front-runner to succeed H. H. Asquith as Prime Minister at some time in the future.

He was born in 1863 – in Manchester, ironically, where his father, William George, was briefly a headmaster. But his upbringing was entirely Welsh. His father died when he was still a baby, and he was raised by his uncle, his mother's brother Richard Lloyd, a master shoe-maker and Baptist preacher, bearded like an Old Testament prophet, in the Caernarvonshire village of Llanystumdwy, near Criccieth. His mother, Elizabeth Lloyd, is by comparison a shadowy figure, though she lived until her son was thirty-three. David, or Dai – outstandingly

---

* More than any of the other peoples of the British Isles, the Welsh have always attracted English distrust, exemplified in the children's rhyme 'Taffy was a Welshman, Taffy was a thief . . .' Lloyd George's pride in his Welsh ancestry was an essential part of his political charisma, but also the butt of some unpleasant racial snobbery.

precocious from an early age – was brought up primarily by his uncle, who taught himself Latin and French (and to an extent probably English too, since his first language was Welsh) to keep one step ahead of his nephew. As a boy, David took his uncle's surname and eventually joined it with his father's – unlike his younger brother, who remained all his life plain William George; and he always acknowledged his debt to his substitute father, though Frances in later years wondered if he really loved Uncle Lloyd as much as he piously pretended. One thing, though, is certain: from early childhood LG was used to being the centre of the household – spoiled, waited on and continually praised, physically incapable of doing anything for himself, but accustomed to getting whatever he wanted. This expectation that others were there to serve him stayed with him all his life.

Not that he did not work hard. He certainly did, and that habit, too, never weakened. On leaving school at the age of sixteen – there was no question of going to university – he was articled to a local firm of solicitors in Portmadoc, quickly passed his law exams and in 1885 – three years before Frances was born – set up his own practice, in which he was soon joined by his brother. (The firm was called Lloyd George and George, though after David went into politics, William uncomplainingly did most of the work.) Within five years he was elected to Parliament as member for the Caernarvon Boroughs – seven coastal towns, including Criccieth, which formed a constituency separate from the interior of the county – which he continued to represent for the next fifty-five years.* In his early years in Parliament he was virtually a Welsh nationalist, making his reputation as the scourge of English Tory landlords and the Anglican Church. But he gained national prominence in 1899 as an outspoken opponent of the Boer War. He was not a pacifist, as his role in 1914–18 emphatically demonstrated, or even anti-imperialist; but he was anti-militarist and a passionate defender of the rights of small nations. When the Liberals came to power in 1905 he was appointed straight into the Cabinet as President of the Board of Trade; and when Asquith succeeded Sir Henry Campbell-Bannerman as Prime Minister in 1908, he became Chancellor. In this position he introduced old-age pensions; worked closely with his younger ally Winston Churchill to set up employment exchanges; and introduced in 1909 the famous 'People's Budget', which raised taxes

---

* The seven were Criccieth, Conway, Bangor, Caernarvon, Deganwy, Pwllheli and Nevin.

on land to pay for health and unemployment insurance (as well as new battleships) – the first building blocks of what eventually became the Welfare State. This dangerous innovation so outraged the landed interest in the House of Lords that they took the unprecedented step of throwing out the budget, provoking a constitutional crisis that lasted right through 1910–11. At the moment Frances entered his life, Lloyd George was at the eye of this violent political storm.

More than twenty years earlier he had married – after a long and determined pursuit – a local Criccieth girl, Margaret Owen. The only child of a prosperous tenant farmer, from a family that claimed descent from the ancient rulers of Gwynedd in the twelfth century, Margaret was socially a cut above the young Davy Lloyd, and her family were very much against the marriage. LG, however, won her heart and wore down their resistance, and they were married in January 1888, when he was twenty-five, she nearly three years younger. Their courtship was remarkable, as their marriage was to be. Before they were married, LG wrote his fiancée two long letters that set out with astonishing frankness his ambition, his view of the relations between men and women, and his expectations of his wife. Though LG was not in the conventional sense a good husband, certainly not a faithful one, these letters demonstrate the strong foundations of a relationship which, over fifty years, neither Frances nor anyone else was ever wholly able to break.

In the first – probably written in late 1886 – he told her bluntly that his career came before everything else.

Now once and for ever let us have an end of this long standing wrangle. It comes to this. My supreme idea is to get on. To this idea I shall sacrifice everything – except I trust honesty. I am prepared to thrust even love itself under the wheels of my Juggernaut if it obstructs the way – that is if love is such trumpery child's play as your mother deems courtship to be. Now I have told you over & over again that I consider you to be my good angel – my guiding star. Do you not really desire my success? Recollect my success probably means yours . . . I am prepared to do anything reasonable & fair you may require of me . . . Believe me – & may Heaven attest the truth of my statement – my love for you is sincere & strong. In this I never waver. But I must not forget that I have a purpose in life, and however painful the sacrifices I may have to make to attain this ambition I must not flinch – otherwise success will be remote indeed.

Write me your views candidly & in as good & earnest a spirit as I impart mine to you.

With fondest love

From your sweetheart

D.Ll.G.[1]

The second letter — written after they were formally engaged, some time in 1887 — was occasioned by Margaret's suspicions that he was seeing too much of two attractive clients (the daughters of a local fish-monger) with whom he had enjoyed a flirtation two years before. As always throughout his life, Lloyd George's protestations of outraged innocence were absurdly exaggerated; but the burden of his defence was that his 'dearest Maggie' meant infinitely more to him than Annie and Lizzie Jones.

My ideas as to the qualifications of a wife do not coincide with yours. You seem to think that the supreme function of a wife is to *amuse* her husband — to be to him a kind of toy or plaything to enable him to while away with enjoyment his leisure hour. Frankly, that is simply prostituting marriage. My ideas are very different — if not superior — to yours. I am of opinion that woman's function is to soothe & sympathise & not to amuse. Men's lives are a perpetual conflict. The life that I have mapped out will be so especially — as lawyer & politician. Woman's function is to pour oil on the wounds — to heal the bruises of the spirit received in past conflicts & to stimulate to renewed exertion. Am I not right? If I am then you are pre-eminently the girl for me.

Yours lovingly

Di[2]

The implication was clear: there would always be other women in his life, but they would be mere playthings — amusements — compared to his enduring love for Maggie. Prostitution, he almost suggested, had its place (men would be men), but not in marriage. What he demanded from his wife was uncritical support and sympathy in his political struggles. Brutal though it seems today, LG cannot be accused of failing to lay his cards on the table. When she married him, Maggie knew what she was taking on. By the same token, when, in years to come, he felt that he was not getting from her the solace and support he expected, he felt entitled to seek them elsewhere. When he wooed

Frances, he overcame her scruples by telling her that Maggie was no longer a proper wife to him.

There was some truth in that. From the earliest days of their marriage, after he was elected to Parliament, Maggie was very reluctant to join him in London. This was mainly because she was determined that their children – four born in five years between 1889 and 1894, and a fifth in 1902 – should all be born and grow up in Wales. LG wrote her pathetic letters, describing the loneliness of coming home to empty lodgings every evening, with no one to darn his socks or cook him meals, and begging her to join him; but Maggie was adamant. She was in her own way as strong-minded as he, and she would not budge. Again, the modern reader's sympathy may be with Maggie not wishing to give up the fresh air of Criccieth and her own community for the smoke of London; but in the 1890s this was not the behaviour expected of a wife – as LG did not hesitate to tell her, for instance in August 1897:

> Be candid with yourself – drop that infernal Methodism which is the curse of your better nature & reflect whether you have not rather neglected your husband . . . You have been a good mother. You have not – & I say this now not in anger – not always been a good wife . . . You may be a blessing to your children. Oh, Maggie *anwyl* [beloved] beware lest you be a curse to your husband.[3]

Eventually, in 1899, she did agree to come to London more often, and LG rented a house near Wandsworth Common – barely half a mile from where the ten-year-old Frances was growing up in Clapham; and after he became Chancellor and moved into 11 Downing Street she felt obliged to spend a certain amount of time there. But she was always impatient to get back to Wales as soon as she could, so that he was still left on his own a good deal, especially when Maggie fell pregnant again. 'I was never more unhappy by your absence,' he told her in 1902. 'Cold coffee, cold grape nuts & eternal ham help to make you much more popular . . . Come as soon as you can, dear old darling.'[4] At this time her fifth child, Megan, was just four weeks old. He already had the three eldest – Dick, Mair and Olwen – living with him in Wandsworth, where they went to school; and, baby or no baby, he was comically anxious for her to join them as soon as possible.

Why the poor Boer women had often to trek on waggons through sun &
rain over open rough country for days when baby was only a fortnight or
3 weeks old. I am not as hard as that. But the concentration camp on
Wandsworth Common does need your presence.[5]*

The inevitable consequence of his loneliness was that he had affairs
– some serious, some less so. LG thought little of them, because he was
at heart genuinely devoted to his 'old Mag', whom he regarded – as
he had promised – as the rock of his life. He called her 'my round little
wife';[6] and it is true that by her forties she presented a somewhat
homely figure. She has often been portrayed as a homely personality
too, interested only in her children, her chapel and her garden; but that
underestimates her. She was in fact shrewd, humorous and spirited,
active as a political speaker in her own right and, as time went on, a
powerful support to her husband in his constituency. Their letters over
the fifty years of their marriage show that she was no doormat, but
was able to give as good as she got in their frequent wrangles. She was
often furiously jealous of his infidelities; yet ultimately, so long as there
was no scandal, she always forgave him, partly because she valued his
career, but also because she remained equally fond of him, knew his
frailty and recognised that she was not always there when he needed
her.

He in turn recognised the debt he owed her. Years later – the year
before their golden wedding – he recalled her courage in standing by
him at the time of his greatest unpopularity during the Boer War;[7] and
reflected that there were 'two kinds of wives; those who give up everything to their children and those who give up everything to their
husbands'. Maggie was the former. 'All the same, she is the best of the
bunch and when we were on the point of having a frightful row she
stepped in and said: "I will have none of it", and I will always remember
that.'[8]

He had several narrow scrapes that might have ruined him. In 1897
a cousin of Maggie's, with whom he had undoubtedly had some sort
of dalliance, cited him as the father of her child; but the evidence was
inconclusive and the court, while granting her husband a divorce,
dismissed her claim. In another well-publicised case in 1909 LG sued
a Sunday newspaper for alleging that he had paid hush-money to avoid

* This was an ironic reference to the 'concentration camps' that the British had built
to intern Boer civilians in South Africa.

being cited as co-respondent in a divorce case. On this occasion Maggie stood by him, appearing with him in court even though he was almost certainly perjuring himself. She did this to save his career and to preserve the good name of her children, on condition that there should be no recurrence. But of course this did not stop him. His most serious affair – before Frances – was with the wife of a Welsh draper named Timothy Davies, who later became Liberal MP for Fulham. With the surprising complaisance of her husband, who possibly hoped for political favours in return, 'Mrs Tim' gave LG for several years exactly the sort of womanly pampering he always craved. Sex was certainly part of it, since Lloyd George was a highly sexed man, but probably not the most important thing. What he really craved was what he had told Maggie before their marriage that he needed: the pouring of oil on his wounds and the healing of his bruises; and 'Mrs Tim' at her comfortable house in Putney filled that need. But that affair was largely – if not perhaps completely – over by 1911. When Frances appeared in his life there was a vacancy for someone to take her place.[9]

There was another vacancy too, left by the death of his beloved daughter Mair. His second child but first daughter, Mair Eluned had always been her father's favourite. She was by all accounts an exceptionally sweet and lovely girl. LG was devastated by her death in 1907, at the age of seventeen. It is probably unfair to suggest, as some writers have done, that Maggie was any less affected; but LG – lacking her religious faith – took it exceptionally hard, and it certainly widened the growing gulf between them. Decades later he still spoke of Mair's loss as an emotional scar that never healed; and in 1911 the wound was still quite fresh. It is clear that the young teacher who applied for the job of tutoring his youngest daughter in the summer holidays reminded him strongly of Mair: not only was Frances of comparable age and similarly gentle disposition, but she had actually known Mair at school. (The Swiss girl could not compete with that.) Perhaps, if he identified her in some degree with Mair, LG should not have let himself become so drawn to Frances. But unquestionably this was part of her attraction. Frances became many things to him over the years: secretary, lover, confidante, nursemaid and eventually wife. But in the beginning she was partly a replacement for his beautiful lost daughter.

So, in a more orthodox way, was Megan. Born in 1902, when LG was nearly forty, Megan was the spoiled baby of the family, much

younger than her brothers Dick and Gwilym and their middle sister
Olwen. As a father (and a lover of women) LG was always more indul-
gent towards his daughters than his sons. Megan was only five when
Mair died, six when her father became Chancellor. Thus she grew up
in Downing Street, accustomed from childhood to the media attention
which even then surrounded the daughter of a famous man. Clever,
lively, a natural show-off who loved the limelight, she was tempera-
mentally most like her father — though without his application or his
discipline. Particularly after Mair's death, LG doted on Megan, and she
worshipped him in return with an intensity that in the end was not
good for either of them. This was the precious child whom Frances
was hired to teach.

3

THE BEGINNING OF THE AFFAIR

Lloyd George was not able to join his family in Wales for another three weeks. He was detained in London by the House of Lords crisis, his National Insurance Bill and the threat of a national rail strike, which he managed to avert by his usual methods. The government considered keeping Parliament sitting right through to the end of September, though in fact the House eventually rose on 22 August 1911. But LG wrote nearly every day to Maggie giving his usual egotistical account of his battles and triumphs – and complaining when she did not send him 'even a wire of congratulation' on resolving the rail dispute;[1] and on 7 August he wrote also to Megan. Contrary to Olwen's later recollection, it is clear that Frances had immediately made a good impression.

My darling little Megan,

I thank you so much for sending me that sweet little tooth which had smiled so often on me. I hope you will soon get another which will last you at least ten times as long.

I am glad that you like your new companion & that you get on so well together. I knew you would. I want you to learn French & music so that you can talk French like a petite Parisien [sic] and play the piano like Paderewski.

I am so looking forward to seeing your bright face.

Tada[2]

No doubt he was looking forward to seeing her companion's 'bright face' too.

Frances's memory of that summer in north Wales was idyllic, even though LG was there for only two weeks. Even before he arrived the household was 'extremely lively', since all four of the young Lloyd Georges were there: Dick and Gwilym, aged twenty-two and seventeen respectively, as well as Megan and Olwen. Megan she found 'an enchanting child', and Maggie was kind; she also met and was duly impressed by Uncle Lloyd. 'Part of the day was given over to lessons,' she recalled, 'and at other times we bathed, walked, or talked.' The summer of 1911 was famously hot, and the mix of 'sea, sun and mountains' formed 'a combination of beauty I had never before experienced'.[3]

But the fun really started when LG appeared. He always liked to invite political colleagues to share his family holiday and this year he had asked Charles Masterman, then working closely with him on the National Insurance Bill, with his wife Lucy. Her account of their stay fully confirms Frances's description of a wonderfully chaotic and spontaneous household, with no set times for anything and Maggie patiently putting up with her husband's irrepressible enthusiasm. Each day there were picnics and excursions, dazzling conversation at mealtimes and singing in the evening. The only moment LG ever sat still – under protest – was to allow a local artist to paint a portrait of him; then Megan and Frances had to sit and talk to him to keep him entertained. The rest of the time he was the life and soul of the party, leading expeditions around the scenes of his childhood and showing off furiously to Frances and Lucy – who was only four years older than Frances and just as pretty. This is Frances's account:

There were walks up on the golf links, with the most wonderful view in the world; a midnight walk up Snowdon to see the sun rise . . . excursions every day to some place of interest, or a picnic by the river at Llanystumdwy, where we all took off our shoes and stockings, the men rolled up their trousers (I noted that L.G. had a shapely calf), to cross the stream by the large stones in the river bed, careful, on L.G.'s instructions, to avoid the slippery ones . . . We made a fire to boil the kettle for tea. L.G. was always a good improviser and he then conceived the idea of making mushrooms on toast on a tin lid over the fire. I may add that they were uneatable, tasting of nothing but smoke. On another occasion he insisted on climbing

a tree which overhung the river. He dared us to do likewise but I do not
recollect that anyone accepted the challenge.[4]

Lucy, however, thought that she did accept:

He wasn't happy until he had persuaded us all to climb the same tree, stopping at different stages according to our courage or the resisting power of
our under-clothing. I climbed to the top on a level with him. When he was
back on the ground his collar was off, his tie crooked, his hair pointed to
all the ends of Heaven, and he shouted and sang at the top of his voice.[5]

Frances and LG were not able to go back to Caernarvonshire
together until the very end of LG's life; but they always looked back
on these two weeks as a special time. In 1925 he reminded her that
they had climbed a nearby hill with an ancient British fort at the top,
and attended the annual sheepdog trials above Beddgelert, which was
where he had first been 'stricken' with love for her.[6] Later still Frances
likewise remembered 'wandering in your old haunts by the river –
where you and I were first attracted to each other'.[7] A seed had been
planted that would grow and flourish when they got back to London
in the autumn.

LG was briefly back in London by 11 September, but then set off
again almost immediately for Scotland, where protocol required him
to spend a few days with the King and Queen at Balmoral. 'I am not
cut out for Court life,' he wrote to Margaret. 'I detest it. The whole
atmosphere reeks of Toryism.'[8] From there he went on to visit the
millionaire philanthropist Andrew Carnegie at Skibo castle ('I am going
to stay with a much richer man than the King,' he told Megan, '& a
man who made all that money himself'),[9] then home by way of several
of his Cabinet colleagues at their estates in the borders. He returned
to London on 24 September; two days later *The Times* thought it worth
reporting that the Chancellor of the Exchequer had actually visited the
Treasury!

Margaret stayed in Wales until at least mid-October. But Frances
had made such a hit with Megan that at the end of the holidays it was
decided that Megan should change school to become a weekly boarder
at Allenswood, going back to 11 Downing Street at weekends. This
conveniently enabled LG to continue to see Frances on the pretext of
visiting Megan – and sometimes to invite her to Sunday tea at Downing

Street as well, when she would be pressed to play the piano while the whole family joined lustily in singing Welsh hymns; after which, she wrote, 'I took the Tube back to school in Wimbledon.'[10] But already her entrée into high political circles was causing excitement – and doubtless envy – among her friends, one of whom wrote to her at the end of the autumn term:

> I hope you have had a jolly term & aren't frightfully tired. How are the Lloyd Georges? Does Megan still eat with her fingers? You might write & tell me what sort of time you had there. I was greatly thrilled when I heard you had been there.[11]

During 1912 Frances started doing odd bits of work for LG in her spare time. The first thing he asked her to do was to read and summarise a French book on land reform during her Easter holidays. Land was always the subject closest to LG's heart, and that year he was preparing an ambitious campaign on the subject. On the envelope of a letter from another friend, postmarked 10 April, Frances scribbled a note to herself: 'Land Reform. Jesse Collings MP'. Since Collings, President of the Rural League, was an ally of LG in his campaign, this suggests that she was already doing more than just translating.* Soon she was attending debates in the House and passing down the sort of congratulatory notes LG always expected his family and women friends to send him, after which he would discreetly take her out, first for tea and later for dinner. He was adept at playing up his need for her.

> I remember going to the House of Commons to see him for some instructions on the work I was doing for him one summer's evening before the House rose for the recess. He was very tired and his eyes were red-rimmed with late-night sittings. 'I have to flog myself, otherwise I could not go on,' he said to me. My heart went out to him, and I wanted more than anything else to help him.[13]

As their relationship developed, LG used to go down to Allenswood once a week to see Megan and then take Frances out afterwards. He

---

* On the back of the envelope Frances wrote another curiously assorted packing list, presumably for Easter at the seaside. 'Safety pins Blanco Knickers Bathing dress Belt Wh.Petticoat? Listerine Hairpins Ribbons N.& Cottons Stamps Buttons.'[12]

also began writing her letters, which sadly do not survive. In her diary, which she started only in 1914, Frances described his regret that she had taken him at his word and burned them.

> C. said this morning he wished I had kept the love-letters he wrote me two years ago.* But I promised to burn them, and they are all destroyed, though, as he says, 'every word of them meant business'.[14]

He sent these letters quite openly, with 'Chancellor of the Exchequer' embossed on the envelope. Years later Frances still recalled 'the look of strong disapproval' on the face of the headmistress as she handed the staff their letters after morning prayers.[15] In her 1914 diary, however, she implied that they were not yet exactly love letters.

> He is never tired of talking of that summer when he used to come to Allenswood, & we both felt there was something between us, though it was not yet expressed – and of the following autumn, when we used to meet once a week, and I hovered between doubt and longing, dread and desire.[16]

A few early letters do survive. The first definitely dated note was written on 25 July 1912 from the Treasury and addressed to Frances at 17 Alderbrook Road.

> Dear Miss Stevenson,
>   If you are disengaged could you call at 11 Downing St at 6 pm tomorrow (Friday)?[17]

The signature has been carefully cut out, suggesting that this may indeed have been the first letter she ever had from him. The timing is intriguing, since LG also wrote to Margaret the next day and added a slightly defensive note, telling her that 'Rufus and I are going to the opera tonight. Will that suit Madame?'[18] Did he fear that Margaret might suspect he was keeping less innocent company? The two operas he could have seen were Puccini's *La Fanciulla del West* at Covent Garden or – probably more to LG's taste – Léhar's *Gipsy Love* at Daly's in Leicester Square. Both performances started at 8.15, allowing ample

---

* 'C' was code for Chancellor. It was only when LG became Prime Minister that she took to calling him 'D' in her diary.

time to see Frances first – unless of course she came too.

Another puzzling letter, undated, was written on a Saturday from Walton Heath Golf Club and addressed, somewhat oddly, to Royal Holloway to await collection: maybe Frances was attending a college reunion.

> Dear Miss Stevenson,
>
> There is an article in today's Times on agricultural wages which I must reply to at once. I have sent up to town for the papers. Do you think it would be possible for you to run over in the car by about five o'clock or 5.30 this afternoon to assist?
>
> Yours sincerely,
>
> D. Lloyd George

Enclosed is a Treasury card with possible train times scrawled in LG's writing:

> 4.15 Worplesdon
> 4.20 Woking[19]

But if he was sending his car, why did she need the train times? And if she was at Royal Holloway – at Egham – she would not have caught a train from Worplesdon or Woking anyway.

His next note, dated 6 August, is significantly less formal. It was addressed to Budleigh Salterton, in south Devon, where Frances was on holiday, and included a printed copy of a speech on women's suffrage that he had made at Bath the previous November. Clearly they had already discussed it. At Criccieth in August Lucy Masterman had noted in her diary that Miss Stevenson – 'a very nice girl' – was 'slightly bitten with suffragetism, about which George never fails to rag her.'[20] LG's position on the issue was ambivalent. He had long supported the women's cause in principle – he always claimed that he had been converted by seeing A Doll's House more than twenty years earlier[21] – but he wanted a wide extension of the suffrage to women on the same terms as men, not a narrow extension that would benefit only wealthy women (like Mrs Pankhurst) who were likely to vote Tory. This was the rational and democratic line he took in his speech at Bath.[22] But his support for a manhood suffrage Bill that could be amended to include women simply infuriated the militants, who believed he was double-crossing them: illogically they blamed him, their most prominent supporter in the Cabinet, for failing to deliver their demands, more than they did Asquith and others who openly opposed them. LG was bewildered by their hostility. 'I am the only man in the Cabinet who could render them effective help,' he complained to his brother William, '& yet they have pursued me with unexampled malignity.'[23] His meetings were regularly broken up by 'female lunatics'; in July he was attacked with a hammer by a male suffragist; and there was worse to come. Understandably he was finding it hard to maintain his sympathy in the face of the increasingly violent tactics of the suffragettes.

Feminist though she was, Frances too disapproved of the militants. But LG sent her his Bath speech to be sure that she understood his position.

Dear Miss Stevenson,
    Here is the 'Bath bun' I promised you.
    I leave Thursday morning for Marienbad.*
    Will you send me notes on Green's book to
        Hotel Stern,
        Marienbad,
        Bohemia,
        Austria.
    I hope to be back in town first week in September. I trust you are enjoying your Devon visit in spite of the weather.
    Ever sincerely,
    D. Lloyd George[24]

LG's trip to Bohemia – accompanied by Rufus Isaacs – was supposedly for his health, though he always combined holidays with work. He wrote to Maggie regularly while he was away, reporting in characteristic hypochondriac's detail on the state of his kidneys, but insisting after only a few days that he was missing her and wanted to come home.[25] To Megan he complained that it rained as much at Marienbad as it did at Criccieth. 'I do wish I were there with you & Mamie & I wish it every day & all day.'[26] But a few days later he wrote a much longer

---

* Marienbad – now Mariánské Lázně – in what is today the Czech Republic, was then part of the Austrian empire.

and more discursive letter to Frances (who was still in Budleigh Salterton) – their first substantial communication to survive. It is not a love letter, but it breathes an easy familiarity, covering not only her work for him, but his view of the suffrage question and even French literature.

Dear Miss Stevenson,

Thanks for the second note book. They are admirably done. The Attorney General is now perusing your first. I have a few suggestions to make when we all meet in town. The Index is a great improvement.

I fear the 6th will be too late for me. I shall be in town on the 3rd & 4th & may have to leave for Wales that morning. I should like to turn you on to two or three books. Will you let me know whether you can get off.

I never recommended Candide. I do not care for it. It is much too coarse.

I am glad you liked my Bath speech. It represents my genuine convictions on the great question. I had then hoped to be instrumental in bringing about a realisation of the women's hopes for freedom this year & I was looking forward to taking a hand. The militants have however successfully & as I think wantonly & maliciously wrecked these hopes.

There are two of them here annoying me, sent from England for that purpose. That is how I am to be encouraged on the right path, and they expect Cabinet Ministers to love Women's Suffrage.

Weather very mixed here. So delighted to hear you prefer Wales to Devonshire for Devon is a beautiful land.

Ever sincerely
D. Lloyd George[27]

By this time he and Frances had evidently discussed the possibility that she might work for him on a permanent basis. She was keen to get away from teaching, and at his suggestion had started learning shorthand. Her friend Mary Phillips was undazzled by the glamour of working for the Chancellor, however, and suggested that Frances should be careful.

Darling Frances,

I would *love* to see you . . .

I was intensely interested in your Lloyd George news. Are you a Liberal? Do tell me, do you like him? It ought to be a lovely post *if* . . . Personally

I don't admire him . . .
    Lots of love, Mary[28]

In fact Frances continued to undertake odd tasks for LG over the autumn of 1912. He was in London for just two days at the beginning of September before going to Criccieth for another three weeks. (Parliament did not sit again until mid-October.) But Frances was summoned by two telegrams from his personal private secretary, J. T. Davies, to call on him at the Treasury on the 5th;[29] and a week later she received another letter from his official private secretary.

Dear Miss Stevenson,
    The Chancellor wishes me to tell you that he would like the book which you mentioned, ordered and sent to him at Criccieth.
    His bookseller, as you probably know, is Hugh Rees Ltd., 5 Regent St., W.
    You have probably already made arrangements about buying books for the Chancellor but if you like I will order them for you.
    Yours sincerely,
    H. P. Hamilton[30]

On 3 October J. T. Davies asked her to call at the Treasury next day between 5.30 and 6.00; and two days later he wrote again:

Have you made an *author* catalogue of the Chancellor's Library. If not would you like to do it or are you engaged in it at present?[31]

Frances obviously did perform this not very urgent-sounding chore, since three weeks later Davies wrote again to ask: 'Did you take the catalogue with you? I cannot find it anywhere.'[32]

At the end of September LG took Megan and Frances to the theatre to see a comedy called *Little Miss Llewellyn* at the Vaudeville. The following week he wrote to Frances, with a fractionally more intimate greeting:

My dear Miss Stevenson
    I am delighted to hear you enjoyed your visit to the theatre on Saturday with Megan & myself. We both missed you on Sunday.
    I am looking forward to seeing you tomorrow at the Treasury about 5.15. Will you go to Mr Davies' room.

Ever sincerely
D. Lloyd George

I have bought the book on [illegible: possibly 'Germany'] I want you to summarise.[33]

At this stage Frances was still a friend of the whole Lloyd George family. This is clear from two letters from Olwen, who went that autumn to a finishing school in Paris to improve her French. Contrary to her sour memory of half a century later, she had scarcely got there before she was writing a chatty, girlish letter to 'my dear Frances', enclosing another letter for 'my small sister', complaining how bored she was already, and ending: 'Do write soon. Much love, Olwen.'[34] Six weeks later, in mid-November, she wrote again.

177 Rue de Courcelles
Paris XVII

My dear Frances,

Thanks very much for your long letter, which you wrote in spite of your very busy life. My dear! Don't you work too hard, or there will be nothing of you left by the time I come home. Between shorthand & German you will be a very brilliant person. What's the point in learning German though – just for the fun of it or do you mean to do something with it.

I am sorry Allenswood is getting on your nerves. I think I should get sick of it too. My dear! I must tell you what Miss Boyce thinks of me . . .

She then goes on about Miss Boyce and the other girls at the school, where she is now having 'a topping time'. Dick had recently visited her en route to Spain and 'we had a great time together. I simply love Paris now.'

I suppose Megan has been behaving in her usual way. Thank her for all her letters will you – she really has been a perfect brick in writing. Gwilym my beloved brother has not written me a single line since I've been here – isn't he the limit really. Have you heard that it has been arranged for him to go to Cambridge & that he is working for his exams now. I don't suppose he'll get through – he's such a slacker at work. Not like his dear sister . . .

No, I'm not coming home for Xmas as it isn't worth while going home

for 10 days especially as I'm going home Easter. So you simply must come
out here: we would have great sport. But if Father gets a fortnight's holiday
he's going to take me to Biarritz & Dick is coming out to us there . . .

Do write again soon & give me all the news.

Much love to you & Meg.

Olwen[35]

These cannot have been Olwen's only letters from Paris, since she
also told Frances that she wanted to meet more Welsh people and find
a Welsh church there. It happened that Frances had another Welsh
friend – called Sian, another former teacher at Allenswood – who was
also living in Paris at this time. So in early December she wrote to
Sian urging her to get in touch with Olwen. In another long girlish
letter Frances went on to tell her about the work she was doing for
LG and the temptation to follow Sian's example and break away from
teaching.

You are a lucky beggar to go about as you do. I envy you with all my
heart. Aren't you devoutly thankful you left Allenswood, and aren't you
sorry for the poor wretches who are still in the bonds of slavery there? I
don't know how much longer my purgatory is going to last, but at present
I am learning shorthand, as Mr Lloyd George has promised to find me
something to do as soon as I know shorthand. Meanwhile I am doing
some work for him on his Land Bill. It is awfully interesting – I started
it in the summer, you know, & he wants me to go on with it in my spare
time. It is the only thing that keeps me alive here, but it makes all the
difference.

She then described how she was not simply working for LG, but
getting drawn into his family and political world.

I went to the Lloyd Georges the other Sunday, & Miss Dilys Jones was
there. She sang heaps of songs, & I played her accompaniments, & it was
ripping . . . The Greek consul, & Harold Spender [a leading Liberal jour-
nalist] & Mr Masterman were at Downing St that night, so it was awfully
jolly – they talked all about the war . . .*

* That is, the latest Balkan War in which Greece, Montenegro, Bulgaria and Serbia had
come together to fight Turkey.

Did I tell you that the Mastermans were making up a party this Xmas for Switzerland, & that Lloyd George was going, & some of my friends & myself? Well, it is too sickening, but Parliament only has about a week at Xmas, so there is no time to go. I am awfully sick about it. Perhaps it will come off another time, though.*

Frances's life was not entirely taken up with the Lloyd George family, however, since she also told Sian about a 'jolly' dance she had been to, when she got to bed at five in the morning; as well as more school news. She then disclosed a further important step in her emergence as a thoroughly emancipated young woman.

By the way, I must tell you something which may interest you & may not. I have completely renounced any religious ideas which I may have had whatever. I don't believe in anything, that is to say, beyond this mortal life. It is a nice state of affairs, I expect you will think, but it's been coming on gradually for a long time, & that's how things stand at present. I thought I would tell you, as we have discussed things of this kind from time to time – theology & philosophy, I mean. I have been reading some of Anatole France's books lately, & they make me fearfully cynical, but all the same it was not that influenced me, as I had come to my conclusion long before I started on him.

It would be interesting to know whether this renunciation was influenced by her conversations with LG, who claimed to have undergone a somewhat similar loss of faith when he was about twelve – though all his life he loved Welsh hymns and sermons and, as a politician heavily dependent on Welsh Nonconformity for his power base, never ceased to invoke the ethics and employ the language of Christianity. He and Frances certainly discussed their respective paths to religious disillusion many years later, though Frances then dated her loss of faith rather earlier, to the time of her grandmother's death when she was fifteen, when her prayers for her grandmother's life were not answered.[36] Now Frances told Sian that she had discussed the subject at Downing Street that summer with a leading Nonconformist supporter of LG, the

---

* This possibility seems to contradict Olwen's idea that LG was going to take her to Biarritz at Christmas. In the event, neither holiday came off. The Commons did indeed have just a week's break, returning on 30 December.

Revd T. C. Williams, whom she described familiarly as 'a great dear', but unfortunately they were interrupted.

'Do you think we shall ever have our little flat?' Frances asked Sian finally. Living at home with her parents – when she was not at school – was clearly becoming increasingly difficult.

> Megan sends her love and hopes you are behaving. She seems rather doubtful about it – the behaving part . . .
> Ever so much love & a great big kiss from Frances.[37]

Meanwhile LG wrote to Frances on 16 October – a Wednesday – the envelope addressed in his distinctive pencil scrawl.

> Dear Miss Stevenson,
>   Will you bring Olive Schreiner's book with you tomorrow.
>   Come to Downing St – 5 o'clock – for tea.[38]

The book referred to was *Woman and Labour*, published in 1911, which he had presumably lent her. Evidently it was half-term and Megan was back in Downing Street for the week. The previous day LG had written to tell Maggie, who remained in Criccieth, how he was proposing to entertain her.

> Sarah takes charge of Megan. I have tickets for the Winter's Tale tonight. Tomorrow zoo with Percy Illingworth.[39]*

The visit to the zoo evidently did not come off, or else it was such a success that it was repeated a few days later, since on Sunday 20th, LG wrote again to Maggie:

> Megan & I having been for a walk already through the Parks are now starting for the Illingworths & the zoo.
>   Tonight the Mastermans are supping with us.
>   Megan is looking very well.[40]

* *The Winter's Tale* was Harley Granville Barker's ground-breaking production at the Savoy, with Lillah McCarthy as Hermione. Percy Illingworth was the Government Chief Whip; his children must have been much younger than Megan, since he only married in 1907.

LG does not mention Frances, but it is very likely that she was part of these activities.

Also dating from this autumn term is a very curious letter written by the ten-year-old Megan to her parents ('Dear Tada & Mamie'). It was torn up and presumably never sent; but Frances preserved the pieces. After telling them that she had seen Dick on Sunday and had a letter from Olwen 'who is enjoying France', she signs off conventionally enough 'With best love from Megan arfon xxxx',* but then adds a bizarre post-script: 'I will like you all the better if you shorten the holidays. I will see you both less.' To which Frances has added a further note: 'Miss Stevenson will hate you if you shorten her holidays.'[41] One can only guess what childish tantrum occasioned this. But it adds to the impression that Frances enjoyed a position of intimacy and familiarity with the whole family.

It is clear from her letter to Sian that she needed little persuasion to give up teaching in order to work for LG full time. 'When the possibility . . . was put forward,' she wrote, 'it did not take me long to make up my mind. The point of no return had been reached – and passed.' Shortly before the end of the Christmas term, therefore, she gave in her notice to Allenswood, to the displeasure of the headmistress, who already disapproved of Lloyd George. 'That man has upset me enough with his Insurance Stamps,' she raged, 'and now he takes away one of my staff.' She tried to persuade Frances to change her mind, saying that she could have reached 'the top of the tree'. 'But I don't want to reach the top of *this* tree,' Frances replied.[42]

Two days before Christmas LG wrote her an elaborately formal request for help over the holidays.

My dear Miss Stevenson,

I wonder whether you could find time to render me a little assistance over my doctors trouble.

I want someone to go carefully through the file of the British Medical Journal for the past 18 months to extract attacks made by the medical profession on Friendly Society practice.

Should you be free & feel disposed to help a hard-worked & worried Minister would you kindly see Mr Davies at the Treasury sometime in course of tomorrow. I shall be out of town.

* Arfon was Megan's middle name.

I only bar work on Xmas or boxing day!
Wish your parents & sister a merry Xmas & a happy new year.
Ever sincerely,
D. Lloyd George[43]

The greeting to Frances's parents is interesting. Evidently by now she had introduced LG to them. Like the headmistress, they could not have been unaware of the number of letters he was writing her, or of the fact that she was working for him. They could not exactly disapprove, but in view of LG's reputation they must have worried about what she was getting into. LG, for his part, was plainly exerting all his fabled charm to reassure them.

Despite his generous allowance of two days' holiday, Frances clearly wasted no time. The postal service did not stop for Christmas either, and on Boxing Day J. T. Davies wrote again:

Dear Miss Stevenson.
    The Chancellor thinks these extracts are very good so you might go on getting some more . . .

He then explained precisely the sort of material LG was looking for.

I hope you understand all this.
You will be here at 10.30 on Sat. won't you? . . .
How did the hockey match go off?[44]

The Lloyd George family did not go to Criccieth for Christmas that year, but spent the holiday at Tadworth, near Walton Heath in Surrey, where LG's friend and golfing companion, Sir George Riddell – proprietor of the *News of the World* – was building him a house on the golf course.* From there LG also wrote to Frances on Boxing Day.

My dear Miss Stevenson,
    Davies tells me that he has sent you sample extracts from the British Medical Journal & wants me to write you whether these are the sort of thing I want. He is quite right. If you come across more extracts from

* There was not then thought to be anything corrupt in politicians accepting valuable gifts from wealthy supporters.

speeches, articles & letters demanding a *national* income limit against a local income limit which I proposed then you might copy those also please.

Can you bring as many as you have ready to the Treasury to Mr Davies' room by 10.00 on Saturday morning. I shall be in town & should like to go through them. I have a meeting at the Treasury & you might work in Mr Davies' room.

Megan gave me a dear little penknife worked by your clever Dundee friend. I must show it to you.

Ever sincerely,

D. Lloyd George[45]

Megan also wrote to Frances from Walton Heath on 22 December. (Evidently Olwen had come home for Christmas after all.)

Dearest Pussy,

I wish you a merry Xmas & a happy new year. I thought you would like these books. Olwen & Gwilym are going to town tomorrow & Gwilym has got to hang on to Olwen the whole time in case she is kidnapped.* Zulu [the dog] sends his best love to you.

I am going to the theatre on Boxing day . . . It is called 'Sleeping Beauty'† & we are going in the evening & then we are motoring down here afterwards.

Best *love* & kisses

Megan arfon xxxxxxxxxxxxxxxxxxxxxxxxxxxxxxxxxxxxxxxxxxxxxxxx
xxxxxxxxxxxxxxxxxxxxxxxxxxxxxxxxxxxxxxxxxxxxxxxxxxxxxxxxxxxxxx

The kisses fill the whole of the rest of the page.[46]

Then a few days later – possibly on Christmas Day – Megan wrote a thank-you letter, the greeting decorated with a child's drawing of a cat, the word 'pussy' and the request 'Write soon'.

Dearest Pussy

Thank you ever so much for the spiflicating little book you sent me. I hope you have had a jolly Xmas. I have had tons of presents this Xmas . . .

We have been playing whist this evening (ripping fun). I must end because I have got Loads to write.

* Presumably by suffragettes.
† This was not the Tchaikovsky ballet, but a pantomime at Drury Lane.

xxxxxxx With best love from Megan arfon xxxxxxx a hug[47]

But 'jolly' was probably not the word for Frances's Christmas. She was going to Scotland for the New Year to think hard about what she was going to do. LG had made her a proposal. She had a choice to make that would determine the rest of her life.

4

THE CHOICE

Frances went to Scotland on 30 December 1912 to spend the New Year with friends in or near Dundee. We cannot be certain who they were. They may have been the family of a college contemporary, Dorothy Brown; or maybe the Browns were simply another family spending Christmas in the area. We know only that Megan had given her father for Christmas a knife worked by Frances's 'clever Dundee friend'. We do not know whether Frances realised that going to Scotland would force her to face her dilemma in its sharpest form. She may simply have got away from London in order to think.

Towards the end of the year LG had made it clear that they could not continue as they were. It was difficult to go on meeting surreptitiously at Allenswood or the Treasury on the excuse that Frances was doing odd jobs for him. He wanted to be able to see her legitimately every day. This would only be possible if she came to work for him officially as a member of his staff. He had no doubt of her ability to do the job – she had presumably learned shorthand by now – or of her discretion; and female secretaries were beginning to be accepted, in business and (more slowly) in Whitehall. But of course LG wanted more than that: he wanted to make her his mistress.

There is no knowing whether they were already lovers. In view of LG's reputation, it seems quite likely; and we know that Frances had 'nerve enough for anything'. But she also had a proper and conventional side to her character, so she may have held out. Anyway it was a very different thing to put the relationship on an established basis such as he was proposing. He was inviting her, as she put it many years later, to become his secretary 'on his own terms, which were in direct conflict with my essentially Victorian upbringing'.[1]

LG made no bones about what those terms were. He was in love with her, and wanted her to be with him as much as discretion would permit. He told her that his wife neglected him and did not give him the support he needed to carry on his work. But he would not risk any scandal, would not leave Maggie, and could not marry Frances. Just as he had made it brutally clear to Maggie twenty-five years earlier that he was ready to thrust 'even love itself under the wheels of my Juggernaut', so now – at the height of his career, with the premiership itself within his grasp – he told Frances the same thing. He represented this not simply as personal ambition, of course, but as his duty to the great causes he was in politics to serve: his obligation to the poor and downtrodden who looked to him as their champion. To emphasise his point, he gave her a life of the great Irish leader Charles Stewart Parnell.*

Parnell was the charismatic leader of the Irish Home Rule party in the 1880s, whose policy of rural militancy and obstructing business in the House of Commons had persuaded Gladstone to devote his last years to trying to put a Home Rule Bill through Parliament, splitting the Liberal party in the process. But Parnell had fallen from grace in 1890 with the revelation that he had been having an affair with the wife of another Irish Member, William O'Shea. The scandal ended his career and set back the cause of Home Rule for a generation. LG had been a newly elected MP at the time of Parnell's downfall and had no doubt of the moral of his story. As the leader of an historic movement who carried on his shoulders the hopes of millions, Parnell had shown irresponsible conduct. 'Here he is,' he wrote to Maggie, 'quite a young man having attained the greatest career of this century, dashing it to pieces because he couldn't restrain a single passion. A thousand pities . . . We have our spurs to win & this fellow by his idiot misconduct ruins us all.'[2] 'He must be a base selfish wretch,' he added some days later.[3] Over the next twenty years, however, LG himself more than once risked his own career for a woman. In truth he did not condemn Parnell for having an affair with Kitty O'Shea – that was human, or at least male, nature – but for letting it get into the divorce courts. Parnell's crime, in his view, was to have put his love of Kitty before the interests of Ireland. Twenty-five years on again, he was equally critical of

* Presumably the two-volume biography by Barry O'Brien, published in 1898.

Edward VIII for putting Wallis Simpson ahead of his duty as King. Even then, Frances noted, he was still 'very anti-Kitty O'Shea'. But by now she had long experience of LG's double standard of sexual relations. 'He is always inclined to blame the woman when it is a question of a man choosing her or his career – he is always for the immolation of the woman.'[4]

But at least he was brutally honest with her. In many ways it was an uninviting prospect that he was offering her at the end of 1912. If Frances accepted, she would be condemning herself to a life of secrecy, giving up her youth to a much older man who could never publicly acknowledge her and who would deny her at the first whiff of scandal. It was unlikely that she would ever be able to marry him, since his wife was younger than he was. In the meantime she must give up the expectation of a respectable marriage to a man of her own age, or any realistic hope of having children. It was a huge gamble, since he might easily tire of her in a few years anyway. Moreover she would deeply upset her parents.

On the other hand, she was thrillingly in love with LG, and believed that he truly loved her. She was dazzled by the glamour of the world that he opened up to her, the power of his position at the heart of the government, and the prospect of living and working in that world herself. She believed that he was the greatest political figure of the age (he was certainly the most fascinating) and wanted to help him advance his causes and overcome his enemies. If she had qualms about breaking up his family, LG had convinced her that Maggie was not, and had not been for years, a good wife to him. She was no longer binding his wounds, healing his bruises and 'stimulating him to fresh exertion' as he required; nor was 'Mrs Tim'. He needed Frances to take on this role.

Her instinct was to accept. She was twenty-four, mildly rebellious and desperate to escape the life of a teacher in a girls' boarding school. Above all she was an ardent romantic. Her younger brother wrote to her from school that autumn that she was 'much too advanced to believe in the existence of Love'.[5] But Paul was wrong. She liked to be thought 'advanced'. But in reality, if there was conflict between being advanced – with its implication of promiscuity – and surrendering to Love, Frances would always choose Love. Though her feminism resented the unfairness of it from time to time, the core of her being ultimately relished the idea of subordinating herself – like Ann Veronica – to a man who commanded her complete allegiance. She did not want to spend her life as the wife of a respectable doctor, businessman or civil servant. Presented with the chance of a risky but exciting adventure, her instinct was to follow it where it led her, however much her choice might hurt her parents.

But the decision was made more difficult, and more pressing, by the fact that she had another suitor, who actually proposed to her while she was in Scotland for the New Year. Stuart Brown was exactly the sort of son-in-law John and Louise Stevenson would have wished for. Three years older than Frances, he was educated at Dulwich and King's, Cambridge, where he won a Classics prize. He had entered the India Office in 1909, and was already in the private office of the Secretary of State, Lord Crewe. 'He was in every way a desirable "*parti*",' Frances wrote in her memoirs, 'highly intelligent, musical, a civil servant with a future.' He had fallen in love with her the previous summer – when they had presumably met through his sister Dorothy – and now wanted to marry her. His approach, however, was 'academic rather than romantic'.[6] His letters fully confirm her recollection: he comes over as intelligent, thoroughly decent, but distinctly donnish, with a somewhat laboured classicist's humour. The one he wrote the day after he had proposed to her and been rebuffed – but not, he believed, definitively refused – was typically diffident.

Craigie Barn
Dundee

Dear Miss Stevenson,

I can't forgive myself for the strain I must have put on you last night, and I can't go south without knowing that it had not hurt you. If it would not worry you to let me see you, I will just take my chance and not pester you with a single word. Could you give me some chance of seeing you tomorrow and Tuesday? I really will not worry you, and I will try to go back to things as they were before. Only I am going to wait my chance.

If you could tell me that last night has not upset you, it would be a great help.

Yours ever sincerely,
Stuart Brown

I can't be too grateful for the way you treated all I said last night.[7]

The contrast between this nice young man and the imperious Chancellor of the Exchequer could hardly have been more complete.

According to her autobiography, Frances wrote and told LG about Stuart Brown's proposal. 'L.G. replied at once that I must do what I thought right and that he would not stand in my way. He did not try to persuade me against it; the decision was with *me*.'[8] It is hard to believe that she really had time to write to LG – and get his answer – before turning Brown down. But from the evidence of Brown's letter it would seem that his proposal disturbed her, probably because it confronted her so starkly with the choice before her and the implications of the decision she had in her heart already taken, which she might have hoped to postpone a little longer. If LG did write back to her in the generous terms she describes, she must have burned this letter with his others. Anyway his declared willingness to let her go, if that was what she chose, was well calculated to ensure that she did no such thing. And if this ostensible self-abnegation had not already done the trick, he then doubled the emotional blackmail by writing again.

> Almost immediately I received another urgent letter; it simply said that something terrible had happened and that he needed me. I was unable to imagine what the misfortune could be. I returned to London at once. It was the Marconi scandal which was about to break, with all its threat of ruin and disaster to LG's career . . .[9]

This, as A. J. P. Taylor pointed out, is 'a little puzzling', since 'the first outburst of the [Marconi] affair had passed over in the previous autumn; the real storm blew some months later.'[10] There were no fresh allegations at the beginning of 1913. But LG may well have been worried about it, since he was by no means innocent of the charge that he and Rufus Isaacs had used inside information to indulge in a little profitable speculation in American Marconi shares at a time when the British government was considering a contract with the British company. LG was not a wealthy man: he was always on the look-out for quick ways to make some badly needed money, and careless about how he did it. The idea that there was no connection between the American and British Marconi companies was, even if strictly true, naïve and the ministers' speculation was, at the least, extremely ill-advised. LG would have been in serious trouble if Asquith and most of the Liberal press had not stood by him: he was eventually exonerated only because a parliamentary inquiry divided on strictly party lines. In January this outcome still lay in the future. It was characteristic of LG to make the most of his anxiety to persuade Frances that she could not leave him in his hour of need. When she returned to London she tried to help by trawling the papers for any mention that the American shares were available to the general public.

> However, after many weary but hopeful days I could find nothing to help him. I could only comfort him, talk to him, try to cheer him and help him to cross the raging torrent of political hatred which would gladly have compassed his downfall.[11]

Administering comfort was what she was good at, and she went on supplying it for the next thirty years. According to her own later and maybe starry-eyed account, she knew what she was doing.

> When I returned to London from Scotland . . . in response to LG's letter I returned to place myself in his hands unconditionally, that is to say, on *his* conditions . . . He had made me realise that I was necessary to him. I knew instinctively that in the relationship I was contemplating there would be hurts and humiliations, but it seemed to me that nothing I could ever do would be so worth while as to help this man with whom I wished to join my life.[12]

In years to come they fixed the date of their unofficial 'marriage' quite precisely to 21 January 1913, and celebrated their informal anniversary on that day.* Ironically this was just three days before LG's real wedding anniversary: that year he was celebrating his silver wedding. Among Frances's papers there is preserved a form of contract, written in her handwriting on 11 Downing Street headed paper.

> We, the undersigned, hereby pledge our word that we give our love to each other, wholly and entirely, whatever happens; to cherish each other in sick-

---

* Letters from LG to his brother William appear to cast doubt on the date, since they record that Maggie was in London at that time and accompanied him to Windsor on 21 January. But LG returned to London with Churchill for a few hours in the afternoon, ostensibly to work, before returning to Windsor for dinner.[13] Is it possible that he actually snatched a couple of hours with Frances to consummate their 'marriage'? Or did they celebrate the wrong date?

ness and in health; each one to put the other first, before all the world; to give up everything before giving up one another; in addition to this, to give one another a sweet friendship and mutual interest and understanding in the affairs of everyday life; to let none other come between the sacredness of our love, now or ever, till death do us part.[14]

This was of course romantic eyewash, the purest wishful thinking on Frances's part. The whole point and basis of the relationship on which she was entering was that LG was *not* going to put her first before all the world – neither before his wife and family, nor before his career. Indeed, much as she might have wished him to put her before his wife, she specifically did not want him to sacrifice his career: she wanted above everything to help him in his career, in a way that she believed Maggie failed to do. She probably never even showed this soppy document to LG: it was certainly not signed by either of them.

On the other hand there does survive – on the back of a medical bill dated January 1913[*] – a short poem written in LG's best handwriting (though with a couple of corrections):

> The earth & I are filled with tender yearning;
> Our souls o'erflow in mute expectancy.
> These heart-throbs set the passionate spirit burning: –
> The earth for Spring, & I, my love, for thee.

The word 'passionate' in line three was originally 'pent-up'; and 'my love' in line four replaces the original 'dear love'.

That is definitely LG. But equally certainly *not* by LG is another poem that Frances preserved among her papers from this period. It does not sound like Stuart Brown either, and is not in his file. So it is a mystery. Composed of nine four-line stanzas, it is too long to print in full; but parts of it are worth quoting, first as an indication that Frances was never short of admirers, and second as further evidence of the impression she left on everyone who knew her of an exceptionally sweet and loving disposition.

---

[*] The bill, from Dr Winton of 43 Worple Road, Wimbledon, was for professional services and medicine supplied to 'Miss Stephenson' [*sic*] eighteen months earlier, but was dated January 1913, with a note requesting early payment.[15]

To F.L.S.

. . .

(4)   Last night she kissed me thrice – we two alone.
      She talked to me for five brief minutes' space,
      Just for that little time she seemed my own,
      All night I heard her voice, and felt her face

(5)   Warm against mine; and in the cloudy sky
      I saw her, with her own sweet angel's smile.
      Well is she called St Frances; but on high
      Her house should be, that earth may not defile

(6)   Her simple, sweet and child-like innocence.
      She is too gentle on the earth to stay . . .

(7)   Frances! how happy they who call you friend,
      Sure of your love in praise and help and blame,
      You, motherly yet childlike to the end,
      Though changed from day to day, though still the same . . .

(9)   . . .
      So let the concentration of my mind
      Give her more strength, to speak, live as she ought,
      And keep her pure and loving, true and kind.[16]

'Motherly yet childlike' perfectly describes the attraction Frances held
for LG. The idea that she was almost too saintly for this world also
links her uncannily to LG's beloved Mair. LG often said that Frances
in some way filled the gap left by the loss of his favourite daughter. If
the ghost of Mair adds a slightly queasy hint of incest to his relationship with Frances, the sexual element was only one aspect of that many-
layered relationship, which was why it lasted so long. But Frances
clearly knew from the beginning that one of the roles she filled was
that of substitute for the departed Mair, since she too wrote a poem
around this time dedicated to Mair's shade. It is written on the back
of a letter that LG wrote her from Avignon in February 1913 – just a
month after they were 'married'.

O cause of bitterest grief to one beloved!
  Not yet the shadows lengthened on thy way.
When swiftly thou wert drawn to wider spheres,
  To hold more perfect sway.

But oh! If ought the spirits wot of us –
  Still be the guardian angel for my dear,
And let thine aureole's light reflect on him,
  To make his pathway clear![17]

Thus Frances seemed not merely to acknowledge Mair's prior place in her lover's heart, but almost to ask her posthumous blessing for her own relations with him.

When Frances plucked up the courage to tell her parents what she had done, they were predictably horrified.

I decided to make a confession to my mother, to seek from her some form of forgiveness or reassurance that redemption was possible, or might be. But with her strong and definite moral outlook she turned on me the whole of her anger at the thought that her daughter could be capable of such an action . . . It was useless for me to try to defend myself. The excoriating contempt which met my apologia made me deeply conscious of the barrier which had come between us. She actually quoted the classical words: 'I would rather see you dead at my feet.'

To her embarrassment, her parents asked to see LG, so he invited them to dinner in Downing Street. It is not clear whether Frances was present. Presumably he deployed all his charm to try to reassure them. He could usually disarm anyone when he put his mind to it. But on this occasion he failed, and the attempt, Frances wrote, was not repeated. 'I was sorry for L.G. but angry with my parents . . . My mother never forgave L.G., and I think that to the end of her life she was hoping that I would leave him.'[18] In fact an accommodation was eventually reached. The Stevensons were never happy with the situation, and Louise continued to hope that Frances might yet make a respectable marriage. There were occasional storms. 'They think I am his plaything,' Frances wrote bitterly after one such crisis in 1915, '& that he will fling me aside when he has finished with me – or else they think that there will be a scandal and that we shall all be disgraced.'[19] But they did not disown her, or cast her out. Gradually they accepted the choice she had made, and in due course exchanged perfectly civil greetings, and even Christmas presents, with LG over the succeeding years.

Meanwhile Frances started work at the Treasury as one of the Chancellor's private secretaries.

5

A WOMAN IN WHITEHALL

Female secretaries were still fairly unusual in government departments before 1914, but it was typical of Lloyd George to be a pioneer in this respect as in others.* He had already upset the Treasury mandarins soon after he became Chancellor by introducing a female shorthand typist in place of the male writer who used to transcribe his notes in longhand. Frances was evidently more than a typist – and therefore more of an affront. The regular officials, she later recalled, 'definitely resented this intrusion by a young female into their domain'.[1] But LG had now been Chancellor for nearly five years and was in a strong position to overrule them.

His official private secretary was a thirty-three-year-old high-flier called Horace Hamilton, who served successive Chancellors for six years from 1912 before moving on and up, to finish his career as Permanent Secretary at the Board of Trade from 1927 to 1937. A note he sent Frances in May 1913 illustrates the leisurely habits of Whitehall in those pre-war days.

Dear Miss Stevenson,

Will you be good enough to be at the Treasury at 10 tomorrow morning? I hope with luck (!) to rise early enough to struggle there at that hour &

---

* The Foreign Office, for instance, had sixteen lady typists – or 'typewriters' as they were called until 1907 – who were kept strictly segregated. Their numbers expanded during the war, but it was not until 1925 that the first women were admitted to the administrative grade.

perhaps you will speak to me about some things the Chancellor wants
produced by 10.15!

Yours sincerely

H. P. Hamilton[2]

Frances's dealings with Hamilton were purely formal. By contrast
she quickly made a friend of LG's other private secretary, J. T. Davies,
a Welsh-speaking former teacher who had also joined the Civil Service
by an unconventional route. He and Frances shared a room and got
on well from the start. 'JT' – as he was always known – took her under
his wing with great kindness and no trace of resentment. He evidently
knew of her special relationship with his Chief and was happy to act
as a discreet go-between, while ensuring that there were no awkward
confrontations when Maggie came to London. For most of these first
two years, indeed – when letters from LG are still few and before
Frances had started keeping a diary – their relationship is visible mainly
through the letters JT wrote her whenever she was away from the office,
as she was remarkably often.

In fact JT himself went on his honeymoon just a few weeks after
Frances started work. LG too was away in the south of France with
Rufus Isaacs, but wrote from Avignon asking Frances to buy a wedding
present.* (He could never do anything for himself.) He still addressed
her formally, as if a letter sent to the office might not be altogether
private.

Dear Miss Stevenson

. . .

I had no notion that Mr Davies was going off so soon. Will you go to
Carrington's Regent Street & buy him something nice to give him for me.
Ask them to send it to the Treasury for me. You can then hand it over to
him. You might consult him as to what he would like.[3]

Later that spring Frances was ill. JT sent her a get-well note, enclosing
a letter from LG.

---

* Parliament did not meet until 10 March, so LG had plenty of time to go away in
February. It is nevertheless remarkable that at this moment of high political tension,
when LG and Isaacs were embroiled in the Marconi scandal and the crisis in Ulster was
bringing the United Kingdom to the brink of civil war, the Chancellor and the Attorney-
General should have been playing golf in Nice with the Leader of the Opposition, Bonar
Law.

Dear Miss Stevenson,

I hope you are much better. The Chancellor has been enquiring very earnestly about you but doesn't want you to hurry back before you are fit. He wanted to know whether it was toothache again. I said I did not think so as you had no 'ollow tooth.

Very sincerely,

J.T.D.

LG's enclosure is still formally addressed, but light in tone.

My dear Miss Stevenson

I am so sorry to hear you are run down. I fear the great rush we have had recently over the budget which has kept you all late must have been too much for you. As the Land Campaign is not to be started just yet you must take a short holiday so as to be quite fit when the great pressure comes later on.

You must not worry. That is why I sent you some light literature yesterday & I am sending you some more with this letter now. I thought you would like to know what a Conservative thinks of your Chief!

If you are going out of town for a rest perhaps you could call at the Treasury on your way.

Ever sincerely

D Lloyd George

I am writing on the Bench in the House.[4]

Two days later LG wrote again. This time he addressed the envelope himself, but characteristically managed to get it wrong, writing Aldeburgh instead of Alderbrook Road (where she was still living with her parents).

My dear Miss Stevenson

I am off to Wales first thing tomorrow morning but hope to return Monday. I think you would do well to take a few days holiday.

As to Tuesday next will you let me know whether Miss Wolff can come Tuesday at 4. If you write here tomorrow Brynawelon Criccieth & post it early I'll get it Saturday morning.

Sincerely

D Lloyd George

I am taking Olwen & Megan with me.[5]

It is interesting that LG thought it safe for Frances to write to him at Criccieth – in her official capacity, of course.

While LG was away, JT wrote Frances a note that nicely illustrates the friendliness of their relations.

Dear Miss Stevenson,
Chancellor has gone to Criccieth to a funeral. He is coming back Sunday night or Monday. Hope you will continue to improve. The air seems very light with the C of E away. It would be lighter still if you were here.
Yours,
J.T.D.[6]

This letter was followed on LG's return by another – marked URGENT – characteristic of the Chancellor's imperious demands. When he wanted her, she was expected to interrupt her convalescence – she was staying with friends in Worplesdon – and be there.

Dear Miss Stevenson,
The Chancellor came back tonight & is going to trouble you to come up tomorrow (Tuesday) morning just for a short time to the Treasury. He says he will not worry you after that & you can have as long a holiday as you like (perhaps) . . .
I hope you will take one of these trains as I told C of E I would look them up & send them to you. He is rather worried about this letter to The Times and no-one can help him but you he says.*
Thank you for your nice letter. Will tell you all the news in the morning.
Yours very sincerely
J. T. Davies[7]

There is an intriguing possibility here, since LG had arranged to meet Maggie in Downing Street that Tuesday, but wrote apologising for having missed her, saying he had been unavoidably detained. 'I was so disappointed *hen gariad*' (old darling).[8] Assuming that Frances came in to the Treasury as requested, it is likely that she – rather than the

---

* LG does not appear to have written, or replied to, any letter to The Times at this period.

customs officials he blamed – was the cause of his being late. After this Frances returned to Worplesdon and LG went to the house at Walton Heath built for him by Sir George Riddell, where he now spent most of his time.* JT wrote to Frances again on the Friday – a letter that gives a flavour of LG's chaotic methods.

Dear Miss Stevenson

There is no news to give you. Everything very quiet. The Chancellor was up here today & left about 5 o'c . . .

I hope you are having a nice rest. The Chancellor took 3 of your little black books with him, and all the land things are at Walton. I wonder if we shall ever see them again. If you happen to go to Walton you might see to them & to any stray letters.

I haven't heard when Hamilton is returning.

Shall be glad of a few days by the briny.

Yours very sincerely

J. T. Davies[9]

In July Frances was ill again and convalescing, this time in Margate and evidently at a hotel Davies had recommended. He had clearly been having a busy time in her absence, particularly since Hamilton had been away as well; but this letter illustrates their intimacy as well as JT's relaxed awareness of LG's double life.

Dear Miss Stevenson,

Thanks for your letter. Am so glad you are feeling so much better . . .

I had a pretty warm time of it last week but I am alive to tell the tale. I finished at 11 o'c on Saturday night after the Chancellor's meeting at Dulwich. I gave him your love and he was very pleased, in fact I showed him your letter as he asked me if I had heard from you. I miss your sweet and cheery face across the table but I know that someone else gets that pleasure at the Hereward. Do you like the food? It is generally very good . . .

The C of E is in very good form on the whole tho' I don't see so much of him at the Treasury now! I wonder why! He is moving the Third Reading

---

* His occupation of the new house had been delayed by the suffragettes, who planted a bomb in it in February, damaging several rooms. Mrs Pankhurst took responsibility for the outrage and was given a three-year prison sentence. LG and Maggie finally took possession in March. LG always preferred to sleep out of London if possible, and Maggie much preferred Walton to 11 Downing Street.

of the d——n Welsh Bill tomorrow and is going to speak at Caernarvon soon. Mrs Lloyd George is going down with him & she goes off to Criccieth and he returns – don't smile.

I think [Hamilton] is disappointed that the Chancellor didn't miss him more. I told him the Chancellor missed nobody till Thursday morning & that he still feels that void!

I'm keeping just one or two papers for you. I hope you will send me a line again to say you are quite well . . .

Kindest regards.

Yours sincerely,

J.T.[10]

There was a good deal of bickering between LG and Maggie that summer. Each of them complained that the other did not write – LG thought that pressure of work gave him the better excuse – and Maggie complained that he did not come to Criccieth between jaunts to France (with Isaacs) and the Hebrides (with Churchill on the Admiralty yacht). Did she wonder what he was getting up to in London? His retort was typically defiant.

You ask me whether I mean to stay here until my Scotch trip. What else can I do? You don't imagine I could run down tomorrow & return Sunday night for Monday. I have an important conference with Winston to go through the Estimates.[11]

Then Maggie complained that he did not write to her from Scotland, although she was herself away from home making a speech at Llanfyllin (about fifty miles south-east of Criccieth) and probably thought it was her turn for a line of praise and encouragement.* LG merely renewed his old complaints that she did not look after him properly:

So you don't like being a couple of days without letters! Well Arran is further than Llanfyllin & my time there was just as fully occupied as yours at Llanfyllin . . . You might have spared one servant yesterday to make

---

* In her speech she warned the government not to compromise on Irish Home Rule, otherwise 'the Welsh people would have no faith in the Liberal leaders' – a remarkable public statement by the wife of one of those very leaders who was centrally involved in trying to broker a compromise![12]

Walton ready for me & Whitehouse tomorrow. I mean to have 2 days to
do nothing there – but I did want a comfortable & well-aired house – rather
unreasonable of me I admit to expect.[13]

The point of mentioning Whitehouse – presumably another of LG's
secretaries, though there is no other record of him – was transparently to persuade Maggie that he was not alone at Walton, but safely
chaperoned.

A week later LG wrote that he was too busy to come to Wales, but
Gwilym was staying with him and Megan was coming from Allenswood
at the weekend.

You tell me it is my 'fault' that I am not at Criccieth! That is all you
know & care. Whitehouse & messengers are running up & down to
London every day for fresh material & information. I simply could not
get me a yard [sic] at Criccieth. However you are coming on Friday so
that is all right. I shall be genuinely glad to see you & shall kiss you
warmly.[14]

He particularly wanted Maggie there on Friday (11 October) because
he was launching his land campaign that day with a major speech at
Bedford.

Meanwhile Frances was still very friendly with Megan, who
continued to write effusive letters to 'My dearest Pussy', sending 'heaps
of love' and covered in kisses.[15] In September Frances must have visited
Megan at Allenswood, since LG wrote to Megan that 'Miss Stevenson
tells me that she saw you on Saturday and that you looked bonny &
gay as usual'.[16] Megan of course had no suspicion that there was
anything unusual in her father's relations with her former tutor.

At the same time LG was still wooing the Stevensons to try to assuage
their disapproval of Frances's connection with him. He was clearly
having some success with her youngest sister Muriel. Like her contemporary Megan – they were both eleven that year – Muriel was the fifth
child and the spoiled baby of her family. On holiday in August with
Louise and her elder sister Janet, she wrote to Frances complaining that
Seaford was 'shockingly dull', but saying that she was 'writing to thank
Mr L.G.' for sending her a postal order, and hoping that Frances would
be able to join them.

I hope you can, and did you give Mr L.G. my message about his being selfish. Tell him if he lets you come down here I will bring him back a souvenir from Seaford.[17]

Meanwhile a scribbled note shows LG promising to make it up to Louise for stealing Frances away from Alderbrook Road without warning on a Sunday morning.

My dear Miss Stevenson,
   I wish you could spare an hour or two to take down a speech I am preparing this morning. Could you return with the car now?
   Tell Mrs Stevenson that I shall let you off a day this week to make up for it.
   You can get back home by 3.
   Ever sincerely,
   D Lloyd George.[18]

One has to wonder if it was really her secretarial skills he wanted at such short notice.

Also undated, but clearly from this period, there are preserved in Frances's papers various odd notes that count as LG's first surviving love letters to her. The first is a snatch of poetry in LG's writing. Assuming he wrote it himself – or even if he did not – it is not a bad piece of cod-Shakespeare, celebrating the convenient circumstance that allowed them to conduct a love affair under cover of working together.

Beloved, let us love so well,
Our work shall still be better for our love,
And still our love be sweeter for our work,
And both, commended for the sake of each,
By all true workers and all lovers born.[19]

The second, scribbled on a piece of torn card, is an attempt to address Frances in her mother's language: the execrable French is sure proof that this is LG's own composition.

Je desire votre presence a 11 Downing Street a 7.30 se soir pour vous baiser.

Je encore vous aime le plus grand que tout le monde.
Bon jour a la petite amoureuse de ma coeur.[20]

The third is a proper letter, headed 'Treasury Chambers Monday', evidently written during one of Frances's minor illnesses.

My own darling,

You really must not get ill. Every time you do so I get fonder & fonder of you so I beg you for my sake not to contract another illness otherwise the results may be fatal to the shattered remnants of my judgment & direction.

Today I have a series of deputations. Tomorrow I may be free between 4 & 5. Do get me a nice cup of tea ready & your sweetest smile. Meanwhile dismiss me wholly from your mind, read a good [illegible] novel & get well.

I do miss you – oh so much.

Ever and ever,

[Illegible][21]

At the beginning of 1914 Frances went for a few days' holiday to Versailles. We do not know whom she went with: it is just possible that she met up with LG, since he visited Algiers around the same time, passing through Paris on the way. J. T. Davies and his wife had also just been to Versailles. His New Year greeting shows his tactful awareness that 1913 had been an eventful year for Frances.

Dear Miss Stevenson,

We came back on Friday from Paris . . .

My table is simply covered & it will take me a few days to get st[raight]. How you must have longed for a holiday. I do hope you will have a good restful time. Versailles is grand. We spent New Years day there . . .

Best wishes for a nice holiday & a New Year as happy & exciting as the last.

Yrs v sincerely,

J. T. Davies[22]

During the early months of 1914, LG was politically embattled on several fronts. In January he was involved in a major Cabinet struggle over Churchill's naval estimates. He was personally under renewed

attack by the Tories for his uninhibited denunciation of the dukes and
other great magnates in the course of his land campaign, which culmi-
nated in a dramatic Commons debate in March. In April he unveiled
another controversial budget, as contentious as that of 1909, but much
less successful: in fact it turned into a parliamentary fiasco. Finally there
was the still-deadlocked Irish crisis threatening to plunge the country
into civil war. At such times LG demanded consolation and support
from both his women. On 15 January he wrote to Maggie:

> As you may imagine I am very fully involved over this Navy tangle. It is
> serious & may involve the smash of the Ministry . . . Up to the present I
> cannot see the light . . . I wish you were here. Asquith is returning Monday,
> then I must take an important decision.[23]

That is, whether to resign if he did not get his way. In the event a face-
saving formula was achieved.

Then, on 10 March, the Tories put down a motion condemning LG's
'gross and unfounded personal attacks upon individuals' – specifically
the Dukes of Westminster and Bedford. He had to defend himself in a
crowded House and did so brilliantly. Maggie was in Wales, so Frances
was able to take her place in the Ladies' Gallery, which was as packed
and excited as the Chamber below. In her memoirs she vividly described
the scene and her nervousness on his behalf.

> I was on tenterhooks, for I knew that, in fact, LG had committed one or
> two inaccuracies . . . due to faulty information which had not been prop-
> erly sifted, and I could not see how he was going to ward off his enemies.

In fact he launched a typically defiant counter-attack, which successfully took the wind out of the Opposition's sails and – according to
Frances – so infuriated Lady Londonderry in the Ladies' Gallery that
she had to be quieted by the attendant. At the end Frances scribbled
him one of her congratulatory notes. It was signed P. for Pussy.

> *First class.* It was everything I could have wished. Every point, however,
> quietly made, went home, and you had the rapt attention of the House. It
> was a complete success. P.[24]

This was what LG needed to hear after a speech; but Frances's praise was not enough. He would have liked to have heard it from Maggie too, as he told her the next day.

> I am so delighted to know that you are coming up tomorrow. In spite of occasional sulks &c I cannot do without my round little wife. I am so disappointed you were not in the House last night. By common consent I scored the greatest Parliamentary triumph of my life . . . I pounded them flat.[25]

Three weeks later – by which time Maggie had returned to Wales – he wrote from Walton Heath on a Saturday complaining that he could not get out because he was working so hard at his budget. Evidently Sarah – the Lloyd Georges' servant from Criccieth – had stayed at Walton to look after him.

> Sarah manipulating the telephone for me I writing out the messages. She is at the phone now getting at Hamilton to find out some figures on the National Debt![26]

One wonders where Frances was. In fact it is likely that the whole point of this little cameo was an attempt to conceal from Maggie that he was actually with Frances.

The following week LG went to Criccieth for Easter, taking J. T. Davies with him. (He was still working on the budget, which was very late that year.) Meanwhile Frances went to Deal for the weekend, where JT sent her a coded telegram telling her when they would be back.

> Arriving tomorrow night 9.5. Bringing welsh terrier for you. Please see letters addressed to you at Treasury. Will you wait Downing Street till we arrive.[27]

Stuart Brown did not give up his pursuit of Frances during 1913. Clearly he did not realise the true nature of her relationship with LG – had he known he might not have been so keen to marry her – but still hoped that she would come round to him in time and was willing to be patient. In May he invited her to Covent Garden (*Siegfried*), beginning at five o'clock and preceded by 'an early and I hope sustaining tea' at his parents' house in Hampstead.[28] In September she must have made him promise to stop pressing her. He agreed, yet still remained pathetically hopeful.

Dear Frances,

The bargain is accepted; only it does not really leave me with anything else to say after writing the first two words of this letter. But that is against the rules . . .

I shall try to have a chance of seeing you at King's Cross tonight [she had been in Scotland], but will not worry you if I see that you are already being met. In case we don't come across each other, will you let me know whether you will be free at any time before you go away again. My mother would be delighted if you could manage to spend next weekend with us at Hampstead . . .

I do most earnestly hope you will; but it must be possible to arrange to meet before then.

Yours ever sincerely,
Stuart Brown[29]

He continued to write chatty letters from one civil servant to another about their respective political masters – Lloyd George and Edwin Montagu (then Under-Secretary at the India Office) – full of clever nonsense and donnish jokes. But towards the end of the month Frances must have tried to make it clear that he should not be misled by her friendliness towards him.

Dear Frances,

It hurts a good deal to think that you would rather we did not meet just for the present. *Please* do not think that there is the slightest ground for what you say about encouragement. The position has always been perfectly clear ever since Dundee, thanks to your straightforwardness and sincerity; and if you have felt any awkwardness so far it has been entirely due to my own stupidity. I am most deeply sorry for it, but I can profit by this warning if you feel free to give me an opportunity of seeing you now and then.

I never expected, though I may have hoped, that things would change in so short a time as a month. But I had made up my mind to wait. I have not changed my mind either; and you must know that there are some things which it is impossible to forget.

Forgive my writing at all: it must be a great bother to you in the middle of your work. But it means more than I can very well say to me.

Yours with every good wish,
Stuart Brown[30]

On 7 October he sent good wishes not, as one might have expected, for Frances's birthday, but for the launch of LG's land campaign; and two weeks later an intriguing note implying that LG was being hypocritical about women's suffrage. 'What a scandal your not being allowed to go to Swindon,' he sympathised, 'especially considering what he said to the women yesterday. You might rub that in.'[31]* Clearly he and Frances had discussed the 'woman question'. Was Stuart perhaps trying to dent her defence of LG's diminishing enthusiasm for the women's cause?

Then, on 1 December, Stuart was included in some sort of social evening at 11 Downing Street. The next day he wrote Frances two letters. One was a formal bread-and-butter letter clearly intended to be shown to LG:

Dear Miss Stevenson,
    Perhaps you could find time if you are not too busy to thank the Chancellor for me. I enjoyed last night almost as much as anything I have ever enjoyed, and very soon forgot what a ludicrously small excuse I had for being there at all. But that is about the only thing I am likely to forget about the occasion for a very long time.
    Yours sincerely,
    S. K. Brown

The second, more personal, referred again to LG's views about the suffragettes, who must have been discussed the previous evening. Since the Chancellor admired Meredith, Stuart suggested, Frances should get him to read his 'Ballad of Fair Women in Revolt', which he called 'the greatest suff. [i.e. suffragist] poem ever written.† It might just possibly

---

* LG had met a deputation of suffragists at Swindon on 23 October. He told them that he was personally as committed as ever to the women's cause, but that the violence of the militants had made the passage of any measure in the present Parliament impossible.[32]
† Meredith's poem – actually 'A Ballad of Fair Ladies in Revolt' – is a long (forty-eight-stanza) ballad in high-flown Tennysonian language describing an encounter between two knights and some 'fair ladies' seeking a male champion to secure them equal treatment instead of mere chivalry and protection, with the repeated refrain 'He who's for us, for him are we!'[33] Presumably Stuart thought this quaint appeal might stiffen LG's failing feminism.

warm him up about e.g. forcible feeding, about which not many people seem to have clear notions just now.' Stuart clearly considered himself a progressive on this subject, though he insisted, 'I am non-militant, you know, in case you get confused among different members of the family' – a reference presumably to his sister Dorothy, and possibly his mother. He ended – as though he had been tempting the innocent Frances with strong liquor – 'I hope you are convinced now that Chianti is really harmless, though necessary; I know you wouldn't believe me at first. We must try it again some time.'[34]

Three days after Christmas Stuart spent Sunday with Frances's family in Alderbrook Road.

> It was awfully good of your people to let me come over yesterday: I looked forward to it all Saturday and enjoyed it even more when I got there, I am venturing to hope for some more like it some time or other.[35]

Poor Stuart. No doubt Mr and Mrs Stevenson were keen to encourage him, while his parents clearly approved of Frances. Honourable to the last, he was not yet ready to give up hope. He continued to woo her with invitations to the opera and to tea. But it was no use. Frances had given her heart, and no mere junior in the India Office could compete with the Chancellor of the Exchequer.

6

THE COMING OF WAR

The Great War changed everything. It wrenched the history of Britain, of Europe, of the world, onto quite new paths. Nothing in politics, economics or social life was ever the same again. The years before 1914, turbulent as they had seemed at the time, appeared in retrospect a golden age of innocence and tranquillity compared with the era of carnage and conflict that was unleashed that August.

No life was untouched by the war of 1914–18: millions were prematurely ended or permanently ruined by it. Scarcely a career was not diverted, for better or worse, from its predicted course. Men flocked (and later were drafted) into the fighting forces: if they were lucky enough to survive, they lost four years of their youth and returned to a harsher country scarred by unemployment. Women took their places in the factories and did all kinds of voluntary work – for which they were finally granted the vote as their reward; but most had lost lovers, husbands, brothers or sons. In the new world that emerged from the holocaust the relations of men and women to each other, and of both to an increasingly intrusive state, were changed for ever.

Lloyd George and Frances were just two individuals whose lives were altered. Of course LG neither had to fight nor lost his sons or any close relations in the war. Rather he was raised to the pinnacle of power and national acclaim as the architect of eventual victory. But few careers were more drastically reshaped over these four years. His decision, after much agony, to support British participation in the conflict marked a decisive break with his previous reputation as a left-wing radical widely regarded – on account of his opposition to the Boer War fifteen years before – as something of a pacifist; and it impelled him on a very different path, which led him first to the role of national mobiliser for total war and eventually to the premiership – in coalition with, and dependent on, his former political enemies, while his own party was broken and mortally weakened. He achieved his life's ambition (that ambition for which he had been prepared to thrust 'even love itself under the wheels of my Juggernaut'), but in ironic circumstances that made him responsible for a war he hated and detached him from the progressive causes of which previously he had been the leading champion.

And through it all Frances was by his side, providing practical and emotional support, achieving an unprecedented degree of recognition in her own right in a previously male world, witness to great events and increasingly the confidante of many of the leading figures of the day – yet still compelled to lead a shadowy and insecure existence as an unacknowledged mistress, humiliatingly required to fade into the background whenever her lover's wife appeared. Behind the headlines, the military and political dramas of the war were mirrored by some turbulent – and bizarre – domestic dramas.

As the international crisis originating in the Balkans suddenly forced itself on the attention of a Cabinet initially preoccupied with Ireland, LG reported developments in almost daily letters – really no more than brief snatched scribbles – to Maggie in Wales.

27 July: Crisis upon crisis. Ireland is serious but Austro-Servia is pandemonium let loose. I am off to Cabinet now to consider both.

28 July: War trembling in the balance. No-one can tell what will or will not happen. I still believe peace will be preserved. The Great Powers will hesitate before they plunge their countries into the hell of war.

29 July: Foreign outlook most menacing. Very grave Cabinet this morning.

3 August: I am moving through a nightmare world these days. I have fought hard for peace & succeeded so far in keeping the Cabinet out of it but I am driven to the conclusion that if the small nationality of Belgium is attacked by Germany all my traditions & even prejudices will be engaged on the side of war. I am filled with horror at the prospect. I am even more

horrified that I should ever appear to have a share in it but I must bear my share of the ghastly burden though it scorches my flesh to do so.[1]

As a pious daughter of Welsh Nonconformity still living in the heart of that community, one might imagine that Maggie would have been against British involvement in the war. On the contrary – according to her elder son – she played an important part in helping to convince LG that German militarism must be resisted.[2] But Maggie was 300 miles away in Criccieth. Her support may have reassured LG that he would not lose his own people if he backed the war, but the confidante who was with him in London in these critical days was Frances. Young, patriotic – but also half-French – with as little understanding as most of the public of how the conflict would develop, Frances too was all for British participation. Her fear, she recalled years later, was that LG would feel obliged to placate his radical constituency by opposing British involvement. The weekend before his decision was finally made she was with him in No. 11 as he came and went from meetings, 'desperately unhappy . . . at LG's attitude *against* supporting the French'.[3]

The Liberal Cabinet was badly split. The Foreign Secretary, Sir Edward Grey, held that Britain was morally bound to go to the support of France if she was invaded by Germany. He was largely supported by Asquith, by the right-leaning Liberal imperialist wing of the party, and by Churchill. Conversely those who adhered to the Gladstonian tradition were instinctively opposed to war, as were the left-leaning 'New Liberals' whose principal interest was social reform. LG's instincts and political antecedents all inclined him to the latter group. He was very reluctant to go to war for the sake of France alone; and particularly anxious that Britain should not go to war on the side of France's reactionary ally, Tsarist Russia. Nevertheless he accepted that if Germany breached the neutrality of Belgium, then Britain was bound by treaty, as well as by honour and self-interest, to go to her aid. As a result Frances found herself praying that Germany *would* invade Belgium, so that LG would come down on what she regarded as the right side.[4]

When Britain finally declared war on Tuesday 4 August, LG spoke briefly in the House to explain his support. Frances was present in the Ladies' Gallery as usual – with Megan – and sent him her customary note of congratulation.

Bravo! Yours was *the only* inspiring speech. I am glad from my heart that you did it, & so was everyone else. It was a perfect little speech, perfectly suited to the occasion. P.[5]

Megan wrote her father a note too. It was mainly in Welsh, but the English part was precociously formal and grown-up for a twelve-year-old: 'It really was impressive & just the right line for you to take . . . Delighted & proud. Megs.'[6]

As Chancellor, LG's immediate task was to settle the markets and avert a financial panic. By common consent – and to general surprise, since finance as such had never been his forte – he succeeded brilliantly. It was his 'hardest week since the Budget of 1909', he wrote to Maggie, '& the most responsible work I was ever engaged in'.[7] As usual he was not shy of trumpeting his achievement. 'My arrangements to save a financial panic have been a complete success,' he boasted on 7 August, '– a real triumph – the first great British victory of the war.'[8] But it was true. He won universal praise for his handling of the crisis, and the former radical bogeyman was suddenly the hero of the City.

LG was reporting almost daily to Maggie in these early weeks of the war: on the pressure he was under, his reactions to the first military engagements, and his preparation of what he hoped would be 'a rattling good speech' to be delivered at the Queen's Hall on 19 September.[9] But all the time he was closer than ever to Frances. In September they spent a full two weeks together at Walton Heath, working on this speech, which was indeed one of the finest of his life, setting out in exalted language the reasons for Britain's participation in the war. It was at this time that Frances decided she should keep a diary. From the wording of the first entry it sounds as if it was actually LG's suggestion.

I am to make a diary. I began one three years ago when at Criccieth in the summer – life was interesting then, as now. That diary did not last, but this one is in a sense the outcome of that visit.

At first it was simply written on loose sheets of paper; later she bought proper printed diaries, though she never filled them consistently. From now on, however, we get a much clearer picture of their time together and the mechanics of conducting an affair. The first entry – two days after LG's Queen's Hall speech – is a perfect foretaste of what was to follow over the next thirty years. On the one hand, adoring

accounts of LG's battles and triumphs, as related to her by him. On
the other, bitter-sweet reflections on the happiness and misery of their
clandestine relationship. Thus on 21 September she described LG's initial
conviction that his speech had been a flop, until reassured on all sides
that it had actually been 'a tremendous success'. But then she ended
on a more personal note:

> I returned from Walton Heath this morning with C. after the happiest fort-
> night of my life. Have been correcting Saturday's speech for publication.
> The family have returned from Criccieth, and I go home.
>
> C. said this morning he wished I had kept the love letters he wrote me
> two years ago. But I promised at the time to burn them, and they are all
> destroyed, though, as he says, 'every word of them meant business'. It does
> not seem possible that it is two years ago this autumn, and yet such a lot
> of things have happened since then.[10]

Two days later LG accompanied his family to Criccieth for three
days, promising Frances that he would be back on Sunday, as indeed
he was. He wired on Saturday morning to say that he was leaving at
three o'clock, would stay the night in Shropshire and arrive back in
London the next day, when he would call for her – presumably at
Alderbrook Road.[11] They then went back to Walton Heath to work
on another big speech to be delivered in Cardiff on Tuesday. They also
fantasised briefly about his giving up politics to be with her.

> Yesterday we discussed what it would mean to C. if he retired from pol-
> itics. We both know that he cannot do it. It would be treason if he did
> . . . He must go on, and I will help him.[12]

This was a renewal of the compact by which Frances had given
herself to LG in the first place. There was never the slightest possibility
that he would throw up his career for her. Nor would she really have
wanted him to. She knew quite well that he would be miserable without
his work; while for her part, genuinely as she loved him for himself,
she also loved his power and loved sharing with him the adrenaline of
high politics. She believed in his destiny as ardently as he did himself;
now that Britain was at war, she believed the country needed him more
than ever. There was much talk of 'sacrifice' in 1914. Frances believed
that her sacrifice – her form of war service – was to rededicate herself

to LG to help him serve the country to his fullest capacity.

The following weekend, however, Maggie was back in London, so Frances had to keep out of sight. She returned to the office only on Wednesday 7 October (her twenty-sixth birthday). But writing up her diary at the end of the week she recorded that LG had 'turned in' to see her on the Tuesday, 'and we had a long chat together'. Turned in where? Frances was still living with her parents, so again this can only mean that he came to Alderbrook Road to see her on his way between Downing Street and Walton. 'He looked tired & worried, and I found that passing through Clapham had depressed him, calling up sad memories of Mary [Mair]. He avoids Clapham as much as possible.' In reality LG was probably more worried about the siege of Antwerp, which fell to the Germans on 10 October, but he always liked to talk to Frances about Mair. The next day 'C. & I had a very primitive dinner together at No. 11 (which is under repair) before C. departed for W.H. [Walton Heath]'.

> Yesterday (Thursday) we dined again in the same primitive way. He was to have dined with Donald & friends, but decided to go straight to theatre instead.* We had great fun. C. gave me a beautiful set of Barrie's works for a birthday present. It is sweet of him, he was so keen about it, & it gives him such pleasure to give anyone a present. I was very touched. We hated leaving each other. C. said he might have been going to the war, judging from the parting we had. Have not seen much of him today as he has been very busy in Board Room, with occasional flying visits in here. He has left for weekend at W.H. His last words. 'Same address. "Virtuous" – Walton Heath'.[14]

Virtuous he had to be that weekend, since Maggie was there.

The next weekend LG went to France, accompanied by Rufus Isaacs. Frances was terribly worried, though he was gone only two days.

---

* Robert Donald, editor of the *Daily Chronicle*, was one of LG's strongest supporters in Fleet Street. They were accompanied by Riddell, who commented in his diary on LG's ability to switch his mind away from the war. 'L.G. was completely absorbed by the play . . . His gift of detachment is remarkable . . . He does his best, but now and again takes time off which he uses to the utmost advantage. The result is that he keeps a reservoir of freshness and brightness which enables him to cheer and stimulate everyone with whom he comes in contact.'[13] The play they saw was a Jewish-American comedy called *Potash and Perlmutter*. They enjoyed it so much that LG and Riddell went again the following week.

He left on Friday night, & returned on Monday night. I was very anxious all the time he was away, as there was a considerable risk attached to the journey. We received a wire to say that they had landed safely at Dieppe, and another on Monday from General Headquarters in France. I was glad when I heard late Monday night that he had returned safely. I came down here [Walton Heath] with him on Tuesday, & since then he has told me all about the journey.[15]

To Maggie – now back in Wales – LG wrote that he had been within 1,500 yards of the German trenches. He had gained a very accurate view of the military situation, which would not change much for the next four years.

I went to the English headquarters. Had a great time. Gave me a new idea of what is happening. It is *stalemate*. We cannot turn them out of their trenches & they cannot turn us out. They can only frighten Belgians – French & English stand their ground.[16]

Frances's diary continues:

C. has been very busy since his return, & is fearfully tired. I fear that his health will give way unless he slacks a little more . . . Last night in the car coming down I was afraid he was going to be ill, he was so terribly done up. But he is better again this morning, & has gone up for meetings with the Bankers this afternoon.[17]

It was now LG's habit to spend most nights at Walton Heath, going into London to the Treasury, meetings of the Cabinet and other meetings only when necessary. He always claimed that he slept better in the country. Frances too stayed at Walton most of the time, so she was usually on hand to provide a sympathetic audience for his account of his daily battles – particularly at this time with Kitchener.* 'Stand up fight with Kitchener today over Welsh army,' he wrote to Maggie on 30 October – meaning Kitchener's refusal to create a separate Welsh division. 'Cabinet with me. I gave it him quite straight from the

---

* Field Marshal Lord Kitchener had been brought into the Cabinet as Secretary for War. His was the commanding face on the famous recruiting poster 'Your Country Needs YOU'; and in an otherwise civilian Cabinet his prestige initially gave him practically un-fettered power to direct military policy.

shoulder.'[18] With Frances, however, he was not always quite so bullish. The same day that he wrote to Maggie, Frances wrote in her diary:

> He is depressed about the war. He says he feels sometimes that it will overwhelm him & that he must go away somewhere and get out of it all. War is not his work, and he feels that he has not the heart to deal with it. It is all so horrible.[19]

One thing that worried him was the fate of his own sons, now twenty-five and nineteen. Like any other father, LG was torn between anxiety that Dick and Gwilym should be seen to do their duty and fear for their safety; but his natural ambivalence was complicated by the fact that he was eloquently urging 'sacrifice' on others. When Gwilym wasted no time in joining the Territorials within days of the outbreak of war, LG's comments to Maggie were distinctly contradictory:

> Gwilym's choice meets with my complete approval. Any other course would have marked him down as a shirker & he is much too brave & fearless a boy ever to be open to a suspicion of that kind. He must not be rushed by excitable youths around him to volunteering for the front without first consulting me . . . If the country be in danger we must all make sacrifices but we are a long way off that. There is no dearth of men.[20]

A few days later, with Gwilym – but not just Gwilym – in mind, he still hoped it would be possible to limit Britain's commitment to a purely defensive war in support of France and Belgium.

> They are pressing the territorials to volunteer for the war. We mustn't do that just yet . . . I am dead against carrying on a war of conquest to crush Germany for the benefit of Russia . . . I am not going to sacrifice my nice boy for that purpose. You must write Wil telling him on no account to be bullied into volunteering abroad.[21]

In the end he was relieved when Gwilym's Welsh regiment was sent to India, not France. Meanwhile Frances was worried, for the opposite reason, about her brother Paul.

On 20 November Frances recorded that LG had gone to Walton to spend one of his 'virtuous' weekends, but that they had managed an evening together there the following Wednesday – 'quite unexpected, but

enjoyed to the very fullest': probably a discreet euphemism. She went on
to recall again the letters that he wrote her in the autumn of 1912.

> They were indeed very beautiful, but the things he says to me now are
> more beautiful still. Sometimes I am so happy that I tremble for fear it
> will not last. Our love will always last, but there is the dread that he
> might be taken from me. He is never tired of talking of that summer
> when he used to come to Allenswood, & we both felt there was some-
> thing between us, though it was not yet expressed – and of the following
> autumn, when we used to meet once a week, and I hovered between
> doubt and longing, dread and desire: and of the time in the House of
> Commons, when I left him because I would not agree to his proposals,
> but returned soon after to say that I could not face life without him, &
> would do what he wished. I have never regretted the decision. It has
> brought me two years of happiness, & if Fate wills will bring me many
> more.

Frances even persuaded herself that her mother was beginning to
accept her irregular relationship. That week LG introduced a supple-
mentary budget to meet the cost of the war. Frances could not attend
because she was taking a Red Cross exam that day.*

> Mamma went to the Budget Speech instead of me, & thoroughly appreci-
> ated it. C. also got her a ticket for Lord Roberts' Funeral . . . I think she
> is getting more reconciled to the relations between C. & me, as she recog-
> nises it is an honest love which will last, & not just a passing passion. She
> & C. get on very well together.[23]

The lovers managed at least two interludes at Walton in December.
Frances recorded that on Friday 11th 'C. & I spent the day there, alone.
We have been very lucky considering all things. The previous Thursday
& Friday we spent together & had a jolly time.'[24] Then on Wednesday
16th she noted that she was going down there the next day '& C. is
going to make a strenuous effort to come down in the evening'.[25] He
went to Wales for Christmas, but Frances consoled herself that there

---

* She clearly thought she ought to do some more orthodox form of war work. Her
certificate awarded by the British Red Cross Society for First Aid shows that she scored
86/100 in the practical, but only 60/100 in the written exam.[22]

was a Cabinet on Wednesday 30th so he would have to come back on the Tuesday.

> C. has gone and left me desolate. How long before next Tuesday? There will be plenty of work, though, to keep one busy. There seems every like-lihood of my having to come up here [the Treasury] on Xmas day, and certainly on Boxing Day.
>
> Mamma has received a beautiful basket of fruit from C., and she is very pleased thereat. He sent me at the same time a dear little orange tree. He has been giving me Christmas presents since the beginning of the month, and I hope he has stopped now. But he says that it gives him pleasure to do it, & therefore that it is purely selfish. It would be a good thing if self-ishness always benefited others to that extent![26]

In fact Frances was not required to work on Boxing Day, but felt obliged to invite Stuart Brown for the day, though she was still trying to discourage him. In the middle of November she had had dinner with his sister Dorothy.

> She wished to know whether my feelings towards her brother were any different, as he is still very unhappy. I told her that I had not changed my mind. I cannot explain how things really are, but feel that I am doing the right thing in refusing to see him, since he may forget & marry someone else. I am sorry he is unhappy.[27]

Just before Christmas Stuart rang her with the news that the Germans had bombarded Scarborough. 'It was the first time I had spoken to him for months, & I can't think what made him do it.' He was anxious to see her again, and Dorothy was pleading his cause.

> I can't make up my mind to do it, for it seems to be opening up everything again, & I am sure it is far kinder to him to refuse to see him. He may forget about it in time, whereas if we keep up our friendship I don't suppose he will forget.[28]

But she failed to keep this resolution. Rather than accept his invi-tation to tea on Christmas Eve, she probably thought it safer to see him on her home territory.

Stuart Brown has come upon the scenes again: his family had left him alone
for Xmas, so we had to take pity on him & ask him to spend Boxing Day
with us. I fear he is going to seize his opportunity for reopening old topics.
Sarah* pretends she is sure I will marry him, and C. teases me & says that
I shall give in one day out of sheer boredom.[29]

In January, however, her irritation with both Stuart and his sister
found expression in outraged patriotism.

Went out to dinner with Stuart & Dorothy Brown last night and was thoroughly bored. At one point I was angry when they talked about the high-
mindedness of refusing to fight because it is against one's principles as being
more manly than sacrificing all you hold dear & giving your life for your
country. Somehow I never feel myself with them. I always feel as though
they were patronising me as their intellectual inferior.[30]

That was the end of Stuart Brown for the moment.†
In the early weeks of 1915 Frances was more sure than ever that
she had made the right choice in refusing Stuart. 'I fear my diary has
got very behindhand,' she wrote on 17 January.

The last three weeks have been so busy and happy that I have not had the
opportunity for writing things down. C. returned from Wales on Dec. 29th
and from then till now I have been with him at W.H., coming up every
day to town & going back in the evening. It has been like an idyll, but
alas! came to an end yesterday when the family returned from Criccieth,
& I returned home. The longer we are together, the more our love & affection seems to increase, so that it is all the more difficult to part. But we
have resolved not to be miserable at parting, for 'my true love hath my
heart, & I have his' and happy memories will buoy us up till 'the next
time'.[31]

---

* Sarah Jones had worked for the Lloyd George family since 1899 and stayed with
them until after LG's death. She was devoted to LG and shared his view that Maggie
failed to look after him as he deserved. She therefore approved of Frances and played
a key role in facilitating and covering up their affair over many years.
† Stuart was not himself a conscientious objector. Although as a civil servant he could
probably have claimed exemption, he joined up in 1915 and served on the Italian front
until he was wounded. But he was a model liberal. By contrast – aside from her support
for women's suffrage and her attachment to LG – Frances's political instincts tended to
be increasingly conservative.

His family's return brought LG little joy – at least that was the impression he was always careful to give Frances. 'C. is not very well today,' she wrote on Thursday 21st.

He has been working very hard, but personally I think he is suffering from too much 'family'. He was very upset on Monday because not one of them had remembered that it was his birthday on Sunday. They did not think of it until Sir George Riddell came in at 7.30 in the evening & wished him many happy returns, & then it suddenly occurred to them. He always remembers their birthdays, however busy he is, and goes to a lot of trouble to get them something which will please them . . . 'They take me for granted,' he said to me rather bitterly . . .*

By contrast he persisted in identifying Frances with his beloved, idealised Mair (whose name Frances continued to anglicise).

It is just two years since C. & I were 'married', and our love seems to increase rather than diminish. He says I have taken the place somewhat of Mary, 'my little girl whom I lost' as he always calls her. He says I remind him of her & make up a little for her loss. I have always wanted to make this loss seem lighter to him, and he seems now to be able to speak of her with less pain than he used to.[33]

The following weekend (23–4 January) yields another snapshot of time together snatched whenever possible between affairs of state.

On Saturday C. motored down to Walmer Castle [in Kent] to see the P.M. I went with him & we had a jolly run. In London the weather was terrible – a black fog & snowing, but out in the country the scenery was glorious – everywhere white, and so still & beautiful . . . C. remained down at Walmer till Sunday and I came home by train. The journey back was dreary – lots of stoppages, and noisy soldiers everywhere. But still it was worth it for the run down. I went to Downing Street yesterday evening to await his return, & we had a tete-a-tete dinner.[34]

---

* Riddell's diary confirms LG's annoyance at his family forgetting his birthday; but his account of the evening concludes: 'L.G. seemed harassed and worried by business and anxious for some relief. He therefore sang songs for about an hour, Miss Olwen accompanying on the piano. L.G.'s favourites are mostly songs of the Victorian era and earlier; these he sings with great vigour.'[32]

At the beginning of February LG went to France again to meet his allied opposite numbers, the French and Russian finance ministers. He promised Frances that he would not go to the front this time; but she was still anxious about enemy submarines in the Channel and was relieved when he returned safely. While he was away Frances took a few days off work ('trying to cure a bad cold'), but also took the chance to visit Megan at Allenswood, prompting a chatty letter a few days later.

Dear Pussy,

I was surprised to see you on Wednesday. When is your holiday going to end? I have had a fit of writing letters today. That is why I am so energetic. I did not see you for very long, so I thought I would write to you . . . [There followed a lot of school news.]

With heaps of love from

Megan[35]

LG did not come back empty-handed.

C. has brought me back the sweetest little brooch – diamonds – & a big sapphire – from Paris. He said he spent all his spare time walking the streets to find something to bring me home. It gives him such intense pleasure to give presents and he was so pleased with this one. It was sweet to watch him.

At the same time he was furious at a paragraph in a Sunday paper suggesting that he had visited the Latin quarter to see how war had affected the night life. 'If it were true it would be scandalous & the nation would have a right to object.' Laying on the injured innocence a little thick as always, he swore that he 'never went near the Latin quarter the whole time he was there'; and Frances at least believed him.[36]

7

'LOVE JUSTIFIES MANY AUDACITIES'

But now there broke the first real crisis of their relationship. Some time towards the middle of February 1915 – the result perhaps of their idyllic time in January – Frances discovered that she was pregnant. It was not just a 'heavy cold' that she had been suffering from while LG was away. After he returned from Paris she spent several more days at Walton Heath 'not feeling very fit'.[1] By the next weekend she was feeling better. LG collected her from Clapham and they motored down and spent the day together.

> We went for a glorious walk in the afternoon on the Heath, & wandered about for hours together without meeting a soul. It was the kind of afternoon that comes as a herald of Spring . . . There was a feeling of coming life in the air, as though the earth were waiting to give birth to the spring.

And not just the earth. Frances does not mention her own fertility, but her account of their conversation suggests that – whether she told him yet or not – she probed again the fantasy of his giving up politics.

> C. talked again of what he would like to do when the war is over. He sometimes feels that he would like to give up politics & try his hand at writing on his own. 'But the idea I have got now', he said, 'is to be made Governor of Mesopotamia [modern Iraq] when it comes under our rule, and direct operations there, making the desert blossom like the rose.' 'I would love the climate', he continued, 'and there is scope for any amount of energy in a scheme like that, in organising and promoting irrigation, etc.'

'But I know in the end', he said, 'I should never be able to give up this job I have taken up of bettering the lives of the poor . . . I cannot help myself. I see my way so clearly that I should be full of reproach for myself if I turned to anything else, or devoted myself to making money, which would be easy for me now.'

Fantasy apart, the message was as uncompromising as it had always been, from the time he spelled it out to Frances two years earlier right back to the day he laid it on the line to Maggie before their marriage. Even after the war, he concluded, there would still be the war on poverty to be won, 'and it will not be for me to indulge my Mesopotamian dream!' Naïvely, Frances still hoped that he could somehow follow his political destiny outside the framework of conventional politics, though it is not clear how this would have helped her.

What I want him to do is to go outside *party* politics – to direct great reforms from the outside, impartially, & not waste energy on party strife. He could do it now, for his reputation is established, and both sides admit his capacity. He could leave his party & the Cabinet, without it being said that he had been obliged to leave it, as they would surely have said after the Marconi affair, or at any other time when his schemes were meeting with opposition. If he were to leave now, however, he could promote schemes which are favoured in some form or other by both parties, such as land reform. He could earn enough for his needs by writing, for he is a man of simple tastes and prefers a simple life and simple fare to luxury. He has often hinted at this himself, and if he ever does it, this will be the time.[2]

Of course this was wishful thinking. There was no possibility, so long as he was in public life of any sort, that LG would ever acknowledge fathering a child with her. Yet it was not LG directly, but her mother, who insisted that Frances must not have a child at all, as is clear from her long, anguished and impossibly romantic outburst when she finally unburdened herself to her diary at the end of what she called a 'very stormy' week. She had been optimistic in persuading herself that Louise had accepted her relations with LG.

C. and I have wanted for so long to have a child, and we thought this week that our wish was about to be realised. But when I told Mamma of what was going to happen, she was terribly upset, and is still. She says she would rather see me dead than that such a thing could happen. She has raised all sorts of issues to persuade me, but behind it all is the spectre of respectability which haunts her with horrible pictures of what can happen to 'disgraced' women. She does not think it possible for a woman to give a child to the man she loves, but who is unable to marry her, and still be happy and willing to face the criticism of the world. She does not understand that if anything happened to C. my only chance of happiness would be for me to have someone to remind me of him, and to whom I can devote my life. She can only think of the wickedness of it, *his* wickedness she calls it, & will not understand that our only fault is that we love each other too well, and that where love is, the greatest trials can be sustained. If she would only look at things clearly and judge the facts fairly! But she will not – there is one part of her which has never come out into the clear light – which *may* not do so in case the futility of conventions should be revealed, and the crippling bonds of middle-class routine be weakened. She does not understand that I should be proud to have his child, and would be willing to suffer for it, nay, I should glory in the suffering, rather than die childless. I would suffer so that the child should not. I would spend my life that he might be happy, and I would brave the coldness of the world, for I know there are some friends who would stand by me, and I should not be entirely alone.

But it is not to be. I fear that if I insisted upon this, she would be so upset that people would see what had happened, and I cannot be responsible for the ruin of C.'s career. And then too, my love for Mamma makes me hesitate from hurting her too much. I hate myself for inflicting this upon her – and I fear that the wound is a deep one. I know she loves me dearly, and that this is a real grief to her. She cannot bear the thought that the life I am leading is not an open one, that there are concealments and even lies in it. But C. says that in love lies do not pass for such, just as in war killing is not called murder. But the long and the short of it is, that much as I love Mamma and Dada, and hate to cause them pain, I love C. better and will never leave him, and am impelled to put everything else subordinate to his love. But the idea of our love-child will have to go for the time being. I fear, too, that I shall not be able to stay at home after this, for Dada does not yet know what has happened, and I do not know what his attitude will be. I dread hurting him – but one thing is certain, I cannot give up C.

I can't help *hating* myself for making Mamma so miserable. The thought haunts me all day long and I would do anything to prevent it. But what *can* I do? Some years ago Harold Spender said to C. 'You are the most lonely man I know'. I think I have changed all that now, & I cannot think that I have done wrong. I am not vicious or evil, and my only fault in this matter and his, is love. 'Love justifies many audacities.' I think the justification for these audacities is the length of love's duration & I know C. & I belong to each other for ever. I should be so happy were it not for the fact that I am causing unhappiness to two people whom I love and who have been so good & loving to me.[3]*

Again Frances was fooling herself if she believed that LG would have been happy for her to bear his love child, even if its paternity could be kept secret, though he was doubtless happy for her to blame her mother rather than him for the consequent abortion. There is no record of where it was performed – women in Frances's situation often went to Paris for the purpose, but this would have been more difficult in wartime, so it was probably in London; nor of whether LG paid for it. But he was unusually solicitous when she was recovering from her 'illness' and sent her to Walton Heath to recuperate, with the faithful Sarah to look after her. On 11 March she resumed her diary after a miserable two-week gap – though without being quite explicit about what she had been through.

> The last fortnight has been too dreary and unhappy to write of. I am down here now trying to recover from the effects of it. My people have been trying to separate us – trying to make me promise that I will give up his love, the most precious thing of my life. They do not understand – they will never understand – they do not see that our love is pure and lasting – they think I am his plaything, & that he will fling me aside when he has finished with me – or else they think that there will be a scandal and that we shall all be disgraced. I know they are fond of me, and think it is for my good that they are doing this, but I have always held different ideas from theirs, & it was bound to come to this, or something akin to this, sooner or later. I am willing to pay dearly for my happiness, but I will not give it up. I fear that in the end I shall have to leave home, for they will

---

* Some weeks later Frances again defended to herself the morality of her conduct: 'My little god-daughter Nancy is to be christened today. I have undertaken to be her guardian on the strict understanding that it shall not involve any *religious* teaching, but only the responsibility for her moral and material welfare. I scarcely know whether I am fit to undertake even the former of these two; many people would think I am not. But I do not, oh I do not think that I am wicked & unfit to help in the upbringing of a child. Surely my experiences have made me *more* fit for this: for knowledge is safety.'[4]

never cease to urge their views upon me, & it will be almost intolerable. Besides which, they will never speak of C. except in unfriendly & contemptuous tones & that I will not endure. I cannot give up the hold upon life, & the broader outlook, which I have gained since C. & I came together.

In addition to distress of mind I have been ill, which increased my misery. Finally C. insisted that I should come down here & have absolute rest for a few days, & be free from worrying surroundings. I agreed to this all the more willingly as I could see that C. was making himself ill through worrying about me – several times I thought he was on the point of breaking down; but he has been better since I have been down here & have shown signs of recovering.

I do not think I can ever repay him for his goodness to me the last fortnight or three weeks. He has been husband, lover & mother to me. I never knew a man could be so womanly & tender. He has watched and waited on me devotedly, until I cursed myself for being ill & causing him all this worry. There was no little thing that he did not think of for my comfort, no tenderness that he did not lavish on me. I have indeed known the full extent of his love. If those who idolise him as a public man could know the full greatness of his heart, how much more their idol would he be! And through it all he has been immersed in great decisions appertaining to this great crisis, until I have trembled for his health, & loathed myself for causing him trouble at this time.[5]

Blaming herself for her pregnancy, and worrying about the strain of it on *his* health, might seem to be carrying feminine self-abnegation too far. LG's exceptional concern for Frances at this time suggests that he at least recognised some responsibility for her situation. Yet it is not impossible that Frances had deliberately allowed herself to become pregnant to try to bounce him into accepting the love child she believed they both wanted. Many years later she warned her daughter Jennifer that 'precautions are never one hundred per cent reliable'. But Jennifer's own daughter may be nearer the truth in speculating that Frances's 'precautions' in January 1915 'were blatantly inadequate because she did not really want them to work'.[6]

Moreover there is a significant entry in Frances's diary the previous autumn, recording a dinner with Riddell that LG told her about, when the conversation had turned to 'the unmarried mother and her status'.

One of the party said that at a recent gathering on the subject Mary
Macarthur & Violet Markham* had both spoken in support of her, & they
had expressed the opinion that a woman had a perfect right to have a child
from any man she pleases.[7]

These were advanced views by any standard. Unfortunately Frances
does not relate what LG or any of the other men present thought of
them; and Riddell recorded a different part of the conversation entirely.[8]
Nevertheless it is interesting that LG passed on to Frances the sort of
ideas that were being canvassed at progressive dinner tables, and still
more so that Frances latched onto this particular one. One senses that
she already identified with the position of the unmarried mother.†
For the present, however, Frances decided that her overriding duty
was to LG's work. From blaming herself for causing him trouble at
such a time, she took comfort from the fact that worrying about her
actually seemed to stimulate him; then she went on to pen an adoring
hymn to his selfless patriotic dedication.

In the midst of all this he found time to prepare and deliver a speech at
Bangor which many think is the greatest speech of his life.‡ He says that
the anxiety and trouble helped him to make a great speech, for when his
mind is disturbed his whole nature is upheaved, and it stimulates him to
greater power of expression . . .
    I do not think there is any man in England who is working more
unselfishly for our victory in this war, than he is. He does not cease from
one week to the next to devise some means for advancing our interests: and
when a plan is thought of, he does not hesitate until it is carried into practice,
& with the right men to work it, & a word of advice, a hint, suggestion,

---

* Two leading feminists of the day.
† To his credit, LG took a humane line on the irregular relationships of others, even if
he could not acknowledge his own. When the Archbishop of Canterbury objected that
it would undermine marriage to pay unmarried women whose men had volunteered the
same separation allowance as wives, LG persuaded the Cabinet to make no distinction.
'If you are going to take this line,' he argued, 'you ought to inquire into the morals of
the man *before* you accept his life. Once you have accepted it, he has a right to *demand*
an allowance for the woman he has lived with & their children – provided it is a bona-
fide union.'[9]
‡ This speech provided the title given to a book of LG's speeches that was published
in September and sold in enormous numbers. *Through Terror to Triumph: Speeches
and Pronouncements of the Right Hon. David Lloyd George, M.P., since the Beginning
of the War* was 'arranged by F. L. Stevenson, B.A. (Lond.)'.

or word of encouragement, he leaves it in full swing. And the fruits of his tireless brain have been so diverse that it seems impossible that one man should have been responsible for them, & carried them into effect, & still be 'going strong'.[10]

This, she told herself, was what made her sacrifice worthwhile.

Tireless and dynamic LG certainly was: all contemporary accounts of the war praise his energy and inspiration. Unselfish he was not. Even his concern for Frances was shamelessly egotistical. His first unmistakable love letter that she did not burn dates from this time: it was written from the Treasury while she was recovering at Walton Heath.

My own sweet pet,

I could not talk to you on the phone as I had ears beside my own in the room but I heard all you told me with inexpressible relief. I have almost made myself ill with worry & anxiety about my darling. Today I have a slight recurrence of my old throat trouble but it will pass away now – *if Pussy* OBEYS ORDERS & rests. But if she is naughty & only does what is pleasing in her own sight then she will break her sweetheart hopelessly.

So *rest* REST REST

Not for your own sake but for mine. Never mind whether you feel well or not – rest. I want you to build up a reserve of strength for Monday.

Tomorrow read pious books – they are much more restful. Think occasionally but not too often of the poor old man whose heart bleeds for every twinge of pain you have suffered.

Fond fond affection & love from that old Man

Scribble one word of reply for Sarah to give me.[11]

8

'PRO PATRIA MORI'

As if Frances's trouble was not bad enough, Mr and Mrs Stevenson had an even greater worry at this time when their only son, Paul, was posted to France on 14 March 1915. Aged just eighteen, Paul was the other clever child of the family and the apple of his mother's eye. He had left Christ's Hospital the previous summer with golden opinions and an exhibition to St John's College, Oxford, which he was destined never to take up. He was indeed the very paradigm of Wilfred Owen's 'doomed youth' – an idealistic public schoolboy, fired with callow patriotism, eager to join up and get into the war before it was all over. His first experience in an officers' training camp was a bit of a shock, as Frances recorded in October.

> I have had a rather disquieting letter from Paul who is not happy at St Albans. He says the other officers are rotters. I expect they are so-called 'men of the world' – and he has known nothing of the world yet, poor little beggar. I know his ideals are high, & respect him for it, but I am afraid he will receive many knocks and bruises. He is tough in body & mind, but he has a sensitive soul.[1]

Two weeks later – the same day she recorded LG's relief that Gwilym would not be going to France – Frances heard that Paul would be leaving in a few weeks' time. 'He is quite happy now.'[2] In fact he was not posted for another four months. Preoccupied with her own problems, however, Frances seems to have been remarkably unconcerned about her brother, except as another worry for her mother. 'Paul is under orders to go to France,' she noted at the end of her passionate diary entry of 11 March.

> Mamma and Dada are naturally upset about it, & it seems very hard for them that their troubles should all come at once. I do not want to add unduly to their trouble, so must make up my mind to a little self-sacrifice for some time to come so as not to upset them too much. Nevertheless I will never, never give C. up. 'Leave all for love!'[3]

Frances went home the next weekend to try to support her mother, but was evidently not much comfort to her.

> She is very bitter as to the disappointment that one's children bring. She says 'Everything is turning out so differently from what we had expected. Dada & I have had 27 years of happiness, and now we have got to pay for it.' Poor Mother! She cannot realise, & I fear she never will, that parents cannot control their children's lives for ever – that children exist for their own and the next generation, and not for that of their parents, which is past. However, it is hopeless to argue with her; but I fear she will never be happy unless she takes a wider view. What is more, if she is not careful, she will lose the sympathy and respect of her children.

She did mention that they had received several letters from Paul, who seemed 'in excellent spirits'.

> The casualties lately have been very heavy & I hope this will not continue. I cannot help thinking of the awful terror that must come over some of these boys when they are under fire for the first time. I pray that Paul may be spared that.[4]

Still she does not seem to have shared her mother's awful premonition that he would never come back.

Paul's letters from France are almost unbearably pathetic. On Easter Sunday 1915 he wrote to Frances:

> Well, we haven't been in the trenches yet, but this week we are starting in real earnest. All the officers are going in turn to the first line of trenches for 24 hours each, so that by the end of the week I shall have had my first taste of the firing line.

I think it is just about time that we started doing something. There is no need to be disturbed about it as I am sure I bear a charmed life.

There is really nothing more to tell you. I hope to have something more exciting to say when I write next.

Please give my love to everyone at home.

From your loving brother

Paul

P.S. . . . Have just heard that the plan of going to the trenches this week has all been cancelled. Just our luck![5]

Three weeks later his frustration was becoming desperate:

When do they seem to think the war will be over? From what I can see out here, all the troops, both English and German, are quite cheerful but hopelessly fed up with the whole affair. In some parts of the line there is a mutual understanding between the troops not to fire at one another in the ordinary way. It is said that the Saxons put up a note in their trenches – 'Don't fire now, we are Saxons. Wait till 6.30 when the Prussian Guard relieves us.'

I am rather inclined to doubt this but it shows exactly the point of view of the troops that have been here for some time. The point of view of the troops that have come out lately is that there ought to be a kind of 'mad minute' of fighting, lasting for about a fortnight, and then peace.

There was little to do, he ended, except eat and sleep, 'but I should think that things would begin to move soon'.[6]

Five days after this he wrote again to thank Frances for sending him a number of books, including Shaw's *The Doctor's Dilemma*. Oddly he asked whose copies they were – his own, hers or LG's? Though naturally he did not know the truth, he must have thought his sister knew the Chancellor pretty well to imagine that she might send him his books. He went on, still resolutely optimistic:

We certainly do seem to have had a nasty bump in Flanders, but I hope things will right themselves. I saw the regular bulletins of news issued by the First Army yesterday, and the prospects seemed to be very bright on the whole.

We are still hanging round about the firing line, waiting to go up there tomorrow evening, and wondering when something really exciting is going to happen.[7]

Something exciting would happen all too soon.

At the beginning of April Frances was still not well. She struggled in to the Treasury on Friday 2nd to see LG, who had come up to attend a funeral ('I was glad to see him . . . for Thursday to Monday is a long time to go & it made all the difference seeing him'), then went home to bed, where she was presumably cared for by her mother. LG had ministerial colleagues with him at Walton Heath, which – he claimed – prevented him phoning her. She pretended to be glad, since she did not want him to know that she was ill. He was coming to London on Monday on the excuse of meeting the Archbishop of Canterbury ('"And a very good excuse, too!" said C.') But for once Frances was a little jealous of his absorption in his work. He was currently obsessed with a scheme to reduce drunkenness – and thereby supposedly increase productivity in the munitions factories – by nationalising the liquor trade.

C. is steeped in drink, as I tell him. He has been drink mad this last week – can talk and think of nothing else. I suppose I must put up with it, as it is a great work, but I tell him that I am very jealous of its occupying his attention so much. However we are looking forward to having a little time together after next week, so it is worth waiting for.[8]

But on Monday she was still feeling 'very seedy . . . I felt I could not go on any longer.'[9] So LG sent her to Brighton for a week, where he wrote to her practically every day. These letters were as indiscreet as those Asquith was simultaneously writing in Cabinet to his platonic lady friend Venetia Stanley. But Frances no longer heeded LG's advice that she should burn them.

Cariad [darling]

I am delighted to hear you are throwing off your physical frailties! I do miss you so much more than I can tell you. But I mustn't talk about that lest it make you uneasy & I want you above everything to be restful . . .

I am getting on well with my Liquor Scheme. The Labour leaders are favourable. My trouble now will be the Cabinet.

So you forgot me altogether for hours at a time did you. So glad. The more of those hours of oblivion you seek & enjoy the better will I be pleased. Forget all your worries – *including me.*

Yes get Muriel down over the weekend. Wire her. She might join you Saturday. Are you alright for cash? I would like you to stay until Tuesday. That would suit me better for Walton. I'll explain when we meet.

PM has overruled K[itchener] peremptorily & put me in command of Munitions of War! God help me . . .

No news. Great row between Winston & K. at yesterday's Cabinet! The temper of the great War Lords is getting worse & worse as their short-comings are getting more manifest. K. has made a mess of Munitions & Winston a muddle of the Dardanelles* & their temper is consequently vile.

Burn this & yesterday's at once. It's dangerous to send these letters through the post as they can open them now. I forgot that so I've had a fit of nerves.

Yrs ever
D.[10]

Frances evidently replied; but unfortunately LG did not keep her letters. He wrote back the next day.

My own sweet

I have already read your darling letter twice over & it is yet but the eleventh hour of the morning. I write now lest I fail to find time later on as I have a bustling day in front of me.

I am so glad you are at the Bedford. A boarding house or rooms would have been so dull but there is always life – of a sort – at a hotel . . . Rest for two days without any physical exertion at all. You must be physically very exhausted after your experiences but you have a rattling good sound consti-tution & give it a fair chance by rest to fill up the depleted reservoir of strength you will soon be alright. But don't expect to find yourself A1 at Lloyd (George)'s in 48 hours. Should not be at all surprised that now you are away from the artificial stimulants & excitements of your life here that you might feel weaker & more depressed. That is the first stage of a real rest . . .

5.25

Overwhelmed with work. Meant to write a long letter. Tory leaders have

---

* Churchill, as First Lord of the Admiralty, was principally responsible for a failed attempt to knock Turkey out of the war by forcing a passage of the Dardanelles in 1915.

decided to support my scheme. Am winning support on both sides. But it will be a tough job. I'll put it through with your help Pussy & then –

Look after yourself – for my sake sweetheart mine. I love you so fondly tenderly *fiercely*.

Ever & ever

Your

D.[11]

By Friday Frances was feeling 'terribly lonely'[12] and was impatient to get back to Walton Heath. But LG did not want her back just yet.

My darling Pussy

I am so full of happiness when I look at the sunshine outside & know that it is healing my sweetheart at Brighton. You must not expect too quick results. Patience must be Pussy's motto. I am so disappointed that it was not possible for me to arrange that you should be up today because I am thirsting for my dear little girl's companionship. But I know you will bear with me when I tell you that I found it absolutely impossible to arrange. I still think you had better be under Dr Brighton's charge until Tuesday then Dr Walton (with his able & experienced assistant) can take you on.

Write to me Sunday c/o J.T.D. . . .

I am very busy & getting on well so far but it will mean a very tough fight . . . Hope to get a day off tomorrow. Need it. Feel much less worried because of the good news from you. Oh Puss it hurts me to see you ill & in pain. I would rather miss your sweet face for another week if necessary than have you back incompletely repaired . . .

Come back Tuesday & go straight to Walton.

For ever & ever.

D.[13]

He wrote again on Saturday, with an abbreviated greeting that became one of his trademarks.

MODP [My Own Darling Pussy]

I tried to get on to you by phone. It took an hour to get through & then you were out. I was disappointed & glad. You know the reason for the first. I was glad because I felt you were carrying out my paternal instructions. D. [J. T. Davies] upset me this morning by telling me you were coming up today. I could not believe it possible after all I had written to you begging you to stay until Tuesday. You must get thoroughly fixed up this time however long it may take. But you sometimes do disobey so I am afraid of writing lest this letter fall into other hands.

I want to see you Tuesday ever so much better but you are not coming to the *office* for another week. You have a great deal of strength to recover & it will take you at least a fortnight to do so. You must follow my directions P. I want you *thoroughly* well. I cannot bear the recurrent anxiety of seeing you ill & depressed. You are a courageous little girl & I know you will do this for me . . .

I wish I could feel free to write all I have in my heart. But you know. *Byth bythoedd* C. [For ever and ever]
D.[14]

The reason LG did not want Frances back at Walton Heath before Tuesday is clear from Riddell's diary: his family was there for the weekend. But he did not tell Frances that. Maggie did not stay long, however, and Frances duly came on the Tuesday and was waiting for him that evening when he got back from London after a dinner. They then spent most of the next week together, commuting between Walton and Downing Street. LG was still very taken up with his liquor scheme and the mounting crisis of the government; but they had some moments of relaxation.

On Thursday we left in the car at 5 o'clock & went down to Walton. There was no-one there to prepare a meal, so we collected refreshments of various kinds at Sutton for an impromptu supper. We left the car at Kingswood & went for a long walk on the Heath. C. was quite mad, & improvised mock sermons for my benefit, taking idiotic subjects for his texts. I love to see him in these mad moods; he is like some wild boy broken loose from school. Moreover, I know when he is like this that he has thrown off all worries and cares for the time being & that his mind is having a rest. It was dark by the time we got to Walton. We passed such a happy evening together.

We drove up to town on Friday morning, C. still as mad as ever, this time composing opera, saying mad things in true recitative style, I helping him with the accompaniment in between. He was so busy all day that I scarcely saw him.

That evening LG took his old flame 'Mrs Tim' – with her husband, Timothy Davies – out to dinner, since she was 'downhearted' at not having seen him for a long time. 'I think he is very kind & nice to her,' Frances wrote with extraordinary forbearance, 'and I would not have it otherwise.'[15]

In May the political crisis came to a head, precipitated by Admiral 'Jacky' Fisher's resignation as First Sea Lord, which forced Asquith reluctantly to take the Conservatives into a coalition government – thus bringing to an end the last purely Liberal administration. After much speculation that LG might take Kitchener's place at the War Office, he eventually agreed to leave the Treasury to set up a new Ministry of Munitions instead. Frances's diary gives a blow-by-blow account of all these events from LG's point of view. At the beginning of the month, on top of everything else, he had the budget to deliver (his eighth) and she recorded that he was 'very touchy' from overwork. Yet he still managed to go to the theatre in the evening after his budget speech – having dined with Frances first! The next evening he was 'frightfully tired when he had finished at eight o'clock, but revived after dinner, & became quite merry, describing to me Tree's effort the night before . . . imitating him in his part as the ardent lover, forgetting his part & out of reach of the prompter.'*[16] On 15 May she wrote that they had 'had a strenuous week, & C. & I have seen comparatively little of each other – just enough to keep us going, however, & for him to tell me the news'.[17] Two days later 'C. had a bomb ready for me':

He had been very busy in the early part of the morning seeing Mr Balfour, Mr Bonar Law, the Prime Minister and others.† When I went to him later with some letters, 'Well, Pussy', he said to me. 'I'm leaving this place!' I would not believe him, but he assured me it was the truth . . . We were very excited about it. C. promised to take me with him to the W.O. [War Office], & we had all sorts of plans . . . I passed a sleepless night thinking of all the responsibilities that would devolve on C. & all the incidental happenings that would accompany a change of office.

Next day LG decided that he did not want to leave the Treasury after all. 'However, I am to dine with him tonight & we shall be able to talk the matter over.'[18]

---

* Sir Herbert Beerbohm Tree was the leading actor of the day. The play was a French melodrama called *The Right to Kill*.
† Though Bonar Law had been Tory leader since 1911, his predecessor A. J. Balfour (Prime Minister from 1901 to 1905) was still an influential figure in the party.

The issue was not settled for another week. There was the possibility that LG might take responsibility for munitions while still remaining Chancellor; or that Asquith might take care of the Treasury temporarily himself, leaving LG free to devote all his energy to munitions. LG even told Frances that Bonar Law and Balfour proposed that he should replace Asquith as Prime Minister; but he may have been gilding the lily to impress her, since there is no independent evidence of this – though he did write the same thing to Maggie. Amid all this excitement, he and Frances still managed to have what she called 'a glorious time over the weekend, in spite of worries and uncertainties'. First a friendly Liberal MP invited them to dinner at his flat and afterwards took them to the theatre – the first record of them going out together in public. The next day they went down to Walton Heath.

> I went home to tea first, as it was Muriel's birthday. [She was thirteen.] C. wanted to give her a Persian kitten, but Mamma would not allow her to have another animal. On Saturday we came up, as there was a meeting on the subject of the Coalition. C. took Megan out to tea, & we both motored down to Walton afterwards. Sunday was a gorgeous day. We started at 11.30 & motored down to Beachy Head & picniced there. Came back through Ashdown Forest & had tea on the common there. It was a perfect day & the sea was motionless.[19]

The composition of the new government was finally agreed on 24 May. Years later, when writing his *War Memoirs*, LG told A. J. Sylvester that it was while having tea with Megan at Newnes' Restaurant in Putney that he had finally made up his mind – against much advice, not least from Maggie and his Uncle Lloyd – to accept the munitions job.[20] The intention was that the arrangement should be only temporary: Reginald McKenna was to fill the Chancellorship in the meantime and relinquish it when LG was ready to take it back. '11 Downing St,' he assured Maggie, 'I still occupy.'[21] The next day Frances and J. T. Davies moved with LG to create a new department from scratch. Their accommodation at 6 Whitehall Gardens, recently vacated by an art dealer, was initially furnished with no more than a table and two chairs. At the end of a chaotic first day they all went out for a meal and then to the theatre to see a popular musical of the moment called *Rosy Rapture of the Beauty Chorus*. During the last act Frances noticed JT pass LG a message. She took no notice at the time; but after the show LG took her back to Downing Street, where he broke the news to her that her brother Paul had died of wounds in France. He then took her home to her devastated parents.

It was nearly three weeks before she was able to write again in her diary, on 12 June:

A year ago today we were down at Christ's Hospital for the last prize-giving that Paul would partake in as a member of the school. We were so proud of him & of all the honours that fell to him. Today we have been taking part in a Memorial Service for him & others of the 23rd London, who have fallen recently in France. Even now it seems incredible that he is dead – that he will never return. It is the first time that I have experienced the death of one who was dear to me, & the hopelessness of it all has thrown a shadow over my life that I do not believe can ever disappear. The nobility of his death takes away some of the bitterness, and the many tributes that we have received from all who ever knew him. But all our hopes and plans have come to nothing, though I know he would have wished for no better end than this. He was so terribly eager to get to the firing line, but I did not worry about him, for it seemed to me that he at least would come safely back, that death at least would spare one so promising & so dear and necessary to us. The shock came cruelly, & has numbed my brain, & the consolation seems to be little for so terrible a loss. They say that time will heal the wounds, & leave only pride instead of grief, but how can we ever do anything but miss him and need him more and more as the years go on?[22]

9

THE DECOY

Frances did not write her diary again until September 1915. As soon as she returned to work after Paul's death she was heavily occupied in helping to set up the new Ministry of Munitions. Now that LG had ceased to be Chancellor, she noted, 'I must no longer call him C., but will substitute D., which has the advantage of being permanent.'[1] On 1 July – surprisingly long after the event – she had another letter from Stuart Brown, expressing sympathy over Paul, but also concern for her.

> I am very afraid you must be dreadfully overworked just now. Perhaps, though, it is more of a relief than a trouble to have too much to do, provided that it does not go too far. It is very impertinent of me, but I hope you won't carry it too far. We have had one of our strongest men here [the India Office] breaking down for three months, almost without warning. It would obviously be a pretty serious thing in your case, not only for your own sake – which is what your people and your friends would most care about – but because of your work as well. If as I gather you and Davies are doing what it took three people to do before, the strain must be very great, and it would be worse if you feel that you cannot afford to slacken off a little now and then so as to have something in reserve. I hope you won't mind my saying this: but you know your Chief does not always consider these things.[2]

LG went to Criccieth, rather earlier than usual, for the first week in August. Frances was evidently still at work, since he wrote to her at the office in an envelope marked 'Personal – to be opened by no-one else'.

My own sweet little Pussy,

I am longing to be back with you. I am becoming more intolerant of these partings month by month. I cannot live now without my darling. I know that better even than I did weeks ago. It is either you or nothing for me *Cariad*.

I have had the dreariest of holidays – rain mist damp. Tonight I motor to Colwyn. I leave Colwyn at 9.19 tomorrow reaching Euston at 2.12 – then –

Now Pussy I have made up my mind to disappoint myself – & you. I have two days of most important & trying work in front of me – conferences & decisions on which the success of the Department depend & I must reserve all my strength for them. I know you will agree. Wednesday we can go to Walton. Meanwhile help me to restrain myself – for I am lost for my passion for you is a *consuming* flame – it burns up all wisdom prudence judgment in my soul. Help me *cariad bach anwyl aur*. [My precious little darling].

I feel as if during the last two months I have not given my very best to the terrible task entrusted to me. My future depends entirely on it. What is much more important – the nation's future depends on it. The distracting events of the past few weeks have half-paralysed me & I must pull myself together. I cannot do so without your wise help. You are everything to me now. My failure or success will depend entirely on you. You possess my soul entirely.

Tomorrow night I dine with Churchill so you can make your own arrangements.

Oh I do want to see you – I want *you* & no-one & nothing else.

Your own

D. – for ever[3]

He was back in London as promised on 9 August, and he and Frances were presumably together for the next fortnight. During this period LG wrote several times to Maggie – partly about his battles, partly about Uncle Lloyd's declining health and partly expressing relief that Dick and Gwilym were no longer in the Welsh Division, which was being 'rather badly cut up' in the Dardanelles.[4] Then on 23 August he went to Folkestone to meet the French munitions minister. From there LG wrote Frances another letter of passionate commitment, ending with his first reference to an extraordinary proposal.

My own sweet child

   I received both your darling letters & they were like nectar for lips parched with a great passion. I have been these two or three days thinking things of unutterable tenderness & love for my little *cariad*. My affection for her has deepened & sweetened beyond anything words can tell. Yours is the tenderest & purest love of my life Pussy *bach anwyl aur*. I could face *anything* with you. I have been thinking of you all day & much of the night & always oh so fondly.

   Returning tomorrow. No time to write any more.

   I've had a talk with D. [Davies]. His view is that O. is moved by a consuming desire to *get on*. That is the line. I believe he would do it unconditionally. There is peril & pollution in any other course. I love my *pure* little darling.

   Ever & Ever
   Your own
   D.[5]

The last paragraph introduces one of the strangest episodes in the whole Lloyd George/Frances saga. It seems that LG had the idea of setting up a cover for their relationship by persuading Frances to marry another man who would be willing – like Timothy Davies – to play the role of the complaisant husband by turning a blind eye to her infidelity. The logic was that a respectably married woman could maintain a lover more easily and with less scandal than an unmarried one: London society was full of such discreet arrangements. Even so it is extraordinary that LG, who was normally furiously jealous if Frances so much as smiled at another man, could have contemplated sharing her, even nominally, with another; even more extraordinary that Frances could have entertained the idea for a moment. Yet it appears that she went along with it for some time, to the extent of actually becoming formally engaged. The only possible explanation is that she was desperate to mollify her parents by adopting an outwardly conventional front, behind which she could continue to devote herself to LG – and maybe even bear his children – without scandal. The person who had least to gain from the arrangement was the unfortunate decoy.

The man chosen for this role was Captain William Hugh Owen, known as Billy. He was inevitably a Welshman, somewhat dismissively described by A. J. P. Taylor as the former stationmaster at Holyhead, but now in uniform (Royal Engineers) and working in the Ministry of

Munitions. He finished the war as the ministry's man in Canada, responsible for purchasing ships for use by Britain, so he was no fool. (He had also been a Welsh hockey international before the war.) He was, as LG recognised in his letter to Frances, ambitious to 'get on'; presumably he thought that marrying his minister's mistress would help him to do so. But he also evidently admired Frances and must have hoped that, once married to her, he would in time be able to win her away from LG, or that LG would tire of her, leaving him in possession of his wife. At any rate while he was willing to woo Frances in the knowledge of her commitment to LG – 'I believe he would do it unconditionally' – it is clear that he did not see himself simply as a willing stooge.

The first reference to Owen in Frances's diary is on 20 September. It may be significant that a few days earlier she recorded for the first time a row between herself and LG. They had been in Bristol, where LG was making a speech, and returned to Walton the same evening. 'Both being very tired, and consequently irritable, we quarrelled, which was a pity. However, we have made it up for this week.'[6] Of course this may have nothing to do with Owen at all; LG was having a hard time politically over his support for conscription, which was dividing him from his Liberal colleagues and forcing him inexorably into alliance with the Tories. Nevertheless the following weekend (18–19 September) Frances notes that Owen was with them at Walton Heath. From a later letter it appears that some 'arrangement' was agreed on this occasion. But Frances does not record any serious conversation; on the contrary.

> D. was in high spirits all day – began at breakfast by a wholesale survey of everything almost that the imagination can call up – a fantasy in which potatoes, damson jam, British patriotism (or the lack of it), French courage, pretty women, German tactics & the daily press were all dealt with in a most sweeping fashion.

There followed an interesting exchange – conceivably for Owen's benefit.

> He ended up with a eulogy on love, quoting as the greatest witness St Paul and the 13th chapter of Corinthians. I gave him my own opinion of St Paul by reading him in turn the 11th chapter, to which he had no answer but

that St Paul must have been badly treated by some woman in order to have
obtained that impression.[7]

The eleventh chapter of Corinthians is all about the subordination of
women. ('Neither was the man created for the woman; but the woman
for the man.'[8]) By reading it Frances was serving notice that she was
not to be treated as an object for male convenience, and evidently
succeeded in putting LG on the defensive.

Two weeks later she rejected the idea that she should marry Billy
Owen – on the grounds that it would make LG unhappy! Her conclusion comes at the end of a long account of his deepening worry about
setbacks on the Western Front and in the Dardanelles, and her own
depression about the war and the reality of Paul's death, brought on
by the approach of winter.

> During the summer it did not seem so dreadful to think of him resting
> under a peaceful sky, with the cornfields smiling around him. But the
> dreary weather makes one shudder & brings a queer depression, and as
> time goes by the shock of realising that he will not come back becomes
> more insistent.

Her mother, by contrast, had 'brightened up' and was busy moving
from Clapham to a new house in Wallington. Frances was finally taking
the chance to set up on her own. 'I am trying to persuade Mary Phillips
[a college friend] to take a flat with me in town, so that I would not
go home every night. I think she will probably do it.' Finally:

> I cannot marry Owen. I have told him so & broken off the engagement. It
> did not last very long. But D. was making himself miserable over the idea
> of my belonging to someone else even in name. Several times he had cried
> & sobbed as a child when speaking of it, begging me all the time to take
> no notice of him. But I could not bear to give him pain, & I know that he
> is relieved now that I have broken it off. I must be free to be with him
> always, & marriage I know would forge new bonds. Owen is very upset,
> but wishes to be friends still. He is very weak, and a very little satisfies
> him.[9]

But that was not the end of the matter. Neither LG – despite his
tears – nor Owen was willing to abandon the idea so easily. On

11 October Owen wrote from Holyhead, where he was home on leave:

> My dear Miss Stevenson
>
> The right to address a more intimate salutation is one I would fain possess. As it is my pen almost committed me, but fear of incurring your displeasure coupled with the thought that the state of, well, shall we say 'benevolent neutrality' which you now graciously extend to me hardly warranted such a liberty deterred me. Some day – well some day you may feel disposed to extend to me the privilege.

He went on to say that he was meeting the Deputy Assistant Director of Movements at the War Office in Liverpool next day and would be back in London the day after that.

> I shall be back in town on Wednesday and hope to be allowed an early opportunity of looking over your flat and incidentally to study 'the pink and blue' effect! . . . I am looking forward very much to seeing you again. You won't mind my ringing you up when I get back, will you?
>
> My regards to your respected Chief.
>
> Yours as always
>
> Billy Owen[10]

In fact he did not get to London on Wednesday. He was ill, was sent home to bed and had his leave extended by another week, as he explained to Frances on the Thursday:

> My dear ——
>
> You will be surprised to know that I am still in the country . . .
>
> Under ordinary circumstances this would have given me much pleasure, but seeing that for nearly a week I have been in anticipation of inspecting certain colour effects and making one (about that) of a party of three 'somewhere' in London tomorrow evening, the concession is received with mixed feelings . . .
>
> I am deeply sorry I shall not be able to join you tomorrow, but I really think I am doing just what you would wish me to do.
>
> You'll explain to Miss Phillips, won't you?
>
> Yours as always
>
> Billy Owen[11]

Evidently Frances had accomplished her move so quickly that she and Mary were expecting Owen for dinner on Friday. The flat was at 41a Chester Square, near Victoria, on the corner of Elizabeth Street, above what is today a bookshop. That week Frances noted that she had already bought, among other things, 'a grand piano, a chester-field and an eiderdown'.[12] It is most likely that LG helped, though she wrote a few weeks later that the expense would make 'a considerable hole in my money'.[13] Either way it was clear whom she really meant to entertain there. 'D. is desperately anxious to get it completed, for he is having a rotten time at home, everyone being against him & making him as miserable as possible.'[14] She did not grudge the cost, since 'nothing can be too good for D., & I want to make it so comfort-able for him'.[15]

The next day Owen wrote again, on the excuse that he had heard reports of Zeppelin raids on London and hoped Frances was all right. 'I'm sure these epistles of mine bore you stiff, so on this occasion I'll not inflict on you the trouble of reading through a lengthy one.' But he told her he was feeling fit again after climbing a hundred-foot 'moun-tain' on Anglesey, and sent his best regards to J. T. Davies.[16] To these letters Frances evidently replied in such terms that Owen – now back in London – responded immediately and forcefully.

My dear Frances . . .

As you say, the present state of affairs is very unsatisfactory and cannot be allowed to continue indefinitely. Your letter seems to indicate that you consider me responsible for the present condition of things, but I am confi-dent that when you have heard my case you will not saddle me with more than my share of responsibility.

Please do not think that I write in a spirit of recrimination but rather with a desire to put to you the matter from my point of view.

To come to the point. You say that, first of all having agreed with you that our engagement should be at an end I subsequently said that I came to this agreement against my will. A brief review of matters will explain my position. Your letter breaking off our engagement was couched in very definite language – in fact the note of finality was so pronounced as to cause me absolutely to despair of ever prevailing upon you to change your mind. You did not then suggest that any action of mine had caused you to write, but very decidedly stated that '*you* could not proceed with the arrange-ment that we had come to at Walton Heath because you were fully convinced that such an arrangement would only bring unhappiness to all concerned etc'. Not a word would convey to me that anything I had or had not done had influenced you in arriving at that decision, and I, desiring at all times and above all things that you should be happy, what course could I take other than to reluctantly acquiesce.

Subsequently, however, a remark let fall by one for whom I in common with you have the deepest regard [obviously LG], generated the hope that some action of mine upon which you had placed a wrong construction had influenced you in arriving at the decision you had taken. Your letter strengthens this hope, for it implies want of keenness on my part. Such is not the case. My apparent inattention during the days immediately preceding the rupture was due to causes entirely beyond my control.

Here he explains that a colleague was on leave, which made it impossible for him to come to her. There was also a second domestic reason, which he said was too personal to write in a letter.

It is not, in fact, an easy matter to *talk* about, but had an explanation of my conduct been demanded I would not as in the present case have hesitated to speak.

All I ask is that you give me a chance to explain.

Yours as always

Billy Owen[17]

From this it is clear that Owen was a genuine suitor who was not merely willing, but eager, to marry Frances even on LG's terms. At the same time Frances was still being pressured by the third partner in this extraordinary proposed ménage. 'D. is now on the marriage tack again,' she wrote on 23 October.

He says there are many advantages to be gained by marriage *provided that Owen understands clearly what our relations are*, & promises to respect them. Am dining with Owen tonight to discuss the matter.[18]

Unfortunately Frances did not record the outcome of this discussion. But the idea clearly remained in play for another month, since not until 24 November did she make another apparently final decision to reject it.

I have come to the conclusion that D. needs all my energies and devotion, and I think that marriage might bring an element of worry and unhappiness into his life, even on the most favourable terms (to him). Owen & I are therefore *not* engaged & I have not seen him for some time.[19]

That seems to be decisive. Yet Owen did not disappear, nor did the pretence that he and Frances were engaged.

Over the autumn Frances settled into her flat and LG – ever more critical of his colleagues and the military over the conduct of the war – found a welcome haven there as the slaughter in France continued with no sign of the promised breakthrough. Frances generally soothed and encouraged him; but she also sometimes argued with him, as on 12 October when Sir Edward Carson resigned from the government and LG wondered whether he should do the same.

Carson has resigned today, & D. does not think he will stay in many days more. I fear it is too late, as it will seem like the rat leaving the sinking ship, as D. says. I spoke rather harshly last night, for I was feeling very bitter at the delay, I told him he should have resigned a fortnight ago, following up his Preface* . . . by speeches all over the country, rousing the nation to a sense of danger. He says, however, quite truly, that if he goes out he will be treated as a pariah by the Liberals, and he will not have the advantage of being able to state his case to the country, as that would give us away to the enemy. Whereas if he stays in, he is at least getting munitions for the troops. Perhaps he is right, but I hate him to be associated with a Government that through sheer inefficiency brought Britain to her ruin and humiliated her throughout the world. He was very sweet to me, though, although I said rather bitter things. But God knows I would not wound him, and I am the first to recognise his courage. He is a little sensible to flattery, though, and it is wretched for him to be cold-shouldered by his colleagues and condemned as a traitor.

Inevitably Frances mainly reflected LG's own views back to him in more emotional terms. She was particularly frustrated by the government's failure to send help to Serbia, which he believed could be the

* That is, LG's preface to *Through Terror to Triumph*, which was strongly critical of the government's lack of grip.

key to victory. Despite the failure of the Dardanelles, LG was still anxious to find a way round the deadlock on the Western Front.

> Today in the Cabinet, they have done *nothing* . . . It would be laughable if it were not so dreadfully tragic. I am afraid I made D. cross again this afternoon, by urging him to make them do *something*. He is the only person of action among them, but he says it is impossible to get the P.M. to do anything. He said if I only saw I would understand. He just sits there and uses the whole of his crafty brain to squash any plan for action that is put forward. D. says that if he were in the pay of the Germans he could not be of more complete use to them. I was in such desperation that I could scarcely keep from crying, & D. was rather upset. I have implored of him to insist on their doing something. Delay is criminal.[20]

LG's conduct of his relationship with Frances at this time was a strange mixture of openness and secrecy – caution masquerading as defiance. One night he took her (with J. T. Davies as chaperon) to dinner at the Hotel Cecil. Afterwards, she noted, 'we walked down the Strand, down the Waterloo Bridge steps, and home along the Embankment. We had a very pleasant walk, D. being easily able to go unrecognised, as the streets are pitch dark at present.'[21] But a few days earlier he was careful that they should not be seen to go to Walton Heath together.

> I had to go by train, as D. does not like taking me about in his Gov. car, in case people fix on it for a scandal. I was rather sick about it, as I love driving with him, but D. made me cheer up, saying, 'Never mind! We are "doing" the world in spite of its spitefulness. There is much satisfaction in "doing" the world! I have defied it for 25 years – treated it with contempt, spat upon its tinsel robes, and I have won through. If you pay homage to it in certain things, you can defy it in others as much as you like.' It is very true: he has often said this to me in many different ways . . . If you respect certain forms and conventions, you may break others to your heart's content, and the world will say nothing.[22]

Despite the war, Frances noted on 15 November that they had had 'some glorious times at W.H. at odd moments during the last few weeks', when he managed to get 'right away from politics'.

He is always very sweet to me on these occasions and we are so utterly happy. Coming up in the car the other day he likened them to the oases which one comes to in a journey across the desert, and which even after leaving it keeps one's mind fresh until one comes to the next. We are going down tomorrow night, all being well, to another oasis![23]

In fact they were prevented because LG had to go – with Asquith, Grey and Balfour – to Paris to confer with the French about the Balkans.

He has promised to come back as soon as he possibly can, and I am to get our little home quite ready by the time he comes back. He said that he tried hard to persuade Bonar Law to go instead; but I am glad D. has gone, as I should not have liked to see him left behind . . . But I do hope D. won't be cold on that wretched destroyer![24]

They were gone only two days, and on his return LG drove straight to Walton Heath where Frances was waiting for him. As usual he had found time to do some shopping.

D. had brought me a sweet brooch with the Lorraine cross on it; in addition to this he had brought a charming Napoleon premier clock, and two candlesticks of the same period, for our new home. D. has excellent taste in these things, and I can only wonder that he can bear some of the things that are to be found in his own houses . . . I took these things straight to 41a Chester Square on Friday morning, & in the afternoon D. came to tea with Mr Davies, & D. stayed on to dinner. I had to prepare the dinner myself, but fortunately nothing too dreadful happened and we had a most happy time. The place is not quite ready yet, but we managed to make ourselves comfortable.[25]

While Frances was making her 'little home' with her lover, Maggie was rather out of the picture for some weeks. But LG still valued his wife's judgement. On 1 November, when he was again contemplating resignation, he wrote asking her advice. 'Wire me Downing St whether you agree or not. Wire early as the Cabinet is at 11.30.'[26] From Riddell we know that Maggie advised him not to resign.[27] Frances was again reminded of her subordinate status in late November, when after a 'very happy weekend together' at Walton, she and LG had to return to

London on Sunday night 'as Mrs Ll.George is ill and all alone. The boys are going away to France this week, and both she & D. are feeling rather miserable about it. I believe D. would be heartbroken if anything happened to Gwilym, to whom he is devoted.'[28] The following weekend they were back at Walton, and Megan came from school to spend Saturday afternoon with them. She at least still had no idea of Frances's true position in the household. 'She is a dear child,' Frances noted, 'and very sweet when she is away from the other female members of her family.'[29]

But Frances was able to spend Christmas – or at least Boxing Day – with LG. Two days earlier he was in Glasgow, trying to settle a strike that was damaging munitions production. He got a rough reception and was shouted down at a meeting of shop stewards. J. T. Davies, who was with him, wondered if they would get out alive. LG told Frances later that Glasgow was 'ripe for revolution' and the men 'completely out of hand'. But he enjoyed a scrap and came home 'quite cheery & nothing daunted'.[30] While he was away he wrote to her with instructions about Christmas.

> My own darling Puss
>
> I am having a very trying time up here. Wrangles dissensions suspicion – all hell let loose. But I mean to go through with it now I have started. I know I shall be amply rewarded by seeing your sweet affectionate loving pretty little face on Sunday.
>
> Go straight to Walton Sunday morning. I hope you have told Mrs Jones to get a turkey.
>
> Bring Muriel.*
>
> Fond tender enduring love
>
> From your old Man[31]

The next day he repeated his instructions in a wire from Newcastle: 'WILL YOU GO TO WALTON FOR SUNDAY AND GET TURKEY.'[32]

He travelled south on Christmas Day, eating Christmas dinner on the train and staging an informal concert at which everyone was expected to perform: 'reporters, messengers, anyone who was capable of doing anything to entertain'. JT told Frances that 'D. was quite mad,

---

* This was an odd suggestion, since Muriel was only thirteen and was presumably spending Christmas with her parents.

and they had a rollicking time'. Frances was waiting for him at Walton
and they spent the next day together 'very happily'.

> D. brought me a most handsome dressing gown, which Mr D. was sent to
> purchase in Glasgow . . . I gave D. my photograph for a Xmas present, &
> we have devised a skilful way of disguising it so that the case looks like a
> pocket book & he can carry it about in his pocket.[33]

The first three weeks of 1916 were so busy that Frances had no time
to write her diary – 'very long hours, and lots to do, & things very
worrying on the whole'.[34] By once again threatening to resign, LG eventually forced Asquith to move some way towards conscription. It was
now increasingly suggested that he should replace Kitchener at the War
Office. To Frances he admitted that he 'had done most of the hard
work at the Ministry of Munitions, and . . . was quite ready to seek
fresh fields. But he said that whoever went to the W.O. would have a
frightfully difficult task, for D. considers that disasters are still to
come.'[35]

Yet Chester Square still provided a refuge, as Frances noted at the
end of the month.

> D. & I manage to spend a good deal of time together now that the flat is
> in existence. He comes along there to dinner from the House of Commons,
> and walks home across the Park. I gave him a birthday dinner on his
> birthday, & we managed by dint of manoeuvring to spend the following
> weekend together.

But then, mysteriously, Billy Owen was with them again.

> On the Sunday we motored down to Eastbourne, & I stayed on the pier
> while D. & Owen (whom we had brought along with us) went to see Lord
> Murray* . . . We had a very happy journey: Owen is a very unobtrusive
> third, & looks after D. very nicely.[36]

Presumably Owen was acting as a cover for LG taking Frances with
him. But then why should he accompany LG to see Murray? And why
did he need to 'look after' LG when Frances was there? The fact is

---

* Lord Murray, a former Liberal Chief Whip, was recovering from a heart attack.

that Owen and Frances were still at some level pretending to be engaged. The position becomes odder still in May with a rash of letters from friends, former tutors and even the principal of Royal Holloway congratulating Frances on her imminent marriage.

Dear Frances,

I have just heard from Mary & she tells me of your engagement and marriage next week. It was most exciting news and I send you every good wish.

What does Mr Lloyd George say? Does he give his consent?

I hope this does not mean you give up your maisonette. I feel most sorrowful if it does & the man must be frightfully nice to be worth such a sacrifice! . . .

With love, yrs affect,

Ruby Rusley[37]

My dear Frances,

I have just heard from Nita that you are to be married next week & to such a nice man, she says. I am *so* glad & this brings you my heartiest congratulations & very best wishes for your happiness. It is nice that you are going on with your work till the end of the war, both from your point of view & that of Mr Lloyd George.

I am so glad to hear the good news & I should like to congratulate him too on having such a happy married life in view for it cannot but be happy, if he is all that I hear of him . . .

Yours affectionately,

Norah Bennett

Do let me know the date of the wedding so that we can have the wedding march in chapel.[38]

Dear Miss Stevenson,

Not knowing of your engagement I called upon you last Thursday at the Metropole to see if you could lunch with me, but you were away. Otherwise I might have heard your news, & been able to congratulate you in person. I do so now; but I congratulate Mr Owen still more – will you give him a message from me? – that I think he is a very lucky young man. Don't forget to let us know (the day before) the date of the wedding, so that we may have the wedding march in Chapel . . .

Yours very sincerely

E. C. Higgins*[39]

My dear Frances,

Mr Cross has just reported the great news!! Heaps of congratulations, the greater part of which please give Capt. Owen. By the way, has he any other name than 'young Owen'!! You were a little vague on that point when I last saw you! I am *awfully* pleased about it as I thought he was a dear. Now do write & tell me *all* about it & when you are going to be married & everything – you must make time to do it. Are you now making munitions, governing Ireland† or on the point of running the army? I should think you are nearly dead with work but I am glad 'Love's young dream' has had time to play its part. Excuse my smiling. Please give my respects and *many* congrats to the 'appy man & keep much love & heaps of good wishes for yourself.

Yours

Grace

P.S. Do you now call your boss 'Cousin David'?[40]

Apart from the last query, which is quite baffling, what emerges from all these letters is that Frances's friends – whether they had actually met Owen or knew him only by repute – all thought him a thoroughly suitable match for her. Grace thought him 'a dear', and Norah Bennett had heard good reports of him from Nita. They are all aware that she is doing important work with Lloyd George, and it is significant that she is not thought to be going to give it up, even though she is apparently to be married as early as next week. The idea that LG might have to give his consent is nearer the mark than its author probably knew. The puzzling question is how the story originated. Ruby got it from Mary; but no one knew better than Frances's flatmate the true nature of her relations with LG. The only conclusion one can draw is that Frances had after all gone along with the pretence of an engagement to maintain her alibi for her real

* Miss Ellen Higgins was the formidable principal of Royal Holloway. The Ministry of Munitions was now housed in the former Metropole Hotel, Northumberland Avenue.
† Following the Easter Rising in Dublin in April, LG had been given the additional job of trying to resolve the Irish problem.

relationship. One would love to know how she replied to all the congratulations.

It is clear that LG was still pressing the Owen charade, even as his political fortunes took another important turn. On 5 June – the same day that he wrote Frances a particularly ardent letter ('I love you so dearly. My heart throbs with tenderness for you. You are all in all to me & I could not now even exist without you'), which he signed off somewhat unusually 'Your own fond old man & father'[41] – came the news that Kitchener had been drowned when the ship carrying him on a mission to Russia was torpedoed. Though he had not wanted it before, LG now realised that the War Office was the job he must have in order to gain any influence over the strategy as well as the sinews of war. He immediately telephoned Frances, who was out of London, to come back next day, and scribbled another quick note to await her arrival.

> *Cariad bach anwyl*
>
> Full up of deputations – but fuller of you.
>
> What a tragedy! Poor K. Looking forward so much to seeing you.
>
> If you cannot get at O. any other way take him into the corridor on the way.
>
> Point out what may happen at W. Office now.
>
> Fond love
>
> Your own
>
> D.[42]

What was Frances supposed to point out to Owen? That with LG moving to the War Office, it was more vital than ever that he should have cover for his mistress? That LG as Secretary of State for War might be in a position to advance his prospects? Had Owen been avoiding Frances, or was taking him into the corridor the only way she could speak to him alone? Tantalisingly we do not know. We know only that within a few months Owen went to Canada on a buying mission for the Ministry of Munitions. Maybe he was tiring of the ambiguity of his situation at home. Maybe in wartime an absent fiancé was just as good cover for Frances as one who would be expected to be around her all the time. At any rate he left the country – though not immediately for Canada, since on 9 September J. T. Davies, visiting France with LG, reported an unexpected sighting:

One bit of news I can tell & that is that we saw Owen at Verdun! So that he was bluffing us as to his going to Canada. The S. of S. [LG] says that he was tired of 'well-paid inactivity' at the W.O. & determined to go to the part of the front where he would be in the thick of it!!!!

On this LG scribbled a teasing note: 'He was the very image of your "finance".'[43]*

Nevertheless Owen was on his way to Canada, where Frances wrote to him the same month. He replied from Ottawa on 29 September.

> My dear Frances
>   . . . I was mighty pleased to get your letter. As is usual with your letters, I opened it with some trepidation but this time there were no 'shocks'.

He continued with news of his work – 'I've met all kinds of people & have seen lots of things. I've worked jolly hard, but I've enjoyed it more than anything it has ever been my lot to do' – then closed by sending his best wishes to JT and LG, and signed himself 'Billy'.[45]

In November he wrote from Halifax, again in reply to a letter from Frances. He was still full of enthusiasm for his mission, but also wanted to hear all about her move from Chester Square to a new flat in Victoria Street, news of Mary Phillips and of Frances's parents and 'my little pal Muriel'. At the end, across the bottom of the page, he added:

> I don't want to inconvenience you in any way, but so far as I am concerned the 'matter' referred to by you need not be touched upon until you yourself wish to. Billy.[46]

A third letter, from Montreal three weeks later, was mainly about where he might be posted next – possibly Egypt. But he also looked forward to seeing Frances's new flat and mentioned that he had had a letter from her mother: 'quite a delightful surprise'.[47]

---

* There is one other letter from JT which suggests that he did not approve of Frances's proposed engagement. It is undated, but was written before the ministry moved from Whitehall Gardens. Evidently Frances had been out of the office, possibly at Walton.

> Owen says you may be coming up, but that if you are not then he is going to write to you and send the letter with the papers this evening . . . You must not consider any proposal from whatever source, which involves leaving the Minister, and I know you will not.[44]

Then, at the beginning of December, it sounds as if some rumour of their relationship had appeared in the press – presumably one that their engagement was off. Frances was clearly upset, since Owen lost no time in cabling from Montreal to the War Office:

LETTER RECEIVED TONIGHT DEEPLY SORRY BUT ANNOYED ABOUT REPORT HAVE SAID NOTHING TO JUSTIFY ON MOST DECIDEDLY WRITING OWEN[48]

When LG became Prime Minister two days later, Owen immediately cabled Frances his congratulations. More curiously, on 30 January 1917, he cabled her again – to 10 Downing Street – with the news that his mother had died and asking Frances to communicate with his sister. On 11 February he had received 'disquieting cables from home' and asked Frances (busy as she was) to 'ascertain exact position' for him.[49] These are all puzzling communications, which suggest a continuing level of intimacy not just between Frances and Owen, but between both of them and their respective families. But on 26 February Owen landed back in Britain after a dangerous crossing of the U-boat-infested Atlantic. That day Frances noted coolly: 'Owen is returning from New York any day now. It will be rather strange meeting him after all this time.'[50] The next day she was more forthcoming:

Heard last night that the *Laconia* . . . had been torpedoed, & received a wire from Owen this morning that he was landed at Queenstown. It is extraordinary how little impression the fact that Owen might be drowned made upon me. What I was worried about was that I should have to *appear* to be so dreadfully upset to everyone, when in reality I did not care at all – not more than if he had been any other acquaintance. However, the engagement will be broken off while he is at home, & there will be no more need for pretending.[51]

While Owen was home, the engagement was indeed broken off. The seriousness with which Frances had maintained the charade is demonstrated by two letters she received from her mother and from her second (now married) sister Ninette.

My darling
    I was very sorry to get your letter this morning but not surprised. I have

known all along that you did not care sufficiently for Owen to marry him – the pity is that you ever engaged yourself to him.

However, I am quite of the opinion that it is quite right not to go on with it if you feel as you say – I must admit that I had looked forward to your being married to a good man who really cared for you, & that I am sure Owen does – however, least said, soonest mended.

I suppose you have well thought the matter over, & that there is no chance of your altering your mind.

I have known that your heart was not in this engagement for some long time, but as you did not say anything to me I did not like to force your confidence, but you must know, my darling, how much your happiness is to both Dada & myself.

Will you be coming home before Saty. I should like to see you. Muriel was very upset.

Ever so much love
from Mama[52]

Dearest Fran,

I am *awfully* sorry to hear that you have broken off your engagement. Why have you?

I thought that probably you would have made up your mind to get married soon, & I didn't dream that anything would have come in the way. And yet somehow I feel that you do care for each other, & its on account of some difficulty which might be got over if only you think it over. Have you quarrelled? Do tell me. I feel that you are very unhappy over it, & I can't bear to think that you are miserable. Of course, if you are *quite certain* you couldn't get on together once you are married, I wouldn't for a minute try to persuade you to get married. But are things really quite so impossible as you think . . .

Doesn't Capt. Owen care for you? He must do. I can't think that that is the reason. I feel sure you care for him, & on the face of it, both of you must be feeling utterly wretched. And it makes me feel so too to think of you unhappy, Fran dear. Of course it's no good my saying much. I don't know any of your reasons, which may be quite good ones. But if you would like to tell me all about it, I'd love to help you if I can. But do just as you think best.

Ever your loving sister,
Ninette[53]

Which just goes to show how little sisters can know one another's hearts.

Owen returned to Canada in 1918, where he finished the war as Lieutenant Colonel, was awarded the CBE, married in 1919 and enjoyed a successful career. He wrote Frances two more letters in the spring of 1918, the latter commiserating on the anxious time she and LG must be having at the crisis of the war. The first was signed 'Billy Owen'; the second 'W. Hugh Owen'.[54] And that was the end of a bizarre chapter.

INTO NO. 10

While this charade was going on, LG was still assuring Frances that he would marry her if ever he could, and she continued to accept her ambiguous existence philosophically. At the end of January 1916, while spending the evening with her before another trip to France, LG even told her that he would be willing to 'face disgrace with me now and still be quite happy'. 'I can understand Parnell now for the first time,' he told her. 'Although it would be bitter grief for me were I to be the cause of his disgrace,' she reflected, 'yet it is comforting to know that he feels like that.'[1] As usual he brought her back a present from Paris – this time 'a most wonderful blouse . . . I don't know when he found time to buy it, but he is most wonderfully pleased with his selection, and so am I.'[2] The probability is that he did not choose it himself at all: but in his private life, as in politics, LG was exceptionally good at delegating.

The following week he came to Chester Square for dinner practically every night. Once he actually cancelled a previous engagement with the Governor of the Bank of England. ('He said the thought of our little room compared with a formal dinner was too much for him.') It was on this evening that they discussed marriage, prompted by the example of Edward Carson, whose temporary withdrawal from politics LG attributed to his having just married a new wife, thirty years younger than himself.

He said he has [sic] been thinking, all the way to Chester Square, of how he wished he could marry me. But we both agreed that we must put that thought out of our minds, for it only leads to bitterness and discontent, and sometimes to injustice and folly. However, he has sworn to marry me if he ever finds himself in a position to do so, & I am content with that. Not that I wished him to promise it, for I am happy as we are – we have our little home now, where we can spend many evenings together in solitude – and how sweet the evenings are! The only thing we lack is children, but I often think that if I were married & had children, then I should not be able to keep in touch with D.'s work to the extent that I do now, & perhaps should be less happy. At present all our interests lie together; he does nothing but what I know of it; I almost know his very thoughts. I don't suppose I should see nearly as much of him if I were married to him.[3]

This was probably true: that is why politicians so often marry their secretaries. Nevertheless Maggie still saw rather more of her husband than Frances can have liked. It is clear from Riddell's diary that Maggie was now at 11 Downing Street and Walton Heath a good deal of the time – making Frances's flat an essential condition of LG's double life. Whatever he might tell Frances, Maggie remained important to him, and Riddell – who knew all about Frances – records several scenes of happy family life. Over the weekend of 12–13 February, for instance, LG spent a nostalgic time at Walton making Welsh toffee 'such as he used to make when a boy'. Doubtless Maggie helped with the ingredients, about which LG 'seemed rather hazy'; but to his great delight it turned out very well. Then, amazingly, 'we discussed the conduct of married people in public'.

L.G. says no couple are entitled to indulge in public demonstrations of affection until they have been married twenty years; until that period has elapsed they cannot be sure that they will not have a violent disagreement which may terminate their relationship. He added, 'We have been married for twenty-eight years, so we are justified in making a public demonstration.' Whereupon he kissed 'Maggie bach', as he calls his wife.[4]

For her part, Maggie knew quite well what went on behind her back, but tolerated it so long as it *was* behind her back. When he slipped up she let him know it, as Frances recorded in March.

D. and I are very, very happy. I do not know what I would do if anything happened to him. D. got into trouble the other day at W.H. Mrs Ll.G. was outside the door while he was talking to me on the telephone, & took him severely to task. 'I know very well whom you would marry if anything happened to me,' she said. D. tried to laugh it off, but he says she knows very well that his affection for me is real.[5]

Frances wrote very rarely about Maggie in her diary, beyond the occasional tart aspersion on her taste in furnishings or an explanation that Maggie's sudden appearance necessitated her hasty withdrawal. But later in 1916 her frustration with her subordinate position suddenly spilled out in an uncharacteristically venomous effusion prompted, curiously, by J. T. Davies. It seems that Maggie had been unaccountably rude to one of his typists; probably LG had been flirting with the girl and Maggie took out her deeper grievance on the target that was to hand. 'It is extraordinary how everyone dislikes Mrs Ll.G,' Frances noted smugly.

> J. T. Davies was talking to me about her this morning: he says that sometimes when he is feeling particularly unfriendly towards her, he tries to find some redeeming feature about her which will compensate for all her unlovely qualities. But it is impossible to find one. I have often felt the same too. She is simply a lump of flesh, possessing, like the jellyfish, the power of irritating. But I am being very nasty. I try as much as possible to refrain from commenting upon her, as she has good reason to dislike me. But she has no pride. D. has told her time & again that he does not want her in London, that he would much prefer her to live in Criccieth – when she has been making a fuss about me. I am sure I would not remain with a man who showed so plainly that my presence was not wanted.[6]

Of course this was only half the story. Frances was naïve if she believed everything LG told her he had told Maggie – or, indeed, his assurances that he really wished he could marry her, such as the letter he wrote her from Paris in September when he claimed to have had 'such a sweet dream last night. Dreamt we were engaged & I taking your hand told them at the dinner table.'[7] Given that there was no prospect of him marrying her, it was almost cruel to tease her with such fantasies. The truth is that he wanted and needed both Maggie and Frances – and by paying just enough lip-service to marital propriety on the one hand, and promises of undying passion on the other, he succeeded for thirty years in keeping them both reasonably content with their half-shares in his life.

Frances did feel qualms of guilt about Maggie, recognising that Maggie

had reason to resent her. But she quelled them by telling herself that
Maggie had brought her situation on herself, and that she – Frances –
was only giving LG in default the sort of love and support he should
have been able to expect from his wife. She was quite wrong, however,
to believe that Maggie had no pride: if anything she had too much –
she had never been prepared to subordinate herself to LG's every whim
as Frances did, but was determined to maintain her own life and her
own identity. It was contradictory to condemn Maggie for not coming
to London and then blame her when she did; and ingenuous to believe
LG when he said he wished Maggie would live in Criccieth all the time.
He did not at all. He loved Maggie: she represented his roots and a part
of himself that Frances had no notion of. He respected her judgement,
too; his need of praise and attention was bottomless enough to require
her more sceptical input as well as Frances's uncritical adoration. Of
course he told Frances what she wanted to hear – just as he doubtless
told Maggie that Frances was no more than an efficient secretary. Just
as Maggie averted her eyes as far as possible from the truth about
Frances, so Frances could not let herself acknowledge the enduring place
that Maggie held in his life. In some ways it is harder for the mistress
than the wife. Over the years Frances persuaded herself that Maggie
was merely an incubus from LG's past who had to be humoured for
propriety's sake. In a draft passage of her autobiography she actually
counted it to LG's credit that he took the trouble to do so.

> She was not unhappy. L.G. would have blamed himself if that had been so.
> He considered her – went to enormous lengths to be sure that she had all
> that was due to her as his wife – except of course himself. He gave her lovely
> presents . . . and humoured her to an extent that was almost undignified.[8]

But this rationalisation was written fifty years later from the security of
respectable widowhood. Her feelings at the time were more accurately
represented in that catty diary entry of November 1916.

It looks very much as if Frances had another abortion in the spring of
1916. Whether this was the result of carelessness, incompetence or bad
luck, or of Frances still trying consciously or unconsciously to force the
issue, we do not know. But her daughter Jennifer believes that Frances
had at least two and possibly three abortions in these years; and
April–May 1916 seems the likeliest time for the second one, after she

and LG were together for much of February. Between 20 April and 26 July she kept no diary, though it was a busy and politically important period when LG was first diverted from the war to try to resolve the Irish crisis after the Easter Rising, then took over the War Office, following Kitchener's death, at the beginning of July. Evidently Frances was 'ill' while he was wrestling with Ireland, then went on holiday in Cornwall and joined him in his new job only when she had overcome another crisis of her own.

> It is a long time since I kept a record. I lost heart after being ill; was very depressed and rundown for a long time, & D. & I had constant quarrels, & got out of tune with each other. I was sick at heart and had no courage to face the future – the result of my illness – & D. sent me down to Walton Heath to recuperate. I was feeling very bitter & sore with things in general, when one night I had a dream. I dreamed that D. had been killed, & the horror that that filled me with drove out every other feeling. I knew then that I loved him better than anything in the world, & that if he were dead nothing else would matter. It is extraordinary what a difference this dream made to my mental attitude. *That is all past however, &** we are now just as we always were, & he says that if I had not come to the War Office he would not have come. But here we are, & D. seems to be getting on very well with everyone. It was rather depressing at first, until we got into things – we felt just like children going to a new school.[9]

In this new job Frances began for the first time to attract attention in her own right.

> People have just woken up to the fact that Ll.G has a lady Secretary, or rather that the Secretary of State for War has a lady Secretary. I have people calling to interview me, & I have my photograph in the papers.[10]

Such publicity was gratifying but also dangerous. George Riddell – not only LG's friend but the owner of the *News of the World* – warned Frances on 28 July that LG's enemies in the Cabinet might use her as a means to bring him down.

> 'They would put poison in his cup,' said Sir George: 'they would stoop to

---

* These six words are crossed out, but still legible.

the trick that was played on Parnell if they thought they would get rid of him that way. The divorce in that case was only brought about from political motives, because Parnell's opponents thought that was the only way to crush him. McKenna and these others would resort to those very means if they thought it would bring Ll.G. down.' I think Sir G. was giving me a hint to be very careful, as D.'s enemies are always on the watch; and the publicity that has been given to my appointment will make it still more necessary for us to be wary.[11]

All through 1916 LG's relations with his Liberal colleagues were building to a showdown. From the moment he embraced the necessity for war in August 1914 he had insisted on the need to fight it with all the resources at the nation's command. Asquith and his closest associates, on the other hand, were opposed in principle to fighting German militarism with what they called 'Prussian' methods. They resisted every step towards total mobilisation forced on them by the Tories, public opinion and a jingoistic press, who increasingly saw LG as the only man of energy and imagination to prosecute the war successfully. LG's second battle was with the generals, whom he rightly blamed for the blinkered and stubborn strategy that was continuing to sacrifice thousands of lives in fruitless offensives for minimal gains. He was always looking for alternative strategies away from the Western Front, which might achieve the defeat of the Central Powers with fewer casualties; failing that, he wanted the generals at least to take the time to build up their resources until they had an overwhelming preponderance to deal a knockout blow. From the very first he had always believed that the war would be a long one.

His attitude to the business of war was complicated. Unlike Churchill, he felt no relish for war as such – though he did have a considerable interest in military history and close knowledge of the American Civil War fought by his hero Abraham Lincoln. He had no innate respect for the military and a deep suspicion of their bloody trade. It was ironic that as Minister of Munitions he should have become responsible for maximising the manufacture of the means of slaughter. As a young backbencher twenty-five years earlier, he had complained to Maggie of 'superannuated old Colonels' in the House of Commons 'talking about musket and cannon bores'.

It is perfectly ghastly to listen to these army men complaining that the guns are not killing enough & that they would be more destructive to human life

if certain improvements were effected in them & all this they talk about as
coolly & as indifferently as if it were a matter of destroying vermin. They
talk far more feelingly about shooting hares than men.[12]

He was still horrified by the generals' indifference to the slaughter in
1914–18, but – while doing everything he could to minimise it – he felt
that he must close his mind to the reality of killing and maiming. He
was always squeamish about illness of any sort. In January 1916 he was
badly shaken, on one of his trips to France, by visiting an individual
case in hospital – the son of a Welsh MP who had been shot in the
head and was in agony and semi-paralysed. 'The horror of what I have
seen has burnt into my soul and has almost unnerved me,' he told
Frances when he got back.

'I wish I had not seen him,' he kept on saying to me. 'I ought not to have
seen him. I feel that I cannot go on with my work, now that the grim horror
of the reality has been brought home to me so terribly. I was not made to
deal with the things of war. I am too sensitive to pain & suffering, & this
visit has almost broken me down.'[13]

Yet he still believed that the war was right and necessary and must
be fought to a finish. He was deeply scornful of the manner in which
it was being fought in 1915–16 and feared, as he frequently told both
Frances and Riddell, that the German generals were better than the
British and French. 'The Germans are cleverer than us, he said, and they
deserve to win.' This was 'very broadminded', Frances commented tartly,
'but not very helpful'.[14] Repeatedly in private he predicted that the Allies
might lose, or at any rate would not win, unless the conduct of the war
was radically overhauled. He talked frequently of resigning, but felt he
could not do so without being accused of disloyalty or cowardice, so
in his frustration he took to staying away from Cabinet instead. ('He
says they never decide anything, and he is absolutely sick of it.'[15]) He
was still personally loyal to Asquith, whom he considered a peerless
chairman, but thought him desperately lacking the initiative and drive
needed in a war leader – the very qualities he himself had in abundance.
He could not be blamed for thinking that he would make a better job
of running the war if he were given a free hand; but one part of him
at least did not want the formality of being Prime Minister, and he was
fearful of cutting himself off from his own party and becoming a pris-

oner of the Tories. But that was the inexorable logic of events in 1916.

'I do not boast,' he told Frances in March – reporting a conversation he had had with a Liberal confidant, Lord St Davids – 'but I will tell you this: if I were put in charge of this war I would see the thing through; as I shall not be, it will end in a bad peace.' When St Davids urged him to 'come out and lead the country', LG demurred, fearing it would ruin him. But Frances, who had heard him so often threatening resignation but always staying put, hoped that eventually he would take the plunge.

> I do not believe it: I think D. would have the country solid at his back. And in any event, even if it is risky, I think he ought to speak his mind. Otherwise, I tell him, he will be classed with the rest of the Cabinet as a body of failures, & when the country *turns* them out, he will be disgraced with the others. I think he is pondering over it, and should not be surprised if he takes action soon.[16]

Then came the distraction of Ireland, followed by his move to the War Office, which theoretically gave him authority over the generals, but in practice only made him responsible for the latest bloodbath on the Somme. From her ringside seat Frances watched his struggle to impose himself on the military bureaucracy.

> No one who has not worked *inside* the W.O. can realise what a hotbed of intrigue and jealousy it is. The officials are powerful, especially in society and at Court, & I realise now what people meant when they talked of the danger of attempting to touch the Army or reform the W.O. . . . I never realised what an all-powerful thing a General is – until he is outdone by another General. It is tragic – it is wicked. But I will back D. up against them in a fight.[17]

Soon LG was coming up with new proposals for the more effective prosecution of the war – a conference of all the Allies to coordinate strategy; 'dictators' with sweeping powers to direct food supply and shipping to combat the growing threat from German U-boats; the conscription of women – all of which were still fiercely resisted by his Liberal colleagues. By early November he was again talking of walking out; but now Frances urged him to stick in there.

D. is feeling very sick with everything and talks of resigning & taking on
the food job outside the Cabinet. He says they have made a muddle of the
whole war, & he fears it is too late to do anything . . . I tell him that if he
resigns he will simply be playing into their hands: but he says: no, he will
simply be letting them go to hell by themselves, for that is where they will
be in two years' time. All the same they want to get him out of things, &
will crow if he does resign. But he will not: he is getting the upper hand
over them even now: he has beaten them on every point & they are afraid
of him. He has not been sleeping the last few nights, & this has added to
his depression. But he will recover & be his old self again.[18]

LG eventually got his conference in Paris, which he attended as one
of the British representatives in mid-November. Frances asked him to
take her with him, since an aunt of hers had just died in Versailles and
she wanted to go and see her French cousin. But LG refused, saying
that his enemies would use it against him and there would be a scandal.[19]
Just a week later, however, he told her that he was planning to make a
tour of the Empire to rally support for the war.

I was very upset when he told me, knowing the dangers that would accompany such an expedition, & thinking of the lonely time I would have, though
of course it would be no worse than for thousands of other women whose
husbands have gone to the front. But D. then revealed the fact that he
intended to take me too. He said if there were two women it would not
matter, & he intended to take one other girl as a typist. At any rate, he has
promised that he will not go without me.[20]

Probably he never intended to go at all, and was just trying to make
up to Frances for his previous rebuff. He could not seriously have thought
of leaving the country for several weeks when the crisis of the war – at
Westminster at least – was clearly coming to a head. Though LG normally
relished a challenge, it seems that part of him was also seeking to evade
the fearful responsibility that was likely soon to fall upon him. Just
before going to Paris he told Frances that Bonar Law wanted him to
become Prime Minister, but said that he had 'flatly declined', since there
was 'nothing but disaster ahead . . . He would simply get blamed for
losing the war, & have the negotiating of an unfavourable peace.' Frances
told him firmly that if he was offered the premiership 'he would be
bound to accept – he could not refuse to do his best to save the country,

whatever the odds against it. But he persists in saying that he would resign.'[21]

Of course Frances was right: three weeks later he was Prime Minister. LG genuinely tried to avoid the office, proposing up to the last minute that he should become chairman of a small executive to run the war while Asquith remained nominally Prime Minister. But Asquith rejected all such proposals, believing that the Prime Minister must have ultimate responsibility for directing the war. In this he was probably right, but since the Tories would no longer serve under him, his bluff was called. Since the Tory leaders – Bonar Law, Balfour, Curzon, Carson and Austen Chamberlain – were happy to serve under LG, that was the inevitable outcome. Asquith chose to split the Liberal party by refusing to take second place under his former subordinate, thereby condemning LG to take office at the head of a government dominated by his former political opponents – a trap he had foreseen, but one that in the patriotic crisis of the war he could not escape.

Through all these fevered intrigues Frances loyally backed her man. 'We are receiving countless anxious letters from all parts of the country, urging D. to take over affairs,' she wrote on 30 November. 'He seems to be the only one in whom the people have any confidence, & I am certain that if he were to resign now he would have the backing of the whole country.'[22] Maggie was at Walton Heath in early December, but LG could not get down there very much in these critical few days, so he probably saw more of Frances. On Sunday morning (3 December), for instance, the two of them drove to Surrey together – she to her parents in Wallington, he to Walton; but he had to return to London after lunch to see Asquith, leaving Riddell to dine with Maggie that evening while LG telephoned to tell her that the result of the interview had been 'satisfactory'.[23] Frances was dismayed when Asquith appeared to have accepted LG's terms. 'I cannot help wishing that Asquith would *not* agree, & then there would be smash, & things would be thoroughly cleaned up.'[24] The next day, 'D. was angry with me . . . because I told him he would disappoint everyone unless he went the whole hog . . . He has the country solid behind him, & I feel certain he could turn Asquith out easily.'[25] She was relieved when Asquith changed his mind, and thought LG was too.

D. is much happier now that his course is clear. We had dinner together last night, & he told me that when once his mind was clear as to the best course to take, he was never unhappy as to the consequences of his action . . . He is now willing to suffer the loss of Office, comparative poverty or whatever comes to him, for it is quite clear that the step he is taking is the right one. I cannot think that the people will suffer him to be out of office for long . . . He says he would not be sorry to be out of Office, so that he could have a rest. But I tell him that he must not think of taking a rest until the War is over . . . It is the greatest moment of his life. All classes seem ready to accept him as Dictator & to leave the direction of the war to him.[26]

Wednesday (6 December) was 'a *terrible* day – we were all nearly sick with excitement and suspense'. Asquith tendered his resignation, Bonar Law declined the King's invitation to try to form a government, and at about 7 p.m. LG was sent for and accepted.

I saw him directly he returned & he was very pale & said he would like to run away to the mountains. 'I'm not at all sure that I can do it,' he said. 'It is a very big task.' However we were at the W.O. till after midnight, D. conferring with B. Law, Carson & others.

Most of the Liberals refused to serve him ('Such patriotism,' Frances noted scornfully); but he hoped to win Labour support the next day.*

We all went home very tired & excited, but happy. There was the light of battle in D.'s eyes for the Liberals had deliberately challenged him. But I think he was confident of victory, though he would not own it. 'I'm not Prime Minister yet,' he said to me. 'Oh yes you are,' I replied. I know he will not fail.[27]

Labour did support him, and he squared some doubtful Tories by giving office to a number of prominent figures whom Frances thought he would have been better off without. By the afternoon 'D. was in high spirits. "I think I shall be Prime Minister before 7 o'clock," he said to me. And he was.'[28]

And Frances was the Prime Minister's secretary.

---

* The Labour party then had thirty-seven MPs.

PART TWO

THE PRIME MINISTER'S
PRIVATE SECRETARY

At the age of just twenty-eight, Frances was the first woman to hold the position of secretary to the Prime Minister. Her formal title was still joint principal private secretary, alongside J. T. Davies. Moreover LG soon expanded the Downing Street secretariat to cope with a greatly increased volume and urgency of business. The additional staff were housed in huts in the garden (known as the 'garden suburb'). But Frances's status was recognised by the fact that she occupied a room of her own next to the Cabinet Room.

It is difficult to form a clear picture of exactly what she did: glimpses of her carrying out specific tasks are rare. She probably acted more as an all-purpose personal assistant, gatekeeper and confidante than strictly as a secretary. The man who really ran the government machine was the extraordinary Colonel Maurice Hankey. Practically LG's first act on becoming Prime Minister, after appointing a small War Cabinet of just five members, was to appoint Hankey to be its secretary. Though he had previously acted as secretary to the Committee of Imperial Defence, this was the first time the Cabinet had ever had a secretary to formulate its agenda and record decisions. Hitherto the Prime Minister had simply written a private letter to the King. Nothing more clearly symbolised the new professionalism that LG brought to the business of government, by contrast with Asquith's gentlemanly amateurism; and Hankey brought to the job an almost superhuman degree of unflappable efficiency. He needed it, however, since LG's manner of working was chaotic. While admiring the new Prime Minister's drive and energy, Hankey frequently despaired that his 'horribly unbusinesslike methods . . . render organisation almost impossible'.[1] He also disapproved of LG's irregular relations with Frances. Nevertheless he worked with her perfectly well in her official capacity and confined his moral strictures to his diary.

Even more than when he was merely Secretary of State for War, the fact that the Prime Minister had a female secretary naturally attracted comment in the press. When they had overcome their amazement at finding a woman in such a responsible position, however, journalists were charmed by her demure and gentle personality, and nothing unfavourable was ever written about her – certainly no suggestion that she was not up to the job or any hint that her services might be more than secretarial. Unfortunately Frances kept very few articles about herself, which are now hard to trace. One that she did preserve – from the Liberal weekly *Truth*, sometime in 1917 – may typify the general lack of investigative rigour. The writer described the Prime Minister's 'lady secretary' rhapsodically as 'a flower of spring in the gardens of the past. She is the spirit of calm, the calm of efficient industry . . . the Priestess of Courtesy.' He claimed – with how much real knowledge one cannot say – to have 'never seen her disturbed or agitated', and attributed this serenity either to 'her own fine training in the classics' or to her mixed Scots-French parentage – 'the nervous imagination of the one country interlaced with the austere industry of the other'. Less fancifully he rehearsed her educational history and the fact that she had been at school with Mair and Olwen. This chance had brought her to the attention of LG, who 'had silently formed his own judgment of her brilliant qualities' and appointed her his secretary at the beginning of 1913, since when she had accompanied him though every change of office on his ascent to No. 10.

> A rich and rare experience, most wonderful of dowries; and it is high tribute, and no more than the truth, to say that she has been equal to the clarion summons of high events in these exalted spheres of service.[2]

Their first few weeks in No. 10 were actually very far from calm. Frances had no time to write up her diary until early January 1917, when LG went to Paris and on to Rome to try to improve Allied co-operation and build up the Italian front, leaving her 'perfectly miserable' and unable to sleep for fear that 'the Germans would try to get at him in some way or another' while he was away. Before he left they were able to enjoy 'a supremely happy week' at Walton '& saw the

New Year in together'. Previously, however, they had been through a tense time.

> We have both recovered from the strain of the crisis, which had made us both very bad-tempered & irritable, specially with each other. The incessant work & worry & excitement, together with the late nights and irregular hours & meals, got on our nerves. D. developed a cold & so, having retired to bed, obtained relief in that way. I, not being ill, merely became more grumpy, until Xmas weekend, when we took a rest. The rest of D.'s family went off to Criccieth, so that he & I were able to go down to W.H. for a few days, & by the time we returned to town we had recovered our normal state of health.[3]*

The worst anxiety was the day of LG's first speech in the Commons as head of the government. 'As the time drew near for the delivery of the speech he was quite pitiful, & almost ill with fright.' But of course he delivered it 'magnificently', it was 'a great speech' and Frances was proud of him, 'though it was impossible for a long time to realise that he was really Prime Minister'.[5]

There was some consolation for Frances from LG's continental trip – apart from his usual presents, this time 'an exquisite little marble model of the child taking a thorn out of his foot: & also a beautiful necklace of corals' – because he proposed that in future she should go too. 'D. made a fuss because there was no one in the party who could write & translate French, so that Col. Hankey told me that I must be ready to go next time there is a journey.'[6] If true, this was an extraordinary failure by the Foreign Office; unfortunately for Frances it was remedied before LG next went to France, and she did not often get to accompany him during the war.

Towards the end of January the Lloyd Georges finally moved into No. 10 – it had taken the Asquiths six weeks to move out. This was a difficult time for Frances, since it underlined her exclusion. Two weeks earlier LG had semi-apologised for not taking her with him to Walton for the weekend, since that would 'not quite be playing the game with Mrs Ll.G. "She is very tolerant," he said, "considering that she knows everything that is going on. It is not right to try her

---

* LG told his family that he could not go to Wales because of conferences with the French on both Christmas Day and Boxing Day.[4]

too far."[7] In her new position as wife of the Prime Minister, Maggie accepted that she should stay in London rather more. She had already established an organisation to supply comforts for Welsh troops, which took up several rooms of 11 Downing Street, and now she took on more such charitable work. But this meant that wife and mistress were frequently under the same roof. Previously, while living at No. 11, LG had always had his office in the Treasury, the Ministry of Munitions or the War Office. Now Frances was installed on the ground floor of No. 10 all day, while Maggie (and Olwen and Megan much of the time) were living in the flat upstairs. The move itself was fraught, if we can believe LG's characteristic complaints to Frances, which gave her the opportunity for some more sharp comments about her rival.

D. has been very unhappy this week owing to the change from No. 11 to No. 10. They did not bother to get a comfortable room ready for him & the first night he came down to my office to work after dinner. The second night he did not go up to dinner at all as he & Mrs Ll.G. were not on speaking terms. She had closed the bedroom windows on the quiet, thinking that the room was cold, but knowing that he always gets a headache when he sleeps with closed windows. He was furious when he found out, as it made him feel seedy all day. She does not study him in the least – has hung up some hideous family portraits painted by some cheap artist, though he has had them taken down more than once before. In fact the whole house is hideously uncomfortable at the present moment, quite unworthy of a Prime Minister & very irritating to him, for he has a keen sense of what is beautiful & artistic & what is not.[8]*

A few days later Frances was stung into further bitter reflections when the Irish journalist/MP T. P. O'Connor wrote in a newspaper article about the 'beauty' of LG's family life.

---

* A much more positive description was recorded by Riddell four months later, when the family had had time to settle into the new house.

L.G. invited me to go upstairs to dinner. It was served in the great dining room. So far as the food, service and appointments were concerned, it looked as if a small suburban household were picnicking in Downing Street – the same simple food, the same little domestic servant, the same mixture of tea and dinner. And yet with all that an air of simple dignity and distinction pervaded the room – no affectation, no pretension, nothing mean, nothing ignoble. Mrs Ll.G. is a quiet, dignified woman and brave as a lion.[9]

T.P. must know D. well enough to realise the conditions of his home life. Of course D. is fond of his children, but as he himself said to me . . . 'Every animal is fond of its young'. As a matter of fact he & Olwen are continually at logger-heads & yet he is always pleased when the papers make a fuss of her, simply because she is his child. Of course D. is very clever in the way he *pretends* at being the happy family man when people visit him at home. He makes me very angry sometimes, but he tells me that it is necessary – it is very useful to him in his public life. I do not believe it is as necessary as all that. Everyone knows that Sir Edward Carson did not get on with his late wife . . . but for all that he was not less popular with his own party. I think it is a good deal the result of D.'s kindly nature too, & the fact that he wants to play the game by his wife & not hurt her feelings in public. I can understand that, but I think he rather overdoes it, & it hurts me when I read articles like T.P.'s when they hold him up to be a model family man. It amounts to hypocrisy.[10]

Frances received another piquant reminder of her position in May, when a journalist writing a biography of LG asked her to get Maggie to dictate some anecdotes for him. Frances thought this astonishingly 'tactless' and hoped he would suggest the same thing to Maggie![11] One might have expected her to welcome this evidence that her relations with LG were not common knowledge. On the contrary, one suspects that while avoiding scandal she secretly wanted the political world to acknowledge her position as *maîtresse en titre*.

As LG immersed himself in his new responsibilities, Frances was frus-trated that she saw less of him than she had done before. The War Cabinet was in almost continuous session – Hankey noted its two-hundredth meeting at the beginning of August, that is a rate of nearly one a day – and LG made frequent visits around the country and abroad. He had little opportunity to escape in the evenings to Frances's new flat in Victoria Street. In addition his family were making increased claims on his time. In February Uncle Lloyd died – having lived just long enough to see his nephew Prime Minister – and LG had to go to Criccieth for the funeral.* Then Megan got measles very badly and he convinced

* Just as he had earlier seen Frances as a replacement for his lost daughter, so LG now wanted her to fill the gap left by Uncle Lloyd. Once again she was happy to oblige.

He will miss the old man very much, and he says I am his only devoted friend now – that I shall have to fill the old man's place. God knows I shall try. D. needs so much someone who will not hesitate to give him everything, & if necessary to give up every-thing, & whose sole thought & occupation is for him. Without that it is hopeless to try and serve him.[12]

himself (with memories of Mair) that it was going to turn into meningitis. In April Dick got married (in Bath); and in June Olwen married (in London).* Yet he still managed to snatch some time with Frances at Walton Heath, even if Hankey was often there too, requiring decisions of him. She was pathetically grateful for every glimpse of him, as for instance on 31 March:

> D. & I had hardly seen each other last week, so we drove down to Walton on Saturday to lunch, & had two hours of bliss together. D. saw I was rather down & lonely, & it was sweet of him to suggest it, for he was very tender & kind & bucked me up again. I feel as though I ought not to mind when he is busy & cannot pay me very much attention, but I suppose I am only human and I get depressed. But he soon puts me right again.[13]

Soon after this LG had to go and inspect the Grand Fleet at Scapa Flow, in the Orkneys, followed immediately by another trip to France; so Frances, to relieve her anxiety, took the chance – with a girlfriend – to spend a luxurious weekend in the country as the guest of Colonel Albert Stern, a wealthy businessman and pioneer in the development of tanks, who had become a friend and was possibly a suitor of hers. Certainly her mother thought so, since she wrote to Frances that she had heard she was to marry him. (This was not long after the ending of her engagement to Billy Owen.) 'Was never more surprised in my life,' Frances wrote in her diary. 'I hope he does not want anything of the sort, as he is quite a good pal, and besides I am quite sure he knows of the relations between D. & me.'[14] He had certainly entertained them together at his house more than once. But 'Bertie' Stern – when not promoting tanks – was too frivolous for her taste: a member of the 'smart set', with what she called 'a considerable reputation'.[15] In truth Frances had no intention of being wooed away from LG by any admirer; but the suggestion is both a measure of her mother's undiminished wish to see her respectably married and a reminder that she had become a very eligible young woman.

On LG's safe return the lovers had another 'perfect weekend' at Walton Heath, marked by an extraordinary proposal on his part. One must hope that he did not mean it seriously – but Frances, in her romantic infatuation, evidently did.

---

* Dick married Roberta MacAlpine, a daughter of the building contractor Sir Robert MacAlpine. Olwen's husband, Thomas Carey Evans, was an urologist. But Frances was no longer a friend of the family, and was invited to neither wedding.

I do not think we have ever loved each other so much. D. says that ours is a love that comes to very few people and I wonder more & more at the beauty & happiness of it. It is a thing that nothing but death can harm, and even death has no terrors for me now, for D. asked me yesterday if I would come with him when he went. He begged me not to stay behind, but for both of us to go together, and I promised him to do so, unless I have any children of his to claim me. So, I am not afraid now of the misery if D. is taken away, for then I shall go too & his end will be my end, and until then everything is happiness, if our love stays.

For a fifty-four-year-old man to propose a suicide pact with a twenty-eight-year-old woman is monstrous, even by LG's standards of self-ishness. It was not even reciprocal, since Frances accepted that if by chance she were to die first, 'he could not leave his work, which is a great one'.[16] Maybe Frances needed this level of romantic fantasy to compensate for the fact that her lover was not wholly hers; but one can only marvel at his ability to persuade her to give such an unequal promise.

His eloquence was not only – or, perhaps it should be said, mainly – employed in the bedroom. In these early months of 1917 LG was fighting one of the critical battles of the war to persuade the Admiralty to accept the principle of convoys to protect merchant shipping from German U-boats: at one point Britain had only a few weeks' food supply remaining, until the success of the convoy system stemmed the rate of sinkings. He was also disappointed by the failure of the latest offensive by the French General Nivelle, on whom he had placed exaggerated hopes (by contrast with his lack of faith in British generals). Nivelle, Frances wrote, had 'let D. down badly'.[17] Altogether the situation was not obviously better than when Asquith was Prime Minister, and the political pressure was mounting again. But LG remained astonishingly buoyant: Riddell's diary is full of references to his amazing vitality in adversity, though he was also often very tired.

Frances's role was to help to keep him fresh. She fussed over him, encouraged him to take a little walk every day – weather permitting – and made him drink 'a wonderful concoction of egg, port wine, honey & cream every morning, which seems to buck him up a lot'.[18] She believed, naturally, that his family had the opposite effect. 'The last two weekends,' she wrote at the end of May, 'he has been down at W.H. enjoying what he calls "domestic bliss", & has come back looking twice

as tired as when he went down. This week I am going to try my hand
& see what I can do!'[19]

Maggie had gone back to Criccieth, and LG tried to ensure that
Olwen should stay in Downing Street with a friend while he went down
to Walton seeking 'absolute rest'.

> However his family with their usual consideration for him (!) wished other-
> wise. Dick & his wife arrived without any warning to lunch on Sunday
> morning, having borrowed the official car for the purpose of motoring down.
> Then they got on the telephone with Olwen & arranged that she & her
> friend should come down in the afternoon . . . [D.] was perfectly furious,
> for not only did it disturb the whole of his Sunday's rest, but as he said,
> they never think about him or consider him in any way, but simply use his
> house & garden & car when they think they will. I saw he was very upset
> by the whole thing, & tried to soothe him by saying it was most natural for
> them to come & pay their father a visit on the spur of the moment; but I
> honestly think the whole thing was engineered & done a good deal out of
> spite, as they knew pretty well he would not be there alone.

At least the weekend finished happily from Frances's point of view.

> They all cleared off after tea & we had the rest of the day to ourselves. We
> went for a jolly walk in the woods . . . and I found 3 four-leaved clovers,
> all of which I presented to D., as he needs luck at present more than anyone!
> . . . D. certainly looks much, much better today for the rest & is in much
> better spirits. I got quite alarmed about him last week, especially as he was
> not at all nice to me, which is always a sign that he is overworked or very
> worried.[20]

Two things should be added about Frances's relations with LG's children at this time. First, she was still friendly with Megan (now fifteen)
and sat next to her at an official lunch in April.

> She is an amusing little person, but is getting rather artificial. D. thinks she
> is growing selfish, but that is not her fault, for she has not been taught to
> be unselfish. I think she is wonderfully unspoilt, considering the way she has
> been brought up. Many children would have been unbearable. She informed
> me that her mother 'reminded her of a character out of Dickens'. 'But this
> is only for your ear,' she added.[21]

Second, she was on perfectly good terms with Gwilym, who – unlike his young sister – must have known Frances's true relations with their father. Gwilym was always the most easy-going of the family. At the beginning of August he joined his artillery battery in France, from where on 18 September he wrote Frances a long and friendly letter.

My dear Miss Stevenson,

Many thanks for your letter. I am glad you liked the Eisteddfod. I wish I could have been there as I'm awfully keen on the singing. I am glad father went down to Cricc. afterwards, as there are not many people there just now & he should have a pretty quiet time . . .

About that advice I gave I'll tell you all about it some day. Meanwhile don't breathe a word to a soul . . .

Must stop now,

Cheerioh!

Yrs, Gwilym[22]

What the secret advice was, of course, we cannot know. But Gwilym's letter confirms that Frances accompanied LG on his annual visit to the Welsh Eisteddfod, which he never missed even when Prime Minister. Previously, when Uncle Lloyd was alive, LG had refused to take Frances to north Wales, saying that the old man would be sure to guess their relationship.[23] But this year the Eisteddfod was held outside Wales, at Birkenhead. Maggie did not attend, so LG and Frances were able to stay together in Cheshire with the soap-manufacturer-turned-philanthropist, Lord Leverhulme, where LG was ill for a couple of days. From there he went on to Criccieth, now accompanied by Riddell and a new recruit to his secretariat, Philip Kerr.* Maggie and Megan came to meet them halfway and they all drove back to Criccieth together. 'As we neared our destination,' Riddell noted, 'the P.M. began to recite Welsh verses with much emphasis and feeling – all the time holding his wife's hand as if they were a newly married couple'.[25] LG then stayed another fortnight in Wales. On 17 September he summoned Hankey and most of the War Cabinet up to confer with him there – so much for Gwilym's hope that he would have a quiet time – and on 21 September he took the whole party to see his boyhood home in Llanystumdwy. But a few

* Philip Kerr, later Marquess of Lothian, was not really a secretary, but an increasingly important policy adviser. He became a close friend of Frances, who once described him as 'the most Christ-like man' she had ever known. (He was an ardent Christian Scientist.)[24]

days earlier he had written to Frances, begging her to come up again. Can he really have meant that Frances should come secretly to Criccieth?

My darling little girl,

How I miss you every hour of the day & every wakeful hour of the night. When I see beautiful sights my thoughts always fly straight to you my darling.

Since I left you I have had a really bad time. Saturday I fell ill. Sunday worse & Sunday night I had a high temperature – the highest I have had for years – & I felt I was in for a serious illness. My old trick of perspiration saved me. I sweated gallons & the morning found me normal but feeble as a kitten. That is my present state. And that is why I long more than ever for Pussy.*

I *must* stay down as long as I can be spared. Otherwise P. will soon have to find another Tom Cat. I am asking Hankey down for a weekend.

Now I have a proposal to make. Couldn't you & Muriel come down here & stay at the Marine Hotel. We might snatch one or two walks along the riverside – you Muriel & self.

You could come Saturday & drop a note to Newnham [his driver]. I could meet you on the cliff under Murian beyond Marine Terrace at 10.30 Sunday morning.

Just think of it sweet. But don't let it worry you if it can't be done. I am simply mad to see you.

You might phone from Treasury on Friday if you can come – don't let Hankey see you.

If Saturday impossible what about Monday?

Fondest love to my own

D.

Kerr opens *all* letters – so beware.[28]

---

* To her credit, Frances was always sceptical of LG's chronic hypochondria. As early as December 1914, when he worried about his health, she was shrewd enough to suspect that he was only reacting to a newspaper article. 'It is always foolish to tell C. that he looks ill,' she wrote, 'for then he always imagines that he is ill; but if you tell him that he is looking well, he bucks up at once. It is fatal to sympathise with him too strongly – it is no kindness to him. After all he *does* know how to take care of himself, & when he ought to throw everything up and rest, & he is sufficiently strong-minded to do so & act upon instinct.'[26] And again in February 1916: 'I do not think D. is as ill as he thinks he is. He always thinks he is dying if he has a bilious attack. But I think men are mostly like that. He is very tired & overworked, but I think a rest would put him right.'[27]

This was an audacious scheme, and Frances probably had more sense than to go. It is all a bit mysterious, however, since Frances was not keeping her diary at this time. For some reason she made no entry between 29 May and 5 November; and when she resumed it – on loose sheets of paper, not in a bound volume – she gave no explanation for the gap. She took it up again, however, to describe an important episode: the first time that LG took her with him to an international conference. This followed the heavy defeat suffered by the Italians at Caporetto on 26 October.* Serious though this was, he immediately realised that he could use it to advance his case for unity of command, and specifically to weaken the stranglehold of the boneheaded General 'Wully' Robertson on British strategy. He lost no time in proposing an Allied conference to be held at Rapallo (near Genoa) the following week, and left on the morning of 3 November, taking with him Hankey, General Smuts, General Maurice and their respective aides, plus J. T. Davies and Frances.† Frances had begged to be allowed to come and this time found that LG needed little persuading, 'for I think he had already made up his mind before I asked him'.[29]

With her French-Italian ancestry, Frances knew Paris reasonably well, but she had never been to Italy. Her diary glows with excitement, partly at attending her first high-level diplomatic conference, but also at the sheer tourism of the trip.

We left London on Saturday morning, crossed in destroyer which was most thrilling. We crossed in ³/4 of an hour, tearing through the water. We were escorted by another destroyer, & passed destroyers & transports on the way, but no submarines! Arrived in Paris about 10 at night . . . We stayed the night at the Hotel Crillon, on the Place de la Concorde.

They stayed in Paris all day, while LG had various meetings, leaving Frances free to explore.

Paris is a very sad city, but it was nice to be there once more. The hotel was

---

* LG was playing golf at Walton Heath with Riddell when he heard the news. War or no war, it is astonishing how regularly he managed to play golf – though it did only take about two hours to play a round in those days. He had always found it a convenient way to do business away from Whitehall, since practically all the leading politicians of the day were keen players.
† Jan Smuts, the former Boer general, had been a member of the War Cabinet since June. General Maurice was Director of Military Operations.

full of soldiers – Americans, French, English, & everywhere in the Paris streets you see the blue of the French uniform. Many of the women are in black. The little theatres & cafés in the Champs-Elysées are many of them closed, or being used for war work . . .

I sought Suzanne [her cousin] out during the day, & luckily found her at Mdme Debray's flat. She quite broke down when she saw me, the surprise was too much for her. We spent a great part of the day together. She is very lonely, but will not come to England. Her mother's death has aged her a lot, & I have not seen her since Paul died, so that many things have changed since we saw each other the Xmas before the war. The world is much sadder.[30]

They took the sleeper south that night and woke to the glorious autumnal scenery of Savoy, then passed through the Mont Cenis tunnel, reaching Turin before lunch and Rapallo in the evening, where they were met by the Italian Prime Minister and cheering crowds. Frances was enchanted with the sights and smells of Italy. 'For the first time in my life I have seen oranges & olives growing in the open. I am thrilled with all the surroundings, but it is a place where one wants to be lazy.' It does not sound as if she had a lot to do, though of course LG was busy. 'I feel rather out of place here,' she noted, 'being the only woman. But everyone is very nice & being able to talk French I get along very well with the French people.'[31]

They stayed two days in Rapallo and managed a surprising amount of sightseeing between sessions of the conference. LG achieved most of what he wanted, including the replacement of the Italian commander-in-chief and agreement in principle to an Allied Supreme Command, though in practice that took another few months to become reality. They returned via Brescia, Milan and Aix-les-Bains, Frances still ecstatic with the beauty of it all and LG well pleased with himself. In later years they always looked back on those few days as a particularly memorable time in their relationship.

'THE MAN WHO WON THE WAR'

After the excitement of Rapallo, Frances failed to write her diary again during the whole of 1918. Unless she destroyed it – and we know no reason why she should have done – this is surprising, since 1918, even more than its predecessor, was a year of great events. In March the Germans finally broke the stalemate on the Western Front and advanced forty miles in a few days, almost taking Amiens: for a moment, until the offensive was halted and then reversed, an Allied defeat seemed a real possibility. Another conference at Beauvais in April finally established unity of command, with the British army placed under the ultimate command of the French Marshal Foch, whom LG always rated more highly than Douglas Haig. In May LG successfully beat off his most serious political challenge in the House of Commons. Then the Allied counter-thrust, reinforced at last by the arrival of American troops in sufficient numbers to turn the tide, drove the Germans back, leading to an Armistice on 11 November and the end of four and a quarter bloody years of war. Finally there was a General Election in December, from which LG emerged with a huge majority and an apparently unassailable position as 'The Man Who Won the War'. It is strange that Frances should have recorded none of this.

In his 1971 edition of her diary A. J. P. Taylor wrote somewhat airily that during this year LG and Frances 'were both struck by the influenza epidemic and saw little of each other'.[1] But this cannot be true. Certainly both were ill in the autumn, but that does not explain Frances's silence for the whole year. LG wrote a lot of letters to Criccieth in 1918 – far more than in 1917 – so Maggie clearly spent more time in Wales, which would have left the field clear for Frances. In the January honours Frances was awarded the CBE, and as a result received a whole file of congratulations, mostly from within Whitehall, but also including letters from such varied notables as the press magnate Lord Northcliffe (proprietor of *The Times* and *Daily Mail*) and the social researcher Seebohm Rowntree, all telling her that the recognition was overdue and well deserved.[2] Also from January there survives a single official minute written to LG by Frances (presumably one of thousands), which offers a rare glimpse of the detail of her work for him. It is striking both for its necessary formality and its self-confidence in recommending a particular course of action, on a subject she knew would strike a chord with him.

> Prime Minister,
>   Attached is a letter from Sir Howard Frank on the subject of taking arable land for aerodromes, also a copy of the Cabinet Minute sanctioning this. Do you not think it advisable to have this minute & decision reconsidered? We have numerous letters of complaint from farmers, & it must be most discouraging for them, especially in view of what you have said to them.
>   F. L. Stevenson
>
> Could not 'pasture' be substituted for 'arable' in the Cabinet Minute.[3]

There is no reason to think that Frances did not continue to work as usual for LG in No. 10 for most of the year and continue to look after him more intimately at Walton Heath and elsewhere whenever they could manage it. There is no hint of anything different in the only other direct evidence that survives from 1918 – a clutch of six exceptionally ardent letters, which he wrote to her in the late summer when she developed an inflammation of the kidneys. They were together at the latest house that George Riddell had taken for LG's relaxation – Danny Park in Sussex – when she was taken ill.* LG arranged nursing care for her and wrote her anxious notes when he was too busy to come and see her. At some point she evidently returned to London. But

---

* An additional reason for LG wishing to be out of London as much as possible at this time was his extreme nervousness during air-raids. This was an embarrassing weakness in a war leader, on which Hankey frequently commented disparagingly.[4]

then she suffered a relapse and in late September she was back at Danny, ill again.[5] None of these letters is dated, so their order is uncertain.

Cariad bach anwyl aur chus mel
    But what a worry you are. Last night I got it into my silly head that you had a bad cold & it kept me waking up from fitful sleep all night. I strolled in the night twice outside your door to find out whether all was quiet. I was so thankful to hear your voice – strong as well as sweet – when I called out.
    Oceans of love to my little sweet Worry from a
    Doting old man who is
    Father lover & husband all in one.

Well how is the dear little girl with the cold in her 'dose'? . . . I have been envying that cold & wishing I were it. In the dead of night I should have crept down to the lips & had a great time – pressing their softness & then scampering along those pearly teeth – then touching the top of the tongue – then back to the lips. Oh that I were a cold.
    How are you *Pussy bach?* – Pussy *bach anwyl* – I mean – not Pussy *bach.*
    Longing to see you & to hug you
    Ever your old
    Dotard

My darling
    This is to warn you at the earliest possible moment that I have once more fallen desperately in love with an *absolutely new girl.* She is the darlingest girl I ever met. I saw her yesterday afternoon for the first time lying (in the most seductive attitude) on a sofa. She was attired in a love of a dressing gown. She had the dearest face I ever saw – the most alluring smile – her neck was simply provoking. Altogether I am clean gone. I hope one day to make her love me as much as if I were a grilled kidney swimming in fat.
    Ever & Ever
    Her lover.

The last sentence is a peculiarly revolting image, in view of Frances's illness. But it seems that she had recovered her appetite and that LG – in one of his most teasingly erotic letters – was pretending to be jealous.

Cariad anwyl

When I woke up at 6 my first thought was of the loving little face engraved on my heart & I had a fierce impulse to go there & then to cover it with kisses. But darling I am jealous once more. I know your thoughts are on roast mutton & partridge & chicken & potatoes & that you are longing to pass them through the lips which are wine & to bite them with luscious joy with the dazzling white teeth that I love to press. I know that today I am a little out of it & that your heart is throbbing for other thrills.

I will not despair though for with a patience which few suspect me of but which has nevertheless borne me through many disappointments I shall bide my time feeling confident I will in the end beat the mutton chops & win back the delight of my fickle little *cariad* and it is worth waiting for.

Your very jealous old

Lover.

How are you today *cariad bach anwyl anwyl*?

I am in love today with two such darlings. One is the little pink sofa girl with the blue dressing gown & the other a little love in pink with braided hair falling on each side of the sweetest face you ever saw nestling on a pillow.

Fond fond tender love

to *both*

D.

The last in the series – if it was the last – is one of LG's most serious declarations of his love, expressed in biblical language reminiscent of the Welsh sermons of his youth.

My sweet loving fond thrilling little worry – the dearest thing I have struck in life after meandering through its marshes plains mountains for over half a century. It was worth such a long strenuous & weary walk to come across you in the end. And now I mean to take you along with me – for ever. We will walk alongside arm in arm or arm around waist as long as we can. When you are weary & footsore I mean to carry you & when I stumble on the way through folly or feebleness you will pick me up won't you darling – you will never leave me behind for the wolves to prey upon.

Oh I am full of things wild but true to tell you sweetheart & I'll tell you them on your lips soon.

Ever & Ever your old
Dai[6]

From the way he ended all these letters it seems that LG was feeling his age. He was only fifty-five; but he was under tremendous strain. 'I could not help noticing how terribly Ll.G. has aged in the last twelve months,' Hankey noted around the time of the German breakthrough in France. 'His hair has turned almost white.'[7] In September he fell ill – seriously, for once. He had been speaking in Manchester when he caught a minor strain of the flu epidemic that claimed around thirty million lives worldwide in 1918 – far more victims than the war itself. LG was sufficiently ill that Hankey at one point described his condition as 'touch and go'.[8] He was laid up for a fortnight with – he complained later – nothing to look at but Manchester Town Hall and the statues of Gladstone and Bright dripping in the constant rain outside his window.[9] Frances was not able to go and see him and there is no record that Maggie did. When LG got back to London, Riddell wrote that his 'nasty illness' had 'shaken him a good deal'.[10] But he was quickly back to normal, returned to Danny for the rest of September and was back chairing the War Cabinet at the beginning of October, before going to Paris on 5 October to discuss armistice terms with his French and Italian counterparts. Before he left he wrote one more letter to the still-convalescent Frances – rather different from the others in that it was written in the form of a mock-memo.

Memo from D. to P.

This is not love-letter – it is a purely business communication or rather a minute from a chief to his Secretary. Instructions how to behave on my departure for & during my absence on the Continent.

1. Look today as if you rather liked my going – cheerful jolly, otherwise we shall *both* be miserable (pure selfish thought for himself as usual says Pussy).

2. After I have left & the whole time I am away you must not get depressed or miserable. Act as if you were right down glad to get rid of an old bore who is always hanging about your room when he is not wanted.

3. Get rid of the cold as soon as you can.

4. Don't be in too great a hurry to get well. It leads to fretting & impatience & overpersuading nurses & doctors to let you do things you ought
   not to do – and ultimate disappointment. Climb back to strength slowly.

5. Seek nor desire any substitute for me (vide First Commandment for para-
   phrase of this).

6. Never forget that there is a fond old man who will not be too full of
   affairs for a single moment of his journey to find room – & the best
   room in his heart for you.

Whatever luggage I leave behind Pussy will be with me for the little witch
has done her own packing long long ago & she never leaves the valise whatever is taken out or put in.

Every morning I shall be eagerly awaiting news from Danny – yes &
every evening & how happy I shall be to know you are getting on my
darling *cariad*.
   Byth bythoed
   D.[11]

As soon as the Armistice was signed on 11 November, LG's attention
switched to the General Election, called for 14 December, and the forthcoming Peace Conference. Already on 22 November Hankey noted that
he was 'in a most excited and irritable condition owing to the General
Election, and it is very difficult to get any serious work out of him'.[12]
On 8 December, Riddell – who almost always dined with LG at Walton
on Sundays, often with Maggie and Megan present – recorded unusually that Frances and Philip Kerr were there instead. (Frances is mentioned
very rarely in Riddell's diary.) Talking about the election, LG hoped for
a majority of 150.[13] But otherwise we have only glimpses of Frances at
this time. Almost certainly she did not accompany LG on his election
travels, but stayed in London minding the office. During the campaign
Nancy Astor wrote her a characteristically forthright letter giving her
views on a variety of matters, clearly intended to be passed on to LG.*[14]

* Nancy was the forceful American-born wife of Waldorf Astor, at that time a junior
minister.

Meanwhile Maggie not only stood in for her husband in the Caernarvon Boroughs, but spoke at meetings in south Wales and northern England as well. On the eve of polling day LG wrote to thank her.

> You have done brilliantly. Your tours have been *the* feature of the campaign. You have been flitting about though so much that I found it impossible to know where to write you.[15]

Mrs Astor was not the only one to use Frances as a sympathetic conduit to LG. Sir John Cowans, who had served as Quartermaster-General throughout the war, now hoped for a colonial governorship (he was another who fancied governing Iraq) and that Frances would help secure him one. 'The PM was kind enough to say that you could keep worrying him on the subject when vacancies occurred,' he wrote to her on Christmas Eve, 'and I was to keep on worrying you in turn!!' Frances must have promised him to do her best, since on New Year's Day he wrote again to thank her.

> I agree with you that the Isle of Man is too – well! I won't say more, but you can guess what you like! I think Mesopotamia sounds more alluring – you will be able to come & spend the winter there!*[16]

Before the days of opinion polls, it was always difficult to predict election results. But in 1918 it was especially difficult, because wartime legislation had almost tripled the size of the electorate since 1910. Not only were almost all men over the age of twenty-one now enfranchised, but women over thirty too – their work in the hospitals and munitions factories having made the women's case more effectively than the antics of the suffragettes; 1918 was thus Britain's first truly democratic election, with more than twenty-one million voters. Nevertheless LG was still cautiously optimistic, as he wrote to Maggie:

---

* Frances evidently had a soft spot for Cowans, whose reputation had suffered in 1916 when he had appeared to use his influence improperly to send to France a young man who had spurned the advances of a society lady. When LG told the King about the case, Frances wrote, he 'roared with laughter. "They tell me that he is a trifle fond of the ladies." "Yes, Your Majesty," replied D., "and I believe the ladies are very fond of him."'[17] Cowans was cleared of the charge; and in her memoirs Frances called him 'as charming a person as could be met'.[18] But she failed to get him his governorship, and he died in 1921 without the promotion he had hoped for.

I think the election is all right . . . I shall be very surprised if we are beaten.
I shall be surprised if we don't get a majority over 100. If it is over 120
then I shall be content. If it is under that I shall be disappointed . . .
Fond love to my sweet old girl – & to the two little girls.[19]*

During the campaign Maggie wrote to her husband, having evidently
read of his plans in the newspapers: 'I see you mean to go to Paris on
the 22nd. That means that you will spend your Xmas there so that we
are not going to get a Peace Xmas at home.'[20] But LG did not spend
Christmas in Paris. He spent it at Walton, where he played golf with
Riddell in the morning, then 'carved the turkey in great style' at midday
dinner and slept for three hours in the afternoon.[21] But on this occasion Riddell omits to mention who else was present. Unless Maggie
had changed her own plans, which is unlikely, the probability must be
that Frances was with him.

On Christmas Day Hankey – allowed a rare day off with his own
wife – recorded his growing ambivalence about the great war-winning
Prime Minister.

Ll.G. has brought the country through the war, but is very anxious lest he
should not get the big majority in the election on which his supporters
count. Consequently he is in a nervous, irritable and difficult frame of mind.
The mistake he is making is to try and absorb too much into his hands.
He seems to have a sort of lust for power; ignores his colleagues or toler-
ates them in an almost disdainful way, and seems more and more to assume
the attitude of a dictator. He takes but little advice, and even Philip Kerr
and I have few opportunities to coach him.[22]

In fact LG's anxiety was needless. When the results were declared
on 28 December, supporters of the government had won 478 out
of 602 non-Irish seats (335 Conservative, 133 Coalition Liberal, ten
Coalition Labour). The Asquithian Liberals were reduced to just
twenty-eight, with Asquith himself and most of his leading colleagues
losing their seats. Labour, with sixty-three, became for the first
time the official Opposition. Since the seventy-three Sinn Fein
members refused to take their seats, the government had an effective

---

* The 'two little girls' were LG's first two grandchildren, Dick's daughter Valerie and
Olwen's daughter Margaret, both born in 1918.

majority of more than 300 – a crushing margin, which LG immediately realised would do him more harm than good. 'We were gathered together in my room in Downing Street,' Frances recalled, '& as defeat after defeat [for the Asquithians] came in to us from the Whip Room, D. became very quiet. "I did not want this."'[23] Hankey wrote that LG was 'almost stunned' by the scale of his victory and 'really upset by Asquith's defeat'.[24] Then he went off to spend the first week of the New Year at Criccieth, taking Hankey and Kerr with him to help construct his new government. With the election safely over, he relaxed. Hankey found him now 'gay and cheery', and thoroughly enjoyed his 'very delightful interlude' in Wales.[25]

But having won the war, LG now faced the still greater challenge of trying to win the peace.

PARIS, 1919

The first half of 1919 was largely taken up with peacemaking in Paris. For six months the leaders of the victorious Allies were closeted together in the French capital, as they tried not just to agree among themselves peace terms to impose on Germany, but to redraw the entire map of Europe and the Middle East, carving new states out of the defeated Austrian and Turkish empires – resolving some problems in the process, but creating others for the future. The 'Big Three' in Paris were the French Prime Minister, the elderly but formidable Georges Clemenceau – known as 'The Tiger' – who had the advantage of hosting the conference; the American President, Woodrow Wilson, who came to Europe bearing the hopes of the world as the idealistic prophet of a new world order based on the proposal for a League of Nations; and Lloyd George as the freshly re-elected British Prime Minister, who found himself the man in the middle. (Initially they were the 'Big Four', until the Italian Prime Minister, Vittorio Orlando, went home in protest at Italy failing to win the gains to which his country felt it was entitled.) Most of the decisions were hammered out with remarkable informality between the 'Big Three' and their respective staffs. But these central figures were besieged by delegations from every other country in the world, all trying to advance their own causes and protect their special interests. It was an extraordinary diplomatic gathering for which the only precedent was the Congress of Vienna following the defeat of Napoleon: but this time it was conducted under the eyes of the world's press, constituting the first global media circus.

It fell to LG to try to mediate between the seventy-eight-year-old

Clemenceau's inflexible determination to ensure that Germany was never able to threaten France again and Wilson's high-minded but impractical vision of democracy and self-determination for all. This was the ultimate test of his fabled powers of persuasion, ingenuity and guile. The verdict on the treaties eventually signed at Versailles has been disputed ever since. Were the terms imposed on Germany too harsh – or too lenient? One way or another they led within twenty years to the rise of Hitler and the renewal of war. The settlement of 1919 also drew the frontiers over which the ancient ethnic conflicts of the Balkans and the Middle East have continued to rage to this day. More recently historians have begun to suggest that LG and his fellow-triumvirs probably made as good a job of reconciling impossible demands as was feasible in the circumstances of the time. Whatever the ultimate judgement on his efforts, however, the first six months of 1919 were no less fraught and momentous than the previous two years.

Yet at the same time they were a very pleasant and stimulating interlude – a holiday from the normal pressures of domestic politics, during which, as well as dealing directly on a daily basis with the other leaders of the post-war world, LG was able to consort relatively openly with his mistress who (in A. J. P. Taylor's words) was 'treated generally as his unofficial wife'.[1] In fact this is an exaggeration. LG and Frances still had to be discreet and were careful not to be seen about too much together. Frances enjoyed a busy social life in her own right. But they both – particularly Frances – looked back on 1919 as the most exciting period of their long relationship. Frances resumed her diary in March and kept it up fairly regularly until July, so their life in Paris is relatively well documented. Instead of writing on loose leaves as before, however, she bought a small printed diary, which gave her only limited space for each day.

LG was the last of the 'Big Three' to arrive in Paris, a week before the Conference formally opened on 18 January. Initially both Maggie and Megan came with him, though Maggie stayed only until 8 February. The sleeping arrangements were complicated and revealing. While most of the British Empire delegation – including Frances – was housed in the Hotel Majestic, near the place de l'Étoile, with offices nearby in the Hotel Astoria, LG was provided with a flat of his own in the rue Nitot, filled with classic French furniture and hung with English paintings: Gainsborough, Thomas Lawrence and the like. Arthur Balfour (now Foreign Secretary) occupied the flat upstairs. Later, after Maggie had gone home, Megan – now sixteen and eager for the bright lights

– was allowed to move out of the rue Nitot and share Frances's room
at the Majestic, where she thought she would have more fun. Megan
still did not realise that Frances was any more than her father's confidential secretary. 'It was difficult for me,' Frances wrote in her memoirs,
'to add the duties of a chaperone to those of a secretary, but a chaperone was the last thing Megan wished for.'[2] It was also, of course, the
last thing she herself wanted: in practice Megan was chaperoning her
as much as the other way round. Later LG and Maggie decided that
Megan was having too much fun at the Majestic and sent her to a
finishing school in Paris. Thereafter Frances was able to spend more
time at the rue Nitot.

In his unreliable biography of his mother, Dick stated that Maggie
did not go to Paris at all. 'To her,' he wrote, 'it was a Heaven-sent
opportunity to get out of London and spend a few months of glorious
peace among her own people . . . To her the decisions of Criccieth
Urban District Council were more vital and lasting.'[3] This is doubly
misleading, since Maggie not only did go to Paris for three weeks, but
also fulfilled a large number of public engagements in London over the
following months, so she must have stayed in Downing Street quite a
lot of the time without LG. Indeed, an undated letter from this period
suggests that she was having a high old time quite contrary to her
homely reputation.

> I had a great many visitors here yesterday 15 ladies to tea, & I am lunching
> & dining out very often so that I am very well treated in your absence. I
> have had an offer to go to America for a trip free of charge & I am going
> yatching [*sic*] in Scotland.
>
> I was sorry to miss you on the phone last night. Ring up as often as you
> feel inclined. I am always pleased to hear 'Paris wants you'. I am dining to
> meet the Duke of Connaught & lunching to meet the Prince of Wales so I
> am very gay.[4]

While the statesmen were settling the future of the world during
the day, Paris was one big party in the evenings. After four years of
war, the restraints were off and the survivors were determined to enjoy
themselves with an unprecedented freedom. The restaurants and cafés,
clubs and theatres that Frances had found closed or requisitioned in
1917 were back in business, catering to a huge cosmopolitan influx
of diplomats, their aides and secretaries, socialites and hangers-on. For

the British the Majestic was the centre of this social whirl. Two years later Frances wrote – but published anonymously – a starry-eyed description:

> There never was an institution so entirely democratic as the Majestic. It was the home of famous diplomats, of titled people, of world-renowned statesmen. It was also the home of humble clerks and typists and secretaries. The social barrier, if it existed at all, was reduced to a very thin thread. The gathering at the Majestic reminded one of nothing so much as a large family, the elder members of which had attained distinction and importance, the younger members still being kept in their proper places, but throughout existing a feeling of kinship and brotherhood, the sense that they all stood for the same thing and were working for the same end.[5]

The Saturday-night dances at the Majestic became particularly famous – or notorious. The 'Roaring Twenties', one might say, started here. Elderly statesmen and diplomats came to ogle the girls in their revealing dresses doing the latest dances.* The Prime Minister's younger daughter was conspicuous among them, to the extent that it was suggested that the Majestic should be renamed the 'Megantic', until her mother got to hear of it and her father put his foot down. 'I am glad you stood out against Megan dancing at the Majestic,' Maggie wrote – adding a trifle ingenuously, 'but of course Mlle Arbel would never allow her.'[7] Frances's diary reflected a mixture of fascination and underlying puritanism at these goings-on.

> The dance at the Majestic last night was an amazing affair – a most cosmopolitan crowd – the last touch was put on it when Lord Wimborne [Churchill's cousin] arrived with a crowd of wonderful ladies. People rather resent this invasion of the Majestic on Saturday nights, & steps are to be taken to put a stop to it, otherwise the thing will become a scandal.[8]

In her published account, however, Frances was at pains to deny that anything improper went on – or, if it did, maintained that it was the fault of gatecrashers like Wimborne, not the hard-working members of the delegation.

---

* Marshal Foch was one fascinated spectator. 'Why,' he asked, 'do the British have such sad faces and such cheerful bottoms?'[6]

Exaggerated stories were spread about at home of the orgies which took place on these occasions, of the expensive dresses which were displayed by members of the female staff; so that one might almost get the impression that dresses and dancing occupied most of the attention and thought of members of the Peace Conference Delegation. It was to the interest of some newspapers to make a scandal out of the simple amusements of the Majestic; and the small allowance given to members of the Delegation in order to cover the expenses which they would naturally incur in living away from home for a prolonged period was immediately seized upon as a basis for a series of stories about the extravagances and absurdities of the Conference . . . Anyone who witnessed the Saturday evening dances at the Majestic . . . would have seen instantly that such stories were the product of malicious tongues and were entirely without foundation.

But she did not dispute that they drew a crowd of eminent voyeurs.

They were simple scenes, these Saturday evenings, but how attractive and unusual! . . . Mr Lloyd George would come for a short time to contemplate the bright scene; Lord Milner, Lord Robert Cecil, Lord Curzon were often spectators; I have seen Mr Balfour studying the jazz band with a rapt intentness, entirely oblivious of everything else. Lord Fisher [Admiral 'Jacky' Fisher, then aged seventy-eight] came specially one evening to take part in the dancing, and danced with as much energy and enjoyment as the youngest member of the Delegation. The Maharajah of Bikanir . . . never took part in the dancing, but would gaze with a look half-puzzled, wholly absorbed, on these Western rites . . . Anyone who paid a passing visit to the Majestic, or who was summoned to give evidence before the Conference, was taken as a matter of course to the dance on Saturday evening.

Again, Frances insisted, it was 'a truly democratic scene', where the youngest typist and the highest official mixed 'without a trace of snobbery or awkwardness'.

Some of the girls' frocks were simple ones, made often by their own hands; some were more expensive and elaborate, according to the means of the wearer. The only ones to which exception might have been taken were those worn by members of the fashionable world outside, who sometimes came to take part in the dancing.

'There will probably never be another gathering,' she concluded, 'quite like the British Delegation in Paris during these months.'[9]

Frances threw herself into this heady world with enthusiasm. As an unmarried young woman with close access to the Prime Minister, she was in considerable demand. Of course her first loyalty was to LG whenever he was free; but when he was not – which was much of the time – she was happy to be squired around Paris by numerous eligible (often titled) younger men, any one of whom would have gladdened her mother's heart. Her somewhat brief diary, one suspects, tells only a fraction of her giddy life. Twice in early March she went to the opera – first *Les Contes d'Hoffman*, then *Carmen* – with Esmond Harmsworth, son and heir of the newspaper baron Lord Rothermere, who was acting as an aide to LG. 'I like him,' she wrote, 'but he is not very popular with the other young people of the party, partly I think because he is so serious & does not like playing the fool.'[10] (He had lost two elder brothers in the war.) A few days later she added that Esmond was 'extraordinarily handsome'.[11] He was only twenty, however, whereas Frances was now thirty.

Another gilded young man buzzing around her was Evan Morgan, son of the third Baron Tredegar. Five years younger than Frances, Morgan was a poet, traveller and aesthete who had served briefly in the Welsh Guards before finding a political role in the latter part of the war as private secretary to a Tory minister. A typed note in Frances's papers – presumably taken from a newspaper paragraph – describes him thus:

The Hon. Evan Morgan has become *persona grata* in Downing Street where he aspires to the position of literary adviser to the Government . . . As mentor in poetics and personalities to Mr Lloyd George, the wealthy exquisite of the Café Royal, whose second volume of verse . . . has just been published, will fill a congenial role ingenuously.[12]

It is not clear why LG should have needed a literary adviser, but Morgan had been friendly with Frances for some time; when travelling in North Africa the previous year he had bombarded her with letters and telegrams asking her to tell his family of his movements.[13] Now he was in Paris as a member of the Foreign Press Bureau. On 1 April Frances dined with him at the Majestic. (They had actually been invited to join another party that included LG, but 'D. thinks it better that I should not be seen dining with him in public. I think he is right. We joined the party afterwards for some music.')[14] On another occasion Frances wrote to her mother that she was going with Morgan and others to the opera (*Samson et Dalila*). But many years later she wrote that this was 'the last time I accepted an invitation from the future Lord Tredegar'. He had managed to obtain tickets by giving the impression that LG would be coming: the red carpet was laid out for the Prime Minister and the management was not pleased when he turned up with just Frances. 'I was very angry.'[15] But she remained fond of his mother, who was always kind to her. Later that summer, when they were back in London (and LG was in Criccieth), Frances wrote that she was going to Lady Tredegar's 'for a quiet weekend', in terms that suggested there had been at least the possibility of something between herself and Morgan.

> Evan will be there & things may be a little strained, as he is such a hopeless liar that I have given up altogether. He is very clever, but thoroughly degenerate. It is a great pity, as Lady T. is devoted to him, & she is a dear.[16]

A third, rather older suitor who reappeared in Paris was Sir Albert Stern. Frances's mother was not alone in hoping that she might marry Stern, as Frances admitted in her diary on 16 May.

> Went to lunch at Armenonville with Bertie Stern, who has just come to Paris & says he is going to have a good time, which means he is going to give other people a good time. He is a most generous & thoughtful person & the best host I have ever met. One of his friends asked me the other day why I did not marry him. 'One excellent reason,' I replied, 'is that he has never asked me.' But all the same I think he might ask me if he did not know perfectly well that I would not leave D.[17]

Five days later – a Wednesday, which suggests that the work of the Conference was not too pressing – she saw Stern again, with another man who also made some impression on her.

> Played tennis this afternoon & dined with Bertie Stern & Major Crankshaw & others at the Ambassadeurs. Thoroughly enjoyed it. Major C. is a darling, quite one of the nicest people I have ever met. Danced afterwards at the Majestic.[18]

Evidently LG was a little worried by Stern's attentions and exerted all his charm to ensure that Frances did not succumb to them.

D. & I had a long talk. I know Stern would marry me if I gave him the slightest encouragement & if he thought I would leave D. It is a great temptation in a way for although I don't love him we are good friends & I know he would be very kind to me. It would mean a title & wealth, whereas now I may find myself old & friendless & having to earn my own living, if anything should happen to D. People will not be so anxious to marry me in 10 years' time. On the other hand I know I should not be happy now away from D. & no-one else in the world could give me the intense & wonderful love that he showers on me. He was very sweet about it, & says he wants to do what is best for me. But I can see that he would be unhappy if I left him, so I promised him I would not.[19]

Two days later again, LG secured his victory – as though it was entirely his decision.

D. told me this morning that he had definitely made up his mind that he could not let me leave him. So that is final, & I am very glad. I need not worry about it any more. It would be very foolish to spoil for material prospects the most wonderful love which ever happened.[20]

So Frances recommitted herself to a life in the shadows. She was always complaining that LG was taken up with the Peace Conference; yet they still managed to spend a good deal of time together, if not often alone. Her diary constantly records that 'Churchill came to lunch', 'Paderewski came to lunch', 'Painlevé came to dinner' – which implies that she was present – or sometimes that 'Sir Rosslyn Wemyss came to breakfast' or 'General Smuts came to breakfast', which suggests that she was now sleeping in the rue Nitot.[21]* Just occasionally 'D. & I had dinner quietly together'[22] or 'D. very tired after a heavy day & we dined very quietly & went to bed early';[23] and once 'D. stayed in bed with a cold & a bit of a temperature, & I stayed in to nurse him'.[24] But more often Frances was just one of a larger party around the Prime Minister, and they would have to be careful not to betray any undue

---

* Ignace Paderewski, the former concert pianist, was Prime Minister of Poland; Paul Painlevé was a former (and future) Prime Minister of France; Sir Rosslyn Wemyss was the First Sea Lord.

intimacy. 'We had a very jolly little dinner,' she wrote on 24 March, 'some young people up from the Majestic & D. was on very good form – absolutely mad. When he gets to the point of trying on other people's hats he is always most amusing.'[25]

Once Frances recorded that 'we all went to see *Figaro* at the Opéra Comique'; but LG was recognised and vowed never to go to a theatre again. 'It really is hard lines that he should not be able to enjoy himself quietly without becoming the centre of attention.'[26] More often they dined in – LG was provided with an excellent French chef who catered cheerfully for large impromptu parties – followed by private entertainment. LG liked nothing better than a rousing sing-song (for which Frances often played the piano), but sometimes they invited a professional pianist or singer to perform for them. The sing-songs took place in LG's flat, the serious music usually in Balfour's on the floor above. Many years later President Wilson's doctor reminisced with Frances about these happy days.

> Grayson made me play to him the tunes I used to play in Paris in 1919 – Missouri Waltz and the old S. American songs: Dixie, Swanee River etc. He reminded me of the evening at the Rue Nitot when I played Chopin for Balfour, & Grayson made me end up by playing *his* tunes, at which Balfour was slightly puzzled & quizzical. 'I didn't understand the music he liked,' said G., 'and he didn't appear to appreciate mine.'[27]

But Frances could cater equally to them both.

Sometimes LG did dine out and even danced, though not at the Majestic, judging from Frances's diary for 17 May.

> Dined at the *Pré Catalan*, Evelyn Fitzgerald being the host. D. & Churchill & CIGS [Sir Henry Wilson] & others were there also, & we had a very merry time. D. thoroughly enjoys dining out like this, & loved the dancing. He is a thorough Bohemian. We stayed till quite late, & some of us went on to the Majestic to dance. The Saturday evening dances there are great fun, but I do not say much to D. about it, as he gets rather jealous.[28]

LG also managed several games of golf at Saint-Cloud, with the ubiquitous Riddell – who was in Paris to act as intermediary between LG and the press (in effect a prime ministerial spin-doctor) – and anyone else, from Philip Kerr to the Canadian Prime Minister, whom he could press to play. Frances would sometimes go too, but once LG became 'very jealous, because he says I walked with Esmond Harmsworth all the time, & he took me there to walk with him'.[29]

On Sundays (or any time he had a free afternoon) LG liked to lead his whole entourage on motor trips outside Paris – sometimes to see the battlefields and devastated regions, sometimes just for picnics in the country. For instance, on 13 March:

> In the afternoon we went for a run to Fontainebleau. It was a delicious, springlike afternoon, & the Chateau looked beautiful. We took along one of the girls from the Majestic, 'the Peach', & D. flirted with her to his heart's content. However, he was quite open about it & I think it did him good, so that I did not mind.[30]

Fidelity for LG was always a one-way street. Three days later they were off again:

> We went on an excursion to the devastated area around Soissons . . . The place is a desolation, simply a series of shell-holes . . . We had to walk warily, because of the unexploded grenades and shells which were lying about everywhere. We lunched in the woods beyond Senlis, where the ground was carpeted with daffodils and primroses. D. was in his best form, as he always is on these occasions.[31]

And on 13 April: 'We went for a short run round St Germain & Versailles, picnicking in the woods . . . Lord Rothermere came too.'[32]

Riddell was almost invariably of the party, and his diary normally corroborates Frances's, except that they rarely mention the presence of the other. Just once – on a visit to Pontoise in June – Riddell notes that Megan came along: she travelled with her father and Frances in one car, Riddell with Bonar Law in another, and J. T. Davies, William Sutherland (LG's parliamentary secretary) and Esmond Harmsworth in a third.[33] Frances does not record this outing at all. But in her anonymous book about the personalities of the Peace Conference she included a warm portrait of Riddell, whom she regarded as a good and discreet friend – despite his owning the foremost scandal-sheet in Fleet Street. 'He has a natural aptitude for acquiring news,' she wrote:

He never forgets a fact, and his brain is a store of information . . . It is difficult to mention a person or subject of which Lord Riddell is not able to give you a complete encyclopaedic account.* . . . His eyes are grey and searching, and you feel that they are probing to discover the very secrets of your soul, the very weaknesses of your character – in fact you feel . . . that here is a masterly lawyer putting you through a cross-examination, and that from him very few secrets can be hid![34]

It is difficult to understand how this encyclopaedic inquisitiveness squared with his discretion; but the fact is that Riddell never betrayed Frances's secret. Even when he published his diaries fifteen years later, his references to 'Miss Stevenson' were few and formal.

Over the Easter weekend (19–20 April) LG had planned a two-day trip, spending the night at Amiens; but this had to be curtailed due to the crisis with the Italians. ('Very disappointed, but still, "duty first",' Frances noted.) Next day 'D. arranged for the meeting to be at 10, so that we could start before lunch for a run, & picnic out of doors.' This was a famous meeting at which Orlando broke down and wept, before walking out of the Conference; but LG's mind was already on his picnic. According to Riddell, they did not get away until twelve; but for once his account does mention Frances.

L.G., Miss Stevenson and I drove in one car, the others following in three more cars. We lunched in a wood, L.G. dilating as usual on the pleasure of taking meals in the open air. The other members of the party were Sir Auckland Geddes, Freddy Guest, Philip Kerr and Mrs Flower, one of the secretariat.† I don't think either Geddes or Guest enjoyed the outing. Guest said dejectedly, 'This is a sad way of taking one's pleasure – rushing through the country at sixty miles an hour and lunching in a wood!'[35]

But Frances loved it. 'We had a glorious day – went to Noyon & Lassigny & surrounding places – most interesting. D. so sweet & in such good spirits.'[36]

The next day – despite the Italians – Frances had another happy time.

---

* Riddell was given a peerage in 1920.
† Sir Auckland Geddes, Minister of Reconstruction, and Freddy Guest, Coalition Liberal Chief Whip, were both cronies of LG.

D. came to meet me on my way up to breakfast, & we went for a short sharp walk up to the Arc de Triomphe. Who would have thought that when I made the same visit with Suzanne one morning before breakfast 14 years ago, that I should one day be coming there with the Prime Minister of England, after a terrible war! There is nothing to compare with these little walks with D., when we unburden our hearts to each other & feel that we are about 10 years old!

In the evening we dined with Sir George Riddell at Fouquet's & D. enjoyed himself immensely. He has very little opportunities [*sic*] for these little pleasures, as he cannot go about very much, but he thoroughly enjoys it when he does. Before leaving he asked the orchestra to play *Sambre et Meuse* which they did with great zest.[37]

Philip Kerr was also present, and Riddell adds that they did some work – in typically informal style – over dinner. The Germans had just agreed to send not, as first proposed, mere 'messengers', but 'great personages' to receive the Allied peace terms. This LG considered 'a regular climb-down and very significant', and he wanted Riddell to make it public at once.

'Now let us see – how shall we put it? Shall we call them "great personages?"' Miss Stevenson suggested 'high personages', which was accepted. We then tore some sheets of paper out of the Head Waiter's account book and Miss Stevenson wrote the message in pencil.[38]

Riddell gives another glimpse of this mixture of work and play when he dined at the rue Nitot the next evening.

When we went into the drawing room, L.G. called upon Auckland Geddes to sing, which he did with great effect, producing Scottish soldier songs with gusto. L.G. was much pleased with the singing and joined in the choruses with an imperfect Scottish accent. The Scottish songs were interspersed with pianoforte solos by Spring-Rice.*

About 10 o'clock a letter arrived from Orlando stating that he was leaving tomorrow . . . L.G. said that Orlando must be asked to breakfast and that he must try to get him to continue the negotiations. Then he, Philip Kerr, Hankey and Miss Stevenson went into another room, where he dictated a

---

* A junior member of the British delegation.

letter to Orlando inviting him . . . to breakfast. I drove Davies into Paris
with the letter.[39]

Orlando declined the invitation. LG called on him instead, but failed
to dissuade him from returning to Rome.

Though she occasionally admitted to having some fun on her own,
Frances still hated it whenever LG had to be away. In mid-April, for
instance, when he had to go back to London to answer critics in the
House of Commons, she wrote that she was 'desolate without him,
& I don't enjoy my freedom a bit'.[40] He in turn told her that he was
'very sick' that she was not in the gallery to send him her usual congratulatory note. 'Nevertheless,' she concluded, 'I think it was wise for
me not to travel backwards & forwards with him, as he was away
such a short time. It is jolly, too, to meet again after even a short
parting.'[41]

They had a minor falling-out in mid-May, when the usual party
drove to Barbizon, near Fontainebleau, for the weekend. 'A lovely spot,'
Frances wrote, 'ideal for lovers, & specially beautiful at this time of
year.' But now it was her turn to be jealous.

Spent a very happy day wandering about the woods, though was annoyed
by Mrs Clement Jones,* who expected D. to pay a lot of attention to her,
& I was cross in consequence . . . Of course all women are fascinated by
D. & he in turn is nice to most of them, & once having started they expect
him to go on. The silly ones get their heads turned immediately & there is
no doing anything with them. It is most amusing to watch. But I got rather
angry with Mrs C.J., having had rather too much of that sort of thing lately.
However D. & I made it up in the evening.[42]

During the week in April when LG went to London, Frances made
an excursion of her own to visit her brother's grave near Béthune. She
was accompanied by Nancy Astor, who was going to Ypres and took
Frances with her in her car. They stayed the night at Amiens and went
on the next day.

Left soon after 9 & arrived at Béthune soon after 12, passing along the
Vimy Ridge & through Arras & Lens – a region of horror & devastation.

---

* Clement Jones was secretary to the British delegation.

Annezin is just beyond Béthune, & we found the cemetery quite easily, & also the old woman who has been looking after Paul's grave. She took me to it: it is beautifully kept, but it was a terrible moment to see it for the first time. The pathos of it all swept over me, & the regret that his young life should have been cut off before it was scarcely begun . . . Nevertheless, I was glad to have seen the place where his body lies, & to think of it as something that I have seen; though as I stood there I knew it was not *he* that lay there, but only so to speak a relic or memorial of him. Indeed, I have often felt him close beside me, especially in times of trial when a difficulty or danger has been overcome. Still, the wave of regret sweeps over one from time to time, that he is not here to enjoy the good things of the world, & to live his life to the full.[43]

A few weeks later Mrs Astor – as she still was: Waldorf did not inherit the title until October – wrote from London:

My dear Miss Stevenson,

I was so glad that I could be with you that day, but it was terribly hard to be so little use. My heart just sank when I saw that little grave. You were wonderfully brave . . .

I hope all goes well with you in Paris . . . Behave yourself.

Yours,

Nancy Astor[44]

'I saw a great deal of Nancy in Paris,' Frances recalled in her memoirs, 'and she was kind and helpful to me.'[45] Very soon, however, Frances concluded that Lady Astor – a highly moralistic Christian Scientist – was 'treacherous and not to be trusted. In spite of her repeated protestations and friendship & goodwill towards me, I find that she takes every opportunity of saying spiteful things about D. & myself. It is almost incredible, but it is true.' When later that year Nancy took over Waldorf's Plymouth constituency to become the first woman MP to take her seat, Frances noted cattily that she would 'get her reward in the House of Commons! I do not think any *wise* woman would choose to sit in the House.'[46] This is a somewhat startling observation from a formerly ardent suffragist; and indeed Frances qualified it two days later when she watched Lady Astor's debut with more of the feminist excitement that one would expect.

It really was a thrilling moment, not from the personal point of view, but from the fact that after all these hundreds of years, this was the first time that a woman had set foot upon that floor to represent the people – or a certain number of them. I had a lump in my throat as I saw her come in at the far end – a very graceful, neat figure – & wait for her turn to walk up the floor.[47]

The fact that she had counted Nancy Astor as a friend at all is just one example of the social circles in which Frances was now moving. Not only was she working and relaxing, lunching and dining every day with all the leading figures of British politics, either permanently based in Paris (like Balfour) or frequently passing through (like Bonar Law, Churchill – whom she never liked – and the Geddes brothers). She also met and observed at close quarters all the foreign and imperial leaders who came to the rue Nitot, from Wilson, Clemenceau, Foch and Smuts to glamorous supporting players like Paderewski (whom she thought one of the most impressive people she had ever met)[48] and T. E. Lawrence (whom she found fascinating, but 'a little conceited').[49] With many of these 'high personages' she was on very easy terms. Admiral 'Jacky' Fisher – with whom she danced at least once at the Majestic – 'would drop into my office with ideas for solving all difficulties', and also frequently came to lunch or dinner at the rue Nitot with his friend the Duchess of Hamilton, and told stories – so Frances told her mother – 'until everyone was crying with laughter, and my sides ached'.[50]

She also met the artists who were drawn to Paris by the Conference – among them Augustus John, who gave particularly scandalous parties, which LG forbade Frances to attend. She sat for Sir William Orpen, the official artist of the Peace Conference, who showed her some of the sketches for his huge group portrait of all the leaders. Maybe he drew Frances because he thought of including her in the picture, or maybe he just liked her. She found him 'a charming little man . . . not so terrifying as John', and they became very friendly, judging from the chatty and sentimental letters he wrote her back in London the following year and throughout the 1920s.[51]

The Marquess of Cholmondeley had also become a great patron during the last year of the war, bombarding her with letters and frequently inviting her out to lunch or dinner. He was a big landowner in Cheshire and a racehorse owner, very upset by the suspension of racing during the war. He presumably hoped that Frances would pass on his concerns to LG; but he also took a fatherly interest in her, as evidenced by a letter he wrote her during the Peace Conference, acknowledging her congratulations on the arrival of his grandson.

Dear Miss Stevenson,

Many thanks for your letter. It is *ages* since I heard from you, was thinking of putting an advertisement in the agony column of Times [*sic*] to ask what had happened. I can quite understand how *very* busy you must be, *dancing* and your work – not much time for letter writing . . .

Perhaps you will write again, if you ever have a few minutes to spare from the pleasures of Paris . . .

Yours very sincerely,

Cholmondeley

Is Sir G. Riddell still with you, is he a good dance partner.[52]

Letters like this one show much more clearly than her memoirs, or even her diary, the sort of social status Frances now enjoyed in her capacity as the Prime Minister's confidential secretary. It was a remarkable transformation, which she seems to have taken in her stride with astonishing ease, as though she had been born to this life. Her secret lay in her exceptionally sympathetic nature. Years later Megan – not intending a compliment – likened her to 'a thick pile carpet into which one's feet sank gratefully'.[53] Women sometimes felt Frances's sweetness to be a bit sickly. But men – all sorts of men, both young and old, aristocrats and adventurers – felt they could confide in her, and that she would respect their confidence. They did confide in her and she did not betray them: even her diary is very discreet where gossip about others is concerned. She did not flaunt her relationship with LG, though it must have been obvious to everyone who saw them together that they were very close. She was attractive and accomplished enough to hold her own in any company; she spoke good French and played the piano; but she looked too prim to be anything so improper as a mistress: she did nothing to draw attention to herself and so was welcomed in the highest political and social circles without scandal, though LG's many enemies might have been expected to use any means to attack him. It is an extraordinary tribute to her personal qualities that there was so little gossip.

The Peace Conference eventually concluded with the signing of the

Treaty of Versailles on 28 June. Frances recalled a crisis in the British delegation when it was discovered that LG had no seal.

> I rushed to the Rue de la Paix at the eleventh hour to secure him one & to have it engraved . . . It was an insignificant little object for so great an occasion, but it was the only thing I could get at such short notice.[54]

She attended the signing ceremony, but was disgusted by the way it was – even then – turned into a media circus.

> I am glad I was there, yet the thing as a whole was rather disappointing. It was very badly stage-managed by the French . . . The Press is reducing everything that is noblest and impressive in modern life into terms of Press photographs and Press interviews. In fact they try to dominate everything. How can you concentrate on the solemnity of a scene when you have men with cameras in every direction, whose sole object is to get as near as they can to the central figures? . . . One or two reporters, for the sake of preserving a record, would not be so bad. But they have to be dealt with in armies nowadays. The Press is destroying all romance, all solemnity, all majesty. They are as unscrupulous as they are vulgar.[55]*

President Wilson left Paris that evening, LG the next day. As the train left the Gare du Nord, LG said to Riddell: 'That's over! There's always a sense of sadness closing a chapter of one's life. It has been a wonderful time.' Riddell was with him on the boat as well.

> As the ship steamed out of the harbour at Boulogne, I stood on the deck by his side, as he acknowledged the plaudits of the crowd on the quay. I said, 'Now for the next chapter!' 'Yes,' he replied, 'now for the next chapter . . . Let me have a fortnight's holiday, and then I will decide what to do.'[58]

King George V came with the Prince of Wales to meet his Prime Minister at Victoria, and drove with him in an open carriage through

---

* Riddell agreed, writing that 'the part allotted to the journalists [became] very much like a bear-garden'.[56] He also recorded a wonderful example of French priorities, when Clemenceau dismissed his request that the signing should be at 11 a.m., 'so that the press could get their telegrams off in good time. He said, "No, impossible! The function would last five hours. You must have *déjeuner*. If you fix eleven you will get nothing to eat. It must be two o'clock!"'[57] Perhaps it was lucky for LG that it was not earlier.

cheering crowds back to Buckingham Palace. Flowers were thrown at them, and one wreath landed in the carriage, as Frances proudly recorded.

> It fell on the King's lap but he handed it to D. 'This is for you,' he said. D. has given it to me, & though it will fade, I will keep it all my life.* I know better than anyone how well he deserves the laurels he has won. He is very tired however & will go away to Criccieth as soon as he can for a little rest.[59]

---

* She did keep the wreath, and after LG's death gave it to the museum she established at Llanystumdwy, where it is still displayed – along with the seal she bought in the rue de la Paix.

'MY FATHER & LOVER & BROTHER & FRIEND'

Returning from Paris to London was painful for Frances, It had been, as LG said, 'a wonderful time', and all her life she looked back on it as an unrepeatable experience. It was particularly galling that LG almost immediately went off to Criccieth, though she knew it was inevitable. For the last six months she had had him virtually to herself: now she must go back to sharing him and taking second place whenever his wife asserted her prior claim. As her Parisian idyll ended, Frances vented her frustration in another bitter outburst about Maggie, whom she believed would now be less able than ever to care for her husband in the style to which he had become accustomed.

> D. hates returning home. He has been well looked after in Paris – has had every comfort – the best food – the best attendance. He has been able to entertain at will. When at Downing St, or Walton Heath it is another matter. There is never enough to go round & what there is, is very inferior. I have never seen anyone with such a capacity for making a place uncomfortable as Mrs Lloyd George. Her meanness forces the household to economise in coal & food, & everything that makes for comfort. The servants would be a disgrace to any house, & the P.M. is rightly ashamed of them. But it is no use his protesting – he says he gave that up long ago, because it had no effect & only caused unpleasantness.[1]

In fact Maggie joined LG in London that week to share in the celebrations and host a reception at No. 10. On 3 July 1919 LG recommended the Treaty to the House of Commons, and received warm tributes from all sides. He had planned to have dinner with Frances afterwards, but 'family manoeuvres made it impossible'.[2] The next day he and Maggie left for Wales. 'He needs the rest dreadfully badly, so I cannot grudge him his holiday,' Frances wrote, 'though everything is so dreary when he is not here, & time hangs so heavily. However I must bear up for a fortnight, & just look forward to the time when he comes back again.'[3]

LG's idea of a holiday was to summon first Hankey and then Riddell up to Criccieth: Frances could at least console herself that he did not care to spend time alone with his family. Hankey found him 'dead beat' – and even confessed to being 'a little tired' himself. For the first week they 'did little except read the Cabinet papers sent down to them and draft various telegrams and letters'.[4] In the second week they were joined by Churchill and Sir Henry Wilson – LG's favourite soldier – to discuss the creation of a unified Ministry of Defence. But separation from Frances meant that within three days LG was writing her his first letter for some time, typically managing to make Criccieth in July sound like midwinter.

My own sweet darling

I have missed your loving presence more than ever – & more than ever I can tell you. Your letter warmed me & brightened me up on a raw cheerless day with a raw cheerless fire in the grate.

I hope my sweetheart you have been able to get away for I shall be most disappointed if I don't find you looking fit & well when I come back. You needed a holiday just as much as I did. I saw it in your sweet tired face & it worried me. The fact of the matter is that neither you nor I realise how tired we are when we are together. We act so much as a stimulant to each other. How exhausted so ever I may be the sight of you calls up all the reserves of my nature . . .

As to my return I would return tomorrow were it not that I know in my heart it would be the worst thing in the world for you & for me . . .

Get as much open air as you can pussy *bach anwyl aur glws ariam mel.* You & I must get the worry blown out of our veins . . .

Fond fond tender affectionate love

D.[5]

Frances had not gone away, but replied immediately from 10 Downing Street – at enormous length. This is the first substantial letter of hers that has survived. 'I would have written before,' she wrote at the top of the page, 'but was not sure if you wanted me to, especially as J.T. was not with you.' Presumably JT would have acted as cover had he been at Criccieth. But LG had evidently managed to telephone without being overheard.

My own darling man

It was just heaven to hear your voice today, & it has given me the necessary courage to keep up my spirits till you return. I really have been trying to be cheerful, but I cannot help counting the days, which is a very bad plan; for I try all sorts of ways to try & make the days seem shorter, but all I do only seems to have the reverse effect. However, the first week has nearly gone, & next week I shall be torn in uncertainty as to whether I shall have to wait till the *end* of the week, or whether I must drag on till the beginning of the following week. I want you to have all the rest you can, sweetheart, but oh! I do miss you so dreadfully, & I get such awful fits of loneliness. There isn't anyone or anything who can drive the thought of you away even for 10 minutes, my darling, & I am just aching for the touch of your hand & lips . . .

I really am being very good. But that is just the worst of it – I never seem to be able to enjoy my freedom! I went to see 'Madame Angot' on Monday night with General Macready, & wished so much you could have been there too.* It was awfully good, & I enjoyed it, but even when I am enjoying myself that is just when I want you most . . .

I have been reading a lot since you have been away, all sorts of things – in fact I seem to have revived the passion for reading which I had before I knew you, dearest, but which the 'exigencies' of a very busy life since seem rather to have arrested. Have you read the love-letters of Abelard & Héloïse? They are wonderful, but rather sad, so I won't send them to you to read. Abelard & Héloïse were 12th Century lovers – he was a world-renowned philosopher & logician, & she was just a beautiful & intelligent girl. All sorts of misfortunes overtake them, & they end their days in a monastery & a convent respectively. They did not manage things very well,

---

* Sir Nevil Macready had been Adjutant-General during the war and was shortly to become commander of the British forces in Ireland. He was an unusual soldier, son of the famous actor William Charles Macready and a talented amateur himself. But his love life was unhappy. 'The poor old man is very depressed,' Frances told LG (though Macready was only fifty-seven, just a year older than LG). 'I will tell you all about it when I see you. I feel so sorry for him, for he simply idolises her.'[6] Clearly LG had no need to be jealous of Macready.

La Fille de Madame Angot was a comic opera by Charles Lecocq, then being revived at Drury Lane.

& I think I know two people who would have arranged things better.

Are you having lots of lovely walks, sweetheart, & plenty of real rest? Don't do too much work, as you deserve your short rest, & will come back all the fitter for a complete holiday. Every single person that one talks to, no matter who or what they are, has but one word for you – 'wonderful'. Indeed, your wonderfulness is becoming a legend. I am glad everyone knows now that you are wonderful, darling, for I always knew it, & I knew the whole world would know it one day. But even they don't know just how wonderful!

I have such a beautiful photograph of you before me all the day long, that sometimes I can almost imagine that you *are* here, & that you are going to talk to me. But you *are* here, beloved, in my heart, and that will content me till you come yourself to surround me with your love. I am impatient for that moment, and time stands still in the expectation of it. It frightens me now, *cariad*, when I realise how you are all in all to me, & how nothing, nothing in the world matters to me but you. Is it not a terrible thing to have staked your all like that on one person? It would be, but I know that that person is mine, & that he will not fail me, & that I can lean on him, & trust in him, & that he is my father & lover & brother & friend. You are all that to me, my beloved, and much more, and a thousand times over, & oh! I love you so! I kiss you a hundred thousand times.

PUSSY

PS. I am feeling very, very fit. The medicine Dr Beauchamp gave me has done me a great deal of good, I think.[7]

LG lost no time in responding to this ecstatic effusion.

My own darling little girl

I loved your letter – & I loved you for your letter & beyond everything I loved your letter because it was you – full of sweet gentle passionate true love. After reading it I took you in my arms & assaulted your dear [illegible] with fierce kisses – every bit of it – brow – chin – cheeks – ears – eyes & especially your sweet lips. Now get away Pussy! How do you expect me to rest here until the end of the week when you talk like this!! My little sweetheart, I want to see you quite fit when I get back. I shall be so disappointed – & a little angry – if you are not . . .

When I come back I shall be returning to the most fearful welter any Minister ever faced. It appals me to think of it. I have even had fits of running away & let them clear up their own mess. But those fits soon pass away. I must have a real try, & if the public impatience upsets things before I can work out my plans then the fault won't be mine & I shall retire happily to fulfil other plans.

I mean to return on Friday. They are all coming back – except Olwen. We must run down to Cobham next week. I want to see you so badly. The desire to see you is sometimes so overwhelming that I feel like rushing back to town by the first available train. You are my constant joy – my *cariad*. Ever & ever your fond

D.[8]

The mention of Cobham refers to the fact that LG and Maggie had acquired a new house, close to the London–Portsmouth road between Esher and Cobham. They had sold the Walton house, according to Hankey, in order to escape 'the prying eyes which make Walton Heath and Criccieth so public'. The new house by contrast, called The Firs, was 'quite a nice little property, separated from the road by a ten-acre field . . . with stables, a big lawn carved out of the woods, a nice kitchen garden and an easy exit to Cobham Common'.[9] Frances claimed that the move had nothing to do with her; but since she was going to be there at least as much as Maggie, she took a close interest in the furnishings. It was a curious situation, with wife and mistress competing to put their stamp on the house. On 12 July, with LG still in Wales, Frances wrote in her diary:

D. comes back next Friday. It seems months since he went. Talked to him over the telephone, which cannot often be managed. He says he is much better. I went down to Cobham to see how the new house is getting on, & trying to make things as comfortable as possible for D. Stopped them hanging a picture of Mrs R.Ll.G [that is Dick's wife, Roberta] in the Front Hall, which I think was great cheek.[10]

Frances went to Lady Tredegar's for the weekend, then received LG's second letter on the Monday morning.

Had a darling letter from D. which makes me want to see him more than ever. But it is not very long till Friday now – and then . . . He is much better, it seems. All he needed was a little rest. Unfortunately the family are coming back with him. We had hoped to have the weekend together.[11]

On Friday LG came back to London, to take part in another victory parade on Saturday, followed by a firework display, while the family went straight to Cobham.

> D. has returned – Oh! What joy! He says the last few days have been terrible to go through. I thought they would never end, & that his return was too wonderful a thing ever to come true. But here he is, back again, & as loving as ever. Tomorrow we have a great plan. I hope it will come off.[12]

Next day:

> Our plan came off, & we are so happy. D. is going down to Cobham to join Mrs Ll.G. there today. He is speaking in the House tomorrow . . . D. & I watched the fireworks together last night. They were wonderful. It is sweet to be with him again.[13]

Evidently LG only spent a few hours in Cobham on the Sunday. Doubtless for Frances's benefit, he came back full of complaints.

> D's first impressions of the Cobham house were not very good. It was wet & cold & they had not even bothered to light a fire for him . . . That is how he is always served. So that he is not very favourably impressed. However, I think it *will* be very nice, if only they make it warm. He would not even have had a room of his own if J.T.D. & I had not insisted on the billiard room being turned into a dining room, & the latter being made into a study for D.[14]*

During August LG summoned the long-suffering Hankey to The Firs

---

* A curious letter from Maggie, back in Criccieth that August, suggests that she was making some changes in Wales too.

> My dearest D.,
>   I have one question only to ask you today & that is this. I went up the ladder to the new bedroom yesterday. It is a most pleasant room, but smaller than our present room, & I fear it will not take 2 beds. Will you be satisfied with one large bed, because I have ordered 2 & must at once cancel that & get one bed 6 ft. 4. Let me know by return.
>   Fond love,
>   M[15]

The implication is that the Lloyd Georges had hitherto slept in twin beds. One wonders why they were moving to a smaller room – a better view perhaps? One might assume that this letter referred to the Cobham house, except that it was written on Criccieth notepaper and we know that Maggie was there, while LG was in London in August and already spending every weekend at Cobham.

every weekend, along with a procession of colleagues and advisers and inevitably Riddell (who did not seem to mind that LG had sold Walton Heath).* On 3 August Riddell thought that LG seemed 'quite worn out'.

It is true he talked with his accustomed vivacity, but underlying it all was a sense of weariness and effort. Also he seemed physically tired, and I noticed that when he got up from a low couch his face flushed up as if the effort were considerable. He has aged greatly during the past six months.

As always, what he needed was another holiday.

He took me aside and told me that he was taking a house in Brittany for September. He asked me to accompany him, which I said I would gladly do. He said, 'I must have peace and quiet. There is no real peace in this country. I cannot get away from people. There is a fresh crisis every day. Now sometimes we have two in a day.'[17]

LG actually went to Normandy rather than Brittany – a village called Hennecqueville near Deauville – for more than three weeks from 20 August to mid-September. Moreover, it was Riddell who found the house for him. But LG's idea of peace and quiet was to surround himself with a large party, which included at different times nearly half the Cabinet and their womenfolk. Bonar Law came with his daughter, Hamar Greenwood with his wife, and Eric Geddes with a lady tactfully described by Riddell as his housekeeper. Meanwhile LG was accompanied, most unusually, by both Maggie and Frances – at least for the first week. Maggie had been keen to go with him to Brittany because, as she wrote, 'I want to see how like the Welsh people they are.' She thought she could manage a week before coming back to supervise the finishing of the new house.[18] Frances's presence was presumably covered by the fact that Hankey, his assistant A. J. Sylvester, Philip Kerr and Ernest Evans, another of LG's secretaries, were also of the party.

Yet she was not confined to her secretarial role, since on 22 August Riddell recorded an excursion with LG, twenty kilometres down the coast to Dives-sur-Mer, on which Frances was not only present, but able to gossip indiscreetly about a lady who was said to be Rother-

---

* 'Ll. George had gone down on the Friday,' Hankey noted one weekend, 'and had already dictated the first draft of his speech to a bevy of lady stenographers working under Miss Stevenson.'[16]

mere's mistress. 'I should not care for him to be my lover,' she remarked.[19] How on earth could Maggie have allowed LG to go for a drive with Frances, even chaperoned by Riddell? Perhaps she felt she could not object without drawing attention to the situation. At any rate she did not stay long in France. It sounds as if they may have had a row. A few days later she was back in London and writing to him with unusual emotion.

> My dearest D,
>   We arrived safely & had a good passage. I am going home in the morning . . . I was never so uncomfortable & unhappy at leaving you at any time in my life as I was yesterday . . .
>   My fondest love,
>   Your ever loving
>   M.[20]*

After Maggie had gone home, the party was enlivened by the arrival of the Astors, who proceeded – in Riddell's words – to make up to the Prime Minister 'in the most ardent and unblushing way'. Riddell took a dim view of Nancy's brash vulgarity.

> Mrs Astor is a typical American of a certain class – a sentimental boisterous thruster. Tonight she gave a display as a dancer, ending up with a sort of orgy in which she impersonated an Apache, attacking all the men present and carrying on like a mad woman. Underneath all this she is pretty shrewd and never misses an opportunity.[22]

Vigorous sing-songs were LG's preferred form of entertainment, with Frances at the piano. He also played golf every day. But a good deal of work was done at Hennecqueville too, with various generals in attendance to brief LG on events in Russia and Mesopotamia, as well as a lot of talk about how best to secure his political future by perpetuating the Coalition. 'LG as usual very active with his affairs, dictating letters and telegrams and dispatching messages over the telephone

* The same day it was announced that the Scottish-born philanthropist Andrew Carnegie had left LG an annuity of £2,000 a year for life in recognition of his contribution to winning the war. Though the government had made large cash awards to Haig, Robertson and others (including £25,000 to Hankey), LG had felt obliged to refuse an official grant. Maggie's reaction to Carnegie's bequest suggests that she thought he had been too scrupulous. 'What luck,' she wrote. 'You can't refuse this, that's one consolation.'[21]

through the secretaries.'[23] LG himself confirmed this picture in a letter to Megan, with a hint of an olive branch to Maggie:

> I have had a [illegible] mixed holiday – like all my holidays – half business, half relaxation . . .
>
>   I missed your mother so much for she was (for a wonder!) exceptionally nice to me. Give her my best love will you?[24]

When the party broke up, LG and Frances drove together – with Riddell – in one car to Evreux, where they all had lunch; then LG with Balfour, Bonar Law and Hankey went on to Paris to see Clemenceau, while Frances returned to England with Riddell and the rest via Le Havre, 'all feeling rather sad at the termination of a very pleasant holiday'.[25]

LG came back to face a national rail strike, which with his customary resourcefulness he succeeded in resolving after nine days. For the next two months the only glimpses of his private life come from Riddell, who played golf with him most Saturdays and dined with him at Cobham every Sunday. Sometimes Frances was there, but more often Maggie. On 16 November Dick and Roberta were there; the next week LG's brother William. Altogether LG seems to have seen more of his family than of Frances that autumn.

But then at the end of November Frances resumed her diary and the picture shifts again – even though Maggie was still in London. Frances had decided that in order to see more of LG she would have to take up golf.

> We had a perfectly wonderful day yesterday. Went down to Cobham Tuesday evening, & played golf at Burhill yesterday morning. It is a beautiful course & it was a lovely sunny morning. The pro & I beat D. & Ernie [Ernest Evans] hollow, so I am rather pleased with myself. I want to be really good at golf as D. has been so sweet about my learning & takes such a patient interest in my progress. Came up in the evening in time for dinner.[26]

While LG and Maggie attended a big function, Frances dined with a friend. But the next evening she and LG dined together in Park Lane at the house of Sir Philip Sassoon – a wealthy young Jewish baronet: his mother was a Rothschild – who had been a Tory MP since 1912 and was about to join LG's private office. Over the next three years

Sassoon became a good friend of Frances (they were exactly the same age) while placing his several grand houses at LG's disposal for holidays and international conferences. But already Frances realised that his generosity was not entirely selfless. 'Philip Sassoon has just dropped in for a chat,' she wrote on 12 December. 'He has been very attentive lately, I think probably because he wants to get an Under-Secretaryship or something of the kind. But he is an amusing person, & as clever as a cartload of monkeys.'[27]

The fact that Maggie was spending so much time in London was clearly getting on Frances's nerves – and possibly on LG's too, though that may just be what he told Frances. At any rate she was happy to record him complaining on 29 November:

> D. & Mrs Ll.G. on very bad terms. D. is giving a big weekend party at Cobham, including the American Ambassador . . . and Mrs Ll.G., instead of helping, is doing all she can to *hinder* D's arrangements. She simply hates him to enjoy himself & will not lift a finger to make the Cobham house comfortable.[28]

Nevertheless an important entry a few days later shows Frances resolving to make the best of her situation, frustrating though it was, rather than risk losing her man altogether. The occasion was a small dinner at her flat – 'a jolly little party to celebrate the third anniversary of his becoming Prime Minister' – to which she invited another man of LG's age who had been having an affair with his much younger secretary.

> Sir George Riddell came, General Macready, & Catherine Brunskill, & it was all a great success. I do feel desperately sorry for the poor General. He is so much in love with Catherine, & now she has gone & married that stick of a man, & is going to have a child by him, & they are both perfectly miserable.* She has made a hash of her life & realises it now that it is too late. I think the General suffers the most, as she is made of fairly hard stuff, & besides the General is just as sweet & loving to her as he always was & obeys her slightest request. However it is a warning to me not to do likewise.[29]

Frances had more offers of marriage over the next twenty years, but remained true to her vow not to repeat Catherine Brunskill's mistake.

---

* Catherine Bennett had married Major George Brunskill in 1918. They had one daughter, born in 1920, and were divorced in 1946.

She did not do too badly in December. First, LG had three days of conferences with Clemenceau in London, which gave the opportunity for reviving some of the camaraderie of Paris: twice he brought 'The Tiger' and his entourage to Frances's room for tea and cake. ('Clemenceau thoroughly enjoyed his cake . . . He was in great form and ragged everyone from D. to Philip Kerr.') A bonus was that the talks prevented LG going to speak at an important by-election in Yorkshire. Maggie went instead, so LG and Frances were able to spend the evening together.[30] Then, when Clemenceau left, LG refused to go to Cobham for the weekend, telling Frances he could not face his family. 'It is a pity, as it simply means that he stays here working or at any rate, in the atmosphere of work, instead of going off & getting a rest.'[31] By Tuesday, however, Maggie had gone home, so Frances 'persuaded D. to cut work this afternoon and come down to Cobham for a rest & fresh air. He has a very hard week in front of him, & is beginning to worry a little about things, which he always does when he gets tired.'

> He is annoyed at having to go down to Criccieth for Xmas, but as Mrs Ll.G. announced her intention of staying here if he does not go, he thinks it best at any rate to make sure of getting her down there! But he is coming back directly after Xmas & then we hope to go to Paris for a meeting & then perhaps go on for a short holiday somewhere.[32]

They duly went to Cobham and had 'a quiet & restful afternoon & evening', with a walk in Richmond Park on the way, 'as it would have been too late for a walk when we arrived there, though we did walk again in the garden after dinner. D. cheered up wonderfully.'[33] A few days later Philip Sassoon came down and he, LG, Frances and Riddell played golf at St George's Hill. ('Very jolly.') Later they returned to town and LG and Frances went to dinner with a Tory MP – 'a very amusing party – P.M. & Mr Birrell, the Austen Chamberlains & some others' – another indication that they were beginning to be seen openly together in society.* After dinner they listened to the Black Syncopated Orchestra, which Frances found 'amazing – all the semi-religious songs of the negroes'. LG thought their songs about oppressed people 'very significant . . . He says a race who can sing these songs like that will cause trouble one day.'[34]

---

* Augustine Birrell had been Chief Secretary of Ireland in Asquith's Cabinet.

An incident on 22 December illustrated the unequal nature of their relationship, when Frances failed to offer her usual congratulation after he had spoken in the House.

I behaved very badly. I was feeling very tired & had a splitting headache, & D. had annoyed me over a trifling little thing, & I quite forgot to say anything to him about his speech, or to compliment him on it. I usually leave a little note on his table in the House in case I don't see him at once. But this time I didn't. And when he came back to Downing Street after 11.00 he came up to me & said: 'You haven't said a word to me about my speech – not a word. And you know how I count on your words to me after my speeches.' I felt a perfect pig at once, & did my best to make up for it, & it ended quite happily. But I hate myself for having behaved like that.[35]

But the next day LG went to Wales, and Frances felt 'wretched' without him.

I get such a terrible feeling of loneliness when he goes, & feel almost frightened at his being so far away. However, as D. says, we have not done badly this year. We had all that time at Paris together, & then a month at Deauville, & as he says, we see each other every day & almost every hour of the day. But I suppose that only makes it all the more hard when he does go away.[36]

Frances joined her family at Wallington for Christmas.

15

'. . . WHO DANCED WITH THE PRINCE OF WALES'

By the end of 1919, with LG back from Paris, political life in London was beginning to get back to normal – and social life had recovered something of its pre-war glitter too. Moreover, Frances was moving out of the shadows. Though the truth of their relationship was still not widely known, her position as the Prime Minister's trusted secretary opened all sorts of doors to her and increasingly allowed her to lead a lively social life in her own right.

She and LG still spent as much time together as they could manage, and she was always there whenever he needed her. But he did not care for the smart life of dinners and dances; whereas she did. At thirty-one she was still young, attractive and unmarried, well connected and potentially influential, making her quite a catch for political hostesses and matchmakers. She had many admirers – both potential suitors of her own age and older men who liked to take her out to lunch, dinner or the theatre in return for her particular brand of sympathetic understanding. The Marquess of Cholmondeley, for instance, still wrote to her faithfully and often took her out when he was up in town. Once she stood him up, when LG wanted her at Cobham instead, but he did not mind. 'Lord Cholmondeley is a good-natured, dear old thing,' she wrote, '& never gets put out at anything.'[1] Another faithful confidant was the love-lorn General Macready, whom LG appointed in 1920 to command the British army in Ireland. The flavour of his letters is well represented by this one from September 1922:

My dear Frances,

You are a regular 'Illusive Pimpernel!' [sic] I am by way of being on leave till Oct 10th providing those beastly Irish stay quiet for that period. Anyway I dare not go too far afield. I was going to see Joan this weekend, but if you will be here on Saturday (16th) I will wait till Sunday & we will have a bit of a beano on Saty night. If I do not hear from you by Thursday morning I will so arrange. Is there any particular play you would like to see? I suppose you have done them all! My deep salaams to the PM & tell him not to put *too* much faith in Messrs Cosgrave, Mulcahy & co. nor to invest money on a long life insurance for them! . . .*

If you can come on Saty I will ask Catherine & I suppose perforce Bruno.
Yours very sincerely,
Nevil Macready[2]

A rather younger admirer – he was forty-two in 1920, but wrote like an old man – was the painter Sir William Orpen, whom Frances had got to know when he was official artist in Paris. Two wistful letters from Orpen in this period survive. One, from February 1920, invites her to lunch at the Ritz Grill and asks if she would like Philip Sassoon or someone else to come too. 'Otherwise we could eat (drink – me) and wonder together alone.' The second is undated: 'I expect you are too busy to have lunch with a little thing like me, but if you would any day I should be delighted.'[3] Some years later Orpen wrote to Frances again, addressing her as 'Most Beautiful Lady', asking 'When may I see you? And perhaps be allowed to hold your hand for a fraction of a second without giving undue offence', and signing himself 'Orpsie'.[4]

Other scraps preserved in her papers offer further glimpses of Frances moving in exalted circles. There is a scribbled note from Emerald Cunard, which must date from either September or December 1920:

Dear Miss Stephenson [sic]

The Duchess of Rutland hopes you will come to her [illegible] dance Monday 20th for Prince of Wales. *Do* come. I'll be there too.[5]

Frances also kept the menu card from a dinner at the Savoy dated 30 November 1920 and signed by, among others, Lord Cholmondeley, William Dudley Ward and her old friend Sir Albert Stern.[6] The

---

* William Cosgrave was the first President of the Irish Free State; General Mulcahy was Sinn Fein chief of staff.

redoubtable feminist composer Ethel Smyth thanked her for some help
with a visa and invited her to come and play tennis at her house in
Surrey.[7] One of her early heroes, H. G. Wells, presented her with a
500-rouble note on his return from visiting Russia in October.[8]

Unfortunately Frances's diary is reticent about her life apart from
LG – she kept it primarily as a record of his doings, and their relationship, rather than her own activities. The glimpses she does give are
frustratingly impersonal. On 6 December 1919, for instance, she notes
that she went dancing at the Grafton Galleries – but does not say with
whom. The French heavyweight boxer Georges Carpentier was there.
Frances thought him 'a wonderfully good-looking man', but she was
sorry that everyone made so much fuss of him that 'he had to spend
nearly all his time giving autographs', which she thought 'unkind and
embarrassing'. The next evening she went to the Lyric Theatre,
Hammersmith, to see a play about Abraham Lincoln – but again she
does not say with whom. She thought it 'a wonderful play & wonderfully acted. You really feel that you have seen and heard Abraham
Lincoln himself'. But she added tartly, 'Mrs Lincoln appears to have
been rather a tiresome person.' Since Lincoln was LG's great hero, she
was surely drawing a contemporary parallel.[9]

But the two people who really launched Frances into society were
Mrs Rupert Beckett and Philip Sassoon. Mrs Beckett was a famous
beauty and a fashionable hostess with a house in Grosvenor Street.
It was at a dance of hers on 18 December that Frances first met the
Prince of Wales. Again she does not name her escort for the evening,
but she was excited at the prospect of meeting the Prince. 'I have
never actually spoken to him & don't suppose I shall tonight for
that matter. But it will be interesting to see him there.'[10] She was
not disappointed.

> Was introduced to the Prince, who was very charming & said he was glad
> to meet me as he had heard such a lot about me! I wanted to ask him what
> he had heard. I congratulated him on his speech in the afternoon, and he
> told me he would never get used to speaking in public – he was far too
> nervous . . . I was terribly nervous, & felt I was trembling all over & I
> hardly know what I said, but I hope he did not think I was a perfect fool.

She was not too overcome to make an expert assessment of the
Prince's infatuation with the then love of his life, Freda Dudley Ward,

the young wife of a Coalition Liberal MP, who was to be his mistress for the next fifteen years.

> He is a dear thing, with beautiful eyes, but such a boy. He danced every dance I think with Mrs Dudley Ward, who is a very sweet little thing, but not much brains I should think. However, she always looks very pretty & the Prince seems very fond of her. Lady Loughboro' is her constant companion & is really a beautiful girl & very charming.[11]

The next evening she saw him again dancing at Philip Sassoon's, though this time she did not speak to him. 'Still very much engrossed in Mrs Dudley Ward,' she noted. 'In fact, no party has any attraction for the Prince unless she is there.' Nancy Astor was furious that she could get him only by inviting Freda too.[12]

Some weeks later Frances encountered the Prince a third time – again at Sassoon's, but this time it was just a small dinner.

> Did not know till I got there that the Prince of Wales was to be there. Just 8 of us. I sat between the Prince and Sir Robert Horne.* Was simply shaking with fright at first. But that soon vanished & we got on quite well. He is really a nice boy, & most amusing when his shyness wears off. He must know about D. & me, because he said: 'Mrs Lloyd George does not spend much time in London, does she?' with a meaning look. I said: 'No; she preferred being in Criccieth', & let him infer what he liked.

He was 'very sick' at having to go off almost immediately on another tour of the Empire, having only just got back from Canada. When Frances agreed that it was hard luck, he told her, 'You tell the P.M. that!' He was 'a cheeky little beggar', she concluded, '& very naughty too, I should imagine'. She did not like his voice, which she thought 'rather hard'; but reflected that 'I suppose after D's, anyone's would sound poor'.[13]

The next weekend Sassoon invited Frances to Trent Park, his house in Hertfordshire, where she met a royal flush of princes – not just the heir to the throne this time, but two of his younger brothers: Albert (the future King George VI) and Henry (the future Duke of Gloucester), whom she liked much less.

---

* Horne, then Minister of Labour but soon to be Chancellor of the Exchequer, was unmarried and an exuberant bon viveur.

The P. of W. and his two brothers were there – also the Dudley Wards &
the Loughboroughs among others. The Prince is very much in love with
Mrs D.W., though they are very like two children together, & I must say
very sweet. Played tennis with Prince Henry, whom I must say I don't like.
I should say he had a rather low nature. Prince Albert is great fun & much
more sporting than Henry. But the P. of W. streaks above them both. I could
fall in love with him myself, but think I should find it rather tame after D.;
& besides it must be wretched to be in love with a 'royalty', & then see
him forced to marry someone else. It's quite bad enough when your lover
was married before you met him!

   After dinner last night we danced & were very merry . . .[14]

So now Frances was dining, dancing and playing tennis with royalty,
and becoming quite blasé about it. In ten years she had come a long
way from teaching in Wimbledon. What if the Prince of Wales's eye
had fallen upon her instead of the already married Freda Dudley Ward?
Instead of being merely mistress of the Prime Minister, might Frances
have become Queen, thus rewriting the history of the monarchy? The
twenty-five-year-old Prince's shy charm and vulnerability evidently
appealed to her mothering instinct, though she would indeed have found
him tame after LG. In reality it was never a serious possibility; but she
– and LG too, who had taken a fatherly interest in the Prince ever since
he had coached him in Welsh for his investiture at Caernarvon in 1911
– continued to feel sympathetically towards him, even in the trauma
of his abdication in 1936.

   But Frances always put LG first. In January 1920 he went back to
Paris – taking half the Cabinet with him as usual – for two weeks of
further talks with Clemenceau, and she went too. As it happened,
Clemenceau was unexpectedly defeated in the presidential election just
before they arrived, an unsettling reminder of the ingratitude of democratic electorates. But LG took a touching farewell of the old boy and
consoled himself that he was now 'the doyen of Prime Ministers – in
other words he is the Dictator of Europe as far as treaties are
concerned', an estimate that proved over-optimistic.[15] He celebrated
his fifty-seven birthday while in Paris: Frances gave him 'a watch-
chain, with which he was very pleased', and noted that 'none of his
family have bothered to write to him' at all, apart from 'a scrappy
wire from Megan'. They played golf at Saint-Cloud and dined with
the Montagus at Ciro's, where Frances sat between Bonar Law and

Jimmy Rothschild.[16]* Otherwise it was 'rather a dreary and depressing week', its purpose stymied by the French change of government. Still Frances was sorry to leave Paris – 'but I don't mind where I go so long as I am with D.'[17]

Three days after they got back they had another game of golf – with Riddell and Olwen, showing that Frances was still on tolerable terms with LG's children.[18] Then they had what Frances called 'a perfectly divine weekend at Cobham – all alone', though in fact they played golf again, this time with Riddell and Sassoon, on the Saturday and Riddell came for dinner as usual on the Sunday, so they were not alone all the time. 'The time simply fled,' Frances wrote. 'It is our last weekend for some time, I am afraid, as Mrs Ll.G. returns soon & will be in London some time.'[19]

Actually Maggie did not come back as soon as Frances expected, so she was able to continue seeing LG regularly during February and March. The second weekend in February he was persuaded to go to the Astors' stately home at Cliveden, but he hated that sort of house party where 'a lot of silly women' (Hankey's phrase) could pester him, and 'fled' after tea on Saturday. Frances got a telephone message that he was returning to Downing Street: she immediately dropped whatever she was doing and hurried to get back there just before he did.[20] Riddell came to dinner at Cobham on the Sunday as usual, when they had some mildly risqué conversation about which politicians were most attractive to women. Riddell nominated LG himself, on the ground that 'you have the reputation (quite undeserved of course) of being a little naughty which always makes a man interesting to women'. LG modestly demurred, proposing Auckland Geddes, at which Frances dissented strongly: 'No! He is a very nice man but does not appeal to women. They would be more likely to choose Eric!' She would have been unwise to mention any more names for fear of arousing LG's jealousy.[21]

It was during the following week that Frances dined with the Prince of Wales at Sassoon's, before going to Trent for her weekend with all three princes. On the Friday evening, however, LG dined at her flat and they had 'a very happy time', though he was tired after a heavy week. He rang her the next morning to say that the American Ambassador had been looking for him urgently with a long dispatch from

---

* Edwin Montagu, who had married Asquith's former girlfriend Venetia Stanley, was now Secretary of State for India.

President Wilson, but no one in Downing Street knew where to find him – a revealing clue as to how it was possible for the Prime Minister to conduct an affair in those days.[22]

Riddell makes no mention of Maggie being at Cobham that weekend; if she was not, it is slightly surprising that Frances went to Trent, but perhaps it was too good an invitation to pass up, even to be with LG. But Frances went to Cobham on the Tuesday and they had another 'very happy time'.

> After dinner D. sang Welsh songs, as I have never heard him sing them before. He told me afterwards that Mair used to play them for him to sing, & that it is only now that he can bear to sing them again. We went for a beautiful walk this morning. It was like a warm spring day. D. very fit, in spite of his strenuous work lately.

Now, however, Maggie did come back, watching her husband, Frances complained, 'like a hawk'.

> She is an extraordinary person. She goes away for weeks & does not bother about him, but when she comes back she is on the watch all the time. Most inconsistent, I call it.[23]

She noted that LG was going to Cobham for the weekend, but 'taking several people with him to take the edge of [*sic*] his "domestic bliss"'.[24]

Left to herself, Frances dined with Muriel Beckett and then went dancing. 'Quite good fun.' At dinner she sat next to the 15th Earl of Pembroke and found herself being questioned about LG's attitude to the aristocracy. 'Years ago we hated him and he hated us; now we admire and respect him – but does he like us?' Frances answered tactfully that of course he respected what they did in the war and appreciated their support; 'but the fundamental point was that socially you have nothing in common . . . I explained . . . how the P.M. loathed big dinner-parties & weekend parties.' 'We hate it too,' Lady Pembroke assured her, 'and I can't think why we do it.'[25]

LG was exceptionally attentive to Frances when he got back from Cobham on Monday morning, bringing her flowers and telling her that he wanted her to benefit from the money he had been left by Carnegie.

He says he wants me to have a bigger flat. Mine is not nice enough now, he says, and he also wants me to have my share of his (Carnegie) luck. I am rather glad he wants me to have a bigger flat, though I love the one I have got, but it is getting too full of treasures (mostly his gifts) & they will look much better in a bigger space.[26]

Frances did move later that year, from 96 Victoria Street just a few hundred yards to a new and larger flat in Morpeth Mansions, a handsome red-brick mansion block in Morpeth Terrace on the west side of Westminster Cathedral. But it is not certain that it was LG – at least directly – who helped her buy it. According to A. J. Sylvester (at this time Hankey's secretary, but later LG's), she was enabled to buy the lease with a gift of £2,000 from Sir Samuel Waring, founder of the furniture store Waring & Gillow.[27] Waring had been created a baronet in recognition of his war work in 1919; he was to be raised to the peerage in 1922. It is notorious that under Lloyd George honours were sold openly for contributions to his political fund. Actually the practice of selling honours had been going on long before Lloyd George's time, and continues no less brazenly to this day. It was just more visible under LG because he had no party organisation to absorb the money, which instead seemed to go into his own pocket – though actually into a political fund that financed his office and political activities after he left Downing Street. LG had no qualms about accepting favours from wealthy supporters – most notably Riddell, who had built him his house at Walton Heath before the war and continued to subsidise him in all sorts of ways, including in 1919 buying him a car when a government economy drive deprived ministers of their official vehicles. Nor, it should be said, did anyone else at this time see anything improper in politicians lacking private wealth accepting gifts: LG was by no means alone. But it seems very likely, if Sylvester can be believed, that LG helped Frances buy a bigger flat not with his own Carnegie money, but by inducing Sir Samuel Waring to cough up in anticipation of his peerage.*

---

* There is some previously unpublished evidence of the sale of honours in Riddell's diary for 1922, where he quotes J. T. Davies boasting shamelessly about how much money he was extracting from various dubious applicants, including Waring. 'Everyone has had to pay up – whatever his qualifications.'[28] LG of course denied any direct knowledge of these transactions, while at the same time defending the system as less corrupt than other ways of financing politics.[29] He always had a healthy disrespect for the House of Lords and did not care whom he sent there.

On 26 February Frances again dined at Sassoon's with the Prince of Wales; but this time LG was there too. No doubt it was she who persuaded him to attend, though on this occasion he enjoyed himself since the entertainment included a showing of the film *The Last Days of Pompeii*.* Frances was growing very close to Sassoon at this time. A few days later she boldly defended him against the jealousy of Nancy Astor, who was riled not only by his success in getting the heir to the throne to dine so often, but also because LG had just appointed Sassoon his parliamentary secretary, rather than her husband Waldorf. Frances's relations with Nancy had deteriorated sharply since the previous spring; now she had the confidence to have 'quite a row' with her, as Riddell recorded on 7 March.

> Lady A . . . objected to Sassoon's appointment on three grounds, 1 because he was a conservative, 2 because he was rich, and 3 because he had not fought in the war. Miss Stevenson replied that Astor is both rich and a Conservative, and that although Sassoon had gone as far as Headquarters in France, Astor had never even crossed the Channel. These feline amenities made Lady A. furious.[31]

This is a rare instance of Frances showing her claws in public.

The last weekend in February LG delayed going to Cobham until Saturday evening because his family were there. (At least this was what he told Frances: in fact he had meetings with the French and Italians that kept him in Downing Street all day.) He then arranged another meeting on Sunday evening so that he should have to come back early. 'I feel really sorry for him,' Frances wrote, 'as he needs a weekend rest so badly, & would take it if it were not that he cannot stand being there with that crowd.'[32] For much of March Frances seems to have been kept away; but on the 18th she was able to go to Cobham to help with an important speech in which LG tried to cajole his Liberal colleagues into forming a new Centre party to secure the future of the Coalition. This was a doomed venture that never got off the ground; but 'D was very excited about it. I have rarely seen him more highly

---

* Hankey attended the same dinner, and disliked what he saw. 'There were four ladies present. Mrs Dudley Ward, Lady —— (I forget the name, an Australian girl), Lady Londonderry and Miss Stevenson. The two first named were very young & very pretty & exquisitely dressed, but like all these society girls painted & rouged – horrible to me.' He noted that the Prince 'eyed' Mrs Dudley Ward at dinner 'in rather a marked way, and after dinner, when we had a private cinema show, he sat next to her'.[30]

strung.'[33] They stayed that night, travelled up to London early next morning to deliver the speech, then went back to Cobham to recover and stayed another 'very happy' night. 'D. & I seem fonder of each other than ever,' Frances wrote. 'He is so sweet to me.'[34]

The next day (Saturday) they had planned to play golf together at Weybridge, but were prevented by a fire at the club house. LG went to Walton Heath instead, where for some reason it was 'better' for Frances not to go with him. Were they perhaps too well known there, whereas at Weybridge they could play unrecognised? 'It seems a long time till Monday to see him,' Frances wrote. 'But Mrs Ll.G. is probably going down to Wales next week, so we shall be able to spend next weekend together.'[35] In fact Maggie was still at Cobham the following weekend, so this time Frances's hopes were disappointed. Then it was Easter and LG went to Criccieth for a week. But here the diary breaks off again for another unexplained gap of just over a year. Since no letters have survived from this period either, we have only scattered mentions in Riddell's diary – and occasionally Hankey's – to chart Frances's movements for the rest of 1920 and the early part of 1921. But that does not mean that she did not continue to lead a full and exciting life.

16

FRENCH WITHOUT TEARS

LG's consuming mission, which preoccupied him through most of 1920 and 1921, was to try to consolidate peace in Europe. The Treaty of Versailles was only a beginning, and it had been fatally undermined by President Wilson's failure to persuade the US Congress to play a continuing role in Europe or even join the League of Nations. LG consequently had to carry almost alone the burden of trying to induce the French to scale down the unrealistic level of reparations imposed on Germany at Versailles and negotiate a comprehensive settlement of the tangled web of inter-Allied war debts. In addition there was still the need to conclude a peace treaty with Turkey. Neglecting domestic politics, therefore, he pursued these objectives through an almost continuous round of international conferences, in England and at various spas and holiday resorts around the continent. Frances increasingly accompanied him on these jaunts – her French once more coming in useful – and managed to conduct some informal diplomacy of her own in the interstices of the official proceedings.

First of all she went with him to San Remo in April 1920, as part of the usual travelling circus comprising Hankey, Kerr, J. T. Davies and Riddell, plus on this occasion Megan, continuing her unorthodox education and still amazingly unaware of Frances's dual role, though she was now nearly eighteen. They travelled by sea to Marseilles (which took a week, with a storm in the Bay of Biscay), from where they were driven via Cannes and Nice in two cars. LG, Hankey noted, was 'always very nervous, especially so in France, of being seen in public with Miss Stevenson', so she started off in one car with Hankey and Riddell; but

as soon as they were out in open country they stopped and she was trans-
ferred to LG's car. The second car then broke down and was late getting
to San Raphael. 'Ll.G was quite furious because he had to go into dinner
alone with Megan and Miss Stevenson . . . He lives in a perfect terror
of gossip.' The next day they stopped for lunch with Rothermere at Cap
Saint-Martin, where Hankey was to have accompanied LG.

> Unluckily we lost our way at Nice, had several tyre mishaps and were other-
> wise delayed. Ll.G. dared not take Miss Stevenson to Rothermere's villa,
> but luckily an A.S.C. officer who was . . . following in his own car came
> up and Miss Stevenson was consigned to his charge for lunch.[1]

If this must have been a bit humiliating, the rest of the conference
– which lasted a week – was 'very agreeable'. Frances and Megan were
the only two ladies, and the whole British delegation, which now
included Lord Curzon (who had replaced Balfour as Foreign Secretary)
and Sir Henry Wilson, 'usually lunched and dined together in the big
dining room'. Moreover, after a sticky start the conference ended up
being quite successful.

On the way home from San Remo, LG caught a heavy cold, supposedly from waiting on a draughty railway platform in Paris. 'He is really
suffering from nervous exhaustion,' Hankey believed.[2] To recover his
strength he retired to Philip Sassoon's palatial house at Port Lympne,
near Hythe, where he seems to have been nursed at different times by
both Maggie and Frances. The puritanical Hankey disapproved.

> I found the P.M. in Sassoon's beautiful house living in a state of luxury
> which to me was a positive surfeit. Everything of the very best and most
> expensive. The best beds, linen, baths, food, wine, cigars, Rolls Royce
> motor cars etc. There was a pool and a fountain in the hall, a swimming
> bath and more fountains on the terrace . . . The P.M.'s bathroom was of
> gold tessellated pavement, the sunken bath being the same as the walls
> and the floor. Sassoon and Miss Stevenson were looking after the P.M. I
> thought him looking old and ill, but he had just had 24 hours of Winston
> Churchill, which is enough to make anyone look old and ill . . . Altogether
> I had a rather disagreeable feeling that the P.M. is getting too fond of
> high living . . . I prefer him in the simple surroundings of Criccieth, or
> Cobham.[3]

Hankey was also put out that LG's doctors had ordered him to take another fortnight's rest, since he had 'a mass of urgent business' to get through before Whitsun. In fact LG always mixed work with rest, and held another weekend conference with the French Prime Minister while he was at Lympne. Now it was Riddell's turn to be amazed by the scale of the arrangements. 'Sassoon,' he wrote, 'has made hospitality an art. He is a restless creature, and flitted about from room to room, and person to person, like a bee in search of honey.'[4] Bonar Law and Austen Chamberlain were also there, and Hankey conceded that LG, 'in spite of his recent indisposition, was in splendid form'. Nevertheless the conference was 'thoroughly unsatisfactory', since all Sassoon's hospitality failed to soften French intransigence over reparations. On Sunday afternoon Hankey motored back to town with Chamberlain, 'leaving the P.M. and Miss Stevenson at Lympne'.[5]

LG clearly had a weakness for Sassoon's brand of pampering luxury, since he held another conference at Lympne in June, conducted in the same extravagant style, as Riddell again described:

> In one room the chiefs conferring, in another the minor officials in conference, in another the secretariat at work, in a fourth a sumptuous tea, cakes, fruit and every delicacy. In the kitchen the French chefs getting ready a magnificent dinner . . .
>
> In the evening, dinner . . . with Philip Sassoon and his sister Lady Rocksavage . . . hovering over the scene like attendant imps conducting a banquet of gladiators . . .* Everything done regardless of expense . . . Sassoon and Lady Rocksavage very useful. They know French perfectly and can keep up a conversation with Millerand etc.

No doubt Frances would have been useful too. She was present, but unfortunately was 'confined to bed with a bad cold'.[6]

This was a more successful conference; and the next day LG crossed to Boulogne to continue the conversations on French soil. The following weekend he and Frances were alone at Cobham – at least until Riddell turned up – before LG set off on his travels again, to another international get-together at the Belgian town of Spa. This one lasted more than two weeks, and Frances went too, along with the rest of his

---

* Sassoon's sister Sybil, Lady Rocksavage, was married to the son and heir of Frances's friend Lord Cholmondeley. Around this time Orpen painted a very striking portrait of her.

familiar entourage. Back in England, Frances was at Cobham one weekend, then Maggie the next, followed by Frances the one after. In August there was yet another conference with the French at Lympne before LG dragged his long-suffering staff, plus members of his family and a curious assortment of friends, on another working holiday, this time in Switzerland – chosen partly for the mountains, but mainly because he wanted to meet the veteran Italian Prime Minister, Giovanni Giolitti.

Frances was again included, though it is difficult to imagine that she and LG can have managed much time alone, particularly as both Megan and Gwilym came too. Probably she did not expect to, since – to Hankey's disgust – she brought with her 'a woman called Mrs Rupert Beckett, a regular society woman with few ideas beyond dress and extravagance' who 'used to tell pornographic stories to men, and to swear before Robin [Hankey's son]'. She 'brought a bad time into what would otherwise have been a very pleasant party'.[7] In fact this Swiss jaunt turned out to be even less of a holiday than usual, since as well as all manner of political problems, LG was pursued by the latest Irish horror: a hunger-strike by the Lord Mayor of Cork, Terence McSwiney, in Brixton prison, accompanied by an IRA threat to assassinate the Prime Minister, so that he had to be guarded day and night by the Swiss police. Writing to Maggie, LG affected a pose of manly resolution:

> You & Megan need not be anxious. There has never been a case of assassination of wives & daughters. Of course they will try to kill me & may succeed. I must do my duty . . . If you let him off you might as well give up Ireland altogether.[8]

Hankey, however, gives a less heroic picture. Whereas Hamar Greenwood – the Irish Secretary, who had joined the party – was 'quite unshaken' by the threats, he wrote, LG 'went in terror of his life'.[9] As with German air-raids, so with the IRA, LG was sadly lacking in physical courage. On his return to England he wrote again to Maggie that the Irish would certainly try to kill him if McSwiney died. 'That makes Cobham a little risky for some time.'[10] McSwiney did die on 25 October and LG duly avoided going to Cobham for the rest of the year, while the newspapers were told only that he had gone to 'the country'.

Most weekends he availed himself instead of Sassoon's ever-open hospitality, once at Lympne, more often at Trent Park, usually accompanied by Riddell. What of Frances? Riddell does not often mention her, but she was always welcome at Sassoon's houses. She was certainly at Trent the third weekend in December, along with Mrs Beckett and Lord Dawson (LG's doctor). The next weekend was Christmas. Hankey complained that LG refused to go to Criccieth 'for a certain object' – obviously that he preferred to spend it with Frances – thus 'spoiling the festival for his private secretary', meaning himself.[11] Yet still he did not go to Cobham, but stayed in Downing Street with another curiously mixed party of colleagues, cronies and musicians. Riddell found it 'rather a gloomy proceeding – the sort of Christmas a shopkeeper spends when he eats his Christmas dinner on the counter surrounded by his goods . . . The P.M. was in fairly good spirits, but the festivity had an unnatural air.'[12]

Had Frances been keeping her diary at this time she would not have been rhapsodising about idyllic weekends with her lover. Yet the signs are that she was still seeing more of him than Maggie was. LG wrote to Maggie instead, usually a sign that he was feeling guilty. He did not go to Wales for the New Year either, but to Lympne with Frances. Churchill was there, too – without Clementine. There was much 'lusty singing' round the piano in the evenings. On the Saturday afternoon, however, LG 'went off to rest with a bundle of official papers'; at which 'Winston remarked on the tireless industry of the P.M.'[13]

The next weekend, however, Maggie was obliged to come down from Wales, and Frances correspondingly obliged to be absent, for a significant little ceremony: Lord Lee's formal handing over of his seventeenth-century Buckinghamshire mansion, Chequers, to become the official country residence of the Prime Minister. In his acceptance speech on behalf of the nation, LG spoke of the increasingly intolerable pressures of the highest office.

> He said he had read the lives of many Prime Ministers, all of whom thought their burdens almost insupportable. He thought he was justified in saying that the task of a Prime Minister at the present time was far more onerous than that of any of his predecessors.[14]

If only he could have foreseen the hours his successors would be required to work seventy or eighty years later! Though unprecedentedly professional by the standards of his time, LG still had Victorian assumptions about the amount of time a Prime Minister should be expected to spend on the job. If he complained of the 'violence and malignity of the Press' in 1920, what would he have made of the unfettered partisanship and intrusive prurience of the newspapers of today? By the conventions that had existed before 1914, LG's post-war government certainly attracted an unparalleled degree of hostile criticism – not least about the sale of honours; yet he should still have counted himself lucky that no paper chose to publish the secret of his virtually bigamous relationship with his secretary.

Maggie did not stay long at Chequers, and during the remaining twenty-one months in which LG enjoyed the use of it she never saw it as her territory. Though only temporary, therefore, Chequers was the first of LG's homes in whose running Frances had a greater hand than Maggie. The histories of the house barely mention her: but Frances was actually the first Prime Minister's lady to preside there. In fact it was probably her quiet assumption of the role – the fact that the staff naturally took their orders from her – that finally awoke Megan to the true relationship between her father and her former tutor. 'I noticed the look on Megan's face when she was not consulted,' Frances recalled many years later, 'and after that our relations became much more strained.'[15] As recently as the previous autumn, after they all got back from Switzerland, Megan was still writing artlessly girlish letters to 'Dear Puss', complaining about the weather in Criccieth and hoping Frances was not working too hard.[16] But from now on she became bitterly hostile to the mistress she felt had usurped her mother's place.

Yet Maggie was not only happier in Criccieth: she was also much more use to her husband there. In Wales she was a prominent personality in her own right, and in February 1921 she threw herself with extraordinary energy into a by-election in neighbouring Cardiganshire. The contest was a particularly bitter one in which one of LG's oldest friends and pre-war colleagues, Llewellyn Williams, was standing against the government as an Independent Liberal. Prime Ministers in those days did not involve themselves in by-elections, but Maggie took up the cudgels on his behalf, 'working like a Trojan in the constituency', according to Riddell, 'delivering fifty-eight speeches in a fortnight'. While the votes were being counted she came to Chequers for the weekend.

While L.G. and I were walking in the park she came running out breath-
less, to tell him that Evans had won by a majority of 3,500. He was delighted
and said that if the result had been the other way it would have been a
serious personal set-back. He warmly embraced Mrs L.G., bestowing several
hearty kisses upon her and telling her that she had won the election.[17]

LG was a lucky man. He needed Maggie in Wales as much as he
needed Frances in London, and astonishingly he retained the loyalty
of both.

In Maggie's absence Frances was also daring to make herself more
at home in Downing Street. After playing golf on 22 January, Riddell
accompanied LG back to No. 10 for tea and found the house full of
Frances's family: her mother, two of her sisters and two of Ninette's
children, with whom LG was immediately 'very busy'.[18] We do not
know whether this was the first time Louise had been to Downing
Street, but her willingness to go there – with her grandchildren – suggests
that she had finally reconciled herself to Frances's irregular life. This
is further borne out by letters from around this time, which include
friendly greetings from both Frances's parents to the Prime Minister.*

At the end of January 1921 LG went to Paris again for a week with
his usual entourage, including Frances. Then in February there was
another conference with the French in London. It is difficult to see that
LG had any time for domestic politics at all: like most Prime Ministers, he found the international stage more rewarding than wrestling
with economic problems and trade disputes at home. Moreover he had
forged a good relationship with the latest French Prime Minister, Aris-
tide Briand, a cynical Breton very much like himself. Naturally Frances
was delighted with LG's diplomatic preoccupation and the social round
that went with it – the more so since she had herself struck up an
intriguing relationship with Briand's principal diplomatic adviser.

Philippe Berthelot was Secretary-General at the Quai d'Orsay
throughout the wartime and post-war period while French governments
came and went rapidly: '*le véritable animateur de la diplomatie française
pendant 25 ans*', according to the French dictionary of national

---

* Frances's family were also benefiting from her increasing affluence. In September 1920
her father wrote to thank her for paying their car insurance, and it sounds as though
she had given them the car as well. Both parents, plus Janet and even Muriel, were
having driving lessons. Frances was probably sending them money too.[19]

biography.[20] He was a dark, handsome man with a thick moustache, aged fifty-four at this time, married but with something of a reputation as a womaniser. Hankey, who worked closely with him at all these conferences of 1919–22 and did not praise foreigners lightly, described him in his diary as 'a brilliant, much travelled and interesting man'.[21] Frances, somewhat surprisingly, did not meet him until the San Remo conference in April 1920. But then she sat next to him at a dinner that LG held for Megan's eighteenth birthday, and was immediately 'entranced and enthralled' by him.[22] Berthelot was, it seems, equally attracted by her. 'Behind a manner sometimes abrupt,' his *Times* obituary noted, 'and beneath the metallic ring of a speech in which every syllable was sharply accentuated, there lay a capacity, even a desire, for personal affection, and an emotional quality which rigid self control kept strictly in hand.'[23] Over the next few months Berthelot pursued Frances with extravagantly romantic letters and tokens of his admiration, to the extent that tongues in the French press corps began to wag.

At the time of his death, thirteen years later, Frances tried to describe the nature of her relationship with him.

> Poor Philippe Berthelot is dead. I once had a rather exciting flirtation with him, chiefly through the medium of letters, for we scarcely ever met alone, and our conversations were chiefly at meal times. He was without exception the most fascinating conversationalist I have ever met. It would have been exciting to see more of him, but dangerous from many points of view. Even as it was the French journalists realised his interest in me. Philippe Millet teased me about it one day when I lunched with him and Pertinax.* *'On dit que Berthelot a fait une declaration à Miss Stevenson,'* he said to Pertinax ['It is said that Berthelot has made a declaration of love to Miss Stevenson'] but naturally I pretended not to know what he meant. How those French journalists found out all they did I was never able to discover.

Berthelot, she considered, was 'one of the most interesting and fascinating men I have ever known' – quite a tribute in view of the number of remarkable men with whom her life had brought her into contact over the previous decade.

---

* 'Pertinax' was the pen name of another leading French journalist, André Géraud.

We met a great deal during the post-war conferences, while Ll.G. was still Prime Minister [and] we . . . became great friends. He would enchant me with his stories of his own personal experiences and charm me with his flights of fancy . . . It was pure joy to listen. He wooed me mentally, weaving an exquisite web from mind to mind, speaking no word of love, but taking infinite pains and entirely indifferent to any onlookers. He was profound, amusing, cynical, erudite, provoking. No Englishman could possess this special power of attraction. No Celt would be able to subordinate himself so completely to his task . . .

I think perhaps I became in love with his mind. But in spite of all that has been said to the contrary, he never once spoke a word of love to me, although his letters might be interpreted as an attempt at seduction. In the first place there was no opportunity. Our talks as far as I can remember were all in public – in the drawing room at Chequers and [blank] and in the hotel at San Remo, where I first sat next to him at dinner and . . . he talked to me and no-one else. He would come to my office in Downing Street on the occasions when he came to London, and sit and talk to me there. But in Paris I saw him not at all. He was far too much surrounded for any possible tête-à-tête . . . The Conferences were far too short and far between for any greater intimacy to materialise, though I do not deny that he exercised an uncanny fascination for me.[24]

Frances's contemporary diary tends to support her insistence that there was no more than a flirtation between them – and that more on his side than on hers. Indeed by April 1921, when her diary resumes, she was finding his attentions rather embarrassing. His letters were certainly seductive. For instance, on Sunday 13 March he wrote from the Quai d'Orsay, where he had just returned after three weeks in London and Chequers. He was sorry that he had been unable to say goodbye to her properly, but thanked her for giving him her photograph.

Heureusement que j'ai de l'imagination et que deux ou trois fois j'ai cru apercevoir dans vos yeux lumineux et doux une petite nuance de plus que la sympathie: surtout ne me dites pas que je me trompe.

(Fortunately I have some imagination, and two or three times I thought I could see in your soft and luminous eyes a little hint of something more than sympathy: above all do not tell me that I am wrong.)

After regretting that there were always too many people around them in London, Berthelot expressed disappointment that she seemed not to like a little Norman cross he had given her. It would suit her so well, if she only knew how to wear it.

Un ruban de velours noir autour du cou et le croix pendant sur la poitrine: que vous seriez jolie ainsi! Et comme la finessse discrète, et l'éclair des yeux si beaux, si caressants, mystérieux, et le sourire de la petite bouche iraient au coeur.[25]

(With a black velvet ribbon around your neck and the pendant cross on your breast, how pretty you would look! Just as your unassuming slimness, and the flash of your beautiful, playful, mysterious eyes, and the smile of your little mouth, go to my heart.)

Frances must have written a kind but cool reply, since a week later he wrote again.

Bien chère mademoiselle,
    Votre charmante lettre si délicate et sensible, m'a fait un immense plaisir: ne croyez pas que je suis si aveugle de n'avoir pas compris tout ce qui se cache de précieux et d'original derrière tant de douceur [illegible] *et de discrétion . . .*

(My dear young lady,
    Your charming letter, so delicate and sensitive, has given me great pleasure: do not think me so blind that I have not understood everything that is precious and original behind so much [illegible] sweetness and discretion.)

He told her that he wanted to hold her hand and have long talks with her, but also to keep silent, since silence too was a form of communication between sympathetic people.

Pas un jour, pas un soir, que je n'ai cassé de penser à vous, de regarder votre image et de sourire à vos yeux rêveurs . . .
    Vous ne pouvez vous douter avec quelle ardeur et quelle espérance j'attends notre prochaine rencontre. J'ai si peur que vos amis ne vous plaisent beaucoup plus que moi et que vous ne m'oubliez très vite . . .

Je suis avide de vous avoir près de moi, tout près . . . Mais je n'ose trop dire, de peur de fâcher ma fée anglaise, dont les cheveux doux et les yeux de pervenche ont pris mon coeur, et dont l'exquise petite bouche n'est pas [illegible].

Votre respectueux et si affectionne,
Berthelot[26]

(Not a day, not an evening has passed when I have not fallen to thinking of you, to looking at your picture and smiling at your dreamy eyes . . .

You can have no idea with what ardour and hope I am looking forward to our next meeting. I am so afraid that your friends please you more than I do, and that you will very quickly forget me . . .

I long to have you near me, very near . . . But I dare not say too much, for fear of angering my English fairy, whose soft hair and periwinkle eyes have captured my heart, and whose exquisite little mouth is not [illegible].

Your respectful and loving
Berthelot)

Four weeks later Briand came over to England again, with Berthelot, for what Frances described emphatically as '*a most interesting weekend*' at Lympne. She went down on Friday for dinner, intending to return next day; 'but when it came to the point D. wanted me to stay, & as Lady Rocksavage was there, this was possible'.*

Berthelot very attentive and sweet, but above all remarkably interesting. His is a very powerful brain, capable of intense concentration & industry. He tells me he dislikes politics, which he dissociates from his Quai d'Orsay work, but I think what he really means is that he takes little interest in home politics, whereas world politics are his whole life and interest. He is very witty, but has very little sense of humour . . . Briand on the other hand is both witty and humorous.

She added that Berthelot had 'a very brutal tongue when he likes' and was also strongly anti-Semitic. 'Fortunately he kept off the line he had

---

* There is a rare discrepancy here between Frances and Riddell. While Frances implies that LG spent the whole weekend at Lympne, Riddell has him at Chequers on the Sunday with Maggie and Megan. In every other respect the dates fit – LG was certainly back at Lympne by Tuesday – so it is possible that LG went briefly to Chequers for Sunday dinner with his family before returning to Lympne.[27]

taken in his letters, & was strictly sensible. He is a curious character.'[28]

The French were back in London on 1 May. In the intervening period, as if deliberately to see off a possible rival, LG was particularly attentive to Frances. On Tuesday 26 April they went for a walk in Richmond Park while he rehearsed a speech. 'I love these walks and drives with him alone,' she wrote. 'He is such a wonderful companion, & very sweet to me.'[29] Then they spent a happy day at Chequers.

We went down late on Thursday after D. had made his speech in the House on the Irish Debate. Yesterday a perfect spring day, & Chequers was heavenly. D. & I walked about all day all over the place, very lazy, & thinking of nothing in particular. I think it did D. a lot of good, especially as he had no rest last weekend.

I am beginning to appreciate what the Lees must have suffered in giving up Chequers. The peacefulness of the place is indescribable. There is healing in the atmosphere. We were sorry to leave this morning, but had to come up very early . . . as the other Allies arrived last night & the conferences begin today.[30]

But the next entry immediately reverts to Berthelot:

Saw Berthelot at tea yesterday, when the members of the Conference had tea in my room. He presented me with a very sweet letter, a copy of *La Vie des Martyrs*, which he and Briand say is a most wonderful book, and a quaint old Indian necklace, which Berthelot says is '*sans valeur*' ['valueless'], but which I have reason to think is not. I like him much better than I did, since he has ceased to be sentimental, and is just friendly and interesting.[31]

She invited him to dinner the next day, and he accepted, though he had been due to go to the theatre.

Bien chère mademoiselle,

Je suis très heureux de venir diner chez vous demain et de ne pas aller au théâtre: car votre gracieux invitation est, n'est-ce pas, pour huit heures ¼ 33 Morpeth Mansions, Westminster?

Votre ami respectueux et affectionné et admiratif,

Berthelot[32]

(My dear young lady,

I shall be delighted to come to dinner with you tomorrow, instead of going to the theatre; since your kind invitation is, I think, for 8.15 at 33 Morpeth Mansions, Westminster.

Your respectful, loving and admiring friend,

Berthelot)

LG was jealous, and characteristically found a way to sabotage her evening.

Had a little dinner party last night. Philip Kerr and Muriel Beckett & Berthelot. Asked D. to come but he would not. I suspect he did not like my giving the party much, though I told him of my intention before I asked them. But he got his own back by prolonging the Conference till after nine o'clock, so that it was nearly 9.30 when Philip & Berthelot turned up. The latter said, *'Il me semblait que M. Ll. George voulait prolonger la Conférence!'* ['It seemed to me that M. Ll. George wished to prolong the Conference]. Berthelot was in excellent form and told us the most thrilling stories of the war.[33]

The next evening LG and Berthelot both dined at Sassoon's, where LG clearly set out deliberately to eclipse the Frenchman and effortlessly succeeded.

D. in great form, hilarious and very talkative, but keeping everyone amused. Berthelot quite silent & extremely dull, so different from the previous evening. He looked ghastly. D. rather jealous, especially when I suggested we should drive B. home. However, the latter refused saying he would prefer to walk.[34]

The conference went on all the next day and late into the evening. Frances went home at 11 p.m., since there was no sign of a finish.

On arriving this morning found on my desk a note from Berthelot lamenting the fact that they had departed suddenly – also a note from M. Briand saying: *'Les Conférences Inter-Allies ne sont pas les champs de bataille les moins dangereux'* ['Inter-Allied Conferences are not the least dangerous battlefields']. I think there is a double entendre and D. thinks so too. I think he is rather glad B. has gone. He was getting very jealous, though it takes a lot usually to rouse his jealousy.[35]

There is only one further mention of Berthelot in Frances's diary, in late July. By this time LG's priority had switched to Ireland, relations with the French had deteriorated, and Frances's regard for Berthelot had cooled in parallel.

Great trouble also with the French, who have sent a very insolent note yesterday, which is attributed to Berthelot . . . They talk now of a rupture with us, & goodness knows how it will end. Have not answered Berthelot's last letter as I simply did not know what to say, & I certainly shouldn't know what to say now.[36]

In fact she must have replied eventually, and not unkindly, since three weeks later he wrote her one more enigmatic letter:

Bien chère mademoiselle,
    Votre lettre a été un véritable baume sur une pensée un peu arrière de mon coeur . . .
    Je veux vous appliquer les vers de Byron

> Though human thou didst not deceive me,
> Though trusted you did not betray me.[37]

(My dear young lady,
    Your letter was a real balm to a heart which has been thinking back
. . . I would like to apply to you Byron's lines . . .)

What is one to make of this episode? Was Berthelot serious, or just playing up to the stereotype of the gallant Frenchman to add a little spice to international conferences? Frances was clever, French-speaking and single. But did he realise that her heart was already given to LG? Was she ever tempted by the possibility of a discreet *affaire de coeur*? Her 1934 account almost suggests that she might have been, had the opportunity arisen. Unfortunately her diary is silent from April 1920 to April 1921, exactly the period when she was most in Berthelot's company during all those luxurious confer-ences at Lympne; it picks up again only when she was beginning to tire of his attentions, and LG was exerting himself to reclaim her. Is it possible that she abandoned the diary – or even destroyed it for that period – because more had occurred than she later admitted? It is part of the fascination of Frances's story that it is impossible to know.

Berthelot was not her only French admirer. The journalist Philippe Millet wrote to her in almost equally flattering terms in May 1921.

Dear Miss Stevenson,
    You are – may I say so? – the most charming of diplomatists, and I should enjoy my work a hundred times more if, instead of reading dry notes, I had the pleasure of seeing every day your handwriting.[38]

Again in July:

The evil rumour has reached me that Mr Lloyd George is *not* coming next week to Paris, which would mean that we shall not see you either.
    I wish you would ask the PM to let you come as secretary to the British delegation. Really it would be a thousand pity [*sic*] if you did not come . . . We would give a party in your honour . . .
    I have just written a longish article on Chequers for *L'Illustration*. I hope you will like it. It is secretly dedicated to you.[39]

And again a week later, when it appeared that she and LG were coming to Paris after all:

I shall look you up as soon as you will arrive and give you an *aperçu* of the situation here, which requires delicate handling. Of course, you must understand that I cannot prevent certain papers from printing foolish things, but I will do my best to help you.[40]

Does this refer to the diplomatic rupture between Britain and France? Or could it possibly refer to rumours in the French press about Frances? Once again it is impossible to know.

'WE ARE TOO RECKLESS . . . WE SHALL HAVE TO BE MORE CAREFUL'

Easter 1921 was on 27 March. LG and Frances spent the weekend together at Lympne as part of a large house party including the Dudley Wards and the Prince of Wales, back from his Commonwealth tour, who motored nearly a hundred miles from Windsor on the Sunday to see his mistress. Frances had not yet resumed her diary, but Riddell – who had himself risen from humble origins – was struck by the varied antecedents of the company. 'It was a curious party', he noted.

- Prince of Wales;
- Sir Philip Sassoon, wealthy young Jew;
- L.G., formerly village boy, now Prime Minister, at one time advocate of the working classes and antagonist of millionaires;
- Lady Ribblesdale, wealthy American with dress down to her middle, heavily powdered and painted, rather apprehensive of modern day movements; . . .
- Gubbay, a shrewd commercial Jew, a very nice little man with mind chiefly intent on income tax;
- Evelyn Fitzgerald, genial stockbroker, and man of the world . . . great man with the ladies;
- Miss Stevenson, with her wonderful history – descended from French officer who won the Legion of Honour when serving under Napoleon I – began life as a teacher in a small school;
- Horne, political adventurer and son of a Presbyterian minister;
- Dudley Ward, grandson of the late Lord Esher, with long descent, rowed in university boat; . . .

- Mrs Dudley Ward, daughter of Nottingham lace manufacturer – a clever, perceptive sort of woman, but outwardly childish and frivolous, always on the move, always singing, dancing, smoking, talking or playing tennis.

LG felt out of place in this company. He disliked the growing habit of using Christian names. 'I don't believe in being too familiar with people, but it is a way this set have,' he told Riddell. 'They all talk like this.' He took himself off to Canterbury Cathedral on Good Friday with Frances and Lord French, who had joined the party, to hear a performance of *Messiah*; and to a Baptist chapel – with Sassoon, curiously – on Sunday morning. Otherwise he 'spent much time sleeping or in his own room'.[1] Whether Frances withdrew with him Riddell does not say. More likely she joined in the singing, dancing, smoking, talking and tennis.

'The food and amenities' were, as always, 'all of the very best'. But Sassoon was looking for some return on his hospitality. When LG passed him over in a government reshuffle a few days later, he was deeply upset and 'immediately went off for a long conference with Miss Stevenson'. Clearly he had been relying on Frances to put in a word for him. But probably LG did not wish to be seen to reward Sassoon too blatantly; and Frances's advocacy may actually have counted against him. When Riddell commented on the uncanny ability of Jews to win advancement by gaining the ear of the right person, specifically citing the way Sassoon and Stern had 'worked their way into Downing Street', LG agreed: 'Yes. I noticed they paid great attention to a certain personage. Of course they are clever.'[2] LG never liked anyone else paying too much attention to Frances.

That summer Megan started to make difficulties. On 10 May Frances recorded that LG held a small lunch party for Lord French on his retirement as Lord Lieutenant of Ireland.

Lord French came to lunch & I sat by him. Megan on his other side pricked up her ears when he referred to our meeting at Lympne at Easter, & our drive over to Canterbury. She knew her father was there. She is a little too clever, but not clever enough to do her father in, which she is constantly attempting. One of these days they will come to grips over something & then there will be a row.[3]

Megan did indeed engineer a row the next weekend, when LG was entertaining the Crown Prince of Japan at Chequers.

Mrs Ll.G. was down at Criccieth & did not want to come up, so D. did not overpersuade her & thought she was not coming. Megan, however, who is playing her mother off against D. & me, telephoned her mother all day Friday and yesterday morning told her that D. insisted on her coming up! So she got into the next train & came, much to her disgust & very angry with D. [for] making her come. I am left high & dry, everyone else having gone away for Whitsun. However it is the fortunes of war, & cannot be helped. D. frightfully angry with Megan, but of course he hasn't much of a case! However he will pay her out sooner or later and get even with her.[4]

LG stayed down at Chequers the next day, 'scheming to get Mrs Ll.G. back to Wales' as soon as possible. He must have succeeded, since he was back in London on the Tuesday, before returning – with both Frances and Megan – on Wednesday to work on his speech for a dinner on the Friday.*

We walked about all day at Chequers preparing his speech, which was a very good one (Megan had gone back to town early in the morning) and then came back to town after tea. A most peaceful and sweet day.[6]

The next weekend was even better – after a false start – reminding them of the early days of their relationship.

Went down to Philip Sassoon's at Trent on Friday to lunch – found quite a large party there – Lord & Lady Rocksavage, Mr Dudley Ward, & others. D. & I very unsociable & went for a long walk after lunch by ourselves . . . After tea D. said he would go to Chequers, though Philip wanted us to stay the night. But there is always a spirit of restlessness about Philip's houses, always a crowd of people trying to be bright – & D. loves peace & quietness – so we sailed away. D. said it was the same road – from Elstree – that he took the Sunday years ago when he came to Allenswood to see

* Meanwhile on Thursday of the same week Frances went with LG, Sassoon and Muriel Beckett to *Othello*, with Godfrey Tearle in the title role and Basil Rathbone as Iago. 'A wonderfully good show, & very well acted,' Frances noted. 'What a marvellous man Mr Shakespeare was!' Then she added, without apparent irony: 'The references by Desdemona to women who deceive their husbands were rather embarrassing in view of Muriel B.'s presence!'[5]

me – the first Sunday in July 1912 – when we both of us realised for the first time that something serious was happening – when I asked him to come to the garden party the following Saturday & he said he would. From then we never lost touch with each other & events marched more or less rapidly! However this is back history. We got to Chequers in time for dinner – a glorious evening, & then walked in the garden till bed-time.[7]

Political pressure was now mounting on LG from every side: the French being difficult over Silesia; a vicious guerrilla war in Ireland; unemployment rising; industrial disputes multiplying; and some of his colleagues becoming increasingly restless. 'D. very worried & cross all day yesterday,' Frances noted on 31 May. 'Things are not going very well & he does not quite see his way.'[8] 'Poor old thing,' she wrote the next day, 'my heart aches for him sometimes.'[9] On 2 June (a Thursday) they had 'a lovely walk in Richmond Park' where he picked bluebells for her, which she carefully preserved – they still survive in her papers – before LG went on to the House and 'a very heavy afternoon'. 'We *think* we can manage to be together at Chequers on Sunday but it doesn't do to count on it.' In fact she could not go because his family were there; but they went down together on Friday afternoon instead.

D. *very* cross and irritable all the way down, but made it up very sweetly before we arrived, explaining that he felt very tired and overstrung. He looked it, & I was so sorry for him, and though I can't help being upset when he is cross to me, it is almost invariably when he is over-tired. When we got to Chequers, D. went straight out into the garden & picked me some red roses as a peace offering, & was very sweet to me the rest of the evening.

Next morning he was unwell, so Frances sent for Lord Dawson, who duly declared that he was over-strained and must cancel all his engagements for the next fortnight – though he was allowed to go to Wales for Gwilym's wedding.* Frances was relieved, 'as the next 10 days were going to be very heavy ones for D., & I was getting very worried about it'. She left him to his family while she went off to watch polo with Albert Stern.[10]

But then she was unexpectedly able to return because 'the family' –

---

* Gwilym's bride was Edna Jones, from Denbigh; but the wedding was in Caernarvon.

it is not clear precisely whom she meant – did not stay at Chequers, but went back to town on Tuesday.

> D. was waiting at the station for me – I did not see him until I was on top of him, & was so taken back [*sic*] as he very rarely goes to a station nowadays. We went off in the car and he had brought me some red roses & a basket of strawberries, in case I was hungry! It was a glorious sunny afternoon and we drove to Hughenden to look at Disraeli's house.

Frances was able to stay until Saturday – though they were not alone all the time since LG's idea of rest did not preclude having several colleagues down on the Thursday to talk about Greece and Turkey.

> We have had a heavenly week together. I thought I should have to go away again on Wednesday, but the family did not return, & last night they decided to go by train from London, & to pick up D. at Bletchley, & go on to Wales with him. This was a most delightful piece of luck, as I drove to Bletchley with him early this morning & then returned by train to London. It seems desolate so far from him. He has been so sweet and gentle, and we have had a wonderful time together.[11]

Frances had a gay time while LG was in Wales. First she went to Sussex for the weekend to stay with a Mayfair socialite called 'Cuckoo' Bellville, who had a cottage near Herstmonceux. On Tuesday and Wednesday she went to Ascot with 'Bertie' Stern, who was 'very nice and attentive, arranging that we drove together there & back', though he was evidently no longer wooing her. (The following year he married someone else.) Then on Thursday 'Cuckoo' Bellville gave a party attended by 'lots of celebrities', including the King of Spain, 'who behaved disgustingly with Lois Sturt',* and the Prince of Wales, who was having 'one of his gloomy fits' and looked to Frances for sympathy. His father was insisting that he go to India, but he did not want to.

> They are always having differences. The King is a little harsh, & the Prince very self-willed & a little spoilt & I do not think Philip's influence is very good for him. In addition the poor little boy is very much in love with Freda Dudley Ward, who in turn is simply bored with him. He lives on his

---

* Lois Sturt, a daughter of Lord Alington, later married another of Frances's former beaux, Evan Morgan.

nerves, eats scarcely at all, & smokes & drinks a great deal too much. He told me he never went to bed before two as he could not sleep, and he is up by eight every morning playing games. I don't see how he can avoid a breakdown if he goes on like that.[12]

But amid all these diversions she did not forget to write to LG. Her letter has not survived, but he replied from Criccieth on the Wednesday.

My own girl,

I am sitting outside in a brilliant sun – with a lovely soft breeze playing around me – a sky such as I like – white clouds on a blue background & a prospect of perfectly blue sea & mountains such as I have never seen. And yet I want more than ever to be elsewhere. Do you know why, darling? Can you guess? There is one thing missing in the immediate foreground whose presence alone would make the landscape perfectly beautiful & enchanting to me . . .

I return Friday – I meant to motor straight to Chequers, but as I am accompanied by my family, I shall come up to town.

I want to see you my dearest & had hoped for a weekend – but it cannot be arranged. Very very disappointed . . .

Fond tender enduring passionate love & affection from D.[13]

LG returned as promised on the Friday, complaining that he had not had much of a rest.

Everywhere he went he had to make speeches & this in addition to the wedding & the big meeting at Portmadoc. Also Mrs Ll.G. insists on his seeing & shaking hands with everyone who happens to call. D. intended to go to Chequers (hoping Mrs Ll.G. would stay at Criccieth) but as she returned too, he came to London. We went to P. Sassoon's last night for dinner & as Philip took his guests to the theatre afterwards D. & I had a nice talk. He still has a cold in the head, & I do not think he is as well as he ought to be after a fortnight's rest.[14]

The fact that Maggie came back to London with LG, but was then happy for him to go to Sassoon's that evening – where she must have known Frances would be – is a good example of the freedom she was content to allow him, so long as there was no scandal. She did not stay long: by Monday she had gone again, and Frances was looking forward to dining with LG at the House that evening.[15]

Riddell agreed with Frances that LG was 'much better for his rest, but I think he wants a good long holiday'.[16] Instead he was plunged into an Imperial Conference with the Dominion Prime Ministers, which lasted through the whole of July, and into growing pressure from disgruntled Conservatives to break up the Coalition. Increasingly frustrated in Europe, however, he still had two other major projects in hand, which dominated the rest of 1921: plans for an international disarmament conference to be held in the autumn, and a fresh attempt to settle the Irish problem by negotiation rather than coercion. LG evidently saw the former as a good excuse to get away to some warm spot.

> Several places have been suggested & D. is very keen on Honolulu, but I'm afraid it would be too far. Another suggestion is *Cuba*. It is to be in October and ought to be rather fun.[17]

In fact the conference met in Washington. But LG did not attend in person, sending Balfour in his place; he was too busy at home trying to bring Sinn Fein to the conference table.

Intent on a holiday, LG had previously thought of taking Frances for a motor tour in September 'through the Tyrol and the Italian lakes, ending up at Venice'. But Lord Dawson ruled that this would be 'too tiring' and would not let him go abroad; so LG decided to go to Scotland instead. Frances was given the job – through Riddell, naturally – of finding a suitable house.[18] Meanwhile, with Maggie back in Wales, Frances resumed her position as the Prime Minister's unofficial consort – despite the mounting indignation of Megan.

> Had a divine weekend at Chequers, though Megan rather troublesome, & turning up just before lunch on Sunday resented things being in my hands & was very cross & rude. Everyone noticed how bad-tempered she was. Her frivolous life is taking from her charm and looks. No-one seems to have any control over her or to be responsible for her comings & goings. She just goes wherever she pleases & does what she likes – avoids her father when she has something else to do and resents finding me there when she consents to turn up.[19]*

* There is another conflict of dates here, since Riddell gives the impression that Maggie was at Chequers this weekend. But Riddell's dates are not always reliable, whereas Frances's usually are.

The next day, back in Downing Street, Frances wrote that LG was 'very tired' after 'a terribly heavy day . . . We are going to have dinner quietly with Philip Kerr and then I shall play to him afterwards.'[20] The day after was the same, but with an added worry about Megan making trouble.

Horne has been telling him that people are talking about us, and that we are too reckless. He said someone asked him the other day how long it would be before there was a bust-up in Downing St? Meaning I suppose D. & Mrs Ll.G. Horne says that Megan has been talking to people about me, & criticising her father, thinking I suppose that she would put a stop to it in that way, & not realising that all she would succeed in doing is to discredit her father. But I don't think she would stop at anything to obtain her ends. D. told Horne that he would rather go out of public life than do without me, & that if it came to the point he would do that. I think Horne is right that we are too reckless, & go about too much together, & we shall have to be more careful about that.[21]

Then she added the latest news of General Macready's marital difficulty.

Macready is also having trouble with his spouse, but he has told her that he won't have her back in Ireland, and as soon as things are settled there and he is able to leave he is going to set up a separate establishment. If Catherine had not been such a fool as to get married they would have been able to go abroad and live together.[22]

Is that what Frances would have liked to do with LG? Yet they already managed to live together much of the time – under much greater public scrutiny than Macready – without needing to go abroad. And what would LG have done abroad? Moreover at the time of the Billy Owen episode in 1915, LG had believed that it would have made it easier for them to carry on their affair if Frances *were* married. Anyway, none of these fantasies came to anything: they simply carried on as before, but taking a little more care.

Thus they travelled separately to Chequers the following Friday, pursued by news from Ireland.

To be prudent, I went by train & he came on afterwards by car. He arrived in great excitement and while he was changing, in my room, the telephone rang and D. on answering was told that it was a message from Dublin Castle for me . . . De Valera had agreed to come over this week, was going to issue orders for a truce, & had sent for Macready.* The whole atmosphere was changed . . . D. very pleased, as it looks as though there is every prospect of a settlement.

Frances could not stay the weekend, since LG was entertaining the Dominion Prime Ministers and their wives, so Maggie had to be there. 'D. & I had a very happy morning . . . but I left in the afternoon as the arrival of the family would have made things unpleasant.' She clearly thought that she would have made a better hostess, noting tartly that 'Mrs Ll.G. did not even trouble to be there in time to receive them.' Nevertheless it seems to have been a successful weekend. 'D. took a great deal of trouble so it is not surprising.'[23]

The next few days illustrate Frances's close involvement with events as LG's search for an Irish settlement gathered pace. On Monday (11 July) they had dinner together before LG held a Cabinet meeting at 9.30. The next day he went to Chequers with Austen Chamberlain and others to prepare for his meeting with De Valera, now fixed for Thursday. From there he rang Frances to tell her that De Valera wanted to see him alone. He was 'delighted' – he always preferred to deal one-to-one – but his colleagues were 'rather sticky about it . . . Although they don't object to D. taking the responsibility they hate to be left out of things.' That evening he came back to London in buoyant mood to dine with Frances at Sassoon's.

He was saying what an extraordinary volte-face has happened during the last few weeks. It was not so very long ago that he was politically in deep waters, and in the trough of the wave. But now . . . we are riding up to the crest of the waves, and a very steep and sudden rise too.[24]

Forty-eight hours later:

De Valera has just gone, after having been with D. nearly 3 hours. I have never seen D. so excited as he was before De Valera arrived, at 4.30. He kept walking in & out of my room & I could see he was working out the

* Eamonn de Valera was the uncompromising leader of the Irish republican party, Sinn Fein.

best way of dealing with DeV. As I told him afterwards he was bringing up all his guns![25]

LG wooed De Valera with Celtic flattery backed by warnings of renewed coercion if the talks should fail. Afterwards he was drained – 'utterly exhausted & very highly strung'. He had to speak at a party dinner that evening and did so brilliantly, according to Frances. 'But he was terribly tired, & I was almost afraid he would break down.'[26] He met De Valera again the next day and twice again the following week. On 20 July he was hopeful and started talking about retiring if he could once get Ireland settled. 'I think he really means it this time . . . If he settles Ireland he can go no higher, & the rest would do him good.' That evening he secured the support of the Cabinet and then took the terms to the King – snatching dinner with Frances before going to the Palace. Thursday (21 July) was 'the critical day' and he was 'getting very excited about it'. But then the talks almost broke down: De Valera went back to Dublin with nothing agreed and LG was reduced to threatening that if the Irish refused to come to terms, 'there is only one thing to be done – to reconquer Ireland'.[27]

Frances was able to go to Chequers on the Saturday, but had to return the same evening when the family went there. 'D. very tired,' she noted again, 'and we only walked to the top of the hill, & then sat down and lazed for a long time. He has had a terrible fortnight, & unfortunately there is still such a lot to do to the end of the session.'[28] Yet for Frances social life went on as busily as ever. She attended a royal garden party midweek, where she was introduced to Margot Asquith. 'She was very nice, & I was agreeably surprised in her . . . She is a sort of kind Nancy Astor, whereas Nancy A. is a good looking Mrs A.'[29] Then on Monday 25th she went to 'a topping dance at "Cuckoo" Bellville's', where she met again another of her younger admirers: the Major Crankshaw whom she had liked in Paris two years before:

Crankie has returned from America & is just as sweet as ever, & everyone made a great fuss of him – Sir R. Horne very annoyed because I preferred to talk to Crankie to dancing with *him*. Really very sniffy, & would not look at me or dance with me for the rest of the evening.

Meanwhile LG needed to give some attention to keeping his wife happy.

D. dined 'en famille' as Mrs Ll.G. goes away today, & D. wanted her to go away in a good humour. He intends to take her up to Scotland, going first to Sutherland's wedding & then driving up to Gairloch in short stays, stopping at Glasgow & other places & making a great show of the fact that they are going up there together. He does not expect her to stay long there, however, as she will want to return to Wales.[30]

This visit to Scotland, however, turned into one of the strangest episodes in the whole saga.

18

HIGHLAND FLING

In September 1921 Maggie and Frances, wife and mistress, *both* went to Scotland with LG. For some weeks they were in closer proximity – probably sleeping under the same roof – than at any other time since the summer of 1911. That was extraordinary enough. But the whole situation was bizarre. Riddell had found LG a house at Gairloch, a remote spot on the west coast, fifty miles from Inverness, opposite the northern tip of Skye. LG stayed there for the whole of September. But even in such an isolated retreat he was incapable of having a proper holiday. He continued to conduct critical negotiations back and forth with De Valera in Dublin, attempting to agree terms on which the Irish would be willing to attend a conference, requiring Sinn Fein envoys, as well as a steady stream of colleagues, advisers, secretaries and typists, to attend on him – General Macready turned up in a destroyer – and putting an impossible strain on the primitive local post office and telephone exchange. He even summoned most of the Cabinet to an unprecedented meeting in the council chamber of Inverness Town Hall to consider their response to De Valera's reply to the government's invitation to London. Finally the weather was miserable, with rain practically every day, so that most of the party, including Frances, went down in turn with colds and chills; LG himself got an abscess on a tooth which had to be extracted by a local dentist. Altogether LG's Highland holiday was one of the most surreal chapters in the history of British government.

Unfortunately Frances's diary had now lapsed again, so Riddell is the sole contemporary witness apart from Hankey's deputy, Tom Jones, who went to Scotland only for the Cabinet meeting. There are several surviving letters, some dated, others not; but the dates do not always tally with Riddell's diary, which in turn is not supported by the reports in *The Times* of LG's illness and other activities. The result is that it is not possible to be sure of the order of events or precisely when either LG or Frances was ill.

The potential for embarrassment was apparent before LG's travelling circus even got to Scotland, when they stopped off in Barnsley to attend the wedding of LG's political secretary, Sir William Sutherland, on 26 August. 'Travelled with L.G., J. T. Davies and Miss Stevenson,' Riddell recorded. 'Stopped with Sir Joseph Hewitt, where Mrs Ll.G. joined us.' Hewitt was a Yorkshire coal owner who was knighted in 1919 and had just been raised to baronet: doubtless he paid the going rate for both titles. On Maggie's arrival, Frances presumably faded into the background, merely a secretary attending the wedding of one of her colleagues. Sutherland – known as 'Bronco Bill' – was a colourful character, generally regarded as an unscrupulous wire-puller. Riddell thought him 'the queerest bridegroom I have ever seen'; while LG was 'curious to see whether Sutherland will take even a modified interest in domesticity'. At the reception he described Sutherland as 'my political son' and made a speech full of mildly risqué innuendoes about coalitions and whips.[1] Some of the other speeches gave actual offence and there was very nearly 'a nasty fracas'.

> Wine flowed freely, and Hewitt made perpetual speeches on every possible occasion. At the final dinner he proposed L.G.'s health several times, Mrs L.G.'s health, and finished up by proposing the health of St Frances.[2]

Regrettably Riddell does not say how this appalling gaffe was received.

From Yorkshire, LG and Maggie went on by easy stages via Edinburgh, Blair Atholl and Inverness, reaching Gairloch on 1 September. At Blair Castle they stayed with the Duke and Duchess of Atholl, and the Prime Minister and Riddell went pony-trekking – something LG had never done before. Whether Frances travelled as part of his entourage or separately Riddell does not say. Nor do we know the sleeping arrangements at Gairloch. Frances recalled that 'the house was not a big one, and the resources of the local hotel had to be called in'. She added that 'Dame Margaret, who would much rather have been amongst the Welsh hills than the Scottish, had her hands full . . . in a strange house, especially as none of the visitors was particularly pleased at having to undertake this very long journey to the wilds during the summer recess.'[3] She does not specify whether she herself slept in the house or the hotel. But from the series of surreptitious notes that LG smuggled to her room when she was ill, it would seem that she was in the house.

Either way she was treated as one of the party. When LG arrived on 1 September the Irish envoys were already waiting at the hotel with a letter from De Valera. Over the next four days 'everyone was busily engaged discussing the Irish Question', while Edward Grigg drafted alternative replies.* Then LG consulted the whole party about his preferred draft.

> It was submitted for the opinion of Mrs L. G., Lady Hamar [Greenwood], Miss Stevenson and J. T. Davies. L.G. subsequently took a vote, including amongst the voters himself, Greenwood, Macready and Grigg. The result was a majority of one for the letter.[4]

The Inverness Cabinet took place the next day to confirm the decision. Fifteen members attended, travelling up on the overnight sleeper and grumbling all the way. 'This is outrageous,' Austen Chamberlain complained, 'dragging us to Inverness. Why did the PM not have the meeting in Edinburgh?'[5] But in fact the meeting was a great success, as Tom Jones reported to Hankey in London, particularly since the rain held off for a couple of days.

> The weather was perfect, the town highly flattered, the Provost important, the PM beaming, and even the Ministers who had scowled and growled at Euston melted into friendliness when they saw how delighted the Highlanders were to have them in their midst . . . What the Treasury will say presently we must not anticipate.[6]

The British letter was eventually agreed and given to the waiting Irish to take back to Dublin, while LG returned to Gairloch to await the reply. Riddell went back to London for a couple of days to visit his sick mother, and returned to find 'LG rather seedy and the whole

---

* Grigg was another of LG's political secretaries. He subsequently became a Liberal MP and a minister during the Second World War. His son John Grigg became LG's best biographer.

household rather at sixes and sevens'.[7] A few days later LG 'became seriously ill with an abscess in his jaw, which he tried to treat by domestic methods'. Eventually Maggie telegraphed for Lord Dawson, who said that the infected tooth must come out: it was duly extracted by the local dentist, with the help of a local anaesthetist who rose manfully to the responsibility of putting the Prime Minister to sleep. Then 'an enthusiastic Welsh singer' who was one of the party 'signalised the occasion by indulging in an outburst of "The Men of Harlech" on the piano, just as L.G. was coming out of the gas'.[8]

Soon Dawson had another patient when Frances went down with flu. In her memoirs she made a rare reference to the awkwardness of her position as a guest under Dame Margaret's roof.

> I had a high temperature and had to remain in bed for several days. One morning, suffering from the depression which influenza drags in its wake, I was ruminating on my equivocal position in the house party, some of whose members inevitably regarded me with disfavour; and dwelling on my sins in general I decided to settle down and have a good cry. I was in the middle of it when the door opened and in walked Lord Dawson. He was a marvellous psychologist and took in the position at once . . . I said I would like to go home, but he said that was impossible and would not help L.G. at all. I was soon feeling that my troubles would quickly disperse, and I was filled with gratitude to Lord Dawson.[9]

LG wrote Frances four letters while she was ill at Gairloch – one of which was addressed to 'Ward 2, Flowerdale Cottage Hospital'. (Flowerdale House was the name of the house where they were all staying.) Three of these letters refer to his own dental trouble as if it was over; but since they are all undated it is impossible to be certain of their correct order.*

My own darling girl

   I am so sorry you have got this beastly cold. We have both had bad luck. But I am pulling through mine & you will sooner get through yours. I shall miss you so much. You are my heart's sunshine & even when I cannot talk to you I like to know you are there shining through the storm clouds.

* A. J. P. Taylor dates them to the second or third week of August. But this is clearly wrong, since LG did not arrive at Gairloch until 1 September.

Get a good steaming dish of Allanbury. Insist on it being hot. Pile clothes on until you perspire thoroughly – then sleep dreaming of an old man who loves you more than anything or anybody in the world & would gladly if need be give them all up for you.

Cariad anwyl chus aur melyn.

D.

My sweet,

I heard the doctor's report & it gave me joy. I have been increasingly enquiring about you & I *do* miss you so much.

Police very vigilant today so cannot write but my love is beyond all police supervision.

Ever & ever your own sweetheart & lover & husband

Dai

My own sweet,

I have read your fond letter with thrills of pleasure – but better even than that is J.T.'s news that you are better – temperature in the comforting vicinity of 99. Don't be discouraged – as I was – by fluctuations. The fact that you should be down so soon shows that you are only suffering from a feverish cold which rest & warmth will enable you to throw off. But don't come down for a day or two darling. Get thoroughly well first.

You want to know what I am like . . . [Here LG drew four childish drawings of himself looking first miserable and then happy, before and after receiving her letter.]

Your own

Cariad

My poor little darling

I am so sorry & disappointed but the Doctor had warned me yesterday that he would not let you up until Thursday. It is so dangerous to catch a second chill – that would keep you in bed another week. So be a dear & carry out orders my sweet. You are more deeply rooted in my heart than ever – no gas or forceps can take you out. Except with the last drop of my blood. There are billions of my little girl coursing through my veins – sometimes normally sometimes septically with a high pulse & a very high temperature.

I am longing – oh so much to have you in [my] arms *Cariad bach anwyl aur fe* – you know the rest.

Cheer up darling. Tomorrow will soon come.
Ever & Ever
Your own
D.[10]

While Frances lay in bed, a furious 'telegraphic controversy' was still being conducted back and forth between Gairloch and Dublin, which, Riddell wrote, 'nearly wrecked the small Gairloch post office', though in the end 'the local postmistress rose to the occasion and did the work extremely well'. Once LG had second thoughts about a letter after it had been given to the press. Riddell tried to recall it, but found all the post offices between Gairloch and Inverness closed; he eventually telegraphed the Chief Constable of Inverness to intercept the journalist to whom it had been given and get it back from him.[11] This was diplomacy straight out of Evelyn Waugh, with vital messages practically being sent by forked stick. The experiment of removing the seat of government to the west of Scotland for four weeks was chaotic, as one of the Cabinet Office secretaries, Lawrence Burgis, reported to Tom Jones on 22 September.

The confusion here is indescribable. They are trying to do the work as if they were at No. 10 and with one not very efficient shorthand typist. There is one room as an office into which everyone crowds – *no* telephone and a P.O. with a single line, one mile away. Thirty miles from the nearest railway station which it takes four hours to reach, and only one car!

Noting that LG was still 'by no means well', Burgis added bitterly:

I'm not surprised he is not well in this damnable hole where it rains from morning until night. It has not stopped since I arrived.[12]

The week before, on 15 September, Frances had written similarly to her sister Muriel:

The weather is simply appalling here – raining almost all the time. You simply cannot go out without getting wet. The P.M. caught a 10lb salmon this week and is pleased with his catch. Unfortunately he caught a cold & has been laid up yesterday and today. He really has not had much of a holiday. The Irish question has taken a very serious turn and by the time

you get this it is quite likely that we shall have started for home. It is very
bad luck.[13]

It is odd that Frances does not mention either LG's tooth or her own
flu. Moreover, she must have written a reasonably cheerful letter to her
parents a few days earlier, since the day after she wrote to Muriel she
got one back from her father, glad to hear that she was having a good
time, but mildly satirical about the Prime Minister's problems.

I hope that the PM will be able to settle the Irish Question, the Unemployment Problem, the Silesian Imbroglio, the Turkish Difficulty and a few
other little matters while he is having his well-earned holiday.[14]

Some time towards the end of the month Maggie went back to Wales.
Since Riddell left at the same time, we do not know whether Frances
stayed on to take her place as hostess during the last week. One might
imagine that she did, especially since on 29 September LG wrote Maggie
one of his transparently guilty letters, protesting too much, as he usually
did when he was with Frances.

I miss you so much. I very nearly came with you, & should have done so
but for Dawson's express orders . . . Tomorrow . . . the experts arrive &
I leave Tuesday. Jolly glad to do so though I am back to face trouble . . .
    You don't tell me whether you like the Hindhead site.
    Just received De Valera's acceptance.[15]

The reference to Hindhead, however, indicates that Frances had also
left Gairloch some time earlier – on an important mission. Anticipating
that he might not be in office for much longer, LG had been thinking
for some time of buying or building himself a house for his retirement.
He did not like the Cobham house, and he had long dreamed of
acquiring a farm where he could grow his own produce and live the
open-air life he loved. He entrusted Frances with the task of finding a
suitable one. In July she wrote that she had found 'a lovely little house
at Penshurst [in Kent], but it has no view, so D. won't consider it'.[16]
But very soon they heard of an estate for sale at Churt, near Hindhead
in Surrey, and Frances was sent to investigate it. According to her
memoirs, she left Gairloch before the rest of the party to go down and
inspect the site, and reported back to LG in Scotland that it was perfect:

sixty acres of pine, bracken and heather with wonderful views. LG wired back asking which way the slope faced. She told him confidently that it faced south, so he went ahead and bought it without even seeing it for himself – only to discover when he came down that it actually faced north. Frances was devastated, but LG simply laughed and announced that they would call the house Bron-y-de, meaning 'Breast of the South'. It is a good story, but slightly spoiled by LG's letter of 29 September, which suggests that Maggie too had been to see the site before LG returned from Scotland. We do not know what she told LG at the time; but two years later – after the house was built – she was sarcastic, writing to Olwen that the only thing that faced south was the front door: all the main rooms faced north-west, so 'Backside of the South' would be a better name for it![17] Since Bron-y-de was always more Frances's house than hers, it is not surprising that Maggie was inclined to be sour about it.

Once he got back to London, LG was preoccupied with Ireland for the rest of the autumn. The Irish delegation headed by Michael Collins and Arthur Griffith arrived in London in early October – De Valera stayed in Dublin – and was locked in negotiations for the next two months with a high-powered British delegation that included all the most senior figures in the Cabinet. Frances's diary for November is almost entirely devoted to the progress of the negotiations, with LG veering between excitement and anxiety, though she does record one weekend with Sassoon at Trent Park – largely taken up with Ireland – and, by way of relaxation, two visits to Gilbert and Sullivan operas: *Ruddigore* on 27 October and *Patience* on 22 November. 'D. enjoyed it immensely,' she recorded after the latter. 'He is looking rather tired these days however, & I am a little worried about him.'[18] The next day they 'motored down to Hindhead' to inspect the site again, 'starting at 9.0 & getting back at 1.30. D. wants to start building the house as soon as possible. He is very keen on it & it makes a diversion for him.'[19]

That day LG scribbled a note to Maggie apologising that he could not get away for the weekend. 'The Irish negotiations have taken a turn for the worse – seriously. This time it is the Sinn Feiners. Last week it was the Ulsterites. They are both the sons of Belial!'[20] Eventually, however, by a mixture of bluff, threats, cajolery and a dash of double-dealing, both sides were persuaded to put their names to a treaty, signed at Downing Street in the early hours of 6 December. Frances

had abandoned her diary again, but it is clear from Tom Jones's diary
that she was closely involved in all the comings and goings, drafting
and consultations behind the scenes; she recalled in her memoirs sitting
anxiously in her office next to the Cabinet Room during the final stages
while LG's other secretaries – J. T. Davies, Ernie Evans and Geoffrey
Shakespeare – came in and out pooling whatever information they could
glean.

> Just before 3 a.m. L.G. himself came into my room, exhausted but
> triumphant, and handed me the treaty document with its historic signatures
> and seal. 'Lock it up carefully,' he said, and I did so, in a dispatch box.
> There it lay for many years, until I unlocked the dispatch box again on
> going through L.G.'s papers after his death, and discovered it again. The
> amazing thing was that during all that time it had never been asked for![21]

The Irish treaty was one of LG's greatest achievements. It did not
'solve' the Irish Question. In the short run it provoked a bloody civil
war in Ireland, and in the long run, by partitioning the island, it left
behind the slow-burning fuse that would flare into violence again in
the 1970s. Yet it took the eternal Irish problem out of British politics
for fifty years and, in the circumstances of 1921, that was an extraordinary success. With Ireland resolved, LG frequently told Frances, he
would be happy to retire to his farm, grow fruit and write his memoirs.
Of course he did not really mean it. Like other long-serving Prime
Ministers he could not really bring himself to surrender power voluntarily. But the further strain that the treaty placed on Tory loyalty to
the Coalition meant that his days were numbered. It could only be a
matter of time now before his professed wish would be granted.

19

'THE SWEETEST LITTLE WORRY
IN THE WORLD'

With Ireland settled, LG's attention immediately switched back to Europe. He was set on the idea of one more great conference in the spring of 1922 to deal simultaneously with German reparations and Russian debts, thus – he hoped – bringing both Germany and Bolshevik Russia back into a new concert of nations. This was to be held in Genoa in April. Meanwhile there had to be yet another Allied conference to allay French security fears in the event of a German revival; and this was held in Cannes in January. As usual LG treated the jaunt as a bit of a holiday. Instead of going to Criccieth for Christmas as had been announced, he left for the south of France on 23 December with his usual train of secretaries and colleagues, including Frances. On this occasion Albert Stern put a villa at the Prime Minister's disposal. The conference opened on 6 January and was going well until LG unwisely attempted to introduce the French and Italian Prime Ministers, Briand and Bonomi, to golf, though neither had ever touched a club before. LG thought it a great joke, but the French press was not amused and the pictures of Briand apparently being made a fool of by his British counterpart caused the fall of his government. The Cannes conference was abandoned and Briand, with whom LG had always got on well, was replaced by the much less amenable Raymond Poincaré. Soon afterwards the Italian government fell too.

LG came home to a sea of political troubles. 'D. has been in a very worried & restless condition all this week,' Frances wrote in an isolated diary entry on 3 February. 'He is always like this when he cannot make up his mind.' He thought of resigning, or of calling an election, but actually did neither. 'D. himself has not been very well, & Mrs Ll.G. has been very troublesome & is likely to make more trouble. The net result has not been to improve D's temper.'[1] He was particularly indignant about an article in a Sunday newspaper criticising his allegedly luxurious lifestyle, gadding about Europe playing golf instead of staying at home dealing with domestic problems. 'I live an austere life,' he protested to Riddell:

> I do little else but work. I don't play cards. I don't go out at night. I don't dance – in fact practically the whole of my life is spent in my work. I may do well or I may not, but no one can charge me with neglecting my work.

He knew quite well where his vulnerability lay.

> Then who are these people to attack me? Rothermere is separated from his wife and infatuated with some girl. He wanted to get a divorce so that he could marry her, but Beaverbrook and other friends . . . advised him against it.* Lovat Fraser [the author of the offending article] is given to the bottle. Nice people these to talk about an austere life! I could deal them a shrewd blow.[3]

Riddell's diary mentions Frances only once in February, though she was probably with LG over successive weekends in Trent Park, Chequers and Lympne. The last weekend of the month he came back to Lympne on Saturday night after a tiring day-trip to Boulogne to meet Poincaré again. He stayed in bed until lunchtime on Sunday, then spent the afternoon writing a long letter to Austen Chamberlain offering to stand down in favour of either Chamberlain or Bonar Law, oblivious to the rest of the company – Frances, Sassoon, Sylvester and Riddell – singing revue songs round the piano. His handwritten notes were then transcribed by Frances and typed by Sylvester.[4] To Riddell he insisted that he wanted Chamberlain to accept his offer; but Chamberlain – who, as Lord Birkenhead famously remarked, 'always played the game and always lost' – honourably refused.

---

* Six months earlier, when dining with Rothermere, LG had made a faux pas by complimenting him on the wrong mistress. 'D. had heard of a lady *last* year whom Rothermere was keen on, & naturally thought it was the same one, so started singing her praises. Rothermere broke him off: "Oh, it isn't *that* one," he said. "It's another one."'[2]

In the middle of the following week Riddell played golf with LG at Coombe Hill.

The political crisis in full blast. L.G. evidently very tired, but he played golf better than for some months, holing putts all over the place and driving longer than he usually does. I have however noticed that men who are strung up to a pitch of excitement owing to political or business worries often outshine themselves at golf. The nervous system seems to be preternaturally active, the sight abnormally good, and the powers of concentration abnormal.

That was evidently not how LG felt, however, since the next day Frances rang Riddell 'in great alarm'.

She said that the PM's eyes had been worrying him, and that she had sent for Phillips the oculist. Phillips is a rather gruff man and speaks his mind . . . not like Dawson, who always had one eye on politics and pleasing the PM . . . Phillips had told LG plainly that unless he at once went for a holiday he would have serious cause to regret it. 'Therefore,' said Miss S., 'he is going away now. Don't you think that is right?' Of course I said I did.[5]

In fact he did not go away for another week. Then he went to Criccieth, from where he wrote Frances a series of unusually long letters mixing reports on his health and reflections on his political options with assurances that he was missing her and vows of his undying love. For the first week he did nothing except lie in the sun reading thrillers and recovering his strength.

My own sweet

I have been fretting for days because there was no cheering letter from my little girl. And I said to myself – she is just like the rest of them the moment you turn your back she forgets all about a poor fellow. (I have been very much in the 'poor fellow' frame of mind.) I was therefore so pleased to get a loving letter from you this morning & I am glad you got 2 or 3 days rest. You also needed it my darling. Looking after me is a nerve racking business. I am beginning to find that out myself.

How slowly the first week goes. It just drags along in seconds. The weather is simply wonderful & that does in a measure compensate. But it also makes you more eager than ever for your 'mate' – your one and only mate.

I am sitting now after lunch on the balcony with a warming sun, Chong lying by my side.* By the way Chong is undoubtedly happy here. She has three or four dogs 'squiring' her all day & she enjoys the attention just as much as other friends of mine do & I trust her out of my sight just as little as I do them . . .

Fond fond tender love.

From the battered old warrior who loves you better than anybody or anything else in the world.[6]

My own girl

Here is a completed week of our separation & glad I am that it is gone. I know how the first few days always drag. The weather is still a marvel. J.T. and I walked down to the Llanystumdwy stream this morning. It was like a June day. Your letter darling added a gentleness & a brightness of its own even to this fine spring morning . . .

I hope you are taking advantage of my absence

(a) to leave the office early

(b) to play golf on Saturday & Sunday

(c) *to go to bed early*

Be a good girl. I am always thinking about you & always wishing you were here to go for walks with me – to loll about in the glorious sun – to enjoy the wonderful view – to play golf etc. Pussy – get away or I must take the first train back to London in order to take someone in my arms.

Fond fond love

Your old man.[7]

On 21 March J. T. Davies wrote to Frances that LG was 'ever so much better' and 'much happier', having made up his mind to stick with the Tories until after the Genoa conference.

Personally I regret this & I should regret it the more if he were a younger man. For after all leading a great progressive party of liberals + modern labour requires new stunts, new programmes, new policies, new campaigns, & I doubt whether the PM is fit enough for that now even with six months

---

* Chong was LG's favourite Chow, a present from Philip Sassoon.

rest. I do not mean to say he is getting too old but his great work of the last few years must have told upon him more than he and we realise: I can quite see therefore that a continuance of the present Coalition is what he desires if he can go on with it without suffering loss of prestige or dignity.

Davies added that LG's family had decided to accompany him to Genoa: so he – JT – was trying to get out of going.[8]

The same day LG too wrote that his family were giving him trouble.

My own darling sweetheart

Horne & McCurdy* are entirely responsible for my remissions in writing to my girl these last days. Sunday I could not write. There is no post. But I had a little chat on the phone. How that phone angers me. The moment I get on they start listening & I cannot hear one word – not to be quite sure of it. So I retire in wrath & disgust. Isn't it mean of them? . . .

I mean to come up Monday – leave Tuesday for Folkestone [i.e. Lympne] with a couple of private secretaries. Can you guess the name of one of them? I don't want the big house otherwise there will be a temptation for me to get a house full . . .

I am longing to caress you my own girl. How I look forward to Monday . . .

Fond love to my own darling

D.[9]

LG's next letter suggests that Frances had been seconding JT's view that he needed a long rest. LG was having none of it.

My darling

A day's march nearer Puss. You think I am done for & need 6 months complete rest to be of any use do you? I'll show you as soon as I return. I'll force you to apologise. That is how I feel now about my alluring little Cassandra. I know who will stand most in need of six months rest when I am done with you!

The fat is well in the fire again. Austen writes to say that Winston will resign if I am to recognise the Bolsheviks at Genoa & that he (Austen)

---

* Robert Horne was now Chancellor of the Exchequer; Charles McCurdy was Chief Whip.

cannot face the Tories on a resignation over that issue. If that is the case then I go, & I go on an issue that suits me . . . If the Unionists take Winston's view I go without any hesitation . . .

It is difficult to rest with all these 'crises' hurtling about your head. I have had today a return of those neuralgic pains that worried me.

Fondest love to my pet

D.[10]

It is a pity we do not have Frances's side of this correspondence. Two days later LG replied to her reply:

My sweet

So you were not frightened by my brutal threats – just thrilled. That is all right – for I mean them.

Today is my first day of real storm that keeps me indoors. I have had the luck of a fortnight's wonderful weather.

Riddell arrived this morning before I got out of bed. I am jolly glad he is here.

Megan is off at the Grand National!

As to politics well 'Confound their politics', I wish to God I were out of it without having the process of demission to go through . . .

Tenderest love

Your own

D.[11]

Riddell arrived at midday, so evidently LG was still taking it very easy. The next day they were joined by three distinguished musicians, whom LG had invited to help him with a favourite project, compiling a definitive hymn-book to contain 'all the best hymns'.* LG spent all weekend trying out tunes with them.

The experts were evidently much surprised to see him sing with such vigour. I asked them privately whether he really understood much about it. They said he had a good natural ear and quite good judgment, although his taste naturally tended in favour of the Welsh style of hymn.[12]

---

* The three were Sir Henry Hadow, a composer and academic; Professor Walford Davies of University College, Aberystwyth; and Dr Richard Terry, organist of Westminster Cathedral.

The weekend concluded with a 'great recital' in Criccieth church conducted by Walford Davies, before the whole party returned to London on Monday.

LG survived his showdown with his Tory colleagues on Tuesday 28 March, though only by diluting his plan to recognise Soviet Russia. 'Crisis distinctly off,' he reported complacently to Maggie.[13] After Cabinet, LG went straight to Lympne. His continuing willingness to accept Sassoon's hospitality, however, still did not persuade him to repay his host with the promotion he desperately desired. He had already overlooked Sassoon for a vacant Under-Secretaryship two weeks earlier. Now, despite Frances pleading Sassoon's case, LG gave the Chancellorship of the Duchy of Lancaster to 'Bronco Bill' Sutherland. Sassoon was devastated.

> Oh, Frances! Sir William Sutherland's appointment was a knock-out blow to me . . . *As you know* the PM *promised me a year ago* the very next vacancy, & here I am, with the ever-receding mirage of hope in my eyes & despair in my heart.
>
> I cannot help thinking that you & J.T. who have always shown me sincere friendship will feel a little for me – though I daresay you don't really care a twopenny damn what happens to me.
>
> Yours
> P.S.[14]

Sassoon never did receive any promotion from LG.*

Frances wrote some years later that 'I could not go to Genoa.'[15] This may have been simply because Maggie and Megan went; but there may have been other reasons. For much of the time Frances was busy supervising the building and furnishing of the new house at Churt, still referred to as 'Hindhead'. Amazingly Bron-y-de was designed, built and furnished within nine months of LG buying the land.† At the time LG left for Italy, however, Frances was ill again. During the six weeks LG was away – 8 April to 20 May – he wrote her no fewer than fourteen

---

* He fared better under LG's successors, serving for no fewer than eleven years as Under-Secretary for Air under Baldwin and Macdonald, and then briefly as Minister of Works under Neville Chamberlain.
† The house was designed by the fashionable young architect Philip Tilden, who had previously conceived the oriental splendour of Port Lympne for Sassoon and went on to renovate Chartwell Manor for Churchill.

letters, which are among the most passionate of the whole correspondence. And from his first letter, dated three days after his arrival in
Genoa, it seems that she had been undergoing some sort of operation.
The likelihood is that it was another abortion – probably her third.
Certainly LG was unusually anxious about her. Unfortunately we do
not have her replies, which might have shed some light on the matter;
and once again she was not keeping her diary.

Hen gariad bach anwyl aur chus melyn siwgair mel – yn gariad i gyd. [Like
honey and sugar, loved by all].

You are the sweetest little worry in the world. Oh how I worried about
you. I was quite distracted about 9.30 on Saturday morning when I got no
telegram on my arrival – well you can imagine my state. The world was
black and full of despair. Then came J.T.'s wire & the gloom cleared & the
blue skies appeared. Never saw Italy so beautiful as it looked at 2 pm on
Saturday.

Now make the most of your rest darling. I want to see you look so well
& free from all the lines of care & weariness when I return.

I am working so hard so as to get back as soon as possible to my sweetheart. Oh I do miss her so much. Every hour of the day I miss you *cariad
bach* . . .

If I am here beyond the end of April you must come along. If not I meet
you at Hindhead.

Fondest tenderest surest & most passionate love

Your own

D.[16]

It was more than a week before he wrote again: evidently Frances
had sent him a poem she had written. In the meantime the conference
had been all but wrecked by the bombshell that the two outcast nations,
Germany and Russia, had come together to sign a bilateral treaty of
their own on Easter Sunday. LG had to spend the next four weeks
battling to recover something from the wreckage of his hopes.

My own darling

Been reading your delicious letter & its Enclosure. What a farewell. I
wonder whether you really meant it. It looks uncommonly like it. What a
good thing it is only a 'fragment' – interrupted by my kisses. All the same
it is good poetry – uncommonly good stuff. Write another sweet on the

pangs of separation. I am glad you are going to Chekers [*sic*] altho' I succumbed to temptation & wired for you. J.T.'s wisdom saved you. The journey would have been most dangerous to you until you are completely recovered. I do want to see your dear face looking well & bonny.

The Conference is once more in serious peril. Damn German stupidity. I am working as I never worked in my life to save it . . .

Have you received my letter? You do not say a word about it. I have a horrible fear it may have wandered into other hands.

If the Conference is not through by next week I shall send for you. If it is then I should like to meet you at Chequers or Hindhead. Have you got the furniture in?

Fondest love
My own darling
D.[17]

His next, four days later, is a familiar mixture of self-pity, hypochondria and boastful defiance.

My own sweet
Had to sacrifice my Sunday rest to smooth over another French crisis. I am so glad dearest you are not *all* French otherwise you would be so difficult to handle. As it is I get a French crisis now & again dont I even with our Entente.

The Conference is still labouring heavily & without a boast I am the only man who can pull it through – but it is going to take such a lot out of my frame. If my health holds out I shall win . . .

I do so want you here. I passionately long for you & yet I know it would not be wise. The feeling is getting very bitter among the enemies of the Conference. They are ready to do anything to hit & to hurt me. If they bring me down the Conference goes.

Another week may see an improvement. I'll let you know at once. Be patient & brave my own *cariad bach anwyl*. You are all in all to me.

Ever & Ever your
D.[18]

Again, three days later:

My darling
I have had a simply diabolical day of work & worry. The Conference is

trembling on the edge of a precipice & I am doing all I can to save it – & I am just now very tired & wishing – oh so much – that my little girl was here to help me bear up . . .

If we stay here long you must come here. Can't bear it any longer – my own life & joy.

Fonder than ever of you. Need you here more than ever. More resolved than ever that you are mine & I am yours

Ever & Ever

Your weary old

Man.

Don't you worry my darling. I'll stand by you *whatever happens*.[19]

By the end of April LG had been in Genoa three weeks. His family were getting restive, which held out the possibility that he might be able to get Frances out instead. But that was easier said than done.

My own girl

Your darling letter cheered me up so much in my worries & troubles. You apologise for the length. Why my sweet I would not have missed one drop of its cordial. Keep writing until you can come here.

The French I could overcome were I certain of the Russians. But I am far from sure of them. They are fanatical Orientals . . . Never mind I'll go on fighting as long as the muzzle of a gun is out of the water. Then I shall have nothing to reproach myself with.

Domestic crises in addition to the International perplexities. Megan is getting very sick of this place. Worrying her mother for permission to return to London. It wouldn't do for you to come the moment they go. On the other hand if you come while they are here Megan is quite capable of taking advantage of that to say she insists upon returning because you are here. That would create a first class scandal as the place is a hotbed of gossip & rumour. I have never been so perplexed before what to do. *I want you here more than ever* because my troubles are greater. On the other hand the dangers of your coming are greater. What am I to do sweetheart? Do talk it over with J.T. & make up my mind for me. I am utterly incapable of decision . . .

If I could induce them to take a prolonged trip to Rome that would do.

Hiraeth mawr – cariad laserir [Huge longing]

Your old Pop.[20]

Evidently LG was feeling his age. But his next letter holds out – if only in fantasy – the dream that Frances might one day be able to bear his children. Perhaps in the misery of losing a third she had been pressing him about this.

My sweetheart

I am having the struggle of my life foot to foot & face to face. But I am still on the hopeful side. In a few days I can tell you whether I am off next week or whether I am booked for another three weeks. In the latter case I *must* have my dear little girl here. It is as much as I can do now not to wire for her. It is sometimes insupportable to be without her sweet face to soothe encourage stimulate – and reward. My sweetheart I do want you every moment of my troublesome days. With you I can face anything. Without you I care for nothing. If this Conference were to fail I should like to take Pussy to an obscure island in the South Seas where there are no cables letters or newspapers & then come back in 5 years – with the kittens – & see what has happened . . .

Be ready next week *cariad bach anwyl* . . . I am organising a trip to Rome for my family should we be staying on. Is that alright sweet? . . .

Fondest tenderest most eager love & affection to my girl

Papa.[21]

The next letter is full of LG's attempt to reach agreement with the Russians, in the face of French objections. He was now waiting for the Russian reply.

My girl

Don't apologise again for sending me too long letters. Apart from the fact that it is you & that when I read them I feel as if I were talking to the girl I love best in the world – your letters are full of interest. I want *all* the gossip political and otherwise. The political news is valuable to me – & the rest is most entertaining . . .

I see from the Sunday Express that the attacks made upon me by the hostile press both in France & in England are specially vicious – and of a personal character . . . They are out to down me if they can. They are getting desperate. That is why I hesitate so much darling about your coming – for I want you more than ever – & need you more than ever. Let the Bolshies reply first then I shall know where we are. If they refuse I shall be back next week – and *then*

If they give a favourable answer I shall remain & you can come – & *then* . . .
Fondest dearest love to the girl of my heart
Pop[22]

The next day he was still waiting, distracted by rumours of intrigues against him at home, plagued by flies and frustrated by inactivity.

I hate this waiting. Especially as my girl is not here. I want her more & more – & more. I am in a mood to chuck politics altogether and retire to Italy like Byron & Shelley who told work to go to the devil. I pass Byron's house every day.
Oh I am pining for your sweet happy companionship. I am angry this very day that I cannot get it – yes this very moment. Too angry to write.
My own love
Ever & ever & ever.

I am in a very bad temper with everyone around me. I have come to the end of my shilling shockers. The consumption is unparalleled. Can you send me Byron's poems (unexpurgated please) and such Ridgwell Cullum* as I have not read – & any other tales of adventure. I am so delighted to hear the news of Hindhead . . . Your descriptions of the place are thrilling. It was a lucky find. The often[er] I see the place the better I am pleased with the *Southern aspect*.[23]

The following week he still felt embattled, appealing to Frances for sympathy in his toils. He did not say whether his family were still there. But if they had gone home, he would presumably have summoned Frances to join him.

My own sweet girl . . .
Your letter cheered me greatly. They always do. They are well written & so full of life & interest apart from the sweet affection they breathe. They breathe into my nostrils the breath of life. That is why I am a living man . . .

---

* Ridgwell Cullum was a prolific British-born writer of westerns, to whom LG was particularly addicted. His books have titles like *The Twins of Suffering Creek*, *The Sheriff of Dyke Hole* and *The Tiger of Cloud River*.

When I return I will satisfy you as to my state of health! *Longing* to reassure you on that point – my own sweetheart.[24]

My own life sweetener

It is very hard to go through all this worry & perplexity without the partner I rely upon for comfort solace encouragement support counsel & joy. I have never felt the lack of your inspiration & love as much as I have the last 3 or 4 days. I have felt several times as if I could not stand it any longer. I have no one here who thinks it worth their while to cheer me up when I am oppressed & almost overwhelmed with anxieties.

The Russians difficult . . . The French selfish – the Germans impotent – the Italians are willing but feeble – the little countries scared. The Times devilish . . .

I am fighting the most difficult battle of my life – & the most decisive – for better or for worse. My girls letters give me a strength you can hardly appreciate – you modest little joy of my life. You don't know how much your words mean to me. Keep writing darling. Your letters thrill me like wine & I leap on to the fray with renewed strength.

To my love
Your own
Lover[25]

The next two letters are very brief. He was now busy again – though clearly Frances did not entirely trust him in her absence.

Cariad bach anwyl aur

Looks like my being back middle of next week. I am going to get something through but not all. Still it will mean a great advance. I am up to my eyes preparing it.

My fondest love to the little sweetheart. I am longing so much to clasp you in my arms.

Ever your own
Cariad[26]

Cariad bach anwyl aur chus melyn

Very hard day – but a very good day. Beat French hip & thigh. Looks as if we were going to get something substantial after all. It has been & still is a terrible fight.

Good boy? I should think so. I have been too busy for mischief had I
felt so inclined & I am not in the least disposed.

Thursday or Monday next.

My own love

D.[27]

LG remained defiantly optimistic. Hankey still admired his tireless
ingenuity and resourcefulness. But back in London J. T. Davies gave
Riddell a shrewd assessment of his dwindling power to square circles
and pull rabbits out of hats.

J.T. of course defended the Russian excursions, but then went on to say
that L.G.'s methods had rather worn out. No one believed in him when
acting as a negotiator. His methods were becoming too well known. They
worked in the early days. He would take one party into one room and tell
them one thing, and the other into another room and tell them another,
and thus influence their minds and bring them together. Now his methods
were so well known that this scheme did not work. Everyone was too suspicious of him, not only employers and labour in this country, but the statesmen
in other countries.

'I am bound to admit the truth of this criticism,' Riddell concurred.
'The real point is that you cannot rely on what L.G. says . . . He may
not actually tell a lie, but he will lead you to believe what he considers
will induce you to do what he wants. The consequence is that you
never know where you are.'[28]

LG's deviousness had worked with the Irish just six months earlier.
But it did not work with the Russians. By the time he wrote his last letter
from Genoa he was trying to set up a commission to study the whole
question of war debts; but this was no more than a fig leaf to cover the
failure of his initial hope of achieving a comprehensive settlement. The
great conference by which he had hoped to restore his position had
proved a failure. But he still had his homecoming to look forward to.

My own darling

I feel as if you were now almost in my arms. Saturday night. I could
dine with you either that night or Sunday. I would prefer Saturday. That is
the best we can do for a few days.

The fight is still desperate but I am hopeful of saving my last scheme
. . . The fight for peace will continue.

Next week I shall have to make a speech in the House. That bothers me
– but I shall see *& seize & squeeze & scrunch* my girl before that & after
that. So all will be well.

I stand by every word & syllable of that written declaration & more
now than Ever.*

My own
Your
Sweetheart etc etc[29]

Presumably Frances had been writing as frequently as LG, but only
her last letter survives, written from 10 Downing Street on 17 May,
three days before LG's return. Much of it was political gossip; but she
also reported on the progress of the building work at Churt – and for
the first time dared to try on the role of wife.

My own darling little man

Your return seems to be once again postponed, & I am despairing of
ever seeing you again. But it does look as though you were going to get
something out of the Conference after all, & you deserve it after the fight
you have put up . . .

I went down to Hindhead again yesterday. The wing is finished & the
furniture in, & Mrs Munton goes down tomorrow. They are getting on
very well with the rest of the house & it ought to be finished by the middle
of June. Your bedroom is going to be awfully nice – a lovely large room
. . . I came back with some produce – eggs & rhubarb & flowers, so that
I felt as if I were already Mrs Ll.G., or that at any rate I had developed in
advance some of the characteristics of your illustrious consort!

It is raining today, however, & that will delay the building again. It is a
great nuisance – altogether I am feeling very depressed, what with the
weather & your return being continually put off. I feel as though I simply
can't endure another weekend without you, *cariad,* I have simply got to the
end of my tether.

The struggle at Genoa seems to be continuing right up to the last. My

* What written declaration? Does this refer to the form of contract that Frances copied
out in 1913 (see Chapter 4)? Does this mean that LG did sign it after all?

heart goes out to you, my darling, for it must be terribly trying for you. But I will try to make up for all your worries, best beloved. You will let me, won't you? I only wish we could go right away together.

Till we meet, love of my life
P.[30]

The outcome of Genoa was disappointing, but LG was still met at Victoria by large crowds, half the Cabinet and the Duke of Atholl representing the King. Presumably he slipped away to dine with Frances that Saturday evening as planned, since the next day he went to Trent Park (where Bonar Law was also staying). But he did not arrive there till four o'clock, so maybe Frances took him to Churt earlier to inspect the progress of Bron-y-de. He spent the next two weeks in London catching up with domestic business and reporting to the House of Commons, before going to Criccieth for the first week of June to recharge his batteries yet again, for what would turn out to be his final effort to save his premiership.

20

DECLINE AND FALL

While LG was at Criccieth he was warned by the Home Secretary, Edward Shortt – one of the more obscure occupants of that post – that Irish terrorists were at large again (despite the 1921 treaty) and therefore Chequers might not be safe for him. LG responded that Criccieth was not safe either. 'It would be easy for anyone just to walk up to the house & kidnap or assassinate him' – even though there were always two or three policemen on guard duty and two detectives living nearby'.[1] Less than three weeks later, in June 1922, this threat came very much closer when Sir Henry Wilson, who had just been elected as an Ulster Unionist MP, was shot dead on his front doorstep in Belgravia. The shock impelled Frances to take up her diary again, for the first time in several months.

Just heard the sad news about Henry Wilson. Will the Irish trouble never end? D. very upset, as we all are. Whatever he has done lately, he was a most lovable person, & we were very near him during the war. Can scarcely believe the news. It will put the whole Irish question back into the melting pot again. D. had been warned by Shortt that there were dangerous Irishmen in London, & S. advised him not to go to Chequers, but we had been rather inclined to discount the warning at this juncture. However Shortt was right.[2]

'Isn't it a terrible thing about Sir Henry Wilson's murder?' Frances wrote to her sister Muriel. 'We have just heard that one of the men [that is, one of the IRA gunmen who were arrested at the scene] is a messenger at the Ministry of Labour, so it makes one feel a little uneasy.

We are all very upset about it.'[3] Three days later the German Foreign Minister Walter Rathenau was also murdered in Berlin. 'It makes one frightened,' she confessed in her diary. She consoled herself that 'one good effect of these murders will be to make Scotland Yard more careful and to increase the protection of Ministers & prominent people.'[4] But did she consider that increased protection would make it more difficult for the Prime Minister to visit his secretary's flat and go for quiet walks *à deux* in Richmond Park?

Another unwanted benefit Frances derived from Wilson's murder was that the *Sunday Times* reprinted a sketch of him that she had written – anonymously – the year before as one of a series about the personalities of the Paris Peace Conference. Probably intended as a counter to Maynard Keynes's hugely influential polemic *The Economic Consequences of the Peace*, with its critical portraits of LG and the other leaders, Frances's sketches were published in book form under the teasing title *Makers of the New World, by One Who Knows Them*. The identity of the author was in fact practically given away by the opening essay, a gushing and wholly uncritical portrait of LG. It not only paid tribute to his political genius, but was lightened with more personal insights, including a rebuke to those who imagined that the Prime Minister was not a great reader.

> I was fortunate enough to meet a short time ago someone who was in the process of putting Mr Lloyd George's library in order, and I was told that the number of books he has collected is remarkable . . . Grote, Gibbon, Mommsen, Macaulay, Froude, Green, Bagehot – these well-worn volumes have been his companions for many years, and he constantly refers to them. Carlyle, Scott, Dickens, Thackeray, Smollett, Fielding, Sterne, are familiar friends to him, and of the more modern authors his favourites are perhaps Meredith, Stevenson and Wells; but Mr Bernard Shaw would probably learn with surprise . . . that Mr Lloyd George has read every one of his books as they appeared . . .
>
> He has dipped, too, into the classics, not in the originals, of course, for that he does not aspire to, but in translations. Cicero's letters he reads over and over again. Thucydides he read from cover to cover for the first time during a long sea voyage, and has since re-read many times. He has read much French literature, both in French and in the translations. Victor Hugo is one of his favourites, and he has read most of the novels of Anatole France . . .

Last, but not least, his knowledge of the Bible is thorough, and he can give you chapter and verse of almost any quotation . . .[5]

The last, at least, was true. For the rest – even though LG was indeed better read than he was often given credit for – Frances was outrageously gilding the lily. We know that during the Genoa conference all he wanted was an unending supply of thrillers, plus the unexpurgated bits of Byron. This public paean to her beloved (even if anonymous) was carrying loyalty a little too far.

The rest of the book, however, is not at all bad. Naturally the portraits of Woodrow Wilson and Clemenceau, Briand and Foch, Bonar Law, Balfour and others reflect LG's views. Some are admiring and affectionate, some critical, others no more than perfunctory; but the best are well written and perceptive, showing that Frances could have been an excellent journalist. Moreover several of them could only have been written by a woman. Briand, for instance, she describes as 'the most fascinating man in French politics . . . especially attractive to women', and asks how this can be.

A pale, somewhat haggard face, with a large untidy moustache and great black brows. The latter half-concealing sleepy grey eyes, half-closed and suggesting a cat in repose but nevertheless on the alert. His features are irregular, his hair is unkempt, his shoulders are round and his chest is narrow. His general appearance is of an untidy and badly groomed man, with a heavy, frowning, almost sulky face. Such a man fascinating? Absurd. But one understands the enchantment when he becomes interested and animated. His face lights up and a beautiful smile illumines and transfigures the countenance; the sleepy eyes begin to flash fire, and the heavy flabby features become expressive and mobile. One understands when he begins to speak and one hears his beautiful voice – deep, resonant, able to express every emotion and arouse every feeling of which his audience is capable.[6]

It was often said that Briand was very like LG. But several more of these portraits suggest a woman decidedly susceptible to older men – Henry Wilson, for instance:

Tall and lanky, almost gaunt in appearance, he walks with loose limbs and stooping body. But his face is attractive in its ugliness, with the lines and cross-lines that cover it, running contrary to the direction taken by any other wrinkles on any other face . . . It is a face that makes you feel you can never know enough about it. It arrests the attention and fascinates, and when you have looked at it long, you feel you must turn and look again, to be reassured on some particular point.

His eyes are blue, piercing blue, and almost turquoise at times . . . He has a scrubby moustache which does very little to cover a large, large mouth, a sensitive tender mouth . . . His voice is deep and musical . . . full of rich expression and quite uncommon . . . He is whimsical, daring, deadly in conflict, but withal intensely human, intensely sympathetic, mischievous, imaginative. No danger could frighten this man, morally or physically.[7]

No wonder she was upset when Wilson was killed.

As well as the statesmen and the generals, Frances's gallery of Conference characters included Hankey, Philip Kerr and Riddell – further clues that the author was close to LG – as well as the description of the family atmosphere in the Hotel Majestic and the risqué Saturday dances already quoted. The articles began appearing in the *Sunday Times* in May 1921 and ran for eight weeks. LG was 'very pleased', Frances noted in her diary, '& of course is telling no end of people that I have written them! Then he will be surprised when it gets known.'[8] Some journalists clearly knew the author's identity, because when Bonar Law became Prime Minister the next year, her friend Philippe Millet reprinted Frances's appreciation in *Le Petit Parisien* and told her it was 'the best thing he had seen on Bonar Law'. ('So I feel rather flattered,' Frances wrote to LG.[9]) Her articles were evidently well regarded by the *Sunday Times* as well, since soon after they appeared the editor, Leonard Rees, wrote her an intriguing letter, which suggested that she was supplying him with inside information on a regular basis.

Many thanks for your notes. I've used all I've had from you up to the present (one is standing over till next Sunday), two having gone in our 'Political Notes', and am asking for more. Also for any light and leading you can give me each week.[10]

How long had Frances been feeding Rees titbits? And did LG know about it? Almost certainly he did, and her information was more in the nature of spinning than leaking. LG had an early grasp of the importance of steering the press and may well have used Frances for this purpose. The *Sunday Times* 'Political Notes' column was indeed notably sympathetic to the Prime Minister, and several stories that summer – specifically from Gairloch – show clear traces of her input. We do not know how long it went on. But the connection was consolidated the following year when Frances's sister Muriel – now twenty – became Rees's secretary. She later became secretary to the literary editor, Leonard Russell, and worked for the *Sunday Times* in various capacities, on and off, for many years.

Makers of the New World received mixed notices. Though several reviewers felt that it came late to an already crowded field, *The Times* wrote that there was 'still room for such a crisp and pungent volume of short studies'.[11] The *Times Literary Supplement* likewise thought that 'One Who Knows Them' did 'little to extend our knowledge', but nevertheless showed 'an undoubted gift for concise and caustic character-etching . . . Impertinent the author often is, but sometimes the impertinence is clever.'[12] Only *The Nation* was wholly dismissive: 'There is not a line of portraiture to make the subjects clear to the mind, the artist trying to get his picture by tangling together vague and woolly phrases.'[13] But then the chairman of *The Nation* was Maynard Keynes. *The Times* critic, noting correctly that the 'real hero' of the book was the Prime Minister, suggested slyly that 'to his thirteen portraits of politicians, soldiers and journalists the author has unconsciously added a fourteenth, that of himself'.

> He is one who sets the man of action above the abstract theorist, who prefers a shrewd sense of realities to the parade of idealism, who prizes initiative and despises routine . . . Through impatience with the doctrinaire he grows tolerant of the opportunist; to escape hypocrisy he falls into cynicism; he is sometimes too dazzled by 'success' to weigh its real value.[14]

It is almost as if the reviewer thought LG had written them himself.

Meanwhile Frances was handling negotiations with publishers for the rights to LG's memoirs. It was clear by 1922 that his lease on Downing Street was running out. He was constantly declaring that he wanted to retire to write his book, partly to tell his side of the story of the war, partly to cash in on the large amounts of money being offered to him. He actually started writing before he left office – he showed 15,000 words to Riddell at the beginning of September – and it was not only British publishers who were taking an interest, as Frances recorded.

> Last Friday Marshall, representative of The New York Times, came to see me with a view to getting D's book. I think they will make a substantial offer. I lunched with Butterworth the previous Tuesday. He said the most he would be able to offer would be £40,000. Marshall told me that Butterworth had subsequently approached him & offered him the *American* rights for £50,000![15]

At the same time Frances was busy putting her stamp on Bron-y-de. Riddell went there for the first time on 29 July.

> To Churt, L.G's new house high up among the heather – a pretty but lonely spot with fine views. The house comfortable and well-designed with spacious bedroom and library for L.G. – the other rooms quite small. The decoration and furnishing in good taste. The joint production of Tilden, the architect, and Miss Stevenson – the latter in full charge and very busy. No gardens as yet, but great preparations. L.G. spends most of his time sitting in the loggias, of which there are three, one outside his bedroom window and two on the ground floor. After Genoa, where he considers he derived so much benefit from being so much out of doors, he is keener than ever on fresh air and stays out until quite late. Meals are served in one of the loggias – not an unmixed pleasure during the coldish weather.[16]

It was only sensible that LG should consult Riddell about the marketing of his memoirs. Riddell was both a newspaperman and a lawyer, whereas Frances had no experience of negotiations of this sort beyond the sale of her own articles and book.* Riddell thought LG needed a professional agent.

> LG much concerned about his book, the sale of which is in Miss Stevenson's hands. After a long conference it was agreed to instruct Curtis Brown, the literary agent, and I dictated a letter for Miss Stevenson to write to him.

LG was hoping to get between £80,000 and £100,000, which would

---

* Three months earlier Frances had signed a contract with the literary agents A. M. Heath & Co. to write an 'exclusive' article for *Good Housekeeping* on the position of a Cabinet minister's secretary, for a fee of fifty guineas.[17]

be the largest sum ever paid for a book. 'It is not so much the money,' he boasted, 'but I should like to feel that I have got a higher rate of payment than any other author.' Riddell, however, suspected that Frances had her own agenda.

> Miss Stevenson's sister is now with the 'Sunday Times' and Miss S. who contributes to that paper is of course eager that the Berrys should have the opportunity of acquiring the British serial rights.[18]*

In August it was announced that LG had signed a contract with the American publishers Funk & Wagnall said to be worth £90,000, with serialisation in the *New York Times* and the *Chicago Tribune* and British publication by Cassell (Frances's publisher). Immediately, however, he was criticised for making money from the war, and quickly backtracked, declaring piously that he would give all the proceeds to charity. Maggie took a rather different line from the one she had taken earlier about Carnegie's money.

> I did tell you not to take the money for the book, didn't I? That's a feather in my cap. You can write another book to make money, but not on the war. I could not touch a penny of it.[19]

As a result of this row, LG's literary enthusiasm waned. He decided to forget about the book for the present and write topical articles for the press instead, which were equally well paid and syndicated around the world. The *New York Times* accordingly demanded the return of the advance it had already paid him. Instead of saying that LG was within his rights, as Riddell thought she could have done, Frances let the matter drag on until December, when the paper issued a writ; LG then had to repay the money amid a lot of bad publicity. 'The truth is,' Riddell wrote bluntly, 'that Miss S. is not equal to a job of this sort and the solicitor acting for L.G. did not manage it well.'[20]

Riddell also found LG uncertain about his political future. 'He is feeling the constant strain, but does not want to relinquish the position . . . I doubt if he will go until he is turned out or thinks it impossible to carry on.'[21] In the meantime the government drifted while pressure

---

* William and Gomer Berry – later Lords Camrose and Kemsley – had bought the *Sunday Times* in 1915. They later acquired the *Daily Sketch* and *Daily Graphic* (1926) and the *Daily Telegraph* (1928).

mounted on the Tory leadership to end the Coalition. In August LG
went up to Criccieth, but stayed only ten days, claiming that he could
get no holiday there. 'Criccieth is impossible for me in August & Sept.
I am like a beetle in a glass case or a tiger in a menagerie.'[22]* By the
end of the month he was back in London, writing to Maggie that he
feared the Coalition was 'breaking up over the Tory revolt'. He added,
'I am off with Shakespeare *alone* to Churt.'[24]

If this was true – and LG's very protestation makes one doubt it –
it was so only for a couple of days, for when Riddell went down on
1 September he found the usual crowd of colleagues and secretaries,
including Frances. Over the next few days LG held a series of ministerial meetings, mainly concerned with the escalating war between
Greece and Turkey. Always a passionate Hellenophile, LG had rashly
committed Britain to the side of the Greeks, but they were now in
danger of being overrun. When he wrote again to Maggie on 6
September, he was back in Downing Street and sounded near the end
of his tether.

> I am here for 2 or 3 days for Cabinet conferences. I have not had much of
> a holiday. The Greek situation & Poincaré & the political situation at home
> have occupied me very much . . . I really cannot stand this much longer. I
> don't believe my nerve & spirits can sustain the constant wear & tear. I
> feel depressed, dejected & very much in the mood to chuck the whole thing
> up . . . I don't like the outlook & as I am not clear what to do I am worried
> & unhappy.[25]

The next weekend he was much more cheerful. 'I am tired and have
had a hard day,' he said as he sat down to dinner with Maggie – who
had now joined him in London.

> Beyond this he gave no sign of anxiety or distress at the situation. His
> courage is remarkable and he shows to best advantage when encountering
> 'dreadful odds'. Some of his policies are not happy, but when called upon
> to face a crisis, he is splendid.

---

* On 19 August Geoffrey Shakespeare, who was with LG at Criccieth, wrote to Frances
at the Castle Hotel, Harlech – which suggests that she was spending her holiday there
in order to snatch a couple of secret trysts with LG.[23] This would have been extraordinarily risky, since he was liable to be recognised anywhere he went in north Wales.
But what otherwise would be the point of her holidaying in Harlech?

It was Maggie who on this occasion seemed to Riddell 'depressed and not at all in her usual spirits'.[26]

As the crisis of his government approached, LG was still shuttling between his wife and his mistress, as he had for the whole of his premiership. Maggie might hold sway in Downing Street, but on 23 September Riddell noted again that Bron-y-de was emphatically Frances's domain. As he arrived, his car overtook LG and Frances walking up the drive; he stopped and gave them a lift up to the house. Then over the weekend he noted: 'Miss S. much in evidence. She has planned the house and garden and assumes complete control. We left her at Churt when we departed.'[27] There were a number of other guests, not all members of LG's political family: they included Bonar Law's daughter Ishbel and her husband, Sir Frederick Sykes, who was about to become a Tory MP. Yet Frances was clearly the hostess.

The end came four weeks later. The government was split, with Churchill and Birkenhead backing LG's determination to resist Turkey's advance on the Dardanelles, but most of the rest of the Cabinet, the Tory party, the press and the public strongly opposed to what was widely seen as reckless adventurism. The crisis, which was prudently defused by the British commander on the ground on 30 September, gave the Tory dissidents their chance to strike. The victory of an Independent Conservative at a by-election in Newport was the last encouragement they needed. In a famous vote at the Carlton Club on 19 October, Tory MPs voted by 185 to 88 to withdraw from the government. LG immediately resigned and Bonar Law emerged from retirement to form a purely Conservative administration pending a General Election to be held on 15 November.

LG was remarkably cheerful about his downfall, mainly because after seventeen years continuously in office he needed a rest and was confident that he would be back before long.* All the contemporary accounts – by Riddell, Hankey, Tom Jones and Edward Grigg – describe his high spirits at the release that he had never quite been able to engineer for himself. The person who was least happy at his leaving office was Frances. She was in Downing Street on the day of the Carlton Club vote – she telephoned Riddell to tell him that LG had gone to the Palace – but she could not be with him that evening, even though Maggie

* LG's record of nearly seventeen consecutive years in the Cabinet is still unmatched. Both Kenneth Clarke and Malcolm Rifkind chalked up eighteen years in government between 1979 and 1997, but neither reached the Cabinet before 1985.

somewhat strangely went off to a meeting in East Ham. LG dined in the upstairs flat with just J. T. Davies (who 'hardly spoke a word throughout the meal') and Jones, who recorded his table talk. Did he regret leaving No. 10? Jones asked him. 'Not at all,' LG replied.

> He had no attachment to a house and its furniture. Churt was somewhat different. It was there one was creating something of one's own. He was attached to people like a dog not to a hearth like a cat.[28]

LG did not actually leave Downing Street for another three days. On Saturday 22 October he went to Leeds to make a speech, leaving Frances and Davies with the dismal chore of packing up. On Sunday evening Jones found Frances in her office next to the Cabinet Room 'burning masses of papers in the fireplace, and looking sadder than I have ever seen her'.[29] The next day Jones and Hankey went back to No. 10, where they found LG with Grigg, Shakespeare and Frances, still 'full of fun' and 'absolutely hilarious', imagining himself coming back as leader of a deputation to ask some favour of Bonar Law and play-acting all the parts – 'until we were all in roars of laughter except Miss Stevenson who could hardly conceal her sadness at parting with No. 10'.[30] Then he drove away to Churt, accompanied by Gwilym. Frances had nowhere to go but back to Morpeth Mansions – alone. After ten years at the heart of government her future was suddenly a question mark.

PART THREE

21

INTO THE UNKNOWN

With LG's fall from power in the autumn of 1922, Frances's life was at a crossroads. Up to this point, from the moment she had started doing odd jobs for the Chancellor of the Exchequer in 1912, one thing had simply led to another. She had followed him from the Treasury to the Ministry of Munitions, the War Office and finally 10 Downing Street. So long as LG was in office – before, during and then after the war – the pace of events had left them little time for reflection. He came to rely on her, both as an indispensable member of his staff and as a source of private solace and refreshment; and she was happy to serve his need in both respects, intoxicated by his vows of love and by the heady world of politics to which he had introduced her: the belief that she was helping him to make history. Now, however, outside the bubble of government, everything was suddenly uncertain.

On the one hand, there was her professional position to consider. She had now worked for nearly ten years in Whitehall, six of them as secretary to the Prime Minister. She had considerable experience at the highest level and some public recognition of her work, manifested in the CBE and a growing number of respectful newspaper articles, even the odd fan letter. But she had no official status and no security. Would LG still want her to go on working for him out of office, in opposition or retirement? Or should she take up the opportunity which at that moment was undoubtedly open to her, and become a career civil servant?

A few weeks before LG left office a Canadian newspaper published a perceptive profile, which she thought worth keeping. The writer's expectation was clearly that if the Prime Minister had a female secretary at all, she should be a middle-aged dragon. Frances was then almost thirty-four, but did not look her age.

> There can be few people in the world who know more about the Prime Minister as he really is than his private secretary, Miss Frances Stevenson, and I have seen few young women less like private secretaries to Prime Ministers or other Ministers than this charming pretty young woman. Miss Stevenson looks a mere girl with a rosy complexion, large beautiful blue eyes, fair hair and a slim figure, and her manner is as pretty and feminine as the most confirmed hater of women in affairs could desire. Yet she has an extraordinarily good brain, is the soul of discretion and is said to know all the secrets of the Cabinet without ever breathing a word of them to anyone. She talks like an ordinary, unspoiled attractive girl, and only occasionally one catches a glimpse of the unusual character and knowledge that lie below the surface. 'You do look so young to hold that post,' I said to her. Miss Stevenson dimpled most pleasingly. 'Perhaps I am older than I look,' she suggested, and we let it go at that.[1]

The exceptional nature of her position is further highlighted by a letter Frances received just after she left Downing Street, from a woman writing from Eaton Terrace, SW1, diffidently thanking her 'for all you have been & all you have done'.

> It's been a splendid thing for all of us humble secretarial rank & filers to have had you at the top. The height at which women keep their professional flag flying & never once to be lowered matters awfully, I think, in what are still rather pioneer days, & the record of your fine running will, I hope, go down in history. I'd like you to know therefore, that there are many who feel like that about it.[2]

This must have gratified what remained of her youthful, but now somewhat tarnished, feminism. What would the writer have thought had she known that Frances had got to the top only by sleeping with her boss? Once there, she had certainly flown the flag for working women. But in her heart she knew that she was not quite the role model she appeared.

The matter of her future, however, depended on a more important question. How would her relationship with LG adjust to their new circumstances? Could they simply carry on as before? Or, if it changed, would it grow closer, with the hope that she might eventually be able to come out of the shadows? Or might it cool and eventually come to an end? Away from the pressures of office, would he still need her as much as before? And she, without the adrenaline of power, would she still find the same fulfilment in devoting herself to him? Might LG, as he got older, go back increasingly to his wife? Or would he, on the contrary, want to be with Frances more than ever and, as his public responsibilities declined, feel free to leave his wife and acknowledge Frances openly?

Could she really trust his promises of undying love: his assurances over recent months that all he really wanted, when released from office, was to settle down with her? Maybe even have 'kittens' with her? On the one hand, LG's life would now centre on Churt, the house that Frances – far more than Maggie – had helped to create, and Frances could look forward to continuing to shape and run it as their shared home. Moreover she and LG had been making new wills together – a sign of serious commitment on his part.[3] He had no intention of withdrawing from politics (except briefly for a well-earned rest), but was confident of returning to office before long, when he would need her help as much as ever. On the other hand, his marriage was still important to him, rooted in his childhood and his constituency. Though nowadays he and Maggie lived such separate lives, Frances had to accept that there was no chance of LG leaving his wife; and here his unsatisfied political ambition cut both ways. No more than in 1912 was he going to shipwreck his career by risking divorce, still less by fathering illegitimate children.

If she wanted children, therefore – which despite, or because of, her two or three abortions, part of her still desperately did – Frances was heading towards the point of no return. She had already passed up several offers of marriage. Stuart Brown was now married – to a colleague in the India Office – so that option was closed.* So was Sir Albert Stern. One wonders whether she might have married Philip

---

* His wife, formerly Dorothy Freeth, had been a friend of Frances. When their engagement was announced, Janet Stevenson wrote unkindly: 'How killing about Miss Frieth [sic] and Stuart Brown. I wonder who did the proposing?'[4] Stuart had served in the war, which left him somewhat frail for the rest of his life; but he returned to the India Office and finished as acting Permanent Secretary before retiring with a knighthood in 1941. He died in 1952.

Sassoon, of whom she was certainly fond, who would have given her a life of luxury and social position by which she was certainly tempted. Sassoon used to write her effusive letters, addressed to 'Dearest Frances' and sending 'loads and loads of love'.[5] There is a wonderful photograph of him tempting her with an apple at Lympne in 1920 or 1921. Or maybe Philip Kerr, who called her 'Steve' – in which case she would have finished up as the Marchioness of Lothian. In fact neither Sassoon nor Kerr ever married, so perhaps there was no real possibility there. But she was never short of admirers. A widowed banker named Sir Thomas Jaffrey, for instance, asked her to marry him in 1931.[6] When it came down to it, however, Frances had given her heart totally and romantically to LG: the sacrifice of respectability – and motherhood – that she had made only made the sanctity of her commitment more complete: she had regarded herself as unofficially 'married' since 1913, and the more of her life she had invested in that relationship, the less likely she was to break it off – even though she knew that she faced an indefinite future of discretion and duplicity, with no children, an ageing lover and (since Maggie was younger than LG) no realistic likelihood of eventual marriage.

One consolation was that her parents seem finally to have accepted her choice as permanent. As well as the letter from her father in 1921 already quoted, there is one from her mother in May 1922, on the anniversary of Paul's death, in which Louise drew comfort from the fact that she had her other children, 'and what good daughters you all are', which suggests that Frances's wicked life had been forgiven. 'I am glad the PM is better,' she concluded, and ended: 'Is Megan ill down there?' – that is, at Genoa.[7] A few weeks later, at the time of Henry Wilson's murder, she wrote to Frances: 'Tell the PM to take care of himself – it makes me feel quite anxious about you all.'[8] And finally Muriel, on holiday in Kent that summer, asked after LG's dog Chong, whom she obviously knew well. 'I wish she were down here . . . Will you give my love to the PM, or more properly, give him my regards?'[9] They all wrote quite naturally as though LG was part of the family.

In the event LG's loss of office – and even the fact that he was never to regain it – made remarkably little difference. Frances's ambiguous position resumed very much as before and continued that way for another eighteen years: still in public LG's devoted secretary, still in private sharing him with Maggie, the eternal mistress still subordinate to the wife and obliged to make herself scarce whenever Maggie came out of Wales – even when she came to Churt. LG made no attempt to change the status quo, which suited him admirably, but settled down permanently to a life of effective bigamy, divided between Caernarvonshire and Surrey; while Frances attempted to sublimate her frustration in lightly disguised fiction.

When the Lloyd Georges left Downing Street they at first rented – for sixteen guineas a week – Edward Grigg's house in Vincent Square, Westminster, to serve as a temporary London home. Later they moved to Cheyne Walk, in Chelsea, and then to Addison Road in Kensington. But it took more than two weeks to move all their things out of No. 10, as Maggie described despairingly to Olwen.*

We are very busy packing to go away . . . I have never seen such a lot of rubbish collected in all my life. The general election will be a rest after this. I can't see myself oping [sic] all these cases if I live to be a hundred. I leave here for Cric. & B'nawelon after this. We have taken a furnished house . . . & *Tada* [Father] is in such a fever haste to get there but I am not going until I return from Wales . . . I hope we shall have a house of our own by then or back in No. 10 perhaps, I can't see Bonar lasting *too* long.[10]

Megan echoed her mother's account, with equal confidence that LG would be back before long:

We are packing as hard as ever we can. The mess is indescribable – books, photos, papers, caskets, over-flowing waste paper baskets, men in aprons, depressed messengers, abound in rooms in the house in vast numbers . . . *Tada* had wonderful receptions both at Manchester & Leeds & made wonderful speeches in both places. The people are absolutely with him . . . Whatever happens *Tada* will be the power. He will be tremendous in opposition – & Bonar knows it.[11]

While Maggie and Megan supervised the family's packing, Frances's task, with J. T. Davies, was to dismantle the office and remove everything to LG's new headquarters in Abingdon Street, just opposite the Commons.† He wrote her one letter from Vincent Square, which

* From 1919 to 1923 Olwen was away in India where her husband, Tom Carey Evans, was serving as doctor to the Viceroy.
† The street suffered bomb damage in the war and was subsequently demolished.

suggests that they were finding it difficult to make time to be alone: a walk they planned evidently fell through.[12] In her diary thirteen years later Frances recalled 'the quick evacuation from Downing Street' as a 'dreary time', with 'D. sitting distrait in an uncomfortable armchair in Ned Grigg's uncomfortable house . . . But never once did I imagine that he would be in the wilderness for 13 years at least. When D. said "Ten" . . . I laughed & did not believe him or think that he meant it.'[13]

In fact LG did not mean it. He had no more expectation than anyone else that he would be out for long. He fought a vigorous election, rallying his supporters – now known as Lloyd George Liberals – around the country, while Maggie held the fort in north Wales. 'I don't care much who gets in,' he told her, 'as long as Bonar does not get a working majority. I am working for a break 2 or 3 years hence after we have formed a Centre party with a strong progressive bias.'[14] In fact the Tories won a comfortable majority of seventy-five, while Labour with 142 seats became for the first time the official Opposition. LG held on to sixty-two, the Asquithian Liberals fifty-four. But LG's good humour was undimmed. The following weekend Riddell found him at Churt with Maggie and Megan plus a girl called Peggy Lewis, probably a friend of Megan's. Frances might see Bron-y-de as her domain, yet when Maggie exerted her precedence she was banished – and with other young female company to play up to, LG did not appear to be missing her.

> To Churt for the weekend. Found L.G. in wonderful form, laughing and carrying on like a boy . . . serenading and making love to Miss Lewis, as if he had been a boy of eighteen instead of a man of sixty . . .
>
> The change in the atmosphere since he has been out of office is amazing. Now he is working like a little dynamo to break up the Conservative Party by bringing the more advanced section to his flag, to join up with the 'Wee Frees' [the Asquithians], and to detach the more moderate members of the Labour Party – this with the object of forming a Central Party of which he will be leader.[15]

This was to be LG's political objective, in one form or another, for the next ten years. In the meantime, however, he planned to take a long holiday in the sun at Algeciras in the south of Spain (just west of Gibraltar). He managed to contrive that Frances accompanied him for the first fortnight – presumably Maggie wanted to spend Christmas in Wales – before his family joined him, at which point Frances had to go home. It was a sharp lesson that things were not going to be any different for her just because LG was no longer Prime Minister. Nevertheless the two of them (with J. T. Davies as a sort of chaperon) had a full two weeks together before Maggie and Megan came out on 7 January 1923, followed by Riddell and a stream of political colleagues. They had a blissful time, judging from the long letter LG wrote her on 14 January, protesting how much he was missing her since she left.

My own love

The effect of our week's separation has been to deepen the conviction of my heart that I cannot do without you my girl. But as that conviction was already rooted so deeply in my soul that no fingers can tear it out it seems superfluous cruelty to inflict these days of longing pain upon me to teach me something I already knew so well.

But I have changed my mind thoroughly on one or two subjects. I thought Algeciras one of the most heavenly spots I ever alighted upon. I no longer think so. If you remember I thought those walks through the garden so thrilling that it did not surprise me that God – who has lived long enough to know a thing or two – took a walk in the cool of the evening through the garden of Eden. But I take quite a different view of this garden now. It is no longer Paradise for Eve is gone. I constantly find myself reckoning the number of days before I can decently leave this wilderness of frumps . . .

The Chamberlains have been here two days [plus a variety of other guests] but add them all up & throw in a whole hotel full of a most miscellaneous assortment . . . & they dont make one Pussy – no not even a Pussy *bach* at her worst. The sun may be shining here brightly & warmly & England may be cold & wet & forbidding but my own girl will be there & that is worth all the old suns in the firmament . . .

Write soon & write often & write long & tell me all the news. I want to know all about Churt – & any political news of interest – but mostly I want to know all my sweetheart is doing. If she loves me as I love her then I am happy.

To my darling
D.[16]

When Riddell arrived on 11 January he found LG restless and out of sorts, feeling the loss of office more than he admitted.

He is like a pretty woman who has been absolutely all the rage and who is being somewhat neglected. Even the smallest attentions are gratifying, whereas in other times they would have been disregarded or treated as a matter of course.[17]

In Frances's absence, LG's inexhaustible need for female attention was met by Megan's friend Thelma Cazalet, who had become a sort of adopted daughter to both LG and Maggie. Thelma joined him on walks before breakfast when his family were still in bed, and listened as he read her his latest syndicated article. He once told Thelma she was 'one of the only two women who never bored him', and invited her to join his staff – presumably not on the same terms as Frances. Though she had the good sense to refuse ('I loved him, but was never in love with him,' she wrote many years later), she still used to help out a bit, which Frances might have resented. But in fact they were friends until Megan came between them.

Since Megan and I were such close friends, and she and Frances were not, it was clearly too awkward to be girls together with both. I therefore told Frances frankly that it was best and wisest if our friendship ended, and she had the good feeling to understand and agree amicably.[18]

Meanwhile Frances had not gone straight back to England, but had stopped over in Paris, staying at the Hotel Crillon on the place de la Concorde: from now on Frances never stayed at any but the best hotels. There she started trying to write a novel to assuage some of the heartache she felt at her ambiguous situation. Not a trace of her unhappiness, however, leaked into the long and loving letter she wrote LG on 16 January – though it is strange that she failed to catch his sixtieth birthday the next day. He always attached great importance to birthdays.

My own darling little man
    This will not arrive in time for your birthday, but it brings with it every fond wish for a very happy year, & many, many others besides. I cannot grumble at not being with you on your birthday, after the beautiful time we have had together, but I have been thinking very lovingly of you all day, my darling instead. It is only just over a week since we parted, but it seems like a hundred years. When I reckoned it up, it seemed quite incredible that only a week had passed. I do hope that the next two weeks will go a little

more quickly, or you will find me quite grey-haired by the time you return.

I have enjoyed being in Paris – as much as I can enjoy anything without you . . .

There followed a long report of conversations with her journalist friends Millet and 'Pertinax', and the British Ambassador, about the French occupation of the Ruhr and resurgent bellicosity towards Germany. ('People talk here quite openly of going to Berlin.') This resumé was what he had said he wanted, so she provided it; but then she continued:

I am afraid this is a very dull letter, my darling, & you will probably have given it up before you arrive at this. I would like to have occupied all the space in words of love & affection, & then I should not have told you half of what I have been feeling for you. I try & picture to myself what you are doing, but it is difficult as so little news reaches here of your movements. I gather that the sea has not been good enough for you to cross to Ceuta, but perhaps by now you have already gone.

Take care of yourself, darling man, for my sake. I am longing so much already to see you again. I cease to live when I am not with you, & I shall only commence again when we are reunited.

Think of me sometimes, dear heart, & do not let your sweet love for me diminish one little bit by the time you return.

Ever your loving & devoted

P.[19]

This must actually have been Frances's second letter. The day after his birthday, having not yet received it, LG replied to her first.

I have been so disappointed not to receive a second letter from the little girl I have been thinking of & longing for ever since I left her above [the] rocky bastions of Ronda.* This place is too far from everywhere that matters. I never discovered that – at least it never bothered me much – as long as my sweetheart was here. I measure all distance by my distance from her. Abroad for me means far away from Pussy.

Every day I have been growling to J.T. about the insupportable dulness [sic] of this place. I need hardly tell you I poured these jeremiads into most receptive ears! Ever since we left Ronda J.T. has been liverish, at least he

* Ronda is seventy-five kilometres north of Algeciras. LG must have taken her there to catch the train to Paris.

thought it was liver. I made no such mistaken diagnosis of my case for I knew it was heart. Had it not been that Riddell was coming today & the Birkenheads next week & I felt I had out of decency [to] wait for them, & spend some days with them after they came I should have worked my way gradually northward – until I reached Churt. My polar star will be fixed in that neighbourhood by the time this letter reaches England & my ship will be steered to the end by that star. I feel more certain of that than ever after my darling left me stranded on this outlandish beach.

He wrote as if it was Frances's fault that he was there! He went on a bit more about the 'respectably depressing' company he was having to endure and various trips arranged to Malaga, Granada and Ceuta. Then he described his exercise regime – without mentioning Thelma, who specifically says that she accompanied him before breakfast on his birthday.

Long walks in the morning alone – in the evening with J.T. Yesterday – my sixtieth birthday – I walked altogether 12 miles! Not a bad record for an old man of 60 worn out by years of incessant toil & trouble . . . An invasion of 150 Yanks from a touring ship yesterday. One lady after I passed her said in the penetrating drawl of her country 'He looks much younger than I expected'. Look out Puss when I return . . .

   Ever & Ever
   your D.[20]

LG wrote again a week later. By this time Frances had written several more letters, which he did not preserve; whereas we can assume that she carefully kept all of his. Frances was now back at Churt, planning the garden.* Amid news about his visitors, postponed excursions and his newspaper articles, LG complained about the weather and described his plans to return home – now complicated by Megan.

I was delighted to get your letters. Your Churt news of budding bulbs & big winds & rolling white clouds & beyond a warm little heart eagerly awaiting to be quickened with an embrace have all added to my restlessness here . . . The weather has not been good since you left. None of the

* All her life Frances was a keen gardener. Among her papers there are lists of plants and shrubs ordered for 1923 (and again for 1925) with detailed plans and instructions about planting and maintenance.[21]

glorious warm sunshine of the first fortnight. I have quite exhausted my holiday & I want to be back.

As to returning. There is a boat on Wednesday [31 January]. Not a good one. It lands on Sunday. Now comes the difficulty. Megan is returning by land & will not be back until *Tuesday*. If I leave M. on Monday for Churt – whilst she is alone in town the grievance will be doublefold. So in that case you had better be in town Monday & we'll have a day together. What joy. I dare not dwell upon it otherwise it makes me more disaffected than ever. Megan & I are not on speaking terms. Had a row – not over you this time.[22]

The issue was not LG's love life, but Megan's. Not yet twenty-one, she had fallen unwisely in love with the popular novelist Stephen McKenna, a notorious womaniser fourteen years her senior and – worst of all in LG's eyes – nephew of his bitter Asquithian enemy, Reginald McKenna. LG and Maggie were united in opposing this liaison. Doubtless one reason for taking Megan to Spain was to get her away from McKenna. But she was evidently fractious the whole time and as anxious to go home as LG claimed to be. On 15 January – that is ten days before LG mentioned it to Frances – Riddell noted that Megan 'had been crying. She intimated that she had had a terrible row with her father, with whom she was not on speaking terms, but did not disclose the cause.'[23] It was presumably for this reason that Megan chose to make her own way home by land; another reason, too (apart from his wanting to see Frances), for LG not to leave her alone in London. Soon after her return, however, Megan was reluctantly persuaded to give up McKenna.[24]

LG's last letter from Algeciras was written on 28 January.

My own girl

I have received all the letters & have read them so often that I am prepared to pass an exam: in their contents phrases & especially their nuances (is that right?). The Paris letter is so valuable as a report that I mean to keep it.

Your Churt news makes me more impatient than ever to get there. I have finally decided on the 31st boat in spite of its smallness & if as the result I suffer severely in the Bay of Biscay you must make up for 'all the agonies' I have endured in hurrying to the arms of my sweetheart.

The weather had finally relented to make possible his several-times-deferred trip across the Straits of Gibraltar.

> Ceuta & Tetuan came off at last. It was not a trip – it was more like a Royal Reception. Cruiser – military officers – carpets – Grand Vizier – crowds. Here I am still 'the great man of Europe' & they said so . . . Still it was a great strain & I caught a cold in the head which I hope to throw off in a day or two. It is a nuisance. I wish I could have one holiday as myself & not as 'big man of Europe'. You know well don't you *cariad* what sort of holiday that would be.

The arrangements for his return illustrate how careful he and Frances still had to be in front of his political colleagues. It was not only with his family that they had to be discreet.

> Now to business in case I am interrupted before I can finish the letter. You had better stay there. I shall arrive in London on Sunday. On Monday I shall get off to Churt sans MacN. or Mack. or Hilton Young or Sutherland.* Tuesday they can come & just for that evening you might run up to town returning Wednesday. Sutherland & Shakespeare could stay, the others would leave. But Monday only you & I darling girl of my heart.[25]

Presumably Sutherland and Shakespeare knew of Frances's true status, while the others did not.

After LG's return there are naturally no more letters. Frances's diary had lapsed; and Riddell had quarrelled with LG – partly over policy (Riddell disapproved of LG's pro-Greek sympathies) and partly over what Riddell saw as LG's growing intolerance of criticism – and henceforth saw him only rarely: a great loss to the historian. The result is that we lose sight of Frances for a time. Our only knowledge of her state of mind, filtered through the veil of fiction, comes from the novel that she had begun in Paris.

---

* T. J. Macnamara, Thomas Mackinnon Wood and Edward Hilton Young were former Liberal ministers.

22

ROMANTIC FICTIONS

Frances started writing a novel in Paris in January 1923, after she had been obliged to leave LG in Algeciras when his family came out to join him. Some of her notes are on paper from the hotel they stayed in at Ronda; some on the paper of the Hotel Crillon where she was staying in Paris; some on Bron-y-de paper.

There are two quite separate though similar versions, which have become separated in her papers.* Both survive mainly in note form, with some fully developed episodes. One, probably the first draft, is handwritten, mainly in a small looseleaf notebook. The second is longer, with a more ambitious plot, more fully worked out, and mostly typed. Both centre on a clandestine affair between a politician and a younger woman, told mainly from the woman's point of view. In the first draft the heroine is named Ann and her lover usually Michael. In the second the heroine has become Delphine while the politician varies between Michael and Hubert. Both drafts are closely based on Frances's own experience, with unmistakably autobiographical incidents and recognisable characters based on real political figures. The heroine is tortured by an unfulfilled yearning for children, and by a bitter sense of the unfairness of life in which it is always the woman who has to make the sacrifices. But both drafts have happy endings in which the hero gives up his career – or, in the second version, offers to give it up – for love.[1]

The opening of the first draft is transparently autobiographical. Ann is in the Ladies' Gallery of the House of Commons, anxiously watching

* One draft is still in the possession of Frances's granddaughter Ruth Longford; the other is among Frances's papers in the House of Lords.

a debate, exactly as Frances used to watch LG in 1912. The difference
is that Michael is said to be making his maiden speech. Ann finds the
other speakers very boring – '*The old men so old and so dull and so
pompous and the young men so conceited and cynical and so common-
place to a casual observer*' – and is snobbishly patronising about a
Labour Member who '*argued his way through fallacious arguments
and claptrap phrases. The louder he spoke the less heed the House paid
him.*' But then Michael rises to speak:

> *And now Ann's heart beat with great thumps and jerks. She almost wished
> she had not come. She had vowed she would keep away, so great was her
> anxiety and her fear lest her tension, sitting up there and watching him,
> should somehow or other be communicated to him down below, and hamper
> his effort.*

When he sits down:

> *Ann's eyes were bright with excitement and emotion. No doubt as to the
> success of the speech . . . She sat there going over the speech again in her
> mind, [illegible] it in order to retain a permanent picture. How long she sat
> there she did not know, but her trance was interrupted by a touch on her
> shoulder. He was standing behind her and beckoning her out of the gallery.*

The scene continues in note form:

> '*Oh my dear! How splendid you were. I am glad, so glad.*'
>   '*I pleased you?*'
> *She coloured. Not 'it' pleased you, but 'I'.*
> *She nodded. 'I can't tell you how much.' She scarcely knew herself.*

> *Down in the tea room. Admiring glances.*
> *Arrangements for the morrow.*

> *Would she drive with him down to the country? Taking a day off? His
> new cottage.*
>   '*Your wife? . . .*'
>   '*She is away,' he answered shortly. 'I asked her to come up for my speech,
> but she did not see her way to do so . . .*'
>   '*I should like your company, Ann', leaning forward and looking into her*

eyes. 'Give me my reward for today's speech?'

'Of course I'll come, Michael. We'll have a glorious picnic. Where shall it be?'

Arrangements.

Going out almost collided with M. and a young man.

'Hullo, father.' Did not hear speech. She flushed as she looked at Ann, annoyance being obvious. Ignoring her.

Ann felt guilty, for the first time she scarcely knew why.

Here, clearly, we have Megan – though this is the grown-up Megan of 1923, not the child of 1912. LG was always complaining to Frances that his family did not bother to come and hear his speeches. She assuaged her guilt by telling herself that his wife (like Michael's) neglected him.

The third chapter shows Ann in her bedroom, brushing her hair in front of the mirror and reflecting on what she is getting into (though Michael has now become 'A.B.').

Before today she would have been careful on subject of picnic.

Would have looked forward to it like any other treat which had been sprung upon her. Now . . .

What was the change that had come over her? Why had the colour flushed her face when he held her hand at parting?

Slowly, as she stood there, the truth dawned upon her. She realised that she would do anything in the world for A.B., that in his hands her destiny lay, for good or ill.

The crucial scene, in Chapter 5, comes right up to date. Ann and Michael are now enjoying a romantic idyll in – naturally – Algeciras. They are on the hotel balcony, with the scent of orange blossom wafting up from below.

He tells her that he cannot contain himself, that he loves her and if he does not tear himself away he cannot be responsible for the consequences.

'Don't go, Michael. It is heaven here. Don't let's think about the future.'

'It's not the future I'm thinking of,' he answered roughly. 'It's now. My God, Ann, do you know what it means to me to be with you all day and

part from you at night! I can't go on. I've tried, God knows, but I'm at the end of my tether. It must be all, and we must say goodbye.'

'No, no, Michael, anything but that! I make no conditions but do not go away from me!'

They went into the sitting room. He took her arm and drew her to the sofa.

All power of will went from her. She put her hands on his shoulders and hid her face in his bosom. Happiness surged in her heart as it beat against his. Love robbed her limbs of their strength and he caught her and held her in his arms.

'Ann!' he cried hoarsely. 'Ann. Do you realise what this means?'

'Hold me closer, closer,' she whispered, and gave herself body and soul into his keeping.

But then Michael is invited to join the Cabinet – we are not told how long after his maiden speech this is supposed to be. Frances's notes continue:

Unuttered hope that he may refuse. Sees telegram he had already written out – acceptance.

Row between M. and A.

Taunts him that he is selfish. Will not give up anything vital for her.

He replies that he is not his own master – he serves the State, that must be his first consideration. If he shirked he would be a traitor. They must make the best of their lives together. 'That means the best for you – for me a second best.'

'Motherhood is a woman's right. You deny it me. The price is not paid now, but long years ahead.'

He says she is unreasonable, becomes impatient.

She leaves him proud and defiant.

An angry evening by herself.

A later scene elaborates Ann's grievance that Michael is denying her right to bear children. But when he is adamant, she quickly backs down.

'I adore children. There is a mystery about them which attracts and over-whelms me. Perhaps that is because I haven't a child of my own. If I had, I might be more sophisticated in this respect.'

A child of her own! How sadly the words came from her lips. An infinite longing – an unsatisfied tenderness. All the tragedy of a hungry heart. Because he loved her, he ought to be able to fulfil her womanhood. But he knew her mind. He hinted at the possibility.

'No! No! A thousand times no! Bear a child in secrecy and like a haunted thing. Leave it to others after I had brought it into the world, or else resort to some subterfuge in order to have it with me. It would be a fine thing to bear children to you my lover, even without marriage, but a hideous shame to cover the fulfilment of our love with lies and fear.'

'That would mean ruin to me, Ann.'

'I know, so it must not happen. Don't think I'm complaining, Mike darling. I'm perfectly happy with you as I am. Think, if I had a child I would want to spend at least half my time with him, and how jealous you would be.'

He folded her tenderly to him. 'I want you all to myself,' he murmured. 'There must be no-one else.'

Doubly selfish! He felt it in his heart, but how alter it? Fate decreed it, and if something told him that he was trying to get the best of both worlds – well, it wasn't his fault. And she was happy with him, there was no denying that. Every day the light in her eyes grew more beautiful. In her rounded bosom and the subtly curving lines of her figure there was evidence of a requited love and a life-giving passion.

She gave a shrill little laugh, that ended in a sob. She passed her hand quickly from her forehead over her soft curls, always a sign of unrest with her.

'Oh Michael – what a desperately unfair thing life is for a woman – even now.'

Ann is clearly pregnant, but resigned to losing the child – as Frances had herself done so often. The remainder of the story was to show Ann vacillating between accepting her lot and kicking against it. One draft paragraph surely reflects Frances's shame that in subordinating herself she had betrayed her youthful feminism:

She had been so proud, so strong – now her pride was humbled, her strength was broken. Calm was thrown to the winds. She was his slave, his plaything, his chattel. Wild desire drove out every vestige of modesty and pride. She would grovel at his feet. She would beg him to take her back – into his arms – anything – anything but this utter torment of passion and longing.

But by Chapter 21 – in bare outline only – Ann was to regain her self-respect:

> *Ann reflects.*
> *His attitude – work first.*
> *Can sacrifice nothing for her.*
> *Woman always pays.*
> *Surely motherhood and the child first?*
> *Surely some other career but politics?*
> *Never entered his mind.*
> *She decides to go away.*

It is not clear whether she goes away to have her baby or an abortion. But Michael soon realises that he cannot live without her. '*Realises what she is to him. Moves heaven and earth to find her. Fails. Becomes listless and loses interest in his work.*' Meanwhile Ann has gone to Florence, where she meets a man called Paul who asks her to marry him. She refuses: '*She will remain true to her ideals.*' Living in Florence, she begins to find peace. Back in London, however, Paul meets Michael – '*still haggard and distraught, having left his wife*' – and tells him where Ann is staying. At which point Frances's notes abandon all pretence of realism and cut straight to her dream ending:

> '*But Michael, what about your future, your career?*'
> *Folding her closer, tenderly.*
> '*There can be no future, no career, without you.*'

> *The end.*

It is not great literature, but no worse than Barbara Cartland – or Stephen McKenna, or a hundred other slush novelists of the day. With one work of non-fiction already published, Frances would probably have had no difficulty publishing this too (under a pseudonym, presumably), had she ever finished it. But its purpose was rather to vent her frustration and indulge her fantasy. Another note, written on Hotel Crillon paper, so probably a very early sketch written as soon as she reached Paris from Algeciras, is even more bitter about the one-sidedness of a woman's sacrifice.

Would she be happy if he gave up everything for her?

She realises. Always the woman who pays . . . Even the future genera-
tion must be sacrificed to it . . .

It cannot be right the woman should eternally be the victim. 'What a
coward he was, to let her bear all the brunt' . . .

Why cause him anxiety? Had she *no anxieties? Why should the man*
always be considered?

Did Frances actually say all this to LG? Was she accurately repro-
ducing his counter-arguments? Or was she simply putting into her hero's
mouth what she knew was his position, which he had made plain to
her from the start of their relationship. She had accepted it in 1913,
and ultimately she still accepted it. '*Would she be happy if he gave up*
everything for her?' Ann asks herself. Of course she would not. It was
precisely LG's power that Frances loved – the front-row seat in the
theatre of politics that being his secretary gave her; she believed unques-
tioningly that he was a great man, the saviour of Britain and potentially of Europe, and wanted to help him achieve his remaining
ambitions. And yet . . . Now that he was out of office, did the same
considerations apply? Yes, they did, so long as he had a realistic expectation of getting back to power. But Frances was now thirty-four. Her
biological clock was ticking with increasing urgency. If she was ever to
have a child, it would have to be quite soon. This was the tension that
overhung their relationship for the next six years, as the political world
returned to normal after the upheaval of the war years and LG found
himself increasingly marginalised by the emerging Conservative/Labour
duopoly, which left the divided Liberals struggling to regain a role.
Frances was still in love with LG, and still believed in him, but sometimes she must have wondered if she should not make herself a new
life before it was too late.

She may have hoped that she could make an independent career as
a writer. The second version of her book was much more ambitious
and less blatantly autobiographical, an attempt at a proper political
novel, though it is still based almost entirely on her own barely disguised
experience, padded out with obvious portraits of real people. It probably dates from rather later than 1923. If the earlier attempt was written
merely to get her feelings off her chest, this one – typed and much more
fully structured – was plainly meant for publication. In February 1925
the editor of the *Daily Express* wrote to her indicating his interest:

Dear Miss Stevenson,

I am told that you are writing a book. If so would you mind letting me know when it is to be published and what it is all about?

With kind regards,

Yours sincerely,

R. D. Blumenfeld[2]

A little reflection must have told her that publication was impossible. She could never have maintained her anonymity, and a fictionalised account of LG's adultery would have wrecked his career as surely as open exposure of it. Nevertheless this second draft paints a vivid picture of Frances's secret life and of how ambivalently she felt about it.

This time the heroine is called Delphine – the French name an obvious reference to Frances's own ancestry. She is a successful novelist, who owns an idyllic cottage in Surrey where she escapes to write and garden. The cottage is *'proof of the fallacy of the theory that a woman who has an intellectual occupation could not be an interested housewife. The interior was a triumph of elegant simplicity'* – though naturally Delphine has a couple to look after it for her (and a housekeeper in her London flat as well). Some years earlier, *'in a fit of wartime madness'*, Delphine had married *'an attractive ne'er-do-well'* named Archie Somers, who turned out to be *'a sneak and a cheat'*, and also a bully. But Archie went away to the war, never returned and is presumed dead. She has now formed a relationship with Hubert Shiel (alternatively called Michael Armitage), a rising politician, currently Under-Secretary in an unnamed department. The crucial difference from the earlier story is that Hubert/Michael is not married. The complication this time stems from Delphine's marriage. When the novel opens, she and Hubert are together at her cottage, talking about the flowers and enjoying – shades of Churt? – *'the most superb view in England'*. He has to make an important speech in the Commons the next day, and she, wearing her journalist's hat, is going to write about it. Her fiction pays the rent, but she finds politics more exciting.

> Hubert regarded her affectionately. How lucky it was, he thought, that she could combine her talent with an interest in his work. She was the perfect companion.

1. Frances Stevenson as an undergraduate at Royal Holloway College, c. 1910.

2 & 3. New Women: a walking holiday with university friends. Frances is at bottom left in the upper picture and in the middle of the lower one.

4. Family man: Lloyd George with his wife and youngest daughter Megan in No. 11 Downing Street in 1910, the year before Frances came into his life.

5. Megan electioneering for her father.

6. Butter wouldn't melt: Frances in 1918.

7. The Prime Minister's private secretary at her desk in Downing Street.

8. The Prime Minister's visit to Rapallo, November 1917: Frances with Colonel Hankey and J.T. Davies (*left*) and General Sir Henry Wilson (*back*).

9. LG and Maggie in 1918.

10. Still friends: Frances and Megan in Paris, 1919.

11. Frances tempted by Sir Philip Sassoon at Port Lympne, 1920.

12. Gairloch, 1921: the only picture of Frances and Maggie together. Frances sits on the running board with Dick, while LG and Maggie shelter in the car.

13. Cannes, 1922: a rare picture of LG and Frances together. Frances stands at the back with Tom Jones, Lord Riddell and Sir Albert Stern; Lord Curzon seated, right.

14. Lloyd George at play.

15 & 16. Brynawelon, LG's house at Criccieth (*above*); and Bron-y-de, the house LG built for himself at Churt (*right*).

17. The Lloyd George family meeting, Churt, December 1932: A.J. Sylvester stands on the left, with LG, Olwen, Maggie, Tom Carey-Evans and Megan.

18. LG with Megan and Thomas Tweed (and Sylvester, back left).

19 & 20. Colleagues: Tweed and Frances in the office (*above*); and LG sees Frances, Jennifer and her nanny off to Portugal, 1934 (*below*).

21, 22 & 23. Jennifer and Taid in 1932, 1934 and 1935.

24 & 25. Two faces of LG: the orator (*above*), and the farmer with Frances at Churt (*left*).

26. Father and daughter: LG and Megan in the 1920s.

27. LG at Maggie's funeral, 1941, with his sons Dick and Gwilym, and Sylvester (*left*).

28 & 29. LG and Frances
on his 80th birthday,
January 1943 (*right*), and
on their wedding day
nine months later (*below*).

30. Home to die: Mr and Mrs
Lloyd George on the bridge
at Llanystumdwy, 1944.

31. Keeping the flame:
the Countess Lloyd-George
of Dwyfor in old age.

Delphine is equally happy:

> *She looked lovingly at the handsome head, and stretching out her hand touched his fine black hair. She knew he loved these caresses of hers, and in turn she loved the slightest contact with him. They were perfect pals, and had been these last four years. He sought her company at every opportunity, and she had become more and more absorbed in him and his work.*

Chapter Two elaborates the House of Commons scene in the earlier draft, as Delphine listens to the debate from a front seat in the Ladies' Gallery, *'that very inadequate and uncomfortable compartment'*, where suppressed excitement and malicious female rivalry are *'controlled by a firm attendant'*. Like Ann, Delphine finds most of the speakers old and pompous or young and cynical; but now Frances includes obvious portraits of Stanley Baldwin, Prime Minister by the time she was writing (*'a man of uninspiring and insignificant presence . . . A curious and almost unique instance of a man made a statesman by accident'*) and Austen Chamberlain (*'His lean, long, monocled face was impressive even to deathliness . . . he modelled his every word and action . . . upon the pattern of an illustrious father'*). Delphine also echoes Ann's patronising view of the Labour members, though she means to be sympathetic:

> *They had an attraction for her, in their naïve unconventionality, their badly-cut and shabby clothes, their rugged, uncouth faces bearing unmistakable signs of a long acquaintance with the seamy side of life.*

They are all, in her biased view, a poor lot.

> *Did this group of ejaculating and noisy working men represent the hopes and aspirations of an enlightened democracy? Where were their orators? Where were their visionaries? Where were their statesmen? The justice of their cause was so often obscured by fallacious arguments and claptrap phrases.*

The debate comes alive, of course, when Hubert speaks, and Delphine's heart immediately beats faster.

> *'What a voice!' said the woman sitting next to Delphine, an American to*

whom a musical voice, so rare amongst her own countrymen, would doubt-less specially appeal. Delphine looked at her gratefully. At once the matter was lifted out of the rut of party, above the plane of tedious common-places ...

Delphine listens 'with pride tinged with anxiety'.

On the occasions when Michael [sic] was to speak she never knew whether to go to the Gallery or stay away. For her, listening to a speech of his was certainly not an unmixed pleasure. Today, for instance, she had known every turn of the speech, every argument he would bring to bear. But would he make good, or would the effort fall flat? Would he be in form, or would perhaps a chance interruption throw him off his balance and break the thread of his argument? These questions always tormented her and detracted from the pleasure she derived from his eloquence, and the tightening around her heart when he rose to speak did not relax until the applause proclaimed his success.

At the end Delphine, like Ann, feels '*a touch on her shoulder*', and Hubert invites her to tea in his room. '*As she left the Gallery she had the satisfaction of knowing that Lady Cynthia —— was envying and hating her.*'

Over tea – originally on the Terrace, but later changed to Hubert's room – there is more cattiness about wives who are ambitious for their dull husbands; but we meet a new character, Sir Jonathan Mardelon, a kindly old Member with a protective interest in Hubert and Delphine, who is probably a composite of several of Frances's elderly admirers. ('*Mardy loved her carriage, her air of quiet breeding.*') He invites Delphine for dinner. She accepts, but is grateful that they are going to dine early: '*And then she would be home in time for Michael [sic] if he called round after his dinner. Probably Mardy suspected that. He was intuitive as a woman.*' This was so often Frances's situation, waiting for LG to come to her flat at the end of the evening.

The next chapter opens with a moment of pure autobiography. Walking home through the park to her flat in Ebury Street, Delphine is suddenly entranced by the beauty of nature and renews a childhood vow that she will never grow old. In her memoirs Frances describes making exactly this vow to herself in a similar moment of rapture at the age of about twelve.[3] Delphine goes on to reflect on her life:

Perhaps it had been the latent sex within her which in that brief instant gave her the sense of eternal life and indestructible beauty . . . Life was very wonderful just now, with Michael. Not perfect, perhaps, for their love must necessarily be in secret. None the less, beautiful and true for all that.

She recapitulates the story of her *'ghastly marriage'*, which she entered into largely to get away from her repressive parents: an unimaginative father who believed a woman's place was in the home, and a more gifted mother who nevertheless *'moved through life like a character in a Tchekov play, with a vague discontent with life and circumstances, but unable to summon enough willpower and concentration to alter it'*. There are surely elements here of John and Louise Stevenson, though of course Frances did not escape into marriage. After Archie's disappearance, Delphine had established herself in Ebury Street and thrown herself into journalism until she re-encountered Hubert/Michael, whom she had known previously, but now saw in a new light.

Their love-making had been swift and natural. They accepted their new relation to each other without surprise or question. Their happiness seemed perfect. They were companions as well as lovers. Michael Armitage knew something of the world and women. He had had many women friends, and more than one mistress. But in Delphine he found the perfect friend and mistress.

Delphine's flat, just like Frances's, is *'full of accumulated treasures'*.

'I made this home unconsciously for you,' she would say to him. 'I knew all the time I was preparing for someone who would one day come to me, and love me as I wanted to be loved.' He came there often. It was a haven of joy and rest to him . . .

He was glad to exchange the austerity and gloom of his own house for these sweet surroundings. In the mornings he worked perforce at his house in Hertford Street – a gloomy bachelor residence – or in Whitehall, dealing with his daily correspondence with the aid of a secretary and a typist, and preparing for the business of the House of Commons in the afternoon. The afternoons and evenings were taken up at Westminister, with the exception of those rare days on which he was not required, and when he and Delphine could spend whole blissful hours together, either in town or, if the weather tempted them, driving down to the cottage in her little car.

On this evening, Hubert/Michael comes to her after his speech, which naturally was a triumph.

> *Delphine received him radiantly. She had anticipated his mood. After a speech like this he would be curiously depressed, and all her mother-instinct would be called forth in an endeavour to coax and humour him away from his melancholy . . . He was grateful to her for her comfort and her praise. Like a child to its mother, he looked to her for both, and she never failed him.*

As they talk, he appraises Delphine's beauty in surprisingly classical terms:

> *She looked beautiful in her maturing womanhood, thought Michael. The folds of her violet gown showed up the blue-black darkness of her curls, and the creamy whiteness of her throat. The proud curve of her delicate nostrils gave dignity to a countenance which would otherwise have been merely piquante. So might Lesbia have looked, he thought, when she moved Catullus to immortalise her in song; or so might Circe have appeared in enchanting mood.*

Is this simply Frances flaunting her classical education? Was she attempting to disguise her hero with one attribute that LG conspicuously lacked? Or did the licence of fiction perhaps allow her to endow him with a quality she rather wished he had?

Next they discuss his political prospects. Delphine is ambitious for Michael, but realises that promotion to the Cabinet will bring him more enemies.

> *It meant therefore more circumspection in their method of life, more wariness, more dissimulation. It was this last which Delphine loathed so much. It was alien to her nature, which was clear and honest and uncompromising, but she knew that as time went on they would be forced to dissimulate, and if high office fell to Michael's lot, there were people who might use this love of theirs as a weapon to attack him under cover.*

Here Frances is expressing her distaste for her own clandestine situation, rather than her heroine's; because if Delphine's husband is presumed dead, there is nothing improper about Michael seeing her.

There follows what was evidently intended as a key passage.

> *'What is the greatest thing in life, Michael?' she asked him.*
>
> *'Love,' he answered, believing it at that moment and thinking moreover that that was the reply she expected.*
>
> *'No. Guess again.'*
>
> *'Well, sacrifice then.'*
>
> *'Wrong again. I don't think a negative quality could ever be the greatest thing.'*
>
> *'Tell me, dearest.'*
>
> *'It's courage that ultimately counts . . . without it, all the other things will be in vain.'*
>
> *'You're getting far too philosophical for this time of night, my sweet.' Michael laughed and drew her closer to him. Her soft body and the round curve of her breast fired his brain, and he was glad to take her in his arms.*

Now the scene widens to show the whispering to which their love gives rise in society. A political hostess – American and teetotal, clearly modelled on Frances's *bête noire* Nancy Astor – is annoyed when Michael lets her down at short notice and blames his attachment to *'that Somers woman'*, whom she will not invite *'for many reasons'*. Her husband tells her that Delphine is *'a clever woman'* and that Michael is *'very much in love with her'*. This is confirmed by one of her dinner guests, who describes seeing them together at a weekend house party, when *'Armitage had eyes for no-one else'*. Another, more sympathetic, says that Delphine's husband was a bounder and his death *'good riddance'*; the hostess resolves, somewhat alarmingly, to *'take Mrs Somers in hand'*.

The theme of Delphine's social inclusion or exclusion is pursued in the next chapter, when Michael – like LG – complains at having to attend so many weekend parties on top of his ministerial work.

> *He was not always, however, on these occasions deprived of Delphine's company, for her talent and hard work were bringing her increasing notice, and wily hostesses who had divined that Michael Armitage would be more likely to accept their invitations if Delphine were of the party, were able to seize upon her literary distinctions as an excuse for including her in their lists of guests.*

In just the same way her position as the Prime Minister's secretary had opened doors to Frances.

From here on the story gets more sketchy and melodramatic, with draft episodes that do not fully connect with one another. Michael – or Hubert – is now Chancellor of the Exchequer, and trouble arises over a leaked story about a disagreement between him and the Prime Minister over the budget. A Cabinet meeting provides an opportunity for an unflattering sketch of the Colonial Secretary, clearly modelled on Churchill:

> . . . *a man who would surely one day be Prime Minister himself, in spite of a natural disposition for turning an almost certain success into ghastly failure: a man of superlatively brilliant gifts, but who would, Michael thought, skin his own mother in order to make a drum wherewith to sound his fame.**

There is also mention of '*the Puck-like proprietor of a daily journal*', who is clearly Beaverbrook.

After Cabinet, when no one owns up to the leak, Michael realises that the only other person with a copy of his letter to the Prime Minister is Delphine. Impossible, he tells himself: '*The secret was as safe as houses with her.*' He intends to clear the matter up that afternoon. But driving to the country he is tired and preoccupied, and will not tell her what is on his mind. Over the weekend he has '*a hard day's political talk*' with colleagues about some scheme to dish the Opposition: he emerges to tell Delphine, who embraces him excitedly. But they are observed by a '*repulsive*' journalist called Hamilton-Hill, who hurries away '*to consult a Bradshaw*' (that is, the times of trains to London).

There follows a lovers' quarrel. Worried about the leak allegation, Hubert finds Delphine listless and unhappy. She asks what he would do if she went away, perhaps for good. When he asks what is wrong she replies: '*It's nothing in particular, Hubert. Only everything.*' She goes on: '*I feel you'd be better without me. You don't need me now like you used to. Besides . . . people are beginning to talk.*' She names a journalist (not the same one) and he jumps to the conclusion that she was responsible for the leak after all. But he does not want to

---

* This was indeed something LG once said of Churchill.[4] But LG was genuinely fond of Winston, whereas Frances never trusted him.

discuss it now because he has to go to the theatre with his wife; at this point the story suddenly requires that Hubert is married after all! Delphine is angry, and he tries to excuse himself in terms LG must often have used with Frances.

> *'Delphine! Do be reasonable. Sweetheart, you know my difficulties. Do help me with them, instead of making things more difficult for me.'*
>
> *'Difficulties! Difficulties! . . . Do you never think of my difficulties, or my . . .' – there were tears in her voice, of self-pity – 'loneliness?'*
>
> *Even as she spoke she would have given the world to throw her arms round his neck, to tell him that she understood and trusted him, that she would be his true helpmeet and not make any more scenes . . . But his next words drove the impulse from her.*
>
> *'You might give me back the copy of that letter. I need it.'*

Tearfully, she gives him the letter. He takes it and leaves. Delphine knows that he will make no conciliatory move until she makes the first advance.

> *Did he understand, she wondered, her heartache on these occasions? Very likely not. The heart of a man is fashioned differently from that of a woman. Delphine threw herself on the bed in a fit of passionate weeping.*

To stop herself brooding, she goes alone to the Russian ballet, to see *Petrushka*. But of course Michael is there too: *not* with a wife, but in a party including a woman called Norma Hampden, who is openly making up to him. Watching the ballet, Delphine reflects that it is always the same story – *'two men and one woman, or two women and one man'*.

> *Was there going to be a triangle in her case, too? She had thought no-one could come between her and Michael. Surely he was not going to allow that woman to spoil their love.*

She leaves at the interval and wanders miserably through Trafalgar Square, noticing that everyone seems to be in couples – except herself and the prostitutes looking for unattached males.

> *Why should she now be going to her lonely bed, when she wanted him so*

badly? It was unnatural that she should go thus, without her mate, she with her pulses quick with life and her nature in its springtide. Unnatural. Yes, that was the word. And that was what their relationship was – hers and Michael's. How could he not see it? No doubt he did; but Career prevented him from taking notice of the fact. His career and his conventions. How she hated the words! Why should men and women, loving each other as they did, be governed by such absurdities?

She runs into an old admirer named Charles, recklessly takes his arm and asks him to walk her home across the park. She asks him in for a drink. Though Charles thinks he has *'never seen her looking so beautiful'*, he resists the temptation to kiss her; but leaves with a spring in his step – just as Michael drives past. *'Michael's heart froze within him, and he resisted the temptation to stop and make his peace with Delphine.'*

Maybe Frances would not have persisted with this line, which is merely a misunderstanding. Instead she contrives a much more dramatic crisis by having Delphine's husband suddenly reappear, expecting to live with her again. She flees to her cottage to think out what to do. She would rather die than go back to Archie. The only alternatives she sees are to throw herself on Michael, wrecking his career, or to go abroad.

On the one hand, betrayal of Michael. He would go through with it, she knew, to save her from the horror of her husband, but his career would be at an end. No reproach would pass his lips, but an everlasting reproach would lie upon her conscience. How face life with Michael under those conditions? . . .

But the alternative was equally appalling – Loneliness, where before there had been companionship and love.

Delphine is remarkably confident that Michael would sacrifice his career for her. LG had made it absolutely plain that he would not do the same for Frances, so this appears to be another romantic fantasy. More realistic is her realisation that she could not live with herself if she wrecked his career. So Delphine takes herself off – like Ann in the earlier draft – to Florence. Before she goes she has a last lunch with Michael at the Berkeley Hotel, where she forces herself to sparkle while her heart is breaking, then leaves, making him promise to love her always, and sobs as her taxi drives away. (Frances wrote two different versions of this scene.) When he finds that she has disappeared, Michael learns that she had a visitor at her flat the day before. Not knowing that it was her husband, he supposes she has run off with another man.

Very soon, living in exile in Florence, indulging her broken heart by playing Debussy, Delphine is indeed tempted by the attentions of an Italian suitor. Frances makes no bones about 'the desires of the flesh'.

> And now, through it all, this desire of the body came stealing, to unnerve and challenge her mind . . . She liked him, she more than liked him. That he knew. Latin-like, he could not comprehend/understand her reserve and diffidence – the Anglo-Saxon unwillingness to give emotion/passion full rein while intellect holds back. If she had another lover, why was she here? If her lover had deserted her, why could she not take another? . . .
>
> Mario rose and went to Delphine's side. 'Come!', he said softly, pointing/beckoning to the lawn below.
>
> There was no mistaking the look in those dark melancholy eyes. If she went, he would make love to her. She rose and accompanied him, her heart beating a trifle faster. She must forget.
>
> 'Marry me, carissime,' he pleaded. 'I've waited so long for this love, that you could give me – that you will give me.'
>
> 'But you've had a lover before, Mario.' She dallied with him. All the time she was burning for his embrace.
>
> 'The love of chambermaids and courtesans. That I can get from my countrywomen.'
>
> 'You can be my lover, too, Mario, but I'll not marry you.' She turned away from the look of pain and surprise in his eyes.
>
> 'Your lover – and not your husband?'
>
> She nodded slowly, looking him full in the face. 'You have it,' she said. There was silence. She could imagine the tumult in his heart – at the fall of the image of her he had created there. But she did not want his esteem. 'You may come to me tonight,' she said faintly, as she turned from him to mount the terrace steps. But even as she said it her heart was numb with the pain of a lost ideal.

But this moment of weakness is merely an interlude. Back in London, Delphine's husband calls on Michael and tries to blackmail him. Michael realises that this is the reason for her disappearance. From here the story accelerates in a few rough notes to a wildly melodramatic conclusion.

4. *He turns on husband.*
   Furious scene.
   Kicks him out of house.

   How to find her.
   He must.
   Politics can go hang.

   Copy of Spectator.
   Picks it up.
   Begins to read without taking in.
   Phrase catches his eye.
   'Courage that ultimately counts.'
   Who said that to him?
   Reads on carefully.
   Delphine!

5. *Visit to Spectator editor – to find out whereabouts of author . . .*

6. *Goes off to Florence.*
   Motors.
   Accident.
   Kills man.
   Discovers it is Delphine's husband.

So, conveniently, the obstacle to their happiness is removed and Michael and Delphine are presumably free to marry and have the legitimate children she dreams of without damaging his career – assuming that he is not charged with murder! At least this happy ending does not depend on Michael voluntarily sacrificing his career, though Frances does seem to have had him on the point of resolving to do so. But the crude improbability of her alternative outcome suggests that she knew quite well that this was never going to happen.

Of course Frances never finished her fantasy. She was intelligent enough to know that it was not very good, and she could never have published it anyway. But just writing it enabled her to articulate some of the frustrations of her situation. In addition to the semi-completed narrative there are a number of other draft scenes and snatches of dialogue jotted down in her notebooks, which she did not manage to work into the story but which furnish further glimpses of the way she felt about life and love and the relationship between men and women. With a better novelist than Frances, one could not assume that fiction simply reproduces the author's own views. In this case, however, it is impossible to believe that Frances was not writing directly from her personal experience.

First, there are several more expressions of her central theme, the heartache of motherhood denied. On the train to Florence, for instance, Delphine finds herself sharing a compartment with a young couple and their baby.

> Delphine felt the hot tears start to her eyes. She could not bear to gaze further upon the happy trio, the ideal trinity. They represented too poignantly all that she longed for so passionately and that seemed to be denied her for ever – all that she was mourning in her flight from love and life as she wished it.
>
> 'It is still the woman who pays,' she said bitterly to herself, 'in spite of all our modernity.'

In another fragment, Delphine has a sympathetic heart-to-heart with Michael's elderly servant, who has looked after him throughout his career and now loyally guards the secret of their relationship: a character clearly based on LG's faithful Sarah. The two women, old and young, share the same maternal protectiveness towards Michael, as Frances explicitly spells out: 'Both of them looked upon him as all they had of children, their care for him was all they had of motherhood.'

Frances made several stabs at the critical conversation in which her heroine confronts her lover with his selfishness. This one, handwritten on Bron-y-de paper, illustrates what she was up against.

> 'The difficulties of our relations seem to cause you no unhappiness. It is only I who suffer, while you continue quite happily – at least so it seems.'
>
> 'Why should you suffer? I do not understand.'
>
> He was not pretending. He was honestly seeking an explanation of her statement, astonished at it.
>
> 'Perhaps it is because you do not understand that I have the heartbreaks,' she said sadly.

In another telling fragment, Delphine hesitantly raises the possibility that they might have a child.

> 'Dearest, if you ever thought of that, could it be now?'
> He looked at her blankly. The next moment she had pulled herself together and was laughing gaily, as though it was a good joke.

There is one echo of how much Frances must have resented LG's occasional infidelities, when Delphine sees Michael kissing another woman. She leaves angrily; he telephones her later to apologise, but she is stiff. Unlike the rest of the book, this episode is told from Michael's point of view, as if she were trying to understand him.

> 'Delphine!' His voice pleaded, besought her. Her restraint deserted her. 'Oh, Michael . . . Why?'
> There were tears in her voice, and he heard it no more. She had put down the receiver.
> 'Why?' That was just what he asked himself.

Frances's abiding sense of the inequality between the sexes emerges in a dialogue between Delphine and Michael's sister, who tells her that she should get out in society and entertain more. Frances's youthful feminism still burns in Delphine's reply:

> 'Look here, Ethel, if I were a man you would not advise me in this way or suggest such things to me. Simply because I am a woman I must fritter my time away in absurd conventionalities. I really believe that is why women do not produce more solid work. A serious man – a man who wants to be taken seriously – has his few friends and lets the rest go. And because a woman does the same thing she is blamed for neglecting her social duties and not doing the best for herself. It's not reasonable or logical.'
> 'When you start with reason and logic, Delphine darling, I'm off. I can't compete. Au revoir.'

In this mood Frances saw herself as a professional woman. But there was another side to her that acknowledged the relative weakness and natural subordination of women to men – as in this handwritten addition to the chapter introducing Delphine's relationship with Hubert, which surely reflects her own experience of working with LG.

Delphine had discovered she could not concentrate on her work when she was with Michael/Hubert. She supposed women were made like that – love seemed to take away their inspiration, or else it was that the presence of the man, like a magnet, drew all the vitality to himself. Delphine certainly found she could do nothing constructive while Hubert was there. She supposed that was why sewing and knitting had been invented for woman, by someone who knew something of the psychology of love and work. With men it seemed different. Her presence did not have that effect on Hubert.

The more Frances felt she had sacrificed and suffered for her love, the more intensely she needed to believe that it was worth it. Her romantic faith in the vocation of love inspires another statement of the 'courage' theme when Delphine is screwing herself up to leave Michael. She pours out her misery to her elderly confidant, Sir Jonathan Mardelon, and unexpectedly releases in him a spasm of grief for the lost love of his life, long ago. He tells Delphine that if she and Michael have truly loved, they will never forget each other: they must have courage, and all will come right in the end. This was a faith that Frances, having committed herself irrevocably to LG, clung to through happy times and some unhappy ones over the next twenty years.

Finally another snatch of dialogue – possibly intended for another scene with Michael's sister – puts into Delphine's mouth a somewhat desperate rationalisation of Frances's realistic acceptance that she could never hope to marry LG: an attempt to convince herself that it was actually better to be a mistress than a wife.

'My dear, I don't want to marry him. I love him so much that I should be afraid of marrying him. He might get used to me as he has done to his tooth brush or his shaving stick, or some other object which is absolutely necessary to him, that he would miss terribly if it weren't there, but whose presence he takes for granted and doesn't think about.

This is immediately followed by another passionate expression of repugnance for the idea of bearing a child whom they could not acknowledge.

I only don't want to bear a secret child – a thing unknown and unowned – an object that I should love dearer than my life but whom I should have

to treat as a stranger, or at best as somebody else's child – and one whom
his father at any rate would be forced to ignore.

Yet before the end of the decade Frances had done exactly this.

One naturally wonders what LG thought of Frances's literary undertaking. He certainly knew about it, since in a letter written on Boxing
Day 1924 she told him that she had started it, and they had evidently
talked about it before.

> I hope you have had a happy Xmas, *cariad* mine. I was thinking of you so
> much & hoping that you were having a rest. I have already made a good
> start with my novel, & am rather pleased with what I have done. You were
> very cute to tell me I should be pleasing you! There is a real definite interest
> in it now for me![5]

It was typical of LG to see himself as her hypothetical reader! But
clearly he approved, though it is hard to see how he could have allowed
her to publish anything so transparent. Presumably Frances showed
him some, at least, of what she wrote. At just one point in all these
drafts and scattered notes, however, is there any sign that he had read
them. This occurs not in one of the obviously autobiographical episodes,
but in a chapter about another character entirely, a woman named
Cynthia, who is first seen falling in love with a crippled ex-soldier, then
at her dying father's bedside. In the margin is a note in LG's distinctive scrawl: 'Good idea but wants rewriting'.[6] One would love to know
if she showed him any of the other chapters. That surely would have
destroyed the therapeutic purpose of the exercise. Maybe in approving
it he killed it. All we know is that, for whatever reason, her book was
never finished.

23

THE GOAT IN THE WILDERNESS

LG's move from government to an indefinite period of opposition made for a major shift in the pattern of his life, and therefore also of Frances's life. One important change was in the personnel of his office, now established at 18 Abingdon Street.* J. T. Davies, with whom Frances had got on so well, left – rewarded with a knighthood and a cushy seat on the board of the Suez Canal company (though he retained a connection with LG's affairs as a trustee of his political fund, which he had done so much to augment). After a short gap he was replaced by A. J. Sylvester, who had previously been Hankey's secretary, but joined LG's personal staff in 1922. When LG left office he stayed on briefly in Downing Street with Bonar Law, but was now lured back to serve LG again. This was the cause of some tension with Frances.

Previously Frances had been clearly junior to J. T. Davies, and they worked well together. Now Frances had ten years' experience and had been the senior secretary for several months, but Sylvester – a champion shorthand typist in his youth, with a considerable sense of his own importance – insisted that he must have the title of Principal Private Secretary; and LG agreed, which was a snub to Frances. LG never cared anything for titles and probably thought it necessary to flatter Sylvester's vanity. In fact Frances worked reasonably well with Sylvester for the next twenty years; but there was no warmth between

---

* This was just a few doors from the Asquithian Liberal headquarters at 21 Abingdon Street. A few years later – in 1926 – LG moved his personal headquarters to 25 Old Queen Street; and then, in 1932, to new offices in Millbank.

them and a permanent undertow of potential blackmail.* Like Davies, Sylvester was expected to make most of the practical arrangements that facilitated LG's double life, moving continually between London, Criccieth and Churt, dealing tactfully with Maggie, Megan, Gwilym and Olwen on one side and with Frances on the other, covering up LG's movements when necessary, posting his letters to Frances and receiving hers to him. He was as devoted, efficient and discreet as Davies; but at the same time he observed everything that went on and recorded it with the unspoken threat that he knew too much to be sacked or in any other way offended.

Eighteen months after coming back to work for LG, Sylvester set down a creepily candid statement of his intentions.

> Reading Boswell's Life of Johnson. Much inspired . . . Henceforth I hope to make copious daily notes in my journal . . . One day L.G. will pass away and, should I remain with him till that unhappy time, then I shall have to make the best of myself. That will be the time to put something on the American market in the shape of a few gleanings of this great man. I know American taste: I shall not forget it. Now I must cater for it steadily.[2]

Having made this resolution in November 1924, however, Sylvester kept up his diary only for the rest of that year; then, inexplicably, he let it lapse for the next six years. In view of his frankly commercial purpose in keeping it, it is hard to see why he would have destroyed the intervening entries. From 1931, however, he kept it up meticulously until LG's death in 1945, recording the old man's increasingly demanding ways, his rows with his family and tensions with Frances, in often prurient detail, with a particularly beady interest in LG's occasional pursuit of other women. Sylvester was an impeccable secretary and an invaluable witness for the historian; but he was not a very attractive man.

Frances's life now settled into a routine that must have been a little dull after the excitement of the previous decade, divided between the

---

* Frances and LG laughed at Sylvester behind his back; they mocked his Staffordshire accent and his Uriah Heep-like demeanour. 'Did he become contemptible because he was treated with contempt by the people to whom he gave excellent service?' Jennifer Longford later wondered. 'Or was he innately contemptible, and they saw through his obsequiousness? I don't know'. Yet she added that Sylvester was always kind to her and she felt guilty that LG and Frances treated him so badly.[1]

office in Abingdon Street, her flat in Morpeth Mansions, where she stayed when LG was up in London, and Churt, where LG now spent most of his time – not only at weekends, but often during the week as well. Frances was normally there too whenever he was – except when his family prevented it – and sometimes when he was not. (More than once he described it as 'our little home'.[3]) He was still frenetically active, but the politics of opposition, particularly in a divided and squabbling third party, were increasingly wearisome. Instead he threw much of his energy into developing his farm. The estate at Churt consisted originally of sixty acres of scrubby, sandy soil, declared unsuitable for growing fruit. But LG was as determined to succeed at growing apples as he had once been to produce munitions or win the war. He would make it pay, he vowed, 'whatever it cost' – and he did.[4] Over the years he bought more and more of the surrounding land, installed expensive irrigation systems and grew several varieties of apples as well as cherries, currants and other fruit and vegetables, which regularly won prizes at local shows. He also kept bees and sold honey to Harrods and Fortnum & Mason (labelled 'From the estate of D. Lloyd George, OM, MP'), and opened a shop to sell his produce at the roadside. Frances had no direct responsibility for the farm, though she enjoyed walking about the orchards with him. He employed a succession of managers and other specialists; but he was such an interfering employer, with so many pet ideas of his own and the conviction that they were all cheating him, that none of them stayed very long and there were frequent crises that Frances did have to sort out. The turnover of housekeepers was equally high, which must have been a continual headache for her – not least because their irregular ménage made them unusually dependent on discreet servants. It is amazing that none of these employees talked after they had moved on, especially since they often left after an argument. Altogether, as time passed and LG became more and more demanding as he got older, it is clear that Frances had an increasingly difficult time with him.

There were also substantial periods when LG was away with his family, either in Wales or further afield, seeking the sun. To Frances he complained incessantly about having to go to Criccieth so often – he complained about the weather, he complained about his family, and he complained about being constantly on show – but he still went, usually several times a year, so his complaints must be taken with a good deal of salt. He still needed the spiritual refreshment of his native haunts, and he still loved showing visitors around them. He always invited members of his staff and colleagues with him: the only person he could not take there was Frances. During his absences, however, they wrote to each other regularly. Since Frances's diary is so sporadic, their letters are the principal source of our knowledge of their relationship in these years; fortunately many more of hers have survived than in the early years, so we get more of her side of the story. They are unfailingly loving, often rapturously so; but there is a sense sometimes that she protests her love too much – as indeed does he: that both of them are desperately anxious to ensure the other's continuing commitment, and that in these ardent letters that fill their periods of separation they are consciously making up for the tensions that arose when they were together.

Only one letter survives from the spring of 1923, when LG spent a few days in Wales between a speaking engagement at Llanfairfechan on 22 May and another at Edinburgh on the 27th. In that time Frances evidently contrived to write to him at least twice. The 'crisis' referred to in LG's reply was the resignation of Bonar Law after only seven months in office – he died within a few months – and his replacement by Stanley Baldwin.

> My own sweet girl
>   My little girl of the sweet face & sweet heart – in fact the little girl who is all sweet to me. I have never longed as much for her. I have never been so desirous of getting back to her & refolding her in my arms. I tried to find an excuse in the political crisis for coming up on Friday – just for one kiss before I left for Edinburgh – or perhaps two or more likely two thousand. But Winston didn't play up. He was always a disappointing colleague! Never mind darling Monday is getting nearer.
>   I phoned last night to Churt & was so disappointed to find you had returned to London after lunch. This morning I phoned to London & found you had left for Churt, *Pussy bach* you have dodged me. Why *cariad*?
>   But I received your delicious letters. I have read them over & over again & they thrill me each time – but they have an unsettling effect & I must read them no more . . .
>   Fond fond fonder than ever love
>   Your own
>   D.[5]

But there was a major flurry of letters in August, when LG next went to Criccieth and Frances simultaneously went on holiday to Beattock in the Scottish borders. They had clearly been through a bad time before LG went away, since Frances wrote him a long apologetic letter before she left London herself.

My own beloved little man,

It is very late, but I feel I cannot leave without sending you a line to await you on your arrival at Criccieth. I want to tell you again & again how much I love you & how desperately sorry I am for any pain I have caused you. I can only say that I was very tired too – more tired than I realised, as I am just beginning to find out. But when you return, my darling, you will find a completely renewed and rejuvenated young woman awaiting you, who will spare no effort to make life sweet and happy and who wants to be such a help to you. Will you believe that, dear sweetheart, and look forward to the time when you will see her?

I do not think you can realise how heavily the time drags once you have gone. At the end of this first day it seems that you have been gone so long that it must surely be time for you to return. The next fortnight will be interminable. I can only bear it if you will promise me that you will make good use of it by resting. You work far too hard, *cariad*. I should be so happy if I thought you were going to have a short time free from work & worry. I fear you will not, though. But do try – my darling.

In the meantime I am thinking loving thoughts of you night and day and thinking often of that wonderful little episode in the sun-flecked lane. You are such a beautiful lover – can you wonder that I scarcely survive when you are not here? . . .

All my love, best and dearest of men. You have my soul and mind and body in your keeping.

Ever your own
P.[6]

Three days later she wrote again from Beattock.

This is a beautiful place, with hills all round – rather like Wales, except that there is no sea. The air is wonderful for jaded nerves – I am feeling a different woman already! (Don't wire me the obvious reply!) . . . I think a place like this would have suited you far better than Gairloch! But to my mind no place is as good for you as Churt. I am looking forward so much,

sweetheart, to spending a little time there with you. It is quite a long time
since we had two whole consecutive days there together!

Do you think of me, sometimes, beloved, and sweetly? I want you to
love me more as the time goes on, just as I love you increasingly with every
day that passes – love you more passionately, more tenderly, and long for
your presence more urgently and desperately. I want you at this moment,
so that I feel I must come straight to you now & beg you to take me in
your arms. But I must not say these things to you, little man, or you will
be reproving me for disturbing your holiday! So I will now get ready for
the kirk, where I shall sit & think of you all the time!

Take care of yourself, belovedest, & write me a little line when you have
time.

Your very devoted

P.[7]

LG replied two days later – a typical moan about the miserable
weather, relieved only by Frances's letters ('two shafts of light that pene-
trated the gloom'), and about the continual sightseers peering through
the privet hedge and climbing the walls to try to get a look at him. As
usual he swore that he only wanted to be back with her: 'I am longing
for my Surrey heath with its sweet heather & the sweeter companionship of the dear little fairy of the lane'. But he too suggested that she
had recently been under stress.

Enjoy yourself darling. I want a renovated calmed little girl. I want nothing
sweeter nor more loving – but just a little less exacting now & again. No
I dont I'll take her exactly as she is & has been & will be – world without
end. Amen . . .

So there you are. But get well – not to change but to be more like your
darling self.

Fond fond fonder than ever

D.

Crowds now on the wall looking at me – in bed. Only just discovered it.
Had they known what I was doing.[8]

The next day he wrote again – an important letter in which he tried
to express his appreciation of what Frances gave him. Maybe they had
been having some of the arguments she reproduced in her novel.

I am so pleased to hear that you have found such delightful quarters & that it is doing you good.

Your nerves have been sorely tried my sweet. You have lived through my worries as well as your own & you have felt mine with an exquisite torture coming from a tender loving heart. I know it is my own love. Don't you imagine that I have not seen it & that it has not filled me with wonder that I should ever have won such an affection. It is my greatest achievement in life – & I mean it. Nothing else gives me such joy to think of. But there is another side – my selfish acceptance of it. I know how much you have been torn in the most susceptible fibres of your heart – *cariad* mine. You need a real rest – free from care which means free from me.

Then he reflected that the uncertainty of his political situation – doubtless the cause of the strains between them – was not really so bad.

We'll pull through. We are passing through the worst time – immediately after the fall. But it is nothing to Asquith's. He retired an accepted failure – without a triumph to redeem his fame. As you say nothing can rob me of what I have accomplished . . . And everything that has happened since my retirement has justified my policy . . .

As I assume you leave Monday or Saturday for Hindhead I shall not risk another letter but you can go on writing me here – until well – until when. I mean to try and escape some time about the end of next week. And *then* . . .

Fondest tenderest love
Your
D.[9]

These letters crossed with another from Frances, giving more news of her holiday. As well as playing a lot of tennis and golf, she had been grouse shooting: she had even sent a brace to Criccieth, which must have been received with mixed feelings. Then she went on:

But it is the next part of my holiday I am looking forward to, when I shall be walking over the *Surrey* hills with my beloved, & when there will be no limit to my happiness, & everything will be perfect. It is only with you, my darling, *darling* man, that I am really happy. Just now underneath everything I feel depressed, & I know it is because you're not there. I seem to feel the need of you more and more, until sometimes I feel frightened at my absolute dependence upon you . . . To be separated from you is to be dead for the time being – oh, it is worse than death – it is a form of purgatory. There could be no purgatory though, if you were there, and heaven without you would be hell . . .

Am looking forward to hearing from you soon, beloved. The sight of your handwriting fills me with joy. I love every letter of it. Meanwhile love me, my darling, & don't let yourself be influenced by anything *they* say about me. Think of me as the little girl who feels such a tender affection & love for her darling old man that she would gladly lay down her life for him.

Ever your own
Pussy[10]

The next day LG's letters arrived and her love overflowed:

My beloved sweetheart,

Imagine my joy at finding *two* letters from my darling this morning. And such wonderful letters too! When I read the second, I just broke down and cried! I don't deserve half the beautiful things you say, *cariad*. I know I don't. I feel I ought to have been far, far sweeter to you, and tried to lighten things for you much more than I have. I will try in future to be a hundred times more tender and thoughtful, & to deserve the wonderful love you give me. As I read the letters, I felt it wrapping me round, and as I carry them about in my breast, with all they imply, I feel I am the richest woman in the world – as I am. How can I ever repay you for all the happiness you shower upon me, *cariad*? Only by giving you all my devotion and love and affection – as I do now & will ever do, more and more. Your loving words have made me thrill with happiness, & I shall now be impatient for the consummation of that happiness by your return & our sweet communion together . . .

I shall go straight to Churt [on Monday] and get things ready for my beloved little man, so that he can complete his holiday there. I feel you have still to learn the art of doing nothing, *cariad*, & as things are at present it looks as though you never will be able to have the chance!

Cariad, I love you so much, & I love you for writing me such sweet letters. Every time I read them the tears come – but tears of happiness and pride – pride at my wonderful lover. You see, nothing matters to me so long as life means walking by your side, wherever we have to walk. But my heart goes out to you when I see you tired and worried . . .

If you do not write again here, I shall look forward to getting a line from my darling at Hindhead, where I shall wait for him (or perhaps I will come up to London & drive down with him). And *then* – oh, my darling ——

Ever your loving & devoted & longing

P.[11]

The next day she wrote again, describing her dreams – with once again a clear betrayal of her insecurity:

My own darling little man,

This is just a little line to let you know that I am always thinking of you and loving you more than ever. I slept with your letters under my pillow last night, and had such a wonderful dream, the poignant sweetness of which was marred by the fact that when I awoke, I found I was not in your arms, beloved! But unlike most dreams, it was one which has the possibility of being fulfilled & at no distant date, I hope, *cariad*. I shall count the days now till you return, darling, and I hope that perhaps by this time next week that dream may have come true! The dreams I had been having up till then, had been all sad ones – you were always cross with me, or else behaving badly with someone else! But last night showed a distinct improvement! . . .

I am putting off quite a lot of weight, though I don't think that you will, even so, find a shadow awaiting you!

Fondest, tenderest & most devoted love from your own

P.[12]

In his next LG warned her not to write again, 'as it takes two days to travel & the post is very late in coming every morning'.[13] But Frances did, telling him about her journey south and some gossip about Lord Birkenhead's affair with the twenty-year-old Mona Dunn: LG was always interested in other people's illicit relationships. After a good deal more political news she concluded:

I am afraid this is a very 'sloppy' letter, best beloved. I have left myself no room to tell you how I am longing to see your darling face again. Don't stay away too long sweetheart. The days are dragging horribly now, and it seems an age since you went away. In fact, you will have to start your wooing all over again, but you will find a very willing seducee! one who has been waiting for you since a previous existence! . . .

> Goodbye for the present, *cariad* mine.
> All my love & tenderest kisses.
> Your loving
> P.[14]

At the beginning of October, LG set off on a triumphant five-week
tour of the United States and Canada. Not since Dickens eighty years
earlier had a British visitor enjoyed such acclaim in America; not until
the Beatles forty years later would his reception be surpassed. He was
met with brass bands and a ticker-tape parade in New York, then travelled around the Midwest and the old South in a special train, speaking
to the crowds that gathered to see him at every wayside station and at
vast rallies in twenty-two cities – which he addressed for the first time
with the help of electronic amplification. Some of them were also broadcast. Everywhere he went he urged the Americans to recommit themselves to helping to preserve the peace of Europe. But he also indulged
his private interests by visiting the famous log-cabin home of Abraham
Lincoln and walking the battlefields of the Civil War. In Washington
he lunched with President Coolidge in the White House, and took tea
with Woodrow Wilson, now crippled by a stroke and near to death.

Frances obviously could not go with him. LG was accompanied by
Maggie and Megan, plus Sylvester, who was responsible for making all
the arrangements and sent back daily cables reporting their progress.
Frances meanwhile took the opportunity to visit Paris and Florence.
She had always loved Paris, but her going on to Florence is intriguing
in view of the romantic association the city evidently held for her. Unlike
her fictional heroines, however, Frances did not travel alone, but with
a woman friend (unfortunately unidentified). From Paris – where she
again stayed at the Hotel Crillon – she wrote a long, anxious letter on
9 October:

> My own darling, beloved little Man,
>   I know I am not going to have one minute's peace until you are safely
> back home. I worry about you every hour of the day and lie awake at night
> thinking about you too, and praying that you may have the strength to
> achieve what you have set out to do . . .
>   I am sending cables to Sylvester every day, or every other day. They are
> really meant for you, *cariad*, but I thought it wiser to send them to him. I
> hope he is showing them to you. I don't sign them.

She was delighted with press reports of his tour, but worried that the enthusiasm might tempt him to overstrain himself.

Darling, *do* look after yourself. The greatest success it is possible for humans to achieve would not be worth while, to my mind, if you knocked yourself up – I suppose it is frightfully selfish in a way to think of it in that way, but all love is selfish to a certain extent, & I want you back above all safe and sound.

Reading of his triumph, she went on, brought tears to her eyes.

How I wish I were there to see it! But you will tell me all about it when you return, won't you, darling one, and in the midst of it all you do stop & think sometimes, don't you, of the little girl here who is following your every movement & every word with anxiety and love. What a talk we shall have when you come home, beloved! You won't have changed at all, will you, *cariad*? I am so afraid that what you see over there will make you dissatisfied with what is over here, & that the charming people you are meeting may distract your love from me – No, I don't really think that – I know now that you do not change and that when you come back you will be just the same sweet lover, and perhaps with an added tenderness, to meet the increased tenderness I am feeling for you after all your endeavours and achievements.

Paris is wonderful as usual . . . We leave here on Thursday . . . Everyone says we shall go no further than Florence, as it is so wonderfully interesting – but we shall see.

I am writing this in bed – *cariad* – and I shall go to sleep & dream about you – sweet dreams that will be realised when you return, but which fill me with longing until I feel your arms round me once again. I have never loved you so much, or been so happy in your love, as now, my darling, when you are going through this ordeal. I am so proud of my little man, so terribly proud, and yet I still have in my heart all the time that poignant anxiety which a mother must feel for her son. It seems to dominate every other feeling, & it is only when you are safe on your homeward journey, my darling, that the wild tumult of passion in my heart will be allowed to have full play . . . Take care of yourself, beloved, & hasten back to the longing breast of your devoted, & loving,

P.[15]

This letter was enclosed under cover of one to Sylvester, whom she addressed far more formally than she had been used to addressing J. T. Davies.

> Dear Mr Sylvester,
>   It is nice of you to send me telegrams & I am very grateful to know all that is going on. You seem to be having a marvellous time. Will you give this letter to the Chief, please? . . .
>   Kindest regards,
>   Yours sincerely,
>   F.L.S.[16]

We know that in Florence Frances stayed at the Hotel d'Italie, since her father wrote to her there, thanking her for a letter from Paris and giving family news.[17] She clearly did not waste her time, since she had armed herself with letters of introduction to various prominent Italians.[18] And, yes, there is preserved in her papers just a hint that she may have enjoyed a bit of a flirtation, if no more, in the form of a wonderfully romantic letter, begging her forgiveness, from a man signing himself 'Your faithful Italian guide'. It was posted from Livorno on 23 October and addressed to the Hotel Crillon, where Frances had stopped again on her way home.[19] Did she, like Ann in the first draft of her novel, virtuously refuse this suitor? Or did she perhaps, like Delphine in the second draft, surrender briefly to her Mario? Either way, it was not only in her imagination that Florence was where one went to meet ardent Italian lovers.

From Indianapolis on 22 October LG wrote his only letter of his American trip.

> My own darling girl,
>   This is my first chance to get one word through to the girl of girls for me – the one & only girl of my heart. I have literally not one minute to myself. It has been a terrible experience although a triumphant one . . . Had I been their own general returned victorious from the Wars they could not have been more enthusiastic . . . Every little station on the route with great gatherings come to see & cheer . . .
>   But I do want to get back to Pussy *bach anwyl aur chus melyn siwgr mel yn gariad I gyd bob tamaid o honi* & all the rest which I dare not commit to writing.

Fond fond yearning love
D.[20]

LG returned on 9 November to another phenomenal reception – first at Southampton and then at Waterloo – only to plunge straight into a snap General Election called by Baldwin to try to win a mandate to tackle the growing unemployment problem by introducing protective tariffs. This had the immediate effect of reuniting the two wings of the Liberal party, with LG once again accepting Asquith's leadership. LG spoke all around the country, drawing enthusiastic crowds that encouraged him to believe he was on the way back. Frances stayed behind in Abingdon Street, reading the reports of his meetings and sending over-optimistic accounts of the view from London.

Am longing to get you back again, best beloved, safe and sound. It is diffi-cult for me to wait patiently here, when I want to be with you so desper-ately. I would give anything in the world to be coming round with you now. Fondest greetings, *cariad*, & all my love
P.[21]*

The result of the election was a hung Parliament. The Liberals won 159 seats, but they were still the third party behind Labour with 191 and the Tories with 258. Though the Tories were easily the largest party, Baldwin's policy had clearly been rejected, so Asquith and LG had little choice but to support the experiment of the first Labour government, led by Ramsay MacDonald, which duly took office in January 1924. In fact it lasted just nine months before the Liberals combined with the Tories to defeat it over its attempts to make a trade agreement with Russia – something LG himself had been keen on only two years earlier. Another election was held, in which the Tories were returned with a landslide majority over Labour, while the Liberals were reduced to just forty seats. Divided more bitterly than ever between the Asquithian and Lloyd George factions, they were caught in an electoral trap from which they would not begin to escape for another sixty years. LG bore some share of blame

* She added the unwelcome – to her – bit of family news that Olwen was back from India with her three children, Margaret (five), Eluned (two) and the new-born Robin. 'I suppose Cheyne Walk will be turned into a nursery now. Whatever you do,' she begged, '*keep them away from Hindhead*!'[22]

for this debacle; but his hopes of an early return to office were now severely damaged.

Still he was not cast down. 'The Goat' was so obviously the biggest beast in the political zoo that most people could not believe that he would not return in one way or another, sooner or later.[*] Frances certainly did everything she could to encourage him in this confidence, constantly reassuring him that he was still 'a towering figure among all the little pigmies who are strutting about at present, & can afford to be amused at them & look on them with contempt'.[23] This was of course what he wanted to hear; but the idea that he was somehow above party politics, and actually better off without a major party behind him, was bad advice, which, as it turned out, would serve to keep him in the political wilderness for the rest of his life.

---

[*] The nickname 'the Goat', popularised by Keynes, referred variously to LG's political agility, his sexual energy, his Welshness and his shaggy white hair. A *Punch* cartoon in October 1922 portrayed him as a defiant scapegoat refusing to go quietly into the wilderness.

24

'TO ME YOU ARE EVERYTHING'

The next year, 1924, is a thin one for surviving communication between LG and Frances. He wrote more often to Maggie in Criccieth and to Megan, who was on a year-long visit to India, than he did to Frances: presumably therefore they were together most of the time, working in Abingdon Street and relaxing, when they could, at Churt. In fact the most remarkable letter he wrote this year was to Maggie in July, when they had evidently had one of their periodic rows in which she had rebuked him for spending so much time with Frances. Her letter is lost; but it drew from LG a characteristically defiant remonstrance, protesting his enduring loyalty to her, despite what he called his 'weakness':

> You talk as if my affection for you came & went. No more than the sea does because the tide ebbs & flows. There is just as much water in it . . . You like me better sometimes when I am nice to you. So do I when you are nice to me. But if at the worst moment anybody is not nice to you I am as murderous towards him as Patrick Mahon.* I would readily hit them with an axe.
>
> You say I have my weakness. So has anyone that ever lived & the greater the man the greater the weakness. It is only insipid, wishy washy fellows that have no weaknesses. Would you like to marry Tim!! [Timothy Davies] He is sober & sternly good in all respects.
>
> You must make allowances for the waywardness & wildness of a man of my type. What if I were drunk as well? I can give you two samples you

---

* Patrick Mahon was a notorious axe-murderer who had been convicted a few days earlier.

know of both the weaknesses in one man & the wives do their best under those conditions. What about Asquith & Birkenhead? I could tell you stories of both – women & wine. Believe me *hen gariad* I am at bottom as fond of you as ever . . .

On this argument Asquith and Birkenhead were even greater men than he was! He added a word about money. Though he was now earning more from journalism than he had ever done as Prime Minister, Maggie was evidently fearful about what might be left for her if he died. Perhaps she knew that he had made a new will.

I am doing my best to cut down expenses. I agree with you about that. You have always been frugal & careful & in that respect *as in many others* I am grateful to you & I recognise it in my will. I certainly mean to return with you in September.[1]

Meanwhile his other wife wrote him thoroughly domestic letters from Churt while he was away during the election campaign. She told him that not only had his favourite Chong produced puppies, but that the sow had produced a litter of nine piglets – with the intriguing comment: 'So you see Churt is keeping up its record for fertility, in your absence.' What could she have meant? Frances would surely not have referred so lightly to her own frequent pregnancies. She went on:

I shall try to run down there tomorrow, but there is a good deal to do here & I feel it is a good thing for me to be on the spot . . . I wish I could do more to help you, *cariad*. I like to think that my loving thoughts are perhaps reaching you in some mysterious way, and may be helping you a little. Although I must say you appear to be doing very well on your own, without anyone's help! But I know it will make you a little happier to know that I am following your every word, and rejoicing with you at your successes, and loving you from the depth of my heart, more than ever before. I am feeling more than ever, darling man, that we are nearer to each other than we have ever been, although there are hundreds of miles between us.

Take care of my lover for me & see that he comes to no harm – for if he did his sweetheart would break her heart.

P.[2]

On 26 November Sylvester recorded a pleasing picture of LG and Frances going to Slough together to buy fruit trees, returning for lunch in the office 'with a cut of beef and a bottle of beer'.[3] But the following week, ever alert for good copy, he suspected that LG was misbehaving with one of his typists, suitably named Miss Cheek. On 6 December LG came up to London to meet Megan on her return from India, then went back to Churt: 'Miss Cheek there alone!'[4] Five days later Sylvester 'dealt with Miss Cheek and told her she could stay if she could do as she was told'.[5] Then, on 18 December, LG was due to dine with the Asquiths and attend a Liberal ball at the Hyde Park Hotel before travelling to Edinburgh the next day to make a speech. He did dine with the Asquiths, and wrote to tell Maggie how it had gone. But he did not go on to the ball; instead he went back to Cheyne Walk 'to concentrate on his Edinburgh speech' – with Miss Cheek. Sylvester arrived at Cheyne Walk soon after nine the next morning.

Found that Miss Cheek had not finished Chief's speech and that he had not finished dictating it. She had been there all night. She said Chief asked what I thought about her going to Edinburgh. Having ascertained that the speech was nowhere [near] finished I arranged for her to go.

LG then continued dictating to Miss Cheek on the train.[6]

So where was Frances? Why was she not helping with the speech, and why did she not go to Edinburgh? There is no hint in a letter she wrote LG on Boxing Day of any quarrel or any explicit suggestion that she suspected hanky-panky – though she does sound a little anxious. LG was by then at Criccieth; Frances had presumably spent Christmas Day with her parents, but was now back in Morpeth Mansions.

My own beloved sweetheart

This is just a line to tell you that I am thinking of you all the time and loving you more than ever. I really don't know what will happen if I go on like this! I miss you terribly, but I am happy in thinking that you love me too – more than you did, I think! Just go & talk to the river a little, for I feel sure it will tell you what I have already told you, & I want you so much to believe that it is true . . .

Longing to see you again, my beloved & hoping the time will pass quickly. Take care of yourself & love me a little.

> Your ever devoted & worshipping
> P.[7]

She had never used the word 'worshipping' before.

When LG returned from Wales, with Sylvester, on 31 December, Frances met them at Euston. Sylvester's account implies that Frances did not quite trust LG.

> L.G. was in good form. Related how he got wet through walking on Saturday: that 'they' had to seek shelter in the gorse.
>
> Frances asked who 'they' were. Chief said Gwilym – and jokingly said that if it had been 'anybody' else he would have been all right and the prickly gorse would not have been his concern.
>
> I quitted the car on the Euston Road and went to the office. They went to Churt.[8]

Is it possible that Miss Cheek had been at Criccieth? Unfortunately Sylvester's diary now falls silent for the next six years, so we never hear of her again.

Instead Frances made a couple of brief entries in her own diary in March 1925. There is no explanation of why she suddenly took it up again – having bought a new printed volume for the purpose – but then abandoned it again almost immediately. Maybe it was because LG had been ill for three weeks, but was now on the mend. Like her fictional alter ego, Frances was playing with the fantasy that he might give up politics – if not for her sake, then from weariness with the Liberal factions.

> Came up today for the first time since D's illness . . . He is by no means fit for strenuous work yet, and has given up the idea of going to Manchester on Saturday. Am very glad, as was worrying about it. Churt is the happiest place of all now, D. I think for two pins would give up politics – at any rate party politics for a time. The dissensions at H.Q. make him sick & the behaviour of the Radical group in the House is also nauseous.
>
> We returned to Churt tonight until next week. D. is superintending emptying the fishponds.[9]

Three weeks later LG went away with Maggie and Gwilym for a short holiday in Madeira. He had not been abroad at all in 1924, and clearly felt the deprivation. From Madeira he wrote Frances a long letter filled initially with his usual protestations about the pain of separation, but ending with an important restatement of his commitment to her.

> My own girl for ever and ever
>   Here I have brilliant warming sunshine which penetrates to the marrow after two years of chilling weather. I have underneath my balcony a garden radiant with bougainvilliers [*sic*] wisteria & flowers I have never heard of – the evening air laden with their perfume – little birds cheeping & caroling in their branches . . . All this ought to content the most sensuous soul but it leaves me with a craving for a misty, grey damp & shivering island under whose murky clouds dwell[s] the darling of my heart whose companionship brings me more sunshine colour & joy than all these foreign delights . . .
>   I am reckoning up the days until I can return to something which beats Madeira & all its beauties, permanent and transient – to fits. This is five days gone & five less days of separation. I am more impatient of it than ever this time . . .
>   Although I have no delusions as to the past – none – neither have I any regrets. It is all to me like a previous existence. A new birth came in October 1922. A new tenderness & a new clear & firm purpose came to us both. Before that – to use a legal term applicable to the law of domicile – there was a certain *animus revertendi*. More marked in your case than in mine – naturally. Since then we have definitely settled our domicile. Your love is henceforth my country & mine is yours. So we have a right to expect loyalty & patriotism to our new domicile. We did not quite feel it was due before. I love you more tenderly than ever – in a different way altogether. I cannot think of life apart from you now. I could give up everything for you without a qualm – even with some relief.
>   Fond love to you my own girl
>   D.[10]

There are several things to be said about this. First, of course, LG had no intention of giving up everything for her, so his continual harping on the possibility was no more than a cruel tease. Second, he and Frances had been together now for twelve years, vowing mutual and eternal love from the beginning. The suggestion that it had all been provisional on both sides up to now is a bit breathtaking. At the same time their situation *had* changed since October 1922. It was not only that LG was no longer in office. He was also aware that he was getting old – he was now sixty-two – while she, at thirty-six, was no longer a girl, but a woman in her prime whose options would soon begin to run out. If she was ever going to leave him to make a new life with someone who might give her the children he knew she wanted, she would have to do so soon. Her novel was her way of telling LG how torn she was. He may also have realised that playing around with Miss Cheek or anyone else made her doubt his fidelity. He had evidently calculated that if he wanted to secure her continued companionship to comfort his old age, he needed to bind her to him now. Hence the quasi-legal attempt to suggest a fresh contract, with promises of good behaviour on his part the price of being able to demand reciprocation on hers. If Frances was really showing signs of restlessness, this letter was cleverly framed to persuade her to recommit herself to him.

On his return LG threw himself back into politics more strenuously than ever: he was busy with a new plan to restore British farming by nationalising agricultural land, and was increasingly critical of the government's failure to tackle unemployment. In the second half of May he spoke no fewer than seven times in the Commons, then went to Criccieth for Whitsun, from where he wrote Frances a characteristic catalogue of complaints.

My own girl,

I am getting more & more to find life, without your sweet & loving companionship, unbearable. I have gone through days of boredom. On Monday I took a picnic ride over these gorgeous mountains to see one of the loveliest valleys in Wales but as we drove towards the East I felt I must go onwards to the spot where my girl was waiting for me. I leapt towards you. I cannot repeat these domestic holidays. They are getting unendurable. I want you my darling. You talk about the time being nigh when I shall be called back. My thoughts have been all the other way – about retiring somewhere from the confusion & din & worries of the aimless battling somewhere to enjoy the endless felicities of your love. To me you are everything.

I am coming up *Saturday* night. Hope to get the train arriving Euston about 9. Meet me at the station & we can drive home together. We can stay at Bron-y-de until Monday afternoon . . .

Until Saturday I shall continue thinking of you and all you mean to me.
Ever & Ever
Your D.[11]

In August, despite all his grousing, LG went to Criccieth again as usual, and Frances took her holiday in Wales as well. She stayed at Llandrindod Wells with her sister Muriel – evidently his idea – but since this was still sixty miles from Criccieth it is difficult to see what the point was. Maybe the post was quicker, since they wrote to each other practically every day; this was one of the most intense (and sexually charged) exchanges in their entire correspondence. Frances's first letter is lost, but it is plain that she was having a dull time – which was doubtless his intention. He did not want her getting up to any more adventures such as she may have had in Florence. They were both now playing a game – outwardly teasing but anxious underneath – of mistrusting the other's fidelity while protesting their own.

My own girl

I have been looking forward so longingly to receiving one letter from you my own girl. I wanted to know how you were & what you were doing & how you were getting on – how you liked Llandrindod Wells, & especially whether you still liked me.

You don't tell me much about your sweet loving & lovable self. I want to hear more. And I gather that you are not in love with Llandrindod or anyone that dwells therein. Only old frumps of 50 or even 60. So you think 60 is past the dangerous age! I am so encouraged to think so for I need not worry now to keep watch on myself. I can concentrate all my vigilance on my sweet little naughty. However you know now why I thought Llandrindod was so good for your health *cariad*.

But chaffing apart you don't tell me what you really think of it. What about the golf course? What about the waters? Did you see the doctor & what did he tell you? I want to see you looking so well & fit that I shall bless Llandrindod for ever more. Do you want to know any thing about your lame & safe sexagenarian lover? Well he loves you still with an affection & devotion & tenderness – & ferocity which is unchilled by the snows of age or the glaciers of domesticity. I am counting the days. It is not now a fortnight before I shall be able to show you my overwhelming demonstration that it is not wise to presume too much on the decrepitude of 60 . . .

Keep on writing my sweet. Do look after yourself. I want my recommendation to be a success. Give it a good chance to succeed.

Give my love to Muriel & tell her not to flirt too much but that *all* the flirting that is permissible to the party must be done by her.

Ever & Ever

Your own

D.[12]

Frances replied at even greater length. She did not seem to mind his chaffing, but responded enthusiastically in kind.

My own beloved darling

It was a joy to me to receive your sweet, sweet letter this morning. My heart has been singing ever since, & I feel as though I were walking on air. You are a *darling* to write me such a loving letter, & you make me feel more than ever that my man is the most wonderful lover in the world, & that no one could give me such tenderness and affection & love as you do. When you write me such a thrilling letter, beloved, I feel so incapable of telling you in return all that I feel for you, for I have not the gift of words as you have, and I cannot express all that I feel for you in my heart. But you know, don't you, that I am thinking about you all the time, and that I am longing & longing to see your darling face again. And I want your *lips*, today, *cariad*. I have been thinking of their sweetness & their thrilling-ness, & of course that leads me to think of other things! I am counting the days too, & it seems such a terrible long time to wait still. But in the mean-time I am being so good & taking such care of myself that you will see an entirely new girl when you return. The Doctor told me to take the saline waters in the morning (which I do) and the sulphur water in the middle of the day (which I also do) and to take the mild sulphur baths every other day (which I am doing & which I enjoy very much). I am already feeling the benefit, & my skin is beginning to look like a two-year-old's, & by the time you come back I shall be a vision of youth & loveliness! I am so grateful to you, beloved, for sending me here, for it really is an ideal place for a rest. The air is wonderful, & we have been playing golf in the morning & tennis in the afternoon.

I thought my description of the hotel, & the visitors over 60, would rouse you to wrath! But darling it *certainly does not mean* that you can relax your watch on yourself, for I would back you for naughtiness against any man of any age, that I know! There are exceptions to every rule, you know, & though the old men here may be bald and rheumatic & perfectly virtuous, there is an old man I know in North Wales who is none of these things, but who is a most dangerous character, & not one to take liberties with! So do be careful, sweetheart mine, and come back to me without a spot on your escutcheon . . .

In his letter LG had sent her two sprigs of white heather picked on the top of an ancient hill fort that they had climbed together back in 1911. Frances remembered it well.

I simply *love* the white heather, darling. It is sweet of you to send it. I will wear it next to my heart . . . I remember so well the old fort, & the walk with you. I remember so vividly the details of that time, whatever I may have forgotten since! It was just this time of the year, 14 years ago! I was happy that summer, but it is nothing to the deep happiness that possesses me now . . .

I am really feeling tremendously fit already, & am going to lay in stores of energy & vitality in order to cope with the vigour of 62 the week after next! Not an easy job, I can tell you, but such a thrilling one!

Muriel sends her love, & was much amused at your message. She asks me to send you hers, & to say that she won't have any chance of a flirtation here . . .

Write me another tender little note if you can, beloved, & tell me about yourself. I am loving you always, always, & always more tenderly & truly.

Ever your own
P.[13]*

LG's reply harked back again to the summer of 1911.

My girl
Am off to see the annual sheep trial. Do you remember? 14 years ago. I was stricken then & the disease has obtained complete hold of me body & soul. Worst of all I like it – yes I do my own darling little rascal.

Delighted to get your letter – full of your doings. It is what I wanted to know. You are doing just what I want. Get well. You will need every ounce of your strength . . .

Write tomorrow. I loved your letter today. Just the stuff for me.

Fond Fond affection love tenderness & *Naughtiness*

---

* She added a note about their postal arrangements. Hitherto she had addressed her letters to Sylvester; but he was now leaving Criccieth, so she proposed to address them in future to LG, but get Muriel to write the envelopes. 'So look out for them! (I will put a double envelope.)'[14] It is unlikely that Maggie was fooled.

Ever & Ever
D.

Love to Muriel. Tell her to cut in at once if she sees you flirting.[15]

Frances's next two letters are missing, so the next one we have is
from LG again. By now his imagination was getting quite heated.

My own darling girl
    The glowing account you give me in both your letters . . . of the effect
upon your body and spirit of golf tennis baths waters & laughter excite me
to look forward to meeting on my return a slim bright girl of Philippian
grace. I shall therefore enjoy all the enchantments of falling in love with a
new girl. A girl this time of the latest fashionable type with all the curves
& roundnesses worked off. But darling – do keep some of them. I never
cared for the new type as you know. They stimulate no interest in me. They
may be alright for Lympne but they won't do for Churt. You know the
Venus I love.
    When I hear how you are enjoying that place & how much good it is
doing my sweetheart I feel ashamed to take her away to look after her very
exacting & adoring old lover. You ought to have at least another fortnight
there. You have had a hard time recently & Sarah has been [illegible] me
to compassion & self-reproach by telling me how tired you looked the last
few days before you left. But I promise you to do my best to look after
you at Churt so that it shall be a time of continued recuperation for you
as well as of real enjoyment . . .
    I felt in my bones that Llandrindod would be the place for you. The air
is tonic wine. It is full of vitamines [sic]. I am also glad the quality of your
fellow hotellers has improved – but do leave the flirtations to Muriel &
Catherine B. I am getting more & more jealous of your flirtations. I want
them all to myself my own *cariad*. I want your thoughts your dreams –
your naughty impulses – every one of them. You have captured mine to the
last particle of mischief. Keep clear of the tropics in your excursions & if
you do then you cannot cross the line. A good motto for both of us my
sweet . . .
    I hope to reach town Monday afternoon & if you can arrange for a
nice girl (*my* style) to accompany me then I can pick up & drive her down.
You know my style – not too slender or flattened out please. I am not
one of these morbid creatures who experience a delight in committing an

unnatural offence (I am afraid you must burn this letter also) . . .

Give my love to Muriel & tell her to keep away from the Equator unless she has very good company to cross it.

And my tenderest for you my sweet girl

D.[16]

This letter crossed with one from Frances in which she reported, with remarkable unconcern, that his old flame 'Mrs Tim' had turned up at her hotel. 'I hope it won't be too awkward,' she wrote. 'I think it's most amusing. This hotel seems to attract your sweethearts.'[17] But as soon as she got his letter Frances wrote again.

My own beloved sweetheart

Your long letter was so welcome. I simply devour them, & your sweet words thrill me as I read them. For a moment, when you talked about my needing a longer holiday, I thought perhaps you were not coming back, & I was so disappointed, & so relieved to find that that was not the case. I *was* tired when I came away, beloved, but this fortnight will have put me quite right again, & as you say we can still continue to have a little holiday at Churt. In fact from what you tell me I think you may have a quieter time there – though perhaps a little more strenuous in some respects! . . . There will still be a few curves for you to caress, & I'm not exactly flat even now! Still, I want you to fall in love with me again, & I hope you will like the new silhouette . . .

After giving more news of her fellow-guests – 'Mrs Tim' did not stay long and Frances did not speak to her – she reverted to the theme of mildly erotic titillation.

I am arranging for someone to accompany you to Churt on Monday, and I hope she will be to your liking. She will be a little slighter than those you have been accustomed to (for the last few years) but in other respects I think she fulfils your requirements. She is very loving & devoted. She will thrill to your touch & to your voice. She will give you everything that is in her power of affection & passion & desire, & she will look after her old lover & try to make life happy for him. Do you think I have chosen well? You must tell me when you see me.

I will write again tomorrow, *cariad*. I am loving you & thinking of you all the time, & I love these little daily talks of ours. They rejoice my heart

& keep me happy, even in our separation, through the knowledge that you are turning to me to tell all your thoughts & hopes & plans.

Fondest kisses, my darling, darling man, from your little girl who is looking forward so eagerly to seeing you – & embracing you again.

P.[18]

Once again LG's comments on her news crossed in the post.

My girl

Your letters are a real joy & a packet of thrills. You beat me leagues in letter writing & you have never written me nicer letters. I know from them that so far you have been a good little girl thinking lovingly of me in the intervals of tennis golf & dining with Tory MPs – & even now & again in the sulphur baths.

Well well fancy Mrs Tim turning up. You will be able to compare notes together! . . . I know you will be nice to her. She is a good soul . . .

Only five more days . . . I leave here at 10.30 for Euston so if you bring Weller [LG's chauffeur] to meet me at the Station we can drive straight to Churt. Bring a bundle of letters & papers in case Mr & Mrs Ernest Brown are with me* . . .

Love to you my dearest

D.[19]

LG also mentioned that he had been bathing in the sea. ('First time for years and years. I liked it.') Frances's response in her next letter was positively maternal.

Darling, I don't think you ought to bathe after not having bathed for so many years. I was very worried when I read that you had done so, and I do hope it hasn't had any evil consequences. Don't do it again, sweetheart. I wouldn't have let you if I'd been there.

She then teased him by telling him that she had been invited to drive to Brecon with a naval captain and his two boys.

All three of them are rather in love with me (the boys are only 16 & 20) but I'm quite impartial so it's rather amusing, & the wife is becoming quite

---

* Ernest Brown, a former (and future) Liberal MP who had been staying at Criccieth, was a prominent Baptist lay preacher.

fond of me! So you needn't be jealous, *cariad*. I'm keeping my promise so nicely, & intend to do so. I'll be waiting for you so impatiently on Monday. I shall get almost delirious as the hour draws near . . .

Ever your own adoring & loving
P.[20]

The same day LG replied to her previous letter:

My darling little girl

It is so good of you to have made arrangements for Monday evening. They suit me down to the marrow. In fact they fill me with a quiver of expectancy bordering on impatience. I wonder how you succeeded in executing such an exacting order so promptly. That is what it is to have a staff of efficient private secretaries. I have no doubt the other members of the staff would have done equally well – for they would have chosen exactly the same girl. They know my taste so well.

But LG's mind was turning back towards politics, and most of this letter was about his hopes of a Liberal recovery at the next election – for which he apologised.

But here I am maundering about politics when my little girl wants rest from them & I ought also to be seeking rest from their buzz & bother.

Never mind darling we will discover other & sweeter things when we meet on Monday.

Oh my love I do want to see you once more & to revel in your wonderful companionship.

Ever & Ever
Your Old Man

No more letters – except one *from* you tomorrow.[21]

There was indeed one last letter in this remarkable sequence.

My beloved man

I am so glad you approve of the young woman who has been told off for duty on Monday evening. There never was a duty that was so gladly done or more eagerly looked forward to. But how long now the time seems till that moment arrives! However, I suppose it will pass . . .

Muriel sends her love to you. She has been thoroughly enjoying herself, and one married man is completely gone on her. The Stevenson family seem to have an attraction for married men!

All my love to you, darling of my heart. I am just living for Monday, & for the time when you will take me in your arms & say such wonderful things to me, & when I shall give you all the love I have been storing up for you for the last fortnight, & which has been increasing in geometrical progression from day to day.

Your own loving & devoted little girl
P.[22]

These letters suggest that LG and Frances had indeed made a renewed commitment to one another in the summer of 1925. Moreover at the end of the year Frances accompanied LG on a trip to Italy. It was a large party, which provided the necessary cover for her to travel ostensibly as a secretary; but it was definitely more of a holiday than a working visit, though LG did plan to meet Mussolini.* From Naples on Christmas Day he sent a telegram to Criccieth; and the next day he wrote urging Maggie and Megan to join him in Rome.

Do come. We could spend a week there seeing the ruins – the catacombs where the early Xtians worshipped . . . Wire that you are coming both of you . . . Miss Pitt will make all the arrangements. You get a through carriage to Rome from Folkestone.[24]

Had they called his bluff, Frances would have had to disappear. But doubtless LG was confident that Maggie had already decided to stay at home and would not change her plans at short notice. At least he could say that he had tried.

---

* Unfortunately this meeting with Mussolini never took place. According to Sylvester, LG cut short his holiday and went home early because Megan had appendicitis, though there is no other evidence of this.[23]

'THE CHILDREN OF NOAH'

The year 1926 held two dramas for LG and Frances: one public and political, the other private and domestic. The first was the General Strike in May, which caused the final rupture between LG and Asquith and ended with LG at last in control of the Liberal party. The second was a family row over LG's relations with Frances, which erupted in October.

During the General Strike LG took a resolutely moderate line, criticising the government for mishandling the coal crisis while insisting that the TUC's reluctant action in support of the miners had no revolutionary purpose, but was merely 'an honest trade dispute where the parties have been unable to come to an agreement'.[1] 'He took a line peculiarly his own,' Frances wrote after it was all over, 'and for this he has been howled down by the Tories, and cold-shouldered by all the Liberals' – with a few exceptions. But his stance was part of a deliberate strategy.

> D's idea is to go definitely towards the *Left*, and gradually to co-ordinate and consolidate all the progressive forces in the country, against the Conservative and reactionary forces. Thus he will eventually get all sane Labour as well as Liberalism behind him . . . D. will not leave the Liberal party. I begged him not to offer himself to Labour, saying that he must be solicited by them.[2]

The Asquithians, however, who had never forgiven LG for displacing their hero in 1916, saw their opportunity to drive him out of the party.

A new development. Last night D. dined with me. I left the office about 6.30 & he was to come on at 7.30. He was a little late & came in very excitedly, so that I could see something had happened. He said to me: 'I have been expelled from the Party.' And handed me Oxford's letter to read* . . . It was a shock to both of us, & I don't think we discussed it very connectedly . . . but rather speculated as to the influences which had led up to it . . . My chief concern last night was to get D. into a calm frame of mind . . . He has now before him a fight for his political life.[3]

After consulting various of his political friends, LG went off to Wales the next morning to consider his reply, while Frances went to Churt. From Criccieth he wrote her a defiant letter:

My own darling girl

I was so disappointed when I woke up yesterday afternoon & found Sylvester had posted the letter without enclosing a word from me to you. But he had to post very early & he didn't like waking me up. I have had a straining time what between one thing and another but I have a feeling in my bones that I am winning through . . .

As to my [illegible], I *do* want to see you my sweet. I miss you so much in all this – more than I can tell you in words alone. You are my comfort – my solace – my inspiration & my reward. When I say I don't care a damn it only means that I know I've got you.

They insist on returning to town with me. I shall probably motor back on Thursday. If in time I'll be at the office but I doubt if Churt is feasible this week. Morpeth [i.e. Frances's flat] on Friday. How I look forward to it. I dare not dwell on it . . .

Fondest deepest tenderest & most endearing – & fiercest Love
D.[4]

But Asquith had miscalculated, as Frances described in her next diary entry on 30 May:

An exciting week. On Sunday D. telephoned from Criccieth saying he had posted a draft reply to Oxford, & he wanted me to get it in the morning & take it round to Masterman. I went up to town early Monday morning, got the letter & took it round to M. who made several corrections and

---

* Asquith had become the Earl of Oxford after losing his seat in 1924.

alterations, which I subsequently telephoned to Criccieth. D. sent the final
letter that night from Criccieth, but it . . . did not reach the office till 6.15.
At 5.30 we heard that Oxford's letter had been sent to the Press, & so we
were relieved to get D.'s reply, which could now be published simultaneously with the other.

On Wednesday everything in a ferment of excitement . . . Hosts of
telegrams and letters from all over the country supporting D. . . . He himself
returned on Thursday, outwardly very cheerful & determined, but inwardly
trembling with excitement, keyed up to the highest pitch – higher than I
can remember – and deep down hurt, almost like a child unjustly punished,
at the treatment he had received. He will not resign. His tactics are perfect.
He is giving them a long rope with which to hang themselves . . . It is quite
likely that D. will eventually succeed in driving *them* out of the Party.[5]

So it turned out. Asquith it was who had to resign the leadership.
LG spent the summer energetically trying to consolidate his advantage.
'The split has opened a new vision and started a new era in British
politics,' he wrote optimistically on 13 June. 'Liberalism may soon again
take the lead in the march of progress.'[6] In July he spoke twice to the
party conference in Rhyl, and spent a few days in Criccieth preparing
his speeches and writing on familiar lines to Frances.

My one & only love,
   I have been looking forward even more than usual to a letter from the
girl of my heart. I expected one on Saturday & I was so disappointed when
there was nothing in the morning or afternoon delivery. I tore Sylvester's
parcel open today long before he arrived & now I am alright. But I shall
expect another tomorrow . . .
   I am looking forward more than I can tell you to Monday. My meetings are Friday & Saturday afternoon. I hope to reach Churt by lunch on
Sunday. Will you tell them my sweet – my own sweet? Oh I do miss you
every hour of the day . . .[7]

There is something unusually frenetic about LG's letters from Criccieth
that August. (None of Frances's survive.) He harps more than ever on
the theme of their fidelity to one another while they are apart – warning
Frances repeatedly against flirtations while assuring her that he is being
'amazingly good'. His first letter – signed 'your own Old Man' –
mentioned that he has been on 'a motor run up to the mountains' with

a senior Liberal MP and his wife, aged seventy-three, asking ironically: 'Is that safe?'[8] The next day he was complaining as usual about the rain and the 'complete failure' of his attempts at fishing.

> For the moment my chief satisfaction lies in the knowledge that this is the seventh day. I want you my girl. That is the dominant thought of my life. Nothing compensates for your absence – fine views, pleasant weather, delightful country walks – Nothing. I want *you*.
>
> Sarah says it is a good thing for both of us to separate for a few weeks & she wants me to tell you so. Perhaps she is right – but I don't like it & I shall be glad in my heart when it is over . . .
>
> I want to see you looking fit when I return and I will do my best to acquire a fitness that will match yours. Your story of my letter thrilled & entertained me. Of course it took full advantage of the strategical position in which you had placed it. That is just what its creator would have done – & please God will do when he gets a chance – & the sooner the better.[9]

Frances had presumably been keeping his letters next to her breast. But his next is harder to interpret. Note the emphasis of his greeting.

> *My* girl
>
> You are charging me with batteries of impatience which are increasingly difficult to switch off when I want to settle down to the prosaic tasks in front of me.
>
> How can I wait for Friday next? I envy those letters so much that I mean to displace them or crush them the first chance I get.
>
> Do you think I could trust you on the 18th at L. Even if I were there? It would be murder this time. You little d——l. I cannot now spare one thrill for anybody else – not one. I want them all. Stormy day – driving rain. I tried to utilise it to prepare my two speeches. But the naughty little fairy swam about & took my thoughts away. Do you know her? I'll tell you all about her when we meet . . .
>
> Store up all your strength for you will need it I vow to you my sweetheart.
>
> Ever & Ever
> Your own
> *Cariad*[10]

A. J. P. Taylor surmised that 'L' was 'an obscure reference to Llandrindod Wells'.[11] Were they perhaps trying to meet there? Had they met there secretly the previous year? It makes no sense, particularly since this year Frances spent her holiday on the Isle of Wight. Maybe she visited Sassoon at Lympne. All we can say is that LG did not trust her out of his sight. There is no surviving letter for another week. Then on Saturday 21 August:

> My sweet
>   Got your two loving longing letters this morning & they made me more rebellious than ever against the conventions that keep us apart. I wish I had been there to comfort & shield you in the storm. It would have added to the thrills of the tempest . . .
>   Write me Monday darling girl – but not after as the post is too uncertain. You can phone from Churt on Wednesday morning about 10 . . .
>   I cannot trust myself to dwell on our meeting next week. As it is I cannot concentrate on my speeches.
>   Ever fond love
>   My sweet [illegible]
>   D.[12]

The next day he wrote again, becoming highly fanciful. Why did he wait so long before telling her of his 'dream'? LG's writing tended to reflect his taste in reading.

> My own girl
>   I write to tell you of a most enchanting dream I had last week. I fell asleep on Wednesday & I dreamt I was summoned to London to meet Cook the Miners Leader* – that on the way there I turned into a beautiful house perched on a hill & embowered in roses & clematis – that there I met the loveliest girl I ever saw in my life. That she smiled on me & said she was expecting me & she opened her arms & & &&& I dare not tell you what happened then – but I spent two days & nights of rapture with her – & then I woke up on Sunday morning & found myself in bed at Brynawelon with a tempest of rain beating on the window. I miss that fairy damsel more than ever & I mean to seek her out until I

* A. J. Cook was the firebrand leader of the Miners' Federation – the Arthur Scargill of his day.

find her. Will you help me darling for my heart is set upon her. She is the Queen of ecstasies . . .

Do you really mean . . . what you say about your never having enjoyed yourself much at L. Surely that is not quite accurate is it? But is Churt better – tell me that my sweet. This is only the vanity of an old lover . . .

Fondest love to my love. How I look forward to next week. I dare not dwell upon it.

Ever your

D.[13]

Finally, the day before he left Criccieth, LG wrote a particularly intriguing letter, which suggests that Frances was entertaining at Churt in his absence. It is also his most explicit recognition that he had – or had had – rivals for her love, whom he believed he had seen off.

My own sweet

Your account of things there makes me wish I could be one of the guests – for two reasons. You are enjoying beautiful weather whilst we are locked in today by driving rain. That is one reason. Can you guess my girl what the other reason is. I think you can . . .

What a worrying troubled old love you have. The others were never fussed about things. They just enjoyed life. Never mind darling. I love you more than all of them put together & I love you more now than even then – & more & more the more I know you. I know you are now mine & I am yours & I shall tell you all that in word & prove it to you in deed – when we meet . . .

Ever & Ever & Ever

Your own *Cariad* my own[14]

Meanwhile LG's relations with Frances caused a major row with his family. It was occasioned, somewhat incongruously, by the affairs of the *Daily Chronicle*. This was LG's tame newspaper, which had been bought by a syndicate of his supporters at the end of the war. He had subsequently invested in it most of his notorious political fund derived from the sale of honours; the paper's success then further swelled the size of the fund. But by 1926 the *Chronicle* was failing and LG was beginning to tire of it, as he wrote to Maggie on 22 September:

I am up in town trying to put a little spunk into the Chronicle & Sunday
News . . . In the end I gave a fairly plain intimation that unless immediate
steps were taken to put things right I should reconstruct the Board – that
is sack the lot . . . McCurdy is lazy & flabby, Gwilym indolent. They have
too many duds in high places.[15]

This was where the affairs of the *Chronicle* overlapped with family
politics. Charles McCurdy was chairman, but Gwilym was managing
director, and the rest of the Lloyd George family, and Frances, all owned
shares. Faced with LG's demand for a shake-up, McCurdy – rather
daringly for the time – suggested bringing a woman onto the board.
Rather less sensibly he proposed Frances. LG jumped at the idea (maybe
he instigated it). But this was too much for his family, who dug in their
heels. Gwilym resigned, and Dick refused to take his place. Objecting
not only to Frances joining the *Chronicle*, they also took the chance
to demand that she be removed from LG's secretariat – 'or else'. Unfortunately, if this ultimatum was ever written down, it has not survived;
neither has the 'terrible letter' that – according to Frances – LG wrote
in response, offering Maggie a divorce 'which he said he would
welcome'.[16] This is almost certainly a wishful figment of Frances's imagination, some forty years later. It is more likely that she was remem-
bering an angry letter that LG certainly did write but possibly did not
post, since it is not with the rest of his letters to Maggie in Aberystwyth,
but still among his papers that were left to Frances. (There is an original in LG's handwriting, plus a typed copy.) It is a characteristically
blustering effusion, which stops well short of offering a divorce.

Dearest M.
    Your Criccieth letter had nothing to do with the unhappy break with G.
He never mentioned the subject to me either during the quarrel or before.
On the contrary he seemed to be on the best of terms with the person he
now pretends to you was the cause of the quarrel. They always – & up to
the last moment chatted & chaffed together. I have seen it myself many
times.

In other words, LG was saying, Gwilym had always been perfectly
friendly with Frances. The 'unhappy break' was due to LG's criticism
of Gwilym's performance as managing director of the *Chronicle* and
nothing to do with Frances at all. Gwilym, egged on by his mother,

his sister and his wife, had brought Frances into it only as a way of hitting back at his father. LG had a biblical precedent for this sort of behaviour.

> However I know now too well what has been going on the last few days. G. in his new mood of ranting hysteria has told three or four persons all the details of the 'family councils' which have taken place. It appears that my children are following the example of the children of Noah by exposing their father's nakedness to the world. It is not the reputation of Noah that has suffered. But his children have gone down the ages as first-class skunks for turning on the old man.* Edna might turn her attention to her own father. As to G.: I have offered him good terms & I do not propose to recede from them whatever the consequences. I will be neither bullied nor blackmailed.

There followed a fierce indictment of Gwilym's failings.

> G. drew £3300 last year from the Chronicle. I never earned ¹/₄th of that amount at his age, in spite of hard work. G. never worked. He is quite frankly a slacker – at the Chronicle & in politics . . . I am giving him one more chance to show what he can *do* on his own. He has the offer before him. If he does not take it I cannot help him and I must let things take their course.

Finally he turned to Maggie herself:

> I must tell you how deeply pained I am to learn that you & *Megan* have turned against me. I have been for some time sick of public life. I work hard – very very hard – & get nothing but kicks. I have been contemplating clearing out & writing my book in retirement. I propose on Thursday to tell them to find another candidate. I am an old man. I mean henceforth to enjoy the leisure which is my due.
>
> Yours
> D.[18]

---

* In fact it was only one of Noah's sons, Ham, who saw his father naked when he was drunk and asleep (and that was scarcely his fault). Ham told his brothers, Shem and Japheth, and they covered the old man up. Nevertheless Noah cursed Ham when he woke up.[17] LG's rage was as unwarranted as Noah's.

The last was of course an empty threat. LG had no intention of giving up politics at the very moment when Asquith had finally ceded him the leadership of the Liberal party. On the contrary, he was gearing up for a major effort. Nor was he an old man: he was just sixty-three. Moreover he probably did not send this letter at all. Nevertheless he doubtless conveyed to Maggie and his children his anger and his fierce sense of what was due to him as the founder of all their fortunes. They all had as much to lose as he had if they were to expose his relationship with Frances: he was not going to give her up. This démarche cleared the air for some years ahead. His family knew that they must continue to put up with Frances – and they did.

At the same time, and probably as a result of this rumpus, LG decided to sell the *Chronicle*. With the advice of Beaverbrook he managed to dispose of his controlling interest to another consortium, which maintained the paper's Liberal identity, installing his old friend Rufus Isaacs (now Lord Reading) as chairman. After three years it merged with the *Daily News* to form the *News Chronicle*, which survived as a Liberal paper until 1960. In the meantime most of the proceeds of the sale went back into LG's fund, to be used to finance his various political campaigns; but LG, his family and Frances all made a tidy personal profit.

For LG 1927 was another busy year. He maintained a high level of speaking all round the country and in Parliament, as well as writing his weekly articles for the *Chronicle*. It is not clear whether Frances ever accompanied him out of London; probably not often. He also set up a high-powered committee to come up with ways of tackling unemployment, comprising leading Liberal businessmen and economists, including Maynard Keynes. Its report, published in February 1928, represented the first practical exposition of Keynesian economics – even though Keynes did not fully work out the theory for another eight years. LG did not dominate the inquiry, even though he financed it. But he often entertained its members for working weekends at Churt, where he delighted in feeding them entirely on home-grown produce from his farm. Frances was present at many of these weekends, though she took no part in the discussions and probably could not be seen to play too obviously the role of hostess.

She wrote only two diary entries in the year. The first, on 3 February, opens with a glimpse of their simple companionship when she and LG were able to be alone together.

D. & I walked in Richmond Park in the morning yesterday, & then picnicked
on sandwiches & fruit which we had bought in Putney on the way down.
A bright cold morning. D. benefited much from the air, he had left the office
feeling rather rattled owing to numerous petty worries.

Now that he had achieved the Liberal leadership, LG could not be
bothered with its chores, and wanted to give up the chairmanship of
the party in the House. His supporters thought it would be mad to
give it up just when he had gained it. 'But D. thinks that is the time
when he can do it best.' Frances was torn.

I don't know what to advise – I always think it best on these occasions for
him to follow his own instinct – it is rarely wrong. I know he is not entirely
happy in his present position, & I hate to see him bothered & wasting his
energy & mind over trifling little matters, when it is the *big* things he is
made for.[19]

In fact LG stuck to his post, and was rewarded with a string of by-
election victories over the next two years, which were a tribute both
to his own energy and to the pioneering methods of his new election
organiser, Thomas Tweed. There were now real grounds for thinking
the party was back in serious contention for power.

In August LG went to Criccieth as usual. Frances and Muriel went
to Wales again too, but this time much closer to him – just across
Tremadoc Bay in Harlech. Risky though this was, they seem to have
managed at least one meeting. LG's letters are full of his usual gripes.
Megan was once again not speaking to him. 'Olwen alone is my sole
pal. She is behaving very nicely . . . Old girl behaving well so far. I am
off for a walk to Llanystumdwy.'

Today I am beginning to feel very tired. Last week the tarantella was still
in my blood & brain & I felt restless. Today the reaction has arrived & I
am at nadir. Depressed miserable heavy not wanting to see anybody or talk
to anybody in the world – except one & I cannot get at her.

If this weather lasts . . . I shall be unmanageable. Oh how I wish you
were here my little comforter & consoler & cheerer. My joy & delight &
solace & sustainer . . .

Love to Muriel. I gazed at that hotel last night across the bay & wished
to God I were there.

We must have another meeting this or next week if we can somehow manage it.

Glad your fellow guests are of the duller sort. Feel more assured.

Fondest love to my darling girl.

D.[20]

His next letter illustrates the complex juggling required to balance LG's obligations to his wife with his desire to see Frances.

MoS [My own Sweet]

I asked Miss R to phone you last night the new development.*

Yesterday Maggie told me she meant to return with me at the end of August in order to see how the new house was getting on & proposed to stay a few days. That would not do as Megan would probably accompany her & stay. So I said I would go up next week . . . & she would accompany me & we could return by Thursday.

There is no-one at Cheyne Walk so she wants to stay at Churt.

This is the plan. We go up on Monday as far as Churt. London Tuesday & *possibly* Wednesday. If you are up I could see you lunch Tuesday. But that would curtail your holiday & I don't think you ought to do that. It would not be fair to you. But I wanted September *all* for ourselves. So I had to save that disaster anyhow. And I am sick of this place . . .

Tenderest love to my dearest little girl – the girl of my heart.

D.[21]

LG and Maggie were just then in the process of moving their London home again from Cheyne Walk to Addison Road, Kensington (just south of Holland Park Avenue). Dwyfor Lodge, as they renamed it (after the river at Llanystumdwy), was a handsome detached villa with a fine staircase and a large garden; they kept it until 1940. Clearly they could not stay at Cheyne Walk at this time because there were no servants there; but it was obviously a nuisance for Frances that Maggie intended to go to Churt. LG was semi-apologising to her with the promise that they would have September together, and showing unusual consideration by saying that she should not interrupt her holiday. But of course she did, as is clear from LG's next letter giving detailed directions – all for a quick lunchtime meeting.

* Miss R. was Winifred Russell, one of LG's longest-serving secretaries, based at Churt.

Next Monday.

You must leave *early* on Monday so as not to clash on road. *Or* as the alternative you could go part of the way on Sunday – if you motor. If not you might go by train on Monday.

If you leave at 8.30 on Monday that will do. I could leave about 9.15. You go London. I drive to Churt.

Office Tuesday 11.30. Morpeth 12.30. Lunch 1. Dessert to follow.

Looking forward very much to seeing you my own sweetheart.

Frances Stevenson is & will always remain the sweetie of Davy Lloyd.*

So you think Harlech Sands a suitable place for a rendezvous! Oh you little devil.†

Ever & Ever,

D.[23]

In fact they managed more than a lunchtime quickie. They actually met on both the Tuesday and the Wednesday and went to Churt together. So what had happened to Maggie? We do not know. Back at Harlech on Friday, Frances merely recorded another spasm of LG's habitual restlessness.

He is in a mood now to retire from politics & write his book. I do not think he will do this. He has had these moods before, & now he is less able to leave the Party to itself . . . D. says he wants to leave the Party to get on without him for the present . . . I don't think he will be allowed to do it, however. Besides, things are going so much better now, it would be a pity.[24]

Unlike her fictional heroines, Frances did not really want LG to give up politics. She knew he could not live without the stimulus of political battle. But nor could she. Perhaps more seriously than LG himself – who, as he got older, increasingly wanted power without the responsibility of government – Frances longed for him to get back into office, so that she would again be at the centre of events. In 1927 this still looked a real possibility. No wonder she thought this was no time for

---

* Davy Lloyd was the name by which LG was known as a boy; the name by which he wooed Maggie. It is a curious throwback that he now used it to pledge his love to Frances.

† Many years later LG made a curious reference to Harlech, 'the scene of one of your too numerous triumphs'.[22] Did he suspect Frances of having had an adventure that summer?

him to take a back seat. But she may have had another reason for wanting LG to maintain his political campaigning at a high level. For the fact was that she was becoming seriously attracted to his campaign organiser.

26

ENTER COLONEL TWEED

Thomas Tweed is a figure still surrounded by a certain mystery. He was born in Liverpool in 1890 the son of a provision merchant, and attended the Liverpool Institute and Liverpool University, but as a young man he was said to have worked as a dock labourer and door-to-door salesman. At university he was remembered as a militant socialist, but he quickly became a Liberal, and was already agent for the constituency of Eccles at the outbreak of war. He enlisted immediately and served in France almost throughout, until invalided out in April 1918. Starting as a second lieutenant, he finished as one of the youngest colonels in the army and won the Military Cross.* With the return of peace he joined the Territorial Army reserve, but returned to politics as secretary of the Manchester Liberal Federation: he was described in one obituary as the 'Tammany boss' of Manchester Liberalism.¹ In 1921 he played some part in setting up the Liberal Summer Schools – the party's unofficial think-tank, which originated many of those Keynesian ideas that LG was to take up in 1927–8.

Here he would have met LG, who attended regularly from 1923. But it was Asquith who promoted Tweed in 1926 to be the party's chief organiser; and LG's first impression of his performance was unfavourable. In a letter to Frances he wrote that Tweed was 'not a patch on' his predecessor; he particularly objected to Tweed going on holiday that August when he should have been at work.² Nevertheless Colonel Tweed, as he was always known, was a gifted campaigner and

---

* He was also said to have been court-martialled, but acquitted, for refusing to obey an order. But I can find no record of this.

soon became the driving force of LG's effort to put the Liberal party back in contention before the 1929 election. Indeed, he can be credited with inventing in the 1920s many of the techniques of intensive canvassing and leafleting that have served the Liberals and the Liberal Democrats so well since the 1960s: at by-elections between 1927 and 1929 the party gained five seats from the Conservatives and one from Labour. But Tweed was more than just a political operator. He was also a serious traveller, and in the 1930s he became a successful novelist. So he was an able and interesting man.

In appearance he was tall, dark and saturnine, with penetrating eyes, glossy hair and a military moustache. But his private life was blighted. In 1912 he married a woman named Louise Hatton, who bore him two children before he discovered that she was nine years older than she had pretended. Tweed felt that he had been tricked – though the marriage certificate shows that he too pretended to be older than he was. They stayed together, but henceforth Tweed felt free to wander. The combination of the war and his bitter marital experience had left him disillusioned and emotionally crippled, though he was also said to be 'a brilliantly witty conversationalist, whose air of cynicism hardly served to conceal his genuine kindness of heart'.[3] Another obituarist wrote that 'he liked to assume the role of cynic, and when he was in that mood his comments on politicians and their motives were entertaining. But in fact he was a genial, good-natured fellow who loved his pipe and a good gossip.'[4] Be that as it may, there was evidently a wounded quality about him that aroused Frances's maternal feeling. And he fell in love with her.

Frances was naturally guarded in what she wrote about Tweed in her autobiography.

He was a man of strong Liberal principles and a splendid war record – and sometimes uncompromising in character. There were often clashes between Colonel Tweed and L.G. on principles and tactics, for the former was fearless in expressing his opinions; but the common cause of Liberalism usually settled their differences.[5]

This was euphemistic: there were indeed 'clashes' between Tweed and LG, and not just about politics – particularly after 1931 when Tweed remained on LG's private payroll after LG had ceased to be leader of the Liberal party. Even before 1931 there were evidently ructions, since LG was increasingly intolerant of independent-minded subordinates who argued with him. Moreover, since he was always paranoid about Frances having anything to do with other men, he cannot have been unaware that she was in daily contact with a handsome war-hero of her own age.

We do not know what exactly occurred between Frances and Tweed at this time. But the evidence of two passionate letters that he wrote her in August 1928 suggests that it was significant. The most likely period when they could have had extended time together was around Christmas 1927 into early January 1928, when LG went with his family on a five-week cruise to South America – leaving Frances to her own devices. His letters from the SS *Avelona* reiterated his usual themes: that he was missing her and that she must behave herself.

> If I miss you as much as I do now this voyage of pleasure will be one of prolonged torment . . . Cold fog outside – & inside my heart I am sailing not towards the sun but from it.

Over Christmas, at least, Frances could not misbehave since she had her family staying with her at Churt – further indication of how much Bron-y-de was her house.

> Give my love to the Xmas company at Churt. Thank your father for these delicious cigars. As you know they are just what I want.
> Be good my girl – until I come back but not one hour longer.

LG added that Sarah, who was travelling with him, was worried about her sister, and asked Frances to invite her for Christmas too. 'She worships you & so do I.'[6]

On Christmas Eve his ship was delayed by a storm off Lisbon, to which 'Sarah succumbed badly'.

> Reading cowboy stories keeps my mind more or less content. But 31 more days! Why did I plan such a holiday.
> Take care of yourself my darling . . . By the time this reaches you $^1/_4$ of our separation will be over.[7]

By 29 December he was nearing St Vincent, in the Cape Verde islands:

There is just a chance that a homeward ship may also call there. So I am
scribbling these few words of unquenchable affection to my sweetheart . . .

As always, he claimed to be having a miserable time.

I am bored sometimes to the point of utter wretchedness. This is no holiday
for me except for health & recuperation . . . I have ploughed through most
of my wild & woolly west stories.

Actually there were two Tory MPs on board, plus the Under-
Secretary at the Ministry of Agriculture, Lord Bledisloe, so LG was not
entirely without political conversation – though he claimed to have
spent the time talking with Bledisloe about pigs. At least part of his
mind was still on politics, since he had left Frances with the task of
editing a collection of excerpts from his speeches.

I am more than ever convinced of the importance of having my book out
as soon as possible. But we can judge better on my return after you have
had an opportunity of perusing the material.[8]*

Unusually he makes no mention in any of these letters of his family.
But LG did not get home until 25 January. What had Frances been
doing meanwhile, apart from spending Christmas with her family and
working through LG's speeches? We do not have her letters to LG, and
she was not keeping her diary. Some clues may be gleaned from the
first of two breathtaking letters that Tweed wrote her the following
August, when he was away cruising in the Baltic.

Darling,
    A few moments of peace as we are sailing down the Skatterack
[Skagerrak? Kattegat?] towards Copenhagen gives me the long wanted, but
hitherto seemingly impossible chance to get into spiritual communion with
you – at least so far as the written word is concerned.
    There is no real need for visible tokens of our love – you are with me
at all times and sometimes I feel your presence so overwhelmingly that I
expect to see you by my side when I open my eyes. There is one girl on

*Frances had already edited two volumes of LG's speeches during the war. This latest,
entitled *Slings and Arrows* and nominally edited by the historian Philip Guedalla, was
not in fact published until 1929.

board who looks very like you – and I hate her – not because she looks like you, but because she dares to be a constant reminder and yet is not you.

I am writing with some difficulty under an indifferent lamp on the back of a magazine and would get along a great deal faster if I did not leave off for long spells to gaze into vacancy – or at least into the inky blackness of the waste of waters across the deck, but I love just sitting and thinking of you. I suppose I ought to be thinking of magic casements and gazing on perilous seas forlorn, but there ain't no magic casements and the seas are not a bit perilous and the only forlorn beings are you and I.

Still I don't need magic casements to picture little dream idylls in my heart and mind – funny little mixed up pictures all jumbled together but every bit of every one a caress and a balm to my loneliness and longing.

Tweed seems to have no doubt that Frances loves him as much as he loves her. The next passage suggests that their relationship had already been going on for some time.

I wonder if you can recollect and place the odd pieces of the jigsaw – Cambridge and a starless night – wind and snow at Lynton – Red Chimney Pots and Cocktails – Riversmeet – the Grey and Red of the Howard – Victory and defeat at Barnstaple – a funny little teashop near Beaux Art [sic] – Churt and thrown kisses before a door closes – ivory flesh and love lit eyes – and over all harmony and an abiding peace and one man's – your man's great thankfulness for your love and the wonderful happiness you have brought him. Good night my beloved. You are very very near to me tonight.

Your sweet heart Chico[9]

Cambridge? The Liberal Summer School had been held in Cambridge in 1927. (LG had spoken there on 1 August.) Lynton and Barnstaple? There is no record of any political reason that might have taken Tweed and Frances to north Devon – but maybe they went there for New Year while LG was on the South Atlantic: that would be consistent with the wind and snow. 'Thrown kisses' at Churt is clear enough. And ivory flesh . . . ? There can be no doubt that this was a true love affair, of reciprocated emotion, pursued over many months.

Five days later Tweed wrote a second letter, still more explicit:

Darling,

Just a short note. We are approaching Stockholm and the dominating thought in my heart and mind is that this is the ultimate point on the cruise.

From now on every mile and every minute brings me nearer to holding you in my arms again – at least nearer to your physical self – because you have never been away from my side, when the sun goes down and in the morning I have stretched out my arms and almost felt the warmth and sweetness of your body within them.

In a curious sort of way I have almost enjoyed this forced severance because it has quickened my realisation of what your love means to me. I never realised quite so vividly my rich happiness and the joyous promise of the years which are yet to come, as much as I do at this moment when hundreds of miles of land and water separate us and yet we are together.

I am very much in love with you my sweetheart, my love, my wife and darling.

Your sweetheart, Chico[10]

Here, anticipating 'the joyous promise of the years which are yet to come', Tweed seems confident that Frances will leave LG and make her life with him. Knowing that she did not, we have to wonder how close she really came to doing so. There is no doubt that she reciprocated his love. The difficulty in practical terms was that Tweed, too, was a married man. His wife was unlikely to give him a divorce; he still had two teenage children to support; and he was not wealthy, though he had evidently made a good deal of money playing the Stock Exchange. Moreover his employment prospects were closely bound up with LG. Nor – though still under forty – was he in good health. For Frances to leave LG for the security of a respectable marriage would have been one thing; to leave him for the uncertainty of life with Tweed was quite another. Apart from the secrecy of their relationship and his refusal to allow her to have his children, LG gave her a good life: certainly a comfortable life, surrounded by servants and creature comforts, staying in the best hotels at home and abroad. Even if it was no longer such an exciting life as previously, there was still the possibility that he would get back into office and take her once more into the heart of national life. Of course he was getting old, and there stretched before her the prospect of nursing an increasingly demanding old man; but that in itself placed on her an obligation – she could not leave him now, when he needed her most, after all they had shared since 1912. And she was nearly forty herself; she needed to be thinking about her own future, not throwing up what security LG gave her for a second, even more uncertain affair with a man with no steady prospects at all. In the end she could not do it.

Apart from these two tantalising letters of August 1928 we do not know what else passed between Frances and Tweed over the next three or four years. He continued to work for LG, so they must have seen each other in the office nearly every day. Presumably he still hoped to win her away from LG; maybe she still led him to think that he might succeed. Maybe she played the two of them against each other. Certainly her life must have been exceedingly complicated around this time; because when she fell pregnant again, in January 1929, she did not know which man was the father.

27

'NO TRANSACTIONS'

LG took his summer holiday later than usual in 1928: he did not go to Criccieth until early September. While he was in Wales, Frances went on a walking holiday in Devon. We do not know who with: probably not Muriel, but possibly Felicia Brook, her closest friend at this time. Felicia was another woman in an irregular relationship – she was the mistress of Charles McCurdy, with an illegitimate child – which was probably what brought them together. But the likelihood must be that Tweed was somewhere around. We know that he was back from the Baltic, because he was at Churt the last weekend in August, discussing political prospects with LG and Keynes. After the ardent anticipation of his two letters, written just a couple of weeks earlier, he would surely not have missed the opportunity of seeing Frances while LG was away. There is no reason to think that LG had any worries about Tweed at this stage. But whoever was with her, LG was more anxious than ever that Frances should behave herself – especially since she had evidently changed her plans.

Ten days. But my heavens how slowly the last 4 or 5 days have dragged their weary feet. Ernest Brown bawled salvation down my ears twice on the Sabbath day but the glad tidings failed entirely to cheer me up. My Paradise was on the tramp in Devon & my heart was in it.

How come you [plan] to be back so soon. I thought you meant to gad about till next week. Are you going to Churt. Now keep out of mischief my sweet heart. You are [an] enticing little devil & you know it & you like to exert your power & to enjoy the rewards. Don't – I beg of you . . . I promise to be good if I feel confident you are . . .

Fondest & most longing thoughts to my girl

D.

Your letters kept me alive darling. I [illegible] them.[1]*

Two days later it seems that she was back in London.

> My own sweet
>
> I was glad to get your letter from A.J. I always am & I tore it open like a hungry wild beast. I always do – & then I talked to A.J. about you. There was a satisfaction in talking to someone who had seen you so recently. He told me he had never seen you looking so well. You evidently have profited from sea breezes & (I trust) total abstinence! . . .
>
> You seem to have had a glorious time on your trip & I am looking forward to enjoying the full benefit of it . . .
>
> Continue to write me my own girl – who is not & who never has been naughty – my girl who thro' life has resisted temptation! Oh you little devil. I'll pay you out – in person & scrag it out of you.
>
> Fondest Love
>
> Your own
>
> D.[2]

The next weekend LG came south to speak at a by-election in Cheltenham. He snatched at least one night at Churt with Frances before going back to Wales to speak for Megan, who had just been selected as Liberal candidate in Anglesey.† But the Liberals failed to win Cheltenham because the intervention of a Labour candidate split the anti-government vote. When he next wrote to Frances on 28 September he was seething with frustration, both personal and political.

> My own darling girl,
>
> A bitter & biting Nor-easter outside & a grumpy old fellow longing for his girl inside the house . . . I was so rebellious this morning that I almost

---

* The last sentence could be 'I loved them'. But it could equally be 'I burned them' – which would explain why Frances's letters from this summer do not survive. Perhaps they were unusually indiscreet. Perhaps she was protesting too much to cover her infidelity.

† The suffrage – and with it the right to stand for Parliament – was finally extended to women over twenty-one in 1928. (In 1918 it had been limited to women over thirty.) Megan, now twenty-six, was one of the first to take advantage. LG and Maggie together pulled out all the stops to secure her selection; but the choice aroused some opposition locally, which LG now needed to defuse.

phoned you to wire me . . . Sarah persuaded me not to. 'Punish yourself
for one week,' she said. I think she is right so I have made up my mind to
do penance . . .

Cheltenham was a blow right between the eyes . . . If Tavistock goes the
same way then it means that Labour . . . are more intent on doing us in
than in putting the Conservatives out . . . So for another five years of Tory
domination with a miserable & ragged group of divided & dejected Liberals
in the House. Then for me – not Westminster but Churt, & Pussy (if she
can bear me) . . .

Fondest & tenderest affection for you my girl.
D.[3]

Tavistock did go the same way. Again Labour's intervention allowed
the Tories to hang on to a traditional Liberal seat: a sharp reminder
of the third-party trap in which the Liberals were now caught. That
autumn LG continued to call for a major programme to regenerate the
economy on the lines set out in the report of his Industrial Inquiry.
'These are extraordinary times and conditions,' he told the House of
Commons, 'and you must have extraordinary measures to deal with
them.'[4] His model was the war, when he had been able to recruit the
ablest men, regardless of politics, to direct shipping, food supply, transport and munitions under his leadership. But barring some similar crisis,
he could not see how he was going to re-create that situation in peace-
time.

Uncertainty often made LG ill. He duly took to his bed in November,
and went down again with flu in late December. He did not go to Criccieth for Christmas, but spent both Christmas and the New Year at
Churt, where Frances nursed him. In fact they were alone there together
for an unprecedentedly long period – five weeks – until the middle of
January; and it seems to have been a particularly happy time. Then LG
left, on 13 January, with an unusually large contingent of his family
(Maggie, Megan, Olwen and Gwilym, with the latter's wife Edna) for
his usual winter holiday in the sun, this time a cruise to Italy. The
previous day – or possibly a day or two earlier – Frances had gone
with Muriel to Torquay. She may already have been pregnant. Her
daughter Jennifer was born just under nine months later on 4 October.

When A. J. P. Taylor edited the LG–Frances correspondence in 1975,
he believed he had established beyond doubt that LG was Jennifer's
father. The dates seemed conclusive, and the letters between Torquay

and Italy that January of 1929 show that Frances's pregnancy was deliberately planned. LG had evidently been persuaded that Frances could now safely bear a child, so long as he was not named as the father. He certainly took it for granted that the child was his, and Frances encouraged him to believe it. When Jennifer was born he took a doting and possessive interest in her, and continued to do so for the rest of his life. Yet the truth is not as clear as Taylor believed. There have always been whispers – encouraged by LG's other children and their descendants – that Jennifer's father was Thomas Tweed. The letters already quoted establish beyond much doubt that Tweed and Frances had a physical relationship around this time. The fact that Frances was with LG at Churt until early January only proves LG's paternity if Jennifer was a full-term baby. But there is one piece of evidence (not known to Taylor) which suggests that she was actually two weeks premature. If that is the case, then Tweed comes back into the picture – since it is possible that he was with Frances in Devon in mid- or late January.

The only near-contemporary evidence for this comes from A.J. Sylvester, who wrote in 1932 that there was 'a good deal of suspicion that Tweed was down in Devon' at the relevant time, when LG was away.[5] Frances's letters seem to prove that she was in Torquay for the whole period, first with Muriel and then with Felicia. Many years later, however, Jennifer seems to have accepted that Frances 'had a holiday with T. F. Tweed . . . at Lynmouth', which suggests some basis for the story.[6] If so, someone else was posting her letters to LG from Torquay, fifty miles away; but that is not impossible.

For once LG seems to have kept all Frances's letters from Torquay. They could scarcely have been more loving. The Palace Hotel was a huge luxurious establishment, opened in 1921, with all modern comforts plus a swimming pool, tennis and squash courts, golf course and gym, its own cinema and a ladies' orchestra. Frances should not have been bored there. Nevertheless her first letter, dated 15 January, was full of her usual assurances that the company was very dull.

My own darling sweetheart,
    This is just a little note to let you know that I am here & that I am thinking of you all the time . . .
    But do not worry, my darling, I really have no other thought but you, & my heart is following you all through your journey. Be careful not to

take unnecessary risks, my darling . . . I do hope they are looking after you well, though I am quite sure I should do it far better myself! . . .

I am sure this place will do me good, & I think I was more tired even than I realised . . . But perhaps that is partly the effect of the separation from you, my darling. I am missing you so sorely – all the more because we have been so constantly together lately. Are you missing me a little, beloved? . . .

You must give up all thought of politics for the first fortnight of your trip at any rate, & take every possible advantage you can of the change (but I don't mean what *you* mean, as George Robey would say).* Send me a little line, my darling, to cheer me up – for I shall be very desolate while you are away, & am counting the days till you return. I think I shall long more than ever to see you again, for I am quite convinced that I love you more than I have ever done.

Tenderest & most loving kisses from your own devoted
P.[7]

LG's first letter was from Monte Carlo:

My own darling girl

Just one week of the chasm between my sweetheart and myself already bridged. That is how I reckon my pleasure cruise. All the same she is with me night & day. I never loved her more tenderly than I do now. The last five weeks of loving care have added many strands of affection to my attachment for her. They revealed to me depths of sweetness in her nature which leave me fonder than ever of my little girl. How I should have enjoyed this trip had she been here.

His reading matter was rather more elevated than usual: Virginia Woolf's *Orlando*, which had just been published. The book is a fantasy about a young Elizabethan nobleman who changes sex and lives on into the twentieth century. Why LG should have been reading it is hard to imagine: maybe he thought it was erotic. It was not at Frances's recommendation, anyway, since he commended it to her, and especially told her to read the top of page 200. 'It bears on the discussion we had on interchangeability. It is a very clever book.' The passage in question is about Orlando's change of sex.

* The comedian George Robey was famous for his suggestive innuendoes.

She had, it seems, no difficulty in sustaining the different parts, for her sex changed far more frequently than those who have worn only one set of clothing can conceive; nor can there be any doubt that she reaped a two-fold harvest by this device; the pleasures of life were increased and its experiences multiplied. For the probity of breeches she exchanged the seductiveness of petticoats and enjoyed the love of both sexes equally.[8]

What on earth is going on here? Why had LG and Frances been discussing 'interchangeability'? It is, as A. J. P. Taylor wrote, 'difficult to think of Lloyd George as a transvestite' – or Frances either.[9] Maybe the relevance was to her friend Felicia.

LG's letter continued on more familiar themes:

But there is one preoccupation for my thoughts. How am I to get through another 25 days without my girl. And it is so difficult to arrange for letters . . .

I trust you will stay there [at Torquay] during this month. You also must have a thorough rest. Besides I shall be less anxious if you move out of London. If you are bored there go to Bron-y-de darling. Do be good my sweet. I promise you faithfully for my part.

Fondest tenderest love to my sweet.

Ever yours,

D.[10]

Frances wrote again on LG's birthday, to greet him when he reached Genoa. Again she stressed the dullness of the hotel and said the weather was very mild. Then she added, significantly: 'The mildness has the effect of making me feel very sleepy – an unusual thing for me!' The rest of the letter looks both forward and back.

I hope you got my birthday wire, sweetheart. You are very much in my mind today, & I am praying for many, many, many happy returns of it for you – for you & me together, & for much happiness & prosperity for you, my darling. I feel this year is going to be a big one for you, & I feel you are going to have a reward for your patience & your forbearance & for the difficult time you have been through the last few years . . .

I think of you so much and so lovingly, my darling, & though I resent very much not being with you, & hate the people that are – still, perhaps it will be worthwhile when we have our sweet reunion . . . One thing I am glad about is that I have been with you to share the last few years & perhaps help you a tiny bit, and I shall rejoice more than anyone if this year brings you good luck as I think & hope it will.

Think of me sweetly, *cariad*, and love me all the more that there is this distance between us.

Take care of my sweetheart for me.

Your own very loving & devoted

P.[11]

Four days passed before Frances wrote again, by which time she had received his letter and obtained a copy of *Orlando*.

My own beloved darling,

It was sweet to get your letter, & I have read every word of it over & over again. The sweet things you say made me so very happy. I loved looking after you, my darling, & I will always look after you & cherish you & take care of you. When you are ill like that you are my little child. Besides, all I can do for you and give you can never equal all your sweetness to me . . .

I am simply counting the days, like you, my darling, & they do seem to go very slowly. Don't worry about me, sweetheart. I am being very good. I shall stay here if you would like me to, & then if I get too bored, I will go to Bron-y-de as you suggest . . .

I have just got 'Orlando', & have not had time to read it yet, but have glanced at the bit you mention, & understand what you mean! It is amusing and I will call Felicia's attention to it when she comes.

I think of you so much my darling, & I do miss you so very much, especially after the weeks we have spent so close together. And when you come back we will be closer together than ever in more senses than one! . . . I am storing up love & affection & tenderness to lavish on you when you come back, my own darling, whom I love & adore.

Ever your own,

P.[12]

Even before she knew she was pregnant – though she already suspected it – Frances does seem in these letters to be more than usually loving towards LG and to be looking forward to a future of redoubled intimacy with him. It is very difficult to believe that she could still have been sleeping with Tweed while writing so devotedly to LG. Could she really have been so duplicitous? Yet the doubt remains. Did she protest too much to cover her infidelity? Or was she recommitting herself so passionately to LG because she had made up her mind to drop Tweed and needed LG's protection more than ever?

LG's next letter is an important one in several respects: for an intriguing reference back to a flirtation that he believed Frances had indulged at the Rapallo conference in 1917; for his clear statement of his political hopes for 1929, seeing himself in characteristically biblical terms as Moses; and above all for the unambiguous indication that he was awaiting confirmation of her pregnancy. It was written somewhere off the coast of Tuscany between Elba and Civitavecchia.

My own sweet girl . . .

I lunched on Sunday at the Rapallo Hotel. Do you remember it. Of course you do. Oh you little devil. No more hanky-panky – please my little darling. I beg of you. But what times they were . . . Wish I could feel after the next election that I had succeeded in achieving a similar result out of the muddle of 1926. I have attained a certain measure of unity of command. June may give us victory. Then we can dictate the terms of the Treaty to the Government of the day. Whether we do or not I shall not fret. I shall have my little girl. If it is not reserved for me to lead the people for whom I have fought all my life to the promised land I shall feel a pang of disappointment – but what a sweet *consoler* I shall have on Mount Pisgah. I have no doubt that from that happy retirement I will make occasional raids to harass the foe – & then come back for my reward . . .

I have been thirsting for a letter from you. I have had two wires. They were like two cocktails – stimulating & cheering – but I want a letter with a full detailed & necessarily true account of *all* your transactions.

By the way I shall be expecting an interesting wire from you next Monday week. You know what I mean. If the usual thing happens wire 'transactions'. If not then 'no transactions'. I am hoping for the latter. Monday may be premature. If so wire on the critical date . . .

I do hope my darling you are having a real rest. You will need all your nervous reserves the next few months. We shall have a trying time.

Fondest love to you my sweet

D.[13]

Frances replied the next day. (If their dating is accurate, it was not just the Italian trains but the postal service that Mussolini had made to run on time.)

> My own darling little man
>
> From what I can gather, it does not look as though your original plans will be carried out as regards your itinerary, and it certainly does not look as though I am going to get my Turkish delight! It will have to be some other kind of delight – Welsh perhaps . . .
>
> I promise to be good, & I only hope you are keeping your promise, too. I know you will say there are no opportunities, but I don't trust you not to get into mischief anywhere . . .
>
> Yes, my darling, I will wire you on Monday week, & I very much hope it will be 'no transactions'. I have a feeling that that may be so, but then I have had that feeling so often before. Only, although I feel so much better in myself, I still feel very lazy, & sometimes I think my eyes are a little tell-tale. However we mustn't be premature. I have so often been disappointed!

This suggests that they had been trying for a baby for some time. Whenever Frances had become pregnant previously, she had always had an abortion. This time it was different.

Then she responded to LG's vision of one last political effort before he retired to Churt. As always, she was passionately loyal:

> I know that whatever happens we could always be happy there, sweetheart, but I do hope for your sake that you will be given a chance to do something after the next election. I know in my heart that you could pull the nation out of the morass, & that *only* you can do it, & so many others feel the same thing. Also I know what it must feel like to have to stand by & see others making a mess of things, especially when such vital things are at stake. The election is going to be a terrible struggle . . . but I hope that a victory will emerge for my darling with all my heart. Later on there will be plenty of time for us to retire into happiness at Churt . . .
>
> It must have been interesting to see Rapallo again. You shouldn't tease me about it. I wasn't nearly as naughty there as you think! Yes, what a time that was, & how proud I was, & am, of you for the part you played in it. Nor will the world ever be able to forget what you did . . .
>
> 'Orlando' is a lovely book – but queer. It had an extraordinary effect on

Muriel . . . She said it was so beautiful that it completely upset her! However she has recovered by now & is flirting hard with Felicia's brother!* She sends her love to you . . .

All my fondest love to you, my darling. I must not think too soon of all the embraces I shall be giving you, as that would unsettle me – & if I told you about them, it might unsettle you! But they will be very sweet.

Ever your own loving – more loving than ever

P.[14]

LG received this at Naples, and replied immediately – still anxious that she was not being naughty.

My own girl

I have just finished reading for the third time the darling letter you sent me here. How it thrilled me. It has however one drawback. It has made me so impatient to return to take my sweet little *cariad* in my arms & kiss her & hug her until she pants for breath.

I am so glad you already feel better. Stick there my girl since it is doing you so much good. The western air will enfold you in its softness & give you renewed strength. Mind you that is the only enfolding I permit in my absence – except one for which I have given you special licence . . .

The important factor to me is that tomorrow I am halfway through & that then I shall be returning at a speed of 8 knots an hour [*sic*] to the girl of my heart. I do want to get back to you my girl. I dont like these holidays without you & they must notice how unusually quiet & tame I am . . .

Love & intense longing for you my own girl. It has grown & deepened with absence. Keep off naughtiness my sweet.

Ever & ever

Your man

D.[15]

Frances's next is mainly another outpouring of love and longing, but it includes another intriguing comment on *Orlando*, which she had only just managed to get back from Muriel.

* Frances had already assured LG that Felicia's brother was 'only a raw youth, so you needn't worry, darling!'

I have got Orlando now. Muriel & I are fighting over it – it is a beautiful piece of fantasy & an extraordinary theme. I read p.200 which you recommended to me, & understand what you mean – & what the writer means! Sex & time seem to be equally unimportant to Orlando – it is a somewhat new version of 'The Well of Loneliness!'* . . .

I *do* miss you terribly my sweetheart. Every now & then such a longing for you comes over me, & if I did not realise that the separation is for your good, I should resent it so much. But as it is I am just loving you in your absence, & storing up such quantities of love & affection & tenderness to pour out on you when you return. At the same time I am fortifying my strength for the energy of which I expect and hope you are laying in a store, my darling. You see, I am trying to be philosophical, but oh! It is so hard sometimes to be contented & happy when the man I love best in the world is so far away from me, and when I so long to be with him!

Ever your own loving & longing & devoted
P.

She added a slightly anxious postscript: 'I am hoping to get another letter from you soon. Your wire says "written three today". Can they all be for me?'[16] In his next he hastened to reassure her. 'I wired have written letters "there" not three. No darling you are the only one I write to!'[17] The letter he had written was a long and delighted description of a violent storm that had driven LG's ship back to Naples.

Cook's man is waiting for this letter. I am glad he has to go ashore & not me – even the harbour is heaving. Write me darling. I'll wire address. I am so happy to think that I am half way thro' and that my girl is now getting nearer & nearer the arms that are throbbing with a desire to enfold & crush her against my bosom.

Ever & ever most fond love
D.[18]

Frances had not yet got this letter when she wrote again. She was still at Torquay, and still some days off her period, so she had nothing more to say except that she was missing him, but his letters helped to

---

* Radclyffe Hall's lesbian novel *The Well of Loneliness* had been prosecuted for obscenity and suppressed in November 1928. Frances does not say whether she had read it: it is really nothing like *Orlando*.

bridge the distance between them 'and comfort me a little in my loneliness'. She fussed about his health ('As you say, there are such filthy
smells in all those Italian places'), but rejoiced that he had now turned
for home.

> I will write again to Cannes, but I won't go on writing too long in case
> you suddenly make up your minds to come sooner than you expected! But
> I do hope my darling that you will have fine weather. In any case, I expect
> it will be fine weather in your heart. The weather is improving in mine as
> each day brings my sweetheart nearer to me, until I can really feel him in
> my arms & press my body to his.
>   Ever your own loving & devoted
>   P.[19]

The next day brought more of the same, but also news of comings
and goings.

> Muriel went back yesterday, but Felicia is coming tomorrow & will stay
> until I go back, which will be very nice. I am not lonely here, as there are
> two or three rather nice people in the hotel, but all quite safe, so don't get
> nervous! . . . There have been absolutely no temptations here, so you need
> have no fear!

Since Felicia was coming Frances told LG she planned to stay on in
Torquay; but she promised to be back in London to greet him on his
return.

> And then we can go to Churt together & see all the new developments
> together, which will be much more fun . . . It will be lovely to get back
> there again. There's no place like home! Don't you agree? . . .
>   Tenderest embraces *now* and *in the future* from
>   Your own
>   P.

> Will not forget to show F. 'Orlando', & will let you know what she thinks
> of it.[20]

All this time Sylvester – the discreet go-between in all this correspondence – had been cabling regularly, usually on the lines of 'ALL

LETTERS SAFELY RECEIVED POSTED ONE TODAY CHIEF VERY FIT SYLVESTER'.[21] But on 31 January he wrote Frances a letter saying that LG had summoned Tweed to meet him at Cannes. Could this have been a ploy to get him away from Frances? Or was it merely intended to show Tweed that he was expected to be at LG's beck and call even when he was in the south of France? Sylvester added a mild complaint about the difficulty of catering for LG's unpredictable whims:

> We still have no itinerary of any sort or kind and just move about according to what the Chief fancies, and as we have moved about a very great deal you can imagine the amount of work this creates especially in a country like this where one has to make arrangements usually when everyone has gone to bed. But I think things have gone well and he is thoroughly enjoying himself.[22]

Of course LG would never admit to Frances that he was enjoying himself – though his next letter came close. Begun at 7 a.m. – confirmation, if it were needed, that he and Maggie occupied separate cabins – this was the longest as well as one of the most torrid he ever wrote her.

> To the darling thrilling loving & lovable little girl who is my last thought at night & my first in the morning.
>
> I have read & reread her Genoese letters & I have them now under my pillow. How they delighted – and disturbed – me. I felt I wished the wireless had reached the perfection that it could transport me *bodily* arms lips & all to the Palace Hotel Torquay. There would have been such a scene of kissing embracing caressing enfolding crushing divesting etc etc as the world could produce no parallel at that witching hour of passionate joy. However I must fall back on the poor policy of Wait & See.
>
> At the foot of the bed I have your rug. It has been my constant companion so soft & warm & cuddlesome. It is the only part of my luggage that I worry about when we move about . . . I have slept in it on deck every afternoon.

LG's account of where they had been, and were going next, enlists some sympathy for Sylvester.

> As to the voyage we rejoined the boat at Spezia . . . I spent a couple of days at Pisa as I did not want to stay in Rome. It would have involved a

call on Mussolini & the Pope . . . We are now lying inside the little bay at
Santa Margherita near Rapallo . . . I mean to stay here until your last
possible letter to Genoa arrives. I am hoping you may have written another
on Monday. When that reaches me I shall sail off but whither I cannot be
quite sure. It lies between Corsica and St Remo.

He then turned to Frances and her need for rest – though making
no further reference to her possible condition: on the contrary.

That store of energy you are accumulating I shall want it all. I don't mind
F. [Felicia] but I am getting jealous of that brother of hers with his motor.
Don't darling. It will take the edge off. And I soon know when that occurs
& it saddens me more than you understand . . .

   You seem to be having excent [excellent] weather & I am so glad of that
for I want to see you look well & fit & beaming. You had such a trying
three weeks with me my sweetheart & your patience & tenderness & love
charmed every fibre of my heart into a new love for you. Stendhal whom
I have been just reading says 'The virtue of a woman comes out in sick-
ness'. Yours my darling shone like the Southern sun on a cloudless day. Its
rays warmed me through & through & restored my strength while I basked
happily in its glow. But my sweet I fear it exhausted you & I am glad you
are getting – & *enjoying* within wise limits – a months rest.

Finally he was beginning to think about what he would be coming
home to.

As to politics I am fuddled about them still. I have sent for Tweed next
week so as to pick up the tangled threads before I return . . .

   I am aiming at returning on Saturday or Sunday week. Megan must go
to Anglesea [*sic*] on Monday. If I return Saturday she might want to spend
Sunday at Churt & her mother would stay there. But if I return Sunday I
might be able to go down alone – not quite alone. In any event I spend my
first evening in London with my girl – do you know her. So will you please
warn us? . . .

   With passionate love fanned by reminiscence & anticipation to a white
heat of intense affection & ardour.

   Your own

   D.

. . . Apologise for me to Muriel for taking Tweed away.[23]

The postscript is at first sight puzzling. The implication is that Muriel – not Frances – was in some sort of relationship with Tweed. Could this be a deliberate tease on LG's part, knowing quite well that it was Frances who would be put out by his hauling Tweed to Cannes? Or was it rather Frances who was allowing LG to think there was something between Tweed and Muriel to cover her own involvement with him? In fact Muriel did have a relationship with Tweed some years later; but this is the only suggestion that it might have been developing as early as 1929.* The likelihood is that it suited Frances to let LG think that Tweed's interest was in Muriel.

At last, on 1 February, Frances came back to the subject of her 'transactions'.

My own beloved little man
    I do hope we shall be able to go to Churt together as soon as you return, sweetheart. I am looking forward to it so much – I cannot tell you how much! . . .
    I think this separation has gone more slowly than any other I can remember, my own darling. I expect it is because we grew more tenderly fond of each other before you went away, & while you were ill that I miss you so terribly. But as I told you, I am storing it all up so that when my dear sweetheart comes back there will be a perfect fountain of it to pour out upon him – I seem to feel more deeply & tenderly, & I think joyfully about our love, than I have ever done before. There are no 'transactions' yet, *cariad*, but there are still two days to go, & I am not letting myself be unduly excited in case of a disappointment. But I do most passionately hope that the longed-for thing may happen. It would just put the seal & crown upon our love & be a marvellous fulfilment . . .
        P.[25]

As the critical day approached, LG was getting anxious. From San Remo on 3 February he sent a telegram: HOME SATURDAY WRITE MONDAY

---

* Tweed did send Muriel two postcards from the Baltic in August 1928, at the same time that he was writing love letters to Frances. But they were no more than friendly updates on his movements. Some years later he sent her much more personal cards from his travels.[24]

AND TUESDAY CANNES STOP GIVE FULLER ACCOUNT OF YOUR DOINGS.[26] The
next day – Monday – Frances wired him the good news; but unfortunately she sent it to Genoa, so he never got it. He wired again from
Nice on Thursday asking once more for the latest.[27] In the meantime
she had written him a long ecstatic letter. Thinking that he had already
had her wire, however, she devoted most of it to assuring him again
of her fidelity.

> My own beloved, darling man
>
> I have just had your loving & beautiful letter, which made me almost
> weep with longing for you. I was amused at the time it was written –
> 7 a.m. You must love me very much to write me such a glorious love letter
> at that hour of the morning, my sweet! Your words thrill me & make me
> sad to feel that Saturday is such a long way away. Today when I sent you
> a wire I was rejoicing that this week was the last lap: now I wonder how
> on earth I can wait till Saturday to throw my arms around you & feel your
> thrilling kisses on my lips. And now comes your wire, with a demand for
> a fuller account of my doings! I thought I had written very fully, my sweet-
> heart, but I am afraid perhaps you are a little jealous, from what you say
> in your letter. Let me tell you at once, *cariad*, there is absolutely no grounds
> or need for it, & I do hope you will dispel at once any fears you may have
> on that account. I have seen a lot of the Brook family, & they have been
> awfully kind to me, but they are very numerous, & we always go about
> several of us together, & *never once* have I been alone with her brother at
> any time. So you need not worry there, my darling. I don't feel the least
> inclined to flirt with anyone, & have not flirted with anyone, & I expect
> you have had my telegram by now & will know that the most wonderful
> thing, the thing we have been longing & hoping for, has really happened
> this time. But I will tell you about that in a minute . . .

There followed another incongruous paragraph about comings and
goings with Felicia's family before she came back to the point.

> And now for the great news. It really *has* happened this time, my love, &
> I am so thrilled about it, & hope that you will be too. I told you that I
> thought it *might*, as I had a curious lethargic feeling, & on the other hand
> I thought it might be due to Torquay air. But now it seems that it wasn't
> only that. But I feel extraordinarily well (only a little lazy) and very rested
> & very fit in mind. I have been loving you so tremendously, my darling, so

very completely & tenderly, & what you say about my having looked after you while you were ill makes me so happy. I am so glad I had the opportunity (though it made my heart sore to see you ill) of showing you how really deeply & devotedly I care for you, & that you can depend upon me to love & cherish you 'till death do us part'. You are my husband, & my little child, & you will never cease to be. Do not doubt me, my darling; it upsets me when I think you are doing so, and under the present circumstances I want all your love and trust . . .

But how I wish I could have been with you, *cariad*! How glorious it would have been to sit there on deck with you, & to have shared the rug, & felt your limbs touching mine, & to have had my hand in yours. Your descriptions do really make me envious & I am so glad you have been missing me a little, my darling! Your letters have been so thrilling with their loving messages, & I do feel your tenderness & love enfolding me & protecting me. I am so glad you have had the rug with you & that it reminded you of me, & that it has caressed you & kept you warm *for* me! You will not need it when you return.

With that promise, Frances abruptly switched roles and gave her boss her view of the political outlook.

As to politics, I agree with you that the Tories are going to try the patriotic stunt at the election, & that it will make it difficult for us. You will need all your energy & optimism, my love, in the coming fight . . . I quite agree it is difficult to decide upon a plan of action . . .

Switching back to lover, she concluded with the arrangements for their longed-for reunion:

Well, my darling, I expect this really will be the last letter I send you before we meet again, & I hope that you will be reassured as to my 'doings'. I simply loved your last letter, *cariad*, and am carrying it about with me next to my heart, where you yourself will be before many days are over. I shall prepare dinner for you on Saturday, in case you arrive on time, & we cannot go to Churt till Sunday. Come *straight* to me, my darling. I shall be waiting for you so eagerly and impatiently, & shall hold you close, close to my body, & then we will try to satisfy all the longing & the love & the passion & the affection that we have both been storing up for each other. I have never wanted you back to much or so passionately, darling of my heart. I feel that we really do love each other more than ever, & whatever happens this year, I will be there to help you with my love & devotion, & to soften things a little for you if they go a little wrong.

Till Saturday! I hold you in my arms in anticipation every night & every morning.

Your own loving & devoted

P.

Muriel I gather very happy now she is back. Though she was very sweet to me while she was here. She will be very annoyed with you for getting Tweed out there![28]

Unfortunately we do not have LG's reaction to the news of Frances's pregnancy, when he eventually received it. He wrote one more letter, from Nice on the Tuesday, before hers reached him. It was quite short and mainly described another Mediterranean storm. But there was another ambiguous reference to Muriel and Tweed.

Tweed arrives here tomorrow. It is advisable that I shall be fully informed of the situation before I return so as to make up my mind as to course of action . . . Muriel returned in time to have a few evenings with Tweed so she'll be happy – & so are you – you little d——. But wait until I am back . . .

The last letter I had from you was written Wednesday of last week. I do hope I'll get a few more the next 2 or 3 days.

If all goes well I'll drive with Tweed straight to Morpeth [Mansions]. The train arrives somewhere about 7 pm. Either Tweed will stay at Morpeth or come down to Churt with Muriel of course (in either case the result will be the same). At least I mean to suggest it to him altho' I would so much like to have my Sunday alone. You can bring Felicia if you like – for a rest.

M. [Megan] may try to send her mother down with me – but I want to go with you to Churt.

My fondest love to you my *girl*.

D.

In spite of assurances to the contrary I am not so sure about the conventual severity of your holiday![29]

It must have been a curious homecoming: LG letting his family go to Addison Road while he and Tweed went straight to Morpeth Mansions to see Frances and Muriel; Frances bursting with her news and presumably longing to see each of the two potential fathers of her baby alone – but not together! Did all four of them go down to Churt, or just LG and Frances? Unfortunately we still lack Sylvester's diary to answer these teasing questions.

JENNIFER

Despite his long absence in Italy, LG did not make an immediate return to the political scene. During February he was still unsure how to proceed. Finally on 1 March 1929 he launched his campaign for the coming election with a speech to Liberal candidates at the Connaught Hotel. If returned to government, he announced, the Liberal party was ready with a programme of essential public works, which would 'reduce the terrible figures of the workless' – currently around 1.3 million – 'in the course of a single year to normal proportions', without adding a penny to national or local taxation. The full programme was published a few days later as a sixpenny pamphlet entitled *We Can Conquer Unemployment*. The cover was a picture of LG, arms outstretched, contrasting the busy munition factories of 1915 on one side with the dole queues of 1928 on the other. Both the Tory and Labour parties and most of the press derided the scheme; but three weeks later they were forced to take it more seriously when the Liberals won two more by-elections in previously Tory-held seats in Cheshire and Lincolnshire. LG spoke in both constituencies; but again most of the credit probably belongs to Tweed's efficient organisation. On 26 March LG spoke at the Albert Hall, using the new broadcasting techniques he had picked up in America to carry his words to another thirteen meetings around the country. Had there been opinion polls in 1929 they would surely have shown that a Lloyd George bandwagon was up and running.

Frances was ill during March, doubtless the effect of her pregnancy. She was forty – an advanced age in those days to have a first baby – so she was bound to be careful. The day before his Albert Hall speech LG wrote her a letter of rare apology for putting politics ahead of

looking after her. He wrote from Churt; she was presumably at Morpeth
Mansions.

My own sweet & darling & precious little girl.

One word of love. I could not tell you on the phone what I thought &
felt. It is when you are ill that I realise the depth and intensity of my affection for you. I have missed you so. Janet must have been bored with my
incessant talk about you.* Whatever talk I started I always found myself
saying 'Frances'. And I worried & worried but I did not phone too often
in case I awoke my little girl. Take plenty of sleep my sweet. That is the
best & surest of all healers.

And what a pig I have been feeling. When I was ill my loving & tender
little sweetheart was by me night & day without cease. My only excuse
darling is that I must not disappoint those scores of thousands who are
looking forward to the great meetings tomorrow. It is war & the grand
attack is to be made by me tomorrow & I am practically alone. If I am not
in form I may fail & the meetings will be a setback at a time when ruth-
lessness is essential to success. Will you forgive me my own darling for
seeming to put the fortunes of the battle above you? I have never done so
in my heart. Had I thought for a moment there was danger I would have
chucked everything & rushed to my *cariad*'s side. You know that don't you
girl of my heart? . . .

I have worked very hard on my speech & I think it is alright. But how
I missed your wise & loving help in its preparation. I was always wanting
to ask you 'What do you think of this?'

Tomorrow I must see you sweet. Meanwhile keep quiet sleep as much
as possible, don't fret. If you feel I could help in any way send for me at
once – *today* & I'll fly to my *cariad*.

Love greater than ever

Your Man

Don't forget what I never shall – that the present success of the Liberal
party is due to the advice you gave me about the Connaught rooms speech.
It is the truth.[2]

* Janet was presumably Frances's sister – the second of the four Stevenson girls, who
was a year younger than Frances, was slightly dim and never married. It would seem
that she had been staying with LG at Churt in Frances's absence. 'Janet has been an
ideal companion for a person who does not want to talk. She has been quiet & placid
& never needing to be fussed. She is a nice girl & in her own way I think she enjoyed
the weekend.'[1]

The election took place on 30 May. LG's unemployment pledge dominated the campaign, while Baldwin fought on the uninspiring slogan 'Safety First' and Labour was almost equally unradical. Keynes distilled the Liberal programe into a short pamphlet entitled *Can Lloyd George Do It?*, brilliantly ridiculing the Treasury argument that nothing could be done – far too good for an election campaign. Tweed covered the country with posters and leaflets and bought advertising space in all the provincial papers. Even the diehard Asquithians fell into line. Yet when it came to the last great throw of his career, LG himself fought a strangely quiet campaign. He did not stump the country as he had in 1923 and 1924, but spoke only four times outside Wales – though he drew huge audiences where he did speak. There may have been differences with Tweed, who – as the *Manchester Guardian* later wrote – 'as usual . . . took entirely his own line'.[3] Maybe LG's priority now really was to be with Frances. Or perhaps he was just feeling his age. But there was no sign of tiredness in an optimistic letter that he wrote her from Llandudno on 15 May. Once again her reply has not survived.

My own sweet

   Delighted to get your loving letter & especially delighted to hear you missed me. But what luck to find an excuse of the very best for running up to town & spending two days together. I shall drive straight to Morpeth & breakfast there.

   To all outward seeming things are going well here. Immense meetings & great enthusiasm. The young girls especially so!* But with this amorphous electorate the issue is too obscure for a premature crow. The canvass is only in its infancy, I cannot hazard a prediction. The three-cornered fight muddles everything up . . .

   But what a time I shall have before I see you. Caernarvon – probably 6000 or more without a loud speaker. A day's journey to Cardiff. Huge meeting there – then special to Swansea – thence by special back here. Three meetings Saturday night. Night mail to London – & then . . .

   Yours

   D.[4]

---

* Women under thirty were voting for the first time. LG obviously thought he had a special appeal for the so-called 'flapper' voter.

LG did come back to London that weekend, though it is not clear what his good excuse was. During the last week of the campaign he made some inflated predictions about forming a Liberal government; but realistically he hoped only to hold the balance of power again with a larger number of seats than in 1923–4. 'Whatever the complexion of the next Parliament,' he told his constituents, 'I venture to predict there will be enough Liberals in it to force the Liberal programme through.'[5] In the event the party won 28 per cent of the vote, but only fifty-nine seats: all LG's energy, Keynes's ideas and Tweed's organisation were not enough to prise open the trap that had already closed on the third party. Or, as LG himself put it on his return to London, 'We have been tripped up by the triangle.'[6] He consoled himself that the Liberals did once again hold the balance of power.* Labour was the largest party with 288 seats to the Tories' 260; so Ramsay MacDonald formed another minority Labour government, and LG set himself to prod and harry it into taking constructive action to meet the ever-deepening depression.

Meanwhile Frances's pregnancy ran its course. We do not know how long she carried on working. She would certainly have had to keep herself out of sight when her condition became visible. Her daughter believes she went to France for 'some months'.[7] That may be, but the only surviving letter from LG – from Criccieth in August – indicates only that she was somewhere by the sea. He still failed to keep her letters: most likely he deliberately destroyed them. He fussed like an expectant father; but even now he was still the jealous lover too.

My girl

You have pleased me so much by writing me two long & loving letters. I received both this morning.

You seem to have struck a most charming spot for your holiday. But I beg you not to forget my entreaty that you shall not run any risks in bathing. I do not want anything to happen to my dearest little girl. Don't bathe at all if the sea is rough. Don't swim out too far. Sarah has promised to post this for me if I let her have it in time. So I must not keep her waiting. Did you receive the letter I wrote you on Tuesday?

It is wet & miserable down here. Gwilym is here fortunately & I am

* LG also drew satisfaction from the fact that Gwilym regained the Pembrokeshire seat that he had lost in 1924, while Megan comfortably won Anglesey – making an unprecedented family group in the House.

organising some fishing to commence tomorrow with my own rod – &
Cranky's (oh you naughty little devil) . . .

If you would like to go to Lymne [*sic*] it must be the two days before I
return. Would you like to try it? I'll trust you implicitly. Just as you could
trust me if I gave my word definitely.

Fondest love to you – my girl.[8]

The latter part of this contains two puzzles. 'Cranky' was the Major
Crankshaw whom Frances had met in Paris in 1919 ('a darling') and
danced with again in London ('just as sweet as ever') in 1921. Had he
lent Frances a fishing rod, which she had subsequently given to LG?
Second, Frances had not been to Lympne, so far as we know, for years.
Philip Sassoon had been a minister in Baldwin's government since 1924
and was no longer as close to LG as in the days of the Coalition; but
no doubt he remained friendly with Frances. Was he offering her his
usual pampering hospitality during her pregnancy? Did LG suspect an
opportunity for some 'naughtiness'? Frances was seven or eight months
gone by this time! Anyway he was evidently expecting to see her when
he returned from Wales, which suggests that she was not by then in
France. After that LG took off with his family for a month-long motor
tour of the continent, which kept him out of the country for most of
September. There are no surviving letters from this trip.

If Frances did go to France for a time, she came home to give birth
in a private nursing home in central London: 27 Welbeck Street, just
north of Oxford Street. Maybe there were complications that made it
prudent to come back to England. The baby – christened Jennifer Mary
– was delivered by Caesarean section on 4 October, three days before
her mother's forty-first birthday. LG was speaking to the Liberal conference in Nottingham that day. There is no record of his reaction to the
birth; nor of Tweed's. There is a story that both of them retired to bed
with exhaustion; but this is probably just a family joke.[9] When she left
the nursing home, Frances took Jennifer back to Morpeth Mansions,
where she had engaged a wet-nurse and a nanny to look after her. Some
time earlier she had moved to a larger flat in the same building – from
no. 33 to no. 11, the grandest in the block, on the top floor, with at
least one extra bedroom and an even better view over Westminster
Cathedral and the London skyline. We cannot be sure, but presumably
LG visited mother and child there as soon as he could. Though Frances
had hoped for a boy, he was probably pleased that she had produced

a girl: he always preferred daughters, and was delighted to have another one.

He celebrated Jennifer's birth with some mawkish attempts at poetry. His first effort makes it clear that he hoped motherhood would stop Frances playing around and keep her henceforth on the straight and narrow: he crossed out his original fourth line and substituted a more anodyne version.

> She sought for pleasure high and low
> She found it now and then
> The more she got the less she gained
> By the embrace of men [replaced by 'from festivals and men'].
> One day a cherub came her way
> And lodged in her heart
> Its strings since then sing this sweet lay /out all day
> The twain shall never part.

The second is no more than a fragment, but the sense appears to be the same.

> Her fevered joys are now but dross
> These but a dead
> She counts them all but as a loss
> Her cherub is a delight
> Cherub is all delight.[10]

More significant, however, is another piece of doggerel, apparently written some months after Jennifer's birth. It does not scan, but its implication is important.

> Little Jennifer is thirteen pounds
> Which is much more than it sounds
> For she has a fortnight in hand
> So it is really very grand.[11]

This, surely, can only mean one thing: that Jennifer was two weeks premature. On whatever date this was written, LG was saying that a weight of thirteen pounds might not sound very much, but was actually pretty healthy, since she had been born – presumably underweight

– two weeks early. At a normal rate of weight gain (one or two pounds a month), Jennifer might have reached thirteen pounds anywhere between four and eight months after birth – that is, somewhere in the spring of 1930. If, for the sake of argument, LG wrote this around 4 April, when Jennifer was six months old, he was saying that she was really only due to reach that age on 18 April, so thirteen pounds already was a good weight. But if Jennifer was not due until 18 October, that would suggest that she was not conceived until mid-January – that is, after LG had left for the Mediterranean and Frances had gone to Torquay, thus lending support to the possibility that Tweed, and not LG, was the father. Of course calculations of exactly when a baby was due were not as sophisticated in 1929 as they are today; so it is perfectly possible that Jennifer *was* a full-term baby, even if she arrived earlier than the doctors had predicted. Moreover the Caesarean might have been performed early for medical reasons. Nevertheless it is odd that LG did not apparently see the implication of Jennifer arriving early. Maybe he was simply not aware of the calculations involved, despite having had five children already. But he may have been happy to encourage some doubt over the paternity. He might even have delib-erately promoted the idea that Jennifer was premature to put himself in the clear.

Jennifer's birth was registered in the St Marylebone district on 6 November, with Frances named as the mother and the father's name left blank. Frances gave her own name correctly in the order in which she was christened, as 'Louise Frances Stevenson', but disguised her address; she described herself, a touch optimistically, as 'of Indepen-dent Means' and gave her residence as the Coburg Hotel, Bayswater.[12] But for the moment she did not publicly acknowledge the child as her own. On the advice of her solicitor and family friend John Morris, Frances took out adoption papers for Jennifer: this was quite normal practice for unmarried mothers anxious to deflect awkward questions about the sudden appearance of a child in their household. She main-tained the pretence that Jennifer was her adoptive daughter for many years; later, when Jennifer went to school, Frances invented a story that her parents had been missionaries killed in China. She did not tell Jennifer that she was her real mother until Jennifer was eleven; and even then Frances did not tell her who her father was.

This was probably because she genuinely did not know. This is an embarrassing thing for a woman to have to admit at any time, the more so after Frances had finally committed herself to LG, renounced the other love of her life, and eventually – when Jennifer was fourteen – achieved social respectability by marrying LG, attaining her ultimate apotheosis two years later as the dowager Countess Lloyd-George. From childhood, Jennifer grew up with LG as the ever-present father-figure (or grandfather-figure) in her life. She called him 'Taid', which normally means grandfather, but can also – a useful ambiguity – mean godfather. 'Taid' was what LG's other grandchildren called him. One would have supposed that Frances would be proud to tell Jennifer the truth after LG's death, had she been sure of it. But she was not.

On the contrary, she told Jennifer specifically that she was *not* LG's child: if she had been, Frances would have suggested that she take his name. She told Jennifer that she was Tweed's child and that she and Tweed had been secretly married. By this time in her life Frances was anxious to conceal her irregular past and shield her daughter from the stain of illegitimacy. She feared that Jennifer's prospective husband would reject her if he knew the truth. Later Jennifer wondered how she had ever believed this story; but she did, and went on believing it for many years until she happened to see her mother's marriage certificate, describing her as 'spinster'. Only then did Frances confess that she had not been married to Tweed, since he was already married. But she still told Jennifer that Tweed was her father.

Why should she have done this when she had by then given her whole life to LG – as mistress for thirty years, briefly as his wife and then as loyal widow? Surely their daughter was the enduring fruit of their love, which could now be acknowledged; the crowning blessing for which she had longed in her diary, her letters and her novel? Even if there was an embarrassing possibility that LG was not in fact Jennifer's father, she had been brought up virtually as his daughter, or grand-daughter. He was her 'Taid'. He loved her, and she had loved him. By contrast Tweed never took any interest in Jennifer at all – even though he too believed he was the father. 'If Frances wants a kitten to play with,' he once told Muriel, 'I don't mind giving her one.' He did make some financial arrangement for her, and left her another £500 in his will. But Jennifer has a vague memory of meeting him only once. Whatever the truth, she has no doubt which of them felt like a father to her, and which one she would prefer to have been her father.[13]

So why did Frances persist in this story about Tweed, if she really did not know? Why indeed did she have an affair with Tweed in the first place, in the middle of her lifelong dedication to LG? The first possibility is that she genuinely fell in love with Tweed; knew she could not marry him; could not bring herself to leave LG for him; but nevertheless allowed herself to have a fling, which she was happy to believe had given her at last a long-desired child, whom she then allowed LG to believe was his. A more calculating possibility, however, is that she and LG together deliberately used Tweed – rather as they had once toyed with using Billy Owen – as a decoy to divert the threat of scandal away from LG. On this hypothesis, Frances used an affair with Tweed as a decoy to allow her to have LG's child, so that they could always if necessary deny that LG was the father. When there were rumours about Jennifer in the late 1930s, LG himself used precisely this defence, denying that the child was his and insisting that she was Tweed's – even though he certainly believed that Jennifer was his. There is a third possibility, hinted at in something Frances once told Jennifer after LG's death, which is that Frances was so angered by LG's 'insane' jealousy and incessant accusations that she was flirting (or worse) with every man she saw that she decided to have an affair – just one – to spite him. This might seem far-fetched, but the fact that Frances said something of the sort to Jennifer, many years later, does illuminate some of the tension that undoubtedly existed between Frances and LG behind the teasing of their letters.

The fact is that we shall never know. Jennifer herself takes an astonishingly calm view of the whole mystery. Some years ago she wrote down, for the benefit of her own daughter, her considered guess at what really happened, based on what she had learned from her mother and from Muriel – the closest (but not a disinterested) witness to these events, who lived to a great age and did not die until 1998. She believes, first, that Frances wanted a child: this we know to be true. Second, that LG wanted a child by her; this clearly had not been the case earlier, but he does appear to have changed his mind by 1929. Third, neither wanted a scandal to ruin his career. 'Both – but especially F. – had already sacrificed a lot to that end.' Therefore Frances deliberately used her affair with Tweed as a cover.

> LlG didn't know about it at the time, but F probably had this aspect of things in mind from the beginning. I don't think she would have worried at all about 'cheating' Tweed, who was not intending to marry her, and was not interested in having children.

Jennifer believes that Frances told Muriel that Tweed was the father 'because M obviously would have been bitterly jealous if she thought F was having an affair with Tweed for any other reason than to have a child which was not LlG's'. Muriel did not like LG; she did very much like Tweed. She naturally preferred to believe that her niece was Tweed's child rather than LG's, and used to tell Jennifer that she had many of Tweed's mannerisms – even though most people are struck by her resemblance to LG. Muriel presumably was not jealous, because she had no wish for children of her own: she was quite happy for Frances – rather than herself – to have Tweed's child whom they could both enjoy.

'In any case,' Jennifer continues, 'Frances could not be sure whose child I was.'

I asked her once how she was sure I was TFT's child, and she said she took 'precautions'. But she did not say with which man she took them. LlG was certainly hoping at that stage that she would have his child, so was not aware of any precautions – but nor presumably was TFT. More importantly, precautions in those days were not secure. She told me once . . . that nothing was safe – and she said it with great strength and bitterness . . . I was much struck by the passion of her response.

Despite the uncertainty, Jennifer unquestionably feels herself, in her blood and instinct, to be LG's daughter. 'I would prefer to be the child of someone I loved and respected, and who loved me and enjoyed my company, than of someone I may, or may not, have met on one occasion.'[14] Today, in her seventies, her house is full of Lloyd George memorabilia. Indeed, she is a good deal kinder to the memory of LG than she is towards Frances, who after all her maternal longings turned out not to be a very good parent. And in spite of all the doubts, the evidence of the dates, of Frances's letters and of Jennifer's clear resemblance to LG still points, on balance, to the probability that her instinct is sound.

29

'A MOST FASCINATING
LITTLE PERSON'

Jennifer's first ten months are almost entirely undocumented. Presumably Frances kept her well hidden, while she went back – at least part-time – to work. Even Muriel does not seem to have seen her before August, which is hard to understand. Maybe Frances went abroad again, though that would surely have prompted some letters from LG. At any rate there is no record of her existence during these months, except for three letters from Frances's friend Felicia who was in the United States. She had evidently not yet seen Jennifer, but Frances sent her photographs and she responded enthusiastically, first from Boston in May 1930.

> I already feel proud of my god-daughter & am longing to make her acquaintance . . . She has a nice shaped head. She looks clever, the dear . . .[1]

And then from California in June:

> I wonder . . . how things are going with you. Some how I feel that you are much happier than you used to be. Perhaps it is Jennifer, or perhaps it's just generally a more settled feeling.[2]

Felicia was one person who almost certainly knew of Frances's torn emotions; her view that Frances now seemed more settled is therefore significant.

Then in August there comes a flurry of letters between LG and Frances, which contain his first written comments about Jennifer. He was at Criccieth, and Frances was now staying in a rented house at Felpham, near Bognor Regis in Sussex. She had evidently needed to engage a new nurse – and LG took a close interest, with all the assurance of an experienced parent.

My sweetest little mother

I am so relieved for your sake to find things have gone so well. I never believed in the 'peaking and pining' bogey. The little girl was obviously so devoted to her mother & so perfectly happy with her that I never thought she would miss anybody else. All the same it is a piece of good luck that you should have such an excellent nurse. That is a comfort for you need feel no anxiety now. You are a darling to say that it will enable you to come up to see me without feeling any worry. It was a sweet thought & pleased me so much.

The house seems ideal in every respect & I hope you are getting good milk. So much depends on that.

There are 2 or 3 things I want to hear about

1. The weight. What did she make last week?

2. What did Mrs Dyer say about her? Does she suspect? What story have you pitched to her & how does she really take it?*

3. Any more teeth?

I am not coming up next week. The Government won't be ready!

Weather bad here until today. I am now lying in a hot sun. I read everyday the Bognor weather news & saw 'Sun shining on Jennifer – overcast everywhere else' . . .

LG was not only besotted with Jennifer; he was still anxious about Frances's fidelity – even if on this occasion his insecurity manifested itself only in a dream.

Drat the Government. I do want to see you so much. Yesterday, as I drove over the mountains from South to North Wales . . . I thought so longingly & lovingly of the sweet natured little girl who was then lavishing her tenderness on a helpless but fascinating little monkey sleeping in her pram. And then last [night] I had such an unpleasant dream. You had decided to leave me altogether & were so defiant about it. You promised however to write

* Mrs Dyer was the wife of LG's chauffeur at Churt, which suggests that Frances had been staying there. She must have known Frances's real position in LG's household, but clearly she was one of those who had to be told that Jennifer was adopted.

me an occasional letter & you told me that you had arranged with R. D.
Holt of Liverpool to deliver them to me.* You had been out with R.D.H.
somewhere on Wednesday. It isn't true is it sweetheart? . . .

Fondest love to you both.

D.[4]

Frances's first surviving letter from Felpham is full of baby talk.

My own darling

I have not got very much news for you – just a repetition of my last,
namely that Jennifer is adorable, sweeter than ever, & much more intelligent
even than I thought she was. Muriel came yesterday, determined of course
not to be too enthusiastic but even she now is obliged to keep on saying: 'She
is a darling'. Jennifer fortunately was not very long in taking to her – a bit
shy at first, but soon got over it. So all is well. I think Muriel is very pleas-
antly surprised – she hadn't expected anything nearly so attractive . . .

She then added a scrap of Churt gossip, which suggests that the
chauffeur's wife was less than discreet where other people's affairs were
concerned.

I hear that Carter's baby was born about a fortnight ago. Mrs Dyer says
that every time Carter has 'anything to do' with Mrs Carter a baby has
been the result. Poor Carter! It seems incredible, but apparently Mrs C.
doesn't hold with that sort of thing.

Meanwhile Frances was expecting a visit from LG's daughter-in-law
Roberta, the soon-to-be-divorced wife of his eldest son Dick: an indication that she was on perfectly friendly terms with at least some of
his family. We do not know what story Frances 'pitched' to Roberta;
presumably that Jennifer was adopted. She promised to write again on
Tuesday to tell how Roberta got on with Jennifer. 'In future that will
be my test for people,' she wrote, and immediately added, 'You have
passed that test very well!' She ended in familiar style, but with one
important difference:

---

* R. D. Holt, a partner in a leading Liverpool shipping firm, was a former Liberal MP
once described by LG as 'almost the most implacable of my opponents' – a curious
figure to surface in his dreams as a possible sexual rival.[3]

I do hope you are well, my sweet. Try & take your mind off work for a little . . . You never do, you know – except when you are engaged in the selling of black currants and gooseberries.

Ever so much love, my darling, from us both, & loving kisses, from your devoted

P.[5]

LG's reply was likewise addressed in the plural:

My girls

Your second letter has arrived & I have already read it through. Every word. What a little clockwork of fascination you have with you. I am so pleased to hear that she has already conquered Muriel up to the point of extracting from her an expression of warm approval. That is a real triumph. I am anxious to hear what Roberta, Ninette [Frances's second sister] & Mrs Dyer think of her . . .

How happy you must be my darling with your enchanting little fairy, & you thoroughly deserve it for the happiness you give to others who don't always deserve it. Here lies one of them writing to you now with a grateful heart for all you have done to cheer & sustain him in his tempestuous life . . .

I enclose four more envelopes for I devour all the Bognor News with avidity* . . .

Love to you both.

D.[6]

When Frances wrote back she reported that Ninette had loved Jennifer, but that Roberta had not come on Monday but was coming that day instead. She was also expecting some neighbours from Churt at the weekend, so she was now getting a regular stream of visitors.

I'm sending you the snaps. Don't you think they are delicious, and don't you love the one of Jennifer clapping her hands? She is always doing that now, and makes quite a loud clap. She looks so sweet, I expect we shall take some more snaps soon, and I will send them to you.

Give Sarah my love, & tell her Jennifer sends her a kiss. We both send our fondest love & kisses to you, *cariad*, and wish you were here.

---

* Presumably he was sending Frances pre-addressed envelopes to disguise her letters.

Tenderest thoughts from your ever loving
P.[7]

The last four letters, back and forth, are full of complicated arrangements for meeting in London or Churt the following week. LG's first opens with a curious greeting that was perhaps a warning to Frances to stick to the agreed story.

My girls – both adopted
   I have most reluctantly (!?) to come up to town for a Conference Monday next.* I leave by the night mail Sunday night from Holyhead. I shall certainly not return for a day or two. I shall write you tomorrow with more particulars. You can write me tomorrow morning (Friday) but in order to ensure my getting it Saturday morning post it early.
   I am looking forward
   (1) to getting photos tomorrow
   (2) to have a glimpse of the original next week.
   Fondest love to both
   D.[8]

My own beloved darling
   How exciting to think I shall be seeing you so soon. Where will you be staying (Churt I suppose) and what do you want me to do? Just send me a line as to your plans – I can easily run over to Churt from here, unless you propose to run over here from Churt! Or do you want me to come up to town? I am so looking forward to seeing you, *cariad* . . .
   All love from your two little girls, & more when we meet.
   Ever your own
   P.

Hope you liked the photos.[9]

CB *a a* CM etc etc†
I have not yet had my morning bag. But as I have to leave at 10.30 for Barmouth I thought I had better write you about my movements.
   I travel to London Sunday night. Seebohm [Rowntree] suggesting we

---

* This was the third in an abortive series of meetings at which LG tried to inject some urgency into the government's efforts to reduce unemployment.
† LG liked abbreviated greetings. This is his usual *cariad bach anwyl aur chus mel.*

should return to Criccieth by the 2.25 train the same day. My answer will be emphatically NO. But what shall I do? I must not lure you to the office. The liftman has the mumps. You must therefore shun O.Q.S.* So must I if I am to see you. Addison Road is dismantled. What about Churt? I mean to have a whole day there before I leave.

You can phone to OQ Street whether you can manage to come up. If so then we can lunch at the Metropole at 1 o'clock or you can go straight to Churt & phone them to meet you at Guildford. Let me know sweet at OQ Street. I might be able to run down with you on Tuesday but that is doubtful. But I do want to see you my darling.

No letter this morning. It may come by late post.

Love

D.[10]

My girls

Photos much the best so far. Delightful. Looked at them & studied them over & over again. She baffles me. But all the same she is a fascinating kid. I like very much the pensive photos. They are quite remarkable for a kid of her age.

Now for Monday. If you cannot manage Monday then you might come on Tuesday straight to Churt . . .

I shall drive straight to the N.L.C. [National Liberal Club] for breakfast & be there until 10.15. Tom [Carey Evans] advises me not to go near office. Not safe owing to mumps.

However you can phone me there should there be any message.

Love

D.[11]

That autumn and over the winter LG was still engaged in trying to ginger up the Labour government, trying to hold the Liberal party together while simultaneously exploring all sorts of other possible alliances with all the rogue elephants and young lions in the political circus. On the one hand, he was talking to the newspaper barons Beaverbrook and Rothermere, who were mobilising a dissident Tory campaign against Baldwin, and with Churchill (who in January resigned from the Tory front bench), to see if there was any basis for reconstituting the old Coalition. On the other, he was in touch with Labour

* LG's office was now in Old Queen Street.

rebels from Sir Oswald Mosley to Aneurin Bevan; and with younger
Tories like Harold Macmillan and Brendan Bracken, who were equally
impatient with the passive leadership of Baldwin. There were constant
rumours that LG might join the Labour party, as some senior Labour
figures were privately begging him to do. But he had no intention of
closing his options in that way; his strategy was to hold himself in
readiness, waiting for the nation to recall him to power when the crisis
came.

At the beginning of 1931 LG was still in Wales when Frances, in
secretarial mode, wrote him two letters reporting the latest timid steps
towards cooperation between the Liberals and the government. She
wrote from Old Queen Street, but LG was finally about to move into
the official Liberal headquarters at 21 Abingdon Street. Her first letter
gives a useful glimpse of their working arrangements, before ending in
more personal style.

> I think you will like your room at Abingdon Street. It is a lovely room,
> with beautiful windows & very comfortable, but unfortunately there will
> have to be a bit partitioned off for me, as I don't see where else I could go
> unless I sat in Sylvester's room on another floor. Your present desk here is
> rather big for the room, & I suggest you have it in your library at Addison
> Road. But you could decide that when you come back.
>
> Will you be coming along to dinner with me on Thursday? If Sylvester
> just gives me a message I should love to have you. Someone else will be
> very pleased to see you too, I know, if you are back in time . . .
>
> All my love to you, *cariad*. The days have gone very slowly since you
> left, and I have so hated being parted from you in these first days of the
> New Year. But I am longing for Thursday, when I shall see you again, my
> darling.
>
> Till then I am thinking of you all the time
> Ever your own
> P.[12]

Soon after this Frances caught flu. Typically LG managed to suggest
that he suffered from her illness almost more than she did.

> My own darling girl
>   You can hardly realise my delight when I heard this morning that you
> had passed a good night & were much cooler. I had passed a thoroughly

worrying night thinking of you & bothering how you were. I woke up in snatches & slept in patches, until about 2 this morning. I was so miserable yesterday that I failed utterly to respond to the repeated requests of the photographers to smile. I simply could not. What a worry you are to a fond old fellow who loves you far too much for his peace of mind.

Tomorrow I bring you a tender young chicken for roast & an old hen of Jennifer's age for broth. Tell me what else you would like. I am willing to level down all my farm to restore your strength. Now for great care. No '*yn & wyfn*' [untranslatable] – no getting too gay – flinging your arms about. South coast free from all cares domestic & emotional . . .

Tomorrow about 5.30.

Love – tender & deep

Ever your

D.[13]

Next day Frances went back to Bognor to recover. Jennifer and her nanny joined her there a few days later. Over the next fortnight LG wrote nearly every day with his usual fussy advice to invalids. He even felt able to visit Jennifer in Frances's absence.

My girl

One day almost gone – but I do miss you my sweet. Oh so much. All the same I know it is the right thing for you to get thoroughly renovated & refitted . . . The first few days will be your worst. By Sunday you will feel ever so much better especially if the little tonic will be with you then. After that you will gain resilience day by day . . .

Love to my girl – & to her mother . . .[14]

My girl

I was so busy yesterday that I failed to write my diurnal love letter. I feel quite sore at my failure. I put it off until I had seen [a] little person so as to send you a report. I was there for half an hour the room crowded with Nurse's friends. I forgot you had warned me that her sister was bringing her two little charges to visit J. The latter was glad to see me. She took no special notice of the other kids but went on with her usual task of nursing all the 'ba's' in turn. She came to me sat on my knee opened my coat & asked for 'Ma'. Then I saw [illegible] the pencil. The other little girl wanted me to do for her what I was doing for J. roll the chain round her arm. J. promptly resented this & pulled it off . . .

Next week very busy . . . Hope to get down for the day Thursday or Friday . . .[15]

My sweethearts

It is good to hear & to feel in your letters that you are improving. Another 10 days will make you fit for any mischief then my troubles begin.

I am full of trying to bring this cowardly government up to the mark – a hopeless task. Sisyphus is not in it with me. I am trying to roll a melting sloshing snowball up the hill . . .

I shall hardly know you & J. when I come down.[16]

All being well I shall make tracks for Bognor tomorrow morning. The news you gave me on the phone that no substitutes were needed was very gratifying – & thrilling. Meanwhile I shall possess my soul in impatience & as somebody said about Coolidge 'rest on my morals'.[17]

It is not certain whether LG did get down to Felpham on 6 February. But when he wrote again from Churt three days later Jennifer had become ill.

My darling

I am sending the first heather bloom of the season for your enchanting little wizard. When I picked it the hoar frost was so thick on its petals that I could hardly distinguish between foliage and flower. But here it is with my love to you *both*. Weller will bring you back when you are ready. He can bring papers from the office at the same time.

I was so relieved for your sake my own girl when I heard there was no cause for anxiety. My heart went *all* out to you in your worry.

If the doctor has the *slightest* worry as to the wisdom of her leaving stop it. In any event I would be disposed to postpone it until *Wednesday*.

Fondest love – tender & tenacious

D.[18]

There is one more undated letter, which may or may not belong to February 1931, after Frances's return from Bognor. It does not really matter. Whenever it was written, it clearly refers to some sort of medical report on Jennifer – almost certainly a phrenological analysis. Phrenology was a pseudo-science developed in the nineteenth century, which claimed to determine character by the shape of the skull. It was totally discredited by the 1920s, but LG was still an unrepentant adherent. (He always thought Neville Chamberlain no good because his head was too narrow.) He must have encouraged Frances to have Jennifer tested. With what purpose? Could it have been used to determine her paternity? Without the report his comments are baffling.

> My darling
>
> I have read the Report *thrice*. That shows the interest I take in the document. It is a fascinating analysis of a most fascinating little person.
>
> I have marked it carefully from the point of view of 'the two parents'. The crosses are Semitic. The straight lines are Brythonic. The gaps must be maternal! What do you think of my analysis?
>
> I shall be looking forward so much to seeing one if not two of the wanderers on Friday afternoon – at tea.
>
> Fondest love
> D.[19]

Brythonic means Ancient British (or Welsh), which is clear enough. But then where does a Semitic element come in? And why does LG write 'the two parents' in inverted commas?

There is another important letter that dates from some time around July 1931. It was discovered by A. J. Sylvester when LG dropped his wallet at the House of Commons and it was handed in by a cleaner. Sylvester thought it 'priceless' – in other words, he thought it might be valuable – and shamelessly transcribed it in his diary before putting it back in the wallet. Evidently Frances and LG had quarrelled, and Frances was desperate to make up. Is it possible that she had inadvertently said something that cast doubt on Jennifer's paternity?

> I feel I must write you a little note to tell you how sorry I am about what passed yesterday. I will be so sweet to you to make up for it and we will be so happy together, as ever we were [sic]. There can be nobody for me but you. I could not stop loving you however hard I tried, and I will not make things difficult for you in future, my darling. As to the other thing that upset you, you must put that right out of your mind for my meaning was not what you thought – *you* know this, and it is foolish of you to upset yourself in that way, especially when there is no possible foundation for it. I have been so miserable and depressed and still more for your voice sounded so cold on the telephone. Do say something nice to me sweetheart. I will

be so loving to you and will only remember your sweetness to me in future. I shall look forward impatiently to seeing you on Monday. Take care of yourself, my darling. I do wish I could have stopped with you last night and been with you today.

Ever your loving P.

J. sends a big kiss. She is in great form, singing at the top of her voice.[20]

It always seemed to be Frances who had to make the first move when they had quarrelled.

30

HORS DE COMBAT

From the beginning of May 1931 A. J. Sylvester resumed his diary, which he now wrote diligently for the rest of LG's life. It is in many ways an unpleasant document; but it paints an unrivalled picture of the complexity of LG's bigamous ménage. Sylvester undoubtedly admired LG: he saw him as the Great Man who had won the war and could save the country again, if he could only get back into power. But no man is a hero to his valet. Just because Sylvester admired LG so greatly, he was bitterly critical of his failings – political and moral. On the one hand, he was increasingly exasperated by LG's chaotic working methods, his unpredictable temper, his extreme self-centredness and lack of consideration for his staff; on the other, prurient fascination with LG's rampant sexual appetite alternated with prim disapproval of his immorality and hypocrisy.* Both responses were sharpened by a hard-nosed realisation of the commercial value of what he knew. For this reason one must be careful not to believe everything Sylvester beadily set down. Yet he was by training a shorthand writer. He wrote down what he heard and saw. He often put a censorious interpretation on what he recorded, and sometimes he may have got the wrong end of the stick. But he had not the imagination to make things up entirely. His unflattering commentary on the rows and rivalries that rent LG's

---

* He was also amazed by LG's prodigious physical endowment. For instance, when LG took a bath in June 1931: 'There he stood as naked as when he was born with the biggest organ I have ever seen. It resembles a donkey's more than anything else. It must be a sight for the God's [sic] – or the women – in erection! No wonder they are always after him; and he after them![1] Another time he was equally impressed by the size of LG's testicles.[2]

family and political household in the 1930s provides a salutary coun-
terpoint to the over-romanticised version that can easily emerge from
the letters between LG and Frances and from Frances's diary and autobiography.

Two of Sylvester's earliest entries give typical glimpses of the continuous juggling needed to keep LG's wife and mistress apart. Maggie and
Megan had been down at Churt over the weekend of 9–10 May. On
Monday morning one of the typists there warned Sylvester that LG
was 'very touchy'.

> It seems that he wanted to get Dame Margaret and Megan up to town on
> an early train. Had a good early train booked up, but Dame Margaret found
> it was not necessary after all for her to come up before the afternoon. This
> put out L.G.'s plans terribly! . . . Consequently Frances could not go to
> Churt and he was bound to come up [to London] which he did not want
> to do. He came to the House at 3.30; Frances was waiting in my room. He
> went into his room; she with him, and there he stopped, being 'not avail-
> able'. Then he suddenly appeared with his hat and coat on. Off he went to
> her flat. How I swore . . . I had fixed an appointment for him at 5 p.m.
> which he did not keep.[3]

Next day:

> L.G. did not come into the office until late this morning, having been for
> a walk. I got hold of him as soon as I could and fairly bludgeoned him
> into looking at my papers. Then Frances came in and as soon as he saw
> her he said: 'I have done enough, rather more than usual.' So that ended
> effective work with him of that kind, and back he went to his speech. In
> fact after coffee and biscuits they both went into Richmond Park, and he
> then went straight to his luncheon appointment at Brackens, where he meets
> Winston.[4]

As well as complicated arrangements to meet Frances, Sylvester also
records numerous instances of LG pursuing other women – usually
his employees: typists, maids or farm workers – whether for a harmless flirtation, a quick grope or a full conquest one can never be sure.
Some of these adventures one should probably take with a pinch of
salt. But throughout Sylvester's diary there are repeated references to
one relationship that cannot be dismissed so lightly. Sylvester never

quite spells it out; but he implies unmistakably that LG had some sort of improper relationship with his own daughter-in-law – Dick's wife Roberta. Philandering is one thing; taking advantage of female employees a good deal worse; but cuckolding your own son transgresses one of the most sacred taboos of civilised life. If true, it would put LG utterly beyond the pale.

Yet the whole family – except Dick – knew about it, and Frances seems to have taken it in her stride. Noting that LG was taking Roberta down to Churt with him in June 1931, Sylvester commented that Frances 'knew what he was up to as he had apparently put his underclothes in his little dispatch box. She seems to accept these expeditions now, as a matter of course.'[5] And many years later she told Jennifer, with no particular sense of horror, that LG had once had 'an affair' with Roberta.[6]

Dick had married Roberta MacAlpine in 1917 on the rebound after breaking off a previous engagement. They met in Bath, where Dick was undergoing treatment after being invalided out of the army, and were married within three months. She was the daughter of the building contractor Sir Robert MacAlpine and brought with her a sizeable fortune. They had two children, Valerie and Owen, born in 1918 and 1924, but the marriage was not a success, as their son Owen wrote with filial tact in his memoir *A Tale of Two Grandfathers*.

> My father, a most loveable man, was very easy-going, enjoyed the good things of life, and from quite an early age drank more than was good for him. My mother, ten years younger, had a very strong personality and a quick temper; . . . She worshipped her father and was inclined to measure all other men by his high standards. By these criteria, she frequently found my father lacking in firmness of purpose. And then there were . . . rows over money, which unhappily ran through my father's fingers like water.[7]

Dick was the black sheep of the Lloyd George family, who never settled to anything. Trained as a civil engineer, he worked in Spain and South America before 1914, then served through the war and emerged, like so many others, psychologically scarred for life. Charming but feckless, he tried farming, but failed to make a success of it. Roberta left him in 1931, supposedly over his infidelities; and they were divorced in 1933. Presumably the marriage had already been in trouble some time before this – not that that excuses LG.

July 1931 was the pivotal moment of LG's later career. That summer, as the world recession deepened in the wake of the Wall Street crash, and unemployment in Britain soared to more than two and a half million, Ramsay MacDonald's minority Labour government staggered helplessly towards collapse. LG's moment, it seemed, was surely coming. On 21 July he had dinner with Churchill, Mosley and their various acolytes to concert their tactics. There were already rumours of MacDonald and Baldwin coming together to form an emergency government. 'That moment,' LG told the company, 'must find us all united on the front opposition bench, and . . . we shall not be there long.' The conspirators parted, Harold Nicolson wrote, 'on the assumption that . . . the Great Coalition has been formed'.[8]

The next day LG dined at Simpson's in the Strand with Frances, Sylvester and Tweed and told them about the previous evening's dinner. Sylvester wrote that the story of coalition between Baldwin and MacDonald 'seems fantastic, but there were those present last night who took it very seriously. L.G. said that those two were very friendly . . . it would please both of them for L.G. to be out of it.'[9]

Fantastic it might have seemed, but this was precisely what happened, helped by a cruel blow of fate that – conveniently for Baldwin and MacDonald – put LG out of action at the crucial moment. Sylvester's diary, however, suggests that in these last days before the illness that wrecked all his hopes, LG's mind was as much on juggling his various women as on politics.

Monday: comes up to town and lunches at the flat [i.e. Morpeth Mansions]; goes to the dentist and makes a wonderful speech in the House. Leaves immediately afterwards with Roberta for Churt. I nearly knocked Dame Margaret and Megan down as the car leaves the yard. They could only just have missed it . . .

Tuesday: Still at Churt [presumably with Roberta] ringing up every hour.

Wednesday: Came up and went straight to the flat. Met he [sic] and Frances at Simpsons with Tweed . . .

Thursday: Annie Parry goes to Addison Rd. J.T. [Davies] lunches there; Megan there for lunch also; as soon as Megan leaves for the House, Annie Parry is packed off and Frances Stevenson goes down there.

Ann Parry was LG's Welsh secretary, who also kept the bees at Churt. The implication is that she came up from Churt to act as secretary at Addison Road while Megan was there, after which Frances replaced her. The farce continued the next day:

> Friday: Comes to the office and his nails manicured by Frances. Gets into a Hell of a temper about Bill . . . * Goes to see Addison . . . and makes a speech in the House which probably saves Government. Sends for Frances and then goes to her flat. Changes his mind three times about going home to dinner [with Megan] and in the end leaves Megan to her own resources and he stays to dinner at the flat and decides to go to Churt Saturday morning.
>
> Meantime Tweed sits in his room reading the newspapers and working out crossword-puzzles; his secretary making hats or sewing; Muriel Stevenson doing fancy work, and this is how they reckon they are going to keep Liberalism alive.[10]†

LG's indecision was clearly due to the fact that he was already feeling unwell. He was taken seriously ill that Friday evening at Morpeth Mansions. He presumably managed to get back to Addison Road that night; but he did not go down to Churt as planned on Saturday. Megan left in the morning, leaving LG in the care of Sarah and Frances, who must have rushed to Addison Road as soon as Megan had gone. About midnight he was in great pain and could not pass urine, so Frances sent for Olwen's husband, Tom Carey Evans, who came and 'tapped' him, releasing a pint and a half of liquid, and gave him a sleeping draught. Frances stayed at Addison Road to nurse him. On Sunday Carey Evans called in Lord Dawson and the leading prostate expert, Dr Swift Joly, who agreed to operate on Wednesday after two days of observation and tests.

On Sunday afternoon Sarah rang Sylvester, who arrived at Addison Road about six o'clock, finding Carey Evans, Frances and Gwilym there. Frances and Gwilym had been taking it in turns to read to LG, who was 'very cheerful', now that the pain had eased. He was anxious not to announce that he was having an operation, so as not to give his

---

* This was a Land Utilisation Bill, which was the one measure of the Labour government that LG strongly supported. Dr Christopher Addison, a former Liberal minister in LG's government, was now Minister of Agriculture.

† Muriel was now working at Liberal headquarters as well – with Tweed.

enemies the idea that he was 'done for'. Carey Evans said that LG was in 'a very good physical state . . . His heart was good; also his kidneys were not affected'. It was lucky the condition had been caught in time, or it might have been more difficult to operate. He told Sylvester – but presumably not Frances – that 'he would probably be a much better and stronger man . . . afterwards because he would not be able to "roger"' so much – if at all. 'It was probably a very fortunate thing it had come as it had.'

The next member of the family to arrive was Dick, who came, saw his father and decided to go to Criccieth next morning and bring his mother back with him to London on Tuesday. A night nurse came for the night (and a day nurse on Monday morning); but Frances still stayed Sunday night as well. 'She looks very tired and worn,' Sylvester noted. 'Carey has been friendly for some time; Gwilym accepted the position; but Dick just passed her and took no notice. It will be interesting to see what Megan does and also Dame Margaret.'

Sylvester's account also includes a significant paragraph about Roberta:

Dick then spoke to Roberta, who was at home . . . She had spoken to L.G. on the telephone yesterday and L.G. had been 'short with her'. But that might be according to plan, as Frances was there. It was quite clear from the conversation Dick had on the phone with Roberta that he could not know anything. If only he knew! It was only by the grace of God that she was at home and not in London. She is coming to town tomorrow, but I do not think L.G. will see her. There is great prejudice against her. Carey and Gwilym speak very frankly about her because they know of her attentions. Carey says this will stop all his 'rogering' for a long time, although he is such a wonderful fellow with such vitality.[11]

This suggests that Gwilym and Carey Evans – but not Dick – knew that something illicit had occurred between Roberta and LG; but they appear to blame Roberta, rather than him, for her 'attentions' to LG.

On Monday (27 July) Sylvester was authorised by Carey Evans and Gwilym to put out a doctors' bulletin saying that 'Mr Lloyd George is suffering from an attack of haematurea [blood in the urine] which necessitates his being confined to bed'. There was no mention of an operation; Sylvester was immediately deluged with press enquiries, and was annoyed to learn that Tweed had told the *Manchester Guardian* that LG was suffering from a prostate condition. The same day Frances went to Abingdon Street to see LG's solicitor, John Morris, with 'various instructions' – presumably about his will.[12] On Tuesday Sylvester found Frances and Megan together at Addison Road. That was all right: 'They just have to tolerate the position.' But Frances would have to leave before Maggie arrived that evening. A second bulletin told the press that the patient had passed 'a somewhat disturbed night', although his general condition was 'satisfactory'. Again Sylvester was deluged with 'a perfect avalanche' of enquiries wanting more detailed information. LG was 'greatly touched' to receive a message from the King and Queen. That evening Gwilym authorised a statement that an operation was necessary.

LG was operated on at Addison Road on Wednesday morning by Dawson and Swift Joly, with an equally eminent anaesthetist, Sir Francis Shipway. St John Ambulance men, plus LG's chauffeur, Dyer, were on hand to carry him into Maggie's bedroom, which was used as the operating theatre, and back to his own room when it was over. Special power lines were laid to provide enough electricity for X-rays and other equipment, and blood-transfusion facilities were standing by. Just before he was put to sleep, LG dictated to Megan a message to be read out at the Liberal Summer School. While the operation was in progress Maggie sat downstairs calmly embroidering chair covers with Edna and Olwen. Megan stayed in her room, praying.

The operation went well and the doctors were pleased with themselves: 'A beautiful clean job had been made of it,' Carey Evans told Sylvester. 'His muscles in that quarter were amazing.' They all came downstairs and had coffee with the family. When Dick arrived soon afterwards, 'Dame Margaret . . . just fell into his arms and wept with sheer thankfulness.' Then Sarah told Sylvester that Dawson had said it was all right for him to telephone Frances. 'I went downstairs and she happened to be ringing me at that moment.* So she was actually the first person outside to hear the news.'

Sylvester issued another bulletin to the press, after which 'the telephone started and during the rest of the day never ceased. Callers came by the score as well as telegrams, letters and messages of all kinds in shoals', plus flowers ranging from grand bouquets to tiny nosegays. A

---

* Presumably Sylvester had his own line in the office at Addison Road.

small crowd of well-wishers gathered in the street outside. When he finally got home, Frances telephoned him again just before midnight.[13]

LG had come through a serious operation very well. For a man of his age at that period it was by no means routine. He suffered remarkably little pain and his brain was said to be 'as clear as a bell'. After another good night he teased Maggie: 'You are not going to get rid of me so easily after all!' He also asked Sarah about Frances and Jennifer. Later Sylvester took him a letter from Frances, which Sarah read to him while the family was at dinner.[14]

By Saturday Frances was getting desperate to come and see him. She hoped that Tom Carey Evans, her closest ally in the family, would help her. At the same time she and the family were united in wishing to keep Roberta away.

> There is a nice pickle. Frances asked me to put her in Carey's hands; she wants to see Chief and she says Chief would like to see her; on the other hand how can she come whilst Dame Margaret is there? And Carey won't give his permission and take responsibility. She will have to wait until Dame Margaret is not there. Meantime she told me that L.G. said that Roberta was not to go into 'that' room, and asked me to tell Carey.

Sylvester duly told Carey Evans, who told Gwilym, so that when Roberta went with Dick to the house, Megan prevented her getting to see LG.

> Gwilym says Roberta has got to be told frankly. I have to find out from Frances Stevenson definitely if that was his statement and wish to her. One can never be sure what he *meant*; he might have said it to Frances but what did he mean?[15]

That day Sylvester recorded a further twist of the situation when he noted that Dyer had gone off with the Rolls to take Jennifer to Bognor. 'Bad luck for him because the family think he is having a day off.'[16] One can only suppose that Frances had her summer holiday booked and had decided that Jennifer and her nanny should go anyway – using LG's car – to get Jennifer out of the way so that she could concentrate all her attention on LG. There was never any doubt where her first priority lay.

The next day – with LG making steady progress, eating solid food, reading to himself and listening to the radio – Sylvester went to see Frances at Morpeth Mansions. He asked if LG had really meant that he did not want to see Roberta. ('It was a serious situation and would be more so if L.G. later on should say he had not said anything of the kind.') Frances said she thought he did mean it, but that he might have changed his mind since the operation. In his diary Sylvester wrote that when Roberta had been prevented from entering the bedroom a few days earlier, she had come down to lunch 'a very unhappy person. Olwen told her straight that it was the talk of the place and everybody knew!'

> Several courses were discussed and without doing anything very definite it was thought best to go slow. Frances was to try to see her [Roberta] and advise her not to try to see L.G. on Tuesday – she herself had not even seen him. Then Frances would ask L.G. when she saw him whether he wanted Roberta . . . In the course of this discussion Frances said that the week before L.G.'s illness Roberta had planned to go away with L.G. She had actually had it in her mind to go with him to Switzerland, which of course was impossible and unthinkable . . . Instead it was planned they should go to Churt. Frances says that L.G. did not want to go; I know he did not, but Roberta insisted. He did not want to be naughty at any rate, and she made him so. That is the reason why, when Frances told him on Tuesday that Roberta had been asking about him, and whether he wanted to see her, he said 'Good God, no'. He thinks Roberta is the cause of his trouble. She did no doubt accentuate it; but she was not the only one. Frances said that . . . when L.G. was taken ill Carey went for him and told him that he had brought all this on himself through his relations with Roberta, that it was her disease which was making her like this and that she was as hot as hell. She had been off her head already.[17]

This extraordinary passage implies that the family thought that Roberta was mentally ill ('it was her disease which was making her like this'); and that it was she who had led LG astray, rather than the other way round. He probably did not put up much resistance, even though he knew it to be wrong ('He did not want to be naughty'). The family and Frances both wanted to prevent her visiting LG on his sickbed, yet did not feel able to deny him if he insisted on seeing her. Carey Evans's idea that his prostate trouble could have been caused by his sexual activity, however, would today be thought medically unlikely.

LG continued to make a good recovery, though not without a deal of complaining – making the most, in his wife's view, of the relatively minor discomfort he was suffering. On Tuesday, with Carey Evans's help, Frances did succeed in visiting him while Maggie was out for a drive. She was pleased to find LG looking very fit, and hoped to come again on Wednesday; but unwisely she brought some flowers. When Maggie asked where they had come from, the nurse innocently told her, at which she was understandably furious with Carey Evans, vowing that if she ever found Frances there again she would turn her out of the house. Sylvester therefore had to tell Frances that Carey Evans would not help her a second time. 'She naturally did not like it, but she said it was for L.G. to put his foot down.'[18] Of course LG was in no position to do any such thing, so Frances was unable to visit him again as long as Maggie was there.

The next day (5 August) Sylvester went on holiday with his wife – initially to Criccieth, of all places – so his first-hand dispatches from the domestic battlefield unfortunately cease. But that day LG evidently contrived to telephone Frances surreptitiously, and on Thursday he wrote her a long letter, doubtless posted by the faithful Sarah. He had not given up hope of seeing her again soon, and was definitely planning to convalesce with her at Churt.

I was so disappointed about yesterday. I thought it could so easily have been managed. But she [presumably Maggie] would not budge.

What a topsy turvy world. Here am I passing though the most painful & anxious physical ordeal I have ever yet encountered & I am deprived of the solace & companionship of the one person who can sooth [sic] & sustain me through the trial. And yet she is within a few miles of me anxious to help & her tender & loving heart eager to love me . . .

Today will be impossible because the Eisteddfod broadcasts about three.

Then – m o s d we'll manage to snatch an hour or two soon – & then Churt. Oh it is good to think of – to be with you all the time *m c b a a c m i m yg i gyd*. And to catch a glimpse of your little girl. I am so deeply touched by your devotion. It is a revelation to me & it will be an inspiration.

But I must not go on.

Slept well last night. Sleep so far not good . . .

The Bougainvilliers [sic] are a constant thrill. Never seen a more beautiful flower. Worthy of the darling giver. My darling how I miss you. I could not stand it any longer & must talk to you last night. I *just* missed being caught! Counting the days.

Can you get me *Rowntree's* biscuits?

Fondest & deepest & most yearning affection for you my love & to your enchanting little girl.

D.[19]

Four days later he managed to write again, proud of his excellent recovery. In spite of Maggie, Frances had obviously managed to bring him some more things.

Here I am at the end of the 12th day after my operation & the 18th after my illness. I am so thankful you were with me thro' the most trying time of all – the first days of agony & apprehension & that horrible night of intense agony. Your wonderful calm & your marvellous gentleness of spirit fragrant with affection kept me up without giving way. I never thought it possible I could have faced it all without a tremor of panic. But I did & it is all due to my treasure of a girl helpmate. It is a mocking cruelty that during the most painful days of my convalescence I should have been deprived of such a precious & healing companionship.

All your 'gadgets' (!) have been so useful. The ring is a constant comfort in the dreams lying on your back. The little table is indispensable. The bougainvillea is a joy to me & a source of admiration to others.

One mustn't get too confident as all illnesses have their unexpected jolts & traps on the road to recovery. But so far I have made an exceptionally good recovery. All the doctors speak of my constitution as a prodigy & claim it as a triumph for a careful – otherwise a virtuous life.

Swift Joly the operator anticipates that I may be up in my chair Wednesday or Thursday. Then I can receive visitors. Sylvester can come. Why not both secretaries?

Then if all goes well I can get down to Churt this day fortnight. I mean there to take my stand firmly. They can take me down but must leave me in a couple of days for Criccieth. I mean to talk to Tom about it so as to avoid an unpleasant personal encounter. All the same that is fixed & final so far as I am concerned.

Sarah wanted me to send you a message that I was very happy. She has a queer notion of happiness. But I mustn't grouse. I am free from pain.

Tell little J. 'Tai' is still in byelows but that one day she can come & see him & give him a tiss. She will have changed. It will be 6 weeks from the time I saw her last before I see her again.

Fondest & tenderest love to you both from

D.[20]

LG still hoped that Frances would manage to visit him again; but he was now too well guarded, so she decided to join Jennifer at Bognor instead. On Friday 14 August he wrote again:

> I cannot tell you what a disappointment it is to me not to have one glimpse of your lovely face before you leave for the South. I know how welcome that face will be especially to an enchanting little person that loves the sight of it as much as I do. You must send me full & detailed accounts of all her doings & sayings and tell her *Tai* sends her a big tiss & is looking forward to seeing her at Churt soon.
>
> The failure to see you upset me so much that I slept very badly & a second dose had to be given me about 3.30 to quiet my nerves. But I decided the time had not come to fight it out. It might seriously retard convalescence. Dawson warned me solemnly & repeatedly about keeping the mind quiet & completely free from all excitement. I am not even allowed to read politics.
>
> But I mean to put my foot down as firmly as 3 or 4 years ago come what may.* But I must not write any more about it.
>
> Megan is not here – the old girl is the typical possessive woman.
>
> I have been wheeled to the window – a delightful change. So far the weather is bright. The green grass is a joy . . .
>
> I am looking forward to seeing you my darling girl.
>
> Fond fond tender love
>
> D.²¹

He did not write again until the middle of the following week, by which time he had suffered a setback.

> MODG [My own darling girl]
>
> I have not written the last few days as I did not wish to poison your well deserved & much needed holidays with anxieties which although very real to me I was assured were quite without foundation.
>
> Swift Joly before leaving for his holiday on Sunday morning felt justified in taking out the last artificial appliance that relieved me trusting that the wound was sufficiently healed to permit nature to take its natural course. It turned out that he was not justified in his anticipation. Sunday was a

---

* If he was referring to the row over Frances and the *Daily Chronicle*, that was now nearly five years ago, in October 1926.

complete failure. The usual machinery did not work at all & I drained entirely through the unclosed wound. Sunday was my worst day – mentally. I foresaw an utter failure of the operation & the necessity for another. Monday showed a slight improvement. Tuesday still better. But last night has so far been the greatest success.

You see why I was anxious not to worry you my darling when you could not give any help or what I needed most of all – consolation.

It has put Churt back 2 or 3 days. Dawson says I must give the wound every chance to heal so thoroughly that it won't reopen.

Your letters have been such a comfort to me. I read them & reread them.

What a battery of joy is that little charmer. I am so looking forward to seeing you both – perhaps somewhere about Friday or Saturday week. But we mustn't be impatient – my sweet.

I never needed you more than I did 2 or 3 days of this week.

Love to you both

D.

I'll phone about 8 if I can.[22]

Meanwhile, while LG was *hors de combat*, the political crisis had broken. The Labour Cabinet refused to make the cuts in unemployment benefit demanded by the City; whereupon MacDonald formed a National Government comprising Tories and Liberals, but only a handful of his former colleagues. This astonishing coup – patriotic or treacherous, depending on your viewpoint – split the Labour movement and left MacDonald a prisoner of the Tories, much as LG had been after 1916. It also split the Liberals again. When the National Government was formed (on 24 August, the first day LG was allowed out for a drive), LG felt bound to welcome it. The Liberals had done well in the allocation of offices: LG's deputy Herbert Samuel became Home Secretary, his old friend Lord Reading Foreign Secretary, and a dozen more – including Gwilym – got lesser jobs. Publicly LG praised MacDonald's courage and promised his help later on: 'if the promise of the Doctors is redeemed'.[23] Privately he raged that the 'crisis ought never to have arisen . . . Object strongly to having our domestic policy dictated by . . . foreign financiers.'[24] He knew that his enemies had seized their moment to marginalise him, and that the opportunity he had been working for over the past nine years had come and gone. Very soon his frustration led him to denounce the emergency government as a fraud and to sever his relations with the Liberal leaders who had joined it.

The formation of the National Government was the turning point of the inter-war period. There could not have been a National Government that did not include all three party leaders. As Liberal leader, LG (had he been well) would have had to be offered a senior position, as Samuel was in his absence. MacDonald and Baldwin could not have formed a National Government worthy of the name if they had tried to exclude him. Once back in office, however, a fit LG would either have dominated it or, if his ideas were blocked, obtained a powerful platform from which to resign and take his case to the country. Of course Baldwin and MacDonald did not contrive the crisis in order to dish LG. But they ruthlessly exploited the opportunity when it arose. LG claimed that he was glad to be out of it, and for another ten years – loyally encouraged by Frances – clung to the belief that his hour would still come. But in his heart he knew that the timing of his illness had ended his last realistic hope of regaining the position he had lost in 1922.

On 25 August LG was moved by ambulance to Churt. Sylvester, back from holiday, was 'amazed' to see him walk downstairs quite normally. LG was very anxious to have no photograph taken that might show him looking old and ill, but then 'walked briskly into the ambulance' – accompanied by a nurse – 'and right glad he seemed to be going to Churt'. Sylvester went back to Abingdon Street with J. T. Davies, who told him how 'fed up' LG was with his family:

> They seemed to think that they had got him there all to themselves and regarded him as in a cage through the bars of which they came and peeped with smug complacency and with the attitude 'Ah, now you have got your claws cut and can do no harm.' L.G. had told J.T.: 'But wait, I will show them that they cannot cut my claws; I will do them.' Frances has only been that once to Addison Rd; and Roberta has been once, too, which was effected with considerable difficulty.[25]

Maggie and Megan went with him initially to Churt, but stayed only a few days before going back to Criccieth, allowing Frances to resume the principal nursing role, for which they had little aptitude or enthusiasm. LG wrote a touching if clumsy poem to welcome her back.

> *Cariad* I have missed you so much
> Your sure understanding & your gentle touch
> It is largely due to instinctive art
> But I am sure that it comes straight from the heart.
>
> I am looking forward to seeing you once more
> And your sweet face appear at the door
> It may send my temperature up a degree
> But you cannot expect joy without paying the fee.[26]

Some three weeks after this Lord Dawson warned him that there would indeed be a fee to pay for too much 'joy'. Though more delicately expressed, Dawson's astonishingly candid letter plainly echoed Carey Evans's view that LG should reduce his 'rogering' – though Dawson knew his patient too well to expect total abstinence.

My dear LG

Let me pick it up where we left off. My 'separation' had long been arranged for the long vacation so when I was confident you were not in danger I just slipped away. How wonderfully well you have done, though no doubt you realised that recovery was a tedious process and when the 'slump' days come, not without discouragement. To achieve the complete restoration you need to fulfil the dictates and desires of your active mind, you must keep yourself in a backwater for months, otherwise you will not regain your 100% . . .

About sex – perhaps I can help you a bit – strictly the nearer you can keep to abstention for many months the better – but if the Pauline view about 'burning' obtrudes itself, come what may, the wise plan is to keep to well tried love*. In this way you avoid the emotional stimulus which any new goddess must promote and to the patient's detriment. This view, I think, fulfils the dictates of statesmanship!

Anyhow, the best of luck to you and I shall look forward to seeing you well on the road to being better than ever – 'Paradise regained' . . .

From, with affection

Dawson[27]

---

* St Paul's advice to the unmarried – not strictly relevant to LG – is that 'if they cannot contain, let them marry; for it is better to marry than to burn'. (*I Corinthians* 7, 9).

Dawson thought LG was well out of the National Government, and he was not the only one. At the end of August, Tweed – just back from holiday in Brittany – wrote Frances two long letters strongly expressing the same view. They were typed, addressed to 'Dear Miss Stevenson' and contain no hint of any special intimacy between them. They represent the views of an independent-minded Liberal still committed to LG and disgusted by all the old men of the party lining up to support the 'bankers' ramp'.

> If the Chief had joined the Government they would at least have possessed one man of guts, vigour and real leadership and he might have transformed the situation, but he is not in, and I listened ever so carefully to the carefully guarded but ambiguous utterances of Reading and Samuel . . . and noted the absence of any message and I knew then that it was not illness or the tedium of a long convalescence which kept him out, but that his heart was not in it and that confronted with the serried ranks of vested interests which compose the new Government his sympathies were as always with the bottom dogs . . .
>
> I have your account of LG's remarkable recovery, but I hope you can persuade him not to try and run the Liberal team in the Government. I feel in my bones that his best policy will be to simulate a very slow convalescence. It would be fatal to openly disavow the action of Samuel & co at the moment, but before many weeks are past the leadership of Labour may be his for the taking and stranger things have happened than that of seeing LG Prime Minister in the next Parliament . . .
>
> My own course is, I think, quite clear. I am LG's man and what he wants me to do, that I will do . . . I will not refuse to do anything I am asked to do by the official Party, but unless and until I am ordered to do so by the Chief I will not take the initiative . . .
>
> Give my love to the Chief,
> Kindest regards,
> Yours ever,
> Thomas F. Tweed[28]

The second letter was similar, stressing that there was 'only one man who can save the nation from this nightmare, not through the ineffective medium of the fading strength of the Liberal Party . . . but by taking a risk which only a giant dare even contemplate'. By dissociating himself from 'the obloquy and shame of the new Government',

Tweed judged, LG would soon dominate the opposition in the House, and 'when the time comes for Labour to resume office he will be in a position either to accept or refuse the Premiership, and either as Premier or in some other position he will be the dominating figure'.

> If it were not for the memory of Gladstone, this would appear to be an impossible task to suggest to a man of 68, but he is only that in years. Actually he is more mentally alert, fitter and stronger than most men twenty years his junior, and even his recent operation, once he is completely recovered, will make him feel fitter and younger than at any time during the last ten years . . . There is no-one else in competition.[29]

This was wishful thinking, but it displays extraordinary loyalty to LG. Tweed fully supported LG's breach with Samuel when the latter backed the government's decision to hold an early General Election on 27 October. LG regarded this as a Tory ramp, blatantly designed to exploit the national emergency for party advantage. When Samuel and another senior Liberal, Donald Maclean, came to Churt to seek his blessing, LG furiously refused it. 'If I am to die,' he told them, 'I would rather die fighting on the left.'[30] 'He let forth the whole blast of his wrath upon them,' Frances recalled, 'and, exceedingly hurt, they left awkwardly and, he hoped, ashamed.' The exertion, however, 'set L.G. back several weeks in his recovery'.[31]

Of the Liberals who had joined the government, only Gwilym resigned, after a first experience of office that had lasted just five weeks. At the same time Tweed resigned from the party organisation: henceforth he worked solely for LG. The election was the most one-sided in British electoral history, with the Tories and their neutered allies sweeping 554 of the 615 seats and Labour reduced to a rump of just fifty-two. LG was left with a family party of four: himself, Gwilym, Megan and Gwilym's brother-in-law Goronwy Owen, who sat for Caernarvon County. Maggie held the fort for her husband in the Caernarvon Boroughs. 'Here she is loved, admired and is the uncrowned queen,' Sylvester noted.[32] 'Thankful peaks of Snowdonia remain above the deluge,' LG telegraphed his agent.[33] He remained defiant, but henceforth he was politically alone.

PART FOUR

31

'MY TWO SWEETHEARTS'

The autumn of 1931 marked the beginning of a third stage in Frances's relationship with LG. She had started out in 1913 – as A. J. P. Taylor put it – as 'his secretary who happened to be also his mistress': that phase lasted right though his premiership until October 1922. For the next nine years she was rather less of one and more of the other: 'his mistress who happened to be also his secretary'. But following his illness and the return of the National Government with a huge majority, LG's interest in politics was much reduced. Aged sixty-eight, he still had not given up hope of regaining office some day; but in the short run he concentrated his energies on writing his memoirs and managing his farm. From now on Frances was 'virtually his second wife'.[1] She gave up her flat in Morpeth Mansions and bought a house for Jennifer and her nanny in Worplesdon, about ten miles from Churt; but she herself spent most of her time with LG at Bron-y-de, except when Maggie paid a rare visit.* Later LG gave her the land to build her own house on the Churt estate, and it was here that Jennifer spent most of her childhood – with '*Taid*' a constant loving presence in her life.

Yet there were still times when LG had to give precedence to his first family. As soon as the election was over, he began planning his convalescence in the sun. His first idea was to go to Sicily with Frances to start writing his book. But Sylvester was doubtful – 'I cannot see L.G. getting away to Sicily for three months without the family having something to say'[2] – and he was right. Maggie was not abdicating her prior title. Wherever LG chose to go, she and Megan would go with

---

* Frances sold her flat to Winston and Clementine Churchill, who made it their London base for the next eight years until they moved into 10 Downing Street in 1940.

him. So on 19 November they all set off on a seven-week cruise to
Ceylon (now Sri Lanka) accompanied by Gwilym and Edna (as far as
Suez), the local GP from Churt (who went as LG's personal doctor), a
nurse (respectably elderly) and of course Sylvester.

Throughout the voyage LG wrote regularly to his 'two girls'. Sylvester
was kept busy discreetly posting his letters wherever they docked and
picking up Frances's in return. Before they had even left Marseilles, LG
was protesting that he had never wanted to go away.

> My own girl
>
> Here I am at last after a trying journey which knocked me about a good
> deal. I have been calling myself a d——d fool for listening to these doctors
> who insisted on my leaving a comfortable house where I was exceptionally
> happy for this wretched adventure charged with discomfort. It has left me
> sore & penitent for my foolishness in not realising when I was well off.
> However I am for it now & must make the best of it. I am never happy
> away from you my girl – and now there is another little girl around whom
> my heart strings are twined . . .
>
> Fondest deep & tender love to you both
> Taid[3]

Now that Jennifer was getting older, he clearly wrote with both of them
in mind: this was the first time he signed himself *Taid*.

Frances wrote the same day, from Morpeth Mansions.

> My own beloved darling
>
> I have discovered that I can get a letter to you at Port Said by Air
> Mail, & I am so glad, as I have been feeling so lonely since I left you,
> and have been wanting to tell you how much I love you. I do miss you
> so terribly, *cariad*, after all these lovely weeks at Churt. I have so loved
> looking after you, & being with you constantly, and there is a gap which
> even Jennifer can't fill. She came up from Churt today with Nurse, looking
> so cheerful and well. Nurse said she was asking for you all day yesterday.
> I don't think she quite realised that your going 'on the *big* ship, on the
> *big* sea, far far away' meant being separated from you! But she was terribly
> thrilled at the picture of you & Dr Nicoll when she saw it in the paper
> today . . .
>
> I do hope the journey is going to do you no end of good. My feelings
> of tenderness towards you have increased so much during the last few weeks.

I feel that you too are my baby. I will be very sweet to you, my darling, when you return. I am so glad I have got plenty to do between now and then, as otherwise I should be very lonely; and as it is I shall be counting the hours – I expect you are too, sweetheart, in the intervals of taking out certain little photographs from your pocket & looking at them long & lovingly! One thing you can be certain of, you have captured her little heart, for she adores you . . .

I am thinking of you & loving you always.

Your own

P.[4]

Sylvester confirms that LG carried Jennifer's picture about with him. 'He is tremendously proud of her.'[5] LG's next letter – posted from Aden and addressed to 'dearest Mam-ee & her sweet Denny' – described 'a charming little 2 year old' he had made friends with, 'toddling about and wheeling her baby p'am about the deck . . . You can imagine who I was thinking of.'[6] Meanwhile Frances kept him up to date with Jennifer's progress, the latest political news and her move to Worplesdon. She was very pleased with the young couple she had engaged to keep house for her. 'The only risk is . . . that they may acquire a family, but they seem so good that I am going to risk that. I must introduce them to Marie Stopes!'* She also thanked LG for a car that he had given her. 'The car has arrived & is such a nice one – easy to drive & not too ostentatious but very comfortable. Nurse is practising on it & likes it.' (Frances did learn to drive herself, but never got the hang of it and soon gave up.) 'I cannot thank you sufficiently for it, sweetheart . . . You are so good to me that I often think I cannot repay you.' For the first time she signed off for Jennifer as well: 'Ever & ever your own loving P. & J.'[7]

LG wrote again from Colombo. He was drawing huge crowds wherever he went, but pretended that he just wanted to get home.

My two pets

Nearly three weeks away from them and nearly 5 more weeks to go. I wonder whether they have *both* forgotten me – the big pet as well as the little one . . . They are ever present in my mind & I am constantly reckoning

---

* Marie Stopes was the leading pioneer of birth control – a matter on which Frances was perhaps not an expert!

of the weeks that separate me from my darlings . . . I wonder whether you
mean to spend Xmas at Bron-y-de or Bognor. It seems a very unnecessary
expense & bother to go to Bognor when the nurse told me Bron-y-de suits
little Denny so much better . . .

Fond & affectionate & tender love

Taid[8]

The same day Sylvester recorded that the whole party had been shopping. LG had wanted to buy presents not only for Frances and Jennifer,
but also for Roberta. Or rather he wanted Sylvester to buy them for
him.

Megan watched me like a cat watching a mouse. First there was an elephant
that he liked. I had to bargain for that. Megan came up to me and said;
'Well, A.J., what are you getting?' So I said, 'Oh, much too dear' and walked
away to look at something less noticeable. The same with the silver bull. I
went back later and bought both for L.G. at reduced prices.[9]

LG also got Sylvester to buy an ivory tiger, and a Turkish carpet,
which he arranged to have packed in a zinc-lined box. 'It is not going
to be easy to get these things home without the family knowing.'[10]

While in Ceylon, LG became agitated that he had not had any letters
from Frances, badgering Sylvester constantly and reckoning when they
should have come. On 14 December the party was due to drive seventy
miles inland, into the hills.

If the letters do not arrive, I shall have to stop here and bring them on.
L.G. is all worked up at the mere prospect of getting a letter from Frances.
He is just like a bundle of electricity. He said today: 'Do you realise that
when we leave here we shall have our noses for the first time towards
home?'[11]

But the next day all was well.

I was a little anxious . . . because I knew what a panic L.G. was in . . .
After breakfast, however, there came a letter which was addressed to me
by air mail . . . in Frances's handwriting. Fortunately I got it before Megan
came round the corner.[12]

In fact Frances's letter-writing could not be faulted. She wrote regular long letters full of political news mixed up with wifely cluckings and maternal pride.

My own beloved sweetheart

At last there is definite news of your return, & I am counting the hours & days until Jan 2nd. I told Jennifer that you were coming home soon, & she said '*Taid* tumming home to see Denny'. Little egoist! . . . In my opinion she is sweeter than ever! . . . She talks incessantly, & evidently regards this place [Churt] as her own property . . .

I expect I shall be at Worplesdon when you arrive, as I don't quite know where else to be unless I hear from you differently. The telephone number there is Worplesdon 90. But I will leave it to you to arrange for us to see each other at the earliest possible moment . . .[13]

My own beloved darling

It was a joy to receive your letter posted from Aden, & to know that . . . the journey is doing you so much good. And the wires I have received from you & A.J. during the last week have warmed my heart. It is lovely too to know, my sweet, that tomorrow you will be turning once more in this direction, & that the 'big s'ip' will be less 'fa' fa' away' each day from now onwards. I feel satisfied now that your health is really improved, but for some time I felt anxious, my darling, for I know what a bad journey you had at first. Do be careful in nearing this dreary island to wrap up well & not to take cold . . .

We have missed you so much, Jennifer & I. We often talk about you together, for she can really hold a conversation now . . .

I'll write again, my darling, so that you'll get a letter at Marseilles. And then there will only be a week before I can see you & hear you & hold you & lavish upon you all the pent-up sweetness & affection of the last few weeks. I hardly dare to think of the thrill of beholding you again . . .

Ever your own

P. & J.[14]

My own beloved sweetheart . . .

It was sweet of you to send the little snaps. Your latest sweetheart looks a little darling . . . but I was not so much interested in her picture as in that of her gentleman friend. He certainly looks very fit and happy, but well guarded by his spouse!

I think Jennifer would be very jealous if she knew! She found your photograph in the paper last week . . . and nearly tore the paper to pieces trying to draw their attention to it . . . I am quite sure that she is *much* more intelligent than your little friend! Still I am glad you have found someone to relieve the tedium of the journey – my darling – and there is safety in the fact that she is only a two-year-old! Stick to them in future! . . .

You need not worry at all about my not being good – there is a little person who has full control over my time and thoughts in your absence, and I have no time or desire for anyone else. Also I cannot express to you the additional tenderness & devotion I feel to you since your illness . . .

I was *hoping* you would be able to persuade Them to go to Wales. It will be perfect to be there [at Churt] with you again. I will be so sweet to you, my darling. I looked into your room before I left & tried to imagine you back in it, but it seemed very empty! . . .

You will get this on New Year's day, my darling. I shall be thinking of you so sweetly, *cariad*, & wishing you a year full of health and luck and success, & all happiness in the future. And if the devotion and worship of your two little girls can help you in any way, you have all that we have to give.

Ever your own loving & devoted

P. & J.[15]

Two of these letters were waiting for LG when he got back to Port Said on 27 December. ('That kept him quiet,' Sylvester noted.[16]) He did not reply till the last day of the old year; but then he wrote a long letter full of his impatience to get back to 'my dear sweetheart *& wife*' – with an explicit assurance that this meant Frances ('To be with you is now my home & I hope will continue so to the end') and detailed arrangements involving trains from Plymouth, which would allow him to leave his family at the earliest possible moment.

The quickest train to London is the GWR – that will be taken by my wife Megan & Sylvester. But the S Western stops at Salisbury. The first possible is at halfpast 8 reaching Salisbury at 12.31 . . . The likeliest – weather permitting – is the 10.10 train reaching Salisbury 2.24 or the 11.5 arriving 2.50 at Salisbury. It has a restaurant car. We shall have had our lunch. You therefore shd lunch at the hotel. I'll give you the money. Say we miss this train we can wire you there & you can see the Cathedral & Stonehenge whilst waiting for us – by the next train which arrives Salisbury . . . If we catch this train we'll get to Churt by 4.30 – just in time for 'tose' with Denny.*

Then he looked forward to their life together in the future.

When I return I want you to help me with my book. I want you to give your *mind* to it . . . But above all I want to be with you . . .

As to politics I am less keen to plunge in for some time . . . This is the last day of a very anxious and troublesome old year. Whatever fresh troubles there may be in store for me I am determined that those associated with leading a party shall not be amongst them . . . I am well out of that humiliating morass & I do not mean to step into it again . . . Still events may smash all my careful & cautious plans.

We'll talk it over on our walks at Bron-y-de, my sweet & sagacious pal. There is no hurry . . .

My fondest love to you
both my darlings
Taid[18]

LG wrote one more brief letter from Marseilles before starting on the last leg of his journey home. He confirmed that 'They' would be going from Plymouth straight to London; and hinted that Frances could expect to find his physical vitality fully restored. 'I hope you haven't exhausted all your thrills at Bognor. I mean to have one.'[19] Dr Nicoll confirmed as much, telling Sylvester: 'He is a bloody marvel. He has got the heart of a young man of thirty-five, and the blood pressure too; and he has the chest and expansion of a prize fighter.'[20] For all his chronic hypochondria, LG had made a remarkable recovery.

LG and Frances enjoyed ten days together – with Jennifer – at Churt in early January 1932 before LG went off again to Criccieth, supposedly for three weeks. He had not been to Wales since his illness, so he probably needed to show his constituents that he was fully recovered. There was nearly an awkward encounter when Olwen picked him up at Addison Road to drive to Euston, since Frances was in the house when she arrived and the maids had to be instructed to keep them from meeting.[21] But no sooner had LG gone than Frances – now installed

* Sylvester confirms these arrangements. 'We are . . . working out a plan which will take him from Plymouth to Salisbury, or Basingstoke . . . so that he can get back to Churt and Frances while the poor old thing with Megan and myself find our way back to London.'[17]

in a fine new modern office at Millbank – wrote implying that their reunion had been as blissful as they had hoped.

> I don't think I have ever been happier than this last 10 days at Churt, with you so well & fit again, & doing all the old things! You have been so sweet to us both, darling, & I think of all your sweetness to us with gratitude – I can never, never repay you for all you have done for me . . .
>   Ever your own devoted
>   P. & J.[22]

A few days later she wrote again, saying that Denny 'cannot understand why *Taid* will insist upon going "fa' fa' away" so often!'[23] In fact he returned to London after just ten days, because the government had decided to introduce import duties, which he strongly opposed. In February he and Frances started serious work on his memoirs; but with Jennifer there, Sylvester constantly complained that it was difficult to keep LG's mind focused on work. On 20 February, for instance, 'it was not possible to get anything . . . done because he was playing with Jennifer with her Noah's Arc [*sic*]'.[24] A few days earlier, Sylvester had again had to act discreetly to avert an awkward encounter with the family.

> Jennifer is teething and is not well. Frances phoned to say would I arrange that the family did not come to Churt this weekend. Saw Megan and Gwilym and put them off . . . These arrangements ensured they did not go to Churt as [the] child could not be removed. I had to make out that he [LG] might be coming up from Churt tonight.[25]

In April Sylvester went down to Churt himself and noted the domestic arrangements:

> They have made a day nursery out of one of the bedrooms; consequently plenty of notice is required when the family are going down to Churt for everything has to be removed and taken to Worplesdon. Dyer says he needs a pantechnicon to carry out the removal.

Sylvester walked through the orchards with LG, Frances, Jennifer and her nurse. LG delighted in playing with Jennifer and the watering system.

She turned the hosepipe on *Taid* and *Taid* got wet. I could not help asking myself who was the bigger baby . . . Later he went to see Jennifer put to bed . . . L.G. worships that kid . . . His whole life and being is made up in that child.[26]

But politics still intruded. In May LG made his first public speech since his illness – in Llandudno. Frances was beginning to get impatient that he still had to keep going to Wales so often.

My own beloved darling
   I feel terribly miserable & depressed today at the thought of not seeing you again for so long. We have been so happy together that it seems so senseless that we have to separate for intervals like this. But the only thing to do is to look forward to the time when we can be together again at Churt. It will not be so very long, my darling, but I shall count the days, & expect you will too . . .
   Jennifer sends *Taid* fond love & a butterfly kiss!
   Tenderest love & fondest thoughts from your own devoted.
   P.[27]

Two days later, along with the usual news of Jennifer, she wrote him one of the strongest statements of her dependence on him that she committed to paper:

It is so peaceful here, & I am so glad I have got this place [Worplesdon].
   I miss you though, my sweet, and feel very lost without you. It does make a difference having Jennifer . . . But I want my Old Man, too. I have had him so long now that he is a part of myself, and a very essential part, & I simply cannot do without him. Life loses its meaning for me when he is not here, & I shall look forward so much to his return.[28]

The same day LG told Frances of a dream he claimed to have had, in which Frances had left Jennifer alone in the House of Commons; he had found her and wheeled her out in her pram across New Palace Yard.

I knew I should be noticed. But I did not care a rap. My heart went out to the poor little mite – then I woke up to the reality – that I loved her with all my soul. That's a story for you.

He went on to give advice about Jennifer's nanny. Frances was thinking of replacing Miss Neale, but LG was strongly against it.

> Do nothing in a hurry. J. must come first & I know she will in your thoughts. Nurse is . . . difficult. *But* . . . you will find it very difficult to get another of equally valuable qualities. Be very sure what you do ere you change . . . You are bound to be away a good deal up in town. A careful & reliable nurse who knows what to do in an emergency is therefore vital.

He added that Jennifer was fond of Miss Neale, and 'the disciplinary method will do her good. Her real danger is that she will be spoilt. She is so fascinating that she invites spoiling.' LG knew that he had spoiled Megan, and had some inkling that he should not do the same to Jennifer.[29]

There were several more letters back and forth: she grateful for his advice about Miss Neale, he seeking hers on what to say in his Llandudno speech. 'I meant to deliver a solemn constructive speech,' he wrote on 17 May. 'But I found it almost impossible to keep my thoughts off attack. What do you think?'[30] She replied with her usual loyal encouragement.

> I think if I were you I should try to keep off attacking if you can . . . The most important thing now is to show people that there *is* an alternative to the present Gov, I am sure it will not be very long before the people discover that this Gov is *not* going to get them out of the mess – then they will turn to someone or something else.

Meanwhile she pictured him 'wandering in your old haunts by the river – where you and I were first attracted to each other'.

> I wish Jennifer & I could be there – or alternatively that you could be here, my darling. It does seem useless that we should have to have these separations, but perhaps it makes our reunions all the more thrilling.[31]

LG came back after two weeks; but then at the end of July Maggie fell in the garden at Criccieth and broke her arm, and LG immediately went back again to see her. Sylvester thought this 'the nicest thing he has done for a long time because it would please her so much'[32] – though he may have been planning to go anyway. Frances was naturally less delighted, and wrote almost daily about how much she and Jennifer were missing him. Her first letter contains some unusually direct reflections on Jennifer's anomalous position.

Just as you drove away, she turned to me and said: 'Why aren't 'os going too, Mummy?' She will have lots of strange things to learn as she grows up, poor darling, and we shall have to give her all the love and tenderness we can to compensate for any shocks she may have to suffer! But I agree with you that she *has* all the attention and love & tenderness we can possibly lavish on her, so she ought to grow up without any inferiority complex, I think . . .

Nurse . . . thinks she ought to have more children to play with. I told her we had done our best.

Ever so much love to yourself my darling from two very lonely little girls, who want you to come back . . .

Fondest kisses also

Ever your own

P. & J.[33]

The next day Frances commented tartly that she hoped he was 'being properly appreciated down there' – something she always doubted.[34] LG's only letter (they also managed to speak at least once on the phone*) was mainly about the preparation of his speech at the Eisteddfod; but he included a word about Maggie, doubtless to assure Frances that it was right for him to have gone to her.

The old girl had a bad accident – broke her wrist right across. But it is healing. It is pathetic to see her constant delight in my surprise visits.[37]

Frances did her best to be sympathetic.

I'm so sorry about the old girl's arm. It was probably a good deal more painful than my ankle & that was bad enough. It was rather lucky you had arranged to go down.[38]

---

* They evidently had pre-arranged times for telephoning. In one letter Frances told LG that she would ring at 8.45 on Tuesday morning.[35] But telephoning could be tricky, as Sylvester noted, 'because one is heard all over the house'.[36]

The next day she wrote again, to Port Talbot, where LG was paying his annual visit to the Eisteddfod. This letter was almost entirely about Jennifer.

> You may really feel confident that you have won Jennifer's heart. She has not ceased to talk about you and to ask when you were coming back. I sometimes feel quite jealous. She really feels that she is part of you & you of her, & her little life is not complete without you. No wonder, for you are very sweet to her & I know you love her – I do hope you love me a little too, *cariad*.[39]

Strikingly absent from this letter is even a veiled implication that LG was Jennifer's father. Frances writes absolutely as if he was her step-father, or adoptive father. She reassures him that Jennifer loves him; but it is a love that he has had to earn. In her previous letter she had written of them both needing to love her to compensate for 'any shocks she may have to suffer'. But never in any of her letters does she make any reference to Jennifer looking like LG, or reminding her of him when he was away, which would surely be a natural thing to say, whether it was true or not. Since LG certainly believed that Jennifer was his child, one might have expected Frances to be anxious to reas-sure him on this point. Was she just being careful never to put on paper anything that might implicate him? Or was her reticence an indication that she did indeed suspect that he was not the father?

In September LG went back to Wales, with Sylvester and Tweed, to speak at a by-election in Cardigan; he then stayed another fortnight at Criccieth.* Frances meanwhile spent some days apparently alone at East-bourne, while Jennifer was at Felpham with other children of her own age – Felicia Brook's son and the daughter of Frances's solicitor, John Morris. Evidently Frances had heeded Miss Neale's advice. 'I am sure it is good for Jennifer to have the young society,' she wrote to LG, 'though I feel you are not quite convinced about this!' For herself she complained of the dullness of Eastbourne and hoped that LG would be coming back sooner than he did. As usual it is clear that she wanted to be with LG much more than to spend time with Jennifer.

---

* The Liberals retained the seat with a big majority over Labour. Though Cardigan was a traditional Liberal seat, the result had been expected to be close and LG thought the result 'magnificent'.[40]

When do you think you will be returning? I think I will go over to Bognor on Monday, in case you are returning soon, as I want to get in a few days there. Let me have a little line to say what your plans will be.[41]

Over the next week LG wrote to Frances practically every day: four long letters and one shorter one, full of his usual complaints about the weather and the dreariness of Criccieth. Yet this was his fourth visit that year.

Had it not been for a meeting in my constituency tomorrow week I should have returned this week. I can barely contemplate the slow torture of another 9 days. Criccieth in fine weather is an attractive place but when you have rain – well give me Gehenna. I miss my pal. I miss my daily round. I miss a good deal else which is indefinable. I love Bron-y-de & all that it means & has meant to me. I have *always* disliked Criccieth.

He was also worried about Frances's health – and her safety.

I do hope you will make the most of your holiday darling. Don't wander to any lonely spots on Beachy Head. There are too many prowlers about these days . . . Get thoroughly fit before you get back to J. The little monkey takes too much out of you especially as you have to put up with the old orang-outang as well.

As to politics, he still proposed to lie low:

I don't want to throw myself into active politics before 1934. Tweed agrees that is the sound policy. The economic situation will be better defined by then – & the Govt will be in the third year – only 2 years before the election. All that is on the assumption that there is no serious trouble in Europe before then . . .[42]

A few days later he added, 'I like my regained independence & I mean to stick to it.'[43]

Few of Frances's letters from this separation have survived, though it is clear that she was writing as usual. ('Frances used to send her letters under cover to me,' Sylvester wrote. 'Now she writes to him marked "personal". It is a good thing that I know the handwriting!')[44] Her last letter, on 2 October, was notably upbeat, both personally and politically.

My own beloved darling

It was lovely to get your long letter with all its news. I am feeling more exhilarated as the time for our separation draws to an end. I shall get more & more excited as Wednesday draws near . . . We go back to Bron-y-de this afternoon & I shall be so glad to be back there, with its happy & tender associations . . .

I do feel intensely that politics are going to be more interesting for us from this moment . . . Things will begin to come your way very soon, my darling, & it will make things all the simpler because you are not in a hurry. They will just fall into your lap . . .

We shall be waiting for you so eagerly, my darling, on Wednesday, & you will get such a loving welcome from

Your own

P.&J.

She added a postscript, with what sounds like a sly dig at Maggie. 'Yes I think a Welsh sow would be an excellent idea, provided she is kept in her proper place!'[45]

32

TWEED AGAIN

While LG was leading a double life with his wife and his mistress, Frances was doing the same, rather less blatantly, with her established lover and her other secret love. Despite her repeated assurances to LG that her 'Old Man' was everything to her and she had 'no time or desire for anyone else', there is a good deal of evidence that part of her heart, at least, still belonged to Thomas Tweed. The ever-watchful Sylvester believed that she was still seeing Tweed throughout 1932.

Of course Sylvester's testimony must be treated with some caution – first because it is entirely circumstantial, but also because Sylvester was jealous, in different ways, of both Tweed and Frances. Though he had successfully insisted on the title of 'principal' private secretary, he was naturally in LG's confidence far less than Frances was; while Tweed, though also employed by LG, had the status of a political adviser with an independence that Sylvester could not aspire to. It clearly rankled that when Frances was with LG at Churt she spoke frequently to Tweed in London, but 'she never speaks on the telephone to me'.[1] And when LG was preparing his comeback speech at Llandudno in May, Sylvester thought it 'strange that he should seek the advice of F. so much. Nothing was sent to Tweed, but I will guarantee that he knew all about it, for there is nothing that F. does not communicate to him.'[2]

Sylvester detailed his suspicions in December 1932:

It was her custom, whenever she was in London to go about with Tweed, and often she would return to the office after having seen him [LG] away to dinner, in order to pick up Tweed who ordinarily went away early but always stayed late whenever she was there . . . The whole office knew about it. They were often at the Gargoyle Club!*

He specifically noted a recent evening when Frances had dined with LG and a Tory MP at the Metropole, but then returned to Millbank and 'went away in Tweed's car'.[3] Some months earlier he recorded another suggestive incident when LG left the office to dine with a leading Liberal academic. When he asked Frances what she was doing, she said she was going to visit her mother and would then go and stay with Muriel, so he gave her a lift in his car. Frances could not very well refuse; but a quarter of an hour later she rang, wanting to speak to Tweed, who affected surprise. '"Miss Who?" "Miss Stevenson". "What does she want?" said he in a very nonchalant manner.' Sylvester thought he knew what was going on. 'Their plans had been upset for the moment; they were fixing up where they should meet.'[4]

Maybe he imagined it. In May, when he was with LG at Criccieth, Sylvester phoned Worplesdon one evening as usual, but was answered by Felicia, who told him that Frances had gone to the theatre with Muriel. 'I wonder?' he wrote in his diary.[5] The next day LG himself telephoned to demand of Frances 'with whom she had gone to the theatre and who had she with her today'.[6] This time her story was that she and Muriel had been to see James Bridie's *Tobias and the Angel* for Muriel's birthday. Maybe they had – but Tweed could well have been with them. Sylvester suspected that Tweed's ostensible interest in Muriel was 'only a decoy'.[7] The same month he thought he caught Tweed and Frances lying about which hotels in Oxford they were staying at,[8] and in July he was annoyed, after he had managed to get them all tickets for a Buckingham Palace garden party, first that Tweed declined to go and then that Frances too was doubtful. 'It looks in fact as if they were having a party on their own!'[9]

If Muriel was a decoy, she was a very successful one, since up to now LG does not seem to have suspected Frances's involvement with Tweed. But then in the autumn of 1932, the fat was suddenly in the fire when his family found out and used the information to try to break LG's attachment to her. The revelation was a shock to him; but in one of the greatest crises of their relationship he behaved well.

---

* The Gargoyle Club in Soho was mainly frequented by artists. It cannot have been too risqué, however, since the very proper Sylvester claimed to have seen Frances and Tweed there himself.

Once again it was Frances who was forced to make a choice.

Violent rows were nothing new in the Lloyd George family. LG's relations with all his children were tempestuous. There were rows with Dick over his financial irresponsibility and with Gwilym over the *Daily Chronicle*; constant emotional wrangles with Megan and a bitter dispute with Olwen over land at Churt, which finally led her husband, Tom Carey Evans, to write LG a scorching letter denouncing his 'cruelty' to her.[10] All of them, Megan and Dick particularly, resented their father's relationship with Frances and were anxious to shield their mother from humiliation; while Maggie herself, though pretty tolerant most of the time, was quite capable of fighting her corner when she felt her position was threatened. In public they successfully maintained the image of a close and united family. Yet all these tensions were constantly simmering away beneath the surface, and occasionally erupted. The most dramatic eruption of all occurred in December 1932, when they thought they had found the weapon they needed to expose and discredit Frances.

Relations were already strained after another row in October – unconnected with Frances – when LG snubbed Gwilym by failing to stay to hear him speak in the House. It was not that he was at Churt, or otherwise out of town: he was at Westminster, and had spoken himself the previous day, supporting a Labour motion of censure on the government. Frances was in the gallery as usual for his speech, and sent him her customary note of congratulation afterwards, as she had been doing for the past twenty years:

A magnificent and most powerful speech. Honestly, one of the very best and most statesmanlike I have ever heard you make. The House was very attentive and impressed . . . You were in tip-top form.[11]

LG expected this sort of encouragement for himself. But the next day when Gwilym spoke, LG was conspicuously absent. Dame Margaret was in the gallery, and Megan was in the Chamber to support her brother. Baldwin came in to hear him, but LG inexplicably did not, even though Sylvester 'had kept him informed in detail' and later phoned him to tell him how well Gwilym had done. LG merely asked Sylvester 'to congratulate Gwilym and say he was sorry he had to go away'.[12]

It fell to Frances and Sylvester to try to repair the damage, as Sylvester recorded two days later:

Frances phoned me from Churt saying that the family are very upset about
L.G. not staying for Gwilym's speech on Wednesday night. Would I try to
smooth them down. I telephoned to Dame Margaret. She said it was a
disgrace, and people were talking about it in the House. Gwilym is very
sick; he told me that his father had not listened to him speaking for three
years . . . The family have given him a bad time, and he deserves it.[13]

But then they thought they had found the means to punish him,
when a servant talked. The tale-bearer was a maid called Rowlands,
who had first been employed at Addison Road, but then went to work
for Frances at Morpeth Mansions. Frances was probably unwise to
take her on, since when she sold Morpeth Mansions the girl went back
to the family, taking a position with Olwen in Hammersmith. According
to Sylvester, she was 'very religious and had a strong urge that she must
tell everything that she knew'.[14] What she knew was that Tweed had
been a regular visitor to Morpeth Mansions.

LG's family must have known that Miss Stevenson had mysteriously
acquired a child three years before; and they must have guessed – or
feared – its likely origin. But so long as Jennifer was said to be adopted,
there was little they could do: they preferred the adoption story to the
alternative. Rowlands's evidence changed the picture entirely. They now
had a possible alternative father, which saved them having to believe
that Jennifer was LG's child. Still more important, they had evidence
of infidelity, which they imagined would discredit Frances in LG's eyes
and lead him to throw her over.

On Saturday 10 December, LG summoned Sylvester down to Churt
early the next morning. When he arrived he found Dame Margaret,
Megan, Olwen and Tom Carey Evans all assembled in the library with
LG. But immediately LG took Sylvester up to his bedroom where, after
a bit of business about his memoirs, he came straight to the point. He
reminded Sylvester that 'Your first duty you owe to me'. Sylvester
replied that there had 'never been any doubt about that on my
part – ever'. LG then asked Sylvester directly: 'What do you know
about Frances and Tweed?' This, Sylvester wrote, 'was indeed a poser'.
He did not flinch, however, but told LG that 'of course everybody
knew of their association', though he claimed to know 'nothing
specific'. He described Frances regularly going off in Tweed's car after
leaving the office late, mentioned that they were 'often' seen together
at the Gargoyle and added that there was 'a good deal of suspicion

that Tweed was down in Devon when L.G. was away on the yacht'. The last point clearly refers to January 1929, when LG was away on his Mediterranean cruise and Frances was supposedly at Torquay, around the time that Jennifer was conceived. Though Tweed was 'also very friendly with Muriel . . . it was rumoured that she was only a decoy'. Sylvester was plainly hinting at the possibility that Tweed was Jennifer's father.*

At this point they had to go back downstairs, where a photographer from the *Daily Sketch* had been invited to take a family photograph. Why he was asked on this particular day is not clear; but it could hardly have been a less suitable moment for a happy family group. They were all professionals, so they put on a good show, posed in the library; but the atmosphere does look distinctly tense. LG, seated in his armchair at the centre of the picture, seems to be looking defiantly at Maggie, who looks very sharply back at him, while Tom is also looking sceptically at his father-in-law. Olwen has a far-away expression, and only Megan, in profile in the corner, could be said to be smiling. Sylvester stands beside the fireplace on the other side. It is an extraordinary photograph when one knows the scenes that were going on before and after it was taken.

Immediately afterwards Carey Evans had a word with Sylvester.

Carey asked me whether L.G. had been talking to me about anything particularly; I asked: Do you mean Frances? He said Yes. He said that the kid was not L.G.'s. I inquired whether he knew that. He said Yes. I told him the rumours that were going about particularly some time ago, and that Hutch had often said the kid was Tweed's.

Sir Robert Hutchison – known as 'Hutch' – had been Liberal Chief Whip from 1926 to 1931. One might wonder how he would have known about Jennifer's parentage; but he had been closely associated with Tweed at the time – and it is the business of Chief Whips to know such things.

LG then took Sylvester back to his bedroom to resume their conversation, and Sylvester told him what Carey Evans had said.

* Six months earlier Sylvester had written that J. T. Davies claimed to know that LG was not Jennifer's father, and 'he knew to the very date when Tweed and F. slept together'.[15]

During the whole of this conversation L.G. was terribly upset. I have never
seen him so weighed down with grief in my life. He went to the bottom
drawer of the chest of drawers . . . and took out a painting of Jennifer. He
said: 'Can you see anything of Tweed in her?'

I said: 'No, I cannot.'

He said: 'I do not think Tweed is the father, but at any rate I am not
the father.'

I pointed out that he was so absolutely vital that if he were the father
he would have left his mark. He argued then about his own children; was
there any likeness, for instance of him in Gwilym or Megan or any of them?
Gwilym was exactly like one of his uncles on his Mother's side. I had to
admit that there was 'something' in the way of resemblance nevertheless. I
wish I had thought of it afterwards. I might have suggested that he could
always resort to a blood test. I asked him if there were anything that could
be done and he said 'No'.

What was going on here? LG was clearly upset at the suggestion
that Tweed might be Jennifer's father; yet at the same time he still felt
bound to insist that he himself was not. He questioned Sylvester about
Tweed's relations with Muriel, saying that Tweed was 'a professional
seducer' who had seduced half the staff at Old Queen Street. One
might comment that it takes one to know one! But this would surely
be an argument that Tweed *could* be Jennifer's father. LG seems to
have wanted to have it both ways. He had been happy to use Tweed
as a cover to prevent himself being named as the father; yet he had
not really believed that Frances was being unfaithful to him. He may
genuinely have believed that Tweed's real interest was in Muriel. Thus
the discovery that Muriel had been a decoy, and that Frances had
indeed been deceiving him all along, came as a painful shock.*

We do not know what passed between LG and his family that day.

---

* LG's old but now estranged friend Riddell, who made it his business to know everything, even though he refrained from publishing what he knew in the *News of the World*,
was not sympathetic when Sylvester had tea with him (shortly before Riddell's death)
in October 1933.

Lord R. said it was . . . the most extraordinary thing that . . . L.G. who has had so
many affairs, with whom no woman seemed to be reckoned safe . . . now finds that
his own mistress has been seduced in his own house, almost by one of his paid men.
What retribution! . . . Lord R. said that the reason why L.G. had not got rid of Tweed
was that he feared that T. would tell all the nonconformists about his carryings on.[16]

According to Sylvester, 'There was a great battle going on; the family had learned all about the child from Rowlands . . . Whilst L.G. was trying to smother his feelings Dame M. was fuller of life than I have seen her for years.' But of course Sylvester did not witness the scenes between Maggie and LG. He only knew what he gathered from LG, on the one hand, and Tom Carey Evans on the other. He could see that there was 'a great battle' taking place, and that Maggie was fired up. Yet even in this domestic crisis an air of normality was somehow maintained.

Tonight before dinner L.G. asked Carey and I [*sic*] to go up to his bedroom. Megan joined us later. There we sipped Australian Harvest Burgundy and ate a very thin biscuit. Meantime, he read some Welsh verses. His mind is never still. He is always doing.[17]

Back in London on Monday, Sylvester went into work as usual. Frances and Tweed were both there; but Frances had evidently had a sleepless night.

When I arrived at the office this morning F. was in her room looking very gloomy and with eyes as red as ferrets. I told her that the Chief had asked me to go to Churt and the question of her relationship with Tweed had been raised. I told her that I did not want her to think that I had been telling tales out of school.

But Tweed was unrepentant.

I also saw Tweed and told him that he seemed to have made a mess of things. He did not seem to be at all surprised. I said that I had never seen L.G. so upset about anything before. Tweed said that they could either have met openly or secretly and F. would not tell L.G. because he would have been annoyed. They had not covered anything up.

Sylvester was then out of the office for most of the day, interviewing wartime colleagues for LG's memoirs. But later he spoke to LG at the House of Commons.

He said: 'You talked to Tweed this morning.' I said I did not talk to him, I merely mentioned something to the effect that he had made a mess of things. L.G. asked if he seemed surprised and I said No, he certainly did not . . .

I was told in the office that F. had been in tears all the day and that she and Tweed alternately had been in the chief's room a good deal.[18]

The next day the atmosphere in the office remained tense. LG, forgetting his book, was 'very much on tenterhooks', preparing a speech. 'How he can concentrate on his speech I do not know with all this on his mind,' Sylvester marvelled. 'When he is worried he raps out orders and is buzzing like an electric wire. He cannot remain still.' Meanwhile Frances was frozen out.

F. sits in her room and unless she has something to go to him about he is generally treating her in an off-hand fashion and not giving her anything to do. She remarked to Miss Russell to the effect 'It was all Sylvester now'.[19]

On Wednesday Frances was 'much more attentive to him', but LG remained 'reserved', while Sylvester groused that 'more work than ever falls on me'. That evening, however, it seemed that LG's relations with his family had been miraculously restored. Though 'exceedingly tired' – 'It was not only his speech, but doubtless the anxiety which was on his mind' – he took Sylvester with him to dine with Maggie and Megan in a private room at the Metropole, where he reclined on a settee, drinking champagne, while Megan fed him with soup and whitebait and they all reminisced happily about the Ministry of Munitions. Then LG, with Sylvester still in tow, joined Gwilym and others for another merry party at the House. 'Never was L.G. more brilliant in private conversation,' Sylvester marvelled again.[20]

Unfortunately Sylvester's is the only account we have of these events. Amazingly, two days later it seems that relations with Frances too were back to somewhere near normal. Sylvester and his wife spent the weekend with LG and Frances at Churt. He witnessed no further tension between them: the only conversation he recorded was LG reminiscing again about the war.[21] But the crisis was not wholly resolved: LG went to Churt – not Criccieth – for Christmas. On 22 December Sylvester wrote opaquely that LG 'hurried off to Churt not wishing me or anyone else a Happy Christmas. Knowing how much he is troubled and het up I marvel that he has been able to do what he has done.'[22]

So what had he done? The answer is that, having punished Frances for a few days, LG had forgiven her lapse on condition that she now definitely gave Tweed up. At first sight this is remarkable. Despite his own compulsive womanising, he had always been intensely jealous when he thought that Frances might even be looking at another man. But now, faced with the evidence of a real affair, he was forgiving. Realistically he had little choice. The balance of their relationship had shifted. Nearing his seventieth birthday, LG knew that he increasingly needed Frances more than she did him. He could not now face life without her. Frances had once again to make a choice: once again she decided that her destiny, her duty and her self-interest impelled her to repudiate Tweed and stay with LG.

Among her papers there is a draft of a poem, written in pencil on a small card. It is not signed or dated, but it is Frances's handwriting, and it is in a box of letters mainly from 1932. It looks very like an anguished lament for her act of renunciation. The fourth line is crossed out, but still legible.

> And so, the end. No more
> We revel in imagination, strong
> With dear delight in beauteous things to be
> Desire and passion pressed into the past.
> Heedless of passion past and present pain
> We goad our spirits to the future need
> With sobbing heart.
> Now chastened by the curb of circumstance
> With bended head to fate we must submit
> With senses tortured by her cruel bond.
> Content ourselves with strong affection's chain
> And wring from life the best that it may hold
> Each looking to the other still for help
> And mutual sympathy.
>
> But ah! The passionate regret
> That will not let the soul forget
> The dream that could not be![23]

The evidence is that Frances kept her resolution. It was difficult for her, since Tweed remained on LG's staff and she must have seen him nearly every day. Over the next seven years Sylvester frequently recorded meals – lunches in the office, or dinners at the Metropole or the Savoy – with LG, Tweed and Frances all together: sometimes the four of them alone, sometimes with others present. At least once, in May 1937, Jennifer and her nanny were there. Was this the one time Jennifer remembers meeting Tweed? Just once more, in September 1933, does Sylvester record a suspicion that Frances had been seeing Tweed secretly again. On this occasion LG was 'terribly upset'.[24] Three years later he was still worried; but this time Sylvester assured him that he had no grounds.

> He then asked me if Frances had anything to do with Tweed now. I said 'No'. He said he looked to me to tell him if I saw anything. My loyalty, he said, was first of all to him. He could not understand her. He did not know what to do with Tweed . . . It would suit him if Tweed found another job. On the other hand, he is a good politician and useful in counsel.[25]

Yet Frances still loved Tweed, as she privately confessed in May 1934 when he suffered a serious heart attack.* LG was away at Criccieth, but Frances does not say whether she took the chance to visit Tweed in hospital; only – on a scrap of paper torn out of a notebook and preserved in her papers – that she was desperately afraid for him.

> After the brightness, the dark. My darling T.F.T. is very ill, ill unto death. If he dies, I do not think I shall be able to bear the scent of the gorse and the lilac, when another spring comes round. All day long I have been walking about, trying to staunch the wound at my heart and to relieve my agony. I have never before had to bear pain like this, but I knew it must come one day. People do die, and those who love them live on. But what agony in between.
>
> My little Jennifer came to me, and puzzled at seeing traces of tears, looked at me very searchingly, and said: – 'Grown-up ladies don't cry do they, Mummy?'[27]

A few days later, after describing LG's return, she noted in her diary (which she had briefly resumed):

---

* He was sufficiently a public figure that bulletins on his condition were published in *The Times* until he was out of danger.[26]

Better news of my darling. It looks as though he would live, but it will be a long business. The fierce pain at my heart has lessened, & the grip of panic has loosened.[28]

Tweed did recover, and after a month's convalescence returned to work. But Frances evidently kept her promise to LG – though quite how she managed it is not clear. In October she wrote another anguished note, later deleted but still just legible.

Saw the back of my T.F.T. disappearing down the corridor & my heart bled with longing. It is dreadful to be in the same building and not see or speak to him, but it is better for him that I should be firm, & if I am strong & [illegible] I may get my reward. Yet will I? My heart tells me that in this life there are no rewards [several words illegible] the only thing to do is to take what you want with both hands and pay the price afterwards. That is the only transaction Fate really understands.[29]

This is Frances in romantic novelist mode. First, she clearly *was* still seeing Tweed and speaking to him regularly, though never perhaps alone. Then what was the 'reward' she still hoped for? That she might yet eventually be free to love Tweed after LG's death? What did she mean by taking 'what you want with both hands' and paying later? She had certainly done that in 1913 and had paid a price – though she had also reaped great rewards – ever since. Or did she mean that she had followed her heart between 1928 and 1932 and had paid for that, too? We cannot know.

In February 1933 Tweed struck out in a new direction by publishing his first novel, a futuristic political fantasy entitled *Rinehard: A Melodrama of the Nineteen-Thirties*. The American edition actually appeared two weeks earlier, in a slightly different form and under a different title – *Gabriel over the White House* – flagged as 'A Sensational Novel of the Presidency' – and timed to coincide with Franklin Roosevelt's inauguration. A curious hybrid of quite sophisticated political satire crossed with a formulaic gangster thriller, the book imagines a commanding US President who assumes dictatorial powers to save America and then the world from depression and war by means of free trade, a single currency and universal disarmament, all overseen by a beneficent World Court, imposing his will on corrupt politicians, vested interests and gangsters in the name of true democracy.

The irony is that President Rinehard can do all this only because he is temporarily mad. At the beginning of the book he is just another cynical demagogue who is unexpectedly elected President after a dead-locked Convention. He is only transformed into the far-seeing, all-wise dictator after a car accident. He recovers his senses equally suddenly after another blow on the head, following an assassination attempt, four years later, when he is about to stand for re-election. He has to be forcibly prevented from broadcasting a disavowal of everything he has done over the previous four years; at which point he dies, and we are left to assume that the great experiment in world government is able to continue for the benefit of all mankind.

It is, as the British subtitle suggests, a very 1930s vision of enlight-ened dictatorship: the great leader who can solve all problems simply by knocking heads together, with the saving grace that he is a *demo-cratic* leader, embodying the people's will and the people's interests, while suppressing all the self-serving parasites who have betrayed democracy hitherto. While clearly anticipating elements of Roosevelt's 'New Deal' – it was published just before Hitler came to power in Germany – the novel is an alarmingly anti-democratic vision of a plebis-citary dictatorship, exercised through the new medium of television. The story is narrated by one of Rinehard's aides with a mixture of naïve admiration for the way the President's inspired leadership is able to solve all problems and sweeping contempt for the 'machine politicians' who had gone before. Thus Rinehard fills his new administration with *'men of special aptitude . . . representative of all that was best in Amer-ican public life'*[30] . . . *'men and women of a much higher type and capacity than had been produced by the normal course of election'*.[31] Though the Christian subtext of the American title is not overempha-sised, it is suggested at one point that Rinehard's policy represents *'the fulfilment of an economic philosophy, the teachings of which had first been heard two thousand years before on the shores of Galilee'*.[32] At the same time the book is filled with appalling racial and gender stereo-types – wops, Yids, cruel-eyed villains, drink-crazed hoodlums and their long-suffering but loyal molls – characteristic of contemporary writers like John Buchan and Dornford Yates, but embarrassing today.

The interest of *Rinehard* for the story of Lloyd George and Frances is twofold. First, the fantasy of a great man cutting through the constraints of party politics to push through radical and beneficent reforms clearly reflects what LG – like FDR in America and Hitler in Germany – would have liked to do in Britain in the 1930s, and presumably what Tweed hoped he would do. (LG had used non-political businessmen and others to shake up government in just this way in 1917–18.) Still more intriguing, however, is the relationship between Rinehard and his confidential secretary, curiously named 'Pendie' Malloy. (In the British edition 'Pendie' is short for 'Independence', because she was born on Independence Day; but in the American version it is short for 'Pendola'.)

Pendie is *not* Frances (though there are some similarities), any more than Rinehard is LG; and their relationship is not the same. Though very close, it is stated several times that it is *not* a sexual relationship. Pendie is secretary, companion, nursemaid and mother to Rinehard – everything except his mistress. ('*Was Pendie Malloy in love with Rinehard? It is possible she was, but, if so, then her affections were more maternal than passionate . . . She had no illusions about him whatever.*')[33] Nevertheless the description of Rinehard's dependence on Pendie's support and constant praise unmistakably owes a good deal to Tweed's observation of LG and Frances.

> *Was Rinehard in love with Pendie? Probably he was. But again for a man whose life was hardly monastic, his fondness for her was based on something deeper and more permanent than sexual attraction. It was more sentimental than that of a father for his daughter; more wholesome than that of a man for his mistress; and free of those latent antagonisms and differences of outlook which make life fretful and occasionally irksome for the happiest of married couples.*[34]

Above all, Pendie gives Rinehard the unstinted praise that a man rarely gets from his wife.

> *Every wife thinks it necessary for her self-respect to deflate the public's hero by the administration of a little common sense and a few home-truths. No man is a hero to his wife, but unless he is a hero to his private secretary she does not long remain his private secretary.*[35]

After a speech it was always to Pendie that Rinehard went for her verdict – just as LG did to Frances.

*And whether he had made a good speech or a bad speech, whether there
had been wild enthusiasm or marked coldness, Rinehard never quite relaxed
from the tension of the nervous and mental strain until in the privacy of
his room Pendie had said: 'You were brilliant tonight, my dear; I never
knew you in better form.' A day or two later she would point out the
mistakes and be mercilessly cutting in her comments, but always immediately following the speech, she eased the jagged nerves and soothed the
pent-up soul of the orator with what appeared to be the stock elixir: 'You
were brilliant tonight, my dear.'[36]** ·

Unlike Frances, Tweed was a good enough novelist to be able to
assimilate and transform his own experience into fiction: one cannot
simply read his imagined narrative as wishful thinking. Nevertheless it
may be significant that Pendie is not Rinehard's mistress; while there
is surely an element of autobiography in the fact that the narrator is
himself in love with Pendie and is upset when she marries someone
else. More generally, Tweed's description of the difficulty of serving a
powerful personality like Rinehard is clearly informed by his experience of working for LG. Finally, there is an unmistakable portrait of
LG, not in the character of the stern and saturnine Rinehard – whose
only resemblance to LG is an insatiable *'craving for detective fiction
and Wild West stories'*[37] – but as the septuagenarian British Prime
Minister, an ally and supporter of Rinehard's scheme for world government, whose plans to regenerate Britain are very like LG's.

*The new Premier . . . after years of retirement, had been forced by circum-
stances to take office again. He was a man of invincible courage who definitely refused to admit that Britain was down and out. His speeches had
done more to create optimism and hope than almost anything that had
happened since the crisis in the early thirties . . . Believing that sanity
would and must return, he wanted Britain to be so equipped that it could
take the utmost advantage of any new developments. With an energy and
fervour almost miraculous in a man of his age he had defied the financiers and bankers of the City of London and commenced great schemes
of land irrigation and drainage, of electrification, roads, docks, harbours
and flying ports.*[38]

---

* For some reason these three pages were cut from the British paperback edition.

That, sadly, *was* wishful thinking.

Rinehard won amazingly good reviews. *The Times* thought there was 'little inherently impossible' in the story, and 'much that is wise and even practicable in the author's suggestions', while 'the book as a whole can hardly fail to stir the imagination of all interested in world problems'.[39] *Gabriel over the White House* was a bestseller in America and was immediately made into a sensational Hollywood movie by the studios of William Randolph Hearst, directed by Gregory La Cava and starring Walter Huston as the President.* The following year – before his heart attack – Tweed completed a second novel. *Blind Mouths* (called *Destiny's Man* in America) was another political adventure, set this time in central Europe, and with a stronger Christian theme – 'the advent and mission of an Aryan Christ in a Nazi State'.[40] This too received full and mainly laudatory reviews.

In the second half of the decade Tweed – variously described as 'Mr Lloyd George's able political henchman'[41] and 'Mr Lloyd George's colourful political adviser'[42] – pursued his interest in the problem of dictatorship and democracy by undertaking several fact-finding journeys around Europe: in 1936 to Russia and Germany; in 1937 to Italy; in 1938 a 7,000-mile trip around the Balkans; in 1939 to Berlin and Vienna just weeks before the outbreak of war. According to the *Manchester Guardian*, which in 1937 devoted a long article to 'Colonel Tweed's Totalitarian Studies', he had been 'staggered by the irresponsibility' of the US government in the face of the Depression, and correspondingly impressed by the greater success of authoritarian regimes in tackling it. 'The object of his researches seems to be to find what good qualities of the totalitarian State can be grafted upon humane and independent nations.' He was planning to write a book on the subject: in the meantime 'no doubt Mr Lloyd George will benefit by the data and conclusions which his Chief of Staff amasses'.[43]

It is perhaps surprising that, despite this burgeoning literary career, Tweed continued for the whole decade to work for LG – and thus alongside Frances. But evidently he needed the money: he had lost his pension rights when he had left his job as Liberal organiser to follow LG in 1931, and still hoped to get them back.[44] Outwardly he remained

* The film has recently become something of a cult classic in America. There are articles on the internet that see it as a disturbing anticipation of George. W. Bush.

entirely loyal, capable of simultaneously flattering LG while talking
tough to him – for instance, after a major speech in January 1933:

> My dear Chief,
>   Your speech last night was a fitting conclusion to a most remarkable
> week.
>   I doubt if, in the long history of politics, there has ever been anything
> to equal it.
>   Without leadership, or even a party, you have dominated the press &
> the political scene for days in a way no politician living or dead could equal.
> It is unique – and very significant . . .
>   The ball is once more at your feet – what are you going to do with it?
>   Rusticate at Churt – or kick it & keep on kicking it until it reaches the
> ultimate goal & your return to domination, to the confusion of your enemies
> & the joy of your friends?
>   Ever,
>   T.F.T.[45]

But when LG did try to create a new non-party vehicle to promote
his ideas at the 1935 election – it was called the Council of Action for
Peace and Reconstruction and was based, rather hopefully, on the
Nonconformist churches – Tweed was (quite rightly) unimpressed. And
that summer it seems that he was frankly blackmailing LG: not about
Frances and Jennifer, but about LG's still more scandalous liaison with
his former daughter-in-law Roberta.

Once again the source is Sylvester, who recorded a bitter conversation with Tweed when the latter felt slighted over something to do with
the Council of Action.

> T's face assumed the most extraordinary contortions I have ever seen . . .
> He said he had got to the end of his tether and asked what was L.G.'s
> game. He was not going to be made a scapegoat by L.G. If L.G. was reverting
> to the F-J incident then he knew a lot about L.G.'s relationship with R. and
> he would let these Freechurchmen know about it; that would bust L.G.
>   When L.G. arrived at the office at 10.30 I told him that T. was in an
> ugly mood . . . He asked what for? I said that . . . he thought L.G. had a
> game on, and that he was not going to be made a scapegoat about F. and
> J. I said nothing about R. at this point . . .
>   Later on . . . L.G. asked me exactly what T. had said. I repeated what

I had said earlier . . . and added what T. had said about R. Again he said he did not know what T. wanted . . . but he was clearly thinking hard about what I had told him.

He then disappeared with F. to Churt.[46]

Once again, what does this mean? Tweed was clearly blackmailing LG with his knowledge of the Roberta affair. But does his determination not to be 'made a scapegoat about F. & J.' support the idea that LG and Frances had used him in 1929 as an alibi to protect LG, but that he was no longer willing to be so used? It is difficult to see what else he could have meant.

Later that evening Frances rang to ask Sylvester to offer Tweed an olive branch. Sylvester thought this was 'funk', because LG did not dare to sack him. Three days later Tweed was evidently happy that his blackmail had worked, telling Sylvester that he did not understand why LG had chosen to quarrel with him, 'except that he must quarrel with someone'.

T. said that he could have done (a) resign; which he did not intend to do, because he could not afford to do so; (b) L.G. could have sacked him. He was waiting to be sacked. He would then have been free to do what he liked. He had told J.T.D. that he would then put out what he knew about R . . .

He made no bones about his future; that was what he was definitely for. He said that he had already made it quite clear to J.T. that when anything happened to L.G. the trustees would not be allowed to divide up the fund between the family. T. intended to see that he got his share.[47]

Sylvester's comment on Tweed's behaviour was typically cynical. He did not blame Tweed, since his own motives were no less mercenary. He merely wondered which of them was playing the better game.

In the years that lie before us I shall be very interested to see which has the greater reward; whether T. gets his deserts out of the old firm for threatening blackmail or whether I get mine for the part I have played.[48]

After this the situation settled down for another few years, with Tweed continuing to serve as LG's political adviser and right-hand man. But there was another flare-up in 1938, when the almost simultaneous deaths of two of the trustees raised a question about the future of the Lloyd George fund. Looking to economise, LG talked of putting Tweed on a retainer – that is, effectively sacking him while still paying him a reduced salary – in order to use his room for the Council of Action. Significantly, Frances warned Tweed of what was in the wind. 'Tweed was very angry. He said he would be damned if he would let the family get away with a quarter of a million of money.'[49] Again the implication is that Tweed thought LG was going to distribute the remains of the fund to his family instead of continuing to employ political staff. In fact Tweed did not lose his job – maybe he again reminded LG that it would be unwise to antagonise him. Up to the outbreak of war and beyond he was still advising LG, first on political tactics, then on the 'phoney' war and possible peace terms, until his early death in 1940.

33

DOWN ON THE FARM

In January 1933 LG celebrated his seventieth birthday with a concert at the Memorial Hall in Criccieth. Three days later, after a speech to his constituents in Caernarvon, he declared himself 'fitter mentally and physically now' than before his operation sixteen months earlier.[1] To all appearances indeed, his vitality was undiminished, and for the rest of the decade he continued to work like a dynamo at his various projects, leaving his substantial staff – from secretaries and researchers to farm managers and beekeepers – exhausted in his wake. He divided his energies between his *War Memoirs* (which appeared in six volumes between 1933 and 1935, followed by two more on the Peace Treaties in 1938); his farm (which now comprised some 300 acres under cultivation); and politics, from which he was increasingly detached, apart from a burst of furious activity leading up to the 1935 election. Most of the year he lived semi-openly with Frances at Churt. But he still had his London house in Addison Road; despite his complaints he still went to Criccieth several times a year; and nearly every winter he took a long holiday in the sun – sometimes accompanied by his family, sometimes by Frances, sometimes by one followed by the other. It was still an extraordinarily complicated and effectively bigamous life; yet in 1938 he and Maggie celebrated their golden wedding anniversary amid a remarkable outpouring of national congratulation.

For Frances life had become simpler in one respect, in that she had renounced Tweed; but in other ways it was becoming increasingly difficult and less rewarding, as LG grew older, more cantankerous and more demanding. He was not really the man he had been: the effort of keeping up appearances took more and more out of him; he required constant reassurance that his powers were not failing; and handling his moods became more and more like coping with a tempestuous and often sulky child. Undoubtedly there were still happy times: walking round the orchards, picnics with Jennifer, reading in the evenings and listening to the wireless – times of quiet companionship; but there were also frequent rows and periods of tension (eagerly monitored by Sylvester), followed by apologies and reconciliation. Despite his own undiminished interest in farm girls, maids and typists, which led to a number of awkward incidents, LG was almost insanely suspicious of Frances and constantly accused her of sleeping with every man in his employment, from farm managers to Sylvester! 'He is quite sex mad,' Sylvester noted in 1933;[2] and again six years later: 'On sex matters, L.G. is absolutely mental.'[3] Once Frances simply walked out.[4] Another time she told Sylvester that LG 'was so offensive [that] she refused to have dinner with him and had it upstairs on a tray'.[5] More seriously, Frances told Sylvester's wife in 1936 that LG was sometimes not just mentally but physically cruel.

> Frances told Evelyn that he would hold her down by force in an endeavour to get her to confess to things she had never done. But she now had her remedy. She told him when he was in a bad mood, and when she found herself at the end of her tether, that whatever he said or did could not hurt her any more than she had already been hurt. He had been so cruel to her and had said such terrible things to her in the past.[6]

In 1934 Frances resumed her diary after a six-year gap. It was now less of a consecutive narrative than previously, reflecting the fact that LG was no longer involved in daily politics; it was more a record of an old man's memories of his childhood, his comments about the people and events of whichever episode of the war he was currently writing about, and caustic exchanges about the current situation with various dinner guests. But she still included an occasional telling paragraph expressing her considered view of the big baby to whom she had devoted her life: for instance, a vivid account of the frantic struggle to get volumes three and four of the *War Memoirs* completed. (Oddly, she no longer called him 'D', but the more impersonal 'Ll.G').

> The usual last-minute alterations, corrections, recriminations, leaving everyone utterly exhausted and extremely bad-tempered. Ll.G is incapable of *achieving* anything, without reducing all around him to nervous wrecks.

In this way he *distributes* his own nerves in a crisis, and, I believe, saves himself in the process. I always used to think it was an unnecessary bother and a crisis over nothing, but now I perceive the more subtle psychology of it, and realise that it is necessary for him to produce this state of enervation in everyone else, in order that he himself may derive some sort of nervous energy which fortifies him. Anyhow the MS. is now gone.[7]

A month earlier she had reflected on the origin of LG's extraordinary egotism, and concluded that it was the result of having been spoiled by his mother and uncle as a boy.

I have often wondered how far this early spoiling was responsible for the fact that his presence was – and is – fatal to the smooth conduct of any household. His mere entry to any dwelling has always been the signal for an immediate complete disorganisation. Whether unconsciously or consciously every member somehow or other found themselves pressed into his service for one reason or another & every activity was subordinated to his pleasure . . . It would be interesting to hear the comments of modern students of child psychology upon those early years . . . when there is no doubt that every member of even that humble household combined to make life easier for him while unconsciously encouraging his selfishness.

   Conversely, and strangely, none of his own homes ever seemed to be quite his own.[8]

There is a decidedly bitter paragraph about LG's habit of making instant judgements about people, which surely reflects her resentment of his sexual jealousy and inability to understand her more complex feelings.

He thinks he is a remarkable judge of character and more especially of *motives*. But whereas he is able to detect the more primitive motives and those arising from the lower human instincts, of the more subtle and delicate and complicated motives he has no knowledge at all.[9]

With some despair Frances also noted LG's growing intolerance of anyone who dared to argue with him – for instance, Lettice Fisher, wife of the historian H. A. L. Fisher who had been President of the Board of Education in LG's government and was now a neighbour at Churt.

Ll.G takes it as a personal insult when his friends do not see eye [to eye] with him & do not accept all his tenets as gospel. He has become much more exacting in this respect since his illness, and has alienated many people who would have liked to remain friends with him.

Mrs Fisher had earlier disagreed with him about Herbert Samuel's willingness to join the National Government.

Ll.G took this amiss & as lacking in loyalty to him. [He has] no use for lady friends who do not support him blindly through thick and thin. I fear he will not want to see her again for some time. And incidentally it will make things more difficult for me, as he considers it disloyal on my part to have friendly leanings towards those who have incurred his displeasure. And they, alas! are many, and tend to increase in number.[10]

Another time LG almost came to blows with H. G. Wells about the Paris peace conference. 'It was nearly, if not quite, unpleasant.'

Some of his friends think he would do better sometimes to admit that he has occasionally made mistakes, and been in the wrong, but he seems to be incapable of doing this – possibly because he is able always to make out such a completely good case for everything – the instinct of the clever lawyer at all times.[11]

As well as quarrelling with dinner guests, LG was always suspicious that his workers and managers were cheating him behind his back, so that Frances was forever having to defuse rows, pacify aggrieved employees and try to prevent them from leaving. But her position was tricky, since she was officially only a secretary herself, lacking the authority of a wife – though most of the household must have realised the truth. One farm manager – 'the fourth at Churt in a very few years' – left in 1937 because 'he did not like the moral atmosphere of the place'.[12] There must have been gossip locally about LG's unconventional ménage, but still nothing ever got into the papers.

In 1934 Frances built herself a new house on the Churt estate. Worplesdon was too far away to allow her to nip easily back and forth between Jennifer and LG; and she did not like driving. Moreover

* In later life Jennifer recalled that Frances used to visit Worplesdon 'occasionally, and I visited Bron-y-de quite often'.[13]

LG wanted Jennifer closer to him.* First she bought (or LG gave her) a disused farm building called Old Barn and spent a lot of money doing it up very grandly, creating a vaulted drawing room with a minstrels' gallery. But Old Barn then became too expensive to run, so she let it and built a more modest bungalow for herself, called Avalon.

Designed to Frances's specification by a rising young architect called Anthony Chitty, Avalon was built entirely of wood and dominated by a single long room – much like LG's at Bron-y-de – with French windows looking onto a courtyard, then Frances's garden and the orchards of Bron-y-de beyond. There was also a 'magnificent' nursery for Jennifer. Though uncompromisingly modern, the house was 'amazingly beautiful' and carefully furnished with Frances's accumulated treasures: she always had extravagant but excellent taste.[14] The Arthurian name 'Avalon' was derived from Tennyson; but under LG's influence it was pronounced as if it were Welsh, with the stress on the second syllable.

It was built extraordinarily quickly. In late October 1934 Sylvester was writing that LG wanted Megan to build some cottages on land he had given her at Churt, supposedly to meet the housing shortage; but this, he believed, was 'merely a blind to enable F. to build one at the same time. He is a most audacious man. The whole of his mind is concentrated on Jennifer; Megan is out of it completely.'[15] Less than five months later, on 9 March 1935, Frances and Jennifer – with Jennifer's latest nanny and two Scottish servants – moved into their new home. In practice it was Jennifer's home until she went away to school.

> The pattern became established that Jennifer would walk the mile from Avalon to Bron-y-de in the morning, stay to lunch, talk to Frances in the afternoon when Lloyd George had his usual nap, and then walk back with the nanny, or with Frances, who would leave in order to be back at Bron-y-de for tea with Lloyd George.[16]

Frances continued to spend most of her time with LG at Bron-y-de, and normally slept there. She used to telephone Avalon every evening at Jennifer's bedtime to say goodnight.[17]

LG continued to be besotted with Jennifer – rather more so than Frances herself, who was afraid that he would spoil her. In April 1934, for example (when Jennifer was still living at Worplesdon), Frances wrote in her diary:

Easter Sunday. Jennifer here for the weekend, but unfortunately with a little cold. She & Ll.G. had planned to go out & pick daffodils, & she was disappointed at not having done so, so he went out in his dressing gown before breakfast & brought her back a lovely bunch. He is very sweet to her, but spoils her. I hope it won't do her any permanent harm. But it is a unique thing for her to be receiving all the love and devotion which he lavishes upon her.[18]

Why did she call LG's love for Jennifer 'unique'? Is this a hint that she did not think LG was her father? The next month Frances was comparing the way he spoiled Jennifer with the way he had brought up Megan.

Had Jennifer here for 2 days & she & Ll.G. were very happy together. He adores her but spoils her. He was urging me to let her belong to the country and *not* to get her into the ways of the town. He is anxious that she should learn the management of our orchards and be properly taught the management of fruit. 'Teach her the things that appertain to her peace.' I am sure he is right, & will try to carry out his wishes for J's sake.

But *why* has Ll.G. done what he has done with Megan? An old woman in looks at 32, a mess of nerves so spoiled & impossible that no-one can live with her – that is the result of his upbringing of her. He never thought of bringing her up in the country, or teaching her the loveliness of nature.[19]

Jennifer not surprisingly adored her *Taid*. LG loved children, especially little girls, and was inexhaustibly inventive and funny in playing with her – to the exasperation of Sylvester, who was constantly complaining that LG spent his time with her when he should have been working. In July 1936, for instance, he thought that LG should have attended a Defence debate in the Commons, 'instead of playing about with Jennifer at Churt. That is all he is doing these days, and quarrelling with his workpeople over things he does not understand.'[20] Another time, when Jennifer had whooping cough, LG was 'so upset that he stayed in bed' all day.[21] 'He is 'completely potty about that kid,' Sylvester noted. 'None of his grandchildren come anywhere near her in his eyes.' He was always showing Sylvester photographs and boasting of Jennifer's accomplishments, so that Sylvester found it 'impossible . . . to believe' that Tweed could be her father. But then he added a rider: '. . . or at least for L.G. to believe that'.[22] Sylvester could never quite decide whether he thought Jennifer was LG's child or not.

In a letter of August 1935, when Frances had been visiting Jennifer on holiday with friends in Devon while LG was in Wales, she reported that she had overheard Jennifer telling another little girl that 'she had no Daddy, but that she had a godfather. "My godfather is very strict with my Mummy," she said, "but he is not strict with me."'[23] Out of the mouths of babes! Jennifer spoke perhaps more truly than she knew. Once LG was very cross when Jennifer was not allowed to go for a walk with him because she had to have a rest before going out to tea. 'This infuriated him. He is against her going anywhere or doing anything without him.' He took it out on Frances by ignoring her for several days.[24] Later he became jealous when Jennifer began to make friends of her own and consequently had less time for him.

Naturally LG and Frances wrote to each other only when they were apart, which was less often than before. But still their letters can be puzzling. In January 1934 LG went to Portugal with his family and the usual retinue of maids and typists, plus Sylvester. While he was away he wrote 230,000 words of his third and fourth volumes – a phenomenal output in less than four weeks, even if much of the groundwork had been done for him by Frances, Sylvester and a researcher, Malcolm Thomson. But he also wrote another flurry of letters to Frances. The first was typical of many that he had written over the years: bemoaning his separation from his 'two sweethearts', pretending to be hating every minute that he was away ('the most depressing of all life's pursuits – a holiday'), bullish about the progress of his book, but worried as always about her fidelity.

> Keep writing. I was sick when A.J. received letters from Smithers & his wife on Friday . . . & nothing for me. The letter I received yesterday set me right. I was so pleased to read that you meant to be a good girl. I know you will be happier. The double life is full of worry & apprehension which wrecks the nerves.
> Fond love
> D.[25]

It was a bit rich for LG, after more than twenty years, to be warning Frances about the strain of leading a double life! Once again one can only regret that Frances's letters have not survived. But from this letter and the next it seems that she had made yet another vow of fidelity to him.

> My dearest
>
> Got your 2nd letter. So pleased with it *all*. I know I can trust you not to betray your promise.
>
> I am sending you my Passchendaele revise. I have worked very hard on it. Let me know what you think of it now . . .
> Love
> D.[26]

LG wrote several more long and unusually sunny letters from Estoril, mainly about his golf ('I play golf every day. I am now taking lessons and improving') and his writing, thanking Frances for the raw material she was continuing to send him. 'You have worked well,' he told her on 23 January, adding: 'We work better apart. I want your company when you are about.' Somewhat contradictorily he then wished that Frances could come out and join him for another month. 'But discovered that if I stay M. will also stay.'[27]

Yet there are some curious undercurrents in these letters, too. Most of them are addressed not to 'my girl', or 'my two girls', but by name – which LG had never done before – to 'Dearest Frances' or 'Dearest F.'; and once the words are in inverted commas. What did this ironic formality mean? It seems to mirror her greater formality in referring to him in her diary as 'Ll.G'. The same letter ends: 'Tender love – & understanding. D.' What was he being understanding about? Then the last letter, full of the usual detailed arrangements for his return – wanting Frances and Jennifer to meet him this time at Basingstoke – signs off with the most puzzling last words:

> Love to you both – Mama & child – but not to the papa
> *Taid*

She is bent on ruining my reputation! I wish it was justified.[28]

What on earth is this about? Who was 'the papa' to whom he was not sending love? Tweed? If so, LG was amazingly relaxed about it. Or was he reverting to the story of Tweed's paternity as an alibi for himself? Then who was bent on ruining his reputation? Presumably Megan, who was always threatening to expose him, though she never did. But was she alleging that he *was* Jennifer's father, or that he was not? The family preferred to believe that Tweed was the father. But the implication of LG wishing the allegation was justified would seem to be that he wished he was the father, but knew he was not. These are murky waters, which it is impossible to plumb with any confidence. Once more it is frustrating that we lack Frances's letters, which might have been less ambiguous. No doubt that is why he destroyed them. It was shortly after this that Frances resumed her diary, which, as we have seen, confirms that all was not entirely sunny between them.

Later that year, when LG was in Wales, Frances took Jennifer – with her nanny, of course – to Estoril, where they stayed in the same hotel that LG had stayed at. LG saw them off on 24 August. On 3 September Frances wrote him a long, unusually dull letter, which her granddaughter aptly characterises as 'wifely'.

My own darling little Man

Just a little line to let you know that everything is all right here – Jennifer is quite recovered, and thoroughly enjoying life in every detail and every thrill . . .

It *is* a nice place, and the people are so kind, and thoroughly honest . . . I am so sorry you have not been having very good weather in Wales. It is too bad, and you will have been envying us our sunshine . . .

It has seemed such a long time since we saw you, my darling, and I am longing for a glimpse of you again. I hope all goes well with you, and that you are enjoying your rest, and the change! – and that you are not working too hard . . .

Fondest and most devoted love to you, my darling, from your own P & J.[29]

LG responded by interrupting his holiday in Criccieth, supposedly to attend the funeral of Lord Devonport (his former Food Controller during the war). Sylvester saw what he was really up to:

No one realised the inward meaning of this move; F. and Jennifer arrived back at Churt today. Here was a fine excuse for him to spend the weekend with them . . . Today L.G. is in the bosom of F. and the little Jennifer; his family is his last thought.[30]

At least from Frances's perspective, LG's relations with his family were as fraught as ever – though even she was beginning to see the other side of the picture.

He is bitter about his children, saying that they all now take the line that he is more of a hindrance than an asset to them, after having benefited by all that he has given them. Megan is the worst of them all in this respect, being rude and indifferent to him in private, & in public taking any reflected glory there may be, and playing the 'little daughter' most prettily. They all spend the minimum of time with him, for which he is not sorry. Perhaps they know this and it influences their behaviour. There is always something to be said on both sides![31]

In March 1934 he met several of them at a wedding.

Edna, who thinks Ll.G insulted her at Estoril, scarcely on speaking terms with Ll.G., and cutting Olwen dead, and Gwilym quarrelling with Megan & refusing to spend a weekend under the same roof. A happy family. They keep very clear of Ll.G these days.[32]

Whenever he was with his family LG realised how much he depended on Frances. 'I can forgive F. a great deal,' he told Sylvester with characteristic egoism in August 1933, 'because she was there' – meaning that she had been with him at critical moments of the war when Maggie was not.

'When I am difficult F. understands, and says "Leave him alone; he is worried", but here they never leave me alone and Megan always sides with her mother. Until I had Churt I had no home at all. It is only tolerable to me here when I segregate myself and when Gwilym is here.'

On this occasion he packed up and left Criccieth suddenly at 7.30 on Sunday morning. But Maggie was happy to see him leave. 'Let him go,' she told Sylvester. 'He thinks that will upset us; it won't.' Tom Carey Evans had advised her that it would be better for her nerves to live alone. She had waited on LG when he was ill, and never had any thanks. 'No-one knew what she had been through. They had stood a lot from him and they might not always be able to stand it.'[33]

Despite his own differences with his father-in-law, Carey Evans took a somewhat detached view of these family rows. 'The family had played their cards badly,' he told Sylvester after dinner at Churt in April 1932, 'as they had neglected him. Frances had carefully looked after him. It was astonishing how he always came back to her. Her influence had been good.' It is significant that Carey Evans was prepared to visit Bron-y-de when Frances was there. On this occasion he 'telephoned through to Criccieth' after dinner and spoke to Olwen. Sylvester did not overhear the conversation; but 'it was evident from L.G's remarks and Carey's that she was annoyed because he had come to Churt. Of course, the family knew who was staying there.'[34]

'The fact of the matter,' Sylvester reflected three years later, 'is that L.G. cannot stand his family very long and they cannot stand him. They just rub one another up the wrong way. Being in a unique position I can appreciate both sides; but there is no doubt that Dame M. and Megan have completely lost L.G. by not looking after him. They will fuss him for 5 minutes and neglect him for 5 weeks or months.'[35] By comparison both Sylvester and Carey Evans felt that Frances had earned her reward by looking after him devotedly now for more than twenty years.

Maggie's patience with her husband may have been wearing thin, but she still defended her corner – sometimes in the pettiest ways, as in October 1935.

Meantime there is a barging match going on between Criccieth and Churt as to who shall supply clean linen at Addison Road! Dame M. will not let L.G. have the keys to her linen cupboard. She probably suspects that F. would have them. So L.G. had to bring his own linen from Churt, because what was at Addison Road was six weeks old![36]

Sylvester also witnessed an awkward close encounter at Westminster after LG had come up to speak in a debate about the League of Nations in 1936. Maggie was in London and had presumably been in the gallery to hear him, requiring Frances to keep out of sight – quite literally.

He went off to Churt with F. at 10.20 p.m. nearly clashing with Dame M. in the Speaker's Yard. L.G. rushed to caress Dame M. in her own car, whilst F. hid herself behind L.G.'s. Then when Dame M. had gone L.G. went off to Churt with F.[37]

At times like this the LG–Maggie–Frances triangle descended into something close to farce.

By now LG did not really know if he wanted to get back into government or not. Part of him did, of course, if only from force of habit. He had been in politics for more than forty years, and he could not easily imagine a life that was not directed at winning political office. When Harold Nicolson sought to console him in 1932 that he was 'well out of it', LG replied sadly, 'One is never well out of it. One is just out of it.'[38] He had a poor opinion of those who had succeeded him in office – Baldwin, MacDonald and Neville Chamberlain, but particularly MacDonald – and liked to believe that he could easily sweep these pygmies away whenever he chose. It enraged him to see the fate of the country in the hands of a man he believed to be 'nine-tenths gaga';[39] and he was surrounded by flatterers – including Frances – who constantly assured him that he would soon be recalled to save the country again, as he had in 1916–18. At the same time he half-knew that he was not really up to it any more; as, in her heart, did Frances:

> I doubt . . . whether he would sustain physically a job of work which demands concentration & continual attention. He has got so accustomed to ease and leisure, not to say self-indulgence, since his illness, that he would find daily application to a job very onerous. I think he realises that.[40]

When dissident young Tories like Harold Macmillan came to Churt to try to draw him out of his tent, Frances wrote, LG was 'not very interested . . . He quite definitely shrinks from the possibility of having to go into active politics again.'[41] Instead he fantasised that he could have the power without the responsibility.

> What Ll.G has at the back of his mind is the consolidation of a small block of progressive opinion behind him after the election, in the hope that the Gov. majority will be so small that a block of votes of even 20 or 30 would influence things one way or another. Then Ll.G, with his little party, would be all powerful, and could dictate policy, which is just what he would like.[42]

By the autumn of 1934 he was once again convening conferences of non-party experts to develop 'a vigorous policy of reconstruction on which to fight the election. His idea is to back wholeheartedly any candidate of any party, who will accept his programme.'[43] Frances was privately sceptical, but as LG prepared to launch his own version of Roosevelt's 'New Deal' in January 1935, she could not help being carried along by his renewed enthusiasm.

> The correspondence . . . from all parts of the country is overwhelming . . . It is becoming exciting. Ll.G is in great spirits, & I hope he can see it through. He will have to guard his energies, as he easily gets overtired & overstrained. But it is the moment he has been waiting for all these years. I feel he is staking everything on the results of the next few months. If he fails, he will devote himself to the farm and his writing for the rest of his life. Meanwhile, the book is completely forgotten.[44]

The launch of LG's New Deal – in a speech at Bangor to an audience of 7,000 in the Drill Hall, with another 5,000 listening outside – was of course a 'triumph'.

> Much fluttering of the political dovecots as to Ll.G's position, now & in the future . . . There is no doubt that Ll.G's proposals . . . have caught on in the country. We are overwhelmed with approval from every quarter, & of every political complexion . . . He struck at the psychological moment, & has transformed the political situation.[45]

The government was worried enough to go through the motions of studying LG's ideas. In the spring they invited him to submit his proposals to the Cabinet in the form of a memorandum. 'Ll.G has put all his energy & thought into it,' Frances wrote, 'realising that it is an epoch-making document. His industry on such occasions as these is unflagging . . . one expression of his almost superhuman energy . . . Ll.G himself is looking better than he has done for a long time, & younger.'[46] But three days later it was a different story. 'The New Proposals have gone in, & Ll.G very difficult & on edge. He will be all but impossible to live with in the interval until something more happens that calls for action.'[47]

On 26 March LG went to Tyneside to visit the distressed areas for himself and make several speeches. Frances could not go, since Megan accompanied him; but Sylvester went and wrote a wonderfully vivid account of helping LG correct his text while simultaneously helping him to dress – more often Frances's job. (LG could never do anything for himself.) When Sylvester arrived, LG was still in bed.

> He was using the back of his hand as a backing sheet to the flimsy paper on which he was writing, and he was writing almost madly in his microscopical characters with a huge yellow coloured pencil which resembled a hedge stake – at least a foot long – the point of which was quite blunt thereby adding materially to the illegibility of his hieroglyphics.

Sylvester was then required to read back this scrawl while LG shaved, bathed and dressed.

> At every other line he cried out for some article of clothing . . . I would first read a sentence. Then button up his collar; then another sentence or two and put on his socks. He would try to put on his boots and appeal to me for assistance whilst in the middle of another sentence. And then say: 'Yes, go on', until I was damned glad to come to the end of it.
>
> All the time he was terribly worked up – just like a ball of electricity. When he is in those moods energy seems to ooze from him; he is a colossal fellow. He takes a lot of handling in these moods.

After the meeting, too, Sylvester had to help him unwind. 'Before he could do anything else after his speech I went with him to his bedroom where he changed all his underclothing, for he was wet through with perspiration.'[48] Frances was waiting at Churt when he got back after 'a very strenuous 3 days'. 'Very crotchety and tired,' she wrote. 'It is too much for him to do all that. But a day or two at Churt will put him right.'[49]

To Sylvester, LG repeatedly insisted that he did not want office. 'I don't. I want my proposals accepted. That is all I want.'[50] On the other hand, 'If they won't accept my proposals I will smash them.'[51] Frances, however, still encouraged his belief that he would come back.

> We wandered through the orchards to see the plum blossom. Ll.G wondered, looking at the blossom, what will have passed by the time the fruit is matured. 'I prophesy that before that time you will be in office,' I said.[52]

In April/May he had several surprisingly friendly meetings with Baldwin and Chamberlain. 'He is very happy . . . & in better form than I have seen him for a very long time.'[53] But they were only stringing him along. When Baldwin finally succeeded MacDonald as Prime Minister on 7 June, there was no place for LG in the reshuffled government, and the Cabinet rejected his proposals. His response was to form a Council of Action for Peace and Reconstruction, based rather incongruously on the free churches, as a new vehicle for his ideas in the lead-up to the General Election. Frances wrote in her diary of 'this somewhat comic convention';[54] but LG's optimism was now fired up and he started talking openly of regaining power. He expected Labour to be the largest party with 275–90 seats, but no majority, while the Liberals – whom he still referred to as 'we' – might win twenty to forty seats.

> 'Under those circumstances,' said Ll.G, 'I would form a Government with Lansbury as nominal Prime Minister, but retaining the active leadership for myself. I would then proceed to formulate a devastating progressive programme, & go to the country again immediately upon it with a terrific campaign, & return with a majority of 150.'

This was complete fantasy. George Lansbury was even older than LG. He had been Labour leader since the debacle of 1931, but was now seventy-six and in poor health; he actually resigned before the election. Yet even Frances's scepticism was temporarily suspended. 'I believe he could do it, too.'[55]

The Council of Action was a predictable damp squib: most of the Nonconformist ministers in whom LG had placed his hopes dropped out. 'I *wish* he had not embarked upon this enterprise. I almost wrote this folly,' Frances wrote. 'It seems to me to be the most complete muddle, & scarcely anyone believing in it.'[56] She was so detached from his campaign that she actually went on holiday just as it was gearing up – with Muriel to Germany.* She clearly needed to get away.

> Left for Freudenstadt. *Very* tired and right at the end of my tether. Ll.G very busy preparing for his several meetings in connection with the C. of A. In very good form & extremely optimistic. He is always happy in action. It is doing nothing & marking time that bothers him.[58]

---

* Germany was an odd place to go for a holiday in 1935. On her return she wrote that 'Germany today is rather terrifying in her quiet and earnest preoccupation.'[57]

The result of the General Election dashed all LG's hopes. Labour won only 154 seats – barely half the number he had predicted. Of the 362 'progressive' candidates whom he endorsed, sixty-two were successful (eleven Conservative, seventeen Liberal and thirty-four Labour), but they did not form a coherent group. The Tories and their tame allies won 430 seats, so the so-called 'National' Government's huge majority was barely dented. Frances was philosophical.

> Election over & results out & Ll.G returned to Bron-y-de, not one atom the worse for his strenuous campaign, in which he virtually won three seats – his own & those of Megan & Gwilym. The Gov. large majority is no more than I had expected, or at least not very different. Ll.G nevertheless in good spirits & thinking already of organisation for the future. His resilience is amazing.[59]

She knew that this was the end of his serious political career, though he would continue to go through the motions.

> A *very* quiet weekend. Not a single telephone call for Ll.G from any political source, newspaper or otherwise. One would say that he had suffered a total eclipse. But he is already busy with plans for the future . . . It gives him a semblance of activity & so long as he has this he will be happy. He is already making arrangements to cover the next two years, & it is more than a possibility that at the end of that time he will have become again a political force.[60]

Did she really believe it? If anything, it was a gloomier prospect for Frances. Some time after the election she wrote a long and thoughtful article entitled 'A Parliamentary Impression'. It was a cry of disillusion with the irrelevance of Parliament in the face of the intractable depression. 'Let anyone follow the actual workings of the machine . . . and he cannot but be filled with a sense of fury at the apparent impotency of the House of Commons to deal with matters of supreme urgency.' She claimed to have listened to 'debate after debate' in which eloquent appeals on behalf of the unemployed by socialist Members from Clydeside and the North had 'never so much as ruffled the surface of the deep, deep sea of parliamentary inaction'.[61] She did not mention LG, but she was clearly thinking of the rejection of his plans, and implicitly contrasting the present futility of Parliament with the days of his prime – and her youth. She was probably also reflecting Tweed's ideas about the crisis of democracy and the case for dictatorship. It is not clear if her piece was ever published; but it shows again that Frances could have been a good journalist if her life had worked out differently.

In June 1936 she went to lunch with her old friend Muriel Beckett at her house near Hyde Park. Sir Robert Horne was there, with others who stirred memories of the heady life she had lived fifteen years ago, now lost beyond recall.

Brought back memories of the great days – Ll.G Prime Minister . . . The Peace Conference, with the Pembrokes & Derby & Henry Wilson, & all the glory & excitement of the post-war days.[62]

There was not much glory or excitement left to her now – nearing fifty, still unmarried, stuck in the country helping a demanding old man write his memoirs.

34

'IF LOVE WERE ALL . . .'

At least in the later 1930s Frances could accompany LG on his winter travels. As soon as the 1935 election was over they set off together for a working holiday in Morocco to get on with volumes V and VI of his *War Memoirs*. For once Sylvester did not go, but they were joined by the novelist Francis Brett Young and his wife Jessica, and LG's researcher Malcolm Thomson. LG's family supposedly did not know that Frances was going, so their departure involved some fast footwork by Sylvester.

> There had been a situation. Megan had intimated that she would go to the station with her father. L.G. therefore told her that he was motoring to Tilbury. He did no such thing. At the very last moment only, I had arranged the train journey so that there would be no clashing of the family and Frances.[1]

George Dyer, the chauffeur, told Sylvester that LG was 'miserable at having to leave Jennifer behind'.[2] By contrast there is little sense that Frances minded so much. For her part, Jennifer got used to being left alone at Christmas. Only in later life did she realise why Christmas carols always made her feel unhappy.

> Lavish presents and treats organised by 'Nanny' did not entirely make up for a feeling that she was deserted. Nanny Hackett wrote long letters informing Frances of all these treats and reporting various adorable little sayings of Jennifer. Frances kept and treasured them all, but it was not the same as being there.[3]

In a draft chapter of her autobiography Frances wrote that 'at every turn I tried to put the child's interest before my own.'[4] But in reality she always put LG first – and in her book as published she made no mention of Jennifer at all. When asked in a television interview if she regretted not having had children, she hesitated, then replied, 'Lloyd George was my child.' 'Not, I think, far from the truth' was Jennifer's comment.[5]

From Tangiers the travellers did remember to send a telegram for Christmas Day: JOYOUS XMAS FROM TWO TANGERINES WHO LOVE YOU,[6] followed by a large box of the fruit. In return Sylvester cabled Frances in Marrakesh: JENNIFER HAD ENJOYABLE XMAS AND VERY WELL – SYLVESTER.[7] Meanwhile their party was enlivened by the arrival of Winston Churchill, accompanied by his son Randolph, his daughter Diana with her husband Duncan Sandys, and his egregious scientific adviser 'Prof' Lindemann. Churchill was then writing his life of Marlborough, so he and LG spent the mornings competitively working: LG clocked up 160,000 words in six weeks. In the afternoons LG played golf with Frances while Winston painted. (He had given up golf in 1914 and never played again.) One evening they all had dinner with a local chieftain, and Frances and Jessica were invited to tea with the ladies of his harem, which Frances later recalled 'wasn't nearly as exciting as it sounds'.[8]

Frances went home on 9 January, the day before Maggie and Megan – with Sylvester – came out to replace her. Winston was still there and attended a dinner on LG's seventy-third birthday, when he and LG paid lavish tributes to each other. But the next day King George V became seriously ill, and they had to go home early. LG's party left Morocco on 20 January, the day the old king died, and they were back in time for LG to pay his respects to the new King Edward VIII a week later.

In August 1936, greatly daring, LG took Frances and Jennifer with him to Wales – not to Criccieth, but to south Wales. They stayed at St Donats, on the Glamorgan coast, while LG made his annual visit to the Eisteddfod, this year held at Fishguard. Then LG rejoined them at St Donats and they all visited Porthcawl. Sylvester marvelled at his effrontery.

He is an extraordinary man. He is trying to get the Council of Action going by drawing Nonconformity to him and yet he hawks about his mistress and what he, at any rate, believes is his own illegitimate child all round his native land.[9]

The next month LG went to Germany to see Hitler. This was one of the most controversial episodes of his later career. Hitler was not then universally recognised as the demon he later became. Like Mussolini in Italy, he was widely admired for the way he had restored order and national pride to his defeated country; LG particularly admired – even envied – the way Hitler was putting the unemployed back to work building autobahns and other public works, which was exactly what he himself had wanted to do in Britain for the past ten years. He applauded Hitler's dynamism: unfortunately he averted his eyes from his barbarous racial policies – though in so far as he knew of them, he thought them stupid. LG was not anti-Semitic: on the contrary, he had a romantic admiration for the Jews, was a strong supporter of the establishment of a Jewish national home in Palestine (he had been Prime Minister when Balfour issued his famous Declaration) and frequently praised the incomparable Jewish contribution to European civilisation. Nevertheless in 1936 he overlooked the racial basis of Nazi ideology. Hitler flattered him by receiving him as a great leader, and LG flattered Hitler in turn. This mutual admiration did not make LG an appeaser: he was quite clear, up to the outbreak of war, that Hitler's ambitions in Europe – like Mussolini's in Africa – should be firmly resisted. He strongly condemned Chamberlain's capitulation at Munich in 1938. Only after the war started did he become defeatist; and that was because, without an alliance with Soviet Russia, he did not see how Germany could be vanquished. He never ceased to proclaim that Hitler was a great man.

Frances did not go with LG to Germany, though Sylvester noted that she was 'sick because he did not bring her'.[10] But it was too high-profile a visit to take her safely. Anyway both Gwilym and Megan went, which inevitably ruled her out. LG did not forget, however, to get the Führer to sign a postcard of himself as a souvenir for Jennifer; he also brought her back a little Bavarian dress.

Two months later LG and Frances were off together again, this time to Jamaica. Sylvester came too, with his wife Evelyn, making a somewhat irregular quartet. Before leaving, LG held a family party at Churt, with Maggie and all his grandchildren. ('"All my own," he said laughingly.')

'He was in a rollicking mood,' Sylvester noted, 'for tomorrow he is off with Frances. He wanted to keep the family in good heart, particularly as they had decided to go back to town after dinner.' Having finished his *War Memoirs*, he was now starting his book on the Peace Conference, and took with him 135 books as well as 'piles of documents'.[11]

On the boat out, LG told Sylvester and Evelyn at breakfast one day that on 27 December Frances would have been with him twenty-five years, and paid tribute to her 'patience and toleration in having put up with me for all those years'.* Frances said that it had been 'reciprocal', but asked, 'Why this unusual amount of humility?' L.G. replied, 'It must be very difficult at times. Anyhow I am conscious of it, and that helps me to check myself.' He laughed and added, 'If only you are patient with me.'[12] That said, he continued to try her patience by being manically jealous – especially when Frances was in the swimming pool. 'L.G. . . . behaves like a madman at times,' Sylvester noted. 'Frances cannot be out of his sight for a moment, but that he is after her to see where she is and what she is doing.'[13]

They had barely arrived in Kingston before the Abdication crisis broke on 2 December. This was a question that touched LG and Frances closely. They had both liked the new king when he was Prince of Wales, and supported his right to love whom he pleased. But after fifteen years of discreet adultery with Freda Dudley Ward Edward had abandoned her in favour of a twice-married American, Wallis Simpson, whom he was determined to marry. 'If the little fellow marries her, I shall back him,' LG told Sylvester. 'The only people who will be against it are the aristocracy, and they are the rottenest lot of people.'[14] Yet at the same time he still held to the doctrine that he had spelled out to Frances twenty-five years earlier, that a man had no right to sacrifice his public duty for a woman. He almost decided to go straight home on the next boat, believing that he could help Edward keep both Mrs Simpson and his throne. On 4 December he cabled Gwilym and Megan supporting a morganatic marriage.

HOPE YOU ARE NOT GOING TO JOIN THE MRS GRUNDY HARRIERS WHO ARE
HUNTING THE KING FROM THE THRONE. IT IS FOR THE NATION TO CHOOSE ITS

* This is curiously precise, and puzzling. On 27 December 1911 LG had left for three weeks in the south of France with his old friend Lord Rendel (a Welsh parliamentary colleague from the 1890s). He and Frances dated their 'marriage' to January 1913. LG may simply have mistaken the date.

QUEEN BUT THE KING CANNOT BE DENIED RIGHT OF HUMBLEST CITIZEN TO
CHOOSE HIS OWN WIFE. HAD HE NOT DECIDED TO MARRY THE LADY NOT A
WORD WOULD HAVE BEEN SAID BY THE SCRIBES AND PHARISEES.[15]

Sylvester had actually booked a passage when the news came that
Edward had resolved to abdicate. LG immediately cabled Tweed:
DELIGHTED SQUALID CRISIS OVER. CANCELLED DEPARTURE.[16] He was glad
not to have to go home, but he was disappointed by the outcome.
'The woman Simpson is not worth the price the poor infatuated King
was prepared to pay,' he wrote to Megan. 'All the same if he wished
to marry her it could have been arranged quietly after the Coronation. By that time he might have been persuaded not to make a fool
of himself.'[17] He and Frances listened to Edward's broadcast 'with
wrung hearts', Frances later wrote. She believed that Baldwin had deliberately forced the issue while LG was out of the country. She was sorry;
but she accepted LG's moral code, by which she had lived her life, that
'so long as a man, or a woman, kept the conventions outwardly, the
public would excuse or ignore his private behaviour . . . It is a cynical
point of view . . . but I think it is nevertheless true'.

> 'If love were all . . .' says the Princess in a romantic novel which has . . .
> captured the imagination of all English speaking people.* 'If love were
> all . . .' she says in renouncing her dear lover. So many of the King's subjects
> had been obliged to place duty before love in the service of their country
> that they felt they surely had a right to expect him at least to *follow* their
> example.[18]

No doubt part of her would have liked LG to make for her the sort
of renunciation Edward had made for Wallis Simpson, as she had fantasised in her own romantic novel. But in reality she had adopted the
code of duty and sacrifice and now she held to it. There was romance
in sacrifice too.

Frances and LG seem to have had a happy time in Jamaica. Most
days they played golf on a hilly course that reminded LG of Wales,
with Sylvester playing on his own behind them. (Writing to Maggie,
of course, LG said that he played with Sylvester.) He did not like it

---

* The reference is to Anthony Hope's *The Prisoner of Zenda*, first published in 1893,
where the phrase forms the title of the penultimate chapter.

when Frances beat him, and was correspondingly delighted when he won; but Sylvester noted that he now talked about golf the whole time, and 'has completely put on one side the work he had on hand on his Peace book. I have never known that happen before . . . It shows he is thoroughly enjoying himself.'[19] There were other distractions too:

I must say there was plenty to distract him this morning in the swimming pool – almost naked feminine figures and little children whom he loves to watch. Oddly enough, he took grave exception to the scanty clothing worn by some of the women. An odd trait in a man who does not know the meaning of morality.[20]

By 27 December LG had written only 10,000 words, so they moved to Montego Bay, on the north side of the island, which was quieter. The change was clearly beneficial, as Sylvester described on 4 January 1937:

There he is with Frances every morning early on his own balcony having slept in a cool spacious bedroom with a communicating room with Frances . . . Every morning at some hour about 5 or 6 he wakes up and starts writing more of his Peace Book. He then has his early morning tea and oranges with Frances; then they breakfast, and then walk round the grounds together. There is nobody to interfere with them or say them nay.[21]

Jennifer meanwhile had been left at Churt in the care of Ann Parry, who sent Frances long letters describing her doings and sayings. On 4 December she wrote pointedly that Jennifer was 'now daily waiting for the arrival of a letter from you. I hope she will get one soon!!'[22] And a week later she reported that there was 'a letter in the offing for you and Mr Lloyd George . . . She told me that the beginning of it is going to be "I am enjoying myself but I would enjoy myself much more if you and *Taid* were here."'[23]

Following what was now the usual pattern, Maggie and Megan arrived on 14 January. But for some reason unexplained, Frances and Evelyn left Montego Bay almost a week earlier and returned to Kingston for a few days by themselves before sailing home via New York. It cannot have been that Frances and LG had quarrelled, since the letter she wrote him that evening was her happiest and most loving for years.

My darling man

It was a very sad journey over. I don't think I have ever been so miserable at leaving you. You have been so sweet to me, and the holiday has been such a happy one, that it seemed such a shame to bring it to an end, when I feel that really you and I ought *not* to have to separate! Now I shall just be counting the days until you arrive back in England again . . .

I feel that this holiday has done something definite for us – drawn us closer together and re-cemented the ties, and I am so very happy, my darling, because of this – and I was glad to see you happy too.

Fondest, dearest love to you & all tender thoughts –

Ever your own

P.[24]

LG felt just as desolate. 'There is a big gap now that they have gone,' Sylvester wrote.

L.G. asked me to go for a walk with him. He told me that as soon as they left this morning he started to write doubly hard and he had written 7,000 words since then – a prodigious task. To console us, he called for planter's punches, but he is very sad.[25]

LG wrote back to Frances, on Monday 11th, an ardent, almost elegiac letter written from the balcony where they had breakfasted so happily.

My dearest Jamaican sweetheart

Where are you? I always seem to be looking out for you & on the point of calling you & when I remember I am so sad. I have worked with frenzy in order to forget. But alas I don't. I thought this island the loveliest spot I had ever seen. It is so no longer. The verdure is just the same – the high wind roaring in the cotton tree that used to exhilarate me does so no longer. That delightful walk up the hill which I enjoyed so much is now stony & dreary. I wonder why? It is because the happiest holiday I ever had has come to an end. At first I could not realise it. The empty room – the vacant chair on the balcony. I cannot realise them. I turn round to boast that I have written so many words & there is no Frances to hear me. I seize my pad once more & write savagely in order to forget – but I cannot . . .

My fondest affection to you my sweetest pal. Best regards to Mrs Sylvester.

D.

The joy & glamour of this place have departed and I miss your sympathetic & loving help so much.[26]

Why did they cut short this idyllic holiday before they had to? These letters give no hint. Yet, as so often, Sylvester's diary suggests that all was still not straightforward between them.

This morning at 12 noon he called at the bungalow and asked me to go for a stroll and we walked up the hill as far as he and Frances were in the habit of going. He showed me where she fell down. He said that women were funny creatures. You thought you understood them, but you did not . . . He had at last given up trying to understand them and took things as a matter of course. He had known Frances 25 years; he had seen more of her during that time than any other woman, because she was with him in his work, and yet even now he did not profess to understand her. Tweed had ruined her life.

What on earth can LG have meant by this? That Tweed had spoiled the previously happy relationship she had with LG? He did not elaborate, but went on to speak of Tweed and Muriel, saying that they got on together because they were both selfish! Then he turned his bitterness on Jennifer.

He then talked of Jennifer. When she grew up she would simply use her mother to get out of her all she could. Even now 'Avollon' was hers, and she sort of received her mother for week-ends. She would no doubt welcome her mother's return – but it was only because it was that much excitement, and to know what she had brought her!

It is hard to credit that he could talk this way about a seven-year-old with whom he had always appeared to be besotted; but he was clearly having renewed doubts about whether she was after all his child. He said he wanted to show Sylvester some photographs. 'There was something about her which he could not quite make out.'

When we returned he took me to his bedroom and opened a drawer and took out 48 little photographs in different positions, and asked me what I thought of them. I said they showed a remarkable character in the child; great determination and absolute likeness of Frances. I knew what he was

after; it was as to whether I saw any resemblance of Tweed, and I said: I
see no resemblance whatever. 'Not in the mouth?' he enquired. I said 'No,
I don't' and I really did not. And I might have added but did not that the
chin was more like LG's chin than anyone else's. I think she is LG's kid. I
did not believe she was Tweed's child.[27]

A few days later LG 'wondered again whether there were any traces
of Tweed in those photographs of Jennifer'. Sylvester told him, 'Definitely no, I can see no trace at all'; and wrote that the next time LG
mentioned the matter he would tell him that he saw *his* character in
her.[28] That seems positive enough. Yet by the time he came to type up
his diary, some time later, something had caused Sylvester to change
his mind. He now added in parenthesis after the last sentence of the
previous entry: 'I believe otherwise now.'*

Evelyn Sylvester was taken ill en route from Kingston to New York,
so Frances had to cancel planned trips to Washington and Niagara to
look after her. 'I don't much like the responsibility, quite frankly,' she
wrote to LG, '& only hope I get her home without a collapse.'† Apart
from this, most of the very long letter she wrote from New York –
where she stayed at the Waldorf-Astoria, naturally – was filled with
her impressions of the city ('the sky scrapers have exceeded anything
I imagined – they are far more beautiful than I thought they could be')
and accounts of American opinion about the Abdication and the threat
of war in Europe.

The beginning and ending of this letter, however, repeated her belief
that their time in Jamaica had renewed and deepened their love.

My own darling man
    I was overjoyed to receive your lovely letter – it is the most beautiful
    love-letter I have ever had, & I have read it again & again. I am sorry you
    were so lonely darling, and that Jamaica is no longer so alluring, but perhaps

---

* It is not clear when these words were added. The most likely time is when Sylvester
was typing up the diary to use as raw material for his book *The Real Lloyd George*,
published in 1947, two years after LG's death. Needless to say, nothing of this appeared
in the book at that date, and not much more in the edition of his diary edited by Colin
Cross in 1975.
† LG sent money to pay Evelyn's medical fees. He was not always generous to his
employees, but on this occasion he acted handsomely.[29] He also passed on Evelyn's gratitude to Frances. 'What a dear you have been with her. She is ecstatic in your praise in
the letter she wrote to A.J. But I know how unselfish & considerate you are in your
sweet nature.'[30]

it will give you some consolation to know that you have made me very, very happy – and if I had not gone away I should not have had that wonderful letter! But I would have foregone even that to have been able to remain with you, & be at your side & within hearing of your darling voice. There has been such an aching void since I left you, and I realise now that the entire happiness of my holiday lay in being with you. Well, we shall have to look forward to being together at Churt. But you certainly have turned your loneliness to some account, & I only hope you are not working too hard . . .

Well, my darling, this is a very long letter, & I only hope you will persevere to the end of it! To reward you for getting as far as this (if you do!) I will tell you once more how much, how *very* much I love you, & how I long to be with you again . . .

My fondest love to you, my own darling man, & tender thoughts, & many longings.

Ever your own loving & devoted

P.[31]

Again one wonders if she does not protest too much. Was she exaggerating their happiness to cover some tensions over the previous weeks? Unusually she barely mentioned Jennifer, reporting only that she had heard that she was happy and had been very good at Christmas, which she had spent with Frances's parents. She seems to be straining to reassure LG that she loves him as much as ever.

Meanwhile Maggie and Megan had joined LG in Montego Bay. When they arrived they complained that their bath and lavatory were in the same room. 'By Jove,' he told Sylvester, 'I nearly said it was good enough for Frances, but just stopped myself in time; otherwise the fat would have been in the fire.'[32]

Frances wrote him one more letter before she left New York, mainly about Evelyn's illness and how much she was missing him. 'Churt will seem very desolate without you, my darling, & the days will go very slowly until you are back.'[33] For his part, LG took the opportunity, while his family were at church, to write back an important letter to greet her on her return.* Mostly he reported on the progress of his

---

* 'I am on the Balcony which you & I know so well & always think of so affectionately,' he wrote. Sylvester, however, noted that this balcony had another attraction: it overlooked the swimming pool, 'and no fresh belle went into that pool without his noticing her'.[34]

book. But he too reflected on the strains their relationship had come through and professed a renewed dedication on both sides. Typically he claimed to have had enough of the heat of Jamaica:

> By this time you are revelling in the welcome of Churt. Beware of colds. 80 in the shade for six weeks takes some getting over. I have had just as much as I can carry of it & want to get back – not to the fogs & rains & the damp chills – but to the warmth of a renewed & reinvigorated & I genuinely [believe?] a reformed companionship. Reformed & reconstructed on both sides. Keep off the grass darling & I promise you I will. We have trodden the cinders of hell these last few years – both of us. I more than I can [tell] you. Perhaps also you more than you have revealed to me. Often my heart has been chilled with despair & despondency & I foresaw nothing but a gloomy future with no ray of consolation. Work is only a distraction & I have worked like a maniac to divert my thoughts from poignant memories that sting. Let there be a second spring. The last week here gave me promise of it. I am yearning for light at eventide. Give it my darling. You alone can do so.[35]

There is so much here that requires comment. First, LG looks forward to 'a reformed companionship. Reformed and reconstructed on both sides': a rare recognition on his side, perhaps, that he too needed to change his ways, not just in the matter of sexual fidelity ('keep off the grass'), but also maybe by treating Frances with more consideration and less selfishness than he had sometimes shown her. Clearly he had been deeply hurt by her affair with Tweed: but he acknowledges that she too has 'trodden the cinders of hell these last few years'. One week into his seventy-fifth year he is painfully aware of his advancing age. He still hopes that he may have 'light at eventide', but he knows that he is dependent on Frances to save him from a bleak old age. Finally there is a suggestion that they came to some sort of concordat, with the promise of 'a second spring', in their last week together at Montego Bay – though still no explanation of why Frances left a week before she needed to.

Politically LG declared himself as usual in no hurry to re-enter the fray, but at the same time determined not to be written off.

> The doctor here excellent. He said after examining me – heart & chest – 'I wish all the men of 74 I meet were as fit as you' . . . so there is life in the old dog yet. And the rabbits & jackals & poisonous rattlers at Westmin-

ster will find that out in good time, as they did in Paris with Clemenceau when they thought him down & doomed for ever. He could not sell a thousand copies of his newspaper a few weeks before he became dictator at 78. That is how I feel now.[36]

LG and Sylvester between them give only glimpses of the two and a half weeks that Maggie and Megan spent in Jamaica. LG continued to write furiously, and played golf with Sylvester and Megan; how Maggie passed her time is not recorded. Soon after their arrival, Sylvester noted that LG was more difficult to handle when his family were there, since they wound him up and he would then take out his tension on Sylvester.[37] By the time they sailed for home, however, all was unwontedly peaceful. 'I have never been on any trip where he and his family have been so happy and . . . so free from squabbling. I told him so and he agreed.'[38]

But there was a dreadful row just before they reached Southampton. They were all gathered in LG's cabin for a drink before dinner when Megan raised her glass to thank '*Tada*' for a delightful holiday. LG, however, only raged at her for always being late and never getting up early to walk with him before breakfast, as her mother did (and, of course, as Frances did). 'But then *she* is a lady and you are not.' 'I have never heard you talk like that to Megan before,' Sylvester told him. 'It's about time,' LG replied. Later Sylvester found Megan in floods of tears. '"My God," she said to me, "it will be a long time before I forgive him for that."'[39] When they were filmed disembarking the next day Megan 'appeared with very swollen eyes, as she had been awake all night crying'.[40]

LG came home to face a minor crisis. While he had been away rumours had been circulating, almost for the first time, about his relations with Frances. A Liberal MP, Sir Harry Fildes, warned Sylvester of 'a whispering campaign against L.G. in his constituency about his immoral life. That he had taken Miss Stevenson with him on this trip & that there was a child.'[41] When Sylvester told LG, he snorted and went so red in the face that 'I thought he would have a fit'.[42] He responded with an amazing show of blustering defiance, to be conveyed through the long-suffering Sylvester, mixing outraged denial with a spurious threat to link his case with that of the ex-king, claiming that 'the whole thing had been started by the Government whips'.

He would send private detectives down to the Boroughs to find out who it was who was spreading these slanderous statements and he would take criminal proceedings against them. After all, he could not have done his book without Frances. She was the only person who had been there the whole time. To bring a charge of this kind against an old fellow who had had a serious operation six years ago, which has taken away some of his vitals, was a preposterous and ridiculous thing. The suggestion was that he was the father of Tweed's child . . . 'I have a letter from Tweed saying that he is responsible for the child.'

He recalled the time he had sued the Sunday *People* for making similar allegations in 1909. Now, as then, he was confident that 'the old girl will stand by me'.

'I made him pay £1000 for suggesting that I was capable of anything of the kind, and now I am seventy-four. If they say anything about Frances you can exaggerate. Tell them she is a graduate of London University with honours and that she is very able . . . As long as I am writing these books, Frances is absolutely essential to me. She knows French. She knew Foch, Briand, Clemenceau, Bonar and all the ministers . . .

'I am fighting not only my own battle, but the battle of my late King. I will mix both these things up so that there will be such a stink at the coronation that it will go right through the world, and *they* will be responsible . . . If they do it, I will be like Samson. I will pull down the pillars to kill the Philistines, even if I am overwhelmed.'[43]

Most of this was utterly irrelevant. Of course he did not expect Sylvester to believe a word of it; LG was only rehearsing the smoke-screen of lies he expected Sylvester to throw up on his behalf. Sylvester knew better than anyone that he adored Jennifer and desperately wanted to believe that she was his. Clearly there never was a letter from Tweed admitting paternity; while the claim that LG was not up to fathering a child since his operation is particularly absurd, since Jennifer was born nearly two years before his operation, when he was only sixty-six. There was no comparable scandal in Edward's relations with Wallis Simpson that he could mix up with his own. Nor was there any need to exaggerate Frances's credentials: her degree and her ability were real. The fact that she was his secretary was a legitimate reason for her going on holiday with him, but it in no way precluded her being his mistress as well. Finally it is by no means certain that by this date Maggie would have stood by him again as she did in 1909.

The next day Sylvester dined in a private room at the House of Commons with Fildes and Sir William Letts, the High Sheriff of Caernarvonshire, who was the recipient of the allegations that had been circulating in the county. 'I got off my chest the observations which L.G. had made. I knew that Sir William knew much more than he cared to admit. When we parted I had left nothing to the imagination of either.' Sylvester added, with some self-satisfaction: 'As Sir William said good night, he added: "I don't know what L.G. pays you, but judging the way you have argued tonight he ought to pay you £10,000 a year." I replied, "Will you tell *him* that?"'[44]

Nothing came of this scare: LG got away with it again. Meanwhile he had 'got the wind up' and proposed to go to Criccieth 'to be with Dame Margaret at Easter merely for appearance sake'. He planned to show his constituents home movies taken by Sylvester at Churt and in Jamaica 'to show what a loving family they are', and had the gall to demand why Sylvester had not taken more footage of Maggie and less of Frances![45]*

On 24 January 1938, LG and Maggie celebrated their golden wedding anniversary – in Antibes. But before the family came out, LG had already been there for several weeks with Frances. Unusually, she had returned home to spend Christmas with Jennifer. During the interval Gwilym came out to keep his father company. But there was another interval between Gwilym going home and Maggie coming out when Frances could possibly return. LG begged her to come.

> Latest news. G. leaves Janry 2nd. Maggie arrives January 10th . . . That leaves 8 days for you if you think it worth-while? I certainly do – but then I would not have to leave such an enchanting little companion in order to spend my time with any old grognard – except myself.[47]

It was not likely that Frances would leave LG on his own for eight days. She did go back to Antibes in early January – and on the way home ran into Sylvester at Folkestone, on his way back from escorting

---

* Sylvester was placed in a similar difficulty when Megan asked to see the press cuttings from Jamaica, which were full of references to Frances. He quickly had to rustle up a new scrapbook containing only the references to Megan and her mother.[46]

Maggie and Megan as far as Paris! As if the coming and going was not already farcical enough, Frances then went back a third time at the end of the month. Even as LG was preparing to celebrate his golden wedding, Sylvester wrote, he was already planning how to get rid of his family as soon as possible after the event so that Frances could return.

> Moreover he is quite ready and lying in wait for Megan if she should be at all awkward or difficult. There is all the material for a first-class row to celebrate the day!

'All the above,' Sylvester added, 'was confirmed absolutely by Tweed. Incidentally it shows how complete is the communication between Tweed and Frances. F. gives everything to Muriel and Muriel meets with Tweed and gives it to him. That is why I keep in contact with T.F.T.'[48]

LG marked his seventy-fifth birthday on 17 January more quietly than usual, saving the big celebrations for the following week. Maggie and Megan had arrived on 12 January, followed on the 21st by the rest of the family: Dick with his second wife, June; Gwilym and Edna; Olwen and her elder daughter Margaret. LG was not overjoyed to see them, but only wanted to 'get rid of them', sending them off the next day on a motor trip to Monte Carlo, so that he could get on with his writing.[49] Maybe he remembered that the 21st was the silver anniversary of his second 'marriage' – though as far as we know he did not mark it by writing to Frances.

The golden anniversary was celebrated as a great international event, with Sylvester fielding shoals of congratulatory telegrams and flowers, as well as journalists and photographers from all round the world. The whole family went for lunch with the Churchills at Cannes, where Winston made a speech; then in the evening there was a family dinner – including Sylvester – at which toasts were drunk and an inscribed loving cup passed round; then there were fireworks and home-grown entertainment in which Olwen and Gwilym dressed up as their parents: Olwen as LG and Gwilym in drag as Maggie. 'I have never laughed so much in my life,' Sylvester wrote. There was only one sour presence. Megan was 'very out of it all and very angry'. Sylvester had some sympathy with her distaste for the charade that was being played.

This has been a most interesting day. The world has paid tribute to L.G. and Dame Margaret on their golden-wedding day. What would it think if it knew that for the greater part of every year L.G. lives with another woman and even tonight was only eager to get rid of his family so that she could return to him? Real knowledge of the facts makes these celebrations pure humbug – on his part.[50]

The family stayed on in Antibes for another week, during which LG complained to Sylvester that Megan was making difficulties about returning. 'She liked her fun, but she would not let him have his. He said it was necessary for him to have Frances to help him with his book. J.T. and Frances are the only people who know the papers.'[51]* In the event Megan went home with the others on 31 January.

When L.G. said good-bye to his family, he was much touched and almost wept. Yet I know he was only waiting to get rid of them all and welcome Frances tomorrow. What can one make of him?[53]

Frances arrived back in Antibes on 1 February, and she and LG stayed there for nearly another three weeks, working on his book and playing golf. They returned to England hurriedly on 20 February as a result of a tip-off from Sylvester that Anthony Eden – the glamorous young Foreign Secretary appointed by Baldwin after Samuel Hoare's resignation in 1935 – was at loggerheads with Baldwin's successor, Neville Chamberlain, over the appeasement of Mussolini and was about to resign. LG was delighted, and sent a telephone message via Frances encouraging him in his resolve: 'Tell Eden that the country is on the look-out for a young man with ideals, brains and courage, that Eden has the first two, but he has not yet shown he has courage . . . If he takes a strong line, he is made.'[54] But in the Commons LG showed signs of ageing. He accused Chamberlain bluntly of having been 'beaten by the dictators' and of having sacrificed the only man in the govern-ment who wanted to stand up to them; but then came off worst in a clash with the Prime Minister.[55] 'For the first time in my experience,' Sylvester wrote, 'he made many lapses of the tongue, which the House had to correct.'[56]

---

* This, Sylvester noted angrily, was 'absolute balls. Frances only knows the papers when they are asked for by him and then they are only there because they were sent there by me from London. I said nothing, but thought a lot.'[52]

On 1 March (St David's Day) LG and Maggie visited Cardiff to be presented with a gold plate paid for by the Welsh people. Crowds lined the streets as they drove to the theatre. LG was nervous before his speech, with good reason, as he hymned the institution of marriage to an audience ignorant of the reality of his domestic life.

> I need hardly say that my wife and I are of different temperaments. One is contentious, combative and stormy. That is my wife. Then there is the other partner, placid, calm, peaceful and patient. That is me. But in spite of the fundamental differences in our dispositions, we have lived in perfect harmony for fifty years. Now that is a great tribute to the institution of marriage.

'To this day,' Dick wrote some years later, 'I can hear the peals of laughter with which my mother met this ridiculous statement. It was unquestionably his ability to make her laugh that so endeared my father to my mother.'[57] Sylvester commented that LG's telegraphic address should be 'Audacity'.[58]

LG displayed further audacity a fortnight later when he and Frances visited Paris, taking Jennifer with them, and he brazenly allowed himself to be photographed holding Jennifer's hand, as he would never have done in England. 'It looks as though I was allowed to exist in France even if not in England,' she reflected many years later, 'but I was described, as always, as F's adopted daughter.'[59] LG laid a wreath on Foch's tomb at Les Invalides, showed Jennifer Napoleon's tomb and death-mask, and then went to see Clemenceau's house in the rue Franklin, still trailed by photographers. Sylvester was horrified.

> Hand in hand with Jennifer, he took her from room to room. A very enter-prising French photographer asked me the name of 'the little girl' but I avoided an answer. Frances looked on with evident satisfaction. The result may be a sad page for L.G., especially when the family see it. L.G. said later to J: 'Oh, yes, you will be in the papers all right', & was obviously very much amused at the idea.[60]

The next day he had an appointment with the Prime Minister Leon Blum; but before that he took Frances and Jennifer to Versailles and got back a quarter of an hour late. 'He was late through buggering about with Jennifer at Versailles,' Sylvester complained. 'I thought this distinctly bad taste.'[61] He even took Jennifer with him to his meeting with Blum.[62]

Frances and LG then went back – for a fourth time – to Antibes, while Sylvester accompanied Jennifer and her nanny back to England, where he had to face the family. 'Megan is bloody annoyed about the Paris visit, and so are the rest of the family. Only Dame Margaret is decent to me.'[63] For several weeks Sylvester continued to suffer the family's anger about this Paris jaunt.

35

WAR AGAIN – AND TWO DEATHS

As the shadow of war once again loomed over Europe, LG felt horribly ambivalent. Throughout the 1930s he had been robustly critical of the weakness of Baldwin and Chamberlain in the face of the dictators. In 1935–6 he had been all for sending arms to help the Abyssinians fight Mussolini and had denounced the Hoare–Laval Pact in the Commons in a blistering speech described by Churchill as 'one of the greatest Parliamentary performances of all time'.[1] He had condemned the government's mealy-mouthed neutrality in the Spanish civil war and even proposed to go to Spain himself to lend support to the anti-fascists. But by the time of Munich he feared that Czechoslovakia was indefensible: as one of the architects of the 1919 settlement that was supposed to have enshrined the principle of self-determination, he had some guilty sympathy for the Sudeten Germans. He scorned Chamberlain's self-deluding shuttle diplomacy as 'a ghastly muddle' whose only result had been to leave the country facing the prospect of renewed war with Germany 'without friends'.[2] Throughout 1939 he urged that the only way of effectively containing Hitler was by alliance with Soviet Russia.

But his trumpet gave out an increasingly uncertain sound. At the time of Munich, Sylvester noted, LG was 'sick' at not being consulted by the government; but actually he was 'thinking far more about appointing a new farm manager at Churt than about the international situation'.[3] Several times he went up to London intending to speak in the House, but came home without doing so. Twice he did not even attend important debates because he preferred playing with Jennifer.[4] When he did speak he was a shadow of his old self. 'It is the first time in my life that

I have not been able to formulate a clear idea of my own as to what should be done,' he told Sylvester in July 1939.[5] The Molotov–Ribbentrop Pact cast him into despair. 'I have not seen L.G. so pessimistic, ever.'[6] On 3 September he came up from Churt with Frances, stopping in Richmond Park on the way, to listen to Chamberlain's announcement of the declaration of war on the car radio. In a short speech in the Commons he struck a positive note, recalling the united national effort of 1914–18: 'After four and a half years, terrible years, we won a victory for right. We will do it again.' But over lunch he asked gloomily: 'Can anyone tell me how we can help Poland?'[7] During the months of the 'phoney war' he continued to urge a compromise peace to avert another bloody stalemate, which he believed neither side could win.

His carping pessimism, often slipping privately into outright defeatism, was difficult for Frances. Conventionally patriotic herself, she was embarrassed by his negative attitude and alarmed that he risked tarnishing his reputation as the undaunted leader in the previous war. More than once she was so 'fed up' that she asked Sylvester to arrange appointments for him that would enable her to get away for a few hours.[8] She was anxious for him to return to office – if not in the Cabinet, then at least with a real job to do that would commit him fully to the national cause. Churchill had joined the government on the outbreak of war, and he was keen to get his old friend back in harness, if only as a symbol of national unity and resolve. The two old warriors had lunch in December. 'Tweed has it from Frances that nothing definite was said,' Sylvester recorded, 'but that "It's all right", meaning that Winston intends to get L.G. into the Government when the chance arises.'[9] Five months later LG played an important part in Chamberlain's replacement by Churchill, telling the Prime Minister bluntly – in his last great speech in the House – that he should set an example of sacrifice, since 'there is nothing that can contribute more to victory in this war than that he should give up the seals of office'.[10] But Churchill did not immediately bring LG in. To Sylvester, LG pretended that it suited him to stay out for the moment, still insisting that his time would come. But Frances told a different story.

'There is no doubt that he was very much upset when he realised that the War Cabinet was fixed . . . He had an idea that he would be a member. Since then he has fortified himself with the idea that he will be given Agriculture or Food. Food production is what he wants.'

Lord Dawson had examined LG and pronounced him fit for that level of work, not running a department, but chairing some sort of council. Churchill had asked him to lunch, when he expected to be offered something of this nature; but Frances feared it was too late, and she was right. LG came back looking 'very grim', saying he was 'glad to be out of this War'. But Sylvester thought this was 'sour grapes' because he was not offered anything.[11]

Frances told Sylvester that 'she had had a very straight talk with L.G., who had been talking of nothing but peace'.

> 'If you were in the Government, you would not be talking peace,' she had said to him. She continued to me: 'He talks about giving in without fighting because he thinks we are beaten. The whole point is that he hates Neville and the Government so much he would like to see them beaten, and he would like to see the English beaten. I said to him: "Don't you make any mistake; if you are beaten, Wales will be beaten also."'[12]

This was desperate stuff, born of a sour combination of jealousy and frustration.

In June 1940, following the fall of Paris and the entry of Italy into the war, Churchill did offer LG a place in the War Cabinet. 'Frances and I have both impressed upon him the importance of his accepting,' Sylvester wrote. 'Now the situation has deteriorated so much that it is vital that L.G. should be inside. He has such vision, and I have such faith in him still . . . But he now sticks his toes in and says: "I won't go in with this crowd", which means Neville.'[13] But he was critical of Churchill too, complaining that he had not appointed a proper War Cabinet of experienced men such as he had had around him in 1916–18. 'Winston is an able man but he is not a leader.'[14] On 25 June Frances took him to task again.

> Frances told me that she had had a row with L.G. last night. She had told him categorically that he had done absolutely nothing to help his country in this war. She said that he had been very annoyed with her and had said it was a damned lie . . . What I am afraid of is that it will be thought that L.G. is waiting to play the part of Laval or Pétain, and I am genuinely alarmed about it.[15]

The following year Churchill made the same suggestion in the House of Commons. Sadly, there was a good deal of truth in it.

Meanwhile Frances had another anguish to contend with. In November 1939 Sylvester had written that 'F. is undoubtedly still up to her eyes in love with Tweed'.[16] The only evidence he cited was that she had rung the office wanting to speak to Tweed, but there is no reason to think it was not true. All this time Tweed had remained an apparently loyal member of LG's staff, writing him several long memos that autumn about the war situation and possible peace terms. Yet the threat of blackmail still hung in the air. In January 1940, for instance, LG proposed to cut back his Council of Action to save money.

> Tweed told me that he did not intend to see L.G. shut down the C. of A. merely to save a few more thousands to divide between his children. 'I shall return any retainer he sends to me,' he said. 'I shall insist on being fired: once I am fired, all my loyalties to him cease: I am a free man and I can say all I know.'[17]

But then Tweed fell ill again. He collapsed at home in the early hours of 27 February and was taken to Hendon Cottage Hospital, where Frances visited him – without LG's knowledge – on 3 March.* By 8 March *The Times* was reporting that he was 'out of immediate danger', though unlikely to be able to leave hospital for some weeks.[19] While he struggled to recover, LG celebrated fifty unbroken years as an MP with tributes in the House of Commons and a packed meeting in the Caernarvon Pavilion. Tweed paid his own handsome tribute to his old Chief, which glossed over the ambivalence of their relations over the past fifteen years.

> And amongst those anonymous millions who have not forgotten twenty-five years ago and whose regard and affection is undimmed by neither time nor the fortunes of politics, please include one who in humble duty signs himself, T.F.T.[20]

---

* Frances had been out of London visiting Jennifer, who was now at boarding school in Colwyn Bay. Suspicious that she might be seeing Tweed, LG made enquiries about what time she had left Chester. But she covered her tracks successfully, telling LG that she did not get back to London until 2.15, when in fact she had been at Hendon by one o'clock.[18]

Two weeks later Tweed was dead. He was just fifty.

According to the *Evening Standard*, his death was 'sudden and completely unexpected'.

> He had apparently made a complete recovery from his attack of coronary thrombosis, and was sitting up in bed, smoking his pipe and solving a cross-word puzzle. He was expected to be able to get up next week. His nurse found him dead, with his pipe still burning.[21]

The obituaries – which Frances preserved – were full and generous. One tribute called Tweed 'the wizard behind the wizard'. The *Manchester Guardian* described him as 'an original among political organisers' and regretted that 'his boldness and remarkable fertility of ideas never found their full scope'.[22] LG issued a statement praising his gallant war record and his political work.

> Colonel Tweed was one of the most capable and experienced political organisers in this country. He had an unusual mastery of the political issues of the day and an exceptionally sound and penetrating political instinct. His sudden death is a real loss to the causes with which he was associated.[23]

But privately he told Sylvester: 'He was not a very satisfactory fellow', and added, with staggering ungenerosity: 'I have nothing to thank him for.'[24]

LG gave out that he would not attend the cremation at Golders Green; but then Olwen mysteriously rang Sylvester to ask him to keep two seats for her 'on the left hand side of the chapel'. Sylvester described a bizarre occasion.

> I went to the funeral with Finney, Miss Smithers and Miss Dann. There I met Frances and Muriel in deep mourning. They were obviously terribly upset. No sooner had we taken our seats than L.G. entered, with Lady Carey Evans; they took their seats on the left-hand side. *Never* have I seen him attend a funeral service thus. He is always most particular about his attire on all occasions. Today must have been a studied insult to the dead, and intended to persecute the living in the person of Frances. He wore a blue suit, a blue overcoat, a blue hat, with a dark tie that was not even black. His face was white – knowing him, he was het up. He sat in the front seat, well towards the left. As he looked towards the pulpit on the

right, he could see Frances in the second row and watch her every movement and reaction.

Outside, after the service, he searched the wreaths looking for one from
Frances. There was one – but he failed to find it.

'What was the motive for this extraordinary behaviour?' Sylvester
asked; and answered in a word: 'Jealousy. He is eaten up with it.'

Afterwards, on the telephone, Frances told me that he was literally perse-
cuting her to death. He had twitted her about being upset. He wondered
whether she would be upset when *he* died. He criticised her deep mourning.
In the end, and unwisely as I think, she said she had confessed to L.G. that
she had been very fond of Tweed, that Mrs Tweed had been very kind to
her and had taken her home, where they had had a frank talk.[25]

This must have been another piquant conversation, between the wife
whom Tweed had rejected and the lover he could not marry. The next
day Louise Tweed wrote to LG thanking him for attending the funeral,
saying that nothing would have pleased her husband more than to have
known that he was there.[26] Two days later she and her two grown-up
children wrote Frances a rather more genuine joint letter thanking her
'very deeply' for her 'very charming and sympathetic letter and also
for the beautiful flowers'.

It is a great solace to us all to know that you share equally with us our
grief at this time and we do sincerely trust that you will keep your promise
to visit us . . .
    We are very happy to have had the opportunity of knowing you and
trust that we will continue to do so.[27]

In his will Tweed left £37,348. Most of it went to his family, with
£500 to the Benevolent Fund for Liberal Agents; but he also bequeathed
£2,000 to Frances and £500 to Jennifer. By contrast, Muriel received
only the *income* on £1,000. Even more significantly, one-fifth of any
remaining estate was to be added to an existing arrangement made
between Frances, Muriel and their solicitor John Morris in 1931 settling
money on Jennifer.[28] This is the strongest indication that Tweed
believed Jennifer was his daughter: why else should he feel any responsibility for her? That was certainly Sylvester's interpretation. 'My

impression is that this will prove beyond doubt that Tweed really claims the parentage of the child. If this is true, what a smack for L.G.!'[29]

When the will was published in July the bequest to Frances – '£2000 for L.G.'s Woman Secretary' – was reported to be 'in partial repayment of a loss incurred on an investment taken on my advice'.[30] Did the press really believe this, or were they hinting at more than they could say? Clearly they sensed a story: the London *Evening News* printed photographs of Frances and Tweed, and the phone rang at Churt so much that Frances was forced to tell LG why. 'He was so angry that he went to his bedroom.'[31] Ten days later Sylvester – in London – wrote that he had 'not yet got the real reactions of L.G. on Tweed's Will, but judging by the fact that Miss Smithers [his secretary] can get no instructions because things at Churt are so difficult, it does not look too good'.[32]

With that Colonel Tweed disappears from the story – apart from one sad footnote. When Louise too died, less than four years later, Sylvester attended her funeral at Golders Green. It was 'the most pitiful service I ever attended – only three present, including myself'.[33] By then Frances was married, so she could not easily have attended even if she had wanted to.

In August LG went to Criccieth as usual, and stayed there most of the autumn. The reason was that he was terrified of air-raids. He had been nervous in 1917, but now that he was older it was much worse. 'For a man of L.G.'s distinction and eminence, I have never seen such a funk,' Sylvester wrote scornfully.[34] Publicly he contributed defiant articles to the newspapers with upbeat headlines such as 'Hitler Cannot Frighten Us' and 'Freedom: Let's Fight For It'.[35] But privately he was more and more negative, talking of 'nothing else but bombs and invasion. He is very jumpy.' He continued to insist that Hitler was 'a prodigious genius' and listened carefully to the preposterous Lord Haw-Haw on the radio.[36] Before leaving for Wales he set his workforce to build him a large and embarrassingly luxurious underground shelter at Churt – 'a monumental affair' cut fifty feet into the sand, with brick and concrete walls and steel girders. 'It resembled in every particular a big underground station like Piccadilly tube,' Sylvester wrote.[37] 'It has certainly not cost less than £6,000 and it is the talk of the place.'[38] LG justified himself by pointing out that Churchill slept underground in London. But Frances hated it. 'She frankly did not like being underground as she got claustrophobia'; and she thought it made him look 'a bloody fool'.[39]

Yet LG still imagined that he had a role to play in the war. In one extraordinary letter from Criccieth he actually suggested that he hoped to replace Churchill.

> Hitler does not fear Winston. In his best days he was an impetuous bungler, now he is hesitant – a combination of rashness and hesitating decisions . . .
>
> I am sure Hitler fears him less than he fears me. That seems conceited. But read Mein Kampf and recall what he said to Phipps.[40]*

But Frances was sceptical, as she told Sylvester: 'L.G. has some idea he is coming in on the peace settlement, that he will be able to make peace where Winston won't. But when you see him in the state in which he is you wonder whether he would be capable.'[41]

She did hope that some employment could be found for him, however. While he was still at Churt – with the Battle of Britain raging overhead – Frances wrote to Muriel that she hoped to be able to come and see her.

> On the other hand it is still on the cards that Ll.G. will go into the Gov. & then I don't know what will happen. I feel on the whole it would be the best thing for him to have a job. I shall go crackers if he goes on like this. We spent the whole night in the air raid shelter, & I hardly got a wink of sleep . . .
>
> The air battle was thrilling.[42]

LG came back to Churt briefly in September, but did not stay long, as Frances explained frankly to Sylvester.

> 'I am awfully sad about L.G. too. I have tried my best to persuade him to believe that the chances are that one does not get hit, and that if he takes a proper job of work he would not have the time to think about it. But you cannot budge him. He is more terrified than a child . . . He was not so bad when he came back here, but two or three nights here have reduced him to a doddering old man. He does not want to go. He was almost in

* Sir Eric Phipps was the British Ambassador to Germany who had accompanied LG on his visit to Hitler in 1936. Presumably Hitler had said something flattering to Phipps, which LG took seriously.

tears when he went. It was pathetic. He said: "I cannot help it. You must forgive me for being like this. If I stay here it will just kill me." And of course it would . . . The only thing for him to do is to go to Wales.'[43]

LG stayed at Criccieth until just before Christmas. Shortly before the outbreak of war he had bought a Georgian farmhouse with thirty-seven acres of land near Llanystumdwy, presumably with an eye to his eventual retirement – though it is difficult to see how he could have lived there with Frances, with Maggie just down the road. He wanted to prove that he could grow fruit in Wales as successfully as in Surrey; at any rate, planning the cultivation of Ty Newydd gave him a pretext for staying in Wales. His absence gave rise to the last exchange of letters with Frances, though she also telephoned every morning, presumably on the excuse of discussing business. Between the lines of her usual assurances that she was missing him, she was clearly relieved that he had gone. Her graphic accounts of the bombing certainly did not encourage him to hurry back.

My own darling

I have been so sad since you left, as I hated your going, & would have liked so much to accompany you. But I think you were wise not to stay. We had a most peaceful night on Saturday night – absolute & complete silence, but last night was *very* noisy again, & they have been at it again this morning. We had a warning yesterday from 4.30–6.30, & another one at 8 o'clock, which lasted till 2.0, with wave after wave of aeroplanes, & guns, & bombs somewhere not far off . . . Edna & Gwilym & David* came to supper here, & after supper we went out & watched the fireworks. Edna & Gwilym had an awful time on Friday night – a bomb fell about 50 yards from the Park Lane Hotel . . .

It seems to me that one has either got to stay in the shelter almost continuously, or else ignore the warnings altogether, which we are doing at the moment. Poor London seems to have had a very bad time last night . . .

Do let me have a little line to tell me what you are doing & thinking. I miss you so much, my darling, & do so love being with you & am very lonely without you. But if you are well, & moderately happy (!) that is all right . . .

Fondest & tenderest love to you, my sweetheart, from your devoted P.[44]

---

* David was Gwilym and Edna's elder son, then aged eighteen.

Her next letter gave more details of the bombing ('They seemed to be dropping bombs at intervals all night long, & finished up with a couple at 5 o'clock this morning that nearly brought Avalon down like a pack of cards!'), spiced with criticism of Churchill. Frances had never trusted Winston and now seemed happy to feed LG's jealousy. 'It seems terrible to think of him, with his faulty judgment, as dictator of this country.' She repeated that LG was better off where he was for the present; reported that Jennifer was happy at school*, and ended positively:

All is well here, so don't worry, my darling. If you *could* come back for a flying visit any time, it would of course be lovely, but don't fret about anything – just keep yourself fit for the time when it becomes quite clear that you will have to take a hand in things – which time is not so far off, I feel sure. And the most important thing is that you should be well & fit.
   Fondest & tenderest love to you, *cariad*, & many loving thoughts from
   Your devoted
   P.[45]

LG did not want to come back, but he plainly felt a bit ashamed at staying away.

As to returning I am perplexed. The danger immensely greater than when we left. My present idea is to go up for one day to London & spend another at Churt – then return here for another fortnight . . . Feel that as Father of the House I ought to be there – first sitting under bombardment . . .†
   Love to you all
   D.[46]

On 30 September Sylvester took his courage in both hands and wrote what he called a 'most audacious memorandum' urging LG to put aside his personal feelings and join the government, citing the example of Clemenceau in 1917. 'The country is crying out for the old patriot who rescued it from destruction in the Great War.' He was mortified when LG first ignored it, and then – when pressed – maintained that there

---

* Jennifer's school had been evacuated to Chatsworth, in Derbyshire, when the buildings in Colwyn Bay were requisitioned by the government.
† LG had been Father of the House since 1929.

was no comparison: 'Clemenceau had power; I shall wait until Winston is bust.'[47]

Sylvester was not alone in his urging. A good many people who did not realise how badly he had aged still hoped to see LG – now seventy-seven – back in office. J. L. Garvin, the long-serving editor of the *Observer*, for instance, believed that he might be good for only six hours a day, but 'it would be six hours of radium'.[48] But it is curious that two of the keenest should have been those who knew best that LG was not up to it. In fact Frances and Sylvester wanted him back in office not so much to save the country as to save him from the pitiful decline into which they saw him falling. As for LG himself, his motives were both contradictory and discreditable. His contempt for Chamberlain, his jealousy of Churchill and his fear of air-raids were all very human; his horror of another war and his despair about how Britain alone was ever going to win it were honourable and – until the Soviet Union and America entered the war – quite rational. To be fair he never envisaged surrender to Hitler; he wanted to beat off the invasion threat before he talked peace. But his calculation that he could somehow come in and pick up the pieces when Churchill had failed was unworthy as well as unrealistic. One moment he was saying that he would take only a non-executive role to do with agriculture or food supply; the next he was saying that he must have power. In truth he knew perfectly well that he was not fit for the latter, and it was doubtful whether he was even up to the former; but his pride would not let him admit it. All his blustering prevarications were just excuses for not facing the reality that he was past it.

On 1 October LG wrote again from Criccieth, begging Frances to use the shelter at Churt. 'A piece of shrapnel would tear through the roof of the bungalow & destroy or disfigure you. Do try.' He also reported that German planes had been bombing the Caernervonshire quarries, so 'I am therefore not out of it altogether'.[49] Frances wrote back the next day. She was clearly enjoying running Churt in his absence.

> My own darling man
>   It is nice to hear your voice on the telephone & it sounds very strong & well. Don't worry about us here – I am certain we are all right. There is plenty to do, & I seem to be fully occupied all day long, as there are a good many things to be seen to at Bron-y-de, & although I say it as shouldn't,

I think it gives people there, and here [at Avalon], a feeling of confidence for me to be about, as your representative! . . .

You will have fun planning Ty Newydd . . . It will be good for you to have something to occupy your mind – & it is useful work that you will be doing. So don't worry, darling, any more than you need. It would be lovely, of course, if you could come back here, but I don't want you to do anything that will harm you, & these explosives are very startling – though of course you get used to them. I wish you could see us all here in the shelter tucked up for the night! We have managed to get 5 camp beds in & are most cosy. It is really rather fun, now that we have got used to it . . .

Fondest love to you, my darling, & tender thoughts from
Your very devoted
P.[50]

LG's next letter again made the most of the small amount of enemy activity he was suffering at Criccieth: he was now building another shelter there, large enough 'to accommodate the whole household'. He declined to 'run the gauntlet of the incessant bombardment in & around London merely for the privilege of hearing a speech from Winston explaining the Dakar fiasco'; and still clung to the delusion that he would yet be needed.

I am convinced that I can be helpful if I can preserve my health & nerve for a few more months. The people are not ready to pay any heed to good counsel. They still cherish illusions of 'complete victory' . . . All this may sound UNHEROIC but I am convinced it is sound . . . The nation must have a sense of failure of the existing leadership & of the existing order . . . I cannot serve effectively in the intervening period.[51]

Frances continued to humour him – 'Your time will surely come, & the great thing is to keep fit until that time arrives . . . I have complete faith in your political instinct. I can't remember any time when you have not been right in the long run' – while subtly discouraging him from coming to London with her own version of the Blitz spirit.

There is no point in taking all those risks . . . Even if one escapes unin-jured, the bombs when they drop are really very alarming . . . On the other hand, when you see how very little damage is done – except in the big towns, of course – you realise that there is no need to be frightened – it is the noise that is the worst part of it.[52]

On 15 October LG made a speech in Caernarvon expounding in relatively moderate terms his sombre view of the state of the war. But his letters were increasingly wild. He still refused to join what he called 'the present crowd'. 'Winston,' he wrote jealously, 'now feels that he is God & the only God.' It was no use his speaking in the House unless he could say what he really thought and 'if I did so they would say I was nagging & defeatist'; and 'still less use talking to Winston as he would not listen'.[53]

This was sad stuff. LG had finally become a bitter old man. Cut off in Criccieth, he did not know what he was talking about: he merely raged about everyone and everything, making unsubstantiated predictions of catastrophe in the Mediterranean, which were not fulfilled. Frances was finding it impossible to reason with him; and Sylvester heard that he was becoming more and more difficult with his family too. 'He has not lived with his family so consistently for more years than I can remember: and now they are fed up with him to the back teeth and he with them.'[54] Sylvester himself was finally losing patience with his once-revered Chief. The last straw was LG asking him to get him a copy of Boccaccio's *Decameron*, which provoked from the normally prudish Sylvester an angry obscenity: 'If L.G. gave his mind to thinking out how he could best help his country, instead of thinking cunt and women, he would be a better man.'[55]

In fact LG did pen a more reasoned account of his position in a letter to Jennifer (now aged ten), who had written to him – probably at Frances's instigation – asking why he would not join the government. He paid her the compliment of a serious reply.

Darling Jennifer . . .

Your letter interested me very much. You put your points intelligently and clearly. You want to know why I have declined to join the War Cabinet when I was given the Offer. I have asked Mummy to give you my reasons when you meet this weekend. But I can give you just a hint – for yourself alone. You are not to repeat it to anyone else except of course, your Mummy.

1. I do not believe in the way we entered the war – nor in the methods by which it has been conducted. We have made blunder after blunder and

are still blundering. Unless there is a thorough change of policy we shall never win.

2. I do not believe in the way or in the personnel with which the War Cabinet is constituted. It is totally different to the War Cabinet set up in the last War. It is not a War Directorate in the real sense of the term. There is therefore no real direction.

I am convinced that unless there is a real change in these two matters it would be a mistake for me to join up with the present lot. If I entered the Cabinet I should soon have to resign because of total disagreement with the plans and methods of this lot and that would do no good . . .

I had experience in directing a great war and I helped to win the victory. I am unhappy at the way things are done today and I wish I could be in a position to alter the course of events.

Love and kisses from *Taid*.[56]

In fact LG's last chance to serve his country came in a rather different form from what he had anticipated. On 12 December Lord Lothian – LG's former private secretary Philip Kerr, now Ambassador to the United States – died suddenly in Washington. Churchill offered LG the job. Can he really have thought that LG was the man to bring America into the war? Did he simply want him out of the way? Or did he make the offer as a kindness to an old friend, knowing well that LG would refuse? LG did refuse, pleading that his health was not up to the strain. Sylvester raged. ('I am completely sick of L.G.'s mucking about. The man is doing nothing for his country, and he is just living amongst the clouds, quarrelling with everybody.'[57]) But LG would have been totally unsuited to the job, and he surely knew it. He travelled to London on 15 December – Frances went to Oxford to meet him halfway – and saw Churchill the next day, reinforced by Dawson's medical opinion. This was the end of any serious likelihood of LG taking any form of war-related office. Churchill sent Lord Halifax to Washington instead.

Having once returned to Churt, LG stayed there with Frances for most of the rest of the war: the worst of the bombing was over, and he had had enough of Criccieth. Jennifer was allowed home for Christmas, and the three of them spent the holiday at Bron-y-de, where they were joined by Dick and Gwilym with their respective families: a large party that illustrates the growing acceptance of Frances and her supposedly adopted daughter, at least by the men of LG's family. Megan and Olwen stayed in Criccieth looking after their mother, who had recently had a fall and broken her hip.

The injury was not at first thought to be too serious, but Maggie contracted complications and failed to recover: in the New Year her condition suddenly worsened. By 18 January 1941 it was clear that she was critically ill. First Dawson was sent for, and then LG. Unfortunately there was heavy snow in north Wales. LG decided to travel by car, driven by George Dyer and accompanied by Ann Parry,* but they got stuck in a snowdrift thirty miles short of Criccieth. They had to be dug out by local farmers and towed back to Cerrig-y-Drudion, where they were forced to spend a miserable night in a hotel. Maggie died the next morning, before LG could reach her.

Meanwhile Sylvester and Dawson had gone by train, but managed to get only as far as Bangor. On the way Dawson blamed Dame Margaret's illness on her errant husband. 'L.G.'s treatment of her and his carryings-on had no doubt worried her and this would undoubtedly aggravate the trouble and speed the end.'[59] Nevertheless when Dawson telephoned to break the news, LG was distraught. 'She was a great old pal,' he sobbed pathetically, begging Sylvester to come as soon as he could. 'I want your companionship.'

'My business obviously was to look after L.G,' Sylvester wrote, 'but I could not get to him . . . Outside Canada and America I have never seen such snow.'[60] After considering the options of horseback or even an aeroplane, he and Tom Carey Evans eventually got a train from Bangor back to Chester and another from there to Corwen, while members of the Home Guard cut a passage through the snow between there and Cerrig-y-Drudion – a distance of seven or eight miles – to enable LG's car to get through. He arrived looking near death himself ('his face was an awful colour'), but revived with hot milk and a pick-me-up at the local hotel, greatly touched by the efforts of the men who had turned out to help him. Then Dick and Gwilym, with their wives, arrived from London. 'L.G. fell into Dick's arms and sobbed.' 'I knew,' Dick wrote later, 'that it was as much a sense of guilt towards my mother as sorrow for her that wrung his heart.'[61] By now, Sylvester recorded, 'the Great Western Railway had been very enterprising and had had snow ploughs at work'; and the mourning party was finally

---

* Frances went with him as far as Broadway, in Worcestershire, from where she wrote to Jennifer: '*Taid* is on his way to Wales. He had to go quite suddenly, as his wife is not at all well.'[58] Probably she did not realise the seriousness of Maggie's condition.

able to reach Criccieth. For all the storms and recriminations, the Lloyd Georges were still in some ways a very close family. 'The scenes I witnessed between members of the family,' Sylvester wrote, 'were most pathetic.'[62]

Three days later Maggie was buried after a private service at Brynawelon, the coffin pulled by sixty-five Home Guardsmen. During the service LG 'was overcome with grief and in floods of tears'. Later, as the coffin was lowered into the vault beside the long-dead Mair, LG, 'standing between Dick and Gwilym, trembled and sobbed'.[63] This was not hypocrisy. Doubtless he wept for his own mortality. But in his own way he had genuinely loved his old Maggie. However badly he had strayed, she had been the anchor of his life for fifty-three years. He received shoals of telegrams from all round the world – from the King and Queen, from Churchill, from Roosevelt, and from ordinary members of the public unaware of the true nature of his marriage.

Meanwhile this was the day Frances had never dared to hope would come to pass. Twenty-eight years after she had first accepted LG's terms, he was at last free to marry her. There was just one obstacle: Megan.

36

FRANCES VERSUS MEGAN

Megan was the baby of the Lloyd George family – in more ways than one. She was not only much younger than the other three surviving children (eight years younger than Gwilym), but she had been spoiled from childhood. Born in 1902, she was only six when LG became Chancellor, fourteen when he became Prime Minister. She had thus spent most of her childhood in Downing Street; she was used to the limelight from an early age, and loved it. Petite and pert, she was a born mimic and a lively speaker, with – when she wanted – much of her father's charm and wit; but she could also, like him, be sulky, selfish and demanding, without his redeeming genius. Having been elected to Parliament at the age of twenty-seven, she always attracted attention; but she never made much serious impression on the House, and unlike Gwilym she never held office.*

She was, at least initially, very close to her father, who indulged her shamelessly after the death of his beloved Mair. Her friend Thelma Cazalet-Keir, who was herself a great favourite of both LG and Maggie, wrote of Megan's 'almost telepathic' relations with LG.[1] But Megan was also devoted to her mother; and when she found out – very late in the day, not until 1920 – the truth about her father's relationship with Frances, she passionately took her mother's part. Because she could not bear to think ill of her hero-father, however, she blamed Frances,

---

* Gwilym was Parliamentary Secretary at the Ministry of Food, 1940–2, and Minister of Fuel, Light and Power, 1942–5. He was narrowly defeated for the Speakership in 1943, but went on to become Home Secretary under Churchill and Eden in 1954–7. Gwilym became a Conservative, whereas Megan left the Liberals for Labour in 1955 and sat as a Labour MP until her death in 1966: a perfect working-out in the second generation of the contradictions of the father.

whom she regarded bitterly as a viper nursed in the family's bosom. None of LG's other children, nor indeed Maggie herself, felt the situation so emotionally. This may have been because Megan's own love life was unhappy. She had a number of suitors, but never married. Most people thought this was because she was so much in the shadow of her father. LG believed it was because she was 'married to politics', and would never allow any man to dominate her.[2] In fact from 1936, unknown to any but a few close friends, Megan was herself involved in a long-running affair with a married Labour MP, Philip Noel-Baker, a prominent peace campaigner and champion of the League of Nations, thirteen years older than herself. Noel-Baker treated Megan far worse than LG treated Frances: he was always promising to leave his wife and marry her, but never did so. Then, when his wife finally died, in 1956, he decided that he was too upset to marry Megan. One might think that Megan's own experience would have given her some empathy with Frances's position; but the fact was quite the opposite.

From the moment Maggie was buried, Frances was determined to secure the reward to which after nearly thirty years she felt she was entitled. LG had always promised that he would marry her if he was ever free to do so; now she expected him – after a decent interval – to keep his word. His other children would have made no strong objection: they could see the justice of her claim, and they could see that their father needed her. No one else was going to care for him in his declining years as she would. But Megan set herself adamantly, by every art of emotional blackmail at her disposal, to prevent her father doing any such thing; and she expected them to back her. 'The fight is now ON,' Sylvester wrote two weeks after Maggie's funeral with some lack of perspective, 'not only with Germany, but between Frances and the family.'[3]

At first, Sylvester assumed that Frances was bound to prevail. 'With Dame Margaret's death,' he wrote, 'the last factor has gone which at least caused him to have some slight discipline.' Frances herself told Sylvester: 'Things are different now: I have had a lot to put up with for years.'[4] She lost no time in adopting a more proprietorial manner at Churt. Instead of retiring discreetly to Avalon when Olwen and Megan came, she now stayed at Bron-y-de even when they were there. During the rest of 1941 she did not force the issue; but Sylvester heard that she had 'completely changed'. Dyer the chauffeur told him that she had become 'terribly mean and greedy . . . She interferes with the domestic

staff & is so mean to them'; she also used LG's car and petrol supply
to run Jennifer and her parents around; and used the money from the
sale of his eggs to support Muriel.[5] Sylvester's hitherto suppressed
resentment of Frances now overflowed. In his diary he called her 'a
bitch' and 'a simpleton', and he once referred to Jennifer as 'that little
bastard'.[6]

> If she marries L.G., how long will it be before she interferes in the wider
> sphere and perhaps works against me? I have never trusted her TOO MUCH.
> She has a v. sweet smile, and a v. engaging manner, but my Heavens she's
> HARD! Look at her face![7]

Doubtless this says more about Sylvester than about Frances; but it
does suggest her determination to get her due. By the spring of 1942
she evidently felt that sufficient interval had elapsed since Maggie's
death. In March she asked Sylvester to look up the form of the marriage
service in a Baptist chapel. Then she persuaded LG to take her with
him to Wales. The farm manager at Ty Newydd was instructed to 'get
the place ready for Easter, as L.G. is going to stay there with someone
else'.

> These instructions have been spread around the town. If L.G. takes Frances
> and Jennifer to Ty Newydd, there will be an unholy row. Megan will regard
> it as an insult to the memory of her mother, and Megan tells me that even
> Gwilym would not tolerate that. But, happily, the place is not ready, so he
> cannot go.

Over lunch with Gwilym and Megan at the House of Commons, LG
was 'most attentive' to Megan, trying to win her round. But Megan's
face, Sylvester wrote, 'set like a piece of chizelled [sic] marble'.

> She said not a word. There was SILENCE. L.G. understood . . . I predict . . .
> that he will NEVER 'buy' Megan. She will never acknowledge Frances; it is a
> high principle with Megan. She told me she would rather go on the parish
> relief.

'The situation is not an easy one for me personally,' he added. 'I have
to make sure that I do not find myself between two fires – yet that is
a position in which I daily live.'[8]

Faced with Megan's opposition, LG began to get cold feet. In May Frances asked the ubiquitous Sylvester to act as go-between.

Frances telephoned me and asked me to commit an indiscretion. Would I let it be known to Megan that the thing is contemplated . . . 'I think L.G. is frightened of Megan and her reactions,' said Frances. 'But I do not see how she could quarrel about it. I do not think she would like it, but I do not think she would break off relations.' She asked me to let it be known to Megan that no date had been fixed but that inquiries had been made about a licence and that sort of thing. 'He is so frightened of saying anything to her himself. I think I am justified in taking things into my own hands. Everyone in the neighbourhood is expecting it.'[9]

No more than LG did Sylvester dare tell Megan directly, but he dropped a hint via Olwen.* Megan's response was to get Lord Dawson to tell her father that the idea of him marrying Frances was making her ill. Frances pressed LG to have it out with Megan 'face-to-face'.

I want to know where I stand. I said to him 'If she says to you it is all right so long as you don't marry, what will you say?' 'I have got to be very careful with her,' replied L.G. 'But you have to be careful with me too,' replied Frances. 'Otherwise I shall be the next person to have a nervous breakdown.'[11]

A month later Sylvester described Frances and Megan battling almost physically for possession of the prize. Megan was 'clinging to L.G. like a leach' [sic]. She travelled up with him from Churt to London in the morning; Frances went back with him in the evening. 'I have seen L.G. in many a wangle,' he reflected, 'but never one like this. He is playing a very deep game between Megan and Frances. One of them must be disappointed one day.'[12] Frances, however, remained confident that it would not be her. 'She was quite satisfied that he had not sold the pass and had only promised Megan that he would not do anything until he had discussed the matter with she [sic] and Gwilym';[13] and in July she confided that 'on his own initiative, L.G. had told her that he meant

---

* Frances also tried to use Thelma Cazalet-Keir as an intermediary to Megan. Thelma had not seen Frances for years until she was invited to lunch at the Savoy and asked to undertake what she called this 'uncongenial mission'. She reluctantly agreed, but 'the interview was as unpleasant as I feared', and only damaged her friendship with Megan.[10]

to marry her. She wore a new ring made of a big single diamond on her engagement finger.'[14]

'He wants to wait two years, for the sake of appearances,' she told Sylvester in October. 'After that, I do not think L.G. will bother about Megan.'[15] LG tried to trump Megan's health card by asking Dawson to tell her that 'his marrying Frances is necessary on medical grounds'. But Frances did not trust LG to give his doctor the full picture and asked Sylvester to speak to Dawson too. '"The trouble," said Frances, "is that L.G. is not quite frank."'[16]

> The fact is, she said, that he is in a hell of a mess. Megan understands he has promised her he won't marry Frances, but Frances says she has definitely promised her to do so. He is afraid to marry Frances because he would be so worried about Megan & yet he is worried because he wants to get it over.[17]

All through his life LG had deployed his battery of persuasive arts to bring political antagonists to believe incompatible things: trade unions and employers, Ulster Unionists and Republicans, Frenchmen and Italians, Tories and Liberals. Now, nearing the end, he was trying the same trick closer to home on his daughter and his mistress; and finding it harder to pull off.

His health was a more serious factor than LG himself knew. His doctors had suspected for some time that he had bowel cancer. ('He might go off at any time or he might live a number of years,' Dr Prytherch had told Sylvester in January 1941.)[18] When Sylvester met Dawson on 19 November, Dawson agreed that this 'would strengthen the case for the marriage. He thought that Frances had a case and that she would marry him even on L.G.'s death bed.' That evening Frances said that LG had 'definitely decided to go ahead with the matter & had actually discussed the details with her on his own initiative'.[19] But four days later he was wriggling again. Gwilym had warned him that 'his proposed marriage . . . would not be popular with the people of Criccieth'.

> Frances told me that L.G. had said to her that the present circumstances were all right. They suited him all right, why alter them? Frances . . . reminded him of the chances she had had to be married, which she had given up. 'That is all done with,' L.G. had replied. 'Honourable people think

you should do it,' Frances had said. 'There are no honourable people,' L.G. had said.[20]

This was alarming. Her solicitor, John Morris, advised Frances to tell LG bluntly that her position was 'intolerable'. She should 'go away and let L.G. make up his mind'. He would then realise that he could not live without her. But Frances would not do it. She was not so hard as all that. '"I cannot take action," said Frances. "L.G. is an old man. I do not like to bring pressure on him."'[21]

In December LG asked Dawson to try to mediate. First he had two meetings with Megan, then he saw Frances, who continued – perhaps surprisingly – to confide in Sylvester.

> She said he [Dawson] had been very nice and kind. He had seen Megan again and he told Frances that she had been irreconcilable. He said he had thought after his first interview he might be able to do something, but he now realised that nothing he said made a difference. She just went round and round and came back to this one thing – *her mother*.
>
> Dawson said that apart from Megan there was no reason why it should not go forward. There would be some criticism . . . but for all the people who would criticise him there would be another lot who would say he was doing the right thing. Gwilym would not stand in the way.

'You cannot talk to Megan like a normal being,' Frances had concluded. 'She was not a normal woman. She had this mixture of sex and religion which created the most extraordinary obsession in her.'[22]

Dawson too reported all his interviews to Sylvester. By now he had also spoken to Gwilym, who repeated that the marriage would be unpopular around Criccieth, 'where they had loved Dame Margaret during her life and whose memory was sacred to them'. Nevertheless Gwilym's attitude was that 'his father was at liberty to do whatever he desired; provided that nothing happened that was detrimental to the memory of his mother he had no opposition'. Dawson then said that he had had 'a very frank talk with Miss Stevenson and the impression he had got had been a very favourable one'.

> She was an extremely well-preserved woman, who would be acceptable in any place or circumstance. He had been astonished to find that she had been with L.G. for thirty years. That was a long time. He said that he had

learned that the question of L.G. marrying her had cropped up over and over again, and it had always been understood, even in Dame Margaret's lifetime, that if anything happened to his wife L.G. would marry Miss Stevenson. She had had a number of offers of marriage, all of which she had turned down because of her association with L.G. What she wanted was the name.[23]

Dawson asked about Jennifer, but received 'no definite answer to that question'. Frances seems to have suggested that 'there was someone who was ready to take the responsibility for the Father-hood of the child'; but she did not say who, nor whether he was still alive. She undertook that Jennifer 'would not take the Lloyd George name, which was what the family feared might happen'. She also agreed that 'if criticism were caused by their going to live in N Wales, then she would not insist upon that'. Dawson confirmed that this was a condition of Gwilym's approval. Finally he told Sylvester that 'if L.G. got old slowly it might be very desirable that he should have someone like Miss Stevenson to look after his physical needs'.[24]

January 17th 1943 was LG's eightieth birthday, a milestone that was bound to be marked by family celebrations and public tributes. Dawson urged Megan to use the occasion as the opportunity for a gesture of friendship towards Frances. 'It need not last long,' he told her, but 'it must be warm and really friendly in its quality'.

Now I want you to listen to me. I both understand and sympathise with your feelings and especially those which surround your mother's memory, but I am sure that she would wish nothing but that the evening of your father's life should be made as smooth as possible. He is in need today of physical care and is likely in this respect to become more dependent in the future. Miss S. fills this role and there is no one else at once fitted, avail-able and acceptable for this duty.

But Dawson had somehow got the impression that Frances had given up her claim to marry LG.

If it be a fact that what you feared is off, as it appears to be, it must in justice be said that she has now made a great sacrifice and from what she said to me I think she has made things easy and put aside the bitterness of her disappointment . . . You are not called upon to be a friend but only to be kindly . . . when you meet her in the capacity as a necessary helpmeet for your father today.

He appealed to Megan as 'a matter of Christian charity for your father's sake' to make the gesture he suggested, since 'he has changed his intention mainly for you'. If she did, he assured her that she would never regret it.[25]

The same day Olwen asked Sylvester's advice about going to Churt. 'I said that nothing and no one ought to stop her and Megan going to Churt on Sunday and greeting their father on his eightieth birthday, whether Frances Stevenson were there or not. If he should die in his sleep on Sunday night, and they had not been to see him, how great would be their remorse.' Dawson gave similar advice; and LG made it clear that he would be pleased to see them, on the understanding that Frances would be there as well.[26]

It must have been quite an ordeal for Frances: the first time that she had received the family en masse as hostess of Bron-y-de. Megan attended, but could not bring herself to make the gesture Dawson had asked of her. Gwilym and Edna had always been friendly – indeed they had often stayed at Churt when Frances was there. Olwen and Tom, with their seventeen-year-old son Benjy, made the effort to shake hands; but 'Megan simply ignored her'.* When Frances spoke to her, she turned her back and powdered her nose. Frances withdrew for some of the time to leave the family alone, but they all had lunch together. 'The day passed without any open breach,' Olwen told Sylvester, 'but when Megan got back to Du Cane Road [Olwen's house in Hammersmith] she just cried her eyes out, saying that she could never forgive her father.'[27]

Like Dawson, Olwen evidently thought the family could afford to be civil to Frances since 'Father had told Megan again definitely that he won't marry her'. On that basis, she told Sylvester, she supposed they would have to put up with her. 'Megan has won hands down with the other thing, and we have to consider that.' She was sorry for Megan, but her concern now was to restore relations with her father. 'If I can do anything to help now that he has promised not to do the big thing,

---

* Only Dick was not present. He was already ill with TB, complicated by alcoholism. LG's elder grandchildren were all in uniform and unable to get leave.

I want to help him as much as I can.'[28] 'I am not certain that if Mother knew it would upset her. It is not being disloyal . . . The main thing is to stop him marrying, and that we have done.' Olwen realised that Frances was taking a load off the rest of them. 'You are not prepared to do for Father what Miss Stevenson does,' she told Megan. 'Anybody can do that,' Megan replied; at which Olwen told her 'she could not have her cake and eat it'.[29] But that was precisely what Olwen herself was trying to do. She was happy to exploit Frances as an unpaid nurse to look after their father in his last years, without conceding her her due reward.

Meanwhile Frances remained confident that LG had *not* promised Megan that he would not marry her.

> 'He is willing to delay it for a bit if she would consider being friends with me. Once on speaking terms with me he has an idea that the whole thing will break down. But she has not consented to that . . .
>
> 'I am quite sure that he has not sold the pass. I think he has got it in mind to put it off, not because of Megan at all, but until he resigns from the constituency. I have come to the conclusion that the whole thing is governed by the political situation . . . I am sure he does not intend to stand again . . . I am quite sure, and I have no doubt at all, that he does intend to do it. He is thoroughly honest about that.'

Recording this conversation, Sylvester was sceptical; he suspected that LG was playing a game with both of them, and was inclined to trust his wife's intuition. 'Evelyn has always said that L.G. will never marry Frances. I wonder if she is not right.'[30] For Frances, however, the clinching point was that LG had 'promised Jennifer that it would be THIS year. I have always had it in my mind that it should not be before the middle of this year.' Then Megan would have to choose whether to be friends with her father or 'go to Hell'.[31]

It may well have been at Frances's prompting, therefore, that during the Easter holidays Jennifer – now thirteen – asked LG directly when they were going to get married. 'We were standing, I remember, by the gate that led from the Bron-y-de grounds to the first of the orchards. *Taid* roared with what sounded like very embarrassed laughter at my question and said something fairly non-committal.'[32] Jennifer has always believed that it was she who finally shamed him into doing the right thing.

But even Frances's confidence wobbled around this time. LG was becoming 'impossible', she told Sylvester in April. 'If anybody knew what I have been through . . .' Apart from anything else, even at this stage of the war he continued to be embarrassingly defeatist and pro-German, still refusing to hear a word against Hitler. As for their marriage, he was still making excuses for delay.

> 'I think he does intend to do it. He wants people to think that there has not been anything in our relationship; he thinks that if we were married soon people would think there had been something between us. You can hardly follow it; it is so twisted.'[33]

Finally, in September, she was able to announce that LG had made up his mind.

> 'He never intended to do it before the end of this year, but he did not want to say so. The only thing is will Megan do anything violent? She will do anything she can to stop it. I think he will be one too many for her when it comes to the point.'[34]

The date was set – secretly – for Saturday 23 October. Megan was 'terribly upset'; but Olwen now accepted that 'it was a matter for he himself to decide'.[35] Sylvester made all the arrangements at the register office in Guildford, then went down to Churt the night before. Megan had not yet given up. After supper she rang to speak to her father.

> She threatened that if he did not come to the telephone she would come down to Churt tomorrow. He disappeared and was away for so long that Frances went to see if he was all right. Presently she returned to say that she was certain that Megan would make her father ill. Would I go to help him?
>
> When I reached the new drawing room, I found him somewhat upset and exhausted. I heard him say: 'But Gwilym and Edna agree and Olwen agrees' . . . 'Well, my dear, that shows you are thoroughly selfish.' That was the last word he spoke to her, because I tapped him on the shoulder and he handed me the telephone . . . Megan was crying . . . and saying excitedly: 'It is an anticlimax to a great career . . . People will laugh at him. I could not bear people to laugh at him' . . . She continued to sob . . . 'It will absolutely break my heart . . . He says Gwilym and Edna and Olwen are for it. They are not . . . It is ridiculous.'

'I felt sorry for her in many ways,' Sylvester wrote.[36] But he clearly thought that in the end LG was doing the right thing.

Frances phoned Gwilym and Edna, who promised to come to the ceremony the next day. LG was pleased. He and Frances then retired to his bomb shelter. But in the morning Gwilym rang to say that Megan had been on the phone to him, as a result of which they had now decided not to come to the wedding after all, but would come down afterwards. LG's reaction to this is not recorded: Sylvester noted only that he was looking 'very fit and sparkling'. At 11.15 Dyer brought the car round – such was the secrecy that he had no idea where he was taking them – and LG and Frances left for Guildford, with Sylvester and Muriel to act as witnesses. There were just the four of them in the room.

> Mr Catt, the Registrar, emphasised that though this was not a religious cere-
> mony it was legally binding on both parties. L.G. then repeated after the
> Registrar the oath that he took Frances Louise Stevenson as his wife. L.G.
> spoke in very clear and definite tones, likewise Frances. I produced the ring.
> L.G. signed the register with a special pen we had brought. Then Frances,
> Muriel and I signed. It was a very happy ceremony . . . And so the deed
> has been done, after many months of doubt . . . As we drove back to Bron-
> y-de, L.G. was immensely happy.[37]

So was Frances, as she wrote twenty-three years later:

> The whole countryside was bathed in sunshine, as was my heart, and a
> deep contentment possessed me; contentment, but not the thrills of the usual
> bride. Our real marriage had taken place thirty years before.[38]

When they got back to the house, LG was delighted to find Jennifer waiting for them: she had been allowed home from school for the weekend. (She was now at a school in Oxford.) She immediately noticed that Frances's bed had disappeared from her bedroom; but when she mentioned this to one of the secretaries, she was 'received with lascivi-ous giggles'. 'As *Taid* was 80 and my mother 55 (and I 13) I had not thought of the marriage in terms of sex.'[39] Sylvester recorded that they 'tapped a bottle of champagne and drank the health of the bride and groom, and then lunched on home-grown pork, which was delicious'. When LG retired for his customary rest, Sylvester issued an announce-

ment to the press and spent the afternoon dealing with astonished journalists; while Frances practised writing her hard-won new signature:
'Frances Lloyd George'.[40]

Gwilym and Edna arrived in time for tea. Gwilym said that Megan
was 'much upset and he had had a very bad time with her'. Sylvester
noted that he merely shook hands with his father and did not congratulate him. 'They are a funny family.'[41] Two days later, however,
reflecting on the 'splendid' coverage of the event in all the papers, he
was amazed that it had gone off so well.

I feel that L.G. is an exceedingly lucky man. The gods are certainly with
him to a most remarkable degree. In somewhat similar circumstances as
Edward VIII was dethroned, L.G. is elevated. He has lived a life of duplicity.
He has got clean away with it.[42]

37

A WIFE AT LAST

Four days after the wedding, when Jennifer had gone back to school, Frances wrote her a short happy letter:

> What a marvellous weekend it was, made all the more marvellous by having you here, & watching your joy. Since then we have just been snowed under by letters & telegrams, including one from the P.M.[1]

'My impression,' Jennifer wrote years later, 'was that both F. and Ll.G. were entirely contented in their new marriage, and the only worry – quite a minor one at that stage – was *Taid*'s health.'[2]

In fact another continuing worry was Megan's refusal to accept what her father had done. In November 1943 Frances made a serious effort to reach a reconciliation.

> My dear Megan
>
> I hope you will read this letter through, as it is written in all sincerity, to ask you if you will not reconsider your attitude towards your Father's marriage with me. I am so anxious that you shall not commit yourself to a permanent and irrevocable estrangement from him, both for the sake of his happiness and your own, and that is why I am sure you would not forgive yourself if you were to be the cause of any sadness in his last years, and I know you would never regret it if you could bring yourself to put your own feelings on one side in this matter, and to act generously, as I believe you are capable of doing.
>
> I am depriving you of nothing in becoming his wife, neither of his

affection, nor of any material benefits now or in the future. You must realise how much you owe to him, and how an estrangement would hurt him. Even if you cannot see your way to burying the past as far as I am concerned, I hope you will make this concession to him, and so establish yourself even more firmly in his heart.

Ever sincerely,

Frances Lloyd George[3]

Megan did not reply. Thelma Cazalet assured Frances that she would 'come round in time';[4] but Tom Carey Evans told Sylvester that Megan regarded her father's marriage as 'a closed door'.[5] She had no contact with LG for several weeks after the wedding. In January 1944 he sent her a cheque for the profits from some orchards he had given her on his estate; she acknowledged it in a 'fairly formal' note.[6] A week later – 'speaking with great vehemence' – she made her position crystal-clear via Sylvester.

'I will never, never have anything to do with *her*. I made up my mind twenty years ago and I will never change. Tell him that I cannot be bought. Of course he must go to his constituency, but I advise them not to go to stay at Ty Newydd, because I should not like my Father to be hurt by the attitude of the people.' She said there was 'intense feeling against him for marrying'.

Sylvester delivered this message later that day when LG came up to the Commons for a meeting of the Welsh parliamentary Liberal group – all six of them – of which Megan had just been elected chairman. He picnicked with Frances on the way up to avoid any risk of meeting Megan at lunch. 'His lips curled and like a flash he fastened on to the phrase: "I cannot be bought".'[7] He managed to congratulate Megan, but the meeting was such 'an emotional strain' that two weeks later Frances was still worried about its effect on him.[8] The next day LG wrote to his brother William that he and Frances would be coming to Ty Newydd in April or May. When Megan heard this, Sylvester 'thought she would have dropped through the floor. She was much upset.'[9]

In fact they did not go to Ty Newydd until September; but Frances was keen to go earlier. She was convinced that the local people were *not* all on Megan's side: they had received 'many very nice letters from people in Criccieth' – though she accepted that it might be unwise to take Jennifer on their first visit.[10] Megan apart, the rest of LG's family seem to have accepted Frances's new status pretty well. There is a whole file of letters in her papers from LG's grandchildren addressed to 'Dear Aunt Frances' or 'Dear *Taid* and Aunt Frances'. The boys were all in uniform: but 'Benjy' Carey Evans came to Churt on leave in February and wrote to thank them for a lovely weekend and the best meal he had had in a long time, hoping he could come again.[11] Dick's son Owen wrote from Egypt thanking 'My dear Aunt Frances' for sending cigarettes; he sent his 'very best love to *Taid*' and asked to be remembered to Jennifer.[12] In August his sister Valerie stayed at Churt with her new baby – LG's first great-grandchild. In short, Frances – and Jennifer – appeared to have gained a whole new family. When Gwilym's son William was told of the marriage, he was said to have exclaimed: 'Good God, Jennifer's my aunt!' Jennifer had in fact, as she wrote later, 'acquired five nephews and two nieces, all older than me; all of them were invariably pleasant to me, and I liked them all'.[13]

Nor was it only LG's grandchildren who seemed to have accepted Frances: during his lifetime their parents were equally friendly. Dick, for instance, wrote to her from hospital, thanking her for having Valerie to stay and asking her to send his wife June a line for her birthday. 'She would like it so much from you.'[14] Olwen wrote chatty letters full of family news, signed 'Yrs affec., Olwen';[15] and Gwilym's wife Edna wrote 'my darling Frances' an exceptionally friendly letter regretting that they could not come to Churt because Gwilym was detained in London.

> We are very disappointed, I really feel I shall forget what you look like darling if I don't see you soon . . .
>
> I hear *Taid* made a marvellous speech at the luncheon last week and was full of beans. We are so delighted . . .
>
> What news of Jen? I am looking forward to seeing her . . .
>
> All my love my darling, to you & *Taid* & Ann.
>
> Edna[16]

Family, friends and staff had no doubt that LG's remarriage had been very good for him. Lord Dawson, who had done so much to try to overcome Megan's objections, was now 'very interested to hear that the marriage was turning out so well and that L.G. was happier. He thought Frances had behaved altogether admirably.'[17] In April Olwen

visited Churt and was pleased to find her father 'very happy'.[18] Even
Sylvester now had only praise for Frances. 'I think Frances has behaved
nobly, and I have had a good opportunity of judging. She is dignified,
generous and fair.'[19]

Visiting Churt that spring for the wedding of one of LG's staff,
Sylvester proposed the toast to 'Mr & Mrs Lloyd George, coupled with
the name of Jennifer'. Afterwards he was given a tour of the farm, and
described in idyllic terms what LG had created.

> When I knew that spot in 1921 it was as bare as any common; today it is
> full of the most beautiful fruit trees of all kinds I have ever seen. It is one
> mass of pink and white blossom and the bees are working overtime with
> pollination. It is a veritable Garden of Eden. Although L.G. has put more
> than a fortune into that hungry soil he certainly has a marvellous show.

He also visited Frances's Avalon. 'The front garden is a carpet of
wild violets and primroses, whilst her orchard is full of young fruit
trees and carries a flock of geese as well as goats.' But leaving this
paradise, he felt sad. LG, he finally recognised, 'can never do anything
great again. The sands are fast running out, and he is now past any
effective work or decision, though with great care and the happiness
Frances obviously brings to him, he may last for years.'[20]

LG still went to London occasionally. The first time after his wedding
was to hear Eden make a statement about a conference in Moscow.
'During Eden's speech L.G. sat in his place on the front opposition
bench and often beamed up to his newly-wedded wife, seated in the
gallery right in the front.'[21] One of his last appearances was for a two-
day foreign-affairs debate in May.

> As he walked down the floor, the whole House applauded him . . . Winston
> spoke for one and a half hours. L.G. sat with his mouth open at times,
> listening to the speech and occasionally looking up at Frances.

Afterwards, he left the chamber with Megan. Churchill overtook
them behind the Speaker's chair and the two stood talking for some
minutes until Megan 'suddenly flounced off', having seen Frances
coming. 'Winston received Frances graciously,' Sylvester wrote, but LG
became acrimonious, demanding why the Allies had not yet launched
the second front. 'Winston had not yet answered L.G. when, very

cleverly, Frances turned the conversation to another subject by congratulating Winston on his speech.' LG later said he was pleased that Frances
had congratulated him because he could not do so himself. 'His jealousy is incredible.'[22]

Frances's very last diary entry describes the same occasion. 'The
House,' she wrote, 'gave him a touching welcome. I wonder if they
realise how near it may be to his last appearance.'

> Winston, whom we met in the corridor afterwards, was nice to us both.
> Ll.G was rather inclined to be critical of the Government's policy, but I
> thought Winston very patient & I finally managed to turn the conversation
> to his pictures: we parted very happily. It was a perfect spring day, but as
> we drove through the smiling countryside there was a heavy sadness in my
> heart.[23]*

In January 1944 there was a renewal of German air-raids, after nearly
three years of relative peace. Once again, Frances told Sylvester, LG
was 'frightened stiff . . . He just sat and sat thinking of bombs.'[24] In
February Sylvester's house in Putney was damaged, so Evelyn came to
live at Churt for three months. Then in June flying bombs – 'doodlebugs' – brought a new terror to London and Surrey, so that Frances
felt she could not leave LG alone, as she explained apologetically to
Jennifer.

> My little love . . .
>   Now I have something to say that you will not like, my sweet, and neither
> do I. *Taid* has *begged* me not to leave him next weekend. He is rather
> nervous about these pilotless planes . . . and I can see that he will upset
> himself if I do come to Oxford next Saturday. Will you be very tolerant
> and forgiving, my darling, if I do not come? You know it is not because of
> any lack of love for you – I am just hungry for the sight of you – but
> because, taking things all round, I do not want to upset *Taid* at this moment.
> I will explain more to you when I see you. Don't think hardly of him for
> causing us disappointment – that would be a pity, as you know how very
> fond he is of you. And I think at his age we must give him special consid-
> eration, & forgive him for being a little selfish.[25]

---

* LG actually attended the House one more time, on 6 June, to hear Churchill's statement about the Normandy landings.

Never had she been so explicit about putting LG's need of her first, ahead of her daughter.

Though in principle LG was determined to take his new wife to Wales, he was still nervous of the reception they might get and kept putting it off. The doodlebugs helped make up his mind; and in September he and Frances finally set off, followed by Sylvester and Evelyn. It was intended to be just a visit; but Tom Carey Evans guessed that 'L.G.'s instinct [had] led him to his old home to die, like an old dog returns to his lair.'[26]

Megan was now living at Brynawelon, which had been left to her in her mother's will. No sooner was LG settled at Ty Newydd than he said he wanted to see her, so Sylvester rang her.

> Megan was acid. 'I shall be delighted to see him, but he will come alone,' she said . . . It was arranged that L.G. should go to Brynawelon. He asked me to accompany him. He rang the bell and Megan came dancing to see him. They were alone for some time. Then I helped her find some whiskey, and presently they were arm in arm, walking round the garden.

Meanwhile Sylvester talked to old Sarah, who told him she had been with the family forty-four years. She initially refused to see LG, not because of his remarriage – she had always approved of Frances – but because since Maggie's death he had stopped the allowance he had previously made for the upkeep of Brynawelon. '"I will not go," she said . . . "He stopped my money."' But eventually she did go and spoke to him in Welsh. 'She told me afterwards that he had looked so different that she could not be other than civil.'[27]

LG was now 'just a shrunken old man, looking very delicate and feeble'.[28] 'He talks very little these days,' Sylvester noted, but 'sits for hours saying not a word', staring across the bay towards Harlech through a pair of German binoculars captured in the Great War.[29] But Frances was resolutely upbeat. In October she wrote to Winifred Russell, back at Churt:

> I have been very happily surprised at the warmth of our welcome everywhere & the Chief himself has been delighted at it, I think. I must say we are very happy here, & so comfortable, & the view is simply marvellous . . .
>
> There is plenty of interest in the farm, too, and as Mr Sylvester has

made it his personal interest, you can imagine that we are getting a move on!³⁰*

There was a children's concert in their honour in Llanystumdwy village hall; and each Sunday they attended a different local chapel. 'We are really much more "social" here than at Bron-y-de,' Frances wrote, '& have people to tea almost every day, which is very nice.'³² 'The Chief seems very well these days & obviously loves being here.'³³

Meanwhile it was clear that LG would not be able to contest another election. Sylvester made soundings in London about the possibility of the other parties allowing him a clear run in the Caernarvon Boroughs. 'You can tell them it will not be for very long,' LG suggested, 'rather pathetically.'³⁴ But the local associations would not agree. After fifty-four years, however, LG could not face the prospect of having no plat-form in Parliament. With the end of the war in sight, he still had the idea that he would have something to contribute to the eventual peace settlement; so Sylvester set about trying to secure him the earldom tradi-tionally awarded to former Prime Ministers. In his Edwardian heyday, and as Prime Minister, LG had despised the House of Lords. Even as recently as 1936 he had criticised former radicals who finished up by accepting titles. 'If Ernest Bevin takes an honour in connection with the coronation,' he warned, 'that will be the end of him. Gladstone, Bright, Cobden . . . Joe Chamberlain never made the mistake of taking an honour.'³⁵ Nevertheless when it came to his turn LG could not refuse. At the end of November Frances telephoned Sylvester that the 'thing' would be accepted if offered – though she warned that 'Lady' (that is, Megan) should not be consulted.³⁶

A courier came to Ty Newydd on 18 December to deliver the letter from Churchill containing the offer. LG accepted by telegram the next day, followed by a personal letter to Winston:

> With all my pride in the honour, I cannot help feeling the sadness involved
> in the change in my station; but whilst relieving me of the tediousness and
> embarrassment of an election, it gives me the feeling that for the rest of my
> days I shall still have a voice in the Councils of the Nation.³⁷

---

* Sylvester did inspect the orchards at Ty Newydd, but he found the crop 'very poor
. . . more fit for pigs than for humans'. He reported his view to LG. 'A few years ago
I should have expected him to have skinned somebody. Today he said nothing.'³¹

LG's elevation was announced in the New Year Honours, with the title Earl Lloyd-George of Dwyfor.*

There was some criticism of LG for accepting a peerage, and some suspicion that Frances must have persuaded him so that she might be left with the title of Countess. But there is no basis for this allegation. 'She had been entirely contented with her status as Mrs Lloyd George,' Jennifer wrote, 'and neither wanted or needed anything more.'[38] Sylvester confirms this. 'She said she had made it clear to LG that *he* must decide, and that if he refused she would be perfectly happy.'[39] Even the family, in their later hostility to Frances, never believed that she had manipulated him to gain herself a title. LG wanted it for his own reasons. 'The difference in his health and happines on New Year's Day was enormous,' Jennifer remembered. 'He was radiant . . . at the thought of future achievement through his new position in House of Lords . . . We drank champagne at 11 o'clock in the morning, and it was a kind of resurrection.'[40]

But the resurrection was short-lived, and LG never took his seat in the Upper House. A faltering speech at a children's party was his last public utterance. He celebrated his eighty-second birthday quietly on 17 January 1945; Megan had compromised to the extent of going to Ty Newydd, but she still did her best to ignore Frances (though she was surprisingly civil to Jennifer). In February Dick's wife June wrote sympathetically to Frances.

> I am sorry about Megan's attitude. It is stupid, undignified, and lacking in practical common sense, to say nothing of humanity . . . However, you have too much strength of character to let anything get you down, and I hope everything rights itself soon.[41]

On 9 February LG suffered a bad turn, which brought the whole family up to Llanystumdwy, followed by a ghoulish pack of journalists and photographers, waiting for the end. 'With good judgment & admirable tact,' Sylvester wrote, 'the new Countess offered them every facility and opportunity, & everything worked with a measure of outward smoothness.' But the old man did not go gently: he could still occasionally assert himself.

---

* Garter King of Arms made a difficulty about the title, arguing that LG's surname was properly not Lloyd George at all, but plain George. Sylvester eventually persuaded him to allow the double-barrelled form, but only with the addition of a hyphen.

One day the Countess, who personally attended to his every want, was about to shave him when Megan said she would stop to watch the operation.

'No, you do nothing of the sort: you go away,' said L.G. firmly.[42]

Another time he perked up when Dr Prytherch mentioned that he had a patient in a neighbouring village. 'Oh, yes,' LG recalled, with a flash of his old spirit, 'I used to know a girl up there.'[43]

On 26 February Dr Prytherch wrote to Lord Dawson describing his patient's condition and Frances's devoted nursing.

> I have never known anyone with such remarkable recuperative powers. He rises to the occasion every time . . . I have escorted Megan there twice this week (this still requires patience, diplomacy and time). Each time he has rallied . . . I think he knows the truth, but so far he is unaware or refuses to recognise his condition . . . He is comfortable and placid and extremely well looked after. His wife is doing a grand job of work. She has done so for the last six months, and latterly, with his loss of control, this is no easy task, but she is doing it with all the devotion he deserves, and she is doing it unstintingly and extremely well, and he calls for her constant presence. One cannot say more than that he is one of the best cared for patients I have ever had.[44]*

Jennifer had come to Ty Newydd for the Christmas holidays, but then contracted appendicitis. She had her appendix out at Portmadoc; by the time she was better it did not seem worth her going back to school – with all the difficulties of wartime transport – only to have to return very soon for LG's funeral, so she stayed and had private coaching for the rest of the term. At the same time, unluckily, Frances's mother was dying; but Frances did not feel she could go to her, as she explained to her father:

> I can't tell you how desperately sorry I am not to be able to come to you but the Doctor said it would have a very adverse effect upon LG if I went away, so that I clearly cannot leave him. He is not so well today and the Doctor fears that the end cannot be far off.[45]

Frances was very upset, but characteristically hid her feelings. But when Jennifer, who loved her only grandmother, cruelly suggested that

---

* Dawson himself actually died on 7 March – nineteen days before LG.

she did not care, Frances snapped and, for the only time in her life, actually hit her daughter – making Jennifer realise the strain she was under. When Louise Stevenson died, Frances's old friend Felicia Brook wrote her a letter of condolence, and added: 'How providential that Jen should get appendicitis & have a term off, just when you wanted her most. It must be a great help having her there. She's so sensible besides being devoted to you.'[46]

The end came finally on 26 March. The previous evening Sylvester, who had chronicled the ups and downs of LG's relationship with Frances for so long, witnessed their last hours together.

Tonight L.G's strength is ebbing away. In his sleep he gripped both the Countess's hands as she watched every breath. It was a scene that to me spelt complete happiness.[47]

He lingered through most of the next day and breathed his last around 8.30 in the evening. It was a classic deathbed scene, like a Victorian painting, Frances holding one hand and Megan the other; Olwen behind Megan, Dr Prytherch behind Frances, and Jennifer with Ann Parry at the foot of the bed; Gwilym and Sylvester standing by the window. Only Dick, the bankrupt, alcoholic elder son – and now the new Earl – was absent, undergoing treatment in a sanatorium in Denbigh.

The funeral was arranged for 1 April, which was Good Friday, so that thousands were able to attend a simple service at the spot where LG had instructed that he wanted to be buried – not in Westminster Abbey, but beside his beloved River Dwyfor. Churchill arranged special leave for the four grandsons who were serving in the forces to enable them to attend. As the widow, Frances could not be denied the leading role: due proprieties were observed. But once the formalities were over, hostilities were resumed. Megan never spoke to Frances again, and gradually persuaded the whole family to follow her example. After thirty years as a mistress and just seventeen months as a wife, Frances faced a long and difficult widowhood.

38

OCCUPATION: WIDOW

At first Frances stayed on at Ty Newydd – partly no doubt to defy the family, partly for practical reasons. Under LG's will, Bron-y-de and most of the land at Churt were left to Gwilym. Frances still retained Avalon and enough orchards to comprise a small farm of her own; but Muriel had been living there since 1940 to escape the bombs of London and she was still there. After their mother's death the sisters brought their widowed father to live there too, but he did not last long and died the following year. Meanwhile Frances had several important matters to attend to in Wales.

First she commissioned the architect Clough Williams-Ellis to design LG's grave beside the Dwyfor. He came up with an extraordinarily beautiful circular walled enclosure, built in Welsh slate, with a locked gate. When it was completed Frances sent each of LG's children a key; but only Gwilym acknowledged it. Megan and Olwen would have nothing to do with her after the funeral. Then she busied herself with creating a small museum in Llanystumdwy to which she gave all sorts of treasured memorabilia that she had collected over the past thirty years, plus the elaborate caskets from all the cities that had awarded LG their Freedom after 1918. Finally she tried to establish an enduring memorial to LG's belief in the importance of agriculture by founding an agricultural training college bearing his name. She wrote to all his old friends and former colleagues seeking funds for this project. But Gwilym and Megan had more influence in the Liberal party and in the government: potential donors would not give to a scheme that LG's own family did not support. Frances had the highest expectations of

Lord Beaverbrook. After giving first use of LG's papers to Malcolm Thomson – the researcher who had done much of the work for his *War Memoirs* – to write a rather dull official biography, she sold them to Beaverbrook for a mere £15,000 on the understanding that he would help endow the proposed college. But Beaverbrook too let her down; and the college never came into being.

For a year or two, while working on these projects, Frances tried to play the role of the Dowager Countess in Llanystumdwy and Criccieth. But she was always bound to be seen as a usurper in Dame Margaret's former kingdom. Megan and Olwen did their best to ensure that she was not welcomed in local society and even tried to prevent local tradesmen from serving her. 'The entire neighbourhood seemed to be drawn into one camp or the other,' Jennifer recalled. 'I had never known anything like it.' She kept a 'passionate diary' – which she later destroyed – recording what she called 'the horror of it all'. Among other snubs, Olwen's two sons were forbidden to speak to her – though they had the decency to be shamefaced about it.[1] Frances did have some friends, even within the family. Dick's wife June wrote to her again soon after the funeral hoping that the 'unpleasantness' would soon fade, and meanwhile encouraging her to 'ignore it for what it most certainly is, small-minded and intolerant'.[2] When Tom Carey Evans died suddenly in 1947, LG's brother William wrote to her: 'Poor old Tom, I think he did his best to keep aloof from the vendetta in which some of his women folk seemed to delight.'[3] The same year Frances was delighted to accept an invitation to preside over the Criccieth sheepdog trials. 'I very much want to do it,' she wrote, 'because 1 the sheepdog trials are very thrilling and 2 it will put certain people's noses very much out of joint' – adding wrily 'I expect I ought to have put 2 first'.[4] Eventually, however, she gave up the unequal struggle and decided to make her home in Surrey – where, after all, she had spent most of her life. She sold Ty Newydd in 1948 and moved back to Avalon, which she shared henceforth with Muriel. In 1951 she made a last attempt to launch a memorial appeal, with the unveiling of some grand gates that Williams-Ellis had persuaded her to buy, but the occasion was boycotted by the family and she 'went away feeling I never wanted to come to Llanystumdwy again'.[5]*

Another reason for staying at Ty Newydd initially was that Jennifer started a new school in September 1945 – a Swiss school temporarily

---

* She did in fact go back once more in 1963, when the Queen attended a centenary ceremony at LG's grave.

housed in Aberdovey: Frances wanted to stay in Wales to be near her. But then the school moved back to Switzerland, and Jennifer with it. In May 1946 Frances wrote to Jennifer: 'I realise that you are now the only thing that really matters to me.' But it was a bit late for that. For years she had consistently put her daughter second behind LG, abandoning her even at Christmas to follow LG to the sun. In her daughter's words: 'Jennifer was not inclined to be very responsive to such outpourings. She was sixteen and wanted her own life and she found it inappropriate to have a passionate "Mummy" around now at last when she was almost grown up.'[6] As a child she had learned to be self-sufficient, and now she was keen to assert her independence. She became a committed Christian, read English at St Andrew's and then took a teaching job in Tanganyika, where she met her future husband, a colonial civil servant named Michael Longford; she married him and stayed in Africa to bring up three children, with only occasional visits home. Her relationship with her mother remained sadly distant. It was cruelly ironic that Frances, who had so yearned for a child when she could not have one, should have so neglected the daughter she finally did have that she virtually lost her. Looking back, Jennifer has written very candidly about her relationship with her mother, realising in retrospect that Frances was attractive and clever, 'endlessly kind and enormously generous'. Even so, the legacy of her childhood could not be overcome.

> However much I looked forward to being at home, and enjoyed being there, I quickly got bored with her unadulterated company . . . We quarrelled quite a bit, and it was not always I who started the quarrels. And I didn't like her touching me . . . The first time I kissed her willingly, without some inward reluctance (except perhaps when I was a very small child), was after she was dead.[7]

Jennifer and Michael, with their children, returned to England when Tanganyika became independent (as Tanzania) in 1963. They settled at Witley, just nine miles from Churt. Having never brought up a child herself, however, Frances was not a good grandmother either; she enjoyed spoiling her grandchildren when she got the chance, taking them to the theatre and other treats, but she could not cope with normal childish behaviour.

Widowed in her fifties, Frances declined into a respectable but rather dull old age, sharing Avalon with her youngest sister. After Tweed's death Muriel had found another lover, a Canadian stationed near Churt who promised to divorce his wife and marry her; but when the war ended he returned to Canada and never wrote to her again. Frances eventually brought her other sisters, Janet and Ninette, to live nearby as well: she discreetly supported all three of them, but her generosity drained her own resources. She still had her pension from Carnegie, but she had acquired expensive tastes in her years with LG; moreover she never managed to make her orchards pay. Gradually she had to sell many of her precious possessions; she sold her piano to pay for herself and Muriel to fly to Jennifer's wedding. In 1962 she sold her farm and in 1963 was forced to leave Avalon itself and move – still with Muriel – to a smaller cottage.

Meanwhile she returned to the faith she had boldly abandoned as a young feminist around 1910 and became a pillar of the local church; she was also chairman of the horticultural society, served on all sorts of local committees and was regularly asked to open fêtes. As if to cover her immoral past she became very puritanical, to the point of objecting when an unmarried couple set up house in the village. She worried about whether she should meet them, and tried to prevent Jennifer doing so. The irony of her life was that her instincts were indeed – before they were swept away by LG – 'essentially Victorian'. Muriel and Jennifer thought it very funny when she was invited to open a fête in aid of the League of Moral Welfare: but Frances did not see the joke and saw no reason not to accept.[8]

Yet at the same time she lived on her memories. 'Nothing was as real to her, or as satisfying, as thinking about, talking about and ultimately writing about LG.'[9] After so many years in the shadows she enjoyed being a countess and gloried in being a professional widow: she even gave 'Widow' as her occupation in her passport. She was ever-vigilant to defend LG's reputation whenever it was attacked, as it often was in the years after his death, missing no opportunity to write to the papers to correct what she saw as inaccurate or unfair. She was particularly critical of Sylvester, who – as he had always intended – wasted no time in bringing out a book, based on his diaries, entitled *The Real Lloyd George*. By modern standards it is very tame: he did not tell one-tenth of what he knew. His portrait was overwhelmingly admiring – the first chapter is titled 'The Strength and Audacity of a Genius' – but he included some less flattering details, which in 1947 were widely considered to be below the belt.* Frances wrote angrily to William George:

> I do not know if you have seen Sylvester's book, but it is a terrible piece of work, and I cannot understand quite why it has been given such publicity. It has upset me very much. I imagine he has received somewhat more than his 'thirty pieces of silver' for his effort.[12]

To the *Sunday Dispatch*, which had serialised the book, she wrote that Sylvester's revelations were 'beneath contempt and so beneath comment. Decent people will form their own opinion of a man who, after his master is dead, betrays intimate, if inaccurate, details of his private life.'[13] William agreed that the book told more about Sylvester – pompous, self-important and 'transparently childish' – than it did about LG.[14] In truth they should have been grateful that Sylvester did not reveal very much more.

Almost the only person who defended Sylvester was Dick, now a hopeless and embittered alcoholic. LG had excluded his eldest son entirely from his will, reckoning that he had received and wasted so much already that it was pointless to leave him more. Dick tried to contest the will, claiming that his father had not been himself after Maggie's death 'and his subsequent actions should not be counted as his'.[15] Implicitly he was suggesting that Frances had influenced him unduly. But his doctor at Churt testified that LG was in perfectly sound mind when he made a new will after his remarriage. He was in fact very careful not to favour Frances over his children: she received very little except Ty Newydd, the orchards around Avalon and his papers, plus some of his personal effects, though of course he had given her a good deal in his lifetime. Bitterly as Gwilym, Olwen and Megan now resented Frances, they could not pretend that she had disinherited them, and they were 'appalled' by Dick's attempted challenge.[16]

His revenge – after some years in America – was to come back and lend his name to a scurrilous ghost-written book about his father, published in 1960, potentially far more damaging than Sylvester's, but

---

* The *Times Literary Supplement* was typical. 'Whether Mr Sylvester has rendered a service to the memory of his chief, or to himself, by writing this singular book is a question not lightly to be answered in the affirmative.'[10] The *Spectator* reviewer conceded that 'his reporting is superb: it is a pity that he attempted interpretation'.[11]

so fantastic that it could not be taken seriously. It portrayed LG in his latter years as a sort of oriental despot wallowing in sexual luxury at Churt, and Frances as just one of a harem of nymphs who waited on his pleasure. It made Dick some money, but only embarrassed his sisters and brother. Dick finally died in 1968, when the earldom passed to the steadier hands of his son Owen.

The family continued to ignore Frances as far as possible, though there was a partial softening in 1960 when she was invited to the unveiling of a statue of LG in Cardiff attended by the Prime Minister, Harold Macmillan. She sat on the platform next to William George – who at the age of ninety-three had just published his own book about his brother – and helped look after him. Megan and Olwen still snubbed her, but Gwilym and Edna were 'very nice' to her, and the grandchildren were 'very friendly'.* At lunch after the ceremony she was pleased to be seated next to Macmillan.[17] Three years later there was another ceremony when LG's statue was placed in the lobby of the House of Commons. This time the family did not invite Frances; but fortunately the Speaker did.

In 1966 Megan died, aged sixty-four. Frances had always hoped for a reconciliation: it was after all to tutor Megan that she had been drawn into LG's family in the first place, fifty-five years earlier. But it never happened: Megan went to her grave – her *Tada*'s name on her dying breath – still refusing to forgive.[18] Nevertheless Frances insisted on going to Criccieth for the funeral. She was seventy-seven; her presence was not wanted, and she did not mingle with the other mourners. But she was determined to make the gesture.

Gwilym died next, in 1967, leaving Olwen alone to carry on the feud; but she managed to make herself unpleasant one last time at the unveiling of a plaque in Westminster Abbey in 1970. Frances was invited this time, but was not allowed to take Muriel to the party afterwards, even though – now aged eighty-two – she needed an arm to lean on; so she did not go, either. The service in the Abbey, however, was 'out of this world'. The singing was 'heavenly', she wrote to Jennifer, and Jeremy Thorpe – leader of the Liberal party – gave a 'wonderful' address. 'The blot on the proceedings was the Family, some of whom were revolting, especially Olwen who was throwing her weight about and

---

* Frances's financial generosity had included helping Dick's now estranged wife June; and before Dick died, his daughter Valerie sought her help in trying to find a home for her father.

looked awful.'[19]* But Gwilym's son William was charming, so it was not all bad.

Frances was gratified by the revival of interest in LG after the opening of his papers to scholars at the Beaverbrook Library in 1967, which coincided with the release of the official records of his premiership when the Wilson government cut the period of closure from fifty years to thirty. She contributed to this renaissance by writing her autobiography; then collaborated with A. J. P. Taylor on the publication of her diary in 1971. Before she died she had the satisfaction of being finally recognised as an historical figure in her own right. But she still could not tell the whole truth. When her book came out she was interviewed on television by Fyfe Robertson. Right at the end he asked if she regretted not having had children. She hesitated; but she had not mentioned Jennifer in the book and still did not feel able to do so. So she repeated her standard answer: 'Lloyd George was my child.'

> She recorded it before it went out and she did not mention this to Jennifer. When she came to watch it Jennifer knew this was only being consistent, but it made her feel obliterated – denied existence by her mother. She knew the feeling was not rational, but she did not like it. Frances remained unaware of her feelings: they did not discuss it.[20]

Frances, Countess Lloyd-George of Dwyfor, died at Churt on 5 December 1972, aged eighty-four. 'It was,' her granddaughter wrote, 'a good time to die . . . Physically and mentally she was deteriorating, slowly but irreversibly, and she died while still retaining her dignity and a great deal of her beauty.'[21]

---

* Olwen lived until 1990, finally dying at the age of ninety-eight. She too wrote a memoir of her father, published in 1985, in which she was dismissive of Frances.

SOURCES AND BIBLIOGRAPHY

Manuscript sources

This book is based largely on manuscript sources. Selections from the diaries of Frances Stevenson, Lord Riddell, Lord Hankey and A.J. Sylvester have been published, as have editions of the letters of Lloyd George and Frances Stevenson, and those between Lloyd George and his family. But wherever possible I have gone back to the originals, which are very often fuller, and at significant points different from the published texts, which cannot be considered reliable. The manuscript collections I have used are the following.

House of Lords Record Office, London
- Lloyd George papers (LG)
- Frances Stevenson papers (FLS)

National Library of Wales, Aberystwyth
- David Lloyd George papers (LG/NLW)
- William George papers (WG/NLW)
- Frances Stevenson papers (FLS/NLW)
- A.J. Sylvester diary

British Library, London
- Lord Riddell diary

Churchill College, Cambridge
- Lord Hankey diary

I have also been privileged to see family papers still in the possession of Mrs Jennifer Longford and Ruth Longford (Mrs Ruth Nixon). These are referenced as 'Ruth's box'.

Published sources

Caroline Bingham: *The History of Royal Holloway College, 1886–1986* (Constable, 1987)

David Butler and Gareth Butler: *British Political Facts, 1900–1994* (Macmillan, 1994)

John Campbell: *Lloyd George: The Goat in the Wilderness, 1922–1931* (Jonathan Cape, 1977)

Olwen Carey Evans: *Lloyd George Was My Father* (Gomer Press, 1985)

Thelma Cazalet-Keir: *From the Wings* (Bodley Head, 1967)

Frances Donaldson: *Edward VIII: The Road to Abdication* (Weidenfeld & Nicolson, 1974)

Bentley B. Gilbert: *Lloyd George: The Architect of Change, 1863–1912* (Batsford, 1987)

John Grigg: *The Young Lloyd George* (Eyre Methuen, 1973)

——*Lloyd George: The People's Champion, 1902–1911* (Eyre Methuen, 1978)

——*Lloyd George: From Peace to War, 1912–1916* (Eyre Methuen, 1985)

——*Lloyd George: War Leader* (Eyre Methuen 2002)

Viscount Gwynedd: *Dame Margaret* (Allen & Unwin, 1947)

Mervyn Jones: *A Radical Life: The Biography of Megan Lloyd George, 1902–66* (Hutchinson, 1991)

Thomas Jones: *Whitehall Diary*, ed. Keith Middlemas, 3 vols (Oxford 1969–71)

——*A Diary with Letters, 1931–1950* (Oxford, 1954)

Frances Lloyd George: *Makers of the New World, by One Who Knows Them* (Cassell, 1921)

——*The Years that are Past* (Hutchinson, 1967)

Owen Lloyd George: *A Tale of Two Grandfathers* (Bellew, 1999)

Richard Lloyd George: *Lloyd George* (Frederick Muller, 1960)

Ruth Longford: *Frances: More Than a Mistress* (Gracewing, Leominster, 1996)

Margaret Macmillan: *Peacemakers: The Paris Conference of 1919 and its Attempt to End War* (John Murray, 2001)

Norma Major: *Chequers: The Prime Minister's Country Home and its History* (HarperCollins, 1996)

Lucy Masterman: *C.F.G.Masterman* (Frank Cass, 1968)

John M. McEwan ed.: *The Riddell Diaries: A Selection* (Athlone Press, 1986)

K.O. Morgan: *Consensus and Disunity: The Lloyd George Coalition Government, 1918–1922* (Oxford, 1979)

K.O. Morgan ed.: *Lloyd George: Family Letters, 1885–1936* (University of Wales Press, Cardiff, and Oxford University Press, 1972)

Harold Nicolson: *Diaries and Letters, 1930–1939*, ed. Nigel Nicolson (Collins, 1966)

——*Diaries and Letters, 1939–1945*, ed. Nigel Nicolson (Collins 1967)

Frank Owen: *Tempestuous Journey: Lloyd George, His Life and Times* (Hutchinson, 1954)

Emyr Price: *Megan Lloyd George* (Gwynedd Archives Service, 1983)

Roland Quinault: 'Golf and Edwardian Politics' in Negley Harte and Roland Quinault (ed)., *Land and Society in Britain, 1700–1914* (Manchester University Press, 1996)

Lord Riddell: *Lord Riddell's War Diary, 1914–1918* (Ivor Nicholson & Watson, 1933)

——*Lord Riddell's Intimate Diary of the Peace Conference and After, 1918–1923* (Gollancz, 1933)

——*More Pages from my Diary, 1908–1914* (Country Life, 1934)

Stephen Roskill: *Hankey: Man of Secrets*, 3 vols (Collins, 1970, 1972, 1974)

Peter Rowland: *Lloyd George* (Barrie & Jenkins, 1975)

A.J. Sylvester: *The Real Lloyd George* (Cassell, 1947)

——*Life with Lloyd George*, ed. Colin Cross (Macmillan, 1975)

A.J.P. Taylor ed., *Lloyd George: A Diary by Frances Stevenson*, (Hutchinson, 1971)

——*My Darling Pussy: The Letters of Lloyd George and Frances Stevenson, 1913–1941* (Weidenfeld & Nicolson, 1975)

Philip Tilden: *True Remembrances: The Memoirs of an Architect* (Country Life, 1954)

Thomas F. Tweed: *Gabriel over the White House: A Sensational Novel of the Presidency* (Farrar & Stewart, New York, 1933)

——*Rinehard: A Melodrama of the Nineteen-Thirties* (Arthur Barker, 1933)

H.G. Wells: *Ann Veronica* (T. Fisher Unwin, 1909)

Virginia Woolf: *Orlando: A Biography* (Hogarth Press, 1928)

NOTES

Introduction

1. A. J. Sylvester, *The Real Lloyd George*, p.xi.

1. New Woman

1. Frances Lloyd George, *The Years That Are Past*, p.11.
2. ibid., p.12.
3. ibid.
4. ibid., p.27.
5. ibid., p.30.
6. ibid., p.32.
7. Margaret E. T. Taylor, Senior Staff Lecturer, in FLS/1/4.
8. FLS/1/1.
9. H. G. Wells, *Ann Veronica*, p.10.
10. ibid., p.248.
11. Louise Stevenson to Frances, FLS/1/1.
12. Constance Chattel to Frances, FLS/1/1.
13. FLS/1/3.
14. ibid.
15. *The Years That Are Past*, p.39.
16. ibid., p.40.
17. FLS diary, 10.3.34.
18. MLG to Mrs Woodhouse, 18.7.11, FLS/1/14.
19. Mrs Woodhouse to Frances, 26.7.11, FLS/1/14.
20. LG to MLG, n.d., in K. O. Morgan, ed., *Lloyd George: Family Letters*, p.156.

21. LG to MLG, 26.7.11, NLW 1359.
22. Olwen Lloyd George to Frances, 28.7.11, FLS/1/2.
23. *The Years That Are Past*, pp.42–3.
24. Olwen Carey Evans, *Lloyd George Was My Father*, pp.67–8.
25. LG to MLG, 30.7.11, WG/NLW 3499.
26. FLS/1/2.
27. *The Years That Are Past*, p.43.

2. The Wizard – and His Wife

1. LG to MLG, n.d., NLW, in K. O. Morgan, ed., p.14.
2. ibid., n.d., NLW, Morgan, p.19.
3. LG to MLG, 21.8.97, Morgan, p.112.
4. ibid., 23.5.02, Morgan, p.136.
5. ibid., 24.5.02, Morgan, p.136.
6. ibid., 11.3.14, Morgan, p.166.
7. A. J. Sylvester diary, 13.1.37.
8. ibid., 14.1.37.
9. For LG's affairs, see John Grigg, *The Young Lloyd George* and *Lloyd George: The People's Champion, 1902–1911*.

3. The Beginning of the Affair

1. LG to MLG, 21.8.11, NLW 1378.
2. LG to Megan, NLW, in K. O. Morgan, ed., p.157.
3. *The Years That Are Past*, pp.44–7.
4. ibid., p.46.
5. Lucy Masterman, *C. F. G. Masterman*, p.212.
6. LG to Frances, 11.8.25, 13.8.25.
7. Frances to LG, 19.5.32.
8. LG to MLG, 16.9.11, Morgan, p.159.
9. LG to Megan, 18.9.11, Morgan, p.159.
10. *The Years That Are Past*, p.49.
11. Grace Steenthal to Frances, 18.12.11, FLS/1/1.
12. 10.4.12, FLS/1/1.
13. *The Years That Are Past*, p.51.
14. FLS diary, 21.9.14.
15. *The Years That Are Past*, p.51.
16. FLS diary, 20.11.14.
17. LG to Frances, 25.7.12, FLS/1/2.

18. LG to MLG, 26.7.11, Morgan, p.162.
19. LG to Frances, n.d., FLS/1/2.
20. Lucy Masterman diary, cited in Bentley B. Gilbert, *Lloyd George: The Architect of Change, 1863–1912*, p.464.
21. Riddell diary, 6.10.13; A. J. Sylvester diary, 17.10.37.
22. Speech at Bath, 24.11.11.
23. LG to William George, 29.6.11, WG/NLW 2615.
24. LG to Frances, 6.8.12, FLS/1/2.
25. LG to MLG, 12.8.12, NLW 1435.
26. LG to Megan, 14.8.12, NLW 3134.
27. LG to Frances, 20.8.12, FLS/1/2.
28. Mary Phillips to Frances, 4.8.12, FLS/1/1.
29. J. T. Davies to Frances, 2.9.12, FLS/1/2.
30. H. P. Hamilton to Frances, 10.9.12, FLS/1/2.
31. Davies to Frances, 5.10.12, FLS/1/1.
32. Davies to Frances, 26.10.12, FLS/1/1.
33. LG to Frances, ?4.10.12, FLS/1/2.
34. Olwen to Frances, 4.10.12, FLS/1/1.
35. ibid., 16.11.12, FLS/1/2.
36. FLS diary, 31.10.34.
37. Frances to Sian, n.d., November 1912, FLS/6/19.
38. LG to Frances, 16.10.12, FLS/1/2.
39. LG to MLG, 15.10.12, NLW 1450.
40. ibid., 20.10.12, NLW 1455.
41. Megan to LG and MLG, n.d., FLS/1/3.
42. *The Years That Are Past*, pp.51–2.
43. LG to Frances, 23.12.12, FLS/1/1.
44. Davies to Frances, 26.12.12, FLS/1/2.
45. LG to Frances, 26.12.12, FLS/1/2.
46. Megan to Frances, 22.12.12, FLS/1/4.
47. ibid., n.d., FLS/1/4.

4. The Choice

1. *The Years That Are Past*, p.52.
2. LG to MLG, 25.11.90, K. O. Morgan, ed., pp.38–9.
3. LG to MLG, 28.11.90, Morgan, p.39.
4. FLS diary, 27.4.36.
5. Paul Stevenson to Frances, 27.10.12, NLW X2/1.

6. *The Years That Are Past*, p.53.
7. Stuart Brown to Frances, FLS/1/5.
8. *The Years That Are Past*, pp.52–3.
9. ibid., p.53.
10. A. J. P. Taylor, ed., *My Darling Pussy: The Letters of Lloyd George and Frances Stevenson, 1913–1941*, p.2.
11. *The Years That Are Past*, p.54.
12. ibid., pp.55–6.
13. LG to William George, 21.1.13, WG/NLW 2678.
14. FLS/6/26.
15. ibid.
16. FLS/1/14.
17. *My Darling Pussy*, p.4.
18. *The Years That Are Past*, p.56.
19. FLS diary, 11.3.15.

5. A Woman in Whitehall

1. *The Years That Are Past*, p.57.
2. H. P. Hamilton to Frances, 8.5.13, FLS1/2.
3. ?.2.13, *My Darling Pussy*, p.3.
4. LG to Frances, 29.4.13, FLS/1/2.
5. ibid., 1.5.13.
6. J. T. Davies to Frances, ?.5.13, FLS/1/2.
7. 12.5.13, FLS/1/2.
8. LG to MLG, 13.5.13, NLW 1463.
9. J. T. Davies to Frances, 16.5.13, FLS/1/2.
10. ibid., 7.7.13.
11. LG to MLG, 18.9.13, NLW 1479.
12. *The Times*, 24.9.13.
13. LG to MLG, 30.9.13, NLW 1489.
14. ibid., 6.10.13, NLW 1491.
15. Megan to Frances, 5.3.13, 23.1.13, FLS/1/4.
16. LG to Megan, 30.9.13, NLW 3137.
17. Muriel Stevenson to Frances, ?.8.13, FLS/1/14.
18. LG to Frances, n.d., FLS/1/2.
19. FLS/6/9.
20. FLS papers, Ruth's box.
21. ibid.

22. J. T. Davies to Frances, 5.1.14, FLS/1/2.
23. LG to MLG, 15.1.14, K. O. Morgan, ed., pp.165–6.
24. *The Years That Are Past*, pp.63–7.
25. LG to MLG, 11.3.14, Morgan, p.166.
26. LG to MLG, 4.4.14, NLW 1505.
27. J. T. Davies to Frances, 13.4.13, FLS/1/2.
28. Stuart Brown to Frances, 2.5.13, FLS/1/14.
29. ibid., 8.9.13, FLS/1/5.
30. ibid., 26.9.13.
31. ibid., 24.10.13.
32. *The Times*, 24.10.13.
33. *The Poetical Works of George Meredith* (Constable, 1912), pp.246–56.
34. Stuart Brown to Frances, 2.12.13, FLS/1/5.
35. ibid., 29.12.13, FLS/1/5.

6. The Coming of War

1. LG to MLG, 27.7.14, 28.7.14, 29.7.14, 3.8.14, K. O. Morgan, ed., pp.166–7.
2. Viscount Gwynedd, *Dame Margaret*, pp.159–60.
3. *The Years That Are Past*, p.73.
4. ibid., p.74.
5. LG, I/2/1.
6. ibid.
7. LG to MLG, 6.8.14, Morgan, p.167.
8. ibid., 7.8.14, Morgan, p.168.
9. ibid., 10.9.14, Morgan, p.172.
10. FLS diary, 21.9.14.
11. LG to Frances, 26.9.14, FLS/6/9.
12. FLS diary, 28.9.14.
13. Lord Riddell diary, p.33 [6.10.14].
14. FLS diary, 9.10.14.
15. ibid., 23.10.14.
16. LG to MLG, 20.10.14, Morgan, p.173.
17. FLS diary, 23.10.14.
18. LG to MLG, 30.10.14, Morgan, p.174.
19. FLS diary, 30.10.14.
20. LG to MLG, 6.8.14, Morgan, p.168.
21. ibid., 11.8.14, Morgan, p.169.

22. FLS/1/1.
23. FLS diary, 20.11.14.
24. ibid., 14.12.14.
25. ibid., 16.12.14.
26. ibid., 23.12.14.
27. ibid., 20.11.14.
28. ibid., 23.12.14.
29. ibid., 17.1.15.
30. ibid., 21.1.15.
31. ibid., 17.1.15.
32. Riddell diary, 17.1.15.
33. FLS diary, 21.1.15.
34. ibid., 25.1.15.
35. Megan to Frances, 8.2.15, LG I/3/4/14.
36. FLS diary, 8.2.15.

7. 'Love Justifies Many Audacities'

1. FLS diary, 11.2.15.
2. ibid., 14.2.15.
3. ibid., 23.2.15.
4. ibid., 16.5.15.
5. ibid., 11.3.15.
6. Ruth Longford, *Frances: More Than a Mistress*, p.29.
7. FLS diary, 30.10.14.
8. Riddell diary, 28.10.14.
9. FLS diary, 23.10.14.
10. ibid., 11.3.15.
11. LG to Frances, n.d., March 1915, FLS/6.

8. 'Pro Patria Mori'

1. FLS diary, 23.10.14.
2. ibid., 5.11.14.
3. ibid., 11.3.15.
4. ibid., 25.3.15.
5. Paul Stevenson to Frances, 4.4.15, FLS/1/14.
6. ibid., 27.4.15.
7. ibid., 2.5.15.

8. FLS diary, 4.4.15.
9. ibid., 8.4.15.
10. LG to Frances, 6.4.15, FLS/6.
11. ibid., 7.4.15.
12. FLS diary, 13.4.15.
13. LG to Frances, 9.4.15, FLS/6.
14. ibid., 10.4.15.
15. FLS diary, 25.4.15.
16. ibid., 6.5.15.
17. ibid., 15.5.15.
18. ibid., 18.5.15.
19. ibid., 24.5.15.
20. A. J. Sylvester diary, 6.1.37.
21. LG to MLG, 25.5.15, K. O. Morgan, ed., p.178.
22. FLS diary, 12.6.15.

9. The Decoy

1. FLS diary, 2.9.15.
2. Stuart Brown to Frances, 1.7.15, FLS/1/4.
3. LG to Frances, 8.8.15, FLS/6.
4. LG to MLG, 10.8.15, 11.8.15, 16.8.15, 18.8.15, K. O. Morgan, ed., pp.179–80.
5. LG to Frances, 23.8.15, FLS/6.
6. FLS diary, 15.9.15.
7. ibid., 20.9.15.
8. I *Corinthians* 11, 9.
9. FLS diary, 5.10.15.
10. Billy Owen to Frances, 11.10.15, FLS/1/3.
11. ibid., 14.10.15.
12. FLS diary, 11.10.15.
13. ibid., 24.11.15.
14. ibid., 11.10.15.
15. ibid., 24.11.15.
16. Billy Owen to Frances, 15.10.15, FLS/1/3.
17. ibid., 20.10.15.
18. FLS diary, 23.10.15.
19. ibid., 24.11.15.
20. ibid., 12.10.15.

21. ibid., 19.10.15.
22. ibid.
23. ibid., 15.11.15.
24. ibid., 16.11.15.
25. ibid., 22.11.15.
26. LG to MLG, 1.11.15, Morgan, p.180.
27. Riddell diary, 14.11.15.
28. FLS diary, 30.11.15.
29. ibid., 6.12.15.
30. ibid., 29.12.15.
31. LG to Frances, 22.12.15, FLS/1/2.
32. ibid., 23.12.15.
33. FLS diary, 29.12.15.
34. ibid., 21.1.16.
35. ibid., 31.1.16.
36. ibid.
37. Ruby Rusley to Frances, 19.5.16, FLS/1.
38. Norah Bennett to Frances, 20.5.16, FLS/1.
39. E. C. Higgins to Frances, 22.5.16, FLS/1.
40. Grace (Steenthal?) to Frances, 7.6.16, FLS/1.
41. LG to Frances, 5.6.16, FLS/1.
42. ibid., 6.6.16.
43. J. T. Davies to Frances, 9.9.16, FLS/1/2.
44. ibid., n.d., FLS/NLW FCF2/1.
45. Billy Owen to Frances, 29.9.16, FLS/1/3.
46. ibid., 10.11.16.
47. ibid., 28.11.16.
48. ibid., 5.12.16.
49. ibid.
50. FLS diary, 26.2.17.
51. ibid., 27.2.17.
52. Louise Stevenson to Frances, 7.3.17, FLS/1/4.
53. Ninette Stevenson to Frances, n.d., FLS/1/4.
54. Billy Owen to Frances, 17.3.18, 12.4.18, FLS/1/3.

10. Into No. 10

1. FLS diary, 31.1.16.
2. ibid., 1.2.16.
3. ibid., 8.2.16.

4. Riddell diary, 13.2.16.
5. FLS diary, 12.3.16.
6. ibid., 11.11.16.
7. LG to Frances, 7.9.16, FLS/1.
8. Ruth Longford, *Frances*, pp.135–6.
9. FLS diary, 26.7.16.
10. ibid.
11. ibid., 28.7.16.
12. LG to MLG, 9.8.90, K. O. Morgan, ed., p.33.
13. FLS diary, 1.2.16.
14. ibid., 13.11.16.
15. ibid., 16.2.16.
16. ibid., 1.3.16.
17. ibid., 11.10.16.
18. ibid., 10.11.16.
19. ibid., 13.11.16.
20. ibid., 20.11.16.
21. ibid., 14.11.16.
22. ibid., 30.11.16.
23. Riddell diary, 3.12.16.
24. FLS diary, 3.12.16.
25. ibid., 4.12.16.
26. ibid., 5.12.16.
27. ibid., 6.12.16.
28. ibid., 7.12.16.

11. The Prime Minister's Private Secretary

1. Stephen Roskill, *Hankey: Man of Secrets*, Vol. 1, p.353 (12.1.17).
2. *Truth*, n.d., 1917, in FLS/1/11.
3. FLS diary, 9.1.17.
4. LG to William George, 23.12.16, WG/NLW 3195.
5. FLS diary, 9.1.17.
6. ibid., 10.1.17.
7. ibid., 15.1.17.
8. ibid., 1.2.17.
9. Riddell diary, 5.4.17.
10. FLS diary, 9.2.17.
11. ibid., 19.5.17.
12. ibid., 1.3.17.

13. ibid., 1.4.17.
14. ibid., 14.4.17.
15. ibid., 15.11.16.
16. ibid., 23.4.17.
17. ibid., 12.5.17.
18. ibid., 10.3.17.
19. ibid., 27.5.17.
20. ibid., 28.5.17.
21. ibid., 28.4.17.
22. Gwilym to Frances, 18.9.17, LG I/3/2/11.
23. FLS diary, 1.2.17.
24. ibid., 7.5.21.
25. Riddell diary, 9.9.17.
26. FLS diary, 14.12.14.
27. ibid., 23.2.16.
28. LG to Frances, 13.9.17.
29. FLS diary, 5.11.17.
30. ibid., 5.11.17.
31. ibid., 6.11.17.

12. 'The Man Who Won the War'

1. A. J. P. Taylor, ed., *Lloyd George: A Diary by Frances Stevenson*, p.169.
2. FLS/1/11.
3. Frances to LG, 3.1.18, LG F/93/1/1.
4. e.g. Stephen Roskill, *Hankey: Man of Secrets*, Vol. 1, p.588 (6.8.18).
5. Lord Cholmondeley to Frances, 28.9.18, FLS/1/12a.
6. LG to Frances, n.d., August/September 1918, FLS/6/1.
7. Roskill, Vol. 1, p.522 (9.4.18).
8. ibid., p.604 (22.9.18).
9. Riddell diary, 21.9.18, 10.7.20.
10. ibid., 21.9.18.
11. LG to Frances, 5.10.18, FLS/6/1.
12. Roskill, Vol. 2, p.21 (22.11.18).
13. Riddell diary, 8.12.18.
14. Nancy Astor to Frances, 20.11.18, FLS/1/2.
15. LG to MLG, 13.12.18, in K. O. Morgan, ed., p.188.
16. Sir John Cowans to Frances, 24.12.18, 1.1.19, FLS/1/12a.
17. FLS diary, 8.8.16.

18. *The Years That Are Past*, p.88.
19. LG to MLG, 13.12.18, in Morgan, pp.188–9.
20. MLG to LG, n.d., LG I/1/2/50.
21. Riddell diary, 25.12.18.
22. Roskill, Vol. 2, p.39 (25.12.18).
23 FLS diary, 17.11.35.
24. Roskill, Vol. 2, p.40 (28.12.18).
25. ibid., p.41 (31.12.18–5.1.19).

13. Paris, 1919

1. *My Darling Pussy*, p.26.
2. *The Years That Are Past*, p.149.
3. Viscount Gwynedd, *Dame Margaret*, p.176.
4. MLG to LG, n.d., LG I/1/2/53.
5. *Makers of the New World, by One Who Knows Them*, pp.162–3.
6. Margaret Macmillan, *Peacemakers*, p.158.
7. MLG to LG, n.d., LG I/1/2/53; for the 'Megantic', see Macmillan, p.158.
8. FLS diary, 23.3.19.
9. *Makers of the New World*, pp.175–8.
10. FLS diary, 9.3.19.
11. ibid., 12.3.19.
12. FLS/1/7.
13. FLS/1/11.
14. FLS diary, 1.4.19.
15. *The Years That Are Past*, p.158.
16. FLS diary, 12.7.19.
17. ibid., 16.5.19.
18. ibid., 21.5.19.
19. ibid., 23.5.19.
20. ibid., 25.5.19.
21. ibid., 9.3.19, 10.4.19, 14.5.19, 12.3.19, 10.4.19.
22. ibid., 26.3.19.
23. ibid., 19.4.19.
24. ibid., 6.4.19.
25. ibid., 24.3.19.
26. ibid., 13.3.19.
27. ibid., 17.9.34.
28. ibid., 17.5.19.

29. ibid., 19.3.19.

30. ibid., 13.3.19.

31. ibid., 16.3.19.

32. ibid., 13.4.19.

33. Riddell diary, 8.6.19.

34. *Makers of the New World*, pp.145–8.

35. Riddell diary, 20.4.19.

36. FLS diary, 20.4.19.

37. ibid., 21.3.19.

38. Riddell diary, 21.4.19.

39. ibid., 23.4.19.

40. FLS diary, 16.4.19.

41. ibid., 17.4.19.

42. ibid., 10–11.5.19.

43. ibid., 15.4.19.

44. Nancy Astor to Frances, 17.5.19, FLS/1/12a.

45. *The Years That Are Past*, p.155.

46. FLS diary, 29.11.19.

47. ibid., 1.12.19.

48. ibid., 10.4.19.

49. *The Years That Are Past*, p.156.

50. ibid., p.157.

51. FLS diary, 2–3.4.19; Orpen to Frances, 17.2.20, n.d. October 1926 and 10.10.28, in FLS/1/13a.

52. Lord Cholmondeley to Frances, 12.5.19, FLS/1/12a.

53. John Grigg, *Lloyd George: From Peace to War, 1912–1916*, p.80.

54. FLS diary, 10.4.34.

55. ibid., 28.6.19.

56. Riddell diary, 28.6.19.

57. ibid., 24.6.19.

58. ibid., 29.6.19.

59. FLS diary, 29.6.19.

14. 'My Father & Lover & Brother & Friend'

1. FLS diary, 29.6.19.

2. ibid., 3.7.19.

3. ibid., 5.7.19.

4. Stephen Roskill, *Hankey*, Vol. 2, p.110.

5. LG to Frances, 8.7.19, FLS/6/1.

6. Frances to LG, 10.7.19, FLS/6/1.
7. ibid.
8. LG to Frances, 13.7.19, FLS/6/1.
9. Hankey diary, 25.8.19 [Hankey papers 1/5].
10. FLS diary, 12.7.19.
11. ibid., 14.7.19.
12. ibid., 18.7.19.
13. ibid., 20.7.19.
14. ibid., 21.7.19
15. MLG to LG, 13.8.19, LG I/1/2/40.
16. Hankey diary, 25.8.19 [Hankey papers 1/5].
17. Riddell diary, 3.8.19.
18. MLG to LG, 14.8.19, LG I/1/2/40.
19. Riddell diary, 22.8.19.
20. MLG to LG, undated, LG I/1/2/58.
21. ibid.
22. Riddell diary, 30.8.19.
23. ibid., 8.9.19.
24. LG to Megan, 10.9.19, LG/NLW 3142.
25. Riddell diary, 12.9.19.
26. FLS diary, 26.11.19.
27. ibid., 12.12.19.
28. ibid., 29.11.19.
29. ibid., 8.12.19.
30. ibid., 11.12.19.
31. ibid., 13.12.19.
32. ibid., 16.12.19.
33. ibid., 17.12.19.
34. ibid., 20.12.19.
35. ibid., 23.12.19.
36. ibid.

15. '. . . Who Danced with the Prince of Wales'

1. FLS diary, 23.1.20.
2. Sir Nevil Macready to Frances, 19.9.22, FLS/1/5.
3. William Orpen to Frances, 17.2.20 and n.d., FLS/1/13a.
4. ibid., October 1926, FLS/1/13a.
5. Emerald Cunard to Frances, n.d., Ruth's box.
6. FLS/1/1.

7. Ethel Smyth to Frances, 20.7.20, FLS/1/1.
8. H. G. Wells to Frances, 28.10.20, FLS/1/1.
9. FLS diary, 6.12.19.
10. ibid., 18.12.19.
11. ibid., 19.12.19.
12. ibid., 20.12.19.
13. ibid., 12.2.20.
14. ibid., 16.2.20.
15. ibid., 20.1.20.
16. ibid., 17.1.20.
17. ibid., 21.1.20.
18. ibid., 24.1.20.
19. ibid., 2.2.20.
20. ibid., 8.2.20; Stephen Roskill, *Hankey*, Vol. 2, p.146 (15.2.20).
21. Riddell diary, 9.2.20.
22. FLS diary, 14.2.20.
23. ibid., 20.2.20.
24. ibid., 21.2.20.
25. ibid.
26. ibid., 23.2.20.
27. A. J. Sylvester diary, 20.11.24.
28. Riddell diary, 3.6.22.
29. ibid., 2.7.22, 8.7.22.
30. Hankey diary, 25.2.20 [Hankey papers 1/5].
31. ibid., 7.3.20.
32. FLS diary, 28.2.20.
33. ibid., 18.3.20.
34. ibid., 19.3.20.
35. ibid., 20.3.20.

16. French Without Tears

1. Hankey diary, 1.5.20 [Hankey papers 1/5].
2. Stephen Roskill, *Hankey*, Vol. 2, p.164 (8.5.20).
3. Hankey diary, 14.5.20 [Hankey papers 1/5].
4. Riddell diary, 15.5.20.
5. Roskill, pp.167–8 (23.5.20).
6. Riddell diary, 20.6.20.
7. Hankey diary, September 1920 [Hankey papers 1/5].
8. LG to MLG, 2.9.20, in K. O. Morgan, ed., p.192.

9.   Roskill, p.190 (18.9.20).

10. LG to MLG, 15.9.20, in Morgan, p.193.

11. Hankey diary, 27.12.20 [Hankey papers 1/5].

12. Riddell diary, 26.6.20.

13. ibid., 1.1.21.

14. ibid., 8.1.21.

15. Ruth Longford, *Frances*, p.151.

16. Megan to LG, September 1920, NLW FCF2/1.

17. Riddell diary, 19.2.21.

18. ibid., 22.1.21.

19. John Stevenson to Frances, 25.9.20, FLS/1/2, and other letters from John and Louise Stevenson to Frances, mostly undated, in FLS/1/1/ and FLS/1/2.

20. *Dictionnaire de Biographie Française* (Paris 1954), Vol. 6, p.199.

21. Roskill, p.150 (27.3.20).

22. FLS diary, 23.11.34, in FLS/5/2.

23. *The Times*, 23.11.34.

24. FLS diary, 23.11.34, in FLS/5/2.

25. Philippe Berthelot to Frances, 13.3.21, FLS/1/9.

26. ibid., 20.3.21.

27. Riddell diary, 17.4.21.

28. FLS diary, 20.4.21.

29. ibid., 26.4.21.

30. ibid., 30.4.21.

31. ibid., 1.5.21.

32. Berthelot to Frances, 1.5.21, FLS/1/9.

33. FLS diary, 3.5.21.

34. ibid., 4.5.21.

35. ibid., 5.5.21.

36. ibid., 29.7.21.

37. Berthelot to Frances, 18.8.21, FLS/1/9.

38. Philippe Millet to Frances, 29.5.21, FLS/1/1.

39. ibid., 28.7.21, FLS/1/1.

40. ibid., 3.8.21, FLS/1/1.

17. 'We Are Too Reckless . . . We Shall Have to be More Careful'

1.   Riddell diary, 27.3.21.

2.   ibid., 3.4.21.

3. FLS diary, 10.5.21.
4. ibid., 15.5.21.
5. ibid.
6. ibid., 16.5.21, 20.5.21.
7. ibid., 24.5.21.
8. ibid., 31.5.21.
9. ibid., 1.6.21.
10. ibid., 5.6.21.
11. ibid., 11.6.21.
12. ibid., 18.6.21.
13. LG to Frances, 15.6.21.
14. FLS diary, 18.6.21.
15. ibid., 20.6.21.
16. Riddell diary, 22.6.21.
17. FLS diary, 4.7.21.
18. ibid., 24.6.21; Riddell diary, 3.7.21.
19. FLS diary, 4.7.21.
20. ibid., 5.7.21.
21. ibid., 6.7.21.
22. ibid.
23. ibid., 11.7.21.
24. ibid., 13.7.21.
25. ibid., 14.7.21.
26. ibid., 18.7.21.
27. ibid., 20.7.21, 22.7.21.
28. ibid., 25.7.21.
29. ibid., 22.7.21.
30. ibid., 26.7.21.

18. Highland Fling

1. *The Times*, 29.8.21.
2. Riddell diary, 26.8.21.
3. *The Years That Are Past*, pp.186–7.
4. Riddell diary, 1–6.9.21.
5. Thomas Jones, *Whitehall Diary*, Vol. 1, pp.169–70 (6.9.21).
6. ibid., p.170 (9.9.21).
7. Riddell diary, 12.9.21.
8. ibid., 14.9.21.
9. *The Years That Are Past*, pp.185–6.

10. LG to Frances, n.d., September 1921.
11. Riddell diary, 15.9.21.
12. Lawrence Burgis to Tom Jones, 22.9.21, in Jones, p.173.
13. Frances to Muriel Stevenson, 15.9.21, FLS/NLW FCF/1/1.
14. John Stevenson to Frances, 15.9.21, FLS/1/1.
15. LG to MLG, 29.9.21, in K. O. Morgan, ed., p.194.
16. FLS diary, 13.7.21.
17. MLG to Olwen LG, n.d., in Morgan, p.201.
18. FLS diary, 23.11.21.
19. ibid., 24.11.21.
20. LG to MLG, 24.11.21, in Morgan, pp.194–5.
21. *The Years That Are Past*, pp.190–1.

19. 'The Sweetest Little Worry in the World'

1. FLS diary, 3.2.22.
2. ibid., 29.7.21.
3. Riddell diary, 28–9.1.22.
4. ibid., 26.2.22.
5. ibid., 2.3.22.
6. LG to Frances, 15.3.22, FLS/6/1.
7. ibid., 17.3.22.
8. J. T. Davies to Frances, 21.3.22, FLS/6/1.
9. LG to Frances, 21.3.22.
10. ibid., 22.3.22.
11. ibid., 24.3.22.
12. Riddell diary, 23–8.3.22.
13. LG to MLG, 28.3.22, in K. O. Morgan, ed., p.195.
14. Philip Sassoon to Frances, n.d., FLS/NLW FCG2/4.
15. FLS diary, 7.4.34.
16. LG to Frances, 11.4.22, FLS/6/1.
17. ibid., 19.4.22.
18. ibid., 23.4.22.
19. ibid., 26.4.22.
20. ibid., 30.4.22.
21. ibid., 2.5.22.
22. ibid., 3.5.22.
23. ibid., 4.5.22.
24. ibid., 7.5.22.
25. ibid., 9.5.22.

26. ibid., 10–12.5.22.
27. ibid., 13.5.22.
28. Riddell diary, 'Mid-April and Early May' 1922.
29. LG to Frances, 15.5.22, FLS/6/1.
30. Frances to LG, 17.5.22, FLS/6/1.

20. Decline and Fall

1. Riddell diary, 3.6.22.
2. FLS diary, 22.6.22.
3. Frances to Muriel Stevenson, 23.6.22, FLS/NLW FCF/1/1.
4. FLS diary, 26.6.22.
5. *Makers of the New World*, pp.18–19.
6. ibid., pp.35–6.
7. ibid., pp.121–3.
8. FLS diary, 15.5.21.
9. Frances to LG, 16.1.23, FLS/6/2.
10. Leonard Rees to Frances, 31.8.21, FLS/1/2.
11. *The Times*, 28.7.21.
12. *Times Literary Supplement*, 4.8.21.
13. *The Nation & Athenaeum*, 13.10.21.
14. *The Times*, 28.7.21.
15. FLS diary, 22.6.22.
16. Riddell diary, 29.7.22.
17. A. M. Heath & Co. to Frances, 21.4.22, FLS/1/2.
18. Riddell diary, 29.7.22.
19. MLG to LG, n.d., LG I/1/2/44.
20. Riddell diary, 20.12.22.
21. ibid., 29.7.22.
22. LG to MLG, 8.9.22, in K. O. Morgan, ed., p.196.
23. Geoffrey Shakespeare to Frances, 19.8.22, FLS/1/2.
24. LG to MLG, 29.8.22, in Morgan, pp.195–6.
25. ibid., 6.9.22, in Morgan, p.196.
26. Riddell diary, 15.9.22.
27. ibid., 24.9.22.
28. Thomas Jones, *Whitehall Diary*, Vol. I, p.214 (19.10.22).
29. ibid., p.216 (22.10.22).
30. ibid., p.217 (23.10.22); Stephen Roskill, *Hankey*, Vol. II, pp.299–300 (23.10.22).

21. Into the Unknown

1. *Saturday Night* (Toronto), 23.9.22, in LG F/93/1/2.
2. Jean Scott to Frances, 27.12.22, FLS/1/13b.
3. Rhys Roberts to FLS, 14.1.21, FLS/1/2.
4. Janet Stevenson to Frances, 18.1.20, FLS/11/2.
5. FLS/1/2; FLS/NLW FCG 2/4.
6. A. J. Sylvester, *Life with Lloyd George*, p.177n.
7. Louise Stevenson to Frances, May 1922, FLS/1/1.
8. ibid., June 1922, FLS/1/1.
9. Muriel Stevenson to Frances, summer 1922, FLS/1/1.
10. MLG to Olwen, 25.10.22, in K. O. Morgan, ed., p.197.
11. Megan LG to Olwen, 25.10.22, in Morgan, p.197.
12. LG to Frances, n.d., FLS/6/1.
13. FLS diary, 13.7.35.
14. LG to MLG, n.d., Morgan, ed., p.200.
15. Riddell diary, 16.11.22.
16. LG to Frances, 14.1.23, FLS/6/2.
17. Riddell diary, 13.1.23.
18. Thelma Cazalet-Keir, *From the Wings*, pp.50–1.
19. Frances to LG, 16.1.23, FLS/6/2.
20. LG to Frances, 18.1.23, FLS/6/2.
21. FLS, Ruth's box.
22. LG to Frances, 25.1.23, FLS/6/2.
23. Riddell diary, 15.1.23.
24. For Megan and Stephen McKenna, see Mervyn Jones, *A Radical Life: The Biography of Megan Lloyd George, 1902–66*, pp.50–2.
25. LG to Frances, 28.1.23, FLS/6/2.

22. Romantic Fictions

1. The first draft is in Ruth's box. The second is in FLS/9/1, FLS/9/2 and FLS/9/3.
2. R. D. Blumenfeld to Frances, 16.2.25, FLS/1/5.
3. *The Years That Are Past*, p.18.
4. FLS diary, 13.2.34.
5. Frances to LG, 26.12.24, FLS/6/2.
6. FLS/9/2.

23. The Goat in the Wilderness

1. Jennifer Longford paper FLS/NLW X3/1, p.24.
2. A. J. Sylvester diary, November 1924.
3. LG to Frances, 14.8.25.
4. Philip Tilden, *True Remembrances*, p.77.
5. LG to Frances, 23.5.23, FLS/6/2.
6. Frances to LG, 9.8.23, FLS/6/6.
7. ibid., 12.8.23, FLS/6/6.
8. LG to Frances, 14.8.23, FLS/6/6.
9. ibid., 15.8.23.
10. Frances to LG, 15.8.23, FLS/6/6.
11. ibid., 16.8.23.
12. ibid., 17.8.23.
13. LG to Frances, 21.6.23, FLS/6/6.
14. Frances to LG, 22.8.23, FLS/6/6.
15. ibid., 10.10.23.
16. Frances to Sylvester, 10.10.23, FLS/6/6.
17. John Stevenson to Frances, 18.10.23, FLS/1/1.
18. FLS/1/1.
19. 'Italian guide' to Frances, 23.10.23, FLS/1/1.
20. LG to Frances, 22.10.23, FLS/6/6.
21. Frances to LG, 26.11.23, FLS/6/6.
22. ibid.
23. ibid., 17.8.23.

24. 'To Me You Are Everything'

1. LG to MLG, 24.7.24, LG/NLW 1835.
2. Frances to LG, 20.10.24, FLS/6/2.
3. A. J. Sylvester diary, 26.11.24.
4. ibid., 6.12.24.
5. ibid., 11.12.24.
6. ibid., 18–19.12.24.
7. Frances to LG, 26.12.24, FLS/6/2.
8. Sylvester diary, 31.12.24.
9. FLS diary, 17.3.25, Ruth's box.
10. LG to Frances, 14.4.25, FLS/6/2.
11. ibid., 2.6.25.
12. ibid., 11.8.25.

13. Frances to LG, 12.8.25, FLS/6/2.
14. ibid.
15. LG to Frances, 13.8.25, FLS/6/2.
16. ibid., 18.8.25.
17. Frances to LG, 18.8.25, FLS/6/2.
18. ibid.
19. LG to Frances, 19.8.25, FLS/6/2.
20. Frances to LG, 20.8.25, FLS/6/2.
21. LG to Frances, 20.8.25, FLS/6/2.
22. Frances to LG, 21.8.25, FLS/6/2.
23. A. J. Sylvester, *The Real Lloyd George*, p.98.
24. LG to MLG, 26.12.25, LG/NLW 1853.

25. 'The Children of Noah'

1. Speech at Cambridge, 1.5.26.
2. FLS diary, 15.5.26.
3. ibid., 21.5.26.
4. LG to Frances, 24.5.26, FLS/6/3.
5. FLS diary, 30.5.26.
6. *Sunday News*, 13.6.26.
7. LG to Frances, n.d., July 1926, FLS/6/3.
8. ibid., 10.8.26.
9. ibid., 11.8.26.
10. ibid., 13.8.26.
11. *My Darling Pussy*, p.102, n.1.
12. LG to Frances, 21.8.26, FLS/6/3.
13. ibid., 22.8.26.
14. LG to Frances, 24–25.8.26, FLS/6/3.
15. LG to MLG, 22.9.26, in K. O. Morgan, ed., pp.206–7.
16. *The Years That Are Past*, p.218.
17. *Genesis* 9, 18–27.
18. LG to MLG, October 1926, in FLS/6/6.
19. FLS diary, 3.2.27.
20. LG to Frances, 3–6.8.27, FLS/6/3.
21. ibid., 8.8.27.
22. ibid., 1.10.40.
23. ibid., 10.8.27.
24. FLS diary, 18.8.27.

26. Enter Colonel Tweed

1. *Daily Telegraph*, 1.5.40.
2. LG to Frances, 24–5.8.26, FLS/6/3.
3. *News Chronicle*, 1.5.40.
4. *Evening Standard*, 1.5.40.
5. *The Years That Are Past*, p.220.
6. LG to Frances, 22.12.27, FLS/6/3.
7. ibid., 24.12.27.
8. LG to Frances, 29.12.27, FLS/6/3.
9. Thomas Tweed to Frances, 9.8.28, in Ruth Longford, *Frances*, pp.95–6.
10. ibid., 14.8.28, p.96.

27. 'No Transactions'

1. LG to Frances, 12.9.28, FLS/6/3.
2. ibid., 14.9.28.
3. ibid., 28.9.28.
4. Speech in House of Commons, 9.11.28.
5. A. J. Sylvester diary, 11.12.32.
6. Jennifer Longford paper FLS/NLW X3/1, p.1.
7. Frances to LG, 15.1.29, FLS/6/3.
8. Virginia Woolf, *Orlando*, p.200.
9. *My Darling Pussy*, p.112n.
10. LG to Frances, n.d., *c*.16.1.29, FLS/6/3.
11. Frances to LG, 17.1.29, FLS/6/3.
12. ibid., 21.1.29.
13. LG to Frances, 22.1.29, FLS/6/3.
14. Frances to LG, 23.1.29, FLS/6/3.
15. LG to Frances, 25.1.29, FLS/6/3.
16. Frances to LG, 26.1.29, FLS/6/3.
17. LG to Frances, 31.1.29, FLS/6/3.
18. ibid., 26.1.29.
19. Frances to LG, 29.1.29, FLS/6/3.
20. ibid., 30.1.29.
21. A. J. Sylvester to Frances, 31.1.29, FLS/6/8.
22. Sylvester to Frances, 31.1.29, FLS/6/8.
23. LG to Frances, 31.1.29, FLS/6/3.
24. Tweed postcards to Muriel, 1928 and 1934–9, in Ruth's box.

25. Frances to LG, 1.2.29, FLS/6/3.
26. LG to Frances, 3.2.29, FLS/6/3.
27. ibid., 6.2.29.
28. Frances to LG, 4.2.29, FLS/6/3.
29. LG to Frances, 5.2.29, FLS/6/3.

28. Jennifer

1. LG to Frances, 25.3.29, FLS/6/3.
2. ibid.
3. *Manchester Guardian* obituary, May 1940.
4. LG to Frances, 15.5.29, FLS/6/3.
5. Speech at Caernarvon, 29.5.29.
6. Interview at Euston, 31.5.29.
7. Jennifer Longford paper, in FLS/NLW X3/1, p.1.
8. LG to Frances, n.d., August 1929, FLS/6/3.
9. Ruth Longford, *Frances*, p.99.
10. ibid., p.101.
11. FLS/NLW D/2.
12. Birth certificate, Jennifer Mary Stevenson, 6.11.29.
13. Jennifer Longford paper, FLS/NLW X3/1, pp.1–4.
14. ibid.

29. 'A Most Fascinating Little Person'

1. Felicia Brook to Frances, 23.5.30, FLS/1/12a.
2. ibid., 18.6.30.
3. LG to Frances, 24–5.8.26, FLS/6/3.
4. ibid., 9.8.30, FLS/6/4.
5. Frances to LG, 10.8.30, FLS/6/4.
6. LG to Frances, 12.8.30, FLS/6/4.
7. Frances to LG, 14.8.30, FLS/6/4.
8. LG to Frances, 14.8.30, FLS/6/4.
9. Frances to LG, 15.8.30, FLS/6/4.
10. LG to Frances, 15.8.30, FLS/6/4.
11. ibid., 16.8.30.
12. Frances to LG, 6.1.31, FLS/6/4.
13. LG to Frances, 25.1.31, FLS/6/4.
14. ibid., 28.1.31.
15. ibid., 30.1.31.

16. ibid., 4.2.31.
17. ibid., 5.2.31.
18. ibid., 9.2.31.
19. ibid., n.d., possibly February 1931.
20. A. J. Sylvester diary, 8.7.31.

30. *Hors de Combat*

1. A. J. Sylvester diary, 25.6.31.
 2. ibid., 5.8.32.
 3. ibid., 11.5.31.
 4. ibid., 12.5.31.
 5. ibid., 17.6.31.
 6. Jennifer Longford paper, FLS/NLW X3/1, p.31.
 7. Owen Lloyd George, *A Tale of Two Grandfathers*, p.31.
 8. Harold Nicolson, *Diaries and Letters, 1930–39*, pp.78–9 (21.7.31).
 9. Sylvester diary, 22.7.31.
10. ibid., 24.7.31.
11. ibid., 26.7.31.
12. ibid., 27.7.31.
13. ibid., 29.7.31.
14. ibid., 30.7.31.
15. ibid., 1.8.31
16. ibid.
17. ibid., 2.8.31.
18. ibid., 4.8.31.
19. LG to Frances, 6.8.31, FLS/6/4.
20. ibid., 10.8.31.
21. ibid., 14.8.31.
22. ibid., 19.8.31.
23. LG to Ramsay MacDonald, 30.8.31, LG G/13/2/15.
24. LG to Herbert Samuel, 25.8.31, Samuel papers A 78/12, in John
    Campbell, *The Goat in the Wilderness*, p.298.
25. Sylvester diary, 25.8.31.
26. FLS/6/4.
27. Lord Dawson to LG, 18.9.31, in Ruth Longford, *Frances*, p.106.
28. Tweed to Frances, 29.8.31, LG G/28/2/2.
29. ibid., 31.8.31, LG G/28/2/3.
30. Samuel note of a talk with LG, 5.10.31, Samuel papers A 81/25–6, in
    Campbell, p.299.

31. *The Years That Are Past*, pp.223–4.
32. Sylvester diary, 25.10.31.
33. Reported in *The Times*, 29.10.31.

31. 'My Two Sweethearts'

1. *My Darling Pussy*, p.152.
 2. A. J. Sylvester diary, 30.10.31.
 3. LG to Frances, 20.11.31, FLS/6/4.
 4. Frances to LG, 20.11.31, FLS/6/4.
 5. Sylvester diary, 22.11.31.
 6. LG to Frances, 28.11.31, FLS/6/4.
 7. Frances to LG, 3–5.12.31, FLS/6/4.
 8. LG to Frances, 8.12.31, FLS/6/4.
 9. Sylvester diary, 8.12.31.
10. ibid., 16.12.31.
11. ibid., 13.12.31.
12. ibid., 14.12.31.
13. Frances to LG, 9–10.12.31, FLS/6/4.
14. ibid., 16.12.31.
15. ibid., 21–3.12.31.
16. Sylvester diary, 27.12.31.
17. ibid., 22.12.31.
18. LG to Frances, 31.12.31, FLS/6/4.
19. ibid., 1.1.32.
20. Sylvester diary, 5.1.32.
21. ibid., 19.1.32.
22. Frances to LG, 20.1.32, FLS/6/5.
23. ibid., 25.1.32.
24. Sylvester diary, 20.2.32.
25. ibid., 12.2.32.
26. ibid., 4.4.32.
27. Frances to LG, 13.5.32, FLS/6/5.
28. ibid., 15.5.32.
29. LG to Frances, 15.5.32, FLS/6/5.
30. ibid., 17.5.32.
31. Frances to LG, 19.5.32, FLS/6/5.
32. Sylvester diary, 31.7.32.
33. Frances to LG, 30.7.32, FLS/6/5.
34. ibid., 31.7.32.

35. Frances to LG, 30.7.32, FLS/6/5.
36. Sylvester diary, 24.5.32.
37. LG to Frances, 1.8.32, FLS/6/5.
38. Frances to LG, 2.8.32, FLS/6/5.
39. ibid., 3.8.32.
40. LG to Frances, 23.9.32, FLS/6/5.
41. Frances to LG, 23.9.32, FLS/6/5.
42. LG to Frances, 23.9.32, FLS/6/5.
43. ibid., 28.9.32.
44. Sylvester diary, 28.9.32.
45. Frances to LG, 2.10.32, FLS/6/5.

32. Tweed Again

1. A. J. Sylvester diary, 5.2.32.
2. ibid., 23.5.32.
3. ibid., 11.12.32.
4. ibid., 12.4.32.
5. ibid., 20.5.32.
6. ibid., 22.5.32.
7. ibid., 11.12.32.
8. ibid., 10.5.32.
9. ibid., 21.7.32.
10. Tom Carey Evans to LG, 3.12.40, LG I/3/3/28.
11. Frances to LG, 25.10.32, FLS/6/5.
12. Sylvester diary, 26.10.32.
13. ibid., 30.10.32, 1.11.32.
14. ibid., 12.11.32.
15. ibid., 26.4.32.
16. ibid., 6.10.33.
17. ibid., 11.12.32.
18. ibid., 12.12.32.
19. ibid., 13.12.32.
20. ibid., 14.12.32.
21. ibid., 16.12.32, 17.12.32.
22. ibid., 22.12.32.
23. FLS/6/21.
24. Sylvester diary, 7.9.33.
25. ibid., 23.9.36.
26. The Times, 15.5.34, 22.5.34 and 26.5.34.

27. Ruth Longford, *Frances*, p.113.
28. FLS diary, 23.5.34.
29. FLS diary, 19.10.34, FLS/4/8; see *My Darling Pussy*, pp.210–11.
30. Thomas F. Tweed, *Rinehard: A Melodrama of the Nineteen-Thirties*, p.131.
31. ibid., p.146.
32. ibid., p.237.
33. ibid., pp.29–30.
34. ibid., pp.30–4.
35. ibid., p.32.
36. ibid., pp.33–4.
37. ibid., p.8.
38. ibid., p.55.
39. *The Times*, 3.3.33.
40. Unidentified press cutting, in Ruth's box.
41. ibid.
42. *Evening Standard*, 30.8.38.
43. *Manchester Guardian*, 4.9.37.
44. Sylvester diary, 28.6.35.
45. Tweed to LG, 20.1.33, in LG G/28/2/1.
46. Sylvester diary, 25.6.35.
47. ibid., 28.6.35.
48. ibid., 25.6.35.
49. ibid., 11.4.38.

33. Down on the Farm

1. A. J. Sylvester diary, 20.1.33.
2. ibid., 14.3.33.
3. ibid., 28.6.39.
4. ibid., 14.3.33.
5. ibid., 24.6.35.
6. ibid., 13.12.36.
7. FLS diary, 29.3.34.
8. ibid., 12.2.34.
9. ibid., 24.2.34.
10. ibid., 13.3.34.
11. ibid., 17.3.34.
12. Sylvester diary, 8.6.37.
13. Jennifer Longford paper, FLS/NLW X3/1, p.10.

14. Ruth Longford, *Frances*, p.115.

15. Sylvester diary, 29.10.34.

16. Longford, *Frances*, p.119.

17. ibid., p.149.

18. FLS diary, 1.4.34, FLS/4/9.

19. ibid., 2.5.34, FLS/4/10.

20. Sylvester diary, 20.7.36.

21. ibid., 2.6.36.

22. ibid., 29.11.35.

23. Frances to LG, n.d., August 1935, FLS/6/5.

24. Sylvester diary, 11.5.36, 14.5.36.

25. LG to Frances, 14.1.34, FLS/6/5.

26. ibid., 15.1.34.

27. ibid., 23.1.34.

28. ibid., 26.1.34.

29. Longford, *Frances*, pp.117–18.

30. Sylvester diary, 7.9.34, 9.9.34.

31. FLS diary, 9.3.34.

32. ibid., 21.3.34.

33. Sylvester diary, 11.8.33.

34. ibid., 2.4.32.

35. ibid., 25.3.35.

36. ibid., 21.10.35.

37. ibid., 27.7.36.

38. Harold Nicolson, *Diaries and Letters, 1930–39*, p.120 (21.10.32).

39. FLS diary, 9.4.35.

40. ibid., 18.2.34.

41. ibid., 21.9.34.

42. ibid., 25.9.34.

43. ibid., 8.10.34.

44. ibid., 10.1.35.

45. ibid., 7.2.35.

46. ibid., 11.3.35.

47. ibid., 14.3.35.

48. Sylvester diary, 27.3.35.

49. FLS diary, 28.3.35.

50. Sylvester diary, 9.2.35.

51. ibid., 25.3.35.

52. FLS diary, 1.4.35.

53. ibid., 23.4.35.
54. ibid., 1.7.35.
55. ibid., 17.7.35.
56. ibid., 28.8.35.
57. ibid., 22.9.35.
58. ibid., 9.9.35.
59. ibid., 17.11.35.
60. ibid., 18.11.35.
61. Longford, *Frances*, pp.121–4.
62. FLS diary, 11.6.36.

34. 'If Love Were All'

1. A. J. Sylvester diary, 29.11.35.
2. ibid.
3. Ruth Longford, *Frances*, p.124.
4. ibid., p.131.
5. Jennifer Longford paper, FLS/NLW X3/1 p.1.
6. Telegram, Christmas 1935, Ruth's box.
7. Sylvester to Frances, 27.12.35, FLS/1/3.
8. Longford, *Frances*, p.189.
9. Sylvester diary, 8.8.36.
10. ibid., 1.9.36.
11. ibid., 8.11.36.
12. ibid., 16.11.36.
13. ibid., 23.11.36.
14. ibid., 23.10.36.
15. ibid., 4.12.36.
16. ibid., 8.12.36.
17. LG to Megan, 9.12.36, in K. O. Morgan, ed., p.213.
18. *The Years That Are Past*, p.259.
19. Sylvester diary, 24.12.36.
20. ibid., 20.12.36.
21. ibid., 4.1.37.
22. Ann Parry to Frances, 4.12.36, FLS/1/13a.
23. ibid., 12.12.36.
24. Frances to LG, 8.1.37, FLS/6/5.
25. Sylvester diary, 8.1.37.
26. LG to Frances, 11.1.37, FLS/6/5.
27. Sylvester diary, 9.1.37.

28. ibid., 13.1.37.

29. ibid., 16.1.37.

30. LG to Frances, 24.1.37, FLS/6/5.

31. Frances to LG, 16.1.37, FLS/6/5.

32. Sylvester diary, 14.1.37.

33. Frances to LG, 20.1.37, FLS/6/5.

34. Sylvester diary, 21.11.38.

35. LG to Frances, 24.1.37, FLS/6/5.

36. ibid.

37. Sylvester diary, 16.1.37.

38. ibid., 1.2.37.

39. ibid., 16.2.37.

40. ibid., 17.2.37.

41. ibid.

42. ibid., 19.2.37.

43. ibid., 23.2.37.

44. ibid., 24.2.37.

45. ibid., 2.3.37.

46. ibid., 12.2.37.

47. ibid., 23.12.37.

48. ibid., 12.1.38.

49. ibid., 23.1.38.

50. ibid., 24.1.38.

51. ibid., 26.1.38.

52. ibid., 26.1.38.

53. ibid., 31.1.38.

54. ibid., 12.2.38.

55. Speech in the House of Commons, 22.2.38.

56. Sylvester diary, 22.2.38.

57. Viscount Gwynedd, *Dame Margaret*, p.24.

58. Sylvester diary, 1.3.38.

59. Jennifer Longford paper, FLS/NLW X3/1, p.16.

60. Sylvester diary, 18.3.38.

61. ibid., 19.3.38.

62. Longford, *Frances*, p.134.

63. Sylvester diary, 25.3.38.

35. War Again – and Two Deaths

1. FLS diary, 20.6.36.

2. Speech at the City Temple, 26.10.38.
3. A. J. Sylvester diary, 19.9.38.
4. ibid., 31.7.39, 2.8.39.
5. ibid., 7.7.39.
6. ibid., 24.8.39.
7. ibid., 3.9.39.
8. ibid., 27.11.39, 16.1.40.
9. ibid., 14.12.39.
10. Speech in the House of Commons, 8.5.40.
11. Sylvester diary, 16.5.40.
12. ibid., 15.5.40.
13. ibid., 14.6.40.
14. ibid., 25.6.40.
15. ibid.
16. ibid., 21.11.39.
17. ibid., 'Early January' 1940.
18. ibid., 4.3.40.
19. *The Times*, 8.3.40.
20. Ruth Longford, *Frances*, p.113.
21. *Evening Standard*, 1.5.40.
22. *Manchester Guardian*, undated cutting.
23. LG papers G/28/2/20.
24. Sylvester diary, 7.5.40.
25. ibid., 3.5.40.
26. Louise Tweed to LG, 4.5.40, LG G/28/2/19.
27. Longford, *Frances*, p.142.
28. FLS papers, NLW FB1/1/1.
29. Sylvester diary, 2.5.40.
30. *Evening News*, 26.7.40.
31. Sylvester diary, 26.7.40.
32. ibid., 5.8.40.
33. ibid., 11.1.44.
34. ibid., 27.6.40.
35. 11.8.40, 14.8.40, cited in Peter Rowland, *Lloyd George*, p.777.
36. Sylvester diary, 7.7.40.
37. ibid., 15.1.41.
38. ibid., 10.11.40.
39. ibid., 14.12.40.
40. LG to Frances, n.d., 1940, FLS/1/1/3.

41. Sylvester diary, 23.9.40.
42. Frances to Muriel Stevenson, n.d., 1940, FLS/NLW FCF/1.
43. Sylvester diary, 23.9.40.
44. Frances to LG, 23.9.40, FLS/6/5.
45. ibid., 26.9.40.
46. LG to Frances, 26.9.40, FLS/6/5.
47. Sylvester diary, 3.10.40.
48. Thomas Jones, *A Diary With Letters, 1931–1950*, p.457 (7.5.40).
49. LG to Frances, 1.10.40, FLS/6/5.
50. Frances to LG, 2.10.40, FLS/6/5.
51. LG to Frances, 4.10.40, FLS/6/5.
52. Frances to LG, 6.10.40, FLS/6/5.
53. LG to Frances, 22.10.40, FLS/6/5.
54. Sylvester diary, 28.11.40.
55. ibid., 29.10.40.
56. LG to Jennifer, 11.3.40, copy in LG 1/3/5/4. The original is still in Jennifer's possession.
57. Sylvester diary, 12.12.40.
58. Frances to Jennifer, January 1941, in Longford, *Frances*, pp.147–8.
59. Sylvester diary, 19.1.41.
60. ibid., 20.12.41, 21.1.41.
61. Richard Lloyd George, *Lloyd George*, p.9.
62. Sylvester diary, 21.1.41.
63. ibid., 24.1.41.

36. Frances versus Megan

1. Thelma Cazalet-Keir, *From the Wings*, p.52.
2. A. J. Sylvester diary, 4.4.32.
3. ibid., 9.2.41.
4. ibid.
5. ibid., 28.6.42.
6. ibid., 9.2.41.
7. ibid., 28.6.42.
8. ibid., 26.3.42.
9. ibid., 6.5.42.
10. Cazalet-Keir, pp.51–2.
11. Sylvester diary, 8.5.42.
12. ibid., 9.6.42.
13. ibid., 11.6.42.

14. ibid., 16.7.42.
15. ibid., 23.10.42.
16. ibid., 17.11.42.
17. ibid., 18.11.42.
18. ibid., 29.1.41.
19. ibid., 19.11.42.
20. ibid., 23.11.42.
21. ibid., 30.11.42.
22. ibid., 11.12.42.
23. ibid., 18.12.42.
24. ibid.
25. Lord Dawson to Megan, 15.1.43, in Ruth Longford, *Frances*, p.155.
26. Sylvester diary, 15.1.43.
27. ibid., 17.1.43.
28. ibid., 19.1.43.
29. ibid., 25.1.43.
30. ibid.
31. ibid., 24.1.43.
32. Jennifer Longford paper, FLS/NLW X3/1, p.26.
33. Sylvester diary, 13.4.43.
34. ibid., 8.9.43.
35. ibid., 21.10.43.
36. ibid., 22.10.43.
37. ibid., 23.10.43.
38. *The Years That Are Past*, p.272.
39. Jennifer Longford paper, FLS/NLW X3/1, p.26.
40. Sylvester diary, 23.10.43.
41. ibid.
42. ibid., 25.10.43.

37. A Wife at Last

1. Frances to Jennifer, 27.10.43, FLS/NLW FCF1/2.
2. Jennifer Longford paper, FLS/NLW X3/1, p.26.
3. Frances to Megan, 7.11.43, FLS/NLW FLS/6/8.
4. A. J. Sylvester diary, 25.11.43.
5. ibid., 25.10.43.
6. ibid., 14.1.44.
7. ibid., 20.1.44.
8. ibid., 2.2.44.

9. ibid., 26.1.44.

10. ibid., 21.1.44.

11. David ('Benjy') Carey Evans to LG and Frances, 21.2.44, FLS/1/12a.

12. Owen Lloyd George to Frances, 28.10.44, FLS/1/12a.

13. Jennifer Longford paper, FLS/NLW X3/1, p.26.

14. Richard Lloyd George to Frances, 26.8.44, LG I/3/1/16.

15. e.g. Olwen Lloyd George to Frances, 5.9.44, FLS/1/12c.

16. Edna Lloyd George to Frances, n.d., FLS/1/12c.

17. Sylvester diary, 2.2.44.

18. ibid., 3.4.44.

19. ibid., 28.4.44.

20. ibid.

21. ibid., 11.11.43.

22. ibid., 24.5.44.

23. FLS diary, 24.5.44.

24. Sylvester diary, 1.3.44.

25. Frances to Jennifer, 18.5.44, FLS/NLW FCF 1/2.

26. Sylvester diary, 21.9.44.

27. ibid.

28. ibid.

29. ibid., 23.10.44.

30. Frances to Miss Russell, 9.10.44 FLS/NLW FCG 1/2.

31. Sylvester diary, 7.10.44.

32. Frances to Miss Russell, 5.11.44, FLS/NLW FCG 1/2.

33. ibid., 21.11.44.

34. Sylvester diary, 15.10.44.

35. ibid., 23.10.36.

36. ibid., 28.11.44.

37. LG to Churchill, 20.12.44, FLS/6/25.

38. Jennifer Longford paper, FLS/NLW X3/1, p.27.

39. Sylvester diary, 19.12.44.

40. Jennifer Longford paper, FLS/NLW X3/1, pp.20, 27.

41. June Lloyd George to Frances, 25.2.45, FLS/NLW FCF 2/1.

42. Sylvester diary, 25.2.45.

43. Owen Lloyd George, *A Tale of Two Grandfathers*, p.105.

44. Dr Prytherch to Lord Dawson, 26.2.45, in Sylvester diary.

45. Frances to John Stevenson, n.d., in Ruth Longford, *Frances*, p.160.

46. Felicia Brook to Frances, March 1945, FLS/1/17.

47. Sylvester diary, 25.3.45.

38. Occupation: Widow

1.   Jennifer Longford paper, FLS/NLW X3/1, pp.28, 33.
2.   June Lloyd George to Frances, 3.4.45, FLS/NLW FCF 2/1.
3.   William George to Frances, 15.9.47, FLS/NLW FCF 2/1.
4.   Ruth Longford, *Frances*, p.174.
5.   ibid., p.178.
6.   ibid., p.168.
7.   Jennifer Longford paper, FLS/NLW X3/1, p.34.
8.   Ruth Longford, *Frances*, p.171.
9.   ibid., p.205.
10. *Times Literary Supplement*, 4.10.47.
11. *Spectator*, 3.10.47.
12. Frances to William George, 14.10.47, FLS/NLW FCF 2/1.
13. Ruth Longford, *Frances*, p.172.
14. William George to Frances, 27.10.47, FLS/NLW FCF 2/1.
15. Richard Lloyd George to John Morris, 12.6.45, FLS/1/16.
16. Owen Lloyd George, *A Tale of Two Grandfathers*, p.109.
17. Ruth Longford, *Frances*, p.197.
18. Mervyn Jones, *Megan Lloyd George*, p.320.
19. Ruth Longford, *Frances*, p.208.
20. ibid., p.207.
21. ibid., p.209.

INDEX